THE ENGLISH STUDIES BOOK

Rob Pope

London and New York

First published 1998
by Routledge
11 New Fetter Lane, London EC4P 4EE

Simultaneously published in the USA and Canada
by Routledge
29 West 35th Street, New York, NY 10001

Reprinted 1999

Typeset in Century Old Style/Bell Gothic by Keystroke,
Jacaranda Lodge, Wolverhampton
Printed and bound in Great Britain by TJ International Ltd., Padstow, Cornwall

British Library Cataloguing in Publication Data
A catalogue record for this book is available from the British Library

Library of Congress Cataloguing in Publication Data
A catalogue record for this book has been requested

ISBN 0–415–12866–8 (hbk)
        0–415–12867–6 (pbk)

This one's for you guys.

For Bronwen, Sophie, Ivan and Sasha

With love from Dad.

CONTENTS

List of figures   xiii
Preface and acknowledgements   xv
What the book is about and how to use it   1

PART ONE: INTRODUCTION TO ENGLISH STUDIES   7

      Preview   7
1.1   *Which 'Englishes'?*   8
1.2   One English language, literature, culture – or many?   14
      1.2.1   historically   14
      1.2.2   geographically   18
      1.2.3   socially   19
      1.2.4   by medium   19
1.3   Summary: one *and* many   20
1.4   Activities, reading   21
1.5   *How studied?*   24
      1.5.1   English as a school subject   24
      1.5.2   English as a university degree subject   26
      1.5.3   English and Classics   27
      1.5.4   English and Theology   28
      1.5.5   Rhetoric, composition and writing   29
      1.5.6   History and English   32
      1.5.7   From Literary Appreciation to Literary Criticism   35
      1.5.8   English into Literary Studies   37
      1.5.9   English with Theatre and/or Film Studies   38
      1.5.10 English into Cultural, Communication and Media
            Studies   40
      1.5.11 Critical Theory into Cultural Practice   41
1.6   Summary: pasts, presents and futures   42
1.7   Activities, discussion, reading   43

1.8	Fields of study	44
	1.8.1 Language	48
	1.8.2 Literature	54
	1.8.3 Culture, communication and media	58
1.9	Summary: keeping on course and making your own way	65
1.10	Activities, reading	

PART TWO: THEORETICAL POSITIONS AND PRACTICAL APPROACHES — 67

	Preview	67
2.1	Getting some initial bearings	68
2.2	Theory in practice – a working model	70
2.3	Practical Criticism and (old) New Criticism	77
2.4	Formalism into Functionalism	83
2.5	Psychological approaches	92
2.6	Marxism, Cultural Materialism and New Historicism	102
2.7	Feminism and Gender Studies	111
2.8	Poststructuralism and Postmodernism	124
2.9	Postcolonialism and multiculturalism	135
2.10	Developing positions and future prospects	153

PART THREE: COMMON TOPICS — 155

Preview	155
Absence and presence, gaps and silences, centres and margins	156
Accent and dialect	158
Addresser, address, addressee	160
Aesthetics and pleasure, art and beauty	162
Author and authority	165
Auto/biography and life-writing: self and other	168
Bibles, holy books and myths	170
Canon and classic	174
Character and characterisation	177
Comedy and tragedy, carnival and the absurd	179
Difference and similarity, preference and re/valuation	184
Discourse and discourse analysis	188
Drama and theatre, film and TV	191
Foreground, background and point of view	195
Genre and kinds of text	199
Image, imagery and imagination	202
Narrative in hi/story, novel, news and film	206
Poetry and word-play	212
Realism and representation: fiction, fact, faction and metafiction	216

Speech and conversation, monologue and dialogue   220
Standards and standardisation, varieties and variation   225
Subject and agent, role and identity   230
Text, context and intertextuality   234
Versification: stress, rhythm, metre and rhyme   237
Writing and reading, response and rewriting   242
Your own additions and modifications   251

PART FOUR: TEXTUAL ACTIVITIES AND LEARNING STRATEGIES   253

Preview   253
4.1   Overview of textual activities   254
4.2   Frameworks and checklists for close reading   258
4.3   Writing and research from essays to the Internet   261
4.4   Alternative modes of critical and creative writing   265
4.5   What's (not) in a name? Changing courses   269
4.6   Making anthologies and firing 'canons' yourself   271

PART FIVE: ANTHOLOGY OF SAMPLE TEXTS   275

Preview   275
5.1   **Poetry, song and performance**   276
      5.1.1   Anglo-Saxon poem: anonymous, 'Wulf and Eadwacer'   276
      5.1.2   Fourteenth-century verse   277
              a anonymous, 'Maiden in the mor lay'   277
              b Geoffrey Chaucer, 'General Prologue' (the Knight)   278
              c William Langland, *Piers Plowman*   279
              d anonymous, *Pearl*   280
      5.1.3   Renaissance lyric and sonnet   280
              a Thomas Wyatt, 'They flee from me'   280
              b William Shakespeare, 'My mistress' eyes' (Sonnet 130)   281
              c Lady Mary Wroth, 'Unseen, unknown, I'
                 (from *The Countess of Montgomery's Urania*)   282
      5.1.4   Heroics and mock-heroics, seventeenth–twentieth
              centuries   283
              a John Milton, *Paradise Lost*   283
              b Alexander Pope, *The Rape of the Lock*   284
              c Elizabeth Hands, 'A Poem, . . . by a Servant Maid'   285
              d George Gordon, Lord Byron, *The Vision of Judgement*   286
              e Terry Pratchett and Neil Gaiman, *Good Omens*   288
      5.1.5   John Clare, 'I am'   288
      5.1.6   William Barnes, 'Woak Hill'   289

5.1.7   a William Butler Yeats, 'Leda and the Swan'   290
        b Judith Kazantsis, 'Leda and Leonardo the Swan'   291
5.1.8   Adrienne Rich, 'Dialogue'   292
5.1.9   Some 'New' English varieties   293
        a πO, *7 DAIZ*   293
        b Chan Wei Meng, 'I spik Ingglish'   294
        c Merle Collins, 'No Dialects Please'   294
5.1.10 Queen, 'Bohemian Rhapsody'   296

5.2   Prose fiction, journals and news   298
5.2.1   Letter, diary and life-writing   298
        a Margery Brews to John Paston III, 'A Valentine', from
           the *Paston Letters*   298
        b Samuel Pepys, *Diary*   299
        c George and Weedon Grossmith, *The Diary of a Nobody*   299
        d Janet Frame, *To the Is-land*   300
5.2.2   Slave narratives, seventeenth–twentieth centuries   300
        a Aphra Behn, *Oroonoko*   300
        b Daniel Defoe, *Robinson Crusoe* ('I Call Him Friday')   301
        c Geoff Holdsworth, 'I call him Tuesday afternoon'   302
        d Frederick Douglass, *The Narrative and Life . . . by
           Himself*   303
        e Toni Morrison, *Beloved*   303
5.2.3   Romance, seventeenth–twentieth centuries   304
        a Delarivier Manley, *The New Atalantis*   304
        b Jane Austen, *Pride and Prejudice*   305
        c Mary Shelley, *Frankenstein, or The Modern Prometheus*   306
        d Charlotte Brontë, *Jane Eyre*   306
        e Jean Rhys, *Wide Sargasso Sea*   307
5.2.4   Further post/colonial tales   308
        a Jonathan Swift, *A Modest Proposal*   308
        b Rudyard Kipling, 'The Story of Muhammad Din'   309
        c Joseph Conrad, *Heart of Darkness*   311
        d Zora Neale Hurston, *Their Eyes Were Watching God*   312
        e Amos Tutuola, *The Palm Wine Drinkard*   313
        f Chinua Achebe, *Things Fall Apart*   313
5.2.5   News stories   314
        a *Sun*, '20 Yobs Hold Train to Ransom'   314
        b *Guardian*, 'British Rail's first "steaming" raises calls
           for more staff'   315
        c Headlines, lead-ins and captions   316
        d Tom Leonard, 'This is thi six a clock news'
           (*Unrelated Incidents*)   317
        e Roddy Doyle, *Paddy Clarke ha ha ha*   318
5.2.6   James Kelman, *How late it was, how late*   319

5.3 Scripts and transcripts – conversation, interview and drama 320
  5.3.1 Transcripts 320
    a A supermarket exchange over change 320
    b Family conversation 320
    c Factory Commission interview with millhand, 1852 321
    d Sigmund Freud, *Fragment of an Analysis of a Case of Hysteria* ('Dora') 322
  5.3.2 Early English stages 324
    a Chester Mystery Cycle, *Noah's Flood* 324
    b William Shakespeare, *The Tempest* 325
  5.3.3 Alternative endings 326
    a Henrik Ibsen, *A Doll's House* (1879, Norway) 326
    b Henrik Ibsen, *A Doll's House* (1880, Germany) 327
  5.3.4 Voices with a difference 328
    a John Millington Synge, *The Playboy of the Western World* 328
    b Dylan Thomas, *Under Milk Wood* 329
    c Athol Fugard, *Boesman and Lena* 330
    d Samuel Beckett, *Not I* 330
    e Caryl Churchill, *Cloud 9* 332
  5.3.5 Dramatising 'English' in education 333
    a Toni Cade Bambara, *The Lesson* 333
    b John Godber, *Teechers* 333
    c Willy Russell, *Educating Rita* 335

5.4 Intertextual clusters 336
  5.4.1 Versions of 'Humpty Dumpty', including Lewis Carroll's *Alice Through the Looking Glass* 336
  5.4.2 Versions of Psalm 137, including Salman Rushdie's *The Satanic Verses* 337
  5.4.3 Daffodils? 338
    a William Wordsworth, 'I wandered lonely as a cloud' 338
    b Dorothy Wordsworth, *Grasmere Journals* 339
    c Lynn Peters, 'Why Dorothy Wordworth is Not as Famous as her Brother' 340
    d 'Heineken refreshes the poets other beers cannot reach' (lager advert) 340
  5.4.4 Versions of age 341
    a May Sarton, *As We Are Now* 341
    b 'Clarins the Problem-Solver' (skincare advert) 341
    c William Shakespeare, 'Devouring Time' (Sonnet 19) 342
    d Dennis Scott, 'Uncle Time' 342
    e Billy Marshall-Stoneking, 'Passage' 343
  5.4.5 Death and (not so) grave yards 344
    a Epitaphs by Pope, Gray, Burns, Monty Python *et al.* 344

    b Charles Dickens, *Great Expectations*   345

    c Tony Harrison, *v.*   346

    d Emily Dickinson, 'I felt a Funeral'   347

    e Grace Nichols, 'Tropical Death'   348

  5.4.6 Visions of England at war   348

    a William Shakespeare, *Henry V*   348

    b William Blake, 'And did those feet' (*Milton*)   350

    c Percy Bysshe Shelley, *The Mask of Anarchy*   351

    d Rupert Brooke, 'The Soldier' with Winston Churchill's

     'Speech on Rupert Brooke'   352

    e U. A. Fanthorpe, *Knowing about Sonnets* (with Terry

     Eagleton)   352

    f Theatre Workshop, *Oh What a Lovely War*   353

  5.4.7 Some current genres of small text   354

    a Public notices   354

    b Im/personal adverts   355

    c Mission and customer service statements   356

    d Dialogue with a cash-in-the-wall machine   356

    e Answer-phone messages   357

    f Internet conferencing   357

    g Some contemporary 'I'dentities   358

**PART SIX: GLOSSARY OF COMMON GRAMMATICAL AND LINGUISTIC
   TERMS**   361

APPENDICES   383

A Maps of Britain, the USA and the world   383

B A chronology of English language and literature, culture,

 communication and media   386

C English *and* or *as* other educational subjects   390

Bibliography   393

Relevant journals and useful addresses   403

Index   405

LIST OF FIGURES

1	OED definition of English	10
2	A working model of the text as product/s and process/es	72
3	Postcolonial problems and possibilities with English	144
4	Dominant post/colonial and neo-colonial mind-sets	147
5	Jakobson's model of communication	161
6	Distinctions and connections between drama and narrative	192
7	Textual activities as learning strategies	256
8	Writing and research processes	262
A1	Varieties of English and other languages in the British Isles	383
A2	English in the world: a modern map with some historical underpinning	384
A3	The USA: origins of state names with chief Northern, Midland and Southern dialect areas	385
C	English *and* or *as* other educational subjects	390

PREFACE AND ACKNOWLEDGEMENTS

This book has taken shape over many years and benefited from the generous support of many people. Versions of parts of it have been developed with students at Oxford Brookes University. Those taking 'Language, Literature Discourse I and III', 'Texts, Problems and Approaches' and the 'English Studies Synoptic' have been particularly influential in pointing the present materials. So, latterly, have two students at Anglia Polytechnic University (Aileen Askwith and Alex Taylor) who offered detailed comments on a full draft. All these people have reminded me to keep focused on what is practical and appropriate as well as sophisticated and demanding. Where I have still failed to square this particular circle it certainly isn't for want of being told.

Of the many colleagues and friends who have contributed everything from ideas, corrections and references to word-processors, a place to stay and jolly/stimulating company, it gives me especial pleasure to thank:

♦   the Department of English at the University of Otago, New Zealand for a great year as visiting lecturer, in particular Jocelyn Harris, Colin Gibson, John Hale, Ian Jamieson, Shef Rogers, Paul Sorrell, Elspeth Sandys (the Burns Fellow) and Brian Turner (a former Burns Fellow), as well as co-members of the 'Interactive Learning Group in Languages, Literature and Film', namely Andy Barratt, Claudia Brugman, John Dolan, Thierry Jutel, Chris Prentice, Lesley Procter and Rochelle Simmons; also Graham McGregor.

♦   the Centre for Professional Writing and Communication at the University of South Australia for the privilege and pleasure of being their Visiting Research Scholar, in particular Claire Woods and David Homer; also Bill Corcoran of Queensland University of Technology (a long, hot afternoon with the three of them taking a version of the book apart and putting it back together again – differently – proved both chastening and cheering).

♦   the Departments of English at Massey University (especially Dick Corballis and Warwick Slinn) and at the University of Canterbury, Christchurch (especially Howard McNaughton, Helen Debenham and David Gunby) for brief spells in which parts of the book were trialled; also Graeme Harper, Jon Cook and colleagues at the Centre for Creative and Performing Arts, University of East Anglia, Sharon Goodman of the School of Education at the Open University and Katie Gray of the Department of Continuing Education at the University of Oxford.

♦   numerous participants in lectures, workshops and discussions (formal and informal, in and out of the bar) organised by the British Council, Poetics and Linguistics

Association, Conference on College Composition and Communication (USA), European Society for the Study of English, National Association for the Teaching of English (UK), Australian Association for the Teaching of English, Council for College and University English (UK) and the Humanities and Arts Network for Teaching and Learning in Higher Education (based at the Open University, UK).

All those who agreed to read a rather wild, woolly and overweight version of the penultimate draft (in the event the pen-penultimate draft!) deserve a special mention. Susan Bassnett, Ron Carter, Riccardo Duranti, Stephen Muecke, Rick Rylance, David Stacey, Jean Jacques Weber and an anonymous reader from Holland all gave wonderfully expert and attentive advice on how to restrain and comb the beast without taming it entirely. (If ever I needed reminding that contemporary English Studies is not only alive and well but also deeply contentious it was there in the two hundred or so pages of richly diverse comment supplied by these readers.) Meanwhile, as always, colleagues at Oxford Brookes University, inside and outside the School of Humanities, remain a source of support, stimulation and good humour. Thanks in particular to Nigel Messenger for suggesting the Kipling tale (as well as for countless conversations over the years on English, literature and life in general), to Stewart Young for encouraging me to keep the drama in, and to Archie Burnett for being all that a colleague on jointly designed and taught courses can be. Alan Jenkins, Dave Pepper and Frank Webster have contributed more than they may recall, both on and off the terraces at Oxford United. Felix Lam untangled the cat's cradle which was my computer files, while Bob Pomfret did a great job with computer graphics at impossibly short notice.

Technically and conceptually this was always going to be a challenging book to publish. Moira Taylor at Routledge has met that challenge with rare enthusiasm and expertise; she has encouraged me with just the right blend of patience and push. Working on the detail of design, copy-editing and production with Jody Ball, Beth Humphries and colleagues has also proved a pleasure when it could so easily be a pain. Any mistakes that remain are my fault.

Finally, most important to me personally, there is the dawning recognition that I don't have to become inhuman or a hermit to finish a book. Most of the credit for this must go to my wife, Tania, and to the children. Without their love and laughter none of this could have happened. Nor would it matter that much.

FURTHER ACKNOWLEDGEMENTS

CHINUA ACHEBE, from 'Things Fall Apart', copyright Heinemann Educational Publishers, a division of Reed Educational and Professional Publishing Limited.

SAMUEL BECKETT, from *Not I*, play extract from *Collected Shorter Plays*. Copyright 1973 by Samuel Beckett, reprinted by permission of Grove/Atlantic Inc. and Faber & Faber.

TONI CADE BAMBARA, from 'The Lesson', prose extract from her short story collection *Gorilla, My Love*, published in Great Britain by The Women's Press Ltd, 1986, 34 Gt Sutton Street, London EC1V 0DX, is used by permission of The Women's Press. US rights to reprint are granted by Random House Inc., Alfred A. Knopf Inc., New York, 1972.

CARYL CHURCHILL, from *Cloud Nine*, in *Churchill: Plays One*, copyright Caryl Churchill, published by Methuen, 1985.

Clarins Skincare magazine advert from *Cosmopolitan*, February 1985.

MERLE COLLINS, 'No Dialects Please' from *Singing Down the Bones*, ed. Jeni Couzyn, first published by The Women's Press, 1989.

U.A. FANTHORPE, 'Knowing About Sonnets' from *Voices Off*, 1984. Copyright Ursula Fanthorpe, reproduced by permission of Peterloo Poets.

JANET FRAME, prose extract from *An Autobiography: To the Is-land, vol. 1*. Copyright Janet Frame, 1982, reproduced by permission of Curtis Brown Ltd, London, on behalf of Janet Frame Clutha.

SIGMUND FREUD, Case histories I, 'Dora'. Sigmund Freud copyrights, The Institute of Psychoanalysis and the Hogarth Press, 1905. Permission is granted to quote from The Standard Edition of *The Complete Psychological Works of Sigmund Freud*, translated and edited by James Strachey.

ATHOL FUGARD, *Boesman and Lena*, play extract from *Selected Plays*, 1986, Oxford University Press.

JOHN GODBER, play extract from *Teechers*, from *Five Plays*, Penguin, Harmondsworth, 1989, reprinted by permission of Alan Brodie Representation.

Guardian, 13.2.89, newspaper article 'British Rail's First Steaming' by Paul Keel. Reprinted by permission of the *Guardian*.

TONY HARRISON, interrupted extract from the poem *v.*, from *Selected Poems*, Penguin, Harmondsworth, 2nd edition, 1987. By permission of Tony Harrison represented by Gordon Dickerson.

Heineken: transcript extract from Lowe Howard-Spink's 'Windermere' commercial 'Heineken refreshes the poets other beers cannot reach'.

GEOFF HOLDSWORTH, for his re-write of Defoe: 'I call him Tuesday afternoon'.

ZORA NEALE HURSTON, prose extract from *Their Eyes Were Watching God*, reprinted by permission of Little Brown. US copyright HarperCollins.

HENRIK IBSEN, *A Doll's House*, alternative endings translated by (a) Michael Meyer, *Ibsen: Plays Two*, Methuen 1984, and (b) P. Watts, *The League of Youth, A Doll's House, The Lady from the Sea*, Penguin, 1965. Reprinted by permission of David Higham Associates Limited.

JUDITH KAZANTSIS, 'Leda and Leonardo the Swan', from her *Selected Poems 1977–1992*, 1995, Sinclair Stevenson. Originally in *The Wicked Queen*, 1980, Sidgwick and Jackson.

RUDYARD KIPLING, 'The Story of Muhammad Din', short story from *Plain Tales from the Hills*, 1888. Reprinted by permission of A. P. Watt Ltd, on behalf of The National Trust.

BILLY MARSHALL-STONEKING, 'Passage', from *Singing the Snake*, 1990. Published in *The New Oxford Book of Australian Verse*, 2nd edition, 1991, Oxford University Press, Australia.

TONI MORRISON, prose extract from *Beloved: A Novel*, reprinted by permission of International Creative Management Inc. Copyright 1987, Alfred Knopf Inc.

Nationwide Anglia Building Society TV advert 'At night I dream of many things', November 1990, by permission of Leagas Delaney agency.

GRACE NICHOLS, 'Tropical Death' from *The Fat Black Woman's Poems*, Virago, 1984, reprinted by permission of Little Brown.

LYNN PETERS, 'Why Dorothy Wordsworth is not as famous as her brother', from *The Virago Book of Wicked Verse*, Virago, 1992. Copyright Lynn Peters.

πO, '7 Daiz', first printed in *The Fitzroy Poem*, 1989, Collective Effort Press, P.O. Box 2430V, GPO Melbourne, Victoria 3001, Australia. Reprinted by permission of the author.

TERRY PRATCHETT and NEIL GAIMAN, prose extract from *Good Omens*, Corgi. Copyright Terry Pratchett and Neil Gaiman. Reprinted by permission of Carole Blake of Blake Friedmann.

QUEEN, text of 'Bohemian Rhapsody', words and music by Freddie Mercury 1975. By permission of B. Feldman & Co. Ltd., London.

JEAN RHYS, prose extract from *Wide Sargasso Sea*. First published by Andre Deutsch. 1966. Copyright 1966 Jean Rhys. Reprinted by permission of Penguin UK and W.W. Norton & Co. Inc.

ADRIENNE RICH, 'Dialogue' from *The Fact of a Doorframe: Poems Selected and New, 1950–1984*. Copyright 1984 by Adrienne Rich; copyright 1975, 1978 by W.W. Norton & Company Inc.; copyright 1981 by Adrienne Rich. Reprinted by permission of the author and W.W. Norton & Company Inc.

WILLY RUSSELL, play extract from *Educating Rita*, Methuen, 1988.

MAY SARTON, prose extract from *As We Are Now*. Copyright 1973 by May Sarton. Reprinted by permission of W.W. Norton & Company Inc.

DENNIS SCOTT, 'Uncle Time' from collection *Uncle Time*. Copyright 1973, reprinted by permission of the University of Pittsburg Press.

Sun, front-page story, 13 February 1989: '20 Yobs Hold Train to Ransom' by Michael Fielder. By permission of the *Sun*.

THEATRE WORKSHOP, from *Oh What a Lovely War*, copyright Tessa Sayle Agency.

DYLAN THOMAS, from *Under Milk Wood: A Play for Voices*, reprinted by permission of David Higham Associates Ltd.

AMOS TUTUOLA, prose extract from *The Palm Wine Drinkard*, Faber & Faber, 1987.

WILLIAM B. YEATS, 'Leda and the Swan'. Permission granted by A.P. Watt Ltd on behalf of Michael Yeats. Reprinted with the permission of Simon & Schuster from *The Collected Works of W.B. Yeats, volume 1: The Poems*. Revised and edited by Richard J. Finneran. Copyright 1928 by Macmillan Publishing Company; copyright renewed 1956 by Bertha Georgie Yeats.

Routledge has made every effort to trace copyright holders and to obtain permission to publish extracts. Any omissions brought to our attention will be remedied in future editions.

WHAT THE BOOK IS ABOUT AND HOW TO USE IT

This book provides an introduction to the theory and practice of contemporary English Studies. It combines the functions of study guide, critical dictionary and text anthology, and is designed to support learning and teaching across a wide range of courses. Most undergraduate English courses now have a considerable variety of emphases – literary, linguistic and more broadly cultural. This book aims to recognise and support all, or at least most, of them in a flexible yet coherent way. The choice of the label *English Studies* is calculating not casual. It signals an extremely capacious subject matter (English) and puts equal emphasis on the educational process of understanding it (Studies). Indeed, the book, like the contemporary subject, is in many senses *inter*disciplinary. So any talk of 'the subject' (definite article and singular) can be misleading if it obscures the fact that English (sometimes controversially dubbed 'englishes') is a fundamentally plural and constantly changing series of subjects (Studies). 'It' often turns out to be 'they'.

This is a handbook in that it is designed for flexible handling and for freedom of movement. Don't aim to read it straight through from cover to cover. But do expect to move from one part to another, and from this text in one hand to another text in front of you, or in your mind's eye. Most sections are just a few pages long. They can be used on their own as focuses for a single session, or in interrelated clusters over several sessions. Cross-referencing is copious (see below) and provides constant reminders of connected issues and larger frameworks. The book is also a kind of 'companion' in that it is designed to be of continuing and cumulative use across a wide range of courses right through from introductory to advanced levels. It can be used as a coursebook in its own right or for self-directed study. In all these respects the associated electronic website (see below) offers further materials and continuing support.

Who the book is for: 'You', it is imagined, are primarily a student. You are somewhere between first and final years of a degree or similar programme (perhaps nearer the beginning when you first pick this up). Your programme probably involves a fair amount of English Literature (including Literature in English) and at least some work in English Language. There may also be some dimensions of Communication and Composition or Cultural and Media Studies to what you do. You may be spending most or all of your time in a department called 'English'. However, you may also be studying English as part of a joint, combined, major-minor or modular programme. In any event, it is imagined that you are interested in exploring the rich variety of subjects called 'English' both in themselves and in relation to other subjects that interest you, inside and outside formal education.

But you may also be a teacher or lecturer of English, or perhaps a trainee teacher. An important, albeit secondary, function of this book is to contribute to debate about the present shape and future directions of the subject. It is framed so as to prompt discussion and provide a practical aid to course (re-)design, while also supporting teaching and learning on existing programmes. In any case, whether nominally teachers or learners, we are all in a fundamental sense *students* of English. The past, present and future of our subject is everybody's business and a shared concern – even if it is not, in Leavis's loaded phrase, 'a common pursuit'. Indeed, it is as much the diversity as the unity of English Studies that exercises us here: variations over time, place and social space as much as any supposedly homogeneous object or project.

The book is organised in six distinct yet interconnected parts:

1   *Introduction to English Studies*
2   *Theoretical Positions and Practical Approaches*
3   *Common Topics*
4   *Textual Activities and Learning Strategies*
5   *Anthology of Sample Texts*
6   *Glossary of Common Grammatical and Linguistic Terms*

It is recommended that you read the first part early on to get some initial bearings. Thereafter move around the rest of the book in whatever order and patterns meet your needs.

HOW TO MOVE AROUND

For ease of use the book is variously signposted and cross-referenced. In addition to the general Contents pages at the beginning, there are more detailed *Preview* pages which preface each of the six parts. There is also a comprehensive *Index* at the end where you can find page references for all the main terms, topics, titles and authors, including all the 'hot' terms featured within the body of the text. These 'hot' terms are of three kinds and highlighted in three ways:

- SMALL CAPITALS (e.g., LANGUAGE, LITERATURE, FEMINISM, POSTMODERNISM) refer to the main fields of study and the critical approaches to which whole sections are devoted in Parts One and Two.
- **Bold** (e.g., **discourse, novel, narrative, text**) refers to the common terms and topics featured as substantial entries in Part Three.
- *Asterisks (e.g., *theory, *noun, *pragmatics) refer to terms which are briefly explained in passing or in the glossary in Part Six; they also refer to featured critics (e.g., *Bakhtin).

Many terms are repeated throughout the book; but only when something significant is added by way of definition or illustration are they highlighted. And remember, the index cross-references everything.

Below is a brief summary of each of the six parts of the book. Parts One to Four follow a common pattern of *exposition, example, activity, discussion* and *further reading*. They therefore reinforce the notion that English (like other educational subjects) is best conceived as something we *make* and *do* as well as something we *find* and *find out about*. That is, 'doing English' entails various processes of *telling, showing, doing, reflecting* and *researching*. Turn to the preview pages at the beginning of each part of the main text if you want still further information at this stage.

Part One: *Introduction to English Studies* surveys the many things that 'English' has been, is currently and yet may be. The overarching questions are 'Which Englishes?' and 'How studied?'. In both cases the answer is emphatically 'Many and various', depending upon the times, places, societies and media in play. Beginning with the formation of English as an educational subject in schools, colleges and university during the late nineteenth century, we then trace the ways in which such subjects as CLASSICS, THEOLOGY, RHETORIC and HISTORY all contributed to crucial stages in its development. We observe fundamental shifts from literary *appreciation* to literary *criticism* and literary and cultural *theory* over the course of the twentieth century; and we explore recent constructions of the subject in relation to such configurations as LITERARY, COMPOSITION, CULTURAL, COMMUNICATION and MEDIA Studies. The first part concludes by identifying Language, Literature and Culture (in various permutations) as our main fields of study, and introduces the basic models, methods and tools we need to move across them.

Part Two: *Theoretical Positions and Practical Approaches* offers a 'hands-on' introduction to all the major theories and approaches that inform contemporary English Studies. The emphasis throughout is upon theory that works and on getting you to work (and play) with theory for yourself. This part of the book spans everything from the relatively un- or under-theorised practices of PRACTICAL CRITICISM and (old) NEW CRITICISM to the hyper-theorised (some would say over-theorised) models of POSTSTRUCTURALISM and POSTMODERNISM. Meanwhile, at the core of this section we explore a range of psychological and political approaches that continue to inform and transform critical agendas: PSYCHOLOGICAL, MARXIST and NEW HISTORICIST, FEMINIST and GENDERED, POSTCOLONIAL and MULTICULTURAL. Each section includes simple yet comprehensive advice on *'How to practise'* the theory or approach in question. There are worked examples, further activities and cues for discussion. There are also, finally, pointers to other developing areas such as *ecological criticism and life-writing, as well as further encouragement in developing your own positions and orientations.

Part Three: *Common Topics* features over a hundred common terms such as **author, canon, character, genre, poetry, narrative, text, context** and **intertextuality, writing** and **reading**. These are 'common' precisely because they occur in critical discourses of many kinds, often with competing senses, and are not the exclusive property of any one critical school or movement (**discourse** is itself such a term and therefore included). Again there is an emphasis on using these terms practically, as tools, rather than merely bandying them around for effect. You are also encouraged to carry on building and refining a critical vocabulary of your own.

Part Four: *Textual Activities and Learning Strategies* is especially concerned with the 'study' aspects of English. It provides an overview of ways of reading and writing about texts (including 'alternative' modes of adaptation, imitation, parody and intervention). It also provides guidance on traditional modes such as the essay, and pays particular attention to the impact of computers in research and writing. There is a method and checklist for close reading; suggestions for exploring anthologies and 'canons', and some frameworks for thinking about course content and design. This part of the book is therefore expressly addressed to teachers and lecturers as well as to students. While supporting a considered review of current courses and programmes, it also aims to prompt debate about the shape and nature of future, potential courses and programmes, as well as possible futures for the subject 'as a whole'. Either way, the emphasis is on English as something we *do* (*know-how*, skills, techniques, strategies, interaction) as much as on what English *is* (*know-what*, knowledges, a body of set texts, a hierarchy of textual and social relations).

Part Five: *Anthology of Sample Texts* consists of short texts and extracts recurrently referred to in the rest of the book and often used as focuses for activities. This part of the book also serves as an anthology representing some of the main historical, geographical and social varieties of English encountered on English Studies courses today. We range across poetry, prose and drama, from Old English to contemporary Afro-Caribbean, and from formal elegy and sonnet to 'stream of consciousness' and performance pieces. Placed alongside and amongst these more traditionally 'literary' materials are instances of informal conversation, formal interview and diary, as well as products of the modern media such as news, pop and advertising. The overall aim is to brace literary texts (canonical and non-canonical) against other varieties, and thereby implicitly interrogate as well as illustrate literature's changing relation to the rest of language and culture. Some of the passages (those in 5.4) are gathered in interrelated clusters on such topics as 'death', 'age' and 'England at war'. And again, you are encouraged to explore the possibilities for yourself: in this case to put together a text anthology devised according to your own criteria.

Part Six: *Glossary of Common Grammatical and Linguistic Terms* offers simple definitions and illustrations of all the main terms you are likely to meet on introductory courses in grammatical and linguistic analysis. Most of the terms are traditional and perhaps fairly familiar (noun, verbal group, personal pronouns, subject, sentence, etc.). Some are slightly more technical and perhaps less familiar (e.g., speech acts, context-sensitivity, cohesion, participants and processes). But all are now commonly used and serve practical, often powerful, analytical functions.

There are some *Appendices* at the end of the book. These supply maps and a cultural chronology of English(es); also some diagrams to help plot the subject's changing relations with other subjects and, by extension, the changing constructions of English 'itself'. Thus, at the end, as at the beginning, we are engaging with a subject which may appear to be one but always turns out to be many. The *Bibliography* includes full references for everything in the Further Reading sections. And the *Index*, as already mentioned, is a comprehensive guide to all the terms, topics, texts and authors referred to. This will probably be the part of the book you turn to most.

That returns us to the primary purpose of this handbook. If the whole thing soon looks well thumbed and dog-eared, then it is probably working as intended. Or rather, to put the onus back firmly on you the 'handler', it is probably working as you intend.

THE WORLD-WIDE-WEB site has three main functions. To provide:

- flexible access to further materials and activities organised on the same lines as the book;
- further sections on ecological, global and area-based approaches as well as such topics as **translation**, **editing** and **censorship**;
- regular updates on the most relevant publications, conferences and addresses (including related web sites).

The site is at http://www.brookes.ac.uk/schools/humanities/home.html. When there, just click on *English Studies Book*.

It will be coordinated by Rob Pope in conjunction with Routledge and teaching colleagues from Europe, the USA and Australia. A companion volume, *The English Studies Reader*, is also planned.

Suggestions on corrections, changes and supplements may also be sent to Rob Pope at English Studies, Oxford Brookes University, Headington, Oxford, England OX3 OBP. As far as possible, these will be incorporated and acknowledged in a future edition.

PART ONE

INTRODUCTION TO ENGLISH STUDIES

PREVIEW

This introduces the sheer richness and variety as well as the complexity and contentiousness of contemporary English Studies. *English*, it is shown, can refer to many interrelated things: languages, literatures, peoples and cultures. *Studies*, meanwhile, can involve many interrelated activities: critical and creative, textual and intertextual, engaging individuals and groups. All these issues are framed in terms of two initial questions: *Which Englishes?* and *How studied?*

We then review the development of English in universities and colleges over the past hundred and fifty years, and conclude with a projection into the next twenty. Looking back to the late nineteenth century, we see English as first the competitor and then substantially the successor of Classics, Rhetoric and Theology at the centre of the liberal arts curriculum. Looking to the early twenty-first century, we see English both embracing and to some extent being displaced by Cultural, Communication, Composition and Media Studies, as well as a wide range of other more or less interdisciplinary studies (Women's, Postcolonial, Environmental, etc.). Meanwhile, at the core of contemporary English Studies, we note the complex legacy of certain specifically literary kinds of appreciation and criticism, theory and practice. We also witness the shifts from specifically national views of the subject (centred on Britain, America, Australia, etc.) to conceptions which are at once more regional/local and more international/global.

Part One closes with a provisional mapping of the subject as a whole in terms of three interrelated *fields of study*: LANGUAGE; LITERATURE; CULTURE, COMMUN-ICATION and MEDIA. 'English' is thus recognised to be not so much one fixed subject as a shifting combination of many; not a single discipline but what may be called an 'interdiscipline'. It is also observed that the particular 'English' we practise in the present very much depends upon which of these various pasts we recognise and which of the potential futures we wish to realise (see Figure 1).

1.1   WHICH 'ENGLISHES'?

> The point about 'English' as the name of a subject is that it is an adjective being made to serve as a noun. So 'English' is always pointing towards an absence – the noun. *Is the subject English literature, language, society, culture, people?*
>
> Colin Evans, *English People* (1993: 184) (my emphasis)

> And what should they know of England who only England know?
>
> Rudyard Kipling (1865–1936), 'The English Flag' (1892)

We open with an overview of the many things that go to make up contemporary English Studies. To do this, we make some preliminary sightings (and sitings) of the vast range of subjects that 'English' has been, is and yet may be. In principle these include all the various persons and peoples, times and places, words and worlds – real and imaginary – that may be embraced by that term 'English'. As the first of the above quotations reminds us, this means repeatedly filling and refilling that tantalising absence after the adjective 'English ——'. But with what? What is, are or can be the subject(s) of 'English' – Language? Literature? Culture? People? If all of these in varying measures, then in what proportions and who is doing the measuring?

Should we, for instance, speak of the medium of our subject as 'the English Language' (definite article, upper case and singular) 'varieties of English' (plural features of a single entity) or, more provocatively, 'englishes' (flatly lower case and plural)? When speaking of one of our main objects of study, should it be 'English Literature' or 'literatures in English'? (There's a big difference.) And in either case we need to be sure whether we're talking about canonical and/or non-canonical texts – conventionally recognised 'classics of Eng. Lit.' or something else. Yet again, in a still more challenging vein, perhaps we had better say our subject is 'writings, speeches, performances, films and other media partly in some variety of english'?

It's the same with the 'cultural' dimensions of our subject. Should 'English' be conceived primarily as the cultural heritage, even the property of a specific people located in or identified with just one part of the British Isles (i.e. England)? Or should 'English' be recognised as a global resource, cutting across many cultures and charged with expressing (or appropriating or negotiating) many different kinds of personal, social and historical experience, and many kinds of ethnic, regional, gender and class identity? Alternatively, in another sphere, do we hail 'English' as a conduit for high **art** and 'elite' culture, or as a site where *popular, 'mass media' and other versions of culture can be played out? Finally (or perhaps first) do we see English Studies as a dimension of Cultural or Communication Studies? Do we align it with Humanities or Arts or Education or even Social Sciences? Or do we see it as a pervasively multidisciplinary resource, as in 'English/Writing across the Curriculum' programmes?

Clearly, then, the very act of naming and 'placing' the subject is itself part of the challenge. Simply to say what we are studying turns out to be a remarkably complex business, a source of fascination as well as frustration. Sometimes it is a matter of deciding between a plural and a singular, an upper or a lower case ('English' or 'englishes', say, or 'English Studies *are* . . .' as opposed to 'English Studies *is* . . .'). More often it is a matter of deciding precisely which other words we shall attach to 'English' and thereby get an extra handle on whatever it is we think we are picking up. At any rate English *Studies* is the catch-all term favoured here. It leaves the matter of precisely which English we are dealing with (Language/s? Literature/s? Culture/s?) tantalisingly open. It also allows us to recognise a variety of intellectual and educational trajectories, some converging and some diverging, while not insisting upon identical points of departure or arrival.

At this point we also need to ask how far our ultimate subjects are the people(s) responsible for using (or for being) 'English'. In that case the English we are concerned with is likely to be bound up with a whole range of other subjects: History, Politics, Economics, Sociology, Anthropology and Psychology, for instance. For how can we really understand how and why certain forms of language, literature and culture have come into and gone out of existence unless we also try to grasp who used and made them, when and where and why? At the very least, we must get to know something about English people, past and present, actual and imagined. And this in turn will oblige us to enquire what it means or has meant for specific groups at specific moments to be 'English' or 'English-speaking' (again there's a big difference), as well as what can be called 'English-spoken-to' (i.e., addressed, and perhaps instructed, commanded or labelled, through some form of English). All this is especially necessary in that competing versions and visions of 'England', 'Englishness' and 'English/wo/man' have been highly influential in the formulation of numerous social and historical agendas: political, commercial, educational, technological and scientific. By extension, we must also pay attention to competing versions and visions of 'Britain', 'Briton', 'British', as well as, say, 'America(n)', 'Australia(n)', 'Africa(n)', 'India(n)', 'Asia(n)'. Indeed, the teaching and learning of English (and American, etc.) have often served as sites for the airing (or stifling) of precisely such issues. At any rate it will be clear that *what* we mean by English cannot finally be separated from *who* we mean by English.

The sheer complexity and potential contentiousness of everything connected with 'England', 'English' and 'Englishness' can be confirmed by a few pithy observations and questions. (See the maps and the chronology in Appendices A and B for fuller information.)

England is not Britain. England is only one part of the British Isles

The latter at present include Scotland, Northern Ireland, Eire (the Republic of Ireland), Wales, the Isle of Man, the Hebrides and some of the Channel Islands. This

From the *Oxford English Dictionary* (1928, 1989)

ENGLISH

B. *substantive*
1.a. **The English language.**
First in the adverbial phrase,
on (now in) *English.* Also in
phrase **the King's, the
Queen's English**,
apparently suggested by
phrases like 'to deface the
king's coin'. In ninth century,
and probably much earlier,
Englisc was the name applied
to all the Angle and Saxon
dialects spoken in Britain.
The name English for the
language is thus older than
the name England for the
country. In its most
comprehensive use, it
includes all the dialects
**descended from the language
of the early Teutonic
conquerors of Britain;** but it
is sometimes popularly
restricted to the language
since the close of the
**'Anglo-Saxon' or fully
inflected stage,** sometimes
to the language and dialects
of **England proper as
distinguished** from those
of **Scotland, Ireland, US,
etc.;** and sometimes to the
literary or standard form
of the language as distinct
from **illiterate** or
ungrammatical speech,
etc.

ungrammatical speech But how far does speech have different structures and functions
from the **literary form**? And can or should a single model of 'grammar' be
superimposed on all language use?

Another **etc.** which leaves a lot unsaid. What of the vast and increasingly pervasive
networks of the modern media: TV, film, radio, audio, video, computer interfaces, the
World-Wide-Web . . .? And where will 'English' as language(s) or literature(s) or
culture(s) figure in our as yet unheard, unseen and unlived futures?

The English language or englishes? One or many – historically, geographically, socially and by medium?

the King's, the Queen's English? Or anyone's and everyone's, regardless of rank, sex, age, education, region and nation? Yours and mine, for instance?

The name English . . . the name England . . . So the people(s), language(s) and country need to be carefully distinguished. We/they/it should not be collapsed and simply identified with one another.

descended from the language of the early Teutonic conquerors of Britain. So the origins of English are to be traced beyond Britain – as are subsequent developments. 'It' is always coming from or going to somewhere else. And what of the earlier and later *non*-Teutonic languages and cultures which also conquered or settled Britain: Celtic, Roman, French, Gujarati, Hindi . . . ?

Is **Anglo-Saxon** (i.e. English before the mid-eleventh century) a crucial or incidental part of English Studies? Do we acknowledge or ignore the **fully inflected** stage of the language, the primarily oral poetry, and the peculiar blends of heroic paganism and Christianity?

England proper, as distinguished from . . . Scotland, Ireland . . . Or perhaps we should be 'improper' and recognise British (not English) Studies, and the multicultural diversity of the Dis/United Kingdom, including Scottish, Irish and Welsh cultures in and on their own terms?

as distinguished from . . . US. Where do 'English Studies' end and 'American Studies' begin? And is/are the the United States any more 'united' than the United Kingdom? What of black, white, Native American, Hispanic, Chinese, Jewish . . . cultures? Or is the whole of the world in some respects already 'American'?

What if you are part of this **etc.**? One of the first-, second-, or third-language English speakers in Australia, New Zealand, Africa, India, Singapore, Hong Kong . . . ? What if you are still only represented by ' . . . .'?!

But how **standard** *are* the **literary** forms of various kinds of poem, novel and play? Does standard mean 'of approved quality' (as in 'keeping up standards') or simply 'average, usual' (the 'standard' as opposed to the 'deluxe' model)? Is everything else merely '*non*-standard', including most speech and all less privileged regional and social varieties?

Does **illiterate** mean technically 'without literacy', 'unable to read and write', or is it generally stigmatised as 'uneducated', even 'ignorant'? Either way, what of oral and visual cultures in pre- and post-literate phases of English, and the positive revaluation of communicative practices other than writing and print? What other kinds of technological 'literacy'/competency are also in play – and demand – now?

Figure 1 OED definition of English (For a somewhat different use of this entry, see Ricks and Michaels, 1990: 1.)

casual mistaking of part for whole is widespread. It is readily understandable amongst non-natives but perhaps more remarkable amongst natives. (Predictably, the latter tend to have been born and bred in England rather than Scotland, Wales or Ireland.)

A United – or disunited – Kingdom?

Britain has constantly been subject to the redrawing of national and regional boundaries. It is easy to forget that the United Kingdom is a comparatively recent and very variable geopolitical entity: it was only formally constituted in 1801. Indeed, through the Middle Ages and right up to the twentieth century the internal history of the British Isles has been characterised by internecine wars, exploitation, 'plantations', clearances and migrations, as well as by education policies which had the effect of eradicating or marginalising other native (i.e. non-English) languages and cultures. All these were the subsequently naturalised and normalised effects of *colonisation *within* the British Isles: the consolidation of England and (the) English in Wales, Scotland and Ireland. Henry VIII formally annexed Wales by a series of Acts (1536–43) (there had been 'plantations' of English settlers in Ireland and Wales since the twelfth century). Meanwhile, in Scotland the 'Union of Crowns' (1603) was one attempt to concentrate the monarchy in a single figure (James VI of Scotland / James I of England). However, the Revolution of 1649 cut off its head (in the person of Charles I) and set up a Commonwealth and Protectorate under Cromwell instead. Following the Restoration of the monarchy (1660), it was not until 1801 that the United Kingdom (including Ireland) came into being even as a constitutional entity. But clearances, *enclosures, migration and uneven regional development continued; hence, in the nineteenth and early twentieth centuries, the 'industrial North', the 'rural South' and London as Cobbett's 'Great Wen'. Mutual suspicion and regional/ national stereotyping also persist, as witnessed by the perennial joke formula 'Have you heard the one about the Irishman, the Scotsman, the Welshman and the Englishman ... ?' In some respects, then, none of these 'unions' guaranteed a genuine 'Union of Peoples'. As recently as 1921 the British Isles saw the creation of Eire (Southern Ireland) as a sovereign republic. And even today, in view of their patchy economic development and distinctive political histories, it is still far from certain that Northern Ireland and Scotland (both of which have their own regional/ national assemblies) will always remain parts of the United Kingdom. Finally, notice that the phrase the United *Kingdom* marks the place as residually *male* and *royal*. There is still no 'United *Queen*dom' – nor yet any sign of a 'British *Republic*'. All this is particularly remarkable given the recent preponderance of long-lived *female* monarchs (Victoria and Elizabeth II) and the recurrently shaky position of the British monarchy as a whole.

Britain in or out of Europe?

England, Scotland, Ireland and Wales have all had very specific and to some extent separate historical relations with various parts of continental Europe. Shifting permutations of alliance with France, Spain and Germany have been common – sometimes *against* England. Ireland and Scotland, in particular, have often maintained continental ties and traditions (especially with France and Spain) even when England has broken them in times of war and intense economic competition. Wales, meanwhile, has close linguistic and cultural links with Brittany as well as with Ireland. In recent times, uncertainties about Britain's relations with the rest of Europe have been acutely obvious. Successive post-war governments have prevaricated about membership of the Common Market, the European Community, the European Parliament and, latterly, the European Monetary Union (with its single proposed currency). The following formulas seem to be etched into the language. Should Britain 'go in' or 'stay out'? When 'in' what terms should this be 'on' – purely commercial or also social, legal and political? How far can Britain 'go it alone'? What of some supposed 'special relationship' with the USA? And where, if anywhere, does all this leave that vestige of empire, the British Commonwealth? More generally, what are the pros and cons of Britain joining some future 'United States of Europe'? Would this really amount to a 'loss of sovereignty'? And so on. Whatever the short-term answers to these questions, it is clear that in the longer term precisely what we mean by 'Britain' and 'Britons', as well as 'England' and 'English', will be closely tied up with what we mean by 'Europe' and 'European' (now, again, including the problems and potentials of Eastern Europe). Significantly, for those who see England and Britain from outside Europe (from Japan or Africa or America, for instance), this has long been the perception. They usually speak of 'going to Europe', and casually assume that this includes Britain. In any case, even the much vaunted (or lamented) status of Britons as an 'island race' no longer holds. The road and rail tunnel has linked Britain directly to mainland Europe since 1994. Technically, the British *Isles* no longer are!

Britain and (or as) its empire? America and (or as) its sphere of influence?

When a country becomes as globally extensive and influential as Britain has been and as America is, it becomes difficult to decide where it begins and ends. How far is the empire to be identified with the 'mother land' or the *colonies? Does the sphere of influence have one or many **centres**? For, obviously, in the course of military, commercial and cultural expansion, other centres continually spring up and are recognised. Gradually these new centres compete with the old centre and eventually they may displace it. The margins thereby become independent centres in their own rights, while the orginal centre may itself become marginal or dependent. America's colonial and POSTCOLONIAL relation to Britain is symptomatic in this respect. America was once a dependent colony but is now a superpower which dwarfs the mother country. This process of ceaseless de- and re-location, *de- and *recentring, does much to explain the elusiveness of 'English' when we try to grasp it in a fully historical and global context. If so many English-speaking cultures turn out to be 'elsewhere', then we need to radically rethink our notions of 'here' and 'there', 'inside' and 'outside', as well as centres and **margins**.

English as a national and international resource – local and global

As a result both of earlier British imperial expansion and later American spheres of influence, it is impossible to pin down either the English language or

English-speaking peoples within a single set of national boundaries. English is a massively international resource. It pervades and often dominates areas of global life ranging from technology, science and education to commerce, advertising and pop. Around a third of the world's population (i.e. two billion people) is routinely exposed to some version of English. English is spoken in far more countries than any other language. English is the international language of air traffic control and telecommunications. By the same token, as a system of social exchange and cultural capital, English is the exclusive property of neither Britons nor Americans. (Nor, incidentally, do all British and American citizens speak English as a 'mother tongue' or first language.) One thing, at any rate, is clear. The vast majority of literature, film and performance in English is currently produced by and for people who have *no* direct experience of or association with England. It is *not* made in England: such labels as 'made in America' or 'made in Asia' or 'made in Jamaica' would need to be affixed to most work produced in English now. Indeed, to be even more discriminating, for the work of routinely migrant figures such as Derek Walcott, we would need a label like 'made somewhere between St Lucia, Trinidad, New England, New York, Africa and India'! Of course such labels are crude. Like passports, they tell us little more than places of birth and residence, countries of departure and destination, nominal citizenship. Notwithstanding, they still remind us that texts and utterances in English can be identified with distinct national and regional cultures, even as they transgress, transcend or transform the boundaries of those cultures. English language(s) and literature(s) are at once both national and international, local and global, bounded and boundless. We must therefore ask the next question with persistence, resource and sensitivity. It is perhaps *the* question, and is therefore given a section of its own.

1.2   ONE ENGLISH LANGUAGE, LITERATURE, CULTURE – OR MANY?

This question can be put in four dimensions: historically, geographically, socially and in terms of medium. All these dimensions both converge and diverge, and are simply distinguished for convenience. (Illustrations can be found throughout Part Five.)

1.2.1   Historically one or many?

English, like other languages, changes over time. Gradually it changes into 'other' Englishes. For instance, Britain has long been – and continues to be – home to many other languages, literatures and cultures than English alone. All have contributed to the constitution of the changing thing we call, for convenience, English.

A *Germanic base

Germanic languages form the fundamental substratum of English, which is based on the various Scandinavian languages and dialects introduced by successive waves of Norse invaders and settlers from the sixth to tenth centuries. At this time the language was much more highly inflected and had much freer word-order than modern English. It probably sounded more like modern Norwegian or Dutch, and had some distinctive letter forms based on the older Runic alphabet. Much of the poetry was *oral, had a distinctive **verse-form** based on alliteration and stress (not rhyme and syllable length) and explored a combination of pagan heroic and Christian themes. Society at the time was primarily based on *cynn* (kin, blood ties) and life organised around the village or small town. For a sharp sense of the many linguistic, literary and cultural differences between this form of 'English' and one with which you are more familiar, see 'Wulf and Eadwacer' (5.1.1).

Early *Celtic survivals   in English often have to do with nature, especially the landscape. They include the words 'brock' for badger, 'dunn' for grey, 'torr' and 'crag' for outcrops and high rocks, as well as such names of rivers as Avon (Celtic for 'water'), Exe, Thames, Usk, and names of regions such as Cumberland and Cornwall (both of which feature the names of Celtic tribes) as does *Ireland* (the 'Iershe') and, most prominently, the name *Brit*ain itself (from the 'Britto/Brettas'). Meanwhile, Welsh along with Irish and Scots Gaelic persist to the present day as languages in their own right, latterly sustained by national revival movements and bilingual educational programmes. (Cornish, another Celtic language, disappeared in the eighteenth century.) In conjunction with English, the result has been a wide range of regional/national **varieties** of Anglo-Irish, Anglo-Welsh and Scots which are distinct-ive in **accent** and **dialect**. The associated cultures have their own highly developed and distinctive traditions in writing, performance and the arts, and in the church and education. Some of these features can be found in the work by Burns (5.4.5), Leonard (5.2.5 d), Kelman (5.2.6), Synge (5.3.4 a), Doyle (5.2.5 e) and Thomas (5.3.4 b). Other features of Northern and Southern regional dialects of English, most of them ultimately grounded in Anglo-Saxon distribution, can be sampled in the Cumberland version of 'Humpty Dumpty' (5.4.1 b), Barnes's Dorset poem 'Woak Hill' (5.1.6), and Harrison's mimicking of a Yorkshire skinhead in *v.* (5.4.5 c).

*Latinate traces of *colonisation, Christianity and classical learning
Latin is evident at a variety of levels corresponding to different historical moments. Elements of *Imperial Roman Latin* were already present in the languages of the Norse invaders and settlers. Many had to do with building and settlement ('tigle'/ tile, 'weall'/wall, 'straet'/street); with trade ('pund'/ pound, 'ceapian'/to buy (hence 'cheap'), 'mangian'/to trade (hence fishmonger); and domestic utensils ('disc'/dish, 'cetel'/kettle, 'candel'/candle). In Britain the early Germanic tribes also met some Roman place-names more or less intact (e.g., the elements '-caster/-cester/chester', all derived from Latin *castra* meaning 'camp', as in Lancaster, Leicester, Manchester and Chester). A second, later phase of *Christian, ecclesiastical and educational Latin* began to make its mark in the fourth century with the first Romano-Christian missions, and these were reinforced by the Benedictine revival of the ninth and tenth centuries. The words 'school', 'epistle', 'grammar', 'bishop', 'calendar', 'creed', 'choir', 'cleric', 'demon', 'hymn' and 'paradise' all came into English from Latin at this time. For the third phase of Latin influence we must look to late medieval and especially Renaissance borrowings. These were often of a specifically **classical, learned* nature, chiefly to do with literature and the law. Characteristic examples are '*allegory', 'contradiction', 'encyclopedia', 'equator', 'prosecute', 'suppress', 'testimony', '*imaginary', 'monosyllable' and 'transcribe'. From the sixteenth century

these words were supplemented by specialist words from the recently rediscovered classical *Greek* (e.g., '*absurdity', 'autograph', '*critic', 'presbyter(ian)'/elder). This phase of borrowing, along with the literary and artistic imitations of Roman and Greek models which accompanied it, is generally called *neo*-classical. *Translations of the **Bible** in particular contributed to the naturalising of many Latin and Greek forms as English during this period. Individual writers, and even whole discourses, can to some extent be distinguished in so far as their language is more or less *Latinate. Milton's poetry is quite heavily Latinate, for instance (see 5.1.4 a); whereas the poetry of Clare is not (see 5.1.5). Certain specialist varieties of the language such as those of medicine, the law, science and technology are often characterised by a preponderance of Latin- and Greek-derived elements. So are the generalised varieties of administration and bureaucracy.

*English becomes partly *French.* French influences within English can be identified with two phases: Norman *colonisation and Parisian Court French. First there was the Norman French phase associated with the Norman Conquest and its aftermath (1066–twelfth century). The borrowings at this time signalled the superimposition of a new kind of feudal organisation on the existing social structures of Anglo-Saxon England. The result was the adoption of Anglo-Norman words such as 'master' and 'mistress', 'castle', 'garrison', 'judgement', 'mansion' and 'bailiff'. Also observable during this period is the widespread tendency to differentiate natural objects and cultural practices along lines laid down by the language at its various social levels. Thus, famously, we find the Anglo-Saxon words for 'pig', 'sheep' and 'calf' used to refer to the live or 'raw' animals, while their Anglo-Norman counter- parts were used to refer to the dead, prepared or 'cooked' meats: respectively, 'bacon/pork', 'mutton' and 'veal' (cf. Modern French *porc, mouton* and *veau*). In this way a social hierarchy was woven into the very fabric of the language. There is the low status Anglo-Saxon of the colonis*ed* who tend the animals, as distinct from high status Anglo-Norman of the colonis*ers* who tend to eat the animals! Such sociolinguistic stratification reminds us that a perceived **difference** *between* cultures is often embodied as a perceived difference *within* a culture once those cultures blend. Similar processes can be observed in the later phase of French influence. Court French (also called 'Paris' or 'Ile de France' French) was influential throughout Europe from the twelfth to nineteenth centuries, most notably in the arts, fashion, and food and drink. Thus it is to this period, especially the later Middle Ages, that we can attribute the introduction of a whole range of French words which have come to dominate, even designate, these areas. And they did this by displacing or replacing their Anglo-Saxon equivalents. Of immediate relevance to us is the fact that the following 'key' terms are all French (not Old English: OE) in origin:

'LANGUAGE' (cf. OE 'tongue'); 'LITERATURE' (cf. OE '(ge)writ'); 'CULTURE' (cf. OE 'game(n)', 'play'); 'poet' and **'author'** (cf. OE 'scop/shaper' and 'maker'); 'music' (cf. OE 'glee'); 'conversation' (cf. OE 'speech'), '*story' (cf. OE 'tale'), as well as '*rhyme' and '*romance'. (These last two have no Old English equivalents and signal the distinctive contribution of French literary forms as such.)

Chaucer, for instance, was famed as a remarkable 'translateur' of things French (as well as *Italian) and wrote several romances. Moreover, all his poetry is in rhyme modelled substantially on French and Italian forms, not in the alliterative stressed measure favoured by his Anglo-Saxon predecessors and some of his more northerly contemporaries (compare extracts 5.1.2 b–d).

But French had a much wider and deeper effect on the language and, by implication, the culture as a whole. Witness the French origins of words connected with:

♦   *food and cooking*: appetite, dinner, supper, taste, fry, spice, sugar, cuisine;
♦   *the home*: basin, plate, cellar, chair, chamber, chimney, closet, pantry, parlour, towel.

Also note the French origins of such routine terms in all the major word-classes:

♦   *adjectives*: blue, brown, real, royal, sure and special;
♦   *nouns*: city, country, power, poverty and person;
♦   *verbs*: advise, allow, obey, please, prefer, refuse and receive.

All these lists could be massively extended; for the vocabulary of English more than doubled in size and was throughly transformed between its Old and Middle English phases (i.e. the tenth to the fifteenth centuries).

Anglo-Saxon, French and Latin together provide the main MULTI-CULTURAL foundation of the English language. A handy way of distinguishing the various strains within English is in terms of three levels of *style. Words derived from Anglo-Saxon tend to be more basic and direct and are often monosyllabic; French-derived words tend to be a little more refined and polite or formal; Latin-derived words tend to be more learned and technical and are often polysyllabic.

THREE LEVELS OF 'ENGLISH' STYLE

from *Anglo-Saxon (basic)	from *French (refined)	from *Latin (learned)
holy	sacred	consecrated
ask	question	interrogate
rise	mount	ascend
fire	flame	conflagration
kingly	royal	regal

English continued to change in many ways from the seventeenth century onwards. However, for subsequent developments we must increasingly look beyond, and not just within, the British Isles. At this point, therefore, we slip some 'geographical' lenses on top of our 'historical' ones. This will allow us to see that the *internal* multiculturalism of English (both embracing and being embraced by aspects of French and Latin, as well as Celtic cultures) is supplemented by an *external* multiculturalism involving languages, peoples and ways of life beyond Europe altogether.

1.2.2   Geographically one or many?

English varies from place to place, sometimes beyond recognition. Currently, for instance, there are many highly distinctive national varieties of English, even to the point of competing **standards**: Caribbean, Indian, African, Australian and Singaporean, as well as British and American. Regional **varieties** are also myriad. These range over minor or pronounced differences in **accent**: within Britain alone, the words 'This is the news' may be delivered so diversely in Glasgow, Belfast, Cardiff, Liverpool and London as to confound many native speakers (e.g., 5.2.5 d). Often they extend to marked differences in **dialect**, affecting vocabulary and grammar as well as pronunciation. Cumberland in England, Kingston in Jamaica, Brooklyn in the USA, for instance, can all boast huge differences in word choice, inflection, combination and order, especially when the conversation runs to talk about such basics as food, sex, work, play and death. For examples, see Nichols (5.4.5. e, Guyana); Collins (5.1.9 c, Grenada); Tutuola and Achebe (5.2.4 e–f, Nigeria –Yoruba and Igbo); πO (5.1.9 a, Greek Australian); Chan Wei Meng (5.1.9 b, Singapore); Hurston and Bambara (5.2.4 d and 5.3.5 a – varieties of Black American); Fugard (5.3.4 c, S. Africa). Meanwhile some differences amount to virtually different languages. This is the case with restricted-use pidgins and full-blown *creoles. In the latter we witness new languages in the making from the fusion of old ones, only one of which may be some form of English.

ENGLISH AND EMPIRES FROM THE SIXTEENTH TO THE TWENTIETH CENTURY

The following samples of English vocabulary demonstrate the complex material and cultural **differences** characterising various moments of *colonisation from the seventeenth to the twentieth century. These are just a few of the many verbal traces of past empires which survive in the living language of the present:

- from *Spanish* and *Portuguese*: apricot, armada, banana, cannibal, cocoa, guitar, maize, mulatto, negro, potato, tobacco, yam;
- from *Italian*: balcony, **carnival**, opera, *sonnet, stanza, violin;
- from *Dutch*: cruise, easel, landscape, yacht;
- from *Arabic, Persian and Turkish*: caravan, coffee, harem, sheikh, yoghurt;
- from *North America*: names of states – Virginia (after Elizabeth I, the 'Virgin Queen'); Pennsylvania (after William Penn plus Latin 'woodland'); N. and S. Carolina (after Charles II); Georgia (after George III); California (Spanish 'earthly paradise'); Texas (Spanish for 'allies'); Oklahoma (Choctaw for 'red people'); Kansas (Sioux for 'land of the south wind people'); N. and S. Dakotas (Sioux for 'friends'); also powwow, chipmunk, toboggan, skunk, totem, wigwam;
- from *Africa: South* – Hottentot, voodoo; apartheid, trek, kraal (from Dutch/Boer); *Central* – bongo, bwana, marimba, safari; *North* – assassin, emir, sherbet, zero;
- from the *Caribbean*: barbecue, cannibal, canoe, potato, yucca;
- from *India*: bungalow, chutney, curry, catamaran, guru, jungle, pyjama, pundit;
- from *Australia*: boomerang, dingo, kangaroo, koala, wombat (a third of Australian place-names are from 'Aboriginal' languages);
- from *New Zealand*: haka, hongi, kiwi, pakeha (white) (many place-names are Maori).

1.2.3   Socially one or many?

English varies from group to group and situation to situation, sometimes so as to be hardly recognisable as the same language. We all use different kinds of words, or similar words differently, in different situations: when we speak informally with family or friends as opposed to when we speak more or less formally with someone in authority (the police, doctors, teachers, etc.). The words 'I love you' whispered in private in bed and the words 'I solemnly swear to tell the truth, the whole truth and nothing but the truth' sworn in public in a court of law are clearly worlds apart. So is 'high' in 'high temperature', 'high school', 'high opinion of . . .', 'high time that . . .', 'high on speed', etc. – or 'love' when used of everything from chocolates to people, and pets to God. (You can go through the same operations with most words, drawing on a dictionary and word association. Most words touch on many worlds.) Notice, too, the myriad worlds involved in the languages (i.e. specialist terminologies) of, say, knitting and nuclear physics, skate-boarding and stylistics, computing and greetings cards, instruction manuals and product labels, personal ads and sports commentary, accounting and acupuncture (see 5.4.7 for a tiny sample of the many and constantly evolving **varieties**). These are all ostensibly parts of the same language, but each has its own highly distinctive choices and combinations, forms and functions.

   Moreover, no single person or group ever uses the whole language (in this respect 'the whole language' is an illusory construct). Instead, each of us draws on different parts in so far as we deal with certain topics (common or specialist) or belong to certain social groups (defined by education, occupation, class, gender, ethnicity and region, etc.). Current English has over a million words, and rising. And yet the *active vocabulary of even a highly educated person is scarcely more than 30,000 words (70,000 if we add recognised but not used words: i.e *passive vocabulary). In this sense, paradoxically, 'the whole language' is everybody's and yet nobody's. We all routinely switch from one social variety to another. But still nobody uses more than a tiny fraction of the varieties available. And in any case these are always changing over time and space, being ceaselessly replaced or regenerated. (Do *you* know the technical terms and specialist practices of, say, thatching, basket weaving *and* racing pigeons *as well as* those of maxillo-facial surgery, glue-sniffing, econometrics and 'cyberpunk' . . . ? I'm sure I don't!)

1.2.4   One 'code' many media?

People speak differently from how they write. If for no other reason, this is because sounds in the air and marks on paper or screens have substantially distinct properties and potentialities. The basic linguistic 'code' may be common but it is realised in materially different MEDIA. In this respect the medium *is* the message. Moreover, within **speech** there are clearly crucial distinctions between casual conversation and formal 'speech-making', between scripted and unscripted delivery, between monologue and dialogue. A chat over coffee is different from a class presentation; a 'word in the ear' is different from a sermon; a collectively work-shopped improvisation is different from a film shooting-script.

   Writing, too, takes place in many materials and on many occasions: inscriptions cut into marble or wood or bone; letters dyed or painted on cloth; ink scratched into manuscript or pressed into smudgy newsprint or high gloss paper; shopping lists scribbled on scraps of envelopes with children's crayons; ball-penned postcard messages partly obscured by the stamp; carefully redrafted letters or essays; chalk on blackboards and marker pens on overhead transparencies; meticulously typed and corrected c.v.s or forms for job applications; hastily typed e-mail messages; the embossed lettering on plastic credit-cards; computer-assisted letter-designs which form and re-form on TV and PC screens; letters blazing forth from neon lights or stored away in paper archives or electronic circuits, buried in the ground or circulating in hyperspace. And so on to the last syllable of recordable language.

Moreover, all of these words may be accompanied, shot through – even transformed into – still and moving **images**, as well as music and sounds in general. Clearly, 'the word' leads a hectic and versatile life. It gets around in a prodigious variety of media: on the lips, in the ear and eye, in the air, on the street, on the page, on the screen, in the mind, in the memory (human or machine) – in fact in every conceivable material from fire and sand to brain cells and electronic circuitry. In short, rolling all the above together, English is a prodigiously and increasingly multimedia resource. Of course, the same can be said of other 'world' languages: Spanish, French, German, Russian and Japanese, for instance. But it needs to be said loud and clear with a language as globally, socially and technologically ubiquitous as English. Subject to such diverse pressures and carrier of so many meanings in such diverse materials and contexts, we may well wonder whether we all really are 'speaking the same language' – let alone writing and viewing it.

1.3   SUMMARY: ONE AND MANY

Clearly all the many 'Englishes' referred to above *are* related. All the historical, geographical, social and media varieties are interconnected. They have what Wittgenstein would call 'family resemblances'. They *share* their differences. For one thing, most moderately competent readers of English can to some extent understand most of the varieties of English represented in Part Five. And with only a little assistance, in the way of notes and guidance, they can grasp them quite fully. This can happen because, for all the differences in vocabulary and spelling and grammar, there are enough consistent and commonly recognisable items and structures for us to say 'Yes, this is *some* kind of English!' Even English-speakers who could not read would still recognise and to some extent understand many of these samples if they were read out loud. Many Middle English and Afro-Caribbean varieties (e.g., 5.1.2 and 5.1.9 c), are actually more not less comprehensible when heard rather than read. Many of these texts were built for *oral delivery, and differences of spelling can be deceptive.

For all these reasons it is perhaps best to see English language/s, literature/s, culture/s as one *and* many. Theoretically, we can express this dynamic in a number of ways. *Bakhtin would speak of English, as he also spoke of Russian, as a shifting site defined by the interplay of *centrifugal and *centripetal forces. These forces simultaneously thrust both outwards and inwards, but never with equal force. The system is always 'off balance'. He would also point to the fact that the internal *heteroglossia of a language (its inherent 'varied-tonguedness') is deeply implicated in, and cannot finally be distinguished from, its relations to the external polyglossia (the surrounding 'many-tonguedness'). Languages thus exist and shift through the dialogic interplay of 'internal' and 'external' forces. They are braced against and even within other languages.

   *Chomsky would talk of the 'generative' qualities of language, the fact that an infinite array of permutations can be generated by a finite number of principles. POSTSTRUCTURALISTS would push that idea further and in different directions. They would insist that 'English', like any other system or structure, is a product of its *inter*relations, the relations *between* its elements, and cannot be located in any item or part as such. *Derrida, for instance, would insist that the structure of English is 'open', incomplete, always already in process. Consequently, we must speak of it as having not one 'origin', 'centre' or 'aim', but potentially many and different. Indeed, Derrida would add that, strictly, we have to 'defer' the notion of 'English as a whole', and had better conceive of it as a series of 'holes'. Its infinite **differences** lead to playful plurality not solemn sameness. POSTMODERNISTS would maintain something similar but in another dimension. They point particularly to the contemporary sphere and the sheer multiplicity of media as well as the global heterogeneity of cultures now involved in any communicative activity. English as a 'world language' and, in its American form, a 'world culture' is especially amenable to such global dispersals and localised reconfigurations. In a full-blown postmodernist view, 'English' is a compound of language/literature/culture/media (the terms merge or are no longer relevant); is everywhere *hybrid and nowhere 'pure'; and is consequently constantly reforming under the pressure of other languages/literatures/cultures/media.

   But whatever model we use or theorist we invoke, the main thing is to attempt to grasp English as a process as well as a series of products. It is a system which is interrelated and bound together over time and space and peoples by certain principles of coherence. But at the same time it is a system which is open, always in the making – never closed and never finally made. One *and* many.

'ENGLISH' IS WHAT SOMEONE SAYS IT IS . . .

In a practical and pressing sense, it is the designers and teachers of your courses who will have already framed the main terms of reference within which you will address 'English'. And every department of English, even every person within that department, will frame the subject with slightly or very different emphases. Nonetheless, ultimately and most importantly, it is still only you who can decide 'which English' is most interesting and important to you. With this in mind, work over the passages, maps and diagrams in the activities that follow.

1.4   ACTIVITIES, READING

(a)   *The 'Oxford English Dictionary' (OED) revisited*
      Return to the extract from the *OED* featured at the beginning of this part pp. 10–11. Go on to read the following account of the development of the dictionary then discuss each of the points highlighted on that double-page spread. Go on to read 'The English language – or englishes?'; 'The King's, the Queen's English', etc.

The *OED*, initially called the *New English Dictionary on Historical Principles*, was conceived as a monument of late nineteenth- and early twentieth-century scholarship. First conceived in 1857, it was executed by teams of editors and legions of contributors between 1878 and 1928 (when it was first published). By 1989 it had grown to twenty volumes with supplements integrated, and contained entries on over half a million words illustrated by two and a half million quotations. The *OED* thus constitutes one of the most impressive and informative dictionaries on earth.

However, like all texts, dictionaries are a product of their historical moment. The *OED* is no exception. It emphasises **writing** (chiefly from 'literary' sources) not speech, and older not contemporary forms. It also assumes or asserts the primacy of narrowly native 'English from England' (rather than from the British Isles in general), let alone from America, Australasia, India and Africa. In short, the *OED* is a supreme monument to empire too. Consequently, notwithstanding the thorough revisions of the 1989 edition, it has been estimated that there are at least as many 'English' words which do not appear in the *OED* as ones that do (i.e. a further half-million). The *OED* therefore has to be supplemented by extra entries and alternative definitions from other inter/national and specialist dictionaries: of American, Australian, Anglo-Indian and Afro-Caribbean Englishes; of Anglo-Saxon and Middle English; of dialects and 'slang'; of technology and science; of occupations and hobbies; of linguistics and literature, of cultural theory, communications and computing, and so on. All in all, then, the *OED* offers an extremely powerful but also extremely partial version of English. (For further confirmation, see the very different entries on 'English' in Webster's *New American Dictionary* (1828; third edition 1961) and Ramson's *Australian National Dictionary* (1988).

Such observations may be disturbing to those who casually appeal to 'the dictionary' and 'dictionary definitions' as absolute **authorities** without caring to specify which one. But they would not altogether surprise the editors of the *OED* themselves. Here are some of *their* observations from the 'General Explanations' (1933, pp. xxi–xxii). Use these as focuses for discussion too:

(i)   The vocabulary of a widely-diffused and highly cultivated living language is not a fixed quantity circumscribed by definite limits [. . .] And there is absolutely no defining line in any direction: the circle of the English language has a well-defined centre but no discernible circumference.

(ii)   The Language presents yet another undefined frontier when it is viewed in relation to time. The living vocabulary is no more permanent in its constitution than definite in its extent. It is not today what it was a century ago, still less what it will be a century hence.

(iii)   No one man's English is all English.

(b)   *Putting yourself on the map(s)*
Turn to the maps of Britain, the USA and the world in Appendix A (pages 383–385). Use one or all three, as appropriate.

♦   Mark where you are now, where you have lived, and where you were born.
♦   Where in the world, as far as you know, did your family and ancestors come from or go to? Mark those places too.
♦   Identify those English-speaking cultures that are most familiar to you and those that are more or less remote.

♦   Mark the countries associated with the following writers, using the notes supplied
      in Part Five:

      On the map of the world: Achebe (5.2.4 f); Behn (5.2.2 a); Doyle (5.2.5 e); Tutuola
      (5.2.4 e); Nichols (5.4.5 e); Rich (5.1.8); Dickinson (5.4.5 d); Hurston (5.2.4 d);
      Byron (5.1.4 d); Kipling (5.2.4 b); Ibsen (5.3.3); Fugard (5.3.4 c); Rhys (5.2.3 e);
      Marshall-Stoneking (5.4.4 e); πO (5.1.9 a); Frame (5.2.1 d); Chan Wei Meng
      (5.1.9 b).
      On the map of Britain: Chaucer (5.1.2 b); the 'Pearl' poet (5.1.2 d); Langland (5.1.2
      c); the Chester 'Noah' (5.3.2 a); Austen (5.2.3 b); Barnes (5.1.6); Leonard (5.2.5
      d); Thomas (5.3.4 b); Kelman (5.2.6); Harrison (5.4.5 c); Doyle (5.2.5 e); Nichols
      (5.4.5 e); Fanthorpe (5.4.6 e).

♦   Compare your answers with those of friends and colleagues. Gather them all
      together and superimpose a group map on the one supplied. How much of the
      English-speaking world have you collectively 'covered'? Conversely, what for you
      remains as yet relatively unknown?

READING: Lively and informative surveys of English which combine global and historical
perspectives with attention to language, literature and culture are: D. Graddol *et al. English:
History, Diversity and Change* 1996; R. Carter and J. McRae *The Routledge History of
Literature in English: Britain and Ireland* 1997; R. McCrum *et al. The Story of English*
1992; R.W. Bailey, *Images of English: A Cultural History of the Language* 1992; W.
O'Donnell and L. Todd, *Variety in Contemporary English* 1992; and D. Crystal *The
Cambridge Encyclopedia of the English Language* 1995. The latter is an excellent reference
book and great for browsing too.
     Critical investigations of the role of contemporary English in the world are: J. Cheshire
(ed.) *English around the World: Sociolinguistic Perspectives* 1992; A. Pennycook *The
Cultural Politics of English as an International Language* 1994 and S. Goodman and D.
Graddol (eds) *Redesigning English: New Texts, New Identities* 1996. More conservative is
R. Quirk and H.G. Widdowson (eds) *English in the World: Teaching and Learning the
Language and Literatures* 1985. A previously standard textbook, A.C. Baugh and T. Cable *A
History of the English Language*, 4th edn 1993, is now showing its age in terms of overall
emphasis (first edn 1951) but is still good on earlier periods. Handy collections of discussion
material can be found in D. Burnley (ed.) *The History of the English Language: A Source
Book*, 1992 and C. Ricks and L. Michaels (eds) *The State of the Language in the 1990s*
1990. A good guide and workbook combined is D. Freeborn *et al. Varieties of English*
1993. More specialist studies are: J. Platt *et al. The New Englishes* 1984; L. Todd *Modern
Englishes: Pidgins and Creoles* 1984; P. Trudgill *The Dialects of England* 1990; P. Trudgill
and J. Hannah *International English: A Guide to Varieties of Standard English* 1982 and
B. Kachru (ed.) *The Other Tongue: English across Cultures* 1992.
     Changing notions of England and Englishness, and Britain and Britishness, are explored
in: S. Bassnett (ed.) *Studying British Culture: An Introduction* 1996; J. Lucas, *England and
Englishness: Ideas of Nationhood in English Poetry 1688–1900* 1990; B. Doyle *English and
Englishness* 1989; R. Samuel (ed.) *Patriotism: The Making and Unmaking of British
National Identity* (3 vols) 1989; L. Colley *Britons* 1992; and J. Giles and T. Middleton
Writing Englishness 1900–1950: An Introductory Sourcebook on National Identity
1995. More wide-ranging is E. Said *Culture and Imperialism* 1993 and more theoretical is
H. Bhabha *The Location of Culture* 1994.

1.5   HOW STUDIED?

In the previous section we began to explore how 'English' operates as the name for a variety of languages, literatures, cultures and peoples. We now turn more particularly to the second element in the phrase 'English *Studies*'. The present section is deliberately framed so as to maintain the interrelatedness of *what* is studied and *how* it is studied. We also pay attention to *who* studies, *when* and *where* and *why*. 'Stud*ies*' can thus, if you wish, be conceived as both a plural noun (reminding us of the many things that are done) and a singular verb (reminding us of the actual process of what someone does). Either way, there is an emphasis on studies as a dynamic interplay of *products, *processes, *participants and *circumstances. Most immediately, *they are what we do*. Hence the framing of the following questions:

♦   What are the main materials, methods and models that can be used to study English? Which of them are you yourself currently involved in?
♦   What are the various kinds of *know-how* (i.e. skills, methods, strategies, techniques) through which the various kinds of *know-what* (i.e. 'content', substance, material) identified with 'English' can be realised?
♦   More theoretically, what are the possible **subject** positions that practitioners of 'English' (including learners and teachers) can take up with respect both to our *subject-matters* and to one another as actively participating *subjects*?

Our primary focus here is advanced English, chiefly in tertiary education. But there is much that relates to the teaching and learning of English in other sectors. It should also be added that though the following sub-sections are historical and theoretical in emphasis, they feed directly into the complex fabric of English as it is currently being maintained or unravelled and rewoven. Nor should the pressing significance of the history of the subject surprise us. University and college Englishes, as we see shortly, are hardly a century and a half old. But the traditions they represent are many and various, and often complex and contentious. They inform many actual 'presents' and point to many potential futures. (A practical review of study techniques as such will be found in Part Four: Textual Activities and Learning Strategies.)

1.5.1   English as a school subject

For most of its history 'English' at school has meant the basic skills of *literacy: learning to read and write. For only a small part of that history, from the late nineteenth century onwards, has 'English' meant learning to read and write *about literature*. Latin was the dominant medium of instruction at both school and university during the Middle Ages and much of the Renaissance, and even when English began to take over this role in the sixteenth century the chief languages and literatures studied were still *classical. The emphasis in English was on handwriting and grammar and (as print culture deepened from the eighteenth century) **standardised** *spelling and punctuation. All these were taught chiefly with a view to composing business letters, annotating accounts and drafting routine agreements. Anything more specialist in the legal, medical and scientific spheres, or anything more self-consciously literary, would be developed with classical models in mind, perhaps in Latin. It is interesting to reflect that 'English Literature' did not exist as a school or college subject for Chaucer, Shakespeare, Milton, Wordsworth, Austen or the Brontës; even though their works are now part of what is taught under that name. Women were at a peculiar disadvantage. They were formally debarred from universities till the late nineteenth century and at school generally discouraged from a high degree of literacy (especially knowledge of the classical languages and literatures). Significantly, however, this gave women something of a head start in the writing and reading of such low status **genres** as personal letters and journals, as well as the kinds of vernacular **novel** associated with them.

English, Christianity and a 'civilising' mission

The teaching of English at school has been heavily influenced by the Church for much of its history. It still is in some specifically religious schools and colleges. Therefore, it is to such institutions as the eighteenth- and nineteenth-century Charity Schools, Sunday Schools and Dissenting Academies that we must look for the beginnings of anything like mass education in English. Meanwhile, in the British Empire, education of 'natives' in English was almost wholly under the control of missionary schools of one denomination or another. Many of these schools taught English through – and with a view to – reading the **Bible**, which had been widely available in English *translations since the sixteenth century. The moral and cultural framing of 'English', and indeed its 'civilising' mission, have therefore often been assumed to be in some sense Christian.

The state takes control

Only in the late nineteenth and early twentieth centuries did the state begin to take substantial responsibility for school education of any kind, including schooling in English. (In Britain the most important Education Acts in this respect were in 1870, 1902, 1944 and 1989.) At the same time, significantly, 'English' began to include 'English LITERATURE', and the latter was increasingly charged with a variety of moral roles previously filled by religion. Paramount among these were the three tasks of

- ♦   heightening personal perception and refining sensibility;
- ♦   inculcating social propriety and enhancing public morality;
- ♦   promoting social solidarity and national identity.

One of the first and most influential advocates of this use of Literature in general, and English Literature in particular, was the school inspector, poet and essayist Matthew *Arnold (1822–88). But statements of similar positions on the *value of 'Eng. Lit', sometimes echoing Arnold, resonate throughout the twentieth century: notoriously in the Newbolt Report (1921), and famously in the work of such figures as F.R.*Leavis in the UK and many NEW CRITICS in the USA. Such arguments readily get extended to the function of English in education as a whole whenever and wherever there is talk of some kind of 'national curriculum' and proposed **standardisation**, often in the context of a sense of anxiety about everything from (declining) moral standards to (a loss of) national identity. Typically, especially in the populist media, the arguments are polarised in terms of 'Traditionalists versus Progressives' (in grotesque caricature, 'Rabid Right-wing Reactionaries' versus 'Looney Liberals and Lefties'). Either way, you might like to reflect that *neither* of the following positions, on its own, is likely to result in an adequate programme for English at any level. The two sides need to be combined and refined so as to produce a third which is different again. (The primary focus here is English at school. But the relevance of these arguments to university 'Schools of English' is obvious enough.)

Typically polarised positions on the functions of English in education:

'Traditional'	*'Progressive'*
English for employment	English for 'life'
Vocational training in specialism	Education of whole person
Promotion of single **'standard'** language	Recognition of **varieties**
Emphasis on **writing**	Attention to **speech**
Formal written examinations	Mixed-mode assessment
Dictionary definitions & grammatical rules	Flexibility of usage
Canon of 'great works'	Open or no canon
National curriculum	Local syllabuses
Single dominant cultural identity	Multicultural **differences**

READING: Palmer 1965; Brooker and Humm 1989: 13–72; Dixon 1991; Kress 1995.

ENGLISH LEARNT AS A SECOND OR THIRD LANGUAGE – OR FOR 'SPECIAL PURPOSES'

It is easy for those whose first (and perhaps only) language is English to assume that their language is the natural medium of education, and that all other languages are to be studied separately as 'foreign languages'. However, people for whom English is a second (or third) language, and who are perhaps studying it for 'special purposes' such as Business, Computing, Technology or Science, make up increasing numbers of those who are studying English at schools, colleges and universities worldwide. They tend to have very specific views of the nature of the subject and very specific needs. These needs are not directly addressed in this book. Nonetheless, it is salutary to remind ourselves that we all engage with specific **varieties** of English in more or less self-conscious and specifically targeted ways. In this respect, 'English Literature' or 'Literary Criticism' or 'Textual Analysis' are also kinds of 'English for Special Purposes'. It's simply that native-speaking students and teachers of university English courses (including myself) can easily forget this.

READING: Mercer and Swann 1996: 205–319; also Quirk and Widdowson 1985; Pennycook 1994.

1.5.2   English as a university degree subject

To the astonishment of many contemporary students, university 'English' is little more than a century and a half old. In Britain, the first chair of English Literature was created at University College, London in 1828, while the first chairs in English at Oxford and Cambridge were in Anglo-Saxon and established in 1849 and 1878, respectively. The first chair of English Literature at Oxford was in 1904. In the USA, the first chair of English was at Indiana in 1860, and Harvard got one in 1876. Since then, the university subject called 'English Language and Literature' or simply 'English Literature' has undergone a process of remarkable expansion (though we should add that, latterly, outside Britain at least, there are signs of perceptible contraction). To begin with, university English substantially displaced its pre-decessors, the Roman and Greek CLASSICS and RHETORIC (see below). These had been the areas usually dedicated to linguistic and literary study. At the same time, English substantially displaced THEOLOGY and the study of the **Bible** as a general focus for moral study. Recently, however, there are signs that English in turn is itself being challenged by (or transformed into) other subjects. Notable amongst these are LITERARY, CULTURAL, COMMUNICATION and MEDIA Studies.

Such processes of displacement and transformation appear to be fundamental to the very constitution of the subject. In fact, *paradigm shifts seem to be fundamental to the continuous reconstitution of all subjects, as of scientific knowledges and social **discourses** in general (see Foucault 1986: 31–120). In the following sub-sections we trace the changing nature of university English over the past century and a half. This is not only inherently interesting: it is also immediately urgent. With a subject that is so relatively 'young' much of this history is still with us. Many of the earlier stages are still evident in the contemporary organisation and practice of the discipline. In this respect, the subject is like a long geological fault displaying its multi-layered strata in different configurations and with different degrees of prominence at various places. It is visibly what it *is* because of what it *was*. These 'living histories' are what we turn to next.

READING: Kinneavy 1971: 5–18; Evans 1993: 3–18; Hawkes in Coyle *et al.* 1990: 926–40; Eagleton 1996: 15–46; Doyle 1989; Graff 1987; Baldick 1996: 1–19; Milner 1996: 1–26.

1.5.3   English and Classics

In the first instance, at its inception, the study of English was braced against and heavily influenced by the study of the classical languages, literatures and cultures of ancient Greece and Rome. English was initially viewed as an inferior upstart. Nonetheless, it eventually displaced Classics at the centre of the liberal arts curriculum. Many elements of a (neo-)classical critical agenda carried through, however. Thus among the 'Common Topics' in Part Three you will find a strong classical element in the entries on **art, comedy** and **tragedy** and **genre** (including *epic, *satire and *pastoral), **metre** (see **versification**), *myth and, of course, the term **classic** itself. In short, that older critical agenda is still in part ours now.

There is also the matter of 'classical' models and allusions in English literature. These figure especially in earlier writing for the simple reason that many pre-twentieth-century writers had at least a rudimentary education in Latin (less often Greek), and some had a lot. Thus, when reading Milton's Christian epic *Paradise Lost*, Pope's *mock-heroic *The Rape of the Lock* or Byron's satire *The Vision of Judgement* (see 5.1.4 a–d), it is important to know something about classical epics (such as Vergil's *Aeneid* and Homer's *Iliad* and *Odyssey*) and satires such as those of Horace and Juvenal. For pastoral, meanwhile, we may look to classical celebrations of the country in Theocritus, and especially Vergil's *Eclogues* and *Georgics*. Models such as these supplied a common frame of cultural reference amongst classically aware writers, readers and audiences. Even later poems such as Yeats's and Kazantsis's versions of 'Leda and the Swan' assume (though they do not absolutely require) acquaintance with stories from classical *mythology (see 5.1.7). Many of these stories of classical gods and nymphs are traceable to Ovid's *Metamorphoses* and may be followed up in reference books such as Brewer's *Dictionary of Phrase and Fable*.

At the same time it is important not to overstate the depth and significance of classical culture in English literature. Shakespeare, by Jonson's account, had 'small Latin and less Greek': much of the bard's knowledge of classical mythology, legend and ancient history evidently came by way of *translation (e.g., Golding's translation of Ovid's *Metamorphoses* (1565–7) and North's translation of Plutarch's *Lives* (1579)). Moreover, much of his audience's acquaintance with such things probably came through precisely such plays as Shakespeare's!

However, we must also recognise that there are many other CULTURES upon which English has drawn and in which it has been implicated. These range from early Germanic (e.g., 5.1.1) to contemporary Afro-Caribbean, Indian and Australian Aboriginal (see 5.4.5 e; 5.4.4 e). All of these also have their distinctive mythologies, legends and 'classic' stories, as well as their own characteristic **genres**. A common mistake to avoid, therefore, is simply equating 'classical culture' with 'high culture' and then identifying both of them exclusively with ancient Greece and Rome. The effect of this is to marginalise or romanticise all other (especially non-Western European) cultures as exotic and foreign or, alternatively, to label them as 'folk' and 'popular'. In short, in a global perpective, there are many more 'classic' traditions than one.

Nor need we limit our notions of *classics (see **canon**) and *mythologies to ancient cultures. Many modern commentators would argue that a grasp of the contemporary mythologies and distinctive genres of modern advertising, pop music and film (including 'classics' of all kinds – from 'classic' cars to 'classic' soap operas and cigars, and modern myths from Monroe to Madonna, and Elvis to 'Hovis') is rather more important for an understanding of *contemporary* English Studies than an acquaintance with Greek and Roman gods and heroes and their associated literary and pictorial genres. Significantly, then, the moment English Studies embraces the study of contemporary cultural 'classics' it tends to transform itself into Cultural Studies. And that's certainly not one of the transformation tales told by Ovid in his *Metamorphoses*!

READING: Wynne-Davies 1989: 411–13; Healy in Coyle *et al.* 1990: 964–74; Barthes 1957; Milner 1996 1–11.

1.5.4   English and Theology

In a formally religious age the power to promote and interpret 'good books', notably the **Bible** and commentaries upon it, had been vested in clerics and their academic counterparts: theologians. However, during the nineteenth century, as society became more secular and as education came to be the responsibility of the state rather than the Church, the academic power to decide what was worth reading gradually passed from clerics and theologians to teachers, especially teachers of

English (see above, 1.5.1). For late nineteenth- and earlier twentieth-century critics of CULTURE such as *Arnold, *Leavis and *Trilling, teachers of English were virtually a secular priesthood engaged in spreading 'the word' of a certain form of civilisation. Moreover, many American NEW CRITICS had an aesthetic and ethical agenda which had close ties with a certain form of Southern States Christianity.

Clerics and theologians also bequeathed the notion of a **canon** of permitted (as opposed to proscribed) books. This is still with us in recurrent debates about what should or should not be acknowledged as part of 'the canon of English Literature' (i.e. great works worthy of study). More subtly, theological habits of textual criticism and analysis which had been grounded in interpretation of Holy Scripture and in the practice of biblical commentary carried over into the interpretation of secular works. Partly as a result, it is still common for readers to expect that a text has some hidden meaning or secret 'message' if only they can crack the code. Such a mode of interpretation may fairly be called *allegorical in that it involves a supposed layering of meaning, a reading of the text at various 'levels' (literal, symbolic, moral and spiritual) and, ultimately, a stripping away of all these layers/ levels to get at some essential 'truth'. Much of this quest for ultimate **authority** in texts derives from the underlying expectations of biblical criticism and the orthodox study of Holy Writ. Many of the most systematic and sophisticated techniques of early textual *editing also derive from biblical, along with classical, scholarship. So do many significant strains of early work on *translation; for the first translations into English were often of the Latin, Greek and Hebrew Bibles.

Finally, it should be noted that knowledge of the Bible in any language, and of Christianity in general, can no longer be assumed in those studying English. This poses a major challenge when studying earlier English literature in particular (e.g., the Chester 'Noah' (5.3.2 a), *Paradise Lost* (5.1.4 a), Blake's *Milton* (5.4.6. b). In such cases it is reasonable to expect critical readers to become informed about the stories and language of the Bible, as they would with any other major sources and influences. Confusion only arises when it is implied that a largely secular and potentially MULTICULTURAL body of students should actually believe the doctrine.

READING: Wynne-Davies 1989: 353–4; Prickett in Coyle *et al.* 1990: 653–63, 951–62; Carroll and Prickett 1997: Introduction.

1.5.5 Rhetoric, composition and writing

Rhetoric has been taught in one form or another from CLASSICAL times to the present day. It has always had a close, and sometimes vexed, relation with the study of modern languages such as English. Initially, in a predominantly *oral culture, rhetoric meant 'the arts of persuasive and effective public speaking'. In the ancient Greek city states and the Roman Empire training in rhetoric was reckoned essential for politicians, statesmen and senior administrators, especially in their dealings with a largely *illiterate populace. Influential rhetorical manuals were written by Aristotle, Quintilian, Cicero and Longinus, and these dealt systematically with such matters as:

♦   *invention* – the identification of relevant materials and topics;
♦   *disposition* – effective overall organisation of argument;
♦   *style* – specific choices and combinations of words (including *figures of speech* such as *metaphor, antithesis, parallelism, lists, etc.);

- *the art of memory* – for effective storing and recall of all the above;
- *delivery* – for persuasive handling of tone, manner and gesture.

As literacy became more widespread, the province of Rhetoric was extended to embrace the arts of persuasive and effective written composition.

Clearly, then, Rhetoric initially designated something much more fundamental and powerful than is currently implied by the phrases 'merely rhetorical' and 'rhetorical questions' (i.e. mock-questions to which the speaker already has the answer). The pejorative ring of the latter is the legacy of a comparatively recent *Romantic tradition which sought to privilege personal expression as 'a spontaneous overflow of powerful feeling' (in Wordsworth's phrase) rather than communication as a considered and crafted interpersonal activity. In fact Rhetoric, along with Grammar and Logic, had been one of the three cornerstones of the medieval and early Renaissance academic curriculum (the 'Trivium'). Consequently, just about every recognised writer from the fourteenth to the nineteenth centuries (from Chaucer to Byron) had some training in it, chiefly through classical models. Wilson's *Art of Rhetoric* (1553), a compilation of neo-classical rules and examples, was especially influential in Shakespeare's day. In addition, Oxford, Cambridge and the older Scottish and American universities had Professors of Rhetoric virtually from their inception. Rhetoric was no mere adjunct to the study of language and literature. It was virtually its analytical core, and was in many respects the precursor of modern **discourse** analysis. Moreover, rhetorical training was concerned as much with the actual *practice* of speaking and writing, as with the analysis of what is already spoken and written. Early rhetorical training thus has modern counterparts (and sometimes direct successors) in the teaching and learning of a wide range of written and spoken composition, as well as 'communication skills', at schools, colleges and universities. At any rate it is generally better to approach combinations of critical-creative and analytical-practical activity through broadly 'rhetorical' traditions than through narrowly 'literary critical' or 'linguistic analytical' ones. Another option is to talk of 'language **arts**', with a stress on the practical *artisanal as well as the *artistic side of doing things with words.

Courses in Rhetoric

Sometimes called 'Rhetoric and Composition' or just 'Comp.', for short, such courses are a fundamental feature of colleges and universities in the USA today. They have been for some time. So, increasingly, are courses gathered under the umbrella of 'Writing across the Curriculum' (WAC). These are courses which encourage writing and communication skills rooted in a whole range of departments, not just in an 'English' department as such. Some grasp of the historical development of Rhetoric, Composition and Writing is crucial if we are to understand the particular configuration of university English in the USA. This is also important because certain areas of university English in the UK, Europe and Australasia are beginning to move in the same direction.

'English' in the American academy

English first came into being by detaching and distancing itself from the well-established study of Rhetoric. From the beginning the latter had been charged with the task of schooling a highly heteroglot and multicultural migrant population in the writing and speaking of what was proposed as a 'common tongue': English. (In parts of Canada, French fulfils this role.) The key to English's detachment from Rhetoric was the former's claim to its own specialised subject matter (a **canon** of partly British but also increasingly American writers in English) as well as its own specialised apparatuses of study (variously historical, bibliographical, philological and, latterly, literary critical; see 1.5.6–7). As mentioned elsewhere (1.5.2), English got its first university chair at Indiana in 1860, Harvard in 1876. The institutional result of such differentiation was a hierarchy in which, from the 'English' scholar's point of view, Rhetoric was steadily downgraded to the status of service industry or course prerequisite. Proficiency in writing and speaking were increasingly regarded as someone else's business: what students should do in first-year 'freshman English' or before they enrol at all. The effect on the teaching and learning of English as a whole was cumulative and ultimately divisive. Thenceforth 'English majors' were often writing essays on Shakespeare or Milton (and later Melville and Faulkner), while anyone else who did English at university would be learning how to write reports and letters and be practising formal presentations and debates – maybe with a little 'creative writing' thrown in on the side. There was a fundamental cleavage within both the academic hierarchy and the practice of the subject. English majors talked and wrote about literary classics; students of Rhetoric and Composition analysed and practised many different kinds of speaking and writing.

The hierarchical division of labour between 'Eng. Lit.' and 'Rhetoric and Comp.'

This situation has, however, been strongly challenged over the past decade. As student numbers for straight English Literature have declined (down by 30 per cent in the USA in the past eight years), student numbers and businesss demand for courses in Rhetoric and Composition (now including full MA and PhD programmes) have risen sharply. Funds are tending to follow feet too – and to some extent dictate where they will go. Now many specialist courses in 'English (and American) Lit.' are directly or indirectly dependent for their very existence on the numbers and revenue generated by their erstwhile junior partners. Increasingly, 'Rhetoric and Comp' and 'Freshman English' are not just the bread and butter but also a large slice of the cake in US tertiary education. Similar things are happening throughout the English-speaking worlds: in Australia, New Zealand, Africa, India and the UK. Sometimes these shifts occur *within* a department called 'English'. Sometimes they occur *outside* or *alongside* it, in departments of COMMUNICATIONS or Languages or Applied Linguistics, or in programmes dedicated to Journalism or Professional Writing or Writing across the Curriculum. But whatever the names of the departments or the configurations of the courses, the basic questions are the same:

♦ How far should 'English' include training in effective writing, speech and presentation: verbal and visual, by individuals and groups?

- Can the development of knowledge and critical awareness *about* English be divorced from skills in the use *of* English? And can we really divorce knowledges from skills, and either of them from theory: 'know-what' from 'know-how' and 'know-why'?
- What place is there for kinds of *creative as well as critical writing in English programmes: *script-writing of documentaries and writing of news or advertising copy, say, not only the traditionally 'literary' genres of poetry, plays and novels?
- What, too, of the critical-creative *re-**writing** of texts through such activities as *parody, *adaptation and *intervention (all of which were in fact routine practices in classical and neo-classical Rhetoric)?

READING: *Introductory*: Kinneavy 1971: 6–17; Dixon 1971; Durant and Fabb 1990: 20–2; Elbow 1993: 126–40; Greenblatt and Gunn 1992: 466–520; Pope 1995: 1–30, 183–92; Wooffitt in Maybin and Mercer 1996: 122–61; *Fuller studies*: Nash 1989; Nash 1992: 67–155; Graff 1987; Andrews 1992; Berlin 1996; Nash and Stacey 1997.

1.5.6   History and English

There has long been a 'historical' dimension to the study of English, whether as 'literary history' or 'history of the language'. There has also been a long-standing relationship between the academic subjects called English and History – sometimes close, often vexed, always significant. In fact we can identify most theoretical positions as well as individual practitioners in so far as they are more or less historical. Everyone has a certain version or vision of history, even (and perhaps especially) if they attempt to relegate history to the **background** or ignore it altogether.

Literary History

Mainstream academic History at the close of the nineteenth century was mainly concerned with what have been called 'the biographies of great men' and 'kings and queens and constitutions'. Literary history tended to follow suit. It concentrated on the 'biographies of great writers' (whose 'greatness' was asserted, and whose whiteness, maleness and social respectability were largely assumed). Dr Johnson's *The Lives of the Poets* (1781) was reckoned amongst the major precursors, and that great late Victorian monument to British worthies *The Dictionary of National Biography* (1882 onwards) was one of the chief tools Literary Historians shared with their colleagues in History. Meanwhile, what can be called the 'constitutional' side of Literary History was largely conceived in terms of sources, influences and traditions, often with classical precursors, e.g., Shakespeare's use of Plutarch's *Lives* in his Roman History plays; the influence of Horace, Juvenal and Roman *satiric tradition on Dryden, and of all of them on Pope (see 5.1.4 b). More narrowly, scholars asserted a great *national* tradition of specifically *English* Literature. In poetry this ran from, say, Chaucer to Tennyson; in the novel from Defoe to Dickens. Such studies form an enduring and important strain in contemporary literary history. It should be noted, however, that they often construct a distinctive history *of* literature rather than a sense of literature *in* history. Literature was (and often still is) projected as though existing in its own space and time and changing according to its own inner logic; as though it is not bound up with the pervasive processes of social-historical change. The distinction between a history *of* literature and literature *in* history often turns out to be crucial.

History of the Language

Meanwhile, linguists were laying the foundations of a certain kind of 'History of the LANGUAGE'. Late nineteenth-century Northern European scholars such as Grimm and Verner were expending a great deal of energy and erudition on the study of the early Indo-European 'family' of languages in general and the interrelations among the early Germanic languages in particular. The result was the appearance within English of such subjects as Comparative Philology, History of the English Language, Old Norse and Anglo-Saxon. The sheer linguistic 'hardness' of these subjects along with the teasing fragmentariness of the manuscript record made their study the ideal counterweight to those in CLASSICS and THEOLOGY (see 1.5.3–4) who had tended to dismiss the study of English as 'easy', 'light', 'unscholarly' and 'insufficiently rigorous'. Thenceforth it was possible to maintain (and at many universities up to the 1960s compulsory to learn) that such things as the ancient Indo-European words for 'snow' or 'pine tree', as well as Grimm's and Verner's 'laws' of sound-changes between, say, Sanskrit, Lithuanian and the Romance and Germanic languages, were an essential foundation for the study of English. So, too, it was insisted, was a study of Anglo-Saxon and medieval English poetry and prose, chiefly with an eye to their linguistic characteristics and textual history rather than their 'literary' qualities. In fact, these latter areas were soon re-dubbed 'Old' and 'Middle' English so as to point up the continuity of a tradition leading to 'Modern' English (here meaning English from the sixteenth century onwards). In this way the image of a national language, literature and culture was fashioned 'as a whole': a complete **hi/story** with beginning (Old English), middle (Middle English) and end (Modern English).

New hi/stories for old

Significantly, it is only with the relatively recent recognition of the so-called '*New Englishes' of the Caribbean, Africa, India and Australasia that the earlier, neatly complete history (or story) of English has been challenged and changed. Now, largely under the pressure of POSTCOLONIAL critiques of dominant British and American versions of English, there are seen to be not just one but many possible hi/stories. FEMINISTS have made similarly marked interventions in the older notion of Literary History composed of a 'great tradition' of chiefly male writers. Significant, too, is the fact that courses tracing the previously forgotten or hidden histories of women's writing and post/colonial literature (including slave narratives) are now occupying space in the English Studies curriculum that might once have been filled by courses in 'Old and Middle English' or 'History of the Language'. Medievalists tend to retire or retool, and be replaced by lecturers in later periods and other areas. Thus it is not only the subject's reconstructions of 'external' history which are changing, but also the subject's reconstruction of its own 'internal' history. English is both engaging with and enacting constantly shifting histories. That is precisely why this part of the book (1.5.1–11) offers a historical approach to the subject as presently configured.

The relations between English and History as named academic disciplines are also currently in flux. One sign of this is the appearance of more interdisciplinary programmes involving named combinations of 'English/Literary and Historical Studies'. In part this is made possible by the fact that the historian's and the literary historian's conceptions of history as *social* history have tended to converge. In both subjects the 'great men/writers' versions of history have largely given way to agendas emphasising collective rather than individual agency, e.g.:

- *institutions*: church, state, education, the family, medicine, marriage;
- *movements*: women's, labour, national, ethnic;
- *revolutions*: political, technological, aesthetic and otherwise.

NEW HISTORICIST, MARXIST, FEMINIST and POSTCOLONIAL agendas have all affected the focusing and identification of distinctive, often explicitly political, subject matters in English and History. There is also a common tendency in both these areas to review traditional distinctions between what is in the **foreground** and the **background** of study. Literary historians are now less inclined to approve a text as the expression of some uniquely individual 'genius' and more inclined to explore it as an instance of the interplay of contextual conditions and social-historical forces. Conversely, many historians are much readier to recognise the distinctive value of what would previously have been considered 'soft' sources: diaries, private letters, *oral history, and even poems, plays and novels. These now figure alongside traditional 'hard' sources such as legal statutes, government reports, public records and statistics. They are invoked to help explain people's perceptions and attitudes, their 'mind-sets' and 'interiority' at a particular historical moment. This kind of Literary/Historical interchange is being greatly helped by increased flexibility in the notions of **auto/biography**, **discourse**, **narrative**, **hi/story**, **faction**, **genre** and **representation**. 'Truth' in both subjects is now more likely to be seen as contingent and conditional: as much dependent on who spoke or wrote when, where and why as on what was said.

Periodic border disputes

But there are still many differences between English and History as self-conscious disciplines. There are also plenty of practitioners of both subjects who would reject the interdependence of all the terms highlighted in the previous paragraph. They would insist that traditional distinctions (and traditional discipline boundaries) be maintained. For one thing, there continue to be many different ways of distinguishing historical *periods, depending upon the discipline doing the distinguishing. Thus, where a historian may characterise the late eighteenth and early nineteenth centuries as 'The Age of Revolutions', literary historians are more likely to talk of '*Romanticism'. Meanwhile, the latter term is used by a historian of Music to refer to a somewhat later and different movement. Furthermore, literary historians may talk of Modernism and POSTMODERNISM as both historical periods and cultural movements. Historians, however, are more likely to talk about Modern*isation* and Post-*industrialisation*, and thereby intend only partly similar (or utterly different) processes. Meanwhile, during what is notionally 'the same period', **Art** historians would be busy distinguishing Post-impressionism, Cubism, Constructivism, Pop Art, and the like (or rather the unlike!). The point is that not only does every discipline have its own institutional and intellectual history. It also breaks down and reconstitutes the continuum of history in its own image and through its own apparatuses and terminologies. No period label is easily translatable across disciplines. All processes of periodisation are to some extent discipline specific.

Nonetheless, period labels do change within disciplines; and they do get translated (and thereby transformed) between disciplines. Interdisciplinary work is becoming the norm, not the exception. We now quite routinely have course, book and periodical titles which twenty years ago would have been rare or considered odd, e.g.: 'Writing in Time of Revolution', 'Power and Politics in Renaissance Texts', 'Gender in Popular Discourse in the Postwar Period', 'Representations of Slavery in the 18th and 19th Centuries'. History, then, is very much there for the making as well as the taking. It is still up to each and all of us, individually and collectively, to grasp the kind of history we find most useful in our version or vision of English. That includes the various histories of the subject itself.

READING: *Introductory*: Wellek and Warren 1963: 252–73; Williams 1958; Green and LeBihan 1996: 91–138. *Advanced*: Humm *et al.* 1986; Attridge *et al.* 1987a; Hodge 1990; *Literature and History* (journal); Young 1990. For institutional histories of university and college English, see READING in 1.5.2.

1.5.7 From Literary Appreciation to Literary Criticism

At the same time that one area of English Studies was being fortified as 'hard' and 'rigorous' by philologists and textual scholars, another area was being maintained as 'soft' and 'impressionistic' by devotees of what has been called *literary appreciation*. At best, literary appreciation is a style of commentary on literature which has much in common with a good journalistic review of a book, play, film or concert: it tells you what the reviewer does and does not like and why. At worst, it smacks of after-dinner chit-chat about 'fine' authors, artists, composers, wine and food, or glossy coffee-table books on 'great works'. This approach to LITERATURE is also called *bellettrist (from French *belles lettres*/beautiful writings) or, more pejoratively, dilettantish (from Italian *dilettanti*/delight-tasters). Either way, this way of talking about literature has as its primary aim the division of works into 'pleasing' or 'displeasing', 'beautiful' or 'ugly', 'true' or 'false', 'good' or 'bad', 'major' or minor – depending on the precise criteria in play.

As that loaded phrase literary *appreciation* implies, the expectations of both teacher and learner are presumed to be predisposed towards admiration of 'fine' writing and, conversely, censure of 'bad' writing. Literary appreciation therefore tends to be loosely **aesthetic** and *value-laden. I say 'loosely' because writers in this mode tend not to explore their premises in much detail. Rather, they imply a community of interest and a consensus of belief amongst peers. There is the general air of a gentleman's club or the amiable complacency of an Oxbridge senior common room. The **canon** of great works is not so much argued over as assumed or asserted. One of the most notable critics of this kind was Sir Arthur Quiller-Couch. He was the editor of many highly influential anthologies, including the *Oxford Book of English Verse* (1902) and was appointed Professor of English Literature at Cambridge in 1912. His sweeping gestures and magisterial pronouncements also have something in common with the 'biographies of great writers' kind of Literary History referred to in the previous section. The main difference is that 'Q', as he preferred to be called is more concerned with literary textures than historical contexts. Interestingly, Q's style has much in common with that of a slightly later Cambridge don, F.R.*Leavis. In fact, for all Leavis's avowed opposition to his Cambridge predecessors (as well as many of his contemporaries), his penchant for bold assertion and his vigorous insistence that the critic's task is to '*discriminate' between 'good' and 'bad' writing signal his allegiance far more to the camp of literary *appreciation* than to that of literary *criticism* which superseded it. It is the latter we turn to now.

Professionalising criticism

After the First World War, university English Studies became much more professionalised. The gentleman reviewer and bellettrist gradually gave way to the scholar-critic. The latter insisted that the subject be made more rigorous and technically precise. More particularly, these self-conscious literary *critics urged much greater attention to 'the words on the page' and developed a distinctive critical vocabulary and apparatus for doing just that. These movements were known as PRACTICAL CRITICISM in the UK and NEW CRITICISM in the USA (see 2.3). Here all that need be noted is that Practical/New Criticism aimed to put commentary on literary texts on a new footing. In place of general impressions and loose opinionating, there was to be close and 'objective' analysis of such features as *ambiguity, *irony, **imagery**, **point of view** and integrated or 'organic' structure. The fact that many of these terms are perhaps already familiar, even 'natural', to you as the routine counters of Literary Criticism is a clear measure of just how far Practical and New Criticism succeeded in becoming an orthodoxy for much of the twentieth century.

Criticism can be a confusing concept because 'being critical' and 'being a critic' imply a variety of activities and roles. In fact we can distinguish four basic meanings of criticism:

1 finding fault and pulling to pieces in a negative sense;
2 analysing and pulling to pieces in the neutral sense of taking apart;
3 interpreting with a view to establishing meaning and understanding;
4 evaluating with a view to establishing relative or absolute worth.

Good critical readers and writers are constantly aware of the potential slippage and overlap amongst all these four senses. They also embrace them in so far as they recognise the relation between analysis, interpretation and evaluation. *Critique* is the name for the activity of **rewriting** a text in order to get to grips with it more interactively (see 4.4). (For fuller discussion, see Norris, 'Criticism', in Coyle *et al.* 1990: 27–67.)

Part Two of this book identifies a further dozen or so Theoretical Positions and Critical Approaches. This is a reminder that ultimately Practical/New Criticism is just one kind of movement and historical moment in literary criticism, albeit a highly influential and persistent one. Indeed, for many practitioners of English Studies today it is not the shift from literary *appreciation* to literary *criticism* which is significant, but rather the shift from *literary* study of any kind to *cultural* practices in general. Accordingly, it is not the imperative to 'appreciate' *or* 'objectify' already privileged works of art, literary or otherwise, which engages many cultural commentators and theorists now. It is the very process of evaluation and ceaseless *re*valuation which is now emphasised: not just *what* we value, but also *how*, and *why* values change over time (see below, 1.5.8–11).

READING: Norris and Rylance in Coyle *et al.* 1990: 27–67, 721–35; Graff 1987; Mulhern 1979; Baldick 1996: 20–115.
Also see: Brooks 1947; Leavis 1936, 1948.

1.5.8   English into Literary Studies

One response to the globalisation of English is to drop the 'English' altogether and substitute for it the adjective 'Literary'. This has the effect of at once broadening *and* narrowing the subject matter:

♦ broadening the subject in that many other literatures than English can be openly embraced; e.g., courses on the **novel** which take in nineteenth-century Russian and twentieth-century South American as well as English and American instances; courses on classical Greek and Roman, Elizabethan and Japanese **drama**;
♦ narrowing the subject in that many non-literary forms of speech and writing routinely featured in courses on English Language and discourse then tend to be ignored; e.g., conversation, advertising, news-reporting, historical and philosophical texts.

As usual, there are pluses and minuses all round. The international reach of the course can be attractive (there is an especial grandeur in courses billed as 'World Literature'); but this may be at the expense of a firm grasp of any specific national or regional tradition. 'Cross-cultural' comparisons may be plentiful; but these may turn out to be superficial because of shaky knowledge of local contexts and the specificities of cultural–historical **differences**. The large promise of a totalised view of 'World Literature' may also in practice often come down to a predictable core of Western classics (Homer to Heller, Plato to NATO) duly trimmed with a more or less exotic fringe of token non-Westerners, also classic. It has yet to be seen how far recent attempts at more ideologically sensitive courses and anthologies of World Literature on more genuinely global, or at least less Euro-American lines, will fare (e.g., Caws and Prendergast 1994, Geok-Lin Lim and Spencer 1993).

A further challenge is that a great deal of what is studied under the heading 'Literary Studies' is in English *translation. (The alternative is 'Comparative Literature' courses in more than one language, and for practical reasons these are rare.) Now, 'Literature in translation' or 'World Literature (in English)' are fine – as long as it is recognised that that is precisely what they are: translations. The processes of translation are complex and contentious: they always involve a transformation and dialogue between cultures as well as languages – never a mere transference from 'source' to 'target' languages. In the process, inevitably, distinctive differences get lost, homogenised or exaggerated. Access to the '*other' through translation always runs the risk of appropriating or exoticising it. In other words, courses which use translation extensively need to be informed by at least some work on the theory, practice and implications of translation (see Bassnett 1991).

The term 'literary' can also be a problem when certain notions of LITERATURE are assumed to be universal and transhistorical. Many dominant Western European notions of the literary simply do not apply to other countries and cultures. For instance, traditional mega-genres such as poetry, prose and drama do not easily accommodate the mixtures of verse, song, narrative, dialogue, oratory and performance we find in various Afro-Caribbean and Asian traditions (see 5.2.4 d–f; 5.4.2 e). The printed novel, for instance, is a distinctively modern Western European and substantially bourgeois **narrative** mode. Even such increasingly prominent genres as **auto/biography**, *travel writing, 'science' and 'fantasy' *fiction are not exempt from this risk. No **genre** can apply everywhere and always. Every instance of such apparently universal modes as narrative and drama turns out to be in some sense peculiar; and sometimes it turns into something else entirely (e.g., a performed narrative which enacts a people's place in nature; see 5.4.4 e). Another consequence of a certain kind of narrow 'literary-mindedness' is that alternative ways of describing cultural practices may be ignored. Word-play and language arts, in particular, or *play and **art** in general, can sometimes prove more capacious and productive concepts. So, in another sphere, can the notions of *sign-systems, COMMUNICATION (from face-to-face to multimedia) and CULTURAL practices. But whatever terms and frames are used, the main thing is to avoid imposing an unexamined notion of literature on every performance or text we meet. FORMALIST preoccupation with *literariness and *defamiliarisation or NEW CRITICAL pre-occupations with *ambiguity, *irony and 'organic unity' do not work too well with African folk tale, Caribbean dub poetry and Maori or Aboriginal creation myths. Nor for that matter, do some of the more rigid templates of class, gender and race supplied by certain kinds of Marxist, Feminist and Postcolonial literary criticism.

Nonetheless, the shift from 'English' to 'Literary' Studies is now common and can be well worth making. It all depends what national and international arenas you decide to operate in, and how far the linguistic, literary and cultural frames you work with are themselves held up for inspection and interrogation. It also depends how far you are prepared to bend that frame so as to accommodate some of the kinds of traditionally *non*-literary material featured in the other versions of English which follow (in 1.5.9–11).

READING: Easthope 1991: 3–64; Fowler in Coyle *et al.* 1990: 3–26; Durant and Fabb 1990.

1.5.9   English with Theatre and/or Film Studies

In this case the emphasis obviously tends to be on the text as part of a **dramatic**, filmic or televisual event: not just how words are read from the page but how whole worlds of sight and sound, live or recorded, are realised on stage or screen. In many respects theatre, film and TV are themselves quite distinct MEDIA, both in modes of (re)production and contexts of reception. They are therefore sometimes practised and studied separately. However, the fact that all use sounds and images as well as words often draws practitioners as well as students together. In addition, most films, like most stage and radio and TV plays, are based at some point on a *script (including shooting script and story-board in the case of films). Interestingly, it is only really the *script* as a primarily verbal text which ensures the links between theatre and film studies, and between both of them and English Literature (where plays, novels and poems are traditionally studied as texts not as performances). For the rest, the super-abundantly *non*-verbal nature of theatre, film and TV make them particularly awkward – as well as peculiarly attractive – for students of English. Occasionally, Theatre and Film Studies are closely integrated with English or other Modern Language departments. Sometimes they move within the orbit of Visual Studies, Design or even Education. Increasingly, however, they exist in their own independent spaces, sometimes aligned with Media, Communication and Cultural Studies (see 1.5.10). But whatever the precise configuration, there is a noticeable tendency for English departments to incorporate more and more video and films into their courses. Sometimes this is as a kind of optional extra, the occasional showing of the film of a Shakespeare play or a TV adaptation of an Austen or Dickens novel, for instance. But increasingly there are whole courses built around the relations between literature and film, with the specificity of both media and their various moments of re/production taken into account. Thus we have, say, 'Shakespeare and Film', or 'The Novel and Screen Adaptation', or 'TV Documentary and Drama of the 1970s'. There may even be whole programmes built round English/Literary and Film or TV Studies. (Significantly, such combinations often signal a steady retreat from close associations with practical Drama courses. This seems to be because Drama is perceived as more labour and space intensive, as well as less culturally central than film and TV.) Similar trends towards teaching and learning through film and TV, chiefly by means of video, are even more marked in the (other) Modern Language and Literature departments. In French, German, Italian, Spanish and Russian departments, for instance, the emphasis is increasingly on the Language and Culture sides of the subject. Literature as such (especially earlier literature) is a preciously preserved but relatively endangered species.

Cumulatively, all these shifts are beginning to impact on English in a variety of interesting ways. Collaborative production processes and institutional frames tend to be very much to the fore in film, TV and theatre – both in the materials studied and in the ways of studying them. A film or play is palpably the result of a collective effort, whoever the prominent individuals involved. Many student projects in these areas are also collective and involve team work. Both these facts naturally prompt students of English and Film or Theatre to query the *Romantic notion of the **author** as individual genius. We may, for instance, revise our views of such supposedly individual geniuses as Shakespeare in the light of the palpably collaborative practices of his own theatre (see 2.2). The overall significance of such courses involving theatre and/or film is therefore much greater than a mere change of 'medium', narrowly conceived. What is entailed is a radical revision of what is meant by textual (re)production, as well as a challenge to individualistic modes of learning and assessment.

READING: *Theatre*: Brook 1968; Elam 1980; Aston and Savona 1991; Boal 1992. *Film*: Giddings *et al.* 1990; Bordwell and Thompson 1993; McFarlane 1996. *Television*: Fiske 1987; Allen 1987; Selby and Cowdrey 1995.

1.5.10 English into Cultural, Communication and Media Studies

These are yet other, interrelated, responses to the globalising and technologising of contemporary culture. Here the focus shifts to the processes and products of communication in general, and often the modern print and audio-visual media in particular (i.e. newspapers, magazines, pulp fiction, TV, video, computers and multimedia interfaces). At the same time increased attention is usually paid to MULTICULTURAL and other social **differences**, as well as a concerted challenging or scrambling of traditional divisions between 'high' **art** and '*popular' cultures. This last point is significant because Cultural Studies to some extent takes over where people working on the interfaces between traditional departments of Literature, *Art History and *Music leave off. Until quite recently, if they did interdisciplinary work at all, the latter tended to concentrate on the interrelations amongst **classics** of a more or less elite kind. In earlier periods the emphasis would be on poetry, painting and music produced for aristocrats, often as a result of patronage (e.g., 'The Literature, Art and Music of the Court of . . . '). In later periods the emphasis would be on work of a 'difficult' kind often appealing to small and still privileged minorities of connoisseurs (e.g., 'Modernism, Cubism and Atonality'). In this respect Cultural Studies was initially reactive in that it concentrated on (and was readily confused with) *Popular Studies. There was a deliberate emphasis on folk or popular (rather than court or elite) practices in earlier periods and on mass media or broadcast rather than minority and narrowcast) materials in later periods (e.g., 'Ballads and Broadsheets in . . . '; 'Popular Carnival in . . . '; 'Popular Women's Magazines . . . ').

This balance is currently being redressed, however, especially at postgraduate level. Work within and between traditional departments of English, Art History and Music (often in conjunction with History; see 1.5.6) is now much more likely to embrace the study of a range of material. Popular ballads, songs and images are studied alongside their court and elite counterparts (see 5.4.1; 5.4.6 f). Illustrated newspapers and magazines are studied together with the novels and short stories (often illustrated) which appeared serialised in their pages or circulated in the volumes of travelling libraries (e.g., Dickens). William Blake may be studied in his multifarious roles as poet, engraver, painter and publisher (not solely as poet; see 5.4.6 b). Songs are studied as words and music; **drama** is studied as performance on stage or screen, not simply as words on the page (see 1.5.9). Crucially, most of these courses move beyond the merely supplementary use of art and music as **backgrounds** to the serious business of literature in the **foreground** – as though art were merely illustrative and music were merely atmospheric. The best grapple from the outset with the challenges of perceiving through different media (they do not automatically privilege 'the word'). They also acknowledge the problems of distinct traditions of production and reception, and of different *period and **genre** labels for notionally 'the same' times and places.

At the same time, Cultural Studies is becoming more self-aware and circumspect. It is being recognised that culture operates at a variety of social levels and in a variety of media. Supposedly 'mass' readerships and audiences always turn out to be shifting aggregates and networks of 'minority' interests. There is also a growing recognition that print-culture is not in fact being destroyed by electronic audio-visual media (as various groups have tended to celebrate or lament). Instead, it is being reconfigured. People still speak, and write by hand, even if they also type and tape, film and fax. It's simply that they now do these things in different proportions, on varying occasions and for changing functions. Major cultural practices and communicative modes tend to displace – not utterly replace – one another. The telephone extended the reach of speech, displaced the writing of letters and postcards, and altered people's perceptions of time and distance. But it destroyed nothing except its immediate predecessor and prototype, the telegraph. The same can be observed of many other modes of communication: the car with respect to walking and the horse, or *hypertext and multimedia with respect to the book and newspaper. These are patterns of displacement and replacement not utter destruction and disappearance. All this needs saying loud and clear, both inside and outside education. Otherwise the real complexities and teasing dis/continuities are overwhelmed by the strident strains of 'brave new electronic world' triumphalism on the one hand or 'poor old print world' pessimism on the other.

Practitioners of 'English' therefore have some challenging questions to find answers for:

◆ How dependent is the subject on the medium of the written or printed word? Must its central object of study be the printed book?
◆ Do the boundaries of the 'literary' (as distinct from the 'non-literary') need to be: (i) rigorously policed? (ii) utterly abolished? (iii) maintained so as to be periodically transgressed? (iv) perpetually re-drawn?
◆ Where is 'English' in all this as a national or international culture? and a local and global resource?
◆ Do *hypertext and computerised *multimedia oblige us to recognise much more collaborative (less individualistic) modes of working and much more flexible models of **authorship** (also see 1.5.9)? Is this a total 'revolution' in the making of the subject?
◆ Or is it a gradual, albeit accelerated, 'evolution'– an extension of what we already more or less knew? For haven't we always had a plural, hybrid and flexible sense of the cultures, communicative practices and media in which we are involved?
◆ Or have we?!

READING: *Literature and other arts*: Wellek and Warren 1963: 125–38; Barricelli *et al.* 1990; Open University 1996a. *Cultural Studies*: Brooker and Humm 1989: 236–58; During 1993: 1–28; Grossberg *et al.* 1992: 1–17; Easthope 1991; Green and Hoggart 1987; Graff and Robbins in Greenblatt and Gunn 1992: 419–36; Fiske in Lentricchia and McLaughlin 1995: 321–35; Milner 1996. *Communication and Media Studies*: O'Sullivan *et al.* 1994; Branston and Stafford 1996; Goodman and Graddol 1996; Kress 1995.

1.5.11 Critical Theory into Cultural Practice

This has been yet another set of possibilities opened up by what might be called 'several englishes in search of a **subject**' (where subject means 'discipline', 'subject matter' and 'subject position'). For in this case 'English' has taken several concerted turns towards literary and cultural theory, notably: MARXIST, FEMINIST, PSYCHOANALYTIC, POSTSTRUCTURALIST, POST-MODERNIST, POSTCOLONIALIST and MULTICULTURAL. The resulting prospects are variously arid or exhilarating, shallow or profound. It all depends on the particular theories invoked and how these are related to the actual practices of reading and writing, learning and teaching.

Latterly there have been clear signs that the moment of 'high theory' (i.e. highly abstract theory) has passed. There is now a growing concern with theory in practice, especially the politically and pedagogically urgent question of who learns and teaches what, how and why. All these matters are picked up in Part Two. There each major position is reviewed in turn and its contribution to a transformed practice weighed. The emphasis is on what can be *done* with each theory rather than on what it *is*. There is also an insistence on a flexible yet principled plurality of approach: identifying models and methods appropriate to specific tasks and texts – not arbitrarily imposing one on all.

This principle is extended to modes of writing and study too. Part Four presents a wide range of textual activities and learning strategies which are designed to put a variety of theories into a variety of practices.

READING: Bartholomae and Petrosky 1986; Scholes 1985; Kress 1995; Brooker and Humm 1989: 73–170; Corcoran *et al.* 1994; Green and Hoggart 1987; Pope 1995: 183–202; Eagleton 1996: 169–89; Nash and Stacey 1997: 182–225.

1.6   SUMMARY: PASTS, PRESENTS AND FUTURES

In this section we have traced at least a dozen directions in which the study of English is currently moving. All of these derive directly from the very varied history of the subject as studied in schools, and especially colleges and universities, over the last century and a half. English as we currently know it is constituted by the knitting together of a variety of 'living histories'. Virtually every strand of its past design can be discerned in some aspect of the current fabric. Thus we find that traces of subjects as varied (and themselves as variable) as Classics, Theology, Rhetoric, Composition and History (Literary and Linguistic) and a wide range of 'Studies' (Theatre, Film, Literary, Cultural, Communication and Media) as well as a wide range of critical theories and cultural practices (from New Critical and Formalist to Feminist, Poststructuralist and Postcolonial), can all be discerned in the complex patterning of the discipline(s) we currently call English Studies. Indeed, this patterning is so richly variegated that it has been suggested we recognise English as an 'interdiscipline': a site where old disciplines meet with new, and in their mingling help generate fresh configurations of knowledge. This last aspect is crucial. English as it is currently configured is as much concerned with 'know how' (skills) and 'know why' (critical evaluation and cultural theory) as with 'know what' (content, subject matter).

To be sure, no single department of English – and certainly no single person in it – is practising all of these knowledges. Nor can the present book claim to do more than gesture towards the major ones. And yet, every department and every individual practitioner of English potentially has access to all of them. That is, we all have the capacity (even if we do not always have the opportunity or even the desire) to draw on a variety of traditions stretching from the recoverable past to the as yet unmade future. Put another way, with the emphasis on plurality and choice, we all have some responsibility to identify the pasts of the subject we wish to draw on, and to use these to help articulate the futures we would prefer. In this respect it is desirable, at least initially, to try to think the study of English 'as a whole' (even if it sometimes seems to be no more than 'a series of holes'). No one may be practising all 'English Studies' – but all are practising some. We are all contributing to some features of what is, even if not a common design, a shared fabric. And so are many people who belong to what, nominally at least, are quite distinct disciplines (from Rhetoric to History and from Cultural to Postcolonial Studies). The activities which follow should help you get some provisional bearings on the kinds of 'Studies' you are currently involved in.

1.7   ACTIVITIES, DISCUSSION, READING

(a)   English *and* or *as* a configuration of other educational subjects?
Use Appendix C to help plot the kinds of English Studies in which you are currently engaged. More particularly, use it to discuss:

♦   the main emphases and orientations of your current English programme;
♦   your own main interests within or beyond that programme;
♦   directions or dimensions in which the subject in general seems to be moving;
♦   directions or dimensions in which you would like to push it.
        Go on to modify or completely remodel this diagram as you see fit.

(b)   *What's (not) in a name?*
Use the categories of course titles in section 4.5. ('What's (not) in a name? Changing courses') to initiate a discussion of the shapes and emphases of your own particular courses. Go on to discuss the name of the programme or department as whole. What is implied by such names? How significant or accurate are they in view of what actually goes on? And what, implicitly or explicitly, are *not* the subjects of study?

Discussion

(i)   Interdisciplinary work is not the calm of an easy security; it begins *effectively* (as opposed to the mere expression of a pious wish) when the solidarity of the disciplines breaks down.
                        Roland Barthes, 'From Work to Text', *Image-Music-Text* (1977: 155)

(ii)   English should be reconstituted as the study of how verbal and written fictions have been produced and used, socially channelled and evaluated, grouped together, given social significance, institutionalised, transformed [. . .] The study of English will then provide a creative base for active experiments with cultural production (verbal, visual and aural) which enhance, improve and diversify rather than narrow and homogenise our cultural life.
                        Brian Doyle, *English and Englishness* (1989: 142)

READING: Specific suggestions are attached to each of the above sections (1.5.1–11). The following are of general and recurrent usefulness.
    Brisk and stimulating places to start are: G. Kress, *Writing the Future: English and the Making of a Culture of Innovation* 1995; P. Widdowson, 'W(h)ither English?' and T. Hawkes, 'The Institutionalisation of Literature: The University', in M. Coyle *et al.* (eds) *Encyclopedia of Literature and Criticism* 1990: 1221–36, 926–40; S. Greenblatt and G. Gunn (eds) *Redrawing the Boundaries: The Transformation of English and American Studies,* 1992: Introduction and T. Eagleton *Literary Theory: An Introduction* (2nd edn) 1996: 15–47, 169–208. Many present positions and future possibilities are opened up in the

four excellent volumes of Open University course *U210*: *The English Language: Past, Present and Future* 1996b; especially relevant here are S. Goodman and D. Graddol (eds) *Redesigning English: New Texts, New Identities* 1996 and N. Mercer and J. Swann (eds) *Learning English: Development and Diversity* 1996. These treat developments in India, Australia and elsewhere at a variety of educational levels, while also addressing matters of global standardisation, local identity and high- and low-technology contexts. Also see S. Tweddle *et al.*, *English for Tomorrow* 1997.

The following concentrate on 'English' in tertiary education in Britain and America: Britain – B. Doyle *English and Englishness* 1989 and C. Evans *English People: The Experience of Teaching and Learning English in British Universities* 1993; America – G. Graff *Professing Literature: An Institutional History* 1987; P. Elbow *What is English?* 1993; Greenblatt and Gunn 1992 (as above); Guy and Small, *Politics and Value in English Studies: A Discipline in Crisis?* 1993 and J. Berlin *Rhetoric, Poetics and Culture: Reconfiguring College English Studies* 1996. More historically specific studies are: C. Baldick *The Social Mission of English Criticism 1848–1932* 1983; C. Baldick *Criticism and Literary Theory 1890 to the Present* 1996; P. Parrinder *Authors and Authority: English and American Criticism, 1750–1900* 1991; F. Lentricchia *After the New Criticism* 1980; F. Mulhern *The Moment of Scrutiny* 1979 (on Leavis) and D. Palmer *The Rise of English Studies* 1965.

Collections of relevant essays are: S. Gubar and J. Kamholtz (eds) *English Inside and Out: The Place of Literary Criticism* 1993; P. Brooker and P. Humm (eds) *Dialogue and Difference: English into the Nineties* 1989; J. Batsleer *et al.* *Rewriting English: Cultural Politics and Gender and Class* 1985; C. MacCabe (ed.) *Futures for English* 1988 and M. Green and R. Hoggart (eds) *English and Cultural Studies: Broadening the Context* 1987 and P. Widdowson (ed.) *Re-reading English* 1982.

Relations between 'English' and other subjects are traced in R. Hodge *Literature as Social Discourse: Textual Strategies in English and History* 1990; J-P. Barricelli *et al.* (eds) *Teaching Literature and Other Arts* 1990; A. Easthope *Literary into Cultural Studies* 1991 and Green and Hoggart 1987 (as above); also see G. Landow and P. Delany (eds) *Hypermedia and Literary Studies* 1992.

1.8   FIELDS OF STUDY

Here we take a closer look at the the three main 'fields' in which English is currently studied. For convenience, these are distinguished as LANGUAGE, LITERATURE and CULTURE (this last including Communication and Media). Such labels are crude. But they are initially useful in that they agree with the recent history of the subject and the currently recognised institutional divisions within and around it. That is, individual English courses (and sometimes whole degree programmes) tend to concentrate on 'language' and/or 'literature' and/or 'culture, communication and media'. (The repeated and/ors are a reminder that some courses and most programmes do a mixture, though invariably with a particular emphasis.) At the most obvious level, these distinctions can be observed in the various names we find in prospectuses and over departmental corridors. Aside from the relatively plain and all-purpose *English* and *English Studies*, the current favourites are *English Language & Literature*; *English & Cultural Studies*; *English & Communication*; and so on. Significantly, these names are increasingly hybrid (often projecting English and *or* as something else). Alternatively, they do without the term 'English' altogether, even when many of the materials involve English as an object and a medium of study (e.g., *Literary Studies* and *Rhetoric and Composition*; see 1.5.8, 1.5.5).

A couple of things should be clarified about the notion of 'fields' used here. First, these are better conceived as *force fields* rather than the kind of fields we find in farming. They operate as ceaselessly shifting and mutually shaping energies, not as spatially fixed and mutually exclusive areas. In this sense a 'field' is a force we bring to bear on a particular material, or the conditions in which we place that material. It is also the force exerted by that material. What one person sees and uses primarily as 'language' another may see and use primarily as 'literature', and yet another may see and use primarily as an instance of 'culture' (or communication or media). For instance, think of an extract from a novel and the lyrics of a pop song: e.g., Austen's *Pride and Prejudice* (5.2.3 b) and Queen's 'Bohemian Rhapsody' (5.1.10). Each can be grasped as a series of words (language); as a form of verbal play (literature); and as representation of things going on in the rest of the human world (culture). At the same time, the properties of the material itself predispose (though they do not absolutely predetermine) the ways in which we use and understand it. A novel tends to be read silently and in solitude; a pop song tends to be heard and (if supported by a video or performance) seen, often in the company of other people. We may also be predisposed to classify *Pride and Prejudice* as (classic) literature and 'Bohemian Rhapsody' as (popular) culture. However, the fact the novel can be made into a successful high-street film (and thus shift in medium and cultural location) while the words and music of the pop song have achieved such 'classic' status that they will be readily recognised by most readers of this book (and can thus legitimately be studied as instances of contemporary lyric/poetry), reminds us that these categories are flexible and to some extent arbitrary. What we see in a text is partly a function of what we look for. What it *is* partly relates to what is *done* with it. That is why it is useful to approach all texts, at least initially, as potential instances of language and/or literature and/or culture. For only by grasping the complex interconnections amongst the latter concepts can we wield them effectively, together, as analytical tools.

The following brief examples should help fix the above points. We focus on just a couple of lines: 'I wandered lonely as a cloud' (the first line of Wordsworth's poem of that name; see 5.4.3 a) and 'The rain in Spain stays mainly in the plain' (from the musical *My Fair Lady*, 1956, based on George Bernard Shaw's *Pygmalion*, 1913). Both are used to show how the analysis of a text can operate at a variety of levels, and that, taking all these levels together, we can develop a complexly multilayered comprehension of that text in context and in relation to other texts. The main fields LANGUAGE, LITERATURE and CULTURE are signalled to the left. Meanwhile, the terms *Rhetoric*, *Intertextuality* and *Discourse* have been inserted into the gaps to the right. These simply confirm the overlap between the three fields, while also pointing to other ways in which the analysis might be configured. (More will be said about all these terms shortly; specifically linguistic and grammatical terms can be checked in the glossary in Part Six.) For the moment, simply note the multilayered nature of these analyses:

(a)   **'I wandered lonely as a cloud'**

LANGUAGE: 'I' is a first person singular pronoun (subject); 'wandered' is a simple past tense (verb); 'lonely as a cloud' is an adverbial phrase of manner and comparison. Grammatical structure: (traditional) subject–verb–adverb; (functional): participant–process–circumstance

Rhetoric

LITERATURE: Opening of lyric poem; octosyllabic; embellished by pastoral simile; influential Romantic image of 'poet' and 'poetry'

Intertextuality

CULTURE: Pastoral individualism; 'idle' country classes; subsequently clichéd view of poetry frequently cited and very variously 'sited' in other texts (e.g. 5.4.3)

Discourse

(b)   **'The rain in Spain stays mainly in the plain'**

LANGUAGE: 'The rain' is a noun phrase; 'in Spain' is an adverbial with a named place; 'stays mainly' is a verb and post-modifying adverb; 'in the plain' is an adverbial of place. Nine out of ten syllables are monosyllabic, with recurrent sound patterning. Grammatical structure: (traditional) subject–verb–adverb; (functional) participant–process–circumstance.

Rhetoric

LITERATURE: This is part of a sung conversation based on a stage play. There is a basic pentameter structure (five 'feet' alternating unstressed/stressed and long/short syllables) and there are five internal rhymes on /ay(n)/.

Intertextuality

CULTURE: It is also part of an elocution drill reinforcing 'correct' English (the consequence of a bet between privileged upper-class males (Professor Henry Higgins and Colonel Pickering) about the educability of an underprivileged working-class female (Eliza Doolittle). The line and song were made famous in a Hollywood musical starring Rex Harrison and Audrey Hepburn.

Discourse

Clearly, then, any text may act as the focus for a highly varied yet intricately interrelated set of analytical operations. It can be described at a variety of levels using a variety of *linguistic*, *literary* and *cultural* terms. Picking up those other terms featured to the right, we might also say that every text can be analysed in terms of RHETORIC (its organisation of information and its power to persuade); **inter-textuality** (its relations to other texts) and **discourse** (the particular way of saying and seeing and the values it projects). But whatever the terms and techniques used, it is crucial to observe that analysis can be undertaken in a variety of dimensions and directions and with various frames of reference in mind. It is equally crucial to recognise that all these 'levels' or 'dimensions' contribute to the building of what is notionally a single edifice: a full yet flexible critical understanding of the text. Thus we may roll all the above comments on the first line of Wordsworth's 'I wandered lonely as a cloud' together to produce something like the following.

This text is organised round the notion of the poet as solitary individual, hence the prominence of the first person singular pronoun in the first word and the use of the adverb 'lonely'. The verb 'wandered' (as distinct from, say, 'walked' or 'marched') implies an aimless ramble where there is neither the pressure of work nor a firm destination to direct it. The simile 'lonely as a cloud' points both to the wanderer's aloneness and, at the same time, his oneness with nature. This line is often cited as a quintessential instance of 'poetry'. To be more precise, it exemplifies a certain kind of 'Romantic pastoral poetry' in which some supposedly special and sensitive soul comments upon and communes with nature. However, the susceptibility of this line to ironic and parodic treatment is a measure of just how particular, even peculiar, that vision of poetry and the poet is. Certainly this version of poetry stands at some distance from the largely urban scenes and the highly technologised and commercialised modes of life we encounter in much of modern life. For all these reasons, Marxists, Feminists and Postmodernists would all have different tales to tell about – and with – this material. In fact, the cultural value of this line is endlessly renegotiable, depending upon the texts with which it is identified and the discourses in which it is made to figure. Compare it, for instance, with Dorothy Wordsworth's *Journal* entry about the same outing (5.4.3 b), where other people are present and some are working. Or compare it with the poetic parody (5.4.3 c), where it is the gendered dimension of the text's mode and moment of (re)production that is wittily exposed. Meanwhile, the invocation of the text in the advertising copy (5.4.3 d) quite literally 'trades upon' the poem's status as a familiar 'classic'. This is now palpably poem as commodity.

In all these ways, then, even a single line can serve as the site, or act as the focus, for a wide range of analytical and critical activities. Significantly, these activities are both *in*tensive and *ex*tensive. We look hard *at* the text in hand, but we also attempt to see *through* it. We look closely at 'the words on the page', but also try to see them in relation to other texts and as part of a larger world. We look at what the text *is* but also try to see what it *does*. To be sure, none of this absolutely determines the *value of William Wordsworth's text, or of any of the others touched upon here. Nor does it determine whether we should like it or not. (*Revaluation and dis/likes are matters that can only be weighed through discussion, negotiation and exchange. And in any case these are tiny, merely token samples.) At the same time, it should be clear that getting one's initial bearings in terms of language, literature and culture (or rhetoric, intertextuality and discourse) has some real appeal. It allows us to establish fairly firm ground and provisional conditions upon which to frame a more sophisticated analysis. It also allows us to talk in a number of more or less common critical languages without forcing us to agree. The rest, quite properly, is up to us.

ACTIVITY

(a)　*Conflate the three-tiered comments on 'The rain in Spain . . . '* so as to produce an integrated analysis along the lines of that produced for the line from Wordsworth.

(b)　*Sketch a linguistic, literary and cultural analysis of one of the following lines of text.* Do this in the form of a three-tiered and/or an integrated analysis. The texts for analysis – in their entirety – are:

♦　'Humpty Dumpty sat on a wall / Humpty Dumpty had a great fall' (see 5.4.1);
♦　'If I should die, think only this of me' (see 5.4.6 d)

(Notice that, like the Wordsworth material, each of these lines is presented as part of a cluster of related materials supported by notes. This should help you gesture to broader contexts and conditions.)

Finally, follow up the terms RHETORIC, **intertextuality** and **discourse** in the index. How might these also be used as tools to analyse one of the above texts?

DISCUSSION

> The field cannot well be seen from within the field.
>
> Ralph Waldo Emerson, *Circles* (1841)

READING: All the following approach language, literature and culture as interconnected categories and processes. They often also explore related notions of rhetoric, intertextuality and discourse: Kinneavy 1971: 17–47; Birch 1989; Carter and Simpson 1989; Leith and Myerson 1989; Durant and Fabb 1990; Carter and Nash 1990; Green and LeBihan 1996: 1–48; Short 1996; Fabb 1997; Simpson 1997.

1.8.1 Language

Language can be provisionally defined as 'words', however made and wherever found. Learning to grasp words, both analytically and actively, is obviously a central part of English Studies. And that *grasping*, it should be stressed, means learning both to take language apart and to put it together again – differently. We *use* as well as *analyse* words. As far as language is concerned, English Studies embraces everything from the teaching and learning of basic *literacy skills to the cultivation of advanced skills in comprehension and composition (in reading and writing literary and scientific texts for instance). It includes a knowledge of specific texts and utterances as well as sense of how language in general works. Reading and writing are also best developed in conjunction with listening and speaking, with viewing and presenting. In this way language from the outset is situated in a variety of media (not all of which are exclusively verbal) and is used for a variety of purposes (not all of which are narrowly academic).

Every major theoretical position and critical practice in contemporary English Studies may be 'placed' according to its particular view of language. Each position/practice also has its own partially distinctive vocabulary and even style. Thus American NEW CRITICS, Russian FORMALISTS, and some *deconstructionists tend, in their various ways, to concentrate on language as a system in its own right: they play up the relations between one word and another, and play down the relations between words and the rest of reality. They emphasise the **text** as a self-sufficient construct, more or less independent of **context**, and textuality as a wor(l)d unto itself. Conversely, a number of historically sensitive and politically motivated approaches associated with MARXISM, FEMINISM and POSTCOLONIALISM are much more committed to exploring word–world and text–context relations. They investigate the ways in which people can be liberated or enslaved by the words they use (or which use them), and they treat language as a form of social power (i.e. **discourse**). PSYCHOLOGICAL critics also emphasise the power of words both to express and repress that which is hidden in the unconscious. POSTMODERNISTS, meanwhile, are more engaged by the shifting relations among words, images and sounds in the contemporary media. They often treat words, and especially printed books, as of diminishing cultural significance.

Of course, many theorists and critics combine two or more positions with respect to language. They also develop distinctive approaches to the relations between, for instance, *literary and non-literary or **standard** and 'non-standard' language. Indeed, some linguists contest such distinctions altogether. They use the more neutral terms **text** and **discourse** (without appealing to any essentially literary or non-literary properties) and often prefer to talk of plural **varieties** or versions of English (without insisting on a strict division into standard and non-standard).

For all these reasons, it is important for students of English to develop a good grasp of language, theoretically and in practice.

- What are words? What do we do with them? What do they do to us?
- How and why does language change over time and vary from place to place?
- What's so special (or so common) about the language of each and every one of us?
- Are there really such things as 'literary' or 'standard' language? Or do these change and vary too?

You will not find neat, complete answers in what follows. But you will be encouraged to frame these questions more precisely and to relate them directly to your own experience of using, analysing and reflecting upon words.

What language is and can be

The word *language* derives from Latin *lingua*, through French *langue*, meaning 'tongue'. Conversely, *tongue* is an archaic, ultimately Anglo-Saxon, English word for 'language' (as in 'native tongue', 'foreign tongues'). Either way, language was initially primarily identified with the physical business of **speech**. **Writing**, on the other hand, is invariably a later manifestation of language, both in individual persons and in whole societies. Thus virtually everybody learns to listen and speak before they learn to read and write, and every society is *oral before it is *literate. Moreover, most people continue to communicate orally even when literacy is widespread, even though the relations between oracy and literacy change. For instance, virtually all the readers of this book will use language to talk with other people in corridors, in shops, over meals, in bed and on the telephone as well as to write notes, type essays, write poems, etc. We also routinely use language when listening to the radio and watching TV. This multimedia potentiality of words – their capacity to operate as speech *and* writing, sound *and* sight, in a variety of live *and* recorded modes – is of fundamental significance. It means that words are an extraordinarily versatile and volatile communicative resource. It also means that **variation** and the capacity to generate highly distinct versions of ostensibly 'the same words' are knit into the very fabric of language. That is why some of the activities in the present book work across the speech/writing interface, and involve various kinds of *translation from one medium to another.

'Language' is a term which is used to refer to many different things. It is impor to be aware which sense is in play at any one time. Language can be:

1   *spoken, written, printed and otherwise recorded words*: notionally a single *sign-system but constituted in many materials and media;
2   *the notional totality of all languages*, as well as what is common to them: 'Language' (capitalised and singular);
3   *specific languages* (lower case and plural) e.g., the English, Russian or Yoruba languages;
4   *a distinctive variety, *style or **genre***, e.g., advertising language, journalese, the language of Anglo-Saxon (or Caribbean) poetry, old Church Slavonic;
5   *loosely, by extension, modes of *non-verbal communication and other sign-systems in general*, e.g., 'body language', 'the language of film – or flowers or music or love or advertising' – notwithstanding the fact that each sign-system or communicative practice has its own way of saying/seeing/being which is not wholly explicable in terms of a narrowly linguistic model.

(For descriptions of English in particular, as 'one *and* many' – historically, geographically, socially and by medium – see 1.2.)

What language does and what we do with language

The preceding definitions of language are 'essentialist' in that they aim to explain language in terms of what it *is*. *Functional or *pragmatic approaches, however, set out to explore language in terms of what it *does* and how it is *used*. Here is an overview of functional perspectives.

We use language:

♦   *to interact in a wide range of social situations and material contexts*: immediate and face-to-face (typically through **speech**); indirectly in mediated situations (typically through **writing** and print); in the modern audio-visual MEDIA (typically in various permutations of live and recorded, immediate and remote *sign-systems – only one of which is verbal language);
♦   *to share and shape information collaboratively, through **dialogue**, as well as to transmit and transfer information from one person or group to another, through **monologue***: we thus use words for, respectively, many-way and one-way COMMUNICATION.
♦   *to converse with the rest of the world, others, ourselves and the language itself*, i.e.
    – the *referential/ideational* function: referring to features or aspects of the rest of the world, whether as objects, persons, events or ideas;
    – the *inter/personal* function: expressing and helping constitute individual *identities and social relations, senses of *self and *other;
    – the *metalinguistic* (or *metatextual*) function: drawing attention to the nature of language itself and the status of the specific utterance or text, a comment *in* language *on* language.
♦   *to perform a range of functions which may be further distinguished as*:
    ♦ *declarative*: making statements (e.g., 'It is');
    ♦ *interrogative*: asking questions or making requests ('Is it?');
    ♦ *directive/imperative*: giving directions or issuing orders ('Give it me!');
    ♦ *expressive/exclamatory*: expressing emotions ('It is?!').

(Many of these functions are combined in actual practice, resulting in more subtle kinds of **speech act**: inviting, imploring, insulting, threatening, cajoling, etc.)

♦ *in short – for *power and for *play.*

We use words for all the above functions. The fact that we do not *only* use words – or rarely use words alone – to perform these functions is a reminder that words are always implicated in other communication and sign-systems. Touch, gesture, clothing, car design, cityscapes: these too are ways in which we interact, share and shape, exercise power and explore through play. The advantage (some would say disadvantage) of a functionalist approach to language is that it is much richer (and messier) than an essentialist approach. Either way, trying to establish what we actually *do* with language always turns out to be a much more demanding and potentially rewarding activity than formulating in the abstract what language *is*.

Language *variation and *change

All languages change over time and eventually they change into 'other languages'. Common Latin of the Roman Empire transformed into the various modern *Romance languages: Italian, French, Spanish, etc. Old English transformed into the various kinds of modern English found in Britain, America, the Caribbean, Africa and India, etc. Relatedly, languages vary from place to place and from one social group to another. Even the language of a single person (her or his *idiolect) changes over the course of her or his life and varies according to the company s/he keeps and the situations s/he is involved in. All these processes of change and variation are interrelated. It is obviously important for anyone studying English to understand the principles which inform these processes. These pressures for change and variation may for convenience be categorised under four heads: *historically, geographically, socially* and by *medium* (see 1.2). Here we shall review the main reasons language changes, as well as how people change language and language changes people.

CHANGE – A TRANSITIVE AND/OR AN INTRANSITIVE PROCESS?

A complex formulation of the whole matter of 'change' is necessary from the outset. This applies as much to change in persons, society, nature and life in general, as to language in particular.

- If we see change as something that just happens of itself, we conceive it *intransitively*, independent of any chain of cause and effect (e.g., 'It changes'; 'You've changed').
- But if we see change as something that is bound up with other processes, we conceive it *transitively*, implicated in chains of cause and effect (e.g., 'It changed them'; 'That experience changed you').

The most sensible and sophisticated understandings of change tend to acknowledge that it is in some sense both intransitive *and* transitive: *intransitive* in that we as human beings are never in a position to identify *ultimate* causes and effects; transitive because we as human beings are always able to identify and assign *immediate* causes and effects. Ultimately, change is a sublimely philosophical and spiritual concept; immediately, it is an urgently historical and political matter. Both perspectives are possible and necessary when trying to grasp change in language, as in life in general. Hence the multiplex framing of the next sentence . . .

Language changes / language changes people / people change language because:

- *language communities move around geographically*: people thereby meet the challenge of new conditions and other language communities with old words used in new ways and new words drawn from other languages and cultures;
- *language communities are never socially uniform but are always compounded of* **differences**: differentiation is most evident along the lines of rank, class, status, gender, occupation, ethnicity, religion, age and education;
- *human societies constantly evolve new modes of production and reproduction, of words as of everything else*: changes in technology and material conditions thus underpin shifts between and mixtures of **speech**, **writing**, *print and the modern electronic MEDIA;
- *the human psyche, whether viewed individually or collectively, is constantly exploring new modes of *expression and *repression*: psychologically, words exist on the shifting interface between *conscious and *unconscious states;
- *all *signs are inherently split and unstable*: the material forms of words (signifiers) have no direct and necessary relation to the things they represent (signifieds). For instance, the modern English words 'woman' (Anglo-Saxon 'wifman') and 'black' (Anglo-Saxon 'bla(e)c'), have changed in both form and sense over the past thousand years. The former split to give us modern 'wife' and 'woman'; the latter could mean variously 'black', 'shining' or even 'white' – it all depended upon the reflective property of whatever was shining, not any intrinsic colour.

Overall, then, language change is implicated in every other aspect of change: social, technological, physical and biological. Plenty of big questions remain unanswered, of course. Precisely how and why do communities move geographically? societies become differentiated? new technologies arise? psyches express and repress? signs ceaselessly split and re-form? But at least we can now recognise language change to be no isolated or purely self-sufficient process. It does happen *for reasons* not just 'because it happens'. It is implicated in chains of cause and effect. It is, so to speak, a '*transitive' process. However, not surprisingly, people differ widely as to who or what causes what effect on whom or what. Some people also persist in the belief that language simply changes of itself, '*intransitively', as a kind of self-sufficing process. The following activities and discussion topics will help you weigh these and related matters for yourself.

(Linguistic checklists for close reading can be found in 4.2.)

ACTIVITIES

(a)   *Translate and/or adapt a couple of the following texts* into a variety of English with
       which you are familiar (spoken or written, formal or informal, literally or freely – as
       you wish): (a) Psalm 137 (5.4.2); (b) 'Humpty Dumpty' (5.4.1); (c) one of the Old
       and Middle English poems (5.1.2); (d) Barnes's 'Woak Hill' (5.1.6); (e) Harrison's *v.*
       (5.4.5 c); (f) πO's *7 DAIZ* (5.1.9 a); (g) Chan Wei Meng's 'I spik Ingglish' (5.1.9 b); (h)
       Collins's 'No Dialects Please' (5.1.9 c).

       Go on to make a systematic comparison between your version and the version(s) you
       translated/adapted with respect to: spelling, punctuation and visual presentation;
       word choice; word combination and discourse (see the checklist in 4.2).

(b)   *Put the questions 'What is it?' and 'What does it do?'* to some very different kinds of text.
       Use your observations to prime reflection on the distinctions and connections
       between an 'essentialist' and a 'functionalist' approach to language.
          Suggested genres for comparison are:
       (i)   a brief conversational exchange (e.g., Family conversation (5.3.1 b));
       (ii) news headlines or photo captions on the same event (e.g., Gulf War or IRA
             (5.2.5 c));
       (iii) a brief passage from a novel or short story (e.g., *Heart of Darkness* (5.2.4 c));
       (iv) a short poem, song or advert (e.g., 'Tropical Death' (5.4.5 e); 'Bohemian
             Rhapsody' (5.1.10); Clarins skincare advert (5.4.4 b)).

DISCUSSION

        (i)   no one man's English is *all* English.
                      'Historical Introduction', *Oxford English Dictionary* (1928: xxiii)

        (ii) A system network is a theory of language as choice. It represents a language,
              or any part of a language, as a resource for making meaning by choosing.
                      M.A.K. Halliday, *An Introduction to Functional Grammar* (1985: xiii)

        (iii) As a writer I know that I must select studiously the nouns, pronouns, verbs,
              adverbs, etcetera, and by a careful syntactical arrangement make readers
              laugh, reflect or riot.
                      Maya Angelou, from *Conversations with Maya Angelou* (1985)

        (iv) Language is not decaying due to neglect. It is just changing as it always did.
                      Jean Aitchison, *The Language Web* (1996, BBC Reith Lectures)

       Also see: 1.1; 4.2; **accent and dialect; addresser–addressee; discourse** and
       discourse analysis; *grammar;* **poetry and word-play;** *semiotics;* **speech
       and conversation, monologue and dialogue;** *punctuation;* **standards and
       standardisation, varieties and variation; text, context and intertextuality**.

       READING: Lively and relevant general introductions to language are Andersen 1988,
       Fromkin and Rodman 1997, Montgomery 1996 and Kress 1989. Change and variation are

well treated by Aitchison 1991, 1996 and Graddol *et al.* 1996. Language-based approaches to literature are very well served by Fowler 1996, Short 1996, Fabb 1997, Simpson 1997 and Birch 1989. Traugott and Pratt 1980 is extensive and still very worthwhile. Surveys which combine historical and contemporary perspectives with attention to language and literature include all four volumes of Open University 1996b and Carter and McRae 1997. Ranging collections of essays are Carter and Simpson 1989 and Toolan 1992.

Useful traditional *grammars are Greenbaum and Quirk 1990, Hurford 1994 and Crystal 1996; effective *functional grammars are Halliday and Hasan 1989 (introductory) and Halliday 1985 (advanced).

Recommended theory on language is Williams 1977: 21–44, Voloshinov 1973 and Cameron 1992. For specific reading on 'English/englishes', see 1.4. For glossaries of 'key words' and linguistic/stylistic dictionaries, see beginning of Part Six.

1.8.2   LITERATURE

If you are studying English in tertiary education it tends to be assumed you are doing English *Literature*. And that in turn leads to the common assumption (amongst people outside college at least) that you spend most of your time sitting round reading and making admiring remarks about 'great works of Eng. Lit': poems by Wordsworth and Keats, novels by Austen and Dickens, and plays by Shakespeare and . . . well, more Shakespeare. Occasionally such assumptions turn out to be true. The equation 'English' = 'Eng. Lit.' = 'a small selection of great authors/works' sometimes still holds. Increasingly, however, such assumptions are likely to prove ill-founded, or at best only partial truths. You may indeed spend some of your time studying, discussing and writing about commonly recognised **classics** belonging to a **canon** of supposedly great works. But this is likely to involve something more historically informed and culturally demanding than mere LITERARY APPRECIATION (see 1.5.7). It is also likely to focus on authors, works, genres, social movements and even whole national literatures which have little or nothing in common with the popular – and remarkably persistent – vision of 'Eng. Lit.' as a kind of genteel club.

The shifting multiplicity of subjects covered by the term 'English' is explored earlier in 1.1. The historical fact that Literature, narrowly conceived, has only ever been a part of English Studies, broadly conceived, is explored in 1.2. In the present section we concentrate on the fact that 'literature' is itself a historically variable and theoretically elastic term. We also review past, present and possible future alternatives to it. To be precise, we consider

- the history of the term 'literature', along with cognate terms such as *literary, *literariness and *literate;
- the relative usefulness of alternative terms such as *rhetoric, *poetics, **writing**, **text**, **discourse** and *performance.

What was, is and can be literature?

The word 'literature' ultimately derives from the Latin *littera*, meaning 'letter of the alphabet'. The word came into English, via court French, in the late fourteenth century and for the next few centuries simply meant 'acquaintance with books' and 'book learning' in general. As such it was virtually synonymous with what we now call *literacy (being able to read and write), a word which came into English in contradistinction to 'illiteracy' in the early nineteenth century. Thus a writer in 1581 can talk of 'Ane pure [i.e. poor] man quha [who] hes nocht sufficient literatur to undirstond the scripture' (see *OED*, Literature, 1). By extension, in so far as 'literature' referred to a body of books, as well as the activity of book learning, there was little attempt to distinguish the *kinds* of book. This generalised sense of literature meaning 'anything written on a subject' persists to the present day (e.g., scientific or advertising literature). The only criterion seems to have been that the books be of some *value. Thus Hazlitt (*c*.1825) quotes Ayrton as having dubbed 'the two greatest names in English literature, Sir Isaac Newton and Mr Locke' (Williams 1983: 185). Newton was a scientist and Locke a philosopher; so neither of them would fit into the conceptions of 'English literature' which later came to underpin university departments of that name.

In fact it is only since the late eighteenth and early nineteenth centuries that 'literature' has become narrowed in meaning to its current dominant sense of *creative or **imaginative** writing of a specifically **aesthetic** kind. Thus Dr Johnson in his 'Life of Cowley' (1779): 'An author whose pregnancy of imagination and elegance of language have set him high in the ranks of literature.' Corresponding narrowings and elevations of meaning can be observed over the same period in the terms **artist** (increasingly distinguished from the humbler term *artisan) and **author** (increasingly distinguished from the more general term *writer). Meanwhile, again relatedly, a category of specifically *fictional writing was being increasingly distinguished from a category of specifically *factual writing (see **realism**), just as *story was being separated out from *history (see **narrative**). The overall result of these interrelated changes may be summed up as follows.

'Literature', from the late eighteenth century onwards, was narrowed and elevated so as to mean: certain kinds of **artistic** or **aesthetic** writing which were reckoned to be especially *creative and **imaginative**, *fictional (not factual), *stories (not histories), and to be the product of especially gifted or talented writers called **authors** – in extreme cases *geniuses. Conversely, from this new and narrowly 'literary' point of view, all writing that was reckoned to be *factual and *historical was also implicitly stigmatised as less creative and imaginative – in short, 'non-literary'.

The ramifications of such a division and hierarchy are obviously of fundamental significance. They underpin both the sorting of texts and the sorting of whole subject areas into distinct disciplines. Henceforth (and it is worth repeating that this shift only began to become marked less than two hundred years ago), 'literature' was abstracted from the general continuum of writing practices and book production and put on a special pedestal of its own.

It is the above narrowed and elevated sense of 'literature' which dominated most departments of Literature until quite recently. Now, however, there are signs of a return to LITERARY STUDIES (see 1.5.8), along lines which more and more resemble its pre-Romantic shape. That is, there is a return to a much more capacious view of literature as 'book learning' in particular, and the processes and products of reading and writing in general. This is especially noticeable in the adjacent (and increasingly overlapping) 'field' of RHETORIC and COMPOSITION (see 1.5.5). One symptom of this is that there is now a tendency to talk more neutrally and in less value-laden terms of **texts** (rather than of 'literary works' or even 'poems', 'plays' and 'novels'). Another is that there is a tendency to foreground the social-historical and *power dimensions of various kinds of **writing and reading** by characterising them as **discourses** (rather than compulsively sorting them into the categories of 'literary' or 'non-literary', 'fictional' or 'factual'). In all these ways, contemporary Literary Studies – and even more so contemporary CULTURAL STUDIES (see 1.5.10) – have challenged recently dominant notions of literature and have sought to put the study of texts of all kinds on a different footing. Partly it has been done with the support of the more rigorous models and methods of text and discourse analysis derived from *Linguistics. Partly this has been prompted by more or less explicit and committed political agendas drawn from varieties of MARXISM, FEMINISM and POSTCOLONIALISM. Either way, the result is an approach to literature – and an interrogation of the category itself – which is substantially opposed to the various orthodoxies that dominated the teaching of 'English' (as) 'Literature' for much of the twentieth century. (American NEW CRITICISM in its concentration on the literary work, especially the poem, as 'verbal icon' was one such orthodoxy. Russian FORMALISM with its concentration on *literariness as the *defamiliarisation of ordinary language use and 'routine' norms of perception was another.) In the event, whether they have assumed or asserted, resisted or refused the category itself, every one of the approaches represented in Part Two has had something useful to contribute to the debate on literature.

WHAT IS(N'T) LITERATURE – OPEN DISCUSSION OR HIDDEN AGENDA?

Contemporary students of English quickly become aware of certain things about the continuing debate on what is or isn't literature. For one thing, they recognise that there is indeed a debate (and sometimes nothing short of a pitched battle) when it comes to defending or attacking, maintaining or modifying, certain versions of 'literature'. For another thing, more immediately and as a matter of academic survival, they are usually adept at working out which lecturers hold which views – and perhaps adjusting their own accordingly. This leaves everyone involved, staff as well as students, with opportunities as well as problems.

• At best, the debates on 'what is(n't) literature' are conducted from the outset, in the open, reasonably and for all to participate in, student or lecturer. Regular forums, position papers and round-tables work well in these respects.
• At worst, there is no debate at all: only more or less secret, undeclared and unargued agendas; a sense of faction or mutual incomprehension amongst the staff. Students are thus left with the unenviable task of second-guessing what version or vision of literature, textuality or discourse particular members of staff expect you to engage with.

The suggestions and questions below will not solve any of these problems, intellectually or institutionally. But they will at least help identify areas of common concern and, perhaps, transform them into common interest. The question of 'What was, is and can be literature?' can then be recognised as a challenge and an opportunity – not a threat and an obstacle.

ACTIVITIES

(a)   *What kinds of literature are YOU engaged with?* Go through the following kinds of text and in each case ask how far approaching them as literature is appropriate or adequate. (Some alternative terms and concepts are offered in parentheses.) Does the kind of literature you are engaged with include:

   (i)   *works which are chiefly designed to be read silently by individuals.*

         (Does a 'literary' approach therefore emphasise **reading** more than **writing**?)

   (ii) *works which are primarily designed to be spoken and performed, heard and seen*, e.g., stage and TV plays, films, scripts of speeches?

         (Does a 'literary' approach draw undue attention to the page rather than the stage or screen? What other approaches through **drama and theatre**, performance and other MEDIA are possible and perhaps desirable? How practicable are they?)

   (iii) *texts which are clearly in some sense 'creative', 'imaginative' and 'made-up'* – terms commonly used to designate **poems**, novels and plays – but which also clearly have instrumental social functions: advertising, news reporting, political speeches?

         (How far are notions of rhetoric and, say, play more helpful in these areas? Can poetics embrace more than 'poetry' as such?)

   (iv) **narratives** *of all kinds*: not just novels and short stories, but also instances of **auto/biography**, history, oral anecdotes and jokes, as well as news and magazine stories (printed and televised), films (documentary and otherwise)?

   (v)   *materials from the popular 'broadcast'* MEDIA (e.g., pulp fiction, soap operas, pop song) as well as materials from elite 'narrowcast' CULTURE (e.g., experimental or avant-garde **art** works, modernist writing, **classic** drama, ballet and opera).

         (Is **discourse** a more useful term than 'literature' in such areas? What others are there?)

   (vi) *texts identified with a supposedly single national culture* (e.g., 'English literature' or 'Literature in English') or with a variety of interrelated cultures worldwide (e.g., American, African, Caribbean, Indian, Australian writing)? How far are these literatures/oratures/performances in translation?

         (How far are POSTCOLONIAL and MULTICULTURAL frames more fitting?)

(b)   *Literary and/or non-literary?* Take an actual instance of a supposedly non-literary text (e.g., a bus ticket, a recipe, a news headline, an advert, a note to the milkman, entries in a telephone book). Do two things with and to it.

   (i)   Argue with all the resources and cunning at your disposal that this text is already in some senses creative, **imaginative**, fictional – in short, '*literary*'.

(Compare the reflections on the notices 'Way Out' and 'Dogs must be carried on the escalator' in Eagleton 1996: 6.)

(ii)   Relocate and, if you wish, adapt the 'non-literary' text you chose so that it functions as (part of) a plausible poem, play, novel or short story. Add a commentary exploring what you did and why.

DISCUSSION

(i)   Some texts are born literary, some achieve literariness, and some have literariness thrust upon them.

> Terry Eagleton, *Literary Theory: An Introduction* (1996: 7)

(ii)   It seems, however, best to consider as literature only works in which the aesthetic function is dominant.

> René Wellek and Austin Warren, *Theory of Literature* (1963: 25)

(iii)   Clearly the proper study of literature is – everything else.

> Peter Widdowson, 'W(h)ither English?', in Coyle *et al.* (1990: 1228)

Also see: 1.5.7–10; NEW CRITICISM; FORMALISM; **aesthetic(s)**; **art**; **author**; **canon and classic**; *creativity; *fiction; **imaginative**; **poetry and word-play**; *poetics; **text . . . intertextuality**; **writing**.

READING: For further practical activities playing with (and with the concept of) literature, turn to Durant and Fabb 1990: 1–17; Moon 1992: 72–6, 101–6, 121–4. For further discussion, a provocative pairing is Eagleton 1996: 1–14 with Wellek and Warren 1963: 15–53. Other voices and points of view can be found in Walder 1990: Parts I, IV and VII. Good historical and theoretical overviews of changing conceptions of 'literature' are Fowler in Coyle *et al.* 1990: 30–50 and Williams 1977: 45–54; also see Williams 1983: 183–8 and Williams 1989: 147–56. For alternative reframings of English in terms of critical-creative **(inter)textuality**, see Scholes *et al.* 1995, Pope 1995, and Nash and Stacey 1997; and for English and/as *rhetoric, see Nash 1989, 1992 and Berlin 1996; also Andrews 1992.

1.8.3   Culture, communication and media

The complex and sometimes vexed relations between various kinds of Studies – English, Literary, Cultural, Communication and Media – are introduced from a historical and institutional perpective in 1.5.8–11. In the present section we consider how a practical approach to our subject through Culture, Communication and Media (these terms are differentiated but taken together as a kind of composite 'field') can help redefine and redirect what we are doing in the other two fields of LANGUAGE and LITERATURE (1.8.1–2). We also see that all these relations are reciprocal. Specifically 'linguistic' and 'literary' approaches have their parts to play, too, particularly in the precise and sensitive analysis of verbal materials.

    In certain limited senses 'English' has always been concerned with culture, communication and media. Literary critics from Matthew Arnold in the late nineteenth century to F.R. Leavis and Lionel Trilling in mid-twentieth-century Britain and America, along with many of their successors to the present day, have often insisted upon the 'cultural' dimension of their mission (see NEW CRITICISM). For what is 'the English language', they insist, but a quintessential verbal expression of English (or American) culture? What is 'English Literature' but a splendid way of communicating that culture as a national heritage or spiritual and aesthetic resource? And what are manuscript and print but the primary media in which 'the best that has been known and thought' in that culture have been recorded and transmitted to future generations? In other words, even the most conventional courses in History of the Language and Literary Criticism have always been concerned with such larger issues.

Or have they?

Depending how you look at it, answers to all the above questions may be a qualified ' yes' followed by 'but . . . ', or a disqualifying 'no'. I'll opt for the former.

- ◆   *Yes*, 'the English language' may express 'English culture'

  but which ENGLISHES: old, middle, modern or 'new'? spoken Cumbrian or Caribbean creole? standard printed British or American? (see 1.2.1–2).

  and which versions or sections of those cultures: upper, middle or working class? women or men? the un/employed or the un/educated? Protestants, Catholics, Jews, atheists? non/native Britons, Americans, Australians . . . ?

- ◆   *Yes*, 'English LITERATURE' has had a central role in communicating that culture/ these cultures

  but for a long time (mis)represented by a highly specific **canon** *of texts*, chiefly by men who were almost exclusively white, middle-to-upper class and Western European in origin or orientation.

- ◆   *Yes* with an emphasis on the written and printed words

  but not much attending to manuscript and print cultures in general (including news-papers, popular magazines, bestsellers and pulp fiction) and only very selectively attending to early *oral culture (court songs rather than popular ballads) while roundly ignoring most of contemporary audio and audio-visual cultures (from radio to film, TV, video and, latterly, hypermedia).

  Yes, English Studies has always in some sense been concerned with culture, communication and media – *but . . . but . . . but . . .*

The purpose of this section is therefore twofold:

- to provide some definitions of 'culture', 'communication' and 'media' which both embrace and exceed those current in contemporary English Studies;
- to encourage a range of activities and educational practices which are effective and enjoyable, whether the course be nominally in English, Cultural, Communication or Media Studies.

CULTURE as a word derives via French from Latin *cultus*, primarily meaning 'the nurturing of growth'. The root verb is *colere* – to grow. The history of the term is especially complex and fascinating. Six uses of 'culture' are distinguished below, each of which belongs to a distinct line of development and all of which can be traced in current debates on the subject. Culture has previously meant and still can mean:

1   *the tending of growing things, the nurturing of *nature.* The earliest English senses of 'culture' are tied up with farming, agri*culture* and horti*culture*. *'Cultivation'* is a closely related word which also initially referred to the cultivation of fields, orchards and gardens, and only later (from the seventeenth century) designated the cultivation of people's minds and manners. This radical connection between 'culture' and 'cultivation' and the tending of natural growth is crucial to traditional (especially *Romantic) debates on the relations between 'nature' and 'nurture', and the 'human/nature' debate in general. It is also tapped into by modern *ecological* critics. In these cases, basically, Culture = Nature + Humanity.

2   *human civilisation, set against (rather than alongside or in harmony with) the rest of nature.* From the eighteenth century onwards it became increasingly common to see human culture, for better and worse, as hardly part of nature at all. In these cases, Culture = Humanity – Nature.

3   **artistic** *and* **aesthetic** *activity of a primarily symbolic kind,* as distinct from artisanal and practical activity of a primarily instrumental kind. Such a narrowing and elevation of the sense of 'culture' is observable from the mid-nineteenth century onwards and is closely paralleled by changes in the senses of LITERATURE and **art**.

4   *high culture (variously called court, elite or dominant cultures) as distinct from *popular culture (variously called folk, mass or sub- cultures).* The tendency latterly, largely through pressure from MARXIST, FEMINIST, MULTICULTURAL and POSTMODERNIST critics, has been to resist such fixed polarities, to recognise genuinely plural cultural **differences**, and to argue for constant revaluation.

5   *specific national cultures,* usually in terms of such generalised qualities as 'English reserve' or 'Australian directness', or represented by a few other assorted stereotypes: e.g., 'England' = cream teas, castles and Shakespeare; 'Australia' = the outback, Sydney Opera House and 'Waltzing Matilda'. Such highly selective versions of cultural identity underpin national heritage and tourist industries.

6   *universal or global culture – which may or may not be recognised as rooted in 'the local'.* Thus in the spheres of both high **art** and the mass MEDIA, it is now common for anything from Van Goghs to cans of Coke and from CDs to soap operas to circulate throughout the world as both aesthetic objects and commodities. Celebrants of POSTMODERNISM hail this, along with the Internet and multimedia in general, as the onset of a qualitatively new global culture. Critics of postmodernism recognise the quantity and ubiquity but question the quality and relevance. POSTCOLONIAL, MARXIST and FEMINIST critics all point to continuing imbalances of power and access with respect to this supposedly 'global' culture. (They might also point out that 'colony' ultimately derives from the same verb *colere*, 'to

cultivate', 'to settle', which in its past participle form, *cultum*, gave us the root of *culture* in the first place. Hence the threat of domination – not simply emancipation – through someone else's version of culture.)

These six definitions of 'culture' are neither exhaustive nor conclusive. They often overlap and they sometimes contradict one another. All that is to be expected. Culture is a concept central to so many contemporary debates and practices (including whole disciplines such as English, Art, Sociology and Anthropology) that it would be very surprisng if there were anything resembling consensus. Indeed, that is precisely why we are left with the challenge and responsibility of deciding how debates on culture are to be articulated outside as well as within those disciplines.

COMMUNICATION as a word derives via French from the Latin *communicare* meaning 'to share', 'to make common', as well as 'to impart' (information) and 'to convey' (goods). The distinctions among these meanings are worth emphasising because they point to fundamental differences in the theory and practice of a whole range of activities we now call 'communications'. Basically, there are four interrelated ways in which we can conceive of the processes of COMMUNICATION: one-way; two- or many-way; exchange and change; through medium and context.

1   *In a one-way process*, information is 'imparted' or goods 'conveyed' from one person (or source) to another: **addresser** to **addressee**; A → B. In terms of language this corresponds to **monologue**, and is generally referred to as a uni-directional, linear or *transference* model of communication. This model is properly used in communications engineering where the aim is to transmit a signal from transmitter to receiver in the purest form possible and with the minimum interference or 'noise'. Monologic, one-way modes are also common in social situations where there are marked differences in *power* and **authority** (e.g., in traditional sermons and lectures, where the preacher or teacher is institutionally empowered to speak for long stretches without interruption or audible response).

2   *In a two- or many-way process*, information is shared, goods are made collectively, and they are in some sense held in common. In terms of language this corresponds to **dialogue**, and is in general referred to as a multidirectional, recursive ('feedback') or *interactive* model of communication. In this case the emphasis is on communication as a complexly *inter*active process, not simply *pro*active or *re*active. For instance, addresser A talks to addressee B, who then responds but is interrupted by addresser C. Meanwhile, participant D goes out without saying anything but having heard everything (though she wasn't meant to). She is thus, technically, neither address*er* nor address*ee*, but is still a very important participant. Such many-way modes of communication are the norm in **conversation**, and in this case the activities of interruption or joining in are not merely 'noise' or 'interference' to be eliminated. They may turn out to be a crucial part of the interaction.

3   *Communication as a process of change as well as exchange*. This applies whether the communication system involved is as obvious as a plane full of people or a ship full of cargo (i.e. *transport* systems) or as inconspicuous as a trace on a computer

screen or a movement of air between speaker's mouth and a hearer's ear. In any event – in every event – neither the vehicles which carry the 'message' (the MEDIA), nor the materials themselves nor the participants involved are left unchanged by the process. Nothing arrives exactly as dispatched; it may or may not reach its projected destination, and both senders and receivers are never quite – or at all – the same again. Notice, too, that this notion of communication as ex/change has a *symbolic or *semiotic dimension. *Values are *transformed*, never simply *transferred*, once they are communicated. In this respect all communication is a form of *translation in the fullest sense.

4   *Communication also varies markedly according to* MEDIUM, **context** *and* *participants.* It is convenient to distinguish various kinds of communication in these respects, some of which overlap:

♦   *face-to-face*, where all participants are 'present' in that they are in the same time and place, share an immediate context and can address one another directly (e.g., most conversation);
♦   *mediated*, where one or more of the participants is 'absent' and in a different time and/or place; the contexts are therefore various and some of the communication must be indirect (e.g., all writing, print and telecommunications, including television and the Internet);
♦   *'live'*, where participants communicate at the same time but in different places (e.g., a telephone conversation, an instantaneous broadcast). The inverted commas confirm the mediated aspect of the contact;
♦   *recorded*, where some trace of the message is stored and may be subsequently retrieved. Writing, print, film, audio and audio-visual tape, as well as computer memory and disks are all 'recording' technologies in these respects;
♦   *verbal*, using words (see LANGUAGE, 1.8.1);
♦   *non-verbal*, not using words, but other *signs and sign-systems. (Notice that the treatment of 'verbal' as norm and '*non*-verbal' as marked betrays a word-based, logocentric, bias.)

A couple of further cautions and qualifications may be added. First, all communication is in some sense *interpersonal*, so it can be confusing to talk of specifically interpersonal communication when what is meant is 'face-to-face' interaction. A more precise and useful distinction is that between *inter*personal communication (self with others e.g., 'I' with 'you', 'she' with 'he') and *intra*-personal communication (self with self e.g., 'I' with 'me'). Second, we must beware of treating face-to-face communication as unproblematic and even the norm. Certainly, *face-to-face* communication may be more immediate than *mediated* or *recorded* communication, but it is not necessarily simpler or less problematic. For one thing there are many more *codes to cope with in face-to-face communciation than in writing or print: 'body language' and context as well as verbal language. For another thing the participants may be physically present in the same time and space; but they may have widely varying premises, aims, values and frames of reference. People are still in some respects **absent** from one another even when they are ostensibly 'present'. Moreover, PSYCHOLOGICALLY, no one is wholly 'present' to her or him **self** – let alone to **others**. Ultimately all experiences are mediated by our nervous and perceptual systems. In the process information is transformed and *translated – never simply transferred.

MEDIA as a word derives from the plural of Latin 'medium', meaning 'middle' or 'between' (hence 'mediator'/'a go-between', also *medi*eval, coined in the nineteenth century to label the age *between* the classical period and the Renaissance). From the early twentieth century, however, it has become increasingly common to talk of '*the* media' (definite article and plural). The media thus understood mean two interrelated yet distinct things:

♦ *those specifically *modern technologies and modes of COMMUNICATION which enable people to communicate at a distance*, characteristically through print (especially newspapers and magazines); the various *tele*-communications ('tele-' comes from the Greek word 'far', hence telegraph/'far-writing', telephone/'far-sound', television/ 'far-sight'), as well as *film, video, cable, satellite and the Internet;
♦ *by extension, the institutions which own and control these technologies as well as the people who work for them* (e.g., newspaper proprietors, TV and film companies, advertising agencies and governments, as well as reporters, camera operators, editors, producers, presenters, etc.).

We may therefore say that the media have both *technological* and *social* dimensions. The emphasis on specifically *modern*, often *contemporary*, technologies and organisations is constitutive. Many current courses in MEDIA STUDIES do not reach back to materials much before the mid-nineteenth century and the invention of the steam-driven printing press (see 1.5.10). Often they concentrate on today's (and as far as possible tomorrow's) most pervasive, influential and *popular media. Increasingly these are hi-tech multimedia. For all these reasons, notwithstanding their obvious areas of overlap, the models and methods used in Media and Communication Studies can to some extent be distinguished. Media Studies tend to:

♦ play down face-to-face interaction (e.g., **speech** and **conversation**) and play up technologically mediated modes (e.g., print and TV);
♦ concentrate on TV drama (soap operas and documentary) and film rather than stage plays, theatre and live performance;
♦ within print culture, concentrate on newspapers and magazines rather than books;
♦ generally concentrate on *broadcast rather than *narrowcast media and genres: public letters to 'problem pages' rather than private letters to a friend; bestselling pulp fiction rather than **classics**; general release rather than studio films; magazine and TV advertising rather than **poetry**; etc.

Mediation is the process whereby one person (or group) handles and passes on perceptions and information to another. Some people claim or pretend that the medium and the mediator can be 'neutral', 'impartial', 'objective' or 'innocent'. This is to ignore or suppress the fact that every transference of information involves a transformation, every exchange a change. There is thus, strictly, no such thing as a mediation (or medium or mediator) which simply presents or reflects *reality: all *re-present* and *refract* versions of reality (see **realism** and *editing).

ACTIVITIES

(a)   *What kinds of culture does each of the following represent?* Milton's *Paradise Lost* (5.1.4 a); Yeats's 'Leda and the Swan' (5.1.7 a); Tutuola's *Palm Wine Drinkard* (5.2.4 e); Kelman's *How late it was, how late* (5.2.6); Nichols 'Tropical Death' (5.4.5 e). Are the cultures represented by each piece adequately definable in terms of: (i) high art or popular culture; (ii) literature or non-literature; (iii) class, gender, ethnicity, nationality, age and education? Go on to put the same questions to texts you are studying.

(b)   *Read the entry on addresser–addressee in Part Three* and try to apply Jakobson's model to: (i) a poem; (ii) a piece of prose; (iii) a piece of drama or conversation (see 5.1., 5.2. and 5.3. for examples). In each case go on to consider your own roles as someone who both addresses and is addressed by the text (i.e. is involved in a *dialogue).

(c)   *'Great English Writing' or 'Visions of Empire'?* These are the titles of two radio or TV programmes for which you have been asked to script alternative frames and links using the same material. The material is by Shakespeare (5.3.2 b), Defoe, Behn Douglass and Morrison (5.2.2 a–b, d–e), Swift (5.2.4 a) and Kipling (5.2.4. b). (Substitute others if you wish.) Sketch two very different scripts then consider what this activity shows about the relations between Language, Literature, Culture, Communication and Media.

DISCUSSION

(i)   culture is a whole way of living.
                    Raymond Williams, *Culture and Society 1780–1950* (1958: 148)

(ii)   there is no document of civilisation which is not at the same time a document of barbarism.
                    Walter Benjamin, *Theses on the Philosophy of History* VI (*c.* 1935)
                    in Walder (1990: 363)

(iii)   though cultures have changed and will change poems remain and explain.
                    W.K. Wimsatt and M. Beardsley 'The Affective Fallacy' (1949)
                    in Lodge (1972: 357)

(iv)   communication defined as strict transference of or participation in identical experiences does not occur.
                    I.A. Richards, *The Principles of Literary Criticism* (1924) (1967: 135)

(v)   a scholarly discipline, like literature, cannot begin to do cultural studies simply by expanding its dominion to encompass specific cultural forms (western novels, say, or TV sitcoms, or rock and roll) [. . .] Cultural Studies involves *how* and *why* such work is done, not just its content.
                    Lawrence Grossberg *et al.* Introduction to *Cultural Studies* (1992: 11)

READING: For 'English' students, useful places to start are Widdowson's 'W(h)ither English?' and Hartley's 'Culture and Popular Culture' in Coyle *et al.* 1990: 1221–36, 1098–109, Eagleton 1996: 169–208, Graff *et al.* in Greenblatt and Gunn 1992: 419–36 and Easthope 1991. A wealth of relevant essays can be found in: Green and Hoggart 1987, MacCabe 1988 and Brooker and Humm 1989. Stimulating introductions to the several subjects featured in this section are: for Cultural Studies, Brantlinger 1990, Punter 1986, Grossberg *et al.* 1992 and During 1993; for Communications, Fiske 1990, Corner and Hawthorn 1995; and for Media, Branston and Stafford 1996. Handy reference books are Williams 1983 and O'Sullivan *et al.* 1994. For specifically *rhetorical perspectives on culture and communication, education and English, see Andrews 1992 and Berlin 1996.

1.9   SUMMARY: KEEPING ON COURSE AND MAKING YOUR OWN WAY

There is no single way of summarising the relations between Language and Literature and both of them and Culture, Communication and Media. Indeed the main point of the previous section has been to demonstrate that all these terms are categories and tools, not fixed 'things' at all. We use them to sort and select, work and play with materials which, depending on the very categories/tools we apply, are transformed into specific subjects of study. To be sure, certain texts or other artefacts, because of what we perceive to be intrinsic qualities, may predispose us to work and play with them primarily as 'literary', 'linguistic', 'cultural', 'communicative' or 'media' materials. Nonetheless, it is still arguable how far such qualities are indeed *intrinsic*, and how far they are *extrinsic*: the result of a particular way of looking and handling.

Of course, the main frames and terms of reference within which you are expected to approach 'English' (or whatever it is called) have already been set in the design of the course you are taking. Your teachers have already chosen and combined the materials you will study. They have also, implicitly or explicitly, already decided on the models and methods you will use in handling that material. However, that still leaves you with the fundamental task of recognising what those materials, models and methods are; and then attempting to grasp and wield them for yourself. This can only really happen if you are able to stand back a little from the particular course you are engaged in, and if you can see round – and even beyond – it. Hence the following summary questions:

♦   What *are* the kinds of material you are dealing with?
♦   How far are they being represented to you as language and/or literature and/or culture? And what kinds of language, literature, culture?
♦   Are some kinds of text *valued more than others, and are the criteria of valuation (and perhaps revaluation) made explicit?
♦   Are you concentrating on detailed analysis of 'the words on the page' and/or 'the text in context'? Is it being appreciated as an isolated artefact, a particular series of effects or an ongoing communicative and cultural process? Is the medium (or media) in which it is realised incidental or central to your approach?
♦   Are there visual or audio-visual dimensions to what you do? Are you equipped to deal with these in and on their own terms, or is the emphasis (and your critical apparatus) primarily verbal?

♦   Are you handling this material on your own and/or in groups? Does this 'handling' involve practical work: making, remaking and 'publishing' texts (including your own), as well as analysing and describing those of others?

You are also invited to carry out and discuss the following 'summary' activities, both on your own and with colleagues.

1   Return to the LANGUAGE section (1.8.1). How far is your course concerned with (i) what language *is;* (ii) what language *does;* (iii) how language *varies* and *changes*?

2   Review the kinds and categories of LITERATURE listed in 1.8.2 (esp. p. 57). Which is your course centrally engaged with? Which does it put on the margins? Which does it exclude completely?

3   Review the various kinds of CULTURE identified in 1.8.3 (esp. pp. 60–61). Which seem to be emphasised in your courses, and are there any which you would like to see more (or less) fully represented? Go on to put the related questions to your courses and yourself through the reviews of kinds of COMMUNICATION (esp. pp. 61–62) and MEDIA (esp. p. 63).

PART TWO

THEORETICAL POSITIONS AND PRACTICAL APPROACHES

PREVIEW

This part of the book explores the main theoretical positions available within contemporary English Studies. It shows how they can be used both to approach individual texts and to understand textual and cultural activity in general. The emphasis is on relating varieties of critical theory to varieties of practical activity, and on developing models that really work. The first section (2.1) invites you to get some initial bearings and insists that what ultimately matters is the development of your own positions and orientations. We then consider a general model of textuality and the critical process (2.2). This is framed in terms of *producers*, *texts*, *receivers* and *relations to the rest of the world*. The model is illustrated in action with a specific textual focus (Shakespeare's *Hamlet*) and also used as matrix against which to plot the various theoretical positions and critical practices that follow. Each of these is presented through:

• overview • key terms • major figures and movements •
'How to practise . . . ' • worked example • activities •
discussion • reading

The positions and approaches featured in this part are:

PRACTICAL and (old) NEW CRITICISM (2.3)
FORMALISM into FUNCTIONALISM (2.4)
PSYCHOLOGICAL approaches (2.5)
MARXISM, CULTURAL MATERIALISM and NEW HISTORICISM (2.6)
FEMINISM and GENDER (2.7)
POSTSTRUCTURALISM and POSTMODERNISM (2.8)
POSTCOLONIALISM and MULTICULTURALISM (2.9)

Other approaches are mentioned and cross-referenced in the final section on 'developing positions and future prospects' (2.10).

WHERE TO START

If the idea of a variety of theories and approaches is fairly new to you, begin by 'Getting some initial bearings' (2.1). Then perhaps move to 'Practical and (old) New Criticism' (2.3). The latter approach still informs much of what is done in schools and colleges. It may therefore be the approach you already practise, especially when analysing short passages, even if you are not explicitly aware of it *as* an approach. After that, turn to 'Theory in practice – a working model' (2.2) for an overall framework in which to place other positions and approaches.

2.1   GETTING SOME INITIAL BEARINGS

This brief section is offered by way of both encouragement and warning. It encourages you to see the activity of theorising as a natural and necessary part of being a reflective reader and writer. It warns you against simply mugging up theories so as to sprinkle your speech with flashy phrases that sound clever. Knowing about other people's theories is important, even essential. Opening up that knowledge is precisely what the rest of Part Two is designed to do. At the same time, knowing *about* such things is not necessarily the same as knowing *how* to *do* them. Nor is it the same as knowing when to refine and replace the tools you are working with and pick up others which will do a certain job better. That is why there is particular emphasis on exploring and experimenting with each approach in the various 'How to practise . . .' and Activity sections. Cumulatively, too, as we move from theory to theory, you will see that there is an insistence on bracing one theory against another: sometimes combining them and sometimes leaving them in conflict. Either way, it is insisted that precisely how or whether you use a certain approach (or combination of approaches) will partly depend upon the particular material in hand as well as the hand (and mind and identity) of the particular person who is wielding it. Theories may propose – but it is particular writers, materials and readers that dispose. A number of things are therefore worth stressing:

♦   *No one has a single, pure and fixed position.* Anyone who declares 'I'm a feminist critic' or 'Postmodernism is what it's all about' and merely leaves it at that is naïve or deluded.

◆   *Everyone to some extent has plural, hybrid and shifting orientations.* The person who says 'I have a strong interest in gender from a psychoanalytic point of view, mainly in contemporary film and fiction. But I'm also getting interested in . . .' is likely to be much more self-aware and sensible.

◆   *No-one has an approach identical to other people's.* We are all coming from and going to somewhat different places. The text in hand is grasped by each of us differently, and at different moments differently.

◆   *Yet everyone also has aspects of their approach which interrelate with other people's.* We may not have a 'common pursuit', but we do have some things that we share and can agree as well as argue about.

◆   *A mind which is utterly open is never made up. A mind which is utterly closed is simply not thinking. The most critical and creative minds tend to move between and beyond.* This may be put more abstractly. In theory, critical **differences** are infinite and may be indefinitely delayed and deferred. But in practice we always have to settle on provisional **preferences**. The main thing is to try to keep both the differences and the preferences in play, simultaneously or by turns.

All that said, here is an activity to help you gauge your own present positions as well as the directions and dimensions in which you are currently moving.

ACTIVITY

Turn to the 'Wordsworth' texts gathered in Part Five (5.4.3). Read each of them in order with the following suggestions and questions in mind.

(a)   *William Wordsworth's 'I wandered lonely as a cloud . . .' (5.4.3 a).* Do you normally read such texts with or without the kind of information supplied in the accompanying notes? Does such information make a difference to how you understand the poem?

   (This points to the difference between a purely **textual** and a **contextual** approach. PRACTICAL and (old) NEW CRITICS and FORMALISTS tend to be more purely textual; most other approaches also take contextual information into account. Which are you more used to? Which would you like to know more about?)

(b)   *Dorothy Wordsworth's 'Grasmere Journals' (5.4.3 b).* Do you expect to read journals, diaries and letters as part of an 'English' course? Would you class this piece as 'literature' and/or something else? Go on to weigh how far your reading of Dorothy's journal entry modifies your understanding of her brother William's poem about the same episode.

   (This points to the difference between a purely **literary** and a more broadly **textual** approach to materials. It also suggests that **auto/biography** and **hi/story** may – or may not – be allied areas of study depending how you conceive your notion of the subject. How *do* you currently conceive that subject?)

(c)   *Lynn Peters's 'Why Dorothy Wordsworth is not as famous as her brother' (5.4.3 c).* This text takes a humorously *parodic and decidedly FEMINIST turn. Are you happy with or irritated by this? Does reading Lynn Peters's poem affect your earlier readings of William's poem and Dorothy's journal entry? Or does it leave your responses to them untouched?

(This points up the fact that you may or may not attach importance to the GENDER dimensions of writing and reading. It also points to the use of parody as a form of *critique, and perhaps highlights the question of how serious and reverential or playful and irreverent you expect your subject to be. Many CULTURAL MATERIALIST and some NEW HISTORICIST approaches also sport with this kind of cheerful iconclasm. Might you?)

(d)   *'Heineken refreshes the poets others beers cannot reach' (5.4.3 d)*. Here there's a switch of MEDIA (print to TV screen plus music) and a *hybridising of genres (poem within advert). There's therefore the obvious aim of selling – and not just saying – something: the humour has a commercial as well as a parodic function. The advert is unashamedly populist in appeal. We are thus now firmly within the domain of the POSTMODERN. Though we *could* also be in the domain of, say, MARXIST, FEMINIST and POSTCOLONIAL approaches if we drew attention to the evident class, gender and colour dimensions of this advert and its particular market appeal, along with the cultural, political and economic implication of alcohol production and consumption in general.

      (Again, the basic question is: are you used to studying such texts in such ways? Would you like to know and do more?)

Finally, look through the 'Overviews' introducing each of the main positions and approaches featured in the rest of Part Two: from PRACTICAL CRITICISM (2.3) to POSTCOLONIALISM (2.9). Which of these approaches do you find (i) most familiar; (ii) most interesting; (iii) most forbidding? (Suggestion. After looking at the next 'Theory in practice' section (2.2), go to (i) then (ii). Tackle (iii) later – but do tackle it – bearing in mind that it may turn out to be the most challenging of the lot.)

2.2   THEORY IN PRACTICE – A WORKING MODEL

Theory is still seen as a dubious or even dangerous pursuit in some areas of English Studies; whereas in others it can sometimes be celebrated as an end in itself. Here we shall treat theory as neither a threatening bogey nor a universal panacea. Instead, as far as possible, we shall consider specific theori*es* and theoris*ts* (plural). We shall also engage in activities of theoris*ing* practice and practis*ing* theory (as continuing processes). Some provisional definitions and brief historical explanations of these key terms will therefore be in order:

THEORY AND PRACTICE – A RECIPROCAL RELATION

• *THEORY* involves general and systematic *reflection* upon methods and models. Theory is overtly conceptual, abstract and generalising; it is more of a 'spectator activity'. Theory questions practice.

• *PRACTICE* involves *application* of general methods and models to specific materials. Practice is overtly physical, concrete and particular: it is more of a 'participant activity'. Practice tests theory.

Combining theory with practice, we become reflective practitioners: spectators *and* participants.

The word 'theory' derives via Latin and French from Greek *theoria* (a viewing, contemplation, speculation), *theoros* (spectator, observer) and *thea* (spectacle, sight). Interestingly, all of these words share their root with the word 'theatre' (i.e. a place for spectacle). This combined sense of theory as 'observation' and 'contemplation' was the earliest recorded in English and reminds us that in a certain fundamental sense theory is about both 'observing' and 'contemplating': it embraces both 'spectacle' and 'speculation' (which are also two words which relate to seeing *and* thinking). We may therefore say that theory makes a kind of theatre for events. Theory is a spectator activity.

'Practice', meanwhile, may be conceived as a particular form of *physical* activity. 'Physical activity', 'actual doing' is the root meaning in the Greek word *praktica* from which the English word 'practice' derives via Latin. An alternative, more technical term 'praxis' (again from Greek via Latin) is also sometimes used in English, chiefly in philosophical or educational circles. Praxis specifically denotes a form of 'theorising through doing'. Either way, whether we use the term 'practice' or 'praxis', we are engaged in 'doing', 'application'. Practice is a participant activity.

Figure 2 (over the page) shows a model which will help frame the various theoretical positions and practical approaches that follow. It is adapted from one in M.H. Abrams's influential essay 'Orientation of Critical Theories' in *The Mirror and the Lamp* (1953); also in Lodge (1972: 1–26). Abrams suggests that we may categorise critical positions in so far as they emphasise one of four aspects of the literary-critical process: the *work*, the *author*, the *reader*, the *universe*. In order to make this model more applicable in a contemporary interdisciplinary context, I have modified it as follows. Any text or other human artefact may be understood as a **product** or succession of *products* (Abrams's 'work') and as the result of a number of **processes**. These processes involve three basic elements: **producers** (e.g. authors, artists, performers, publishers – Abrams's 'author'); **receivers** (e.g. readers, audiences, viewers – Abrams's 'reader'); and **relations to the rest of the world** (i.e. everyone and everything else to which the work can be taken to refer or relate – Abrams's 'universe').

Here is some further detail on the key terms:

Every **text** (or other artefact) can be understood both as an array of achieved *products* and as a series of constitutive *processes*. That is why the 'process' arrows are double-headed. They converge on and radiate out from the centre and help us see human activity as both 'product-centred' and 'process-oriented'. They therefore remind us that texts/artefacts are not simply fixed 'things' but are also items we change and exchange. (This may be called the *product-based* or *object-centred* dimension.)

Producers are featured whenever we understand the text as an expression of the design, intentional or otherwise, of particular authors, artists, directors, etc. By extension these include the 'designs' on the text of collaborating or subsequent publishers, performers, adapters, etc. All producers are therefore in some sense *re*producers in that people always make new things out of existing materials in the language, literature and culture. We never make things from scratch, out of nothing. (This may be called the *expressive* or *maker-centred* dimension.)

Receivers are featured whenever we understand the text through its actual or implied effects on various readers, audiences and viewers. Notice that all 'receivers' are also in some sense re/producers; for we always make sense of things actively, not just passively. (This may be called the *affective* or *effects-based* dimension.)

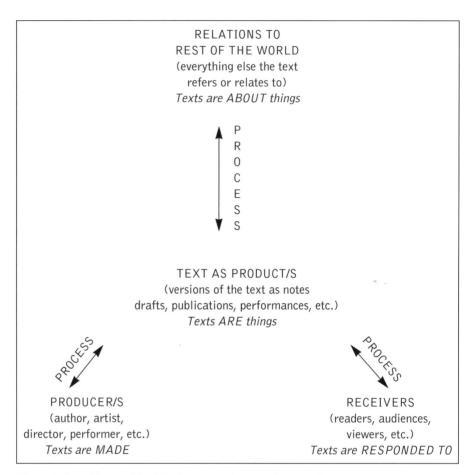

Figure 2 A working model of the text as product/s and process/es

Relations to the rest of the world are featured whenever we understand the text to represent, refer or in some way relate to people, places, events, ideas, beliefs in the worlds behind or beyond it. We say the 'rest' of the world because texts, producers and receivers are also part of the world; we might also say 'worlds' (plural) because there are always many realities (psychological, economic, political, ecological, etc.) to which a text can be related. (This may be called the *representational, mimetic, referential* or *relevance-based* dimension.)

There is a further complication, however. We must also recognise that texts exist in time and space. Every one of these products and processes is therefore constituted in a variety of historical moments. That grand abstraction 'the text' is always potentially deceptive. In reality 'the text' always turns out to be both plural and variable – a series of versions (notes, sketches, drafts, editions, performances, etc.) and not a simple and single thing at all. (Think of your own notes and drafts of essays, for instance.) The text in hand is always a *particular* text – and not just any text or every text. The notions of producers and receivers may be similarly pluralised and extended. They can embrace anyone and everyone who has ever had a hand in the transmission, transformation and reception of the text. Meanwhile, as remarked above, 'relations with the rest of the world' entail locations within and gestures towards all sorts of versions and visions of reality. These stretch from the 'then and there' of an initial moment of production to the 'here and now' of a current moment of reproduction and reception.

BASIC THEORETICAL AND PRACTICAL QUESTIONS TO PUT TO A TEXT

1 *Text as product/s*: In what manuscript, printed, performance, film or otherwise recorded versions has this text existed?
2 *Re/production and reception*: Who has been involved in making and responding to this text at various moments?
3 *Relations to the rest of the world*: What are the various frames of reference and contexts (political, religious, social, etc.) within which this text has been realised historically? What 'world-views' may it be reckoned to uphold?

Example: The not-so-strange case of 'Shakespeare's *Hamlet*'

Here is the above model set to work on a phenomenon known as 'Shakespeare's Hamlet'. The cautious 'scare quotes' round author and title are necessary because, as we quickly see, the whole matter of what we mean by 'Hamlet', whose it is, and where and when it is to be found are themselves the matters at issue. Incidentally, it does not matter whether you already know anything about anybody's *Hamlet*. The same principles can and will be applied to all sorts of other texts and artefacts.

Text as products

'Shakespeare's Hamlet' involves a wide variety of *products* – verbal, theatrical and filmic.

♦   *Verbally*, in a narrow sense, 'Hamlet' exists in three early and substantially distinct printed versions: the First Quarto (1603) – based on a transcript of an actual performance and/or actors' scripts; the Second Quarto (1604) – a much longer text presumably related to a later performance; and the First Folio (1623) – part of the posthumous collection of Shakespeare's plays put together primarily for literary posterity and reading rather than performers. None of these texts bears Shakespeare's signature or is in his hand. All have been used – sometimes singly, often in combination – as the basis for later printed editions.

♦   *Theatrically*, a play called 'Hamlet' (probably written by Thomas Kyd) is known to have existed in the late 1580s. We also know that performances of Shakespeare's earliest version preceded the First Quarto, and various versions have continued to be performed, often highly adapted, from the seventeenth century to the present. Just a few of many notable examples include: a performance for foreign merchants on the deck of an East India Company ship anchored off Sierra Leone (1607–8); Garrick's influential version in which he drops the gravediggers and much of the fifth act as 'indecorous' (1772); Kemble's streamlined version of less than 3,000 lines (early nineteenth century). Meanwhile, outright theatrical parodies, rewrites and extensions are legion. They include Marovitz's *Hamlet: the Collage* (1966; a cut-up, reshuffled version); Stoppard's *Rosencrantz and Guildenstern are Dead* (also 1966, adapted for film 1991, in which two minor characters move centre stage); Hormone Imbalance's *Ophelia* (1979), in which Ophelia is a lesbian and runs off with a woman servant to join a guerrilla commune; Curtis's obscenely funny *The Skinhead Hamlet* (1982) and Jean Betts's *Ophelia Thinks Harder* (1993), in which the heroine acts assertively while the hero dithers.

♦   *Filmically*, 'Hamlet' has existed for film and TV viewers in numerous heavily cut and adapted versions directed by, for instance, Olivier (England, 1947; darkly psychological); Kozintsev (Russia, 1963; darkly political); Zeffirelli (America, 1990; youthfully romantic); as well as the series of half-hour *Shakespeare: The Animated Tales* (English and Russian, 1992; as a brisk folk tale). Again this is to mention only a few.

Producers

'Shakespeare's Hamlet' therefore also involves a wide variety of *producers*, all in their various *moments of production* and *reproduction*. These include: Saxo Grammaticus, the twelfth-century Dane who first recorded but apparently did not invent the Hamlet story; Belleforest, with his retelling of Saxo in the *Histoires Tragiques* (1582, Vol. V); Thomas Kyd, the likely author of the play before Shakespeare; Shakespeare *and* his fellow actors, directors and playwrights (Shakespeare is known to have collaborated closely with all of these as a matter of course, as did virtually all his contemporaries – and as do many subsequent theatrical practitioners); Garrick, Kemble, Olivier, Kozinstsev, Zeffirelli, etc. – along with all the people and technologies (actors, designers, camera-crews, editors, etc.) they worked with. In short, Shakespeare is just one of a vast succession of *re*-producers of 'Hamlet', both named and anonymous. Certainly he is the best known. But he was not the first and is certainly not the last.

Receivers

'Shakespeare's Hamlet' also involves a wide variety of *receivers*, all in their various *moments of reception*. In one sense Shakespeare himself was just another receiver of other people's versions. Whether directly or indirectly, he drew upon Saxo's and Belleforest's versions, the earlier play, and a whole host of influences from other areas of language, literature and culture (widely known works on and beliefs in 'melancholy', ghosts and revenge, for instance). Only through those could he in turn re-produce. Moreover, fellow actors, directors and playwrights are likely to have been his first and most formative 'audience'. Performances of the play will then have been heard and seen by a prodigious variety of early seventeenth-century audiences ranging from artisans to aristocracy, 'groundlings' to grandees (Elizabethan theatre audiences were much more socially variegated than their modern counterparts). Thereafter, we must look to moments of reception (and reproduction) as different as: early seventeenth-century foreign merchants at sea off Sierra Leone; the Restoration and eighteenth-century court and city; the nineteenth-century Victorian music-hall; twentieth-century Soviet, British, Italian, US and world cinemas – and any time, anywhere that a TV has been showing one of the many acted or animated versions. What's more, the awesome – some would say awful – fact is that by far the greatest number of modern 'receivers' of 'Shakespeare's Hamlet' are to be found in formal education. These include students, teachers, scholars, critics – in fact anyone and everyone who has studied 'it' in the classroom or lecture theatre, chiefly from the page, occasionally on the stage, and increasingly from the screen.

Relations to the rest of the world

'Shakespeare's Hamlet' also involves a wide variety of references, representations and kinds of relevance, again in various historical moments and social contexts. These include representations of such matters as: social and psychological order and disorder, families, adolescence, adultery, murder, revenge, love, lust, the supernatural, royalty, nobility, manual labour, scholarship, being a student, returning home, having friends, being alone, and much more. Notice again that all of these issues will be understood slightly or very differently depending on the frames of reference within which they are realised: what they are assumed to relate to in some contemporary world. These worlds will vary between, say, the late sixteenth and early twenty-first centuries, between post-feudal and post-industrial societies. The world-views in play amongst readers and audiences will vary correspondingly: in *religion* across kinds of Christianity, Buddhism, Islam, agnosticism, atheism, etc.; in *politics* across forms of monarchy, absolutism, democracy and dictatorship; in *psychology/physiology* from a vision of the mind–body based on the elements of fire, air, earth and water, along with their associated 'humours', to interrelations of 'ego' and 'id', or 'Oedipus complexes', desire and the 'semiotic'; and so on. For this reason, the most personally pressing questions you are likely to put to Hamlet would be: 'what are my views and experiences of social and psychological dis/order, families, monarchy, being a student, returning home, etc.?' And yet inevitably, at the same time, you are likely to wonder about the historical context: 'what views and experiences of social dis/order, psychological disturbance, families, etc. were available, encouraged, prohibited or unthinkable in late sixteenth- and early seventeenth-century London (England, Britain, the rest of the world)?' Similar questions quickly arise about every other time, place and social context within which Shakespeare's (and everyone else's) *Hamlet* has been realised.

By now it will be clear that 'Shakespeare's *Hamlet*' is a very complex and changeable phenomenon indeed. In fact, 'it' turns out to be a 'they': an apparently single object turns out, on closer investigation, to be an array of *products* and a series of *processes*. These have been plotted systematically and at length (though still far from exhaustively) in four dimensions: *texts*; *re/production*; *reception*; and *relations to the rest of the world*. It has also been pointed out that all of these dimensions are characterised by variation in time, place and social space. Consequently, just whose 'Hamlet' this is remains a highly fascinating and deeply contentious matter: Shakespeare's? his predecessors'? his contemporaries'? his successors'? our own? someone else's entirely? That is one reason why we need theoretical models. It is also why, if they are to be of practical use, we need particular materials on which to try and test them. No model or method is universal and omnipotent. Only by bringing materials, models and methods into dynamic relation can we really know the potentialities of any of them.

ONE MODEL LEADS TO ANOTHER . . .

The above model of *text, producer, receiver* and *relations to the rest of the world* can be used in three ways:

- as a practical tool to help analyse a particular text;
- as a theoretical model of how texts in general come into being;
- as a framework in which to 'place' particular critical movements.

Other related yet distinct models can be found in the entries on **addresser–address–addressee** and **text, context and intertextuality** in Part Three. All are used to underpin the 'How to practise . . . ' sections featured in the rest of Part Two.

ACTIVITIES

(a)   *Applying the model.* Explore a text you are studying (or one of those in Part Five) with the help of the above model of *text, producer, receivers and relations to the rest of the world* (see Figure 2.1). Use the basic theoretical and practical questions on p. 73 to get started, drawing on reference books, critical editions and other resources for relevant information.

   Go on to consider what aspects of the text and your response to it are *not* especially addressed by the present model. Revise or replace it accordingly.

(b)   *'Placing' theories.* Look at the initial 'Overview' sections for a couple of the specific approaches featured in the rest of Part Two (e.g. 'Practical and (old) new criticism' and 'Feminism and gender studies' or 'Postcolonialism and multiculturalism'). Consider how far that approach seems to be text-centred and/or oriented towards producers, receivers and the rest of the world. Which dimensions are you currently most interested in?

DISCUSSION

(i)   [the term] theory is often used derogatorily just because it explains and – implicitly or explicitly – challenges some customary action.

Raymond Williams, *Keywords: A Vocabulary of Culture and Society*
(1983: 317)

(ii)   A man with one theory is lost. He needs several of them – or lots! He should stuff them in his pockets like newspapers.

Bertolt Brecht, in Makaryk (1993: vii)

Also see: 'theory' and 'practice' in *OED*.

READING: Abrams (1953) in Lodge 1972: 1–27 (also see 'Criticism' in Abrams 1993: 39–42); Durant and Fabb 1990: 22–48; Eagleton 1996: Ch. 1; Jefferson and Robey 1986: 7–23; Norris in Coyle *et al.* 1990: 27–65; Selden 1989: 1–15; Selden and Widdowson 1997: 1–9; Wellek and Warren 1963: 38–45; Williams 1983: 84–6, 316–18; Lynn 1994: 1–21; Webster 1996: 1–30; Barry 1995.

For a handy text, critical history and overview of approaches to *Hamlet*, see William Shakespeare, *Hamlet*, ed. Suzanne Wofford (1994) in the series *Case Studies in Contemporary Criticism* (Bedford/St Martin's Press) ed. Ross Murfin. This whole series contains useful introductions to the principal approaches, as well as essays applying them to particular texts. Tallack 1987 and Brooker and Widdowson 1996 are excellent introductions to theory in practice on particular texts. (Section 1 of the latter is also devoted to *Hamlet*.)

'HOW (NOT) TO PRACTISE APPROACH X . . . ': A NOTE ON CRITICAL METHODOLOGY

For each of the theories and approaches featured in Part Two there is a section called 'How to practise': 'How to practise a Formalist approach'; 'How to practise Feminist and Gendered approaches', etc. Each is followed by an example of that particular critical methodology in action. It should be stressed, however, that in each of these examples I have tried to avoid a merely mechanical application of the method. I deliberately do *not* march straight through each text dutifully noting and ticking off every aspect or feature in strict accordance with the suggested questions. Instead, I seek to weave all or most of the issues mentioned into the fabric of a more subtly variegated (though still I hope integrated) response. Thus I start with the 'How to practise . . . ' framework in one hand and with a specific text in the other, but I use the former to help prompt and develop the shape of a response to the latter – not to prescribe its precise design. I treat it as a companion, not a tyrant. That is how I suggest you approach the 'How to practise . . . ' sections too. Look to them for a supporting and occasionally guiding presence. But *don't* treat them too slavishly or solemnly. Good methodologies encourage us to be creative as well as critical, playful as well as principled. What you do with those here – and whether you use some of them at all – is quite properly up to you.

2.3   PRACTICAL CRITICISM AND (OLD) NEW CRITICISM

Overview

Practical Criticism and New Criticism were two highly influential approaches developed during the middle years of the twentieth century in, respectively, Britain and the USA. Both were *text-centred* and required 'close reading' of 'the words on the page'. This was done substantially without reference to context, author's identity and reader's role. Discriminating aesthetic responses and ethical judgements were encouraged among readers. However, students were generally not expected to challenge either the choice of texts (typically, short lyrics and prose extracts from 'classic' English and American authors) nor the critic's and teacher's methods and values (these tended to be assumed or asserted rather than explicitly theorised). The New Critics' emphasis on LITERATURE as a series of finished art objects or 'verbal icons' made them suspicious of (and suspected by) more theoretically explicit and linguistically systematic FORMALISTS and FUNCTIONALISTS. New Critics were also opposed to (and by) many kinds of PSYCHOLOGICAL, MARXIST and, latterly,

FEMINIST and POSTCOLONIAL CRITICS. They assumed that most literature of note was by white, middle- to upper-class males – but that this fact need not itself be noted or was simply irrelevant. It has been suggested that certain strains of POST-STRUCTURALISM (especially *deconstructive criticism) continue the New Critical programme under a different guise; for *deconstruction too can be narrowly text-centred and concerned with paradox, ambiguity and irony (these were all key New Critical concepts; see p. 79 below). Meanwhile, the general practice of 'close reading' has tended to be technically sharpened by the use of *stylistics and politically sensitised by an awareness of RHETORIC (see 1.5.5) and of language as **discourse**.

Key terms: **aesthetic**; *ambiguity; **art**; **canon and classic**; *criticism; *form; **imagery**; *irony; LITERATURE; **narrator** (un/reliable); *paradox; **point of view**; structure, including balance, pattern, tension, (organic) unity and integrity.

Major figures and movements

Practical Criticism as both a critical method and an educational movement was initiated by the publication of I.A. Richards's book of that name in 1929. Its subtitle was 'A Study of Literary Judgement', and it was dedicated to establishing an area of English devoted to LITERARY CRITICISM as distinct from LITERARY HISTORY and philology (historical language study) – both of which had dominated the subject till then. *Criticism as such had often been a dilettanteish form of LITERARY APPRECIATION.

Richards's method was basically simple and is still quite widely practised :

> I have made the experiment of issuing printed sheets of poems [. . .] to audiences who were asked to comment freely in writing upon them. The authorship of the poems was not revealed.
>
> (1929: 3)

The written responses that resulted, what Richards called 'protocols', then formed the subject of his lectures and, subsequently, his book. Through detailed analysis of student responses Richards pointed to many aspects of the **reading** process that had previously been ignored or merely assumed. In particular, he stressed the ultimate *ambiguity of all words, as well as recurring problems which seemed to prevent a sensitive appreciation of the text, e.g., 'stock responses', 'general critical preconceptions' and 'doctrinal adhesions'. Above all, developing a line of argument initiated in his previous book, *Principles of Literary Criticism* (1924), Richards insisted that the reading of poetry was a searching test of and stimulating aid to the cultivation of 'discrimination' in general and 'literary judgement' in particular. In his practice Richards was clearly heir to the eminent Victorian poet, critic and educationist Matthew *Arnold. Arnold advocated that 'short passages, even single lines' of 'poetry belong[ing] to the class of the truly excellent' can be applied as 'touchstones' to other poetry (*The Study of Poetry*, 1880). There is also in Richards's writing a hint of that view of high CULTURE which Arnold famously and influentially described as 'a pursuit of our total perfection by means of getting to know, on all the matters which most concern us, the best which has been thought and said in the world' (*Culture and Anarchy*, 1869). It should be added, however, that Richards was generally more interested in understanding the process whereby literary and cultural judgements were formed, rather than in simply imposing them, In this respect Richards can be distinguished from most of his predecessors as well as many of his successors (e.g., F.R. Leavis, also at Cambridge), who tended to assert their judgements rather than explaining – let alone theorising – them. Richards was unusual, too, in his readiness to engage with larger problems of COMMUNICATION, *value and meaning (e.g., Richards 1924: Chs 4, 21 and Appendix).

In the year of the first publication of *Practical Criticism* (1929), Richards left Cambridge for Peking and then Harvard, where he taught from 1939. This move influenced the development of a partly similar critical movement in English in the United States. This movement came to be called 'New Criticism', after the title of John Crowe Ransom's book of that name (1941). New Criticism and Practical Criticism were to have a pervasive and decisive influence on the critical and classroom practices of the middle years of the twentieth century. In effect, they became orthodoxies which in some quarters persist to the present day. Other key New Critical textbooks were Cleanth Brooks and Robert Penn Warren's *Understanding Poetry* (1939), Brooks's *The Well-Wrought Urn: Studies in the Structure of Poetry* (1947) and William Wimsatt's *The Verbal Icon: Studies in the Meaning of Poetry* (1954). All these texts proclaim themselves in various ways as 'new' criticism in so far as, like Richards, they distinguish their objects and methods from the then 'old' study of literature which concentrated on literary history (including biography) and history of the language (philology) (see 1.5.6). However, in a much more exclusive and self-conscious way than Richards, New Critics insisted that the proper object of study was 'the words on the page' and 'the text itself' or (more often and more narrowly) 'the poem itself'. Consequently, they ruled out appeals both to the supposed intentions or even the life of the **author** on the one hand, and to the actual effects of the poem on particular **readers** on the other. These positions were put most forcefully and influentially by William Wimsatt and Monroe Beardsley in two joint essays attacking what they dubbed 'The Intentional Fallacy' (1946) and 'The Affective Fallacy' (1949). In the former they claimed that 'the design or intention of the author is neither available nor desirable as a standard for judging the success of a work of literary art' (Lodge 1972: 335). In the later essay they asserted that 'The Affective Fallacy is a confusion between the poem and its results (what it *is* and what it *does*)' (Lodge 1972: 345).

New Critics developed a distinctive, though not especially systematic, critical vocabulary. Characteristically, a New Critic would look for the overall principle of *organic unity* or *integrated structure* in a work, often a short lyric poem. This would then be related to the detailed 'particulars' and 'textures' of **imagery**. *Tension, contrast* and above all *balance* in design as well as *ambiguity* in individual words and phrases were reckoned the hallmarks of a fine piece. Thus the overall aim of *the poem as a whole* was to establish *variety within unity*. Where contradictions remained these could be resolved through *irony* (not really meaning what is said) or *paradox* (maintaining two or more contradictory positions simultaneously). According to Brooks (1947: 12), 'the language of poetry *is* the language of paradox'. New Critics were also flatly opposed to any abstraction of what they called the 'prose sense' of a piece of poetry, especially in the form of *paraphrase* (which they considered a 'heresy'). Instead, they preferred to concentrate on the 'poetic sense'. In this, like Richards, they opposed a referential, 'scientific' use of language to an emotive, 'poetic' use of language. They thereby perpetuated that split between the sciences and the 'arts' which continues to divide (and bedevil) much of society both inside and outside education.

A further consequence of the elevation of **poetry** was the marginalising of *prose and the neglect of **drama**. When New Critics did treat prose, it was almost exclusively 'literary' prose (short stories and extracts from novels – and not diaries, letters, newspaper stories and adverts). They also concentrated on formal and structural matters of technique such as **point of view, characterisation**, *narrators (first and third person, partial and omniscient), **narrative** structure and *plot. They were not particularly interested in the worlds represented and the novel's or the novelist's relations with the society at the time (i.e. 'relations with the rest of the world'; see 2.1). Indeed, so pervasive and persistent has been the influence of, for instance, Mark Schorer's essay 'Technique as Discovery' (1948) and Wayne Booth's book *The Rhetoric of Fiction* (1961) that it can sometimes be difficult to recognise that there are any other categories and criteria for analysing and evaluating prose narratives (see **hi/story, narrative** and **fiction** for some alternatives).

How to practise Practical Criticism and New Criticism

(Use texts from Part Five if you wish, but for the purpose of this exercise be sure to *ignore* the attached notes.)

Practical Criticism

Concentrate on short unidentified texts, preferably poems and extracts from novels or short stories, and ask people to 'comment freely' upon them. On the basis of the ensuing discussion or short comments in writing, try to pick out insensitive, clichéd and 'stock' responses. Aim to cultivate greater 'critical discrimination' and 'literary judgement'.

New Criticism

Read an unidentified 'whole' poem, a short story or an extract from a play or novel. Then talk or write about it with respect to the following:

♦   the main tensions or contrasts around which it is organised;
♦   the overall structuring of argument, plot or imagery (including verse organisation for poetry, and types of narrator, characterisation and points of view for story or play);
♦   all the imagery, paradoxes, ambiguities and ironies which contribute to the localised texture and overall variety of the text;
♦   those strategies and devices which, especially towards the close of the text, ensure that it seems to be 'integrated', 'whole' and 'successfully resolved'.

Examples

Read each of the following texts with the above suggestions on 'How to practise Practical and New Criticism' in mind. (Be sure to ignore the accompanying notes in the anthology for the purpose of this exercise.) Only read on once you have sketched a preliminary response along these lines.

Poem: William Wordsworth's 'I wandered lonely as a cloud' (5.4.3 a) The Practical Critical aim here would be to see this poem afresh, avoiding the 'stock responses' that its familiarity as a classic Romantic poem have built up. In a more specifically New Critical vein we would observe that the poem is generally organised around tensions between the sad and solitary poet and joyful teeming nature; between the immediate experience of what was seen and the subsequent memory of it. The argument progresses in three stages: from the poet's solitude ('I wandered lonely ...') to pleasant company with nature ('laughing company') to a later moment of reverie ('when on my couch I lie ...'). Each state dominates one of the verses in turn. Metrically, all the lines are octosyllabic and gathered in verses rhyming 'ababcc'.

Localised ambiguities, especially of imagery, include the observations that even from the beginning the poet is likened to *a part of* nature ('I wandered lonely *as a* cloud') and is therefore not wholly alone and *apart from* it. Notice too that the daffodils and waves are humanised as 'dancing' and 'a laughing company'. The ultimate ambiguity, and perhaps paradox, is that by the close we may not be sure whether the daffodils and waves we have just 'seen' are those of the poet's first moment of vision or his later moments of re-vision: is he – and are we – '[a]long the lake' or 'on my couch'? This may be a paradoxical resolution in that it draws together what are usually recognised as distinct: humanity and nature; inner and outer worlds; past, present and future.

(*Note*: Practical and New Critical readings of this poem would *not* draw attention to many of the historical, biographical, contextual and intertextual aspects featured in the anthology: the redrafting process involving manual and verbal assistance from sister and wife (especially Mary's contribution of 'They flash ... solitude', ll. pp. 21–22); William's transformation of a country ramble evidently involving several people into a solitary act of wandering (see Dorothy's account, 5.4.3 b); the screening out of 'people working' and thus, perhaps, of any thought that William was not. Nor would Practical and New Critics pay anything but slight – and probably slighting – attention to subsequent *re*-productions of the poem in the forms of Feminist critique and Commercial parody (see 5.4.3 c–d). Such things would be considered irrelevant, 'non-literary' or trivial and could not, it would be argued, contribute to an understanding of 'the poem itself'.)

Prose: Kipling's 'The Story of Muhammad Din' (5.2.4 b) The overall tension is between the world-views of adult Englishman and Indian child, the worlds of grown-up work and child's play. The story develops fairly simply, from first meeting with Muhammad Din, through the construction, destruction and reconstruction of his toy palaces, to his death. There is just one, first-person narrator throughout, the Englishman, who seems to play a partly enigmatic role.

Localised tensions include: the illicit but tolerated presence of Muhammad Din in the Sahib's room; strain between father and son; the accidental destruction of the child's toy palace, and the doctor's callous remark on 'these brats'. The precise attitude of the Englishman to the Indian boy is hard to pin down: sympathetic and yet distant, fatherly and yet patronising – in a word (paradoxically) im/personal. All these ambiguous perspectives might be inferred from the narrator's references to 'the little white shirt and the fat little body', 'chubby little eccentricity'. Accordingly, the tone is often ironic, a blend of the (mock-)heroic with the trivial (e.g., the self-conscious formality of 'my salutation' and the 'magnificent palaces from the stale flowers').

The story is resolved sharply, by the boy's sudden illness and death. However, the narrator's ambiguously im/personal, sympathetic and yet distant tone is maintained to the very end: 'wrapped in a white cloth, all that was left of little Muhammad Din'.

(*Note*: Practical and New Critics would probably *not* choose this Anglo-Indian tale in the first place: they rarely feature overtly cross-cultural materials. But if they did they would probably not comment directly on such matters as the specifically political and historical dimensions of the colonial relations between English 'sahib' and Indian servants (e.g., 'servants' quarters . . . any command of mine . . . '); the fanciful, make-believe palaces being built from natural and imperial bric-à-brac in the white man's 'garden'; the total absence of women (mothers, wives, sisters); the occluded 'otherness' of 'Mussulman' burial grounds and customs; Kipling's own deeply traumatic childhood and his – and his age's – general tendency to sentimentalise children; the polyglot mixture of languages, English and Indian, while still observing a hierarchy in favour of the former (all the Indian words are overtly 'power' terms: *sahib*, *khitmatgar*, *budmash*, etc.). In short, there would be no obviously POSTCOLONIAL, MARXIST, FEMINIST or PSYCHOANALYTIC dimensions to such a reading.)

Play: Ibsen's ' A Doll's House' (5.3.3) The overall tension is quite literally a 'marital tension' between husband and wife: should she go or stay? It is also about whether and how far people can really change. The play as a whole moves from apparent domestic felicity through central complications to this resolution. Within this extract, the two very different endings are obviously crucial to how we view the development of the argument and plot.

Localised ambiguities include what the characters mean by 'strangers', '(the miracle of) miracles' and, of course, 'marriage'. Ending 1 resolves the play (and the marriage) in an openly provocative manner: Nora leaves and Helmer is left with a question. Ending 2 resolves both play and marriage with a gesture of token reconciliation: Helmer shows Nora their children and the family unit remains intact. The latter may assert a greater sense of 'wholeness'; but whether it is 'satisfactory' is a moot point.

(*Note*: Practical and New Critics would probably *not* have drawn attention to the existence of alternative endings (these complicate any sense of 'organic integrity'); the particular acting styles, set designs and theatre conditions obtaining at any one moment of production; the scandalised reactions of specific Norwegian audiences and the subsequent pressures on Ibsen to re-write less 'shockingly' for German ones; the vast mass of late nineteenth-century materials relating to the 'marriage' and '(single) woman' questions; Ibsen's own tempestuous relationships inside and outside marriage; his twenty-five-year absence from Norway while writing this and his other social documentary plays about the place; the crucial contribution of these plays to the development of European 'naturalism'; the two very different *translations from which these endings are drawn.)

ACTIVITIES

(a) *Same text, different analyses.* Analyse the same text in two (or more) ways: once using the above 'How to practise Practical Criticism and New Criticism' method; again drawing on the accompanying notes and, if you wish, one of the other 'How to practise . . .' frameworks supplied in Part Two (Feminist, Marxist, Poststructuralist, etc.). (If this is being done in class, different groups can work on different analyses simultaneously.) Go on to compare the various analyses and discuss the strengths and weaknesses of each approach.

  Suggestions: *Poetry*: 'They flee from me' (5.1.3 a); 'My mistress' eyes' (5.1.3 b); 'I am – yet what I am' (5.1.5); 'I felt a Funeral' (5.4.5 d); 'Dialogue' (5.1.8). *Prose*: *Pride and Prejudice* (5.2.3 b); *Heart of Darkness* (5.2.4 c). *Drama*: *The Tempest* (5.3.2 b); *Not I* (5.3.4 d); *Educating Rita* (5.3.5 c).

(b) *Attempt a New Critical analysis of an advert, a news report, a transcript of an interview, a soap opera script.* How far do you get? What problems do you encounter? What other kinds of knowledge and skill do you feel you need to draw on?

  Suggestions: the Clarins advert (5.4.4 b); the *Sun* or *Guardian* stories (5.2.5 a–b); the Factory Commission interview (5.3.1 c).

DISCUSSION

Debate the following positions *for*, *against* and *alternative* (i.e. by fashioning a different proposition). Wherever possible, support your arguments by reference to specific texts, authors, periods, genres and media.

(i)   though cultures have changed and will change, poems remain and explain.
William Wimsatt and Monroe Beardsley, 'The Affective Fallacy' (1949)
in Lodge (1972: 357)

(ii) New Criticism . . . was a recipe for political inertia.
Terry Eagleton, *Literary Theory: An Introduction* (1996: 43)

Also see: 1.5.7 and 1.8.2; FORMALISM; and 'Key terms', p. 78.

READING: *Introductory*: Robey in Jefferson and Robey 1986: 24–45; Eagleton 1996: 37–46; Selden 1989: 23–46; Rylance in Coyle *et al.* 1990: 721–35; Selden *et al.* 1997: 13–28; Lynn 1994: 23–46. *Primary*: Richards 1924, 1929; Ransom, Brookes, Wimsatt and Beardsley, and Schorer in Lodge 1972: 228–40, 292–305, 334–402; Brooks 1947. *Advanced*: Fekete 1977; Lentricchia 1980; Baldick 1996: 64–160.

2.4   FORMALISM INTO FUNCTIONALISM

Overview

Formalism as the name for a specific critical movement is usually identified with 'Russian Formalism'. This developed in Moscow and St Petersburg/Leningrad between 1915 and the late 1920s. The position Russian Formalists adopted was *text-centred* (or, perhaps better, *textuality-centred*) in that they concentrated on those features that make LITERATURE 'literary' and poems 'poetic'. They also systematically studied the devices of narrative fiction. Their aim was thus less the analysis of particular texts (which was the aim of NEW CRITICS) and more the establishment of general principles and theories. Chief amongst the concepts developed by Russian Formalists were *defamiliarisation and **foregrounding**. The idea was that literary texts always in some way challenge and change (i.e. 'defamiliarise') all that is dulled by familiarity and habit: they freshen and sharpen perception. Formalists also observed that literary, especially poetic, texts tend to draw attention to certain aspects of the language (notably through imagery, unusual word combinations, sound patterning, metre, rhyme, inverted or unusual word order) and these elements are thereby 'foregrounded' against a 'background' made up of more routine and 'ordinary' language use. 'Foregrounding' is basically any linguistic feature that, for whatever reason, sticks out. Narrative fiction does this on a larger scale through reshuffling time, space and narrator or character perspective.

Functionalism as the name for a specific movement is usually identified with 'Prague School Functionalism'. This was a distinctive outgrowth from Russian Formalism and was centred on Czechoslovakia, and subsequently Estonia, from the late 1920s to the 1960s. Functionalists took the fairly abstract Formalist notions of 'defamiliarisation' and 'foregrounding' and in effect socialised and historicised them. They insisted that these criteria be seen dynamically in relation to changing notions of 'the familiar' and 'background.' Crucially, the latter were now recognised to be constantly in flux. It was argued that there is no fixed norm of perception nor any absolutely 'ordinary' language-use. Consequently, we have no firm grounds on which to plot that which is universally un/familiar or that which is universally in the 'fore-' or the 'background'. Instead, Functionalists argued, we must recognise that the relation between, say, 'literature' and 'life', or 'art' and 'reality', is always shifting. What we consider literature or art is, therefore, subject to constant renegotiation and revision.

Russian Formalism and Czech Functionalism only really came to prominence in the West from the 1960s onwards, chiefly as a result of the activities of STRUCTURALISTS and *functional linguists.

Key terms: **aesthetics** and **art**; **foreground and background**; *defamiliarisation; *deviation; **dialogic**; *form and *function; LITERATURE; **narrative**; *poetics; **versification**; *period; RHETORIC; *style.

Major figures and movements

Two preliminary warnings should be given about the phrase 'Russian Formalism'. Not everyone associated with the movement was Russian (or constantly based in Russia), and none called themselves 'Formalist'! In fact there were *two* founding groups and movements: the Moscow Linguistic Circle (1915) and the Petrograd – later Leningrad – based group, the Society for the Study of Poetic Language (1916). Members of the former included Roman Jakobson and Petr Bogatyrev; members of the latter included Viktor Shklovsky, Yuri Tynyanov and Boris Eikhenbaum. Several of these (notably Jakobson and Bogatyrev) subsequently moved to Czechoslovakia where they helped found the Prague Linguistic Circle (1926–48). Dominant members of the latter in the 1930s were the Czechs Jan Mukarovsky and Nikolay

Trubetskoy; meanwhile Jakobson and René Wellek, another native Czech member of the Prague circle, emigrated to the USA and became US citizens. In short, the 'Russian-ness' of 'Russian' Formalism was elastic. 'Formalist', meanwhile, was a term of abuse wielded by the opponents – not the proponents – of these groups. The members referred to themselves variously as students of 'linguistics and literature', 'poetics' and, later, 'semiotics'. The name has stuck, however, so we shall stick with it too.

Poetry and *poetics v. 'ordinary language'

One of the most lasting achievements of Russian Formalists was in *poetics. Previously, literary historians had gathered and categorised poems in terms of the various periods, genres and traditions they represented. Formalists, however, sought to codify the underlying rules which made poetry 'poetic'. Central to this project was Jakobson's view of poetry as 'organised violence committed on ordinary speech'. That is, poetry both disturbs and re-forms the patterns of routine language. And it does so at three distinct linguistic levels: (i) *sound-structure* (alliteration, assonance, rhyme, metre, etc.); (ii) *choice of words* (metaphor, archaism, varieties of vocabulary, etc.); and (iii) *combination of words* (e.g., unusual collocations, inverted word-order, marked parallelism, ellipsis). (For a glossary explaining and a checklist applying these terms, see Part 6 and 4.2.) Look at the first verse of Blake's 'And did those feet . . . ', for instance (5.4.6 b). This would be analysed by Formalists in terms of : (i) sound – the succession of eight-syllable, four-beat lines with rhymes in the second and fourth; (ii) word choice – the mixture of pastoral, patriotic and religious vocabularies, including metaphor (e.g. 'Lamb of God'); (iii) word combination – the parallel question structures, including inversion of syntax. Taken together, all these features effectively commit 'organised violence' in that they both disturb *and* re-form what we would find otherwise in 'ordinary speech'. They draw on ordinary linguistic resources (sounds, choices and combinations of words) but pattern them in 'other-than-ordinary' ways. And that, for Formalists, is chiefly what distinguishes 'poetic speech' from 'ordinary speech': not choice of special subject matter, or tone, or a special 'poetic' (e.g., archaic) vocabulary – but a formal *re*-design of routine verbal materials. Formalists said something similar of prose and drama in so far as they exhibit 'more-than-usual design'.

It is therefore important to insist on two further distinctions: one made by Formalists themselves; the other by their critics. First, *poetics is *not* restricted to poetry as traditionally conceived; there is a potential for 'more-than-ordinary' design in all language. It's simply that poems are more obviously locatable towards one end of a continuum which can also include, say, advertising, political speech-making, sermons, wittily pointed conversations, etc. (see **poetry** and **word-play**). Second, the very concept of 'ordinary speech' is problematic. Can we say with confidence that it actually exists? Can we point to an actual instance (a family conversation (5.3.1 b), say, or your last conversation) and say categorically: *that* is ordinary? Ordinary for whom, when and where? Plenty of families in Oxford, England in 1997 would talk in different ways. And if you think your last converation *was* really 'ordinary', then why don't most people speak like that most of the time?! Paradoxically, then, 'ordinariness' is an extraordinarily variable social, geographical and historical matter. As we see shortly, however, this problem was tackled with considerable success by Formalists in so far as they later turned Functionalist. First, however, we must review the other main terms and concepts that early Formalists put in play.

*Defamiliarisation in poetry and narrative

'Defamiliarisation' is a concept that many people find initially useful when asking 'what precisely is it about this text that I find interesting or striking?' The answer, simply yet significantly, is often 'because it makes me see things differently'. Obvious examples are the opening lines of Shakespeare's 'My mistress' eyes are nothing like the sun' (5.1.3 b) and Dickinson's 'I felt a Funeral, in my Brain' (5.4.5 d). In the first, we are treated to an unexpected *non*-compliment about the poet's mistress. In the second, we wonder what kind of funeral this can be 'in' someone's brain.

Formalists also extended the concept of defamiliarisation to **narrative**. They concentrated on its larger-scale 'techniques' and smaller-scale 'devices'. Shklovsky, notably, argued that the crucial aspect of 'literariness' in the **novel** was its tendency to reshuffle and reconfigure elements of the world. Shklovsky's favourite examples from English literature were Sterne's *Tristram Shandy* and Swift's *Gulliver's Travels*. In the former, the narrator overtly and playfully interrupts, accelerates, delays, expands or digresses from his story till we are sometimes sure of nothing except the act and art of narration itself. In the latter, the ceaseless disproportions in size or nature between the narrator Gulliver and the tiny Lilliputians or the huge Brobdingnagians constantly draw attention to aspects of life which might otherwise pass unnoticed. For Shklovsky it was precisely this sense of art, and especially the novel, as 'technique' that openly reconstituted the categories of time, space and persons which was paramount. (The NEW CRITIC Mark Schorer made a similar observation in his 'Technique as Discovery' (1948).) In fact both Shklovsky and Schorer thereby proclaim their affinity with specifically *Modernist techniques. For writers, artists, and film-makers otherwise as diverse as T.S. Eliot, Joyce, Woolf, Faulkner, Picasso and Eisenstein, it was precisely this project of exposing how a work is put together that marks their work as 'Modernist'. Shklovsky's phrase for this activity was 'baring the device'. This is often cited as the chief characteristic which distinguishes **'realist'** work (where devices are purportedly *not* 'bared') from pre- and post-realist work, whether medieval, Renaissance or modern (where they purportedly *are*). A politically motivated version of 'defamiliarisation' and 'baring the device' can be found in the dramatic theory and practice of Bertolt Brecht, notably his '*making-strange effects' (*Verfremdungseffekte*); also in Benjamin's notion of '*shock' (see MARXISM, pp. 103–105).

We meet several other fundamental distinctions in early Russian Formalism which later theorists and practitioners have adapted. Eikhenbaum, for instance, developed a view of narrative as *skaz* (in Russian literally, 'the thing *said*'). English equivalents would be the anecdote or 'yarn', where it is precisely the narrator's visible and audible presence, and her or his palpable relations with the characters and actions that constitute much of the tale's dynamic and appeal. With a similar emphasis, Mukarovsky, later, following Tomashevsky, was to develop an influential distinction between *fabula* and *sjuzhet*. *Fabula is the raw stuff of the narrative imagined as though in chronological sequence, in a continuous space and as yet 'untold'. *Sjuzhet* is the worked-up material of an actual narrative once it has been reconfigured in time and space and been informed by specific narratorial and character voices.

Another influential approach to narrative was that of Vladimir Propp in his *Morphology of the Folktale* (1928). This was more narrowly Formalist in that it concentrated on a body of texts (a collection of classic Russian folk tales) but paid no attention to narrators and narratees. Instead, Propp aimed to discover what he termed 'the underlying principles of the various shapes' (i.e. morphology) of 'the Folk tale' in general. Propp's claims have subsequently been contested with respect to world folk tale in general. His corpus was small and culture-specific; and world story is such a vast and variegated body. Nonetheless, Propp's model and some of his categories have been applied, sometimes very suggestively, in areas ranging from medieval romance to Hollywood feature films, taking in detective fiction, tabloid newspaper stories, cartoons and soap operas on the way. (For further explanation and activities, see **narrative**.)

Foreground and background

But Formalism was not solely concerned with identifying potentially universal structures. Indeed, in so far as it transformed into Functionalism, it came increasingly to focus on particular structures and effects at particular historical moments. The notion of **foregrounding** is a case in point. In the early years of Formalism, drawing on an analogy with the visual arts, 'foregrounding' had referred to those features which are prominent *within* a text in contrast to other elements *within* the text which thereby act as a **background**. Later, Functionalists recognised that there are in fact at least two stages of the 'foregrounding/backgrounding' process:

- foreground and background *within* the text;
- foregrounding *of* the text against the background *outside* the text.

This may be explained in terms of the initial text–painting analogy. Not only must we see what is prominent *inside* the frame, we must also look *behind and beyond* the frame. Only then can we gauge the overall effect (and material fact) of the picture in relation to the room and building in which it hangs, and by extension the world as a whole. To get 'the whole picture', in the fullest sense, we must look *at, through, behind* and *beyond* it.

Similar refinements and extensions of early Formalist positions characterised Functionalism in general. 'Defamiliarisation' came to be more dynamically braced against a notion of the 'familiar' or 'routine' world which was itself recognised as problematic: historically changing, geographically dispersed, socially variegated and politically contentious. It was recognised that what is familiar or unfamiliar in one period and place, or for one group or person, might not be for another. Moreover, if the whole concept of 'defamiliarisation' is culturally relative, so is the whole concept of 'literariness', of which it was the cornerstone. LITERATURE might be different things to different people(s) – not a universal and eternal form but a range of social-historical functions. Its *values would therefore be conditional, not absolute.

*Form into *function

A fully developed version of this Functionalist model can be found in the work of the most influential member of the Prague Linguistic Circle, Jan Mukarovsky. His *Aesthetic Function: Norm and Value as Social Facts* (1936) is a particularly powerful example. As the title makes clear, Mukarovsky was not at all interested in **aesthetics** in some merely formal sense of 'art for art's sake'. He was concerned with aesthetic function: the ways in which aesthetic and social values interrelate according to prevailing 'norms', and shift as those norms shift. For Mukarovsky, what was crucial was whether a work was perceived as having a practical, instrumental function with some other end in mind, or 'aesthetically', as an end in itself irrespective of other purposes. For instance, a picture of a Madonna and child might have a primarily religious function in a certain period or society. But in another, more secular, period or society it might primarily function as an 'art' object or as a 'tourist attraction'. It might also, of course, chiefly function as an educational 'object of study' – in a History of Art course for example. A church or cathedral or mosque can be perceived as a 'house of God' or as an instance of building techniques and architectural styles or, as with Althusser, an '*ideological apparatus'. A rough clay drinking vessel can become a priceless museum exhibit. Unique and potentially precious manuscripts can be used to bind others, light a pipe or wedge the door open. It's the same with any text or other artefact you may be studying. How we *see* it will partly depend upon how we are expected to *use* it. Its value is a product of its function. Mukarovsky summarises the situation thus (1936: 6, 60):

> [W]e can never discount the possibility that the functions of a given work were originally entirely different from what they appear to be when we apply our system of values. . . . Every shift in time, space or social surroundings alters the existing artistic traditions through whose prism that work is observed.

Mukarovsky also insists that there is no eternally present 'norm' in relation to which the value of a work may be gauged (p. 36): 'A living work of art always oscillates between the past and future status of an aesthetic norm.' In all these respects, Mukarovsky clearly anticipated and, indeed, influenced the reception aesthetics developed by later German *reader-response critics such as Iser and Jauss (see **writing and reading**). More immediately, we may recognise some close affinities between positions being developed by Mukarovsky in Czechoslovakia and those being developed by Mikhail *Bakhtin in Russia around the same time. For instance, Bakhtin was interested in:

- the word as 'a two-sided act' suspended between one language-user and another: words are always 'a site of struggle' between contending **value** systems;
- the **dialogic** relations between various moments of production and reproduction: we are constantly refashioning 'another's words in one's own language';
- 'chronotopes' (Greek for 'time-topics'), which he conceived as *hybrids compounded of formal features of **genres** along with their period-specific aesthetic and social values, all of which change according to time, place and persons;
- **carnival** in general and *parody in particular, where one set of cultural and aesthetic 'norms' is overthrown by another which is its obverse.

How to practise Formalism . . .

Concentrate on the overall strategies and localised devices whereby a work which is considered LITERATURE demonstrates its 'literariness'. In particular, draw attention to ways in which it:

◆ *defamiliarises habitual perceptions*, prevents merely 'automatic' responses and promotes a fresh view of familiar things;
◆ *commits 'organised violence on ordinary language'* and thereby establishes a more than ordinary sense of poetic or rhetorical pattern, chiefly through manipulations of sound-patterning, parallelism (repetition with variation), antithesis, imagery and inverted syntax;
◆ *foregrounds certain aspects of language within the text* (e.g. imagery, sound-patterning) and effectively assumes or 'backgrounds' others;
◆ *plays around with dimensions of time and space and narration*: obtrudes or obscures the controlling presence of the writer, and generally 'lays bare' the devices of writing.

. . . And how to turn it into Functionalism

Go on to investigate:

◆ the aesthetic and social norms which the text was confirming or challenging at the time;
◆ the various functions the text has served, or may yet serve, at various moments of (re)production and reception;
◆ the processes of **revaluation** it has been – and continues to be – subject to.

Examples

Draw on the above guidelines to help sketch your own Formalist and Functionalist analyses of each of the following texts. Do this before reading the commentary supplied.

Poetry and poetics: Shakespeare's 'My mistress' eyes . . . .' (5.1.3 b) A Formalist reading of this sonnet might start by drawing attention to the **versification**: how the rigour of the rhyme-scheme (ababcdcdefefgg) and metre (iambic pentameter) supply a 'poetic' framework, and yet the conversational freedom of the rhythms informs it with a sense of 'ordinary speech'. Formalists might then move to consider the witty contrasts and inversions, and the systematically antithetical, parodic argument. All these features would be cited as evidence of the text's self-conscious 'literariness', and its pervasive *defamiliarising of the romantic love experience. A more fully Functionalist reading would compare the various uses the sonnet form is put to here and elsewhere by Shakespeare, with its use by Wyatt, Sidney and Petrarch previously and, say, Milton, Wroth and Brooke subsequently (cf. 5.1.3 c; 5.4.6 d). It would also consider the fact that most sonnets were written by men and passed around among men. The emphasis would thus shift from what the sonnet *is* to what it *does*; e.g. boast, complain, insult, praise, show off, insinuate, admonish, celebrate, etc. It would also be important to gauge the various **foregrounds** and **backgrounds** against which this sonnet can be placed and evaluated: the conventional (Petrarchan) image of 'fair' female beauty which it sports with in the textual 'foreground', and the changing norms and valuations of female beauty (as well as males' roles as observers and judges) which act as 'backgrounds'. The significance and value of this sonnet could thereby be plotted **textually**, **contextually** and **intertextually** – and in a succession of historical moments.

Prose narrative: Pratchett and Gaiman's 'Good Omens' (5.1.4 e) Formalists tend to concentrate on prose texts which sport with language, genre and narrative structure. In the *Good Omens* passage they would draw attention to such features as:

♦ the humorous slippage between different time-frames and world-views, from the nostalgically archaic and rural ('slumbering villages ... honest yeomen') to the patently modern and commercial ('financial consulting ... software engineering').

♦ the playful mixture of different genres, from documentary journalism ('The surveyor's theodolite is one of the most direful symbols of the twentieth century') through biblical parody ('there will come Road Widening, yea, ...) to an apocalyptic blend of estate agent's blurb ('and two-thousand-home estates in keeping with the Essential Character of the Village. Executive Development will be manifest.')

♦ the overt act of narration and acknowledgement of the fact that this is one book amongst many ('Most books on witchcraft will tell you. . . . This is because most books on witchcraft are written by men.')

Functionalists would go on to observe that many of these issues were acutely topical in the late 1980s and early 1990s in Britain, notably the gentrifying and embourgeoisment of the countryside, and the problem of road extension and widening (along with ecological opposition to it). Also acute was – and is – a sense that 'politically correct' male writers might need to apologise for patriarchal literary traditions. Further contextualisation would entail comparison with other contemporary fantasy and neo-Gothic tales, parodic and otherwise. In all these ways, precisely what is being defamiliarised would be recognised as a function of a specific social and historical moment – even while the aesthetic forms and techniques might be recognised as in some sense universal.

Drama: Beckett's 'Not I' (5.3.4 d); Theatre Workshop's 'Oh What a Lovely War' (5.4.6 f) Formalists, like NEW CRITICS, did not devote much attention to drama. In its mode of production on stage or screen, it was less exclusively 'literary' and more obviously and messily social. But when they did treat drama, again they tended to concentrate on *Modernist or experimental works. Beckett's *Not I* would be chosen because it committed to 'organised violence on ordinary speech' through:

♦ the piling-up of truncated or interrupted phrases without much conventional punctuation or sentence-structure;

♦ half-formed thoughts, a sense of 'talking to oneself' and uncertain or scrambled frames of reference in time, space and person;

♦ the patent theatricality of Mouth and Auditor, which are clearly roles and devices not *naturalistic character-parts;

◆   the sheer effort the reader/audience has to put into making familiar sense of what may initially seem crazily incomprehensible. (Is 'Mouth' the 'tiny little girl' or the mother? Is this an inner dialogue with self or an outer dialogue with an other?)

Functionalists would try to gauge the norms of sense and nonsense prevailing at the time and, more specifically, trace the historical development and reception of so-called **absurdist** theatre. Just *how* 'absurd' was it – and is it now – to whom and where?

Oh What a Lovely War would be analysed in terms of its challenging mixture of media and perspectives: the ways in which it defamiliarises war through a clash of voices, news panel, slides and song, and a shifting array of theatrical 'foregrounds' and 'backgrounds'. In view of the media and subject matter, the analysis would probably take a politically engaged turn towards a specifically Brechtian understanding of 'making strange'. For the effect here is to make audiences question the parts played by nationalism, religion and class in war. Functionalists would go on to observe the changes in production, emphasis and response as the show moved venues and was transformed into a film. Indeed, they would argue that this play/film helped establish a satirical, black-comic and even **carnivalesque** view of the First World War (and war in general) which has become commonplace (cf. *Cabaret*, *Blackadder*). Paradoxically, we now perhaps expect to be shocked in these ways.

ACTIVITIES

(a)   *Use the above 'How to practise . . .' framework (p. 89) to develop a Formalist and/or Functionalist analysis of any 'literary' text you are studying.* If possible, include an instance of poetry and prose narrative or drama. Alternatively, analyse one of these: Wyatt's 'They flee from me' (5.1.3 a); Dickinson's 'I Felt a Funeral, in my Brain' (5.4.5 d); Nichols's 'Tropical Death' (5.4.5 e); Swift's *A Modest Proposal* (5.2.4 a); Churchill's *Cloud 9* (5.3.4 e).

(b)   *Take a small sample of what you consider 'familiar' 'ordinary', 'non-literary' language* (e.g. a scrap of conversation, a bit of a newspaper story, a few entries from a telephone directory; cf. 5.3.1 a–b; 5.2.5). Now think how you might re-present or refashion this material so as to make other people see it afresh, in ways not dulled by routine. Consider anything from changes in punctuation, visual presentation and delivery, through tinkering with individual words and phrases, to full-scale transformation of text and context. In short, attempt to **defamiliarise* the piece.

Go on to reconsider just how 'ordinary' the sample of language was that you started with. How far was it already in some sense patterned and structured? And what grounds are there for labelling your transformation of it 'literary'?

DISCUSSION

Debate the following propositions *for, against* and *alternative* (i.e. by finding or fashioning a different one). Support your arguments with references to specific texts, authors, genres and periods, wherever possible.

    (i)   In art it is our experience of the process of construction that counts, not the finished product.

                             Victor Shklovsky, *Art as Technique* (1917), in Lodge (1988: 20)

(ii)   Any object and any activity, whether natural or human, may become a carrier
       of the aesthetic function.

Jan Mukarovsky, *Aesthetic Function: Norm and Value as Social Facts*
(1936: 6)

Also see: LITERATURE; POSTSTRUCTURALISM; above 'Key terms', p. 84.

READING: *Introductory*: Jefferson and Robey 1986: 24–72; Selden 1989: 37–45; Carter
and Nash 1990: 1–19; Makaryk 1993: 53–60, 179–83; Selden *et al.* 1997: 29–46.
Primary: Shklovsky, Tomashevsky and Eikhenbaum in Lemon and Reis 1965; Shklovsky and
Jakobson also in Lodge 1988: 15–61; Propp 1928; Eikhenbaum, Tynyanov, Propp, Bakhtin
and Jakobson in Matejka and Pomorska 1978; Mukarovsky in Garvin 1964; Mukarovsky
1936; Voloshinov 1973. *Advanced*: Jameson 1972; Bennett 1979; Erlich 1981. Bakhtin
1981.

2.5   PSYCHOLOGICAL APPROACHES

Overview

Psychology for our purposes can be initially defined as 'the understanding of mental
and emotional processes as these relate to language, literature and culture'.
Psychoanalysis is the study of these processes in individual people. Psychotherapy is
concerned with techniques for resolving mental and emotional problems and with
people realising their full potential. As distinctly modern practices, psychoanalysis
and psychotherapy are primarily identified with Sigmund Freud (1856–1939). For it
was Freud who aimed to put the study of human consciousness and the unconscious
on a scientific footing. However, the analysis and treatment of mental and emotional
disorders (as well as debate about the very terms 'mental', 'emotional', 'dis/order',
'ab/normality', 'in/sanity', 'non/sense', etc.) have long and complex histories both
before and after Freud. Indeed, one of the main challenges in studying the 'psyche'
is choosing the ground upon which we define it. The term derives from Greek *psyche*
meaning 'breath' and 'soul' as well as 'mind'. Psyche-ology broadly conceived is thus
potentially the study of mental, emotional and spiritual processes.

LANGUAGE, in modern psychological terms, is the primary symbolic system
through which we differentiate and categorise the worlds within and around us. For
*Lacan, the 'subject's entry into language' is the primary condition for the perception
of **difference**. Words are the chief means whereby we distinguish various **selves**
from various **others** (notably through the personal pronouns 'I, me, my, mine; you,
she, he, it, they . . . '; see **auto/biography**). It is also chiefly through language that
we assume or are assigned various subject positions, **roles** and **identities** (e.g.
common nouns such as 'mummy', 'daddy', 'girl', 'boy', 'baby', 'grown-up', 'student',
'lecturer'; and proper nouns such as people's personal and family names). Words are
therefore a primary means of both *expression and *repression. They allow us to say
and see certain things but at the same time they prompt us to ignore or fail to
recognise others. For this reason, psychologists often pay a great deal of attention to
processes of **dialogue**, especially that between analyst and patient, and in psychotherapy the practice of the 'talking cure'. They also look closely at the psychological
implications of **word-play** (see **poetry**), including word association, ambiguities,

puns and slips of the tongue. Meanwhile, educational and developmental psychologists engage specifically with the processes of perception and memory and the relations between learning and play, not only in language but also in other forms of symbolic representation and social interaction.

LITERATURE, and more generally **writing**, figures both as an object of psychological study and as a therapeutic practice. We can study other people's poems, plays, novels, auto/biographies and journals for what these tell us about their 'inner' lives. We can also use these genres and activities to explore our own identities, situations and circumstances. Either way, the focus tends to oscillate between the psychological object (the writer as realised *in* the text) and the psychological subject (the reader or writer's relation *to* the text). Indeed, as with many contemporary approaches, there has been a noticeable shift of emphasis over the past twenty years: from **writer** to **text** to **reader**. The ostensible focus of study is now less likely to be, say, Shakespeare's or Austen's or Dickens's 'mind', or even the 'mind' of the **characters** Hamlet or Elizabeth Bennett or Pip. It is more likely to be the psychological problems and possibilities realised by these figures in the minds of contemporary audiences and readers. In this respect current psychological approaches have much in common with those of *reader response and reception (see **writing and reading**). *Fiction in particular becomes a 'space' in which it is not only the writer but also the reader who plays, 'daydreams', and generally explores and experiments with various versions of reality and the interplay of conscious and unconscious states (see **realism and representation** and **imagination**).

CULTURE figures in psychological approaches in a variety of shadowy yet powerful ways. Civilisation as a whole can be seen as the result (the symptom even) of human beings' struggle to control and redirect their basic animal drives and desires. Viewed negatively, culture is thus a sustained act of collective *repression: it thwarts and distorts our animal natures and alienates us from our bodies. Viewed positively, culture is a celebration of all that it is to be distinctly 'human': it keeps us sane and safe and also allows us to *express and project our bodies in many directions and dimensions. Thus we can conceive of literature, art, clothing, buildings, cityscapes, regimes of work and play (i.e. COMMUNICATION and *sign-systems in general) in at least two ways: on the one hand, they conceal, constrict and contain; but on the other hand, they express, extend and explore. Either way, we are obliged to recognise that our understanding of emotional and mental processes is likely to be tied up with our understanding of bodily ('animal') functions, and that neither can be divorced from arguments about what we mean by culture, civilisation and humanity. For all these reasons, it is now common to find psychological dimensions to MARXIST, FEMINIST, POSTCOLONIAL and POSTSTRUCTURALIST approaches. Conversely, there are several kinds of psychological theory and practice specifically inflected in terms of class, sexuality and gender, race and ethnicity, and the post-humanist subject. Psychological processes of expression and repression are thereby related to social-historical processes of oppression and suppression. The personal is recognised to be public and political – and vice versa.

Key terms: **absence and presence; absurd** (see **comedy**); **self and other** (see **auto/biography**); **character;** *condensation and *displacement; *consciousness and the *unconscious; *content (manifest and latent); *desire; *dream-work; *ego, *id and *super-ego; *expression and *repression; *lack; *transaction; **subjects and agents, identities and roles.**

Major figures and models

Many of the most enduring terms in psychoanalysis were made current by Sigmund Freud. Even where these terms have been subsequently challenged or changed, they still provide a useful initial frame of reference.

The *unconscious and *consciousness; *repression and *expression

The unconscious is everything in our psychological make-up that we are *not* directly aware of: our ultimate biological drives, pre-eminently sex, along with all those formative moments in our personal histories, chiefly from early childhood, which we have forgotten or repressed. By definition, the unconscious is a huge yet hidden power. It drives much of what we do yet remains concealed. Consciousness, meanwhile, is everything about ourselves that we *are* aware of: the sensations and perceptions we can talk about or otherwise express, including those aspects of our personal histories and identities we can recall and explicitly represent. The relation between the unconscious and the conscious is dynamic not fixed. Hence our capacity to *become* conscious of things of which we were previously unaware, as well as the possibility of active 'consciousness raising' in general. Some later writers go on to make direct links between forms of psychological *re*pression, the political *opp*ression of certain social groups, and mechanisms of *sup*pression (i.e. *censorship) of certain kinds of information (e.g. Macherey 1966; Jameson 1981). They argue in effect for a politicised unconscious. We can – or cannot – realise certain things about our **selves** precisely because of our past and present power relations with **others** (see **auto/biography**).

Manifest and latent *contents: *condensation, *displacement and *symbolism

Dreams, for Freud, are 'the royal road to the unconscious'. So too, potentially, are imaginative LITERATURE and **art** in general. In all these areas Freud observed that much more is meant than meets the eye. Put more formally, the obvious 'surface' meaning of a dream (story, play or painting) is a merely *manifest* content. This must be interpreted so as to get at its hidden 'deeper' meaning, the *latent* content. Freud identified three ways in which meanings tend to be embedded and hidden, more or less unconsciously:

- *condensation*, where two or more meanings come to bear on the same word, figure or image (e.g. puns, metaphors, a composite person or event in a dream or painting);
- *displacement*, where one item stands in for another with which it has some perceived connection (e.g. substitution of opposites or part for whole, say, 'girl' for 'boy' or a ring for the person who wears it);
- *symbolism*, where some word, image or object is conventionally identified with a certain meaning or function (e.g. spears with fighting with men, bowls with cooking with women).

This last kind of symbolic meaning is primary for Carl Jung, Freud's one-time collaborator and subsequent critic. It underpinned Jung's notion that dreams and art were storehouses of universal images belonging to a 'collective unconscious' that had been repressed by civilisation. However, the POSTSTRUCTURALIST psychoanalyst Jacques Lacan repudiated the notion of universal symbolism of all kinds. Instead, he insisted that the *sign – whether in literature, art or dreams – is inherently unstable and elusive. Consequently, we are always faced by a *lack of essential meaning and are constantly engaged in processes of condensation and displacement. There is no ultimate 'deeper', 'latent' content at all – only a ceaseless succession of *metaphoric and *metonymic substitutions (for Lacan's notion of 'the *Imaginary', see **image**).

Myth and psycho-drama; *ego, *super-ego and *id

Several of Freud's dramatic representations of psychological processes have become *classics. They draw upon classical *myth and, like the man himself, have become myths in their own right. The *'Oedipus complex'*, for instance, was Freud's name for what he saw as a general developmental process: a phase when the male child wishes to kill the father and sleep with the mother. The prototype was Sophocles's *Oedipus the King* where the hero, Oedipus, unwittingly does precisely that. Female children, meanwhile, according to Freud, are particularly prone to 'penis envy'. They are aware of themselves chiefly in terms of a 'lack' of what little boys so visibly have: physically a penis, and symbolically a phallus. Not surprisingly, many FEMINISTS have taken Freud to task over the male-centred myths at the heart of his psychology. In their various ways writers such as Klein, Chodorow, Kristeva and Cixous all argue for quite different configurations of mother–father, mother–daughter and mother–son relations. Characteristically, they equate the 'good mother' figure with a phase of security and undifferentiated 'wholeness' before the threat of separation represented by the father. Some psychoanalytic feminists, following Lacan, also identify the pre-verbal stage of child development with undifferentiated sexuality and semiotic flux, and the verbal stage with differentiated sexuality and symbolic fixity. Feminists have also been quick to question the vision of female 'hysteria' represented in Freud's case history of 'Dora' (see 5.3.1 d).

Another psycho-drama which has achieved classic status, and even common currency in speech, is Freud's model of the ego, super-ego and id. This later, three-part model of emotional and mental processes both refined and replaced the earlier two-part model of the conscious and unconscious. Now the psyche was conceived as the site where three, not two, forces are in play. The *ego* (Latin 'I') represents that part of the **self** most concerned to gratify the instinctual drives emanating from the unconscious, now renamed the *id* (Latin 'that', 'that **other**'). Meanwhile, the *super-ego* (Latin 'above-I') is that part of the conscious self which acts as censor and judge. The super-ego regulates what shall be permitted or prohibited by way of expression or repression. It has the function of a kind of 'conscience' or self-censor and is identified by Freud with a socially internalised sense of self. (The ego, meanwhile, is identified with a relatively free, pre-social self.) One advantage of this triadic model of the ego, super-ego and id over that of the *binary model of the un/conscious is that it introduces a sense of dynamism within the conscious self. There is now a range of actual and potential 'selv*es*' (plural). The ego is both impelled by the desires of the id from within and imposed upon by the conscience of the super-ego from without. In short, 'I' becomes a site where versions of self and other contend. Henceforth the psychological **subject** is split, the 'individual' is divided, and people's identities can never be wholly identified with their conscious view of themselves.

Freud's models and myths have been extended (or exploded) in many ways. The following have been most influential in English and Literary Studies.

*Transactional analysis

As developed by Norman Holland, this is concerned less with what the text tells us about an individual psyche (that of an author or character, say) and more with the text's function as a form of therapy involving both writer and reader. In this view writers supply frameworks and scenarios to which readers respond and relate in their own ways. The text thereby becomes the site not just of one but of many psycho-dramas. In Melanie Klein's terms, the text is 'projected onto' by the reader and thereby becomes 'introjected into' her or his unconsciousness. Winnicott (1974) develops a comparable notion of *play as the exchange of real or imaginary objects. These *transitional objects* (whether dolls or texts) operate as a kind of 'potential space' in which hopes and fears may be safely realised and released. Such processes clearly have something in common with Aristotle's notion of *catharsis as the 'purging' of emotion by the witnessing of a dramatic spectacle (see **comedy and tragedy**). They also partly overlap with *reader-response approaches, especially those developed by David Bleich (1978) in his model of 'subjective criticism' as a kind of individual and group therapy (see **writing and reading**).

An overtly socio-psychological approach to learning in general and language-learning in particular was developed by Lev *Vygotsky (1934). For Vygotsky language is a form of consciousness which develops through a continuing **dialogue** between the 'inner voices' of the speaker's unconscious **self** and the 'outer voices' of significant **others** in the surrounding world (see **auto/biography**). Learning and development are thus recognised to be *inter*personal as well as *intra*personal processes: articulated on an 'I/we–you' axis as well as an 'I–me' axis. Indeed, the one is a refraction of the other. For *Bakhtin, too, words are always caught in the processes of exchange and change that bind people to one another socially. Every transaction (linguistic, educational and psychological) therefore entails a transformation. People are 'human *becomings*' not simply 'human *beings*'.

Psycho-politics: the personal is political

The progressive socialising and historicising of psychology are a feature of most contemporary approaches. So is a recognition that 'personal politics' cuts both ways. Just as the personal is always political, so the political always has a psychological dimension to it. Michel Foucault (1986: 121ff.), for instance, insists that we understand 'sanity' and 'insanity', 'normality' and 'abnormality', 'sense' and 'nonsense', dialectically and historically. These terms are braced against one another within shifting medical, legal and other **discourses**. They mean subtly or markedly different things at different times. Thus 'madness' is not the same, nor treated the same, amongst medieval mystics, in eighteenth-century French asylums, in Stalinist Russia and in late twentieth-century Manhattan. Diagnosis and treatment also vary according to sex and social status. Sexuality, too, Foucault argues, is inscribed and expressed differently in different cultures. The libido, like the *body in general, is subject to various 'economies' (distributions, values) and is perhaps not the universal instinctual drive often implied by Freud.

Others, meanwhile, as already mentioned, point to the need to read psychological *re*pression in relation to political *op*pression of powerless groups and the systematic *sup*pression of potentially available means of communication and *ex*pression. (In short, all these '—pressions' are interdependent.) Writers such as Fanon, Freire, Macherey, Williams and Jameson see efforts to achieve consciousness as struggles which are personal-political not simply personal. MARXISTS in effect insist on a pluralising and collectivising of Freud's psycho-drama of the 'I', 'above-I' and 'it'. They argue for the recognition of a 'them' and 'us' dimension of 'inner' as well as 'outer' struggle. FEMINISTS too insist on sexually complicated versions of the psyche, even before the gendered differences entailed by the entry into language and the symbolic order. The whole drama of 's/he' (i.e. the psychological subject as 'she' and/or 'he') must therefore be added to that of an otherwise neutered or patriarchally privileged 'I'. So must the dramas (and traumas) of colour in so far as they impinge upon the development of all of us as personal-political **subjects** living through POSTCOLONIALISM. Study of cross-cultural **differences** is a significant feature of contemporary psychology.

The end(s) of psychology

Finally, in the various debates informing POSTSTRUCTURALISM and POST-MODERNISM, it is the radical instability not only of the psychological subject as person but also of psychology as a discipline and practice which is at issue. That is, psychology too, along with its associated practices of psychoanalysis and psycho-therapy, may itself be identified as just one of a range of socially and historically situated discourses. At some point these will be transformed into or superseded by others. After all, modern psychoanalysis and psychotherapy largely took over the 'curative' and 'purgative' functions previously assigned to religion and magic (e.g. confession, spiritual guidance, conscience, exorcism). The question, then, para-doxically, is *What is it that modern psychology itself 'represses'?* What other modes of expression does psychology in some way deny or distort? What disciplines and practices other than dominant post-Freudian models are currently developing inside, alongside and outside psychology? Does the notion of the human 'psyche' as mental, emotional and spiritual construct have a future at all? Or do we need to think, feel, and generally **imagine** in ways as yet undreamt of – at least in main-stream Western traditions? The method which follows tries to take account of these possibilities too.

How to practise psychological approaches

Begin by considering the text in three dimensions:

♦ what it suggests about the *writer's* emotional, mental and spiritual states and processes, as well as those of her or his time;

♦ how you as a modern *reader* relate to – and perhaps identify with or project onto – the events, characters and situations represented;

- what the *language of the text* suggests about the nature of *expression and *repression in general, and the relation of both to our understanding of tensions within the un/conscious.
  In all these areas also be prepared to take into account such complicating factors as: (i) changing notions of the writer's and reader's roles (see **author**), as well as the conventions and **genre(s)** in play. Try to grasp the interplay of a range of psychological subjects (writer, reader, text, language) in a range of social and historical moments. Don't imagine there is just one psychological reading. Further research and reflection are clearly necessary, so go on to consider:
- **auto/biography**: what is known about the writer's life, both from her or him **self** and from **others**? What seems to be revealed or concealed in the work in hand? What are we (not) being told, and why?
- *choice of psychological model*: which of the following emphases seems to best answer both the demands of the particular material and your own particular aims:

  - *manifest and latent *content*, observing and perhaps attempting to 'decode' the text's strategies of *condensation, *displacement and *symbolism*?
  - Freudian notions of a tension between *the *unconscious and *consciousness*; and psycho-dramas such as the *Oedipus complex* and *hysteria*; or the relations between *ego, *super-ego and *id*?

- *transactional analysis* of teacher–learner and learner–learner as well as writer–reader relations, where the text functions as a 'transitional' object and item of exchange at various moments?
- *post- or anti-Freudian models* of 'the good mother'; *lack and *desire; **self and other**; *the Imaginary; the **subject's** entry into language and the symbolic order?
- *social-psychological* **differences** relating to sexuality and gender, rank and class, ethnicity, religion and MULTICULTURALISM in general.

Finally, consider those aspects of the text and your response to it that are underrepresented, misrepresented or completely unrepresented by your choice of psychological approach. What other, potential approaches has it, in turn, repressed or suppressed?

Example

John Clare's 'I am – yet what I am' (5.1.5). Read this in conjunction with the accompanying notes and, if possible, a brief account of Clare's life (e.g. in Ousby 1992). Sketch a psychological analysis using the above 'How to practise' guidelines before reading on.

A psychological approach to this poem might begin with the writer–text relation (how the poem relates to Clare's life) then move to the reader–text relation (e.g. how you and I relate to the poem). Both might lead to larger inferences about language, the un/conscious, and expression and repression in general, as well as to reflection upon the similarities and differences between early nineteenth- and late twentieth-century notions of sanity and insanity, normality and abnormality.

'Identity crises. The profound sense of self-alienation and estrangement from others that pervades the first two stanzas could be traced back to Clare's adolescence. For

it was then that Clare's lifelong love for Mary Joyce, a local farmer's daughter, was thwarted by the intervention of her father. Clare was of farm-labourer stock and apparently not considered a suitable match. It was then, too, in the early 1800s, that land around Clare's native village of Helpstone was 'enclosed' (i.e. taken over by a local landowner for private parkland and conversion to sheep-farming). This resulted in the dislocation, both physical and mental, of many farm-labourers, including Clare and his family. Against all this could be set the idyllic vision projected in the last stanza of early childhood as a time of security and belonging. Such observations might be backed up by appeal to Clare's scattered autobiographical writings (1821–41) as well as to his other poems. All are marked by a sense of a previously pastoral, almost paradisal, childhood state (real or imaginary) that was subsequently subject to personally traumatic and socially dramatic change. We might therefore venture to say that Clare had trouble maintaining a viable sense of **self** when challenged by **others**: his 'super/ego' fragmented under the pressure of an internal or external 'id'.

But whatever the cause, it is matter of record that Clare was first admitted to an asylum at Epping in 1837. He escaped in 1841 and tried to walk back to Northampton, believing he was married to his childhood sweetheart. He was then committed to Northampton General Lunatic Asylum. There he lived for the remaining twenty-three years of his life and wrote many poems, including this one (*c*.1844). All this information may help us explore – even though it can only crudely explain – a number of the poem's recurrent concerns:

♦ the sense of a self divided against itself ('I am – yet what I am . . . the self-consumer of my woes');
♦ the absence of comforting others ('friends forsake me like a memory lost');
♦ a loss of clear distinction between consciousness and unconsciousness ('the living sea of waking dreams . . . '); all that remains is a present sense of longing contrasted with a past sense of belonging: an overpowering desire to fill an irreparable lack.

Thus the whole last stanza (perhaps reread it now) may be variously interpreted as:

♦ yearning for a kind of primordial infantile oblivion;
♦ a vision of a heavenly paradise or utopia;
♦ a throwback to some sexually undifferentiated state;
♦ a desire for reintegration with nature, the 'id' and all that is 'not-I' – a 'death-wish', even.

The 'forming' of desire Psychological readings might move in other directions and dimensions too. Formally, they might point to the expressively irregular rhythms, the moving caesura (right from the first line) and the 'dashing' punctuation. At the same time they would note the controlling, if not calming, influence of the highly regular versification and metre: three stanzas each with six ten-syllable lines, the first with alternating rhymes throughout, the last two concluding with couplets. Such a high degree of patterning might be seen negatively as a symbolic attempt to repress the semiotic flux beneath – a kind of verbal strait-jacket. But it might also be seen positively as a saving vestige of civilisation, turning what would otherwise be an anguished animal cry into a recognisably human harmony. A rather different, contextual reading might relate the poem's substance and structure to the sense of 'confinement' experienced in many early nineteenth-century (and later) asylums. This might even be extended to notions of 'enclosure': the privatisation of fields and property resulting in the privation of bodies and minds. In this way the personal would be realised as political, and vice versa. The psychology invoked would be grounded in society and history, not simply in the notion of the universal human psyche. There might also be some recognition that this poem was written over a decade before the birth of Freud and half a century before the formal institution of psychoanalysis. Perhaps, then, the most appropriate contemporary intellectual framework for the poem *at that time* was religious and spiritual (as in its last verse) and not psychological at all (as in the above analysis).

A personal–political response. All this leaves us, as modern readers, with a crucial responsibility. And this cannot be detached from the ways in which we, collectively and individually, respond to the text (i.e. our '*response-ability'). What sense do we make of the poem? More pointedly, what sense does it make of us? Personal responses will vary of course. But if we regard psychological *transaction as what takes place between reader and reader as well as between reader, text and writer, then we have an obligation to try to tease out at least some of our responses. Inevitably, some of these will turn out to be idiosyncratic; others may be common; and all are in some sense shareable. (I must leave you to decide which are which, for you, in the following). Here 'I' go:

> I too, like Clare in the last verse, associate childhood with a time when I 'sweetly slept'. Now I often don't sleep too well. As I get older I also recognise, perhaps with Clare (ll. 11–12), that friends and family can become 'strange', either through death (the ultimate estrangement) or through changing relationships. (As I revise this piece in October 1996 I remember my mother who died a year ago, and a good friend who died unexpectedly three weeks ago; also my wife and children who are abroad at the moment. Hence the shape of my present response.)
>
> There is also the tricky matter of fears for one's own own sanity, as well as general uncertainty about what 'sanity' and 'normality' actually mean nowadays. After all, I am a member of a species which is armed to the teeth and gradually tearing itself and the rest of the planet to pieces, notwithstanding claims to scientific rationality and progess. ('Enclosure' too, I recall, was hailed as a mark of progress and civilisation – though by the 'enclos*ers*' rather than the 'enclos*ed*'.) In other words, you don't have to have been in a mental asylum or formally certified as insane to have anxieties about your own and other people's sanity. At the same time, as I reread Clare's last verse, I take comfort from its vision of at least potential harmony and (re-)union. Though whether this is saving illusion or crazy delusion I cannot say.

The relevance of this brief autobiographical excursus to your own response to Clare's poem I must leave you to decide for yourself.

ACTIVITIES

(a)   *Draw on the above 'How to practise . . .' guidelines to help frame a psychological analysis of a text and/or author that interests you.* (Suggested focuses in Part Five are: Swift, *A Modest Proposal* (5.2.4 a); Shelley, *Frankenstein* (5.2.3 c); Emily Dickinson,

'I felt a Funeral' (5.4.5 d); Beckett, *Not I* (5.3.4 d); Rich, 'Dialogue' (5.1.8); Queen, 'Bohemian Rhapsody' (5.1.10).) Whatever and whoever you choose, find out as much as you reasonably can about the lives of the people involved.

(b)   *Four 'I'dentities*. The four texts so labelled in Part Five (5.4.7 g) are partly comparable in form and substance. However, they belong to different **genres**, MEDIA and historical moments. They are also by different people. With all this in mind, consider what kind of psychological approach is appropriate in each case. (Is any kind of psychological approach appropriate on its own?)

(c)   *Who's 'Dora'? Whose Dora?!* Try reading Freud's *Fragment of an Analysis of a Case of Hysteria* (5.3.1 d) in various ways, as: transcript of interview; dramatic script; detective story; scholarly case history; word-and-mind game; any other genre you think plausible. Go on to consider how you might re-write the text so as to express alternative positions which may have been repressed or suppressed. What are the implications of all this for a literary approach to psychology – as distinct from a psychological approach to literature?

DISCUSSION

(i)   our actual enjoyment of an imaginative work proceeds from a liberation of tension in our minds [. . .] thenceforward to enjoy our own daydreams without self-reproach or shame.

Sigmund Freud, *Creative Writers and Day-dreaming* (1908) in Lodge (1972: 41–2)

(ii) 'Psychoanalytic criticism [. . .] addresses the genesis of the self as revealed in literature and the arts [. . .] in all of which there is the attempt to insert the subject into the social.

Elizabeth Wright, 'Psychoanalytic Criticism' in Coyle *et al.* (1990: 774)

(iii) literature reveals a certain knowledge, and sometimes the truth itself, about an otherwise repressed, nocturnal, secret and unconscious universe.

Julia Kristeva, 'Women's Time' (1981) in Belsey and Moore (1997: 212)

Also see: FEMINISM; POSTSTRUCTURALISM; POSTCOLONIALISM; above 'Key terms', p. 93.

READING: *Introductory*: Belsey 1980: 56–84; Wright in Jefferson and Robey 1986: 145–65; Wright in Coyle *et al.* 1990: 764–76; Makaryk 1993: 163–70, 320–4; Selden *et al.* 1997: 136–44; Green and Lebihan 1996: 139–81; Eagleton 1996: 131–68. *Fuller studies*: Vygotsky 1934; Winnicott 1974; Wright 1984; Kristeva 1984; Rimmon-Kenan 1987. *Anthologies*: Freud, Jung, Trilling and Holland in Lodge 1972: 36–43, 175–89; Holland 1990; Lacan in Lodge 1988: 79–106 and in Rice and Waugh 1996: 122–7; Ellman 1994.

2.6   MARXISM, CULTURAL MATERIALISM AND NEW HISTORICISM

Overview

All these approaches are concerned with understanding texts in social and historical **context**. LANGUAGE is grasped functionally for what it *does*, rather than essentially for what it *is*. LITERATURE is treated as a problematic, even suspect category, especially in so far as it offers as 'universal' and 'natural' writing which appears to underpin privileged and elitist views of society. Accordingly, the emphasis of these approaches tends to be broadly cultural and specifically *political*. CULTURE is recognised as an arena of conflict as well as consensus, a 'space' where **differences** of interest diverge as well as converge. Access or denial of access to certain modes of COMMUNICATION is also recognised as crucial. Meanwhile, the primary forces of historical change are reckoned to be those of social class as well as latterly, gender and race.

Marxist approaches to language, literature and culture tend to be developed from the models of economic and political change that Marx, Engels and the other 'founding fathers' of Marxism devised, rather than from the relatively few and incidental things they said about literature and art as such. There is thus much attention to:

- *modes of production* – the technologies and social relations whereby goods are produced (including the modes of production, publication and transmission of poems, novels, plays, newspapers, films, TV programmes, etc.);
- relations between the *economic base* and the *ideological superstructure* – how certain economic organisations of labour and materials affect and are affected by institutions such as the law, religion, education, the MEDIA and the state (e.g. the relations between poverty and illiteracy, control of the media and access to political power);
- *power, powerlessness and empowerment* – how far power is maintained by coercion, complicity or consent; and how far those who are the **subjects** of dominant world-views have the capacity to assert themselves as agents in their own emancipation.

Cultural Materialism is a form of Marxist analysis chiefly identified with Raymond Williams, Alan Sinfield and others in Britain. It is marked by a committed socialist critique of literary and cultural artefacts and of the institutions that maintain them. **New Historicism** is a related, socially sensitive but less politically committed form of analysis identified with such figures as Stephen Greenblatt, Louis Montrose and others in the USA. The aim of New Historicists is to recognise the *power relations in play both in a text's moment of production and in its subsequent moments of *re-production (e.g., by academics in universities). Typically, whereas (British) Cultural Materialists tend to emphasise resistant, subversive and sometimes revolutionary readings of texts, their (American) New Historicist counterparts tend to emphasise the ways in which texts and their readers finally 'contain' subversion and promote conformity.

There are very few pure – some would say vulgar – Marxists in academic circles nowadays. But there are many broadly 'Marxian' critics and theorists who would identify with parts of the above agendas. Most do so with an awareness of other socially sensitive and politically motivated approaches, especially FEMINIST and POSTCOLONIAL ones. Marxists also have vexed but often highly productive relations with PSYCHOANALYTIC, POSTSTRUCTURALIST and POSTMODERNIST approaches. Arguments in this area often revolve around differing notions of the subject (conceived as person, subject matter and academic discipline). It all depends how far it (and we) are understood to be individual *and* social, private *and* public, repressed *and* oppressed, coherent *and* dispersed, local *and* global, in *and* out of history.

Key terms: **absence and presence, gaps and silences, centres and margins**; **foreground and background**; class; **text** in **context**; CULTURE; **discourse**; HISTORY (see 1.5.6); **narrative . . . hi/story**; *ideology (dominant, residual and emergent); *popular; *power; **realism and representation**; **subject and agent**, and **role and identity**; *value.

Some major figures and movements

Broadly speaking, there are three distinct yet interrelated approaches to texts practised by critics in the Marxist tradition, each of which we shall treat in turn:

♦   'socialist **realism**', primarily associated with the critical writing of Georg Lukács (1885–1971);
♦   'socialist POST/MODERNISM', primarily associated with the theory and practice of Bertolt Brecht (1898–1956);
♦   'democratic MULTICULTURALISM', spanning contemporary Cultural Materialism and New Historicism, and distinguished by its attention to cultural **differences** and *power in general.

Socialist realism

The Hungarian critic Lukács was chiefly interested in the nineteenth-century novel and the ways in which such '*epic' and 'encyclopaedic' novelists as Dickens, Balzac and Tolstoy could present overarching views of the societies in which they lived. The sheer breadth of these writers' social and historical visions offered imaginary 'totalities'. In effect, they afforded what Lukács termed a 'world-historical' sense of the various classes and sections of society in dynamic tension: caught in the very ebb and flow of social conflict and historical change. **Characters** were thus significant not only as individuals but for their *'typicality'*, their capacity to express the pressures which their social roles thrust upon them. In short, Lukács read fictions for the social-economic conditions and class conflicts they represented. His attachment to **realism** (or rather 'critical realism') as a mode and the nineteenth-century novel as a historical genre was based upon the assumption that the best art both reflects and refracts history 'as a whole': it holds up a large mirror to social changes and at the same time revealingly tilts it.

Socialist post/modernism

This is a very different kind of political and **aesthetic** vision. Though still discernibly Marxist, it was practised by Brecht. He too aimed for what he termed an *epic theatre; but in his case he had in mind a more formal, Aristotelian notion of epic as **dramatic** exchanges framed by **narrative**. More particularly, Brecht practised a politically motivated version of the kinds of *defamiliarisation technique theorised by the Russian FORMALISTS. His 'making-strange-device' (*Verfremdungseffekt*) aimed to prevent audiences identifying too readily with the characters and situations presented. Instead, spectators were forced to stand back from the action and appraise it critically, from a distance. Brecht's mixture of narrative and dramatic modes, sometimes punctuated by song, had the same aim: to make viewers pause for reflection, not just empathise emotionally. The extract from Theatre Workshop's *Oh What a Lovely War* (5.4.6 f) gives a fair indication of 'Brechtian' theatre in action, with its mixture of narrative and dramatic strategies, speech and song, theatrical and other audio-visual devices. The overall effect is to make us question the nature of patriotism and imperialism through the sharp contrast between jingoistic propaganda and the human carnage it veils. There is particular attention to clashes between the **discourses** of the senior and junior officers and the common soldier. In just such ways Brecht sought to produce, not a single and unified illusion of wholeness, but a plural and variegated play of competing realities. Where Lukács stressed totality, Brecht stressed fragmentation. In this respect Brecht practised what Adorno (a theoretician of the contemporary Frankfurt School) preached: a politically charged *Modernism. Indeed, in his use of the then-modern media (back-projection of slides, bursts of audio-recording) and in his attempts to be popularly accessible, Brecht can properly be seen as POSTMODERNIST. Certainly he did not indulge in the kinds of 'literary' difficulty and obscurity practised by such 'high' modernists as Joyce, Kafka and T.S. Eliot. All of these writers and their characteristic qualities Lukács stigmatised as symptomatic of bourgeois decadence.

Shocking change

Walter Benjamin, Brecht's friend and commentator, went on to develop the theoretical ramifications of such a politicised post/modernist **aesthetics**. Key elements in this are the concept of *shock* and the practice of brushing **history** *against the grain*. Benjamin maintained that in times of revolutionary change a traditional, neo-classical aesthetics of 'harmony', 'balance', 'organic unity' and 'reconciliation' (the basic NEW CRITICAL position, in fact) was inadequate and likely to prove politically reactionary. He insisted that genuinely revolutionary art needed to effect a radical rupture with the past. It needed to shock readers and viewers into a recognition of the oppression which underpins even the most apparently civilised society (see Discussion (iii), p. 111). The job of radical writers and readers was therefore to brush official, dominant versions of history against the grain: to expose the many alternative histories (especially of working-class men and women) that had been muted or suppressed. Benjamin also articulated a crucial POSTMODERNIST view of the relations between **art** and modern technology in his essay 'The Work of Art in an Age of Mechanical Reproduction' (*c*.1935). There he pointed out that the capacity of modern technology to reproduce images cheaply and accurately in effect disperses the 'aura' surrounding supposedly unique works of art. What was previously exclusive may be made widely available. What belonged to elite culture may circulate in *popular culture. Moreover, the 'art object' is more clearly recognised for what it always was – a commodity. In this way Benjamin anticipates the end of such institutionally privileged concepts as 'great' – because rare – art and literature.

    The subsequent progress of Marxist criticism can be seen in terms of a tension between the socialist **realist** and socialist Post/modernist positions outlined above. Should history be viewed as a totality or a series of fragments: one grand and continuous narrative featuring the gradual emancipation of the working classes, for instance; or many small and discontinuous narratives involving many intermittent kinds of struggle? Should literature and art seek to *reflect* this historical reality? Or should they present more or less critical *refractions* of plural realities that can never be grasped in their entirety? There are questions to be asked about the nature and status of LITERATURE and **art** too. Have the boundaries between 'high art' and *popular culture been so transformed as to be virtually meaningless? How far does the control of contemporary technologies increasingly turn all cultural products into commodities circulating according to (late) capitalist modes of production, repro-duction and distribution? What are the possible vantage points and points of leverage outside or within that system? Indeed, is it still possible to 'see' capitalism at all as a distinct and potentially transient phase of social and economic organisation? Or is it already so all-encompassing as to seem 'universal', 'natural' and 'inevitable'? All these questions are answered in various ways by the writers we now review.

*Ideological subjects and agents

For a rereading of Marxism through a combination of POST/STRUCTURALIST and PSYCHOANALYTIC lenses, we must turn to the work of Louis Althusser (1918–90), a political theorist who produced a number of influential modifications of central tenets. Most fundamentally, he distinguished the 'Ideological State Apparatuses' of law, religion, politics and education from the 'Repressive State Apparatuses' of the police and the military, assigning to each sphere a 'relative autonomy' both from one another and from the economic base. This opened the way for a kind of culturalism in which **discourses** tend to be detached from modes of production. Cultural **differences** may then be understood without direct appeal to differences in material conditions. At the same time, Althusser insisted that the humanist notion of the unified and integrated '*individual' (i.e., 'the one who cannot be divided') be radically reformulated. In its place he offered a view of each person as a variegated and shifting configuration of ideological **subjects** (plural). Each member of society is in effect assigned a variety of roles depending on the contexts in which s/he operates. In Althusser's terms, each of us is **'addressed'** (i.e. greeted and named) by various institutions and thereby 'interpellated' in a variety of 'subject positions'. Thus I may be addressed as 'father/dad', 'son', 'brother', 'husband' (in families); 'lecturer', 'teacher', 'colleague', 'Dr ——' (in education); 'witness', 'defendant', 'jury' (in law); etc. You too will be addressed in a corresponding variety of ways. Crucially, however, many of these roles or subject positions are not initially of our own choosing. They are thrust upon us and we must then decide to comply and consent, or resist and refuse, perhaps insisting on another role and subject position entirely. A current example would be the tendency among educational managers to speak of students as 'customers' or 'clients', and lecturers/teachers as 'providers' who 'deliver course-packages'. Meanwhile, all of them/us, including employers and the rest of the public, are addressed as 'stakeholders'. In this way a conspicuously *commercial* model of human relations is being superimposed on a traditionally *educational* process. Those involved may then decide to comply, resist, or assert a preferable alternative. *Pro*-active, as distinct from merely reactive, subjects are sometime called **agents** (see **subject**).

Gaps and silences – the 'not-said'

Pierre Macherey's *A Theory of Literary Production* (1966) signals an even more marked convergence of Marxist and POST/STRUCTURALIST models. For Macherey the primary focus of textual study is what the text *does not* – or *cannot* – say (the 'non-dit'). Every text can therefore be characterised not only by what it *does* talk about, its *expressed subject matter (its **presences**) but also by what it *represses or *suppresses (its **absences**). The 'unsaid' or 'unsayable' thus constitutes a kind of unconscious upon which the text draws but which, by definition, it cannot wholly bring to consciousness. The role of the critical reader, therefore, is to search for the **gaps and silences**: the figures and events that have been quickly glossed over, marginalised or ignored. What other stories and histories have been displaced or replaced by the very act of telling *this* **hi/story** in *this* way and not another? Clearly, then, though Macherey's method is dialectical, historical and psychological, it is not exclusively Marxist. This can be said of much of the later work in this area. Fredric Jameson's *The Political Unconscious: Narrative as a Socially Symbolic Act* (1981) is a case in point. Like Macherey, Jameson stresses the psycho-political force of texts. **Narrative** structure can be construed as a double-edged act of repression/oppression as well as expression. At the same time, Jameson insists on appealing to what he terms the 'ultimate horizon of human history as a whole'.

Dominant, residual and emergent *ideologies

Similar tensions can be found, variously articulated, throughout British and American writings in a broadly Marxian tradition. Raymond *Williams, for instance, worked through from a social democratic commitment to CULTURE as 'the whole way of living of a people' (*Culture and Society 1780–1950*, 1958: 83) to 'an argument [. . .] set into a new and conscious relation with Marxism' (*Marxism and Literature*, 1977: 6). In the latter work in particular, Williams developed a dynamic model of *ideology which many students of literature and culture have found very useful. Williams suggests that we see every text (or other cultural practice) as the site in which three phases of ideological development can be traced. These phases he calls *dominant, residual* and *emergent* (1977: 121–8):

◆   The *dominant* refers to those aspects of the text which express the socially privileged and central ways of seeing and saying of its age: the dominant discourses *in the present*.

◆   The *residual* refers to those ways of saying and seeing which were once central but have now been superseded and are only evident as vestiges: these were often the dominant discourses *of the past*.

◆   The *emergent* refers to those embryonic growth points which exist only as half-formed potential but which may be perceived as precursors of new ways of saying and seeing: these may become the dominant discourses *of the future*.

In short, every text can be grasped as a site where the discourses of past, present and future meet and contend. We might see *Hamlet*, for instance, as a play where residual feudal models of society are challenged by emergent forms of individualism, and with both set against the dominant contemporary model of the nation–state. The emphasis is thus not on texts simply reflecting or representing a single fixed ideology, but on texts refracting ideolog*ies* (plural) as part of a continuing process of struggle. Moreover, following *Bakhtin/Voloshinov, Williams points out that such struggles take place in and over words of all kinds. The contest of dominant, residual and emergent ideologies ensures that even a single word, even every utterance of that word (e.g. 'woman', 'black', 'God', 'freedom') is a newly configured site for the collision and coalescence of the past and the future in the present.

Cultural Materialists and New Historicists

All practitioners of these approaches work with these conceptions of ideology as a dynamic process: texts and language are sites of ideological struggle. The chief differences among them are in the kinds and degrees of political commitment each brings to the task; also in the specific academic institutions and national cultures within which each operates. It is initially tempting, and to some extent useful, to offer the broad equations: Cultural materialism = British Socialist tradition = more positive commitment to conflictual politics; and New Historicism = American democratic tradition = more positive commitment to consensual politics. However, it should also be stressed that contemporary practitioners of all these positions are in some sense eclectic and elastic. Terry Eagleton (UK) and Fredric Jameson (US) may exchange comradely blows on their respective analyses of POSTMODERNISM and its relations to 'late capitalism'. But they do so wielding a similarly wide array of models and methods drawn from POST/STRUCTURALISM and PSYCHOANALYSIS. Moreover, many of the most forceful and resourceful proponents of Marxist analysis now do so with an acute awareness of the need to meld it with FEMINIST and POSTCOLONIALIST critical discourses too. Catherine Belsey and Gayatri Spivak are especially notable in this respect. But whatever the labels we apply, one thing is clear: all these writers share a concern not simply with *which* texts are studied and *how*, but also *who* is doing the studying and *why*. The broadly institutional and cultural as well as the narrowly textual dimensions of study are therefore equally emphasised in the method which follows.

How to practise Marxist analyses, as developed by Cultural Materialists and New Historicists

*In general, consider the *power relations in play within and around the text (i)* in its initial moment of production ('there and then'); (ii) in its subsequent moments of reproduction (e.g. 'here and now').*
   In particular, concentrate on such factors as class, rank, occupation and education, then broaden your analysis to take in such complicating factors as *gender, race, nationality and age*. Do this systematically with attention to every major aspect of the text in context and every moment of production and reception. (Use the following as a checklist.)

Start with 'the text in hand' (on the screen, in your mind)

- How did it get there? Who made it as an object and traded in it as a commodity?
- What labour and materials have gone into its making?
- What technologies, social organisations and general modes of production and exchange (including publication and distribution) were involved? At what economic and ecological costs?

Move to the immediate context and participants

- Where and when are *you* receiving (and thereby reproducing) this text?
- Who are 'you' your **self**, the 'I-who-reads', in terms of class, status, occupation and education; as well as gender, race, nationality and age?
- Who are the **others** you are doing this with? What are the kinds of relation involved: reader–text, learner–learner and learner–teacher?
- What kinds of authority and hierarchy are in play?
- How would you describe the social and political functions or aims of the particular course, programme and institution you are studying in? How far do these accord with your own aims?
- In sum, what constructions of the **subject** (i.e. topic and course) as well as yourself/selves as subjects currently apply?

Now consider every major dimension of the 'text as products and processes' (see Figure 2, p. 72):

- *author–reader (producer–receiver) relations*:
    - What do you know, or can you infer, about the author's social relations to her or his readers (audience, viewers, etc,)? (Pluralise 's/he' to 'they', where appropriate.) Was s/he in some way dependent or independent?
    - Did s/he make a living from this, or was it a private activity? Did s/he require or hire others to produce and distribute it?
    - What do we know about his/her ideas, tastes, values and beliefs? And do these make any difference to how we understand this text?

- *text as product(s) at earlier moments of reproduction*:
    - What were the general modes of *economic production and social organisation* at the time (e.g. was the society chiefly 'slave', 'feudal', 'bourgeois', 'capitalist')?
    - What were the specifically *'literary' or 'artistic' modes of production* and distribution in which this text was implicated: (e.g. oral, theatrical, manuscript, print, filmic; libraries, bookshops, studios)? Who owned or controlled them?

- *relations to the rest of the world – then and now*:
    - What sections of society are **represented** as central – or arguably mis- or under- or un-represented? Are there marked **gaps and silences**?
    - Is the society represented contemporary with that of the author, before or after or some other imagined time and place entirely? Does this make for a more or less critical perspective on the author's present?

◆ Which of the *ideologies* in play would you characterise as *dominant, residual* or *emergent*? And does the writer express or imply a preference?
◆ What relevance to your own times and society does the work seem to have? For instance, does it help you to see your relations to other people and to the rest of the world more clearly or differently?

EXAMPLE

Drawing on the above questions and suggestions, sketch an analysis of the representation of Chaucer's Knight in *The General Prologue* (5.1.2 b).

(Be sure to draw on the accompanying notes as well, if possible supplemented by the notes in a scholarly edition such as *The Oxford Riverside Chaucer*, ed. L.D. Benson 1988: 800–1. Notice that even when you lack further information you can still pose questions about context and history. Do this before reading on.)

The 'value' of Chaucer. A Marxist analysis might start by drawing attention to the specific social and political context in which you are studying, and the fact that you are reading Chaucer in a modern printed textbook. It has an educational function and a price. This book is itself both a medium of instruction and a commodity. The social relations, media and technologies involved are therefore very different from Chaucer's initial moments and modes of production. Chaucer probably first read this *orally to other members of the court circle of which he was a relatively junior member (he was the son of a wine merchant). Thereafter the text circulated in manuscript copies amongst members of the aristocracy, richer merchants and senior clergy. Straight away, then, we are involved in a complex socio-historical dialogue. We may be left asking how far the 'Chaucer' (or any other author) we are studying is a modern educational subject and capitalist commodity as well as, say, a feudal subject and court entertainer. What are and were the social relations? What are and were the 'values' in play?

An (un)ideal knight. A Marxist might then observe that the Knight is given pride of place as the first pilgrim to be introduced, thus confirming his status as the most senior pilgrim. This is also, at least at first glance, an idealised and perhaps flattering image of knighthood: 'He was a verray, parfit gentil knyght' (l.72). All this is conventional and perhaps socially conformist. However, on further investigation, the image of the knight perhaps turns out to be not so simple and stable. And here we may bring parts of the historical **background** into the **foreground**. For one thing, by this time in the late fourteenth century, crusading knights were relatively outmoded as well as economically and militarily irrelevant. They were being displaced by yeomen archers and footsoldiers in fighting, and by members of the moneyed merchant classes in the economy. Chivalry was thus largely a *residual* social form. It belonged to the older feudal order, even though it still exerted a powerful symbolic force. For another thing, reading 'between the lines' of the text, we can identify significant **gaps and silences**. We are told the knight was 'At Alisaundre . . . whan it was wonne' (l.51). But we are *not* told that 'Alexandria, in Egypt, was conquered by Peter I (Lusignan) of Cyprus on 10 October 1365 and abandoned a week later, after great plundering and a massacre of its inhabitants' (*Riverside Chaucer* 1988: 801, n. 51). Merely to note this is to brush Chaucer's history *against the grain*. It raises the possiblity of a negative reading of the Knight as a mercenary, and may also make us wonder whether Chaucer was being 'straight' or *ironic in his view of 'many a noble armee' (l.60).

Christians v. heathens: from the Crusades to the Gulf War. There also remains the ideologically vexed matter of Chaucer's specifically Western European version of medieval Christianity. Did he wholly approve of those who 'foughten for oure feith' against the 'he[a]then' (ll.49, 66)? As another historical note tells us, 'only campaigns against Moslems, schismatics (Russian Orthodox), and pagans are enumerated' (*Riverside Chaucer* 1988: 801, n. 47). Perhaps, then, we are justified in discerning a routinely 'anti-oriental' slant to Chaucer's world-historical reality? Obviously no amount of scrutinising of these few words on the page and the extract *out of context* will give us answers. But a reading *in context* will begin to. A reading of the whole of 'The General Prologue' would clearly help too. For there we see Chaucer formally and critically distancing himself from all these observations by placing them in the mouth and mind of himself represented as a naïve and perhaps gullible narrator.

We might then proceed to further reading in Chaucer's (and our own) contemporaries. We could then help establish just how pervasive and deep-seated were (and are) certain Christian and Western antipathies to Muslims and Orientals. We might even draw tentative analogies between medieval crusades and the 1992 Gulf War. Even the archaic and euphemistic names for the Western forces marshalled against Iraq ('Desert Shield') smack of a latter-day crusade, and this imagery was widely reinforced in many of the accounts in the Western popular media. Such an appeal to a medieval/modern analogy would be a characteristic move for Cultural Materialists and New Historicists alike. (Also characteristically, it would probably be put and received differently in Britain and the USA.) Either way, such a transhistorical gesture would complete the interpretive cycle by reading the past both in and through the present. The critical–political and textual–contextual project would thus be integrated but still open and ongoing.

ACTIVITIES

(a)   *Drawing on the above 'How to practise . . . .' framework, sketch a Marxist (Cultural Materialist or New Historicist) analysis of a text that you are currently studying.* Alternatively, focus on one in Part Five. Either way, you will need to find out about the author's life and times and the text's moments and modes of production and reception. Go on to weigh the strengths and weaknesses of this approach. What experiences and values does 'Marxism' itself perhaps suppress, marginalise or ignore?

(Suggested focuses in Part Five: Hands, 'A Poem . . . by a Servant Maid' (5.1.4 c); Kipling, 'The Story of Muhammad Din' (5.2.4 b); Shakespeare, *Henry V* (5.4.6 a); Theatre Workshop, *Oh What a Lovely War* (5.4.6 f).)

(b)   *Rewrite part of a text which you find politically fascinating and yet frustrating.* Attempt to brush it 'against the grain' and explore some of its **gaps and silences**. (This might take the form of adaptation, change in point of view, altered ending, etc.; see 4.4.) Add a commentary saying what you had to find out and what, overall, you learnt.

DISCUSSION

(i)   Traditional literary critics have only *interpreted* the world in various ways; the point, however, is to *change* it.

Adapted from Karl Marx, *Theses on Feuerbach* (1845); 'traditional literary critics' substituted for 'philosophers'

(ii) the histories we reconstruct are the textual construct of critics who are, ourselves, historical subjects.

Louis Montrose, 'The Poetics and Politics of Culture' in Veeser (1989: 23)

(iii) There is no document of civilisation which is not at the same time a document of barbarism.

Walter Benjamin, 'Theses on the Philosophy of History' VI (*c.* 1939) in Walder (1990: 363)

Also see: 1.5.10–11; 1.8.3; FEMINISM; POSTCOLONIALISM; 'Key terms', p. 103.

READING: *Introductory*: Moon 1992: 49–54, 64–5, 75–6, 92–4; Abrams 1993: 241–6, 248–55; Selden *et al.* 1997: 88–108; Greenblatt in Lentricchia and McLaughlin 1995: 225–32; Frow and Wayne in Coyle *et al.* 1990: 708–21, 791–808; Eagleton, 1996 *passim*. *Primary*: Brecht 1964; Benjamin 1970; Lukács 1962; Marx, Williams and Eagleton in Rylance 1987: 197–227. *Advanced*: Williams 1977; Jameson 1981; Veeser 1989; Cohen and Montrose in Greenblatt and Gunn 1992: 320–48, 392–418; Cox and Reynolds 1993.

2.7   FEMINISM AND GENDER STUDIES

Overview

Feminism is a politically motivated movement dedicated to personal and social change. Feminists challenge the traditional power of men (patriarchy) and revalue and celebrate the roles of women. Feminism is informed by critical–political agendas which cut across subject areas and are not limited to education. LANGUAGE and LITERATURE are, ultimately, not treated separately but recognised as part of a larger and deeply contentious CULTURAL project. In these respects Feminism both influences and is influenced by MARXIST and POSTCOLONIAL approaches. Many Feminist writers also have a strong interest in PSYCHOLOGICAL models and methods, especially those which wrest the human **subject** from a narrowly patriarchal, substantially *Freudian frame. Whether as post-Freudians or anti-Freudians, they seek to develop more positively woman-centred and gender-sensitive critical and therapeutic practices. A decade ago it was common to distinguish *psychoanalytically inclined (French) Feminists* from more *socially and historically inclined (Anglo-American) Feminists*. Now, however, though these emphases partly persist, the internationalising of the women's movement has led to a much more flexible and eclectic approach amongst Feminist critics. Notwithstanding, it can still be useful to further distinguish a variety of Feminisms (plural). Current practitioners can often be described in so far as they adopt one of the following positions or a combination of them:

- *Socialist Feminist* – expressly configured with Marxism and CULTURAL MATERIALISM;
- *black Feminist* and *women of colour* – often drawing on and contributing to expressly Postcolonial or MULTICULTURAL agendas;
- *radical separatist Feminist* – often expressly aligned with the *lesbian movement;
- *bourgeois or liberal Feminist* – concerned with selected 'images' of relatively privileged women, but not with the **representation** (in every sense) of working-class women and women of colour or with lesbian and gay politics as such.

Gender Studies is a related but partly distinct area. It investigates cultural constructions of women *and* men as well as the implications of hetero- and homosexuality in general. Some feminists complain that Gender Studies represents a dilution and diffusion – even a neutralising – of sexual politics. Others maintain that it is more open, plural and less dogmatic, and that it also makes more space for lesbian and gay perspectives. It makes more space for men too. Either way, these approaches have much common as well as some disputed ground. Both were initially concerned with 'images of women' (extending latterly to 'images of men' and 'gays') in writing chiefly by 'straight', heterosexual men. Soon, however, critics and scholars set about recovering and *revaluing previously marginalised traditions or suppressed works by women, gays and/or lesbians themselves (for a note on the changing politics of 'gay', 'lesbian' and 'queer' as names, see below, p.114). Latterly, there has been particular emphasis on seeing not only gender roles but also patterns of sexuality in complexly plural rather than simply polarised ways.

Key terms: **absence**; **auto/biography and life-writing, selves and others**; **canon** (alternative, new orthodox); **difference . . . (re-)valuation**; *gender; *power, empowerment; *reproduction (biological and economic); *romance; *sex; *sexuality; **writing and reading, response and rewriting** (resistantly, as a wo/man).

Some major figures and movements

Crucial to any work in this area is the distinction between 'sex' and 'gender'.

- *Sex* refers to our physiological make-up and those *biological* **differences** which determine us as *female* or *male*: differences of chromosomes, genitals, hormones.
- *Gender*, however, refers to our social make-up and those *culturally constructed* differences which distinguish us as *feminine* or *masculine*: differences of dress, social role, expectations, etc.

We are all *born* female or male; but each of us *learns* to be feminine or masculine according to our experience of the prevailing social norms. Thus, sexually, women (not men) are equipped to conceive, carry and give birth to children. However, these functions do not necessarily mean that women and men have to be stereotyped along the following gender lines:

'FEMININE'?	'MASCULINE'?
emotional	rational
private and personal (interior)	public and impersonal (exterior)

home- and child-centred	job- and task-centred
quiet	noisy
passive	active
beautiful	strong
smooth	rough
arts and education	sciences and engineering

Such mutually reinforcing *binary oppositions (homologies) underpin many people's expectations of what it is to be a girl/woman and a boy/man. They also underpin dominant notions of how women and men speak and write, and what subjects or areas of life they speak and write about. Thus, stereotypically, in **conversation** men talk louder (often about sport and politics), swear more and compete with one another; whereas women talk more quietly and more 'properly' (often about children and relationships) and they support one another. In terms of **genres**, again stereotypically, men like war stories and perhaps pornography, whereas women like *romances and perhaps domestic soap opera. Clearly these stereotypes do partly correspond to observable patterns. Equally clearly, however, they by no means apply to all men and women. Nor do they apply to all historical periods and cultures, or to all parts of nominally 'the same' society. Thus the Victorian middle and upper classes may have idolised women as 'the softer sex' and 'angels in the house'. But this characterisation did not extend to the female factory workers who in clothing, manners and even tasks were often virtually indistinguishable from the males (see 5.3.1 c). Similarly, and equally complexly, Westernised women and men may affect the appearance of equality by wearing 'unisex' clothing (e.g. jeans); but this does not guarantee equality as an economic fact. Nor, conversely, does the wearing of the yashmak and their exclusion from public office prevent many Moslem women from having great matriarchal power over the family within the domestic sphere. Gender differences are therefore always inflected with other MULTICULTURAL differences of period, class, caste, nation, religion, age and familial role. Though the sexual 'facts of life' may seem universal and constant, the precise representation and relative *value of the various gender roles are highly variable. That is why many people working in this area concentrate on attitudes to modes of *sexual* *reproduction (e.g. representations of puberty, menstruation, conception, contraception, pregnancy, abortion, birth and child care) as well as the gendering of modes of *economic* production (e.g. nursing, secretarial and housework gendered as primarily 'woman's work'). Sometimes this focus is broadened to include realisations of *sexuality in general (e.g., representations of masturbation, same-sex love and latterly, urgently, AIDS). Such sensitive topics are the object of private self-censorship and *repression as well as overtly public taboo, censorship and suppression. Their coded presence in – and more often their **absence** from – writings by, say, Shakespeare, Austen, the Brontës, Dickens, Hemingway, Roth, Walker and Morrison is a clear indicator of what these writers could or would not say in their own periods and preferred genres.

Battles of (and for) the sexes. Contrary to casual opinion, there has always been an acute awareness that women and men are expected to play distinct roles, and an equally acute awareness that they often fail or refuse to conform. Alternatives are sometimes explored too. Chaucer's 'Wife of Bath's Prologue and Tale' and Shakespeare's *The Taming of the Shrew* as well as his Sonnets are but three instances of earlier classic texts by men in which traditional gender roles are inverted and sported with. Among the ancient Greeks, Socrates was gay, Sappho was a lesbian, and they both wrote of love partly in those terms. Christine de Pisan's *City of Ladies* (*c.* 1405) is a learned and witty attack on the assumptions of medieval patriarchy and a celebration as well as a defence of the unrecognised achievements and supposedly superior morality of women. Mary Wollstonecraft's *A Vindication of the Rights of Woman* (1792) is a powerful plea for social reform of women's lot at a time when the restitution of middle-class *men's* rights was being trumpeted. Ibsen, too, scandalised bourgeois propriety with his head-on tackling of the nineteenth-century 'woman question' in *A Doll's House* (see 5.3.3). Virginia Woolf, too, most famously in *A Room of One's Own* (1929), acted as feminist literary echo to the work of the suffragettes in the 1920s. In particular she pointed to the lack of education, leisure and opportunity which hitherto had precluded most women from writing, and also began to reconstruct a female literary tradition (e.g., Behn, 5.2.2 a). A little later, Simone de Beauvoir in *The Second Sex* (1949) offered a political and philosophical history of women as the institutionalised **other** relative to dominant notions of the male **self**.

All these writers confirm that there has long been an acute awareness, and sometimes a political consciousness, of the constraints of gender roles as well as a need to establish more positive conditions and roles for women in particular. Sexuality, too, male and female, has repeatedly been at issue. Witness the various 'obscenity' trials and *causes célèbres* that have rocked the literary establishment over the past century: Oscar Wilde's imprisonment for homosexuality (1895); the banning of Marguerite Radcliffe Hall's sympathetic and now **classic** study of lesbian experience, *The Well of Loneliness* (1928); the attempt at continuing expurgation of D.H. Lawrence's *Lady Chatterley's Lover* (1959–60), also now a novel and film classic; the attempted prosecution of the director of Howard Brenton's *The Romans in Britain* (1980) for sexually explicit and politically abrasive analogies between the Roman invasion of Britain and British 'occupation' of Northern Ireland, both conceived as homosexual rape. Many other cases could be cited. All attest to attempts to police the boundaries between LITERATURE (or **art**) and life, as well as to deep anxieties about explorations and exhibitions of sexuality. (Though we may also recall that the usual cynical defence of prosecuted pornographers is the claim that 'It's art, isn't it?!')

At any rate, 'sexual politics' is no new thing, especially if we take this to include 'the policing of sexuality' as well as 'the battle of the sexes'. Most immediately, however, it is to the Women's Liberation and Gay Rights movements initiated in the late 1960s and 1970s that most people look for the roots of contemporary Feminism and Gender Studies. Below we retrace these roots through the 'fields' of Language and Literature.

'GAY', 'QUEER' AND A NOTE ON THE POLITICS OF LANGUAGE

Since the 1970s the term 'gay' has been widely used to refer to homosexual women *and* men but, latterly, may be reserved for homosexual men alone. 'Lesbian' is increasingly the preferred term for homosexual women alone. Both 'gay' and 'lesbian', however, are currently covered by the assertively up-front use of 'Queer', as in 'Queer politics' and 'Queer reading and writing' *by* some homosexuals *of* themselves. 'Queer' then becomes a positively charged term for homosexuality, deliberately challenging the negatively charged sense of the earlier and persistent anti-homosexual usage of the term (cf. 'queer-bashing'). Meanwhile, some people continue to bemoan the associations of both 'gay' and 'queer' with homosexuality, nothwithstanding the fact that both have had such associations in the larger culture or in subcultures since at least the sixteenth century.

LANGUAGE is a common place to start exploring the ways in which women and men are culturally constructed through **discourse** and not just biologically determined. We may distinguish four main kinds of approach, all of which to some extent overlap:

♦   The Anglo-American and Australasian approach (represented by such writers as Lakoff, Spender, Miller and Swift, and Tannen) tends to be more practical and overtly political: language is seen as 'man-made' or at least 'man-centred' and it is the task of the feminist language-user to overthrow that order and construct one fairer to women.

♦   The French approach (represented by such writers as Kristeva, Irigaray and Cixous) tends to be more theoretical and politically elusive, and emphasises PSYCHO-ANALYTIC models. Here language is seen as the primary system wherein we learn to construct ourselves and others through **differences** of all kinds, including those of gender. It is therefore the task of each of us to renegotiate our **subject** positions and gender identities as best we can.

♦   'Black', 'ethnic' or 'postcolonial' approaches (represented by such figures as Hurston, Fanon, Smith and Spivak) often combine political and psychological emphases: language is seen as the primary site where gender identity is further vexed by combinations of Western and indigenous versions of patriarchy and matriarchy.

♦   Gay and lesbian writers (represented by such figures as Rich, Kosofsky Sedgwick and Dollimore) attempt to wrest the whole notion of differences constructed on *hetero*sexual lines from its pride of place. Instead they propose radically revised notions of what it is (not) to be, and read and write, from an assertively 'queer' position.

In practice, much of the best contemporary work on language, gender and sexuality attempts to take cognisance of many, if not all, of the above perspectives (see e.g. Cameron 1990, Coates 1993, Mills 1995, Weedon 1996). For this reason, the following review of topics offers a synthesis rather than a segregation of approaches.

The gendered entry into language and the *symbolic order

In learning a language, we learn to label ourselves and others as 'girl' and 'boy', 'daughter' and 'son', 'sister' and 'brother', 'mummy' and 'daddy', 'aunty' and 'uncle', etc. This process of differentiation is strongly gendered in fundamentally binary ways. As a result, we may learn to ignore or repress differences within and the common ground between what nominally pass as 'masculine' or 'feminine': the 'feminine' *within* the 'masculine', for instance, and vice versa. We may also play down sexual differences and preferences which are not just negatively neither (neuter), but alternatively and positively **other**.

Names and titles

Many languages, including English, have a distinctly 'patrilineal' skew to the ways in which they assign family names and titles denoting status. Family names are invariably drawn from the male rather than the female line. Thus my mother's 'maiden name' was Parsons and *her* mother's 'maiden name' was Stephenson and *her* mother's 'maiden name' was Grimwood. But you could not possibly know that from the surname Pope which appears on the front of this book. *That* was my father's name, and *his* father's, and *his* father's. . . . In this way, women's identities and *matri*lineal traditions in general are relatively 'hidden from history'. Titles, too, are generally distributed in ways which betray a gender imbalance. In English, males will be addressed as 'Mr' (short for 'Master') throughout their lives, whether they marry or not. Females, however, are still usually addressed as 'Miss' when girls and unmarried, and then they become 'Mrs' when they get married. In other words, women are sorted into the categories single/available (Miss) and married/unavailable (Mrs), whereas men (Mr) are not. Nor has the relative newcomer 'Ms' solved all the problems. Though technically this simply signals 'female', regardless of marital status, it is commonly understood by many people to mean 'feminist'. Such is the persistent power of patriarchy. Indeed, it is only when women acquire professional status as 'Dr', 'Professor', 'Your honour', etc. that they achieve titular equality with men. And then of course we encounter the pointed matter of how many female doctors, academics and judges there really are.

'Unmarked' men and 'marked' women

Imbalances between masculine and feminine terms are pervasive in English, as in many languages. Usually this takes the form of the masculine term being privileged as 'normal' (unmarked) and often positive, while the corresponding feminine term is 'abnormal' (marked) and often negatively loaded. Familiar examples of masculine as 'norm' are 'man' and 'mankind' (not 'wo/mankind') ; 'the man in the street' and 'chairman' (cf. archaic 'Madam chairman' and modern 'chairperson'). Examples of masculine as positive and feminine as negative are 'master' (cf. 'mistress'); 'dog' (cf. 'bitch'), as well as a motley host of words for genitals: 'cock' (cf. 'cunt'); chest (cf. 'tit'), etc. Moreover, notwithstanding the clamour for and against 'politically correct pronouns', it is still not hard to find people who believe that the masculine pronoun 'he' is perfectly acceptable even when the person referred to may be male or female (e.g. 'The student . . . he . . . '). For some the shift to 'he or she' (sometimes written 's/he') or the plural 'they' seems to be curiously unthinkable.

Women and men in conversation

Robin Lakoff in a book called *A Woman's Place* (1975) claimed that in **conversation**, compared with men, women tend to (i) use more 'hedges', continually qualifying what they say ('It's *sort of* hot', 'I'd *kind of* like to', 'I guess'); (ii) be super-polite ('Would you please . . . ', ' . . . if you wouldn't mind'); (iii) add on 'tag questions' ('Pete is here, *isn't he?*'; 'We'll go, *shall we?*'); and (iv) generally answer questions with a quizzical rise in intonation (e.g. in response to the question 'When shall we meet?' the answer 'Around eight o'clock?'). You may feel there is some truth in these observations. However, later researchers (e.g., Tannen 1992) have pointed out that much still depends upon education, class and ethnicity, as well as temperament.

Sexist syntax

The combination and ordering of words always carry implications for focus and emphasis. The order of precedence in 'Mr and Mrs', 'male and female' and even 'he or she' may *seem* natural; but try reversing these items and consider whether that seems 'natural' too. Conversely, notice the order of deference in the formula of address 'Ladies and gentlemen'. Often it is the overall organisation of the text which betrays a sexist bias in favour of the male subject or the masculine viewpoint. Hence this characteristic story opening from the UK tabloid newspaper, the *Sun*: 'A terrified 19-stone husband was forced to lie next to his wife as two men raped her yesterday' (see Cameron 1990: 17).

Writing as a wo/man

It is sometimes maintained that women and men have different styles of writing and, by extension, different thought processes. Luce Irigaray and Hélène Cixous, for instance, have argued that there is a distinctive form of 'womanly speech/writing' which they call, respectively, 'parler femme' and 'écriture féminine'. Both of them partly take their cue from Virginia Woolf's praise of Dorothy Richardson's development of 'the psychological sentence of the female gender' (1923; see Cameron 1990: 72). The general characteristics of such 'womanly writing/speech' are reckoned to be long and loosely coordinated sentences, fluid changes of topic, a resistance to 'linear' logic and, implicitly, a woman-centred focus on inner feelings and personal relationships. Set against this are the presumably archetypal characteristics of 'manly writing': tightly controlled and heavily subordinated sentences, orderly and linear progression of topic, and a man-centred focus on external actions and public relationships. Three important qualifications need to be made, however:

1   Irigaray insists that ultimately only biological women have facility in 'parler femme', whereas Cixous suggests that men too can open up the 'féminine' in them-selves and their 'écriture' (e.g. Joyce, Mallarmé);
2   many women writers from the fifteenth century to the present have cultivated a 'plain' or supposedly 'manly' style;
3   there therefore remains a big question about how far so-called 'womanly writing' is tied up with contradictory notions of *Modernism and sexual essentialism. Is it a period-specific phase posing as a universal determinant?

LITERATURE, as the above review confirms, is clearly not separated from a fundamental concern with language by most feminists. Nor is it divorced from a larger CULTURAL and political project. Nonetheless, there are distinctive historical phases and critical emphases within feminist and gender-based literary studies. These may be identified under several heads, as long as we remember that these 'heads' sometimes argue amongst themselves and may or may not belong to the same, constantly metamorphosing 'body'.

Gendered *literacies

Most women for most of human history have not been allowed or encouraged to learn to read or write. And when they have become literate this has often equipped them to do no more than keep household accounts, write letters and diaries, and perhaps read the Bible and novels in the vernacular (e.g. English). Women have thus often been denied 'higher' or more specialised learning in the CLASSICS (Latin and Greek) and in the sciences. The results of all this have been complex and many-edged. Though long discouraged from making substantial contributions to traditional **genres** such as **poetry** and **drama**, women developed facility in both reading and writing the 'newer', and initially notionally inferior genre of the **novel** (see **narrative**). They also cultivated forms of recording the interiorised **self** (through diaries) and personal interactions with **others** (through letters) which have latterly been recognised as pre-eminently – but not exclusively – 'feminine' modes of writing (see **auto/biography**).

Representations of women by men

An initial and enduring emphasis in feminist literary studies has been on **images** or **representations** of women in work by male writers. Given the relative absence of women writers from the traditional male-dominated **canon**, this focus was at first inevitable. So, too, was an early insistence on the ways in which male writers *mis-* or *under*-represent women. Modern male writers, chiefly novelists, such as D.H. Lawrence, Ernest Hemingway, Henry Miller, Phillip Roth and Norman Mailer, were the primary targets in the pioneering polemical work by Kate Millett (*Sexual Politics*, 1970). These men were roundly attacked for representing women as stereotypes, often 'sex-objects'. At the same time, 'images of women' criticism was being extended to earlier bastions of the male canon such as Chaucer, Shakespeare and Milton (e.g., Germaine Greer's *The Female Eunuch*, 1970). Behind and informing all these works were discerned a number of powerful patriarchal stereotypes, many of them ultimately identified with **biblical** women. In addition to the main polarities of woman as 'sinful temptress' (the Old Testament Eve, Adam's 'spare rib') and woman as 'holy mother' (the New Testament Mary, 'full of grace' or a grieving *mater dolorosa*), there were woman as 'whore' (Salome, the whore of Babylon) or the 'silent, submissive woman' (Ruth, Martha). It is still common, and often useful, for readers to read with a critical eye trained on precisely such stereotypes, whether they are reading *Beowulf* or 'the Beats'. Increasingly, however, it is recognised that male writers do not always simply misrepresent women; they may also renegotiate and challenge the stereotypes. They may well be exploring masculinity and their own sexuality too.

Rediscovering and revaluing women's writing

The next phase of feminist criticism and research (sometimes called *gynocriticism*) has tended to concentrate less on men's representations of women than on women's struggle to represent themselves. The few established female novelists (Austen, the Brontës, George Eliot, Gaskell and Woolf) have been radically reread, and the numerous previously marginalised or ignored female writers (Bradstreet, Behn, Manley, Wollstonecraft, Mary Shelley, Edgeworth, Barrett Browning, Dickinson, Stein – to mention just a few) have been investigated afresh or for the first time. Their work has also been widely published and promoted, notably by presses such as Virago, Pandora and the Women's Press. At the same time, there has been a considerable commitment to publishing and studying contemporary women's writing, often with an eye trained on specifically female traditions which conventional LITERARY HISTORY had patronised or ignored. Crucial texts in this deliberate and often daring reshaping of the literary landscape include Ellen Moers's *Literary Women* (1976), Elaine Showalter's *A Literature of their Own* (1977), Sandra Gilbert and Susan Gubar's *The Madwoman in the Attic* (1979), Joanna Russ's *How to Suppress Women's Writing* (1983), Dale Spender's *Mothers of the Novel* (1986) and Jane Spencer's *The Rise of the Woman Novelist* (1986). Nor is this simply a matter of putting women in the existing picture. The effect has been to switch the picture and shift the focus entirely. Thus there has been a thoroughgoing critical and historical revaluation of such social phenomena as 'being single', marriage, child-bearing and rearing, 'madness and hysteria', and widowhood. The institutions of religion, education, the law and medicine have been especially explored for the ways in which they relate to women's (and men's) powers over their bodies, minds and property.

Reading and writing by or as a wo/man

Latterly, there are signs that the issues of women's writing, including the activities of women writing and reading, have opened out again. Do you need to be biologically a woman to write or read *as a woman*? Is to be a woman or a man to be locked into certain kinds of sympathy and antipathy? Or is it a matter of learning to identify with certain **subject** positions within and around a given text – and therefore of potentially unlearning and relearning? In short, can women *and* men re(en)gender themselves as certain kinds of writer and reader? Whatever the answers, the point is precisely that there is room for potential agreement, as well as persistent dis-agreement, about who, under what social, political and psychological circumstances, where and when, can claim to write or read *by, for* or *as* a woman (see e.g. Jardine and Smith 1987; Cameron 1990; Mills 1994).

Becoming our bodies ourselves

There are several ways in which 'the *body' features in contemporary cultural debates and practices. The fact that these debates and practices are central to but not peculiar to Feminism and Gender Studies is a measure of the liveliness of the 'bodies' in question.

♦ Women's bodies have long been **represented** as objects of male desire and of the 'masculine gaze' in practices ranging from high **art** nude portraiture to popular advertising, and from rape to *pornography (cf. 5.1.7). It is one of the primary purposes of feminism to reclaim and celebrate that body as an active **subject/agent** in its own right.

♦   Appeals to or displays of 'the body' promise an actuality and **presence** which are supposedly beyond words. According to certain feminist PSYCHOANALYSTS, bodies defy or defer not only a 'logocentric' (word-centred) world-view but more particularly celebrate a pre-Oedipal *semiotic flux before, alongside and even against the symbolic 'order of the father' (i.e., phallo-logocentrism).

♦   The body is the ultimate site and *sign for all **discourses** on gender *and* sex. Therefore it is crucial how far the body is taken to underwrite and guarantee versions not only of femininity and masculinity (i.e., gender) but also of hetero- and homosexuality.

Time and again, then, the argument is whether men and women are 'necessarily', 'essentially', 'biologically' one thing or another. Are we always already some version of 'feminine' or 'masculine' and 'female' or 'male'? Or are we still in the process of *becoming* something and someone else – alternative, other, plural?

How to practise a feminist analysis sensitive to gender and sexuality

Generally, consider the roles and representations of women and men as they affect your understanding of the text (i) in your immediate context; (ii) in its initial moment of production.
    More particularly, consider:

♦   *the sexual composition, orientation and gender roles of the group, course or programme in which you are studying.* How evident are these in terms of the texts and topics highlighted; social hierarchies and dynamics; the kinds and patterns of contribution? Are the atmosphere and critical agenda discernibly feminist or anti-feminist, and hetero- or homosexual?

♦   *the kinds of women and men represented within the text.* What roles do they play? Is there a sense of tension between and within the sexes? What kinds of women's and men's relationships are *not* represented – and are either unspoken or even 'unspeakable' here? Pay special attention to representations of: family roles and relations; occupations outside and within the home; gendered ways of speaking and behaving; clothed and unclothed bodies; sexual activity; childbirth and child care; single or married states; other commercial, legal, medical, educational and religious institutions as they bear on women and men differently; complicating factors of class, ethnicity, age and other cultural differences.

♦   *the sex, sexual orientations and gender expectations of the writer.* Is this ascertainable from the text or from external (e.g. **auto/biographical**) sources? How far are we justified in identifying the author's **subject** position with any of those offered by the text? What aspects of, say, **genre, narration, characterisation** and **imagery** prevent such a ready author–text identification?

♦   *the gender roles and sexual practices current at the time.* Can the text be read as a form of sexual *expression, *repression or negotiation? What behaviour seems to have been considered 'proper' or 'normal', and how far are such proprieties and norms reinforced or challenged? How far were contemporary readers or audiences comforted or shocked, pleased or puzzled in these respects?

♦   *your own reading and writing practices as a wo/man.* How far do you think gender differences and sexual preferences affect the way *you* relate to this text: whom you *identify with, and what you look for and value? Again, consider complicating factors such as class, ethnicity, age and temperament.

Go on to investigate other relatable texts by women and men at the time, as well as other media and modes of representation. How did women and men feature in the performing or visual arts, for instance, either as producers or as objects of representation? How relatively powerful or powerless were women and men, gays and lesbians with respect to publication and broadcasting? How much have things changed now?

Example

Read Adrienne Rich's 'Dialogue' (5.1.8) with the above 'How to practise' questions and suggestions in mind. Go on to compare your responses with the following.

Feeling a way into the conversation. The poem is a 'dialogue' of a particularly open and teasing kind. There is general uncertainty about the nature of the relationship between the narrator and the speaker. The shifting indeterminacy of the 'I's and 'she's, in particular, makes for an especially enigmatic encounter. In fact the whole thing seems to be more of a monologue than a dialogue: there are no 'you's, for instance, and only one 'we'. Perhaps, then, it is the dialogue with us the readers which is most insistent. We are privy to the action but excluded from any sure knowledge of what it means. As a result, precisely how we read this poem in terms of gender and sexuality (and much else) very much depends upon who and what we reckon we are. It also, of course, depends upon what we infer from the text, and what we may know about the author (a little information about Adrienne Rich is supplied in the supporting notes). I shall therefore begin with some tentative questions:

♦ Is the 'old ring' a token of past friendship, a 'marriage' ring perhaps?
♦ What do I read out of and into the persistence and natural violence of 'our talk has beaten / like rain against the screens'? or the studied distance of 'we look at each other'?
♦ Is the second, report*ed* 'I' (who speaks in italics) talking of another event and relationship altogether? If so, why is the first, report*ing* 'I' so obsessed by the memory of what was said as to 'live through [it] over and over'?
♦ Could it be, then, that what is being so elusively spoken of in italics in fact refers to the relationship between the two participants? or does it refer to another?

At this point most readers pause for further reflection and introspection. They may also reach for information about the writer, or at least a sense of who s/he is. Often they return to the brief biographical notes.

Going public through discussion. Here are some observations on my experience of studying this poem in sexually mixed groups. These are the kinds of 'answer' usually forthcoming once people have formulated something like the above questions for themselves. Overtly heterosexual readers (notably men) who have no knowledge of or interest in Adrienne Rich usually persist in the view that the second speaker is speaking of another, female–male relationship, and that she is talking about this to the first. However, readers sensitive to homosexuality (notably women) who are aware of Rich's radical feminist and subsequently assertively lesbian stance tend to read the poem quite otherwise: as a comment on a female–female relationship, probably between the two present participants, the narrating 'I' in the first part and the speaking 'I' in the second part. But other readings are possible too, and these may be voiced by a range of women and men. Perhaps we should not assume the 'I'dentity of either narrator *or* speaker with Adrienne Rich. Or perhaps we should treat this as a dramatised dialogue between two parts of the self: one observing and the other observed. In any event, as the discussion continues there remain many suggestions and questions in play. Is the *'sex'* in question ('I don't know / if sex is an illusion') the biological difference between female and male? the social gender difference? and/or the sexual act? What kind of subject, gendered and otherwise, is the 'I' who asks 'whether I willed to feel / what I had read about'? The willing victim of romantic or of radical feminist literature, perhaps? Or of some other reading entirely?

A 'Rich' tradition. Our sense of the contexts of writing and reading could be important too. Rich has lived through a period of changing gender roles and continuing sexual revolution. Reading the poem around 1967, when it was first published and when Rich had not yet 'come out' as a lesbian, might have entailed a 'heterosexual' response. Reading it in *Poems Old and New* in 1984, when she had 'come out', might have prompted another (perhaps suggesting a 'repressed lesbian'). Reading it in Carol Rumens's controversially titled collection of *Post-feminist Poetry: Making for the Open* (2nd edn, 1987) might even have suggested a *post*-feminist or a *post*-lesbian reading (whatever one might understand that to mean). But whatever your own reading of 'Dialogue', one thing at least should be clear. Gender differences and sexual preferences are themselves caught up in the ongoing dialogue *between* and *within* specific writers and readers. The image and fact of 'woman' or 'man' are never simply a given but always in part remade. Rich, herself, has famously referred to this process as 're-vision' (see Discussion (iii), p. 123).

ACTIVITIES

(a) *Apply the 'How to practise a feminist analysis . . . ' method to a text by a woman and a relatable text by a man (e.g., texts which treat similar topics or belong to the same period but different genres).* Compare your analyses with other people's and consider how far you can or cannot achieve consensus on matters of women and men, writing and reading. (Suggestions from Part Five: Wyatt and Wroth (5.1.3 a and c); Pope and Hands (5.1.4 b and c); Behn and Defoe (5.2.2 a and b); William and Dorothy Wordsworth (5.4.3. a and b); Yeats and Kazantsis (5.1.7 a and b).)

(b) *Looking or looked at? Doing or done to? Speaking, spoken to or spoken about?* Put these questions to the representation of women and men in any text which interests (and perhaps irritates) you. Go on to consider how you might re-write part of it so as to challenge and change the roles and perspectives it offers.
       (Texts commonly chosen in Part Five include: Shakespeare (5.1.3 b); Rhys (5.2.3 e); Conrad (5.2.4 c); Freud (5.3.1 d) and Ibsen (5.3.3).)

(c) *How desirable or practicable is it to insist upon equal representation of (i) female and male teachers and students; (ii) female and male authors on courses?* Focus on your own department and a particular course to begin with. What are the practical options?

DISCUSSION

Support your arguments, where possible, with references to specific authors, texts, periods, genres and movements.

(i) notions of 'women's' or 'feminine' language just aid and abet anti-feminist thinking.

> Deborah Cameron, *The Feminist Critique of Language* (1990: 11)

(ii) when we look at women writers collectively we can see an imaginative continuum, the recurrence of certain patterns, themes, problems and images from generation to generation.

> Elaine Showalter, *A Literature of their Own* (1977: 10)

(iii) revision – the act of looking back, of seeing with fresh eyes, of entering an old text from a new critical direction – is for women more than a chapter in cultural history: it is an act of survival.

> Adrienne Rich, 'When We Dead Awaken: Writing as Re-Vision' (1971) in Humm (1992: 369)

(iv) if in a woman writer's work a sentence refuses to do what it is supposed to do, if there are strong images of women, and if there is a refusal to be linear, the result is innately lesbian literature.

> Barbara Smith, 'Towards a Black Feminist Criticism' in Humm (1992: 375)

(v) men should take seriously at last the 'hetero' in heterosexuality, which means the heterogeneity in us, on us, and ... give up ... that oppressive representation of the sexual as act, complementarity, two sexes, coupling.

> Stephen Heath, 'Male Feminism' in Jardine and Smith (1987: 22)

Also see: MARXISM; POSTCOLONIALISM; PSYCHOANALYSIS; 'Key terms' p. 112.

READING: *Introductory*: Belsey and Moore 1997: 1–20; Cameron 1990: 1–28; Kaplan in Coyle *et al.* 1990: 750–63; Selden *et al.* 1997: 121–49; Stimpson and Sedgwick in Greenblatt and Gunn 1992: 251–70, 271–302; Jehlen in Lentricchia and McLaughlin 1995: 263–74; Thompson and Wilcox 1989. *Anthologies*: Cameron 1990; Warhol and Herndl 1991; Humm 1992; Belsey and Moore 1997. *Fuller studies: On language* – Cameron 1990, 1992; Kristeva 1984; Tannen 1992; Mills 1995. *On literature and theory* – Showalter 1977; Moi 1985; Armstrong 1992; Mills 1994; Weedon 1996. *For re-visions of masculinity*, see Jardine and Smith 1987; Brooker and Humm 1989: 106–18; Boone and Cadden 1990.

2.8   POSTSTRUCTURALISM AND POSTMODERNISM

Overview

Poststructuralism and postmodernism are two relatable yet distinct contemporary movements. Both are concerned with the radical instability of **subjects** (whether conceived as human subjects, subject matters or whole disciplines) and both celebrate kinds of openness, plurality and **difference** in systems of all kinds. Both are also devoted to the play of indeterminacy within and around meanings. But these two movements are also distinct. Poststructuralism grows out of an academic milieu in Linguistics, Anthropology and Philosophy and is primarily concerned with LANGUAGE. Postmodernism grows out of an artistic and literary milieu and is primarily concerned with global COMMUNICATIONS and the commercial multi-media. *Post*structuralism and *post*modernism are both clearly terms that depend on prior concepts for their definition (i.e. Structuralism and Modernism). As with *post*colonialism, however, we must recognise that the prefix 'post-' can mean 'after' in at least two senses: 'after and distinct from' as well as 'after and a result of'. That is, Poststructuralism can be seen as a radical break with Structuralism as well as a natural extension of it. The same can be said of Postmodernism's relation to Modernism and Postcolonialism's relation to Colonialism. We therefore need to know what is being succeeded or superseded in each case.

Structuralism is a grab-bag of a term stuffed with a wide range of writers and writings: the structural anthropology of *Lévi-Strauss; the formal linguistics of *Saussure and of *Chomsky; the early writings of *Barthes and *Derrida; and the writings of the much earlier Russian FORMALISTS as rediscovered and translated in the West during the late 1960s and early 1970s. What all these writers and writings have in common is the understanding of phenomena (words, poems, narratives, myths, customs, social practices) not as discrete entities but as parts of larger structures or systems. The emphasis is on making sense of things as *signs in larger *sign-systems, and on perceiving the ways in which one sign-system relates to another. Hence the close association of structuralism with *semiotics/semiology, the study of sign-systems.

Poststructuralism is chiefly associated with the later writings of Barthes, Derrida and Foucault and is 'post-' in that it both extends and to some extent explodes the premises of Structuralism. Whereas a structuralist approach would tend to treat a sign-system as a complete, finished, potentially knowable whole with a notional **centre**, a *post*structuralist approach would tend to treat a sign-system as an incomplete, unfinished and ultimately unknowable fragment with many potential centres or no centre at all. We may therefore say that Structuralism concentrates on 'whole systems' whereas Poststructuralism concentrates on the 'holes in systems'. Put yet another way, where Structuralism concentrates on 'sense-making' activities, Poststructuralism concentrates on 'nonsense-making activities' or, perhaps better, 'the making of sense other-wise'.

Poststructuralism is probably best known for the analytical techniques of *deconstruction*. This involves breaking down a text (or other artefact) into its constituent **differences** and identifying its notional **centre**, then exploring the procedures whereby certain of these are preferred or 'privileged'. A characteristic deconstructive move is to invert differences and to point to what is marginalised or absent, thereby setting up alternative centres or challenging the notion of centres altogether. Poststructuralists in general, and deconstructors in particular, are especially fascinated by **absences, gaps and silences** and are keen on offering radical inversions (some would say perversions) of the relations between **foreground and background**.

Postmodernism involves something relatable yet distinct. **Modernism*, its precursor, can be broadly characterised as an early twentieth-century literary and artistic movement with an **aesthetic** opposed to that of nineteenth-century 'classic **realism**'. Modernists in English include such figures as Joyce, Woolf, T.S. Eliot, W.B.Yeats, Carlos Williams, Stevens and Beckett. All of these writers developed strategies of 'non-realist' **representation** involving collage, montage, pastiche, 'stream of consciousness', multiple points of view, and other kinds of highly self-conscious, reflexive and apparently fragmentary techniques. What most of these modernists also have in common is their implication in a 'high art' view of CULTURE and their concentration on a traditionally literary medium: the written word. It is in these latter respects that postmodernism most obviously both extends and explodes the premises of Modernism. Postmodernism is broadly **populist rather than narrowly elitist in appeal, and tends to be multimedia rather than purely literary in materials. At the same time postmodernist texts deploy many of the strategies of Modernism and promote an aesthetic which is still palpably non-realist. Thus we find that collage, montage, pastiche, multiple viewpoint, reflexivity and open intertextuality are also characteristic of such pre-eminently postmodern discourses as **advertising**, **popular music, game and chat shows, magazines and magazine programmes, TV and tabloid news reporting, interactive video, computer games and the World-Wide-Web. In fact just about any aspect of modern life has a potentially 'postmodernist' edge to it in so far as it is concerned with the production, projection and consumption of **images** of all kinds, especially those in the commercial, global domains. By this definition, shopping malls and Disneyland are typical postmodern 'texts'.

Relations between and reactions to poststructuralism and postmodernism vary greatly. Some see the two as complementary aspects of a kind of intellectual–commercial 'New Ageism', and get correspondingly excited or irritated. Others see them as utterly distinct in origin and trajectory. Meanwhile, political critiques proliferate. Poststructuralism is attacked by some MARXIST, FEMINIST and POST-COLONIAL critics as a kind of hyper-sceptical game which is finally debilitating and self-defeating. If all differences and centres are arbitrary, then what grounds are there for morally and politically informed preferences? Others, however, recognise the ground-breaking or at least ground-clearing power of deconstruction to challenge all supposedly 'neutral' differences, 'natural' hierarchies and fixed centres. Postmodernism, meanwhile, is regularly mauled for its complicity with various brands of capitalism, patriarchy and neo-colonialism. Though some critics do point to the potentially subversive power of postmodernist texts in so far as they expose and sport with the superficial artifice and glaring contradictions of contemporary life rather than smoothing them over and concealing them.

Key terms: COMMUNICATION and MEDIA; FORMALISM INTO FUNCTIONALISM; **absence and presence, gaps and silences, centres and margins; aesthetics; author** (death of); **authenticity; **differences**; **faction; **image**; **metatextuality; **myth; **parody; **signs; **subject**; **play.

Major figures and models

We now review the main concepts and figures associated with Poststructuralism and Postmodernism in turn. As usual, this is basically a checklist designed to prompt activities and further reading.

*Saussure and sign-systems

The concept of the *sign composed of 'signifier' and 'signified' is fundamental to structuralism and poststructuralism alike. Saussure made it the basis of his General Linguistics and thereby opened up the way for an understanding of COMMUN-ICATION in terms of *sign-systems in general. In Saussure's view, words do not simply mean things in themselves. Words are the product of systematic yet shifting relations between sounds in air or marks on paper (signifiers) and those aspects of experience which those sounds or marks are taken to refer to (signifieds). There is therefore no necessary reason why the English words 'tree', 'blue' and 'walk', for example, should mean what they do (after all, other languages have different words corresponding to comparable phenomena). Rather, words 'mean' by virtue of an assumed and broadly agreed relation amongst people who 'speak the same language' and therefore draw on the the same sign-system. At the same time, there is always a tension between any particular instance or utterance of a word (the 'parole') and the language system viewed as a whole (the 'langue'). Particular people or groups of people always mean slightly – sometimes very – different things by ostensibly the same word. In the above cases the precise meanings would depend on your experiences of 'trees', 'blue' and 'walk' and the contexts in which you routinely meet and use these words. In short, signs are parts of apparently stable but ultimately moving sign-systems.

Many of the crucial differences between Structuralist and Poststructuralist positions can be placed in relation to one of these two polarities.

Structuralists tend to emphasise systems as closed 'wholes'.
Poststructuralists tend to emphasise the 'holes' within and around open systems.

*Lévi-Strauss and a structural model of culture

The anthropologist Claude Lévi-Strauss developed a model which sought to systematise understanding of symbolic interaction within CULTURES. His model is basically structuralist in that he used sets of fundamental oppositions such as 'nature v. civilisation', 'wild v. domestic' and 'raw v. cooked' to produce an overview of how whole societies interact coherently. For Lévi-Strauss, all cultural artefacts and practices have not only a functional but also a symbolic dimension. Everything from pots and buildings to gesture, costume and field layout thereby become 'goods for thinking with' ('bonnes à penser'). The systematic interrelations among these artefacts and practices also encourage a kind of 'thinking by analogy' ('bricolage'). For instance, pots and spears may be associated with, respectively, feminine and masculine in a given culture, and both pairs of terms may then be accommodated within a larger structural opposition relating 'nurture' (maintaining civilisation) and 'nature' (keeping the wild at bay). Lévi-Strauss also pointed to the ways in which *myths, **dramas** and **narratives** in general rehearse and resolve the contradictions experienced within societies, thereby allowing cultures to maintain a sense of coherence. Lévi-Strauss's approach to myth is similar to *Propp's approach to folktale in that both are looking for the constant, underlying structures that relate one narrative to another. They are less interested in the idiosyncrasies of various versions or the peculiar pressures which make each telling in context to some extent unique. In this respect structuralist models have much in common with FORMALIST models, which they partly draw upon.

*Barthes and the opening up of modern myths

Barthes was a structuralist who always had strong poststructuralist tendencies. His early *Mythologies* (1957) was heavily influenced by Saussure and Lévi-Strauss. The concluding section on 'Myth today' argues for an extension of *sign-theory so as to recognise *myth, including narrative and drama, as what Barthes calls 'second-order sign-systems'. That is, not only are they chiefly made of words (a 'first-order sign-system'); they are also made of strings or frames of words which can be aligned with certain **genres** of verbal experience ('second-order sign-systems'). A simple example would be the formulas 'Once upon a time . . . ' and ' . . . and they all lived happily ever after'. These are made up of a series of individual verbal signs ('Once', 'upon', etc.). However, taken together as strings of words, they also signal the beginning and ending of a traditional kind of children's story. Such attempts at formal systematisation recur in Barthes's theoretical work, and they often have a 'totalising' (and therefore structuralist) air about them – attempting to embrace, if not explain, everything. Another instance is his 'Introduction to a Structural Analysis of Narrative' (1977: 79–124). Significantly, however, Barthes's own analytical practice often belies or exceeds his theorising. Many of the essays in *Mythologies* are lively and more or less *ad hoc* meditations on contemporary *popular culture: 'The Face of Greta Garbo', 'The new Citroën' and 'Strip-tease'. They offer playful and often inspiring sallies into what was then a new terrain. And their cumulative effect is to suggest much more that CULTURE is plural, hybrid, many-centred and ultimately 'non-totalisable'. In this Barthes confirms the strongly poststructuralist side to his project. There is a similarly suggestive disjuncture in his later work *S/Z* (1970). This offers a highly complex and elaborate overview of the processes of **reading** and interpretation in terms of just five *codes (proairetic, hermeneutic, semic, symbolic and referential). However, again, in Barthes's own daring and virtuoso readings these codes are seen converging and diverging, coalescing and exploding in ways which are decidedly *post*structuralist rather than structuralist. There is always a sense that the system is open and in process.

*Derrida, decentring and deconstruction

Derrida is the philosopher who has probably done most to challenge dominant Western notions of 'wholeness' and 'centre' in symbolic structures of all kinds, especially in language. Proceeding from the structuralist insight that all meaning is constituted through the interplay of **differences** (Saussure had remarked that language is 'a system of . . . differences without positive terms'), Derrida argues that all meanings are ultimately 'deferred'. (The ambiguity of the French *différance* allows him a pun on 'difference' and 'deferral'). According to Derrida, there is never an encounter with meaning as such, simply a ceaseless play of differences between those terms which are present and those which are absent. Put another way, we only understand things by understanding what they are not. In any given culture there is a tendency to assume a hierarchy of differences, to imply preferences. Thus in dominant Western traditions it is common and conventional to privilege 'white' before 'black', 'male' before 'female', 'up' before 'down', 'reason' before 'the senses', 'the whole' before 'the part', 'presence' before 'absence', 'centre' before 'margin', and so on. These are all instances of what Derrida and other poststructuralists would term 'violent hierarchies'. It is thus the role of *deconstructive* thinkers not simply to invert these hierarchies (for example by now privileging 'black' before 'white' or 'female' before 'male') but actually to reopen the play of differences round the terms and to resist the lure of merely *binary thinking. In the above examples this means radically rethinking our notions of the 'colour' spectrum (both in the physical and the social sense); recognising the plurality of possible gender roles as well as permutations of homo- and heterosexuality, and generally opening up a relativistic sense of alternative – not simply opposed – differences and centres.

Much of Derrida's work is concentrated upon the domain of linguistic philosophy – even while he attacks many of its premises. Characteristically, he is concerned with the vexed relations between **speech** and **writing** and the effect of trying to 'decentre' the human **subject** from the core of philosophical debate. He also offers the challenge of a non-Western approach to issues of **reality and representation** (including problems of **absence and presence**, and *non/sense) which is not simply its traditional obverse, i.e. Eastern. Put another way, Derrida explores the problems and possibilities of 'sense-other-wise' – beyond the binary principle of 'sense' *or* 'nonsense'. Significantly, this project is seen as too radical by right-wing political commentators who accuse deconstructionists of the destruction of civilised (Western) values. Meanwhile, overtly MARXIST, FEMINIST and POST-COLONIAL commentators sometimes complain of Derrida's apparent philosophical distance from pointedly political issues. Either way, Derrida's *deconstructive techniques, like all tools, remain politically powerful or powerless depending upon who they are wielded by and how.

*Foucault, discourse and historical discontinuity

Foucault was chiefly concerned with the interrelations of knowledge and power, especially the ways in which legal, medical and religious **discourses** operate to produce different perceptions of what it is to be 'normal' or 'deviant' ('sane' or 'insane', 'law-abiding' or 'criminal') at various times. Along with Barthes, Foucault was also committed to exploding the dominant Western notion of the **author** as the sole source, origin and guarantor of a text's meanings. Instead, they proposed that the concept 'author' be treated as a historically variable and politically contested site. They also shifted the focus to **texts** in **context** as **intertextual** constructs, insisting that cultures are expressed *through* not simply *by* writers and producers. Foucault articulated various influential historical models of **self** and **other** as well as a radically dis/continuous view of history which has been very influential with NEW HISTORICISTS. He resists the notion that history can ever be understood, let alone told, within a single narrative frame. Instead, he argues, we must recognise that the many localised narratives of history, like the many discourses of culture, do not add up to a single coherent whole. History is always fractured and off balance. Indeed, Foucault emphasises that what most often arrests us in history is a sense of radical rupture with the past. It is the *dis*continuity rather than the continuity of history which is significant.

*Lyotard and the postmodern condition

Lyotard makes a comparable attack on what he calls the 'grand narratives' (*grands récits*) in *The Postmodern Condition: A Report on Knowledge* (1979). By 'grand narratives' Lyotard means all those overarching intellectual schemes which purport to offer a totalising frame in which to understand some aspect of modern life. The Enlightenment belief in progress, Darwinian evolutionism, MARXIST political and economic history, and Freudian PSYCHOLOGY are all seen as potentially repressive and regressive forces in so far as they limit what he calls 'intensities and energies'. Whatever their avowed aims, all these forms of knowledge may become strait-jackets within which the human *body and mind are restrained. In place of such 'grand narratives' Lyotard argues for a politics of 'small-scale narratives' (*petits récits*), working from the immediate and the *local, and without aspirations to any totalising – and potentially totalitarian – grasp of the whole. In the field of **discourse** this means that Lyotard is committed to what Wittgenstein calls 'language games': people playing their roles with all the energies and resources at their disposal – even to the point of bending or breaking the rules and insisting that another game be played – but at no time believing that theirs is the only game, or that there is some grander mega-game of which all games are simply a part.

Another dimension of Lyotard's vision of 'the postmodern condition' is his attention to the implications of contemporary *global communications. Given our increasing capacity to bring fragments of the 'far' near and to incorporate fragments of the 'past' in the present, he argues that *all* knowledge thereby becomes at once global *and* local, timeless *and* timely. Contemporary humanity has thus done something radically paradoxical with the perception of space and time. This line of thinking is taken to its logical (some would say illogical) extreme in the work of *Baudrillard. Baudrillard argues that modern COMMUNICATIONS and MEDIA (including computer-assisted editing and transmission techniques) have become so pervasive and sophisticated that we can no longer claim to have a view of 'the **real**' which is untouched by human hand, mind or machine. Instead we are treated to composite images of images of images – without any guarantee of an 'untouched' reality beyond. These '**images** without originals' Baudrillard calls *simulacra*. Thus, most provocatively, he argues that in a sense the 1992 Gulf War did not really take place for most people in the West. Its communication through an elaborately mediated mix of real life and simulation meant that for many the events existed in 'virtual reality' and 'cyber-space'. It could all just as well have been a daily dose of hi-tech war stories and disaster movies.

Postmodernism attacked and defended

Perhaps not surprisingly, there are many who take exception to this view of the postmodern world. They see the implications and consequences of global communications more positively, as potentially emancipating rather than enslaving, heightening and extending rather than dulling and constraining our senses of reality – virtual and otherwise. Some, however, attack the very notion of 'the postmodern'. Eagleton and Harvey suggest that Postmodernism is finally little more than a fancy label for 'late Capitalism' (see MARXISM, p. 107). Meanwhile, Said, Spivak and others point to the *laissez-faire* complicity of the concept with 'neo-colonialism' and 'coca-colaisation', as well as its casually unreconstructed stereotypes of gender and sexuality (see POSTCOLONIALISM and FEMINISM).

There are those such as Jameson and *Hutcheon who see 'the postmodern condition' as something we should neither dismiss nor acquiesce in. Rather, we must play *in* and work *through* it, engaging actively with its strategies in order to redirect its political agenda. Hutcheon draws attention to the productively disruptive effects of much postmodern practice in writing, art and the media. She cites numerous instances of *parody, collage and non- or anti-realist representations and performances where there is a sense of creative critique from within a postmodernist aesthetic – not simply an uncritical wallowing in consumer culture. More particularly, Hutcheon points to the radical and potentially liberating view of history as **faction** rather than 'fact'. She argues that alternative histories, both actual and potential, can only be generated once the illusion of a single overarching story (Lyotard's 'grand narrative') is fractured, dispersed and re-formed. She is especially interested (as is Waugh) in the capacity of supposedly 'fictional' writers and other imaginative artists to blur and redraw the boundaries between **fact** and **fiction**, notably in the genre she terms *'historiographic *meta-fiction'*. Along with Fiske (1987), Hutcheon also places considerable emphasis on the critical and creative powers (as well as the responsibilities) of **readers**, audiences and viewers. She observes that people generally take what is most useful and helpful for themselves, and ignore or reject what they judge irrelevant or harmful. Overall, then, Hutcheon argues for a recognition of the opportunities as well as the risks of living *through* the postmodern moment: exploring and experimenting, not simply coping or copping out. In this respect her position resembles that of *Benjamin and *Brecht much earlier. For they too urged culturally aware and politically active engagement with all the contemporary media resources at their disposal. And they too counselled against lofty indifference, reactionary disaffection or indulgent immersion (see pp. 103–107).

The account of Poststructuralism in this section emphasises its primarily philosophical concerns. For a specifically psychoanalytic framing of related issues to do with fragmented and displaced subjects, especially Lacan's notion of *lack, see PSYCHOLOGY; also subject identity and role.

How to practise Poststructuralism in a postmodern moment

Begin by considering the various kinds of **subject** in play: the *subject matter* of the text in hand; the *academic subject* within which you are studying it; some sense of yourself as a *human subject* constituted in terms of gender, ethnicity, class, education and personal history. This serves as a preliminary reminder of the interrelated structures and moments within which you and the text are currently constructing meaning. Go on to consider the following:

Binary oppositions and plural **differences**:

♦ *What are the main contrasts and tensions*, especially the *binary oppositions, through which the text seems to operate (e.g. nature v. artifice; passion v. reason; men v. women; order v. disorder; past v. present; individual v. society; etc.)?

♦ *Which polarities seem to be preferred before their opposites*, thus establishing a perceptual hierarchy (e.g. passion before reason, past before present)?

♦ *What* **other**, *plural* **differences** does the text appear to express or suppress (e.g. other ways of seeing and saying 'the same thing' differently)?

Centres and margins, *de-centring and *recentring:

♦ *What is assumed to be central* within the text (e.g. a certain time, place and set of participants; a particular **aesthetic**, moral, economic or political premise)?

♦ *What is treated as marginal or ignored completely* but might nonetheless offer a related yet alternative centre of interest and valuation (e.g. other previously merely implied or excluded places and participants; other relatable times and places; alternative aesthetic and moral premises)?

♦ *Is there in fact any limit to the number of different centres* you can perceive within and around the text? And how do you, individually and collectively, arrive at preferring some before others?

Closed and open structures: 'wholes' and 'holes':

♦ *Try to describe the text as a 'whole'*, complete and unified in itself. Do the same for the language (or other sign-system) in which it is realised. (In effect, this means saying: 'The text is wholly X.' 'The language is wholly Y', and so on.)

♦ *Now try to see the text as a series of 'holes'*, through which can be glimpsed fragments of other words and worlds. Do the same for the language (or sign-system) in which it is realised. (In effect, this means saying: 'Through this text I get glimpses of texts A and B to which it is similar or relatable.' 'Through this sign-system I get glimpses of other relatable sign-systems.')

'Grand' and 'small' **narratives**, local and global **images**, **factional** and metafictional **hi/stories** (this is where we go more obviously 'postmodern'):

♦ *Are there any larger 'narratives'* (general psychological, political, scientific or religious frameworks and regimes) which the text seems to draw on or contribute to? In what sense could it be viewed as an episode in a global cultural history?

♦ *Or would you rather see it on a smaller scale*, as a configuration of peculiarly local and to some extent unique effects?

♦ How far is the text categorisable as **fiction** or **fact**, **story** or **history**? Or would you rather categorise it as **factional** and **hi/story**? Why?

♦ Does the text comment on itself (*metatextually)? Or is such reflection and self-reflexivity also the prerogative of the reader, audience or viewer (e.g. you)?

Example

Read the text of Queen's 'Bohemian Rhapsody' (5.1.10) with the above 'How to practise . . . ' guidelines in mind. Then compare your responses with those below.

Preliminary reflection on the kinds of 'subject' in play within and around 'Bohemian Rhapsody' produces, for me, something like the following. Textually, this is a song about a marginalised figure, an outcast: the protagonist seems to be a 'poor boy' who faces a death sentence for murder. In this respect it is similar to a number of rock songs which express alienation and disaffection. Contextually, from a present perspective, 'Bohemian Rhapsody' is strongly identified with Queen's singer, Freddie Mercury, who died of AIDS in 1991, when the song was re-released. This fact has tended to reinforce the 'tragic' sense of the song as well as, perhaps, the gendering of its protagonist. Meanwhile, from my own subject position as a white, middle-aged, male lecturer in English (and an old Queen fan), I am aware that there are attitudes and perspectives that may not be shared by all present readers. The mere inclusion in this book of the words of a pop song may grate with more traditional proponents of 'Eng Lit' ('It may be English – but is it Literature?!'). This particular choice of song may also clash with the musical interests and tastes of younger, perhaps predominantly female students.

The general point is that all the above 'subjects' (the subject matter of the text and the subject positions of both performer and interpreters) are all implicated in an understanding of 'Bohemian Rhapsody'. Each and all might serve as focuses for a systematic enquiry into not only *what* the song means but also *how* it means. What are the conditions whereby this text operates in the world? What are the social and textual structures and relations within which it can be sited – or cited and sighted? Anything like a comprehensive answer would therefore need to consider the interplay between a number of verbal, musical and (in performance) visual codes. It would also need to engage with a variety of specific yet shifting discourses – commercial and educational, popular and academic. In what follows I shall concentrate on the words of the song as reproduced in 5.1.10. However, as occasion demands, I shall pick up the broader concerns signalled above. A Poststructuralist reading must necessarily recognise that all structures are interrelated yet open, while a postmodern response cannot be limited to words alone.

If we plot the overall structure of the text of 'Bohemian Rhapsody' in terms of *binary oppositions we come up with something like this:

'real life' versus 'fantasy'; life versus death; 'I' (murderer) versus 'he' (murdered); individual versus society; solo voice versus chorus; angels versus devils; aggression versus apathy . . .

This is initially useful because it offers an overall conceptual grid within which to structure an interpretation. Ultimately, however, it is limiting. For what such simple, fixed oppositions fail to catch are the plural and shifting differences that are in play. For instance, 'Mama, (I) just killed a man' involves three (not two) participants: one spoken to ('Mama'), one speaking (I, understood), and one spoken about ('a man'). Meanwhile, the singer modulates – sometimes gradually, sometimes abruptly – through a whole array of postures and emotions (again not just two). He is by turns langorous, aggressive, defiant, terrified, pathetic and apathetic. Binary structures may be a good place to start. They are rarely a good place to end.

In terms of what is explicitly **centred**, the dominant subject position of the text is emphatically male: 'poor boy' (x 4), 'just killed a man', 'silhouetto of a man', 'Galileo'. This is reinforced by the fact of a male singer and an all-male band – and perhaps by me as a male commentator. However, there is also a marginal yet strong female presence signalled by the repeated appeals to 'Mama' and 'mama mia'. Moreover, still other, non-binary possibilities are opened up by the recognition that Freddie Mercury affected an alternately or simultaneously 'gay-macho' persona in performance. He did this increasingly overtly between 1975, when the single was first released, and 1991 when it was re-released. As a result, the gendering of both performer and performance shifted noticeably over a decade and a half, just as it may still do between one viewer/listener/reader and another. Hetero- and homo-sexual interpretations are never absolutely circumscribed. They are always renegotiable.

'Bohemian Rhapsody' is an apparently finished yet in reality open structure in other ways. It is obviously complete and 'whole' in that it lasts six minutes and physically sounds much the same every time you hear it (in Part Five it occupies a determinate space on the paper and is framed as an entire text). It also has a discernible beginning, middle and end. The song opens and closes simply and quietly, but there is a hell of a lot going on in the middle (including full diabolic/ angelic chorus and extended instrumental solos). There is an overall sense of narrative and dramatic structure, too: 'I' (the 'poor boy') is telling others (notably the chorus and us) of the terrible thing he's done and the punishment that awaits him. There are also several key phrases repeated over the course of the piece, many of them passed between singer and chorus, notably 'poor boy', 'any way the wind bows', 'mama (mia)', 'easy come. easy go', 'let me (him, you) go'. In all these ways textual cohesion and a degree of perceptual coherence are achieved.

At the same time the text obviously falls apart in various ways. It is full of 'holes'. For one thing, the 'I' who speaks/sings is either highly variable or inconsistent. He switches from aggression to apathy, terror to languor, with little notice or apparent cause. It is also unclear whether anything has really progressed by the end, or indeed whether the whole thing, as the opening lines ask, is 'real life' or 'fantasy'. (Do 'Galileo', 'piccolo' and 'magnifico-o-o-o-o', for instance, relate to anything else or even to one another – except as series of similar sounds?)

For a combination of all the above reasons we may therefore say that this text is at once 'whole' *and* 'full of holes'. It is a determinate structure with partly coherent meanings and it is teeming with indeterminacies and discontinuities.

'Bohemian Rhapsody' draws upon a variety of 'grand narratives' in that it can be readily aligned with certain recognisable genres and scenarios. It rehearses a classic, perhaps distinctively modern, confrontation between the individual and society: the outsider pitted against everybody else. The 'poor boy' figure obviously keys into popular images of angry and apathetic young men, rebels with and without causes. It also hints at a combination of the figure on death-row with that of the damned soul ('Too late. My time has come . . . '). In all these respects this text can be 'placed' generically and intertextually: it can be viewed as an episode in a larger cultural history. At the same time, this particular text offers a peculiar and to some extent unique configuration of effects. It is a highly distinctive 'small narrative' in its own right. Historically, 'Bohemian Rhapsody' was among the first cooperations between a rock band and full orchestra. It was innovative in its use of a full-length promotional video incorporating computerised graphics. In addition, as already mentioned, the sense of the song was given a bitterly ironic twist because of the fate of the singer. The anticipated death of the 'poor boy' and that of Freddie Mercury through AIDS have tended to be confused in the popular imagination. The death *in* the song gets mixed up with the death *of* the singer. Fiction lends itself to fact, and vice versa. The two combined make up the factional hi/story which is the rock legend that is 'Queen'.

ACTIVITIES

(a)   *Binary oppositions, violent hierarchies and the play of differences.* Begin by analysing Shakespeare's 'My mistress' eyes' (5.1.3 b) or Defoe's *Robinson Crusoe* (5.2.2 b) or Freud's 'Dora' (5.3.1 d) – or any other text that interests you – in terms of binary oppositions (e.g. black v. white, man v. woman, speaking v. spoken to (or spoken about), etc.). Examine how far each of these oppositions is weighted towards one of the polarities, thereby instituting a 'violent hierarchy'. Finally, consider all the ways in which your reading of the text exposes plural **differences** beyond those of simple opposition.

(b)   *Practising Postmodernism.* Speculate how you might turn one of the clusters of texts in Part Five (on the Wordsworths (5.4.3); Brooke (5.4.6 d–e), etc.) into part of a postmodernist multimedia event. Add a commentary explaining your aims and rationale.

(c)   *Attempt to apply the 'How to practise Poststructuralism . . . ' method* to a twentieth-century post/modernist text (e.g. Beckett's *Not I*, 5.3.4 d) and a nineteenth-century classic realist text (e.g. Austen's *Pride and Prejudice*, 5.2.3 b). What strengths and weaknesses show up in the method when you do this? And is there any sense that it suits certain kinds of text – and perhaps certain genres and periods – better than others?

DISCUSSION

(i)   [Poststructuralism is] the joyous affirmation of the play of the world and of the innocence of becoming, the affirmation of a world of signs without fault, without truth, and without origin . . .
            Jacques Derrida, 'Structure, Sign and Play in the Discourse of the Human Sciences' 1966, in Lodge (1988: 121)

(ii)   [Poststructuralist] readings and interpretations have a tendency to end up all looking the same, all demonstrating the ceaseless play of the signifier and nothing much else.
            Jeremy Hawthorn, *A Concise Glossary of Contemporary Literary Terms* (1994: 149)

(iii)   The point is that we are within the culture of postmodernism to the point where a facile repudiation is as impossible as any equally facile celebration of it is complacent and complicit.
            Fredric Jameson, 'Ideological Positions in the Postmodernism Debate', in Lodge (1988: 381)

(iv)   The current post-structuralist/postmodern challenges to the coherent, autonomous subject have to be put on hold in feminist and postcolonial discourses, for both must first work to assert and affirm a denied or alienated subjectivity: those radical postmodern challenges are in many ways the luxury of the dominant order which can afford to challenge that which it securely possesses.

Linda Hutcheon 'Circling the Downspout of Empire' (1989) in Williams and Chrisman (1993: 281)

READING: *Introductory*: Moon 1992: 30–2, 89–91; Mapp in Coyle *et al.* 1990: 777–90; Hawthorn 1994: 106–11, 174–6, 137–8; Abrams 1993: 280–2, 256–63; Selden and Widdowson 1997: 103–88; Green and LeBihan 1996: 49–90; Eagleton 1996: 79–130. *Poststructuralism and postmodernism together*: Sarup 1993. *Fuller studies of Post/structuralism*: Culler 1975, 1981; Hawkes 1977; Harland 1984; Norris 1991; Weedon 1996 (feminist); Young 1981 (anthology); Barthes, Foucault, Lacan, Jameson and Eagleton in Lodge 1988: 79–124. *Fuller studies of Postmodernism*: Hutcheon 1989; Jameson and Eagleton in Lodge 1988: 166–210; Brooker 1992 (anthology); Waugh 1992a, 1992b (anthology); Marshall 1992; Connor 1996.

2.9   POSTCOLONIALISM AND MULTICULTURALISM

Overview

Awareness of the colonial and postcolonial dimensions of English LANGUAGE, LITERATURE and CULTURE has massively increased over the past two decades. So has recognition of the fact that most English-speaking countries (including Britain, America, Australia, New Zealand and South Africa) are fundamentally multicultural – and in some senses always have been. Signal moments in the modern raising of consciousness were the Civil Rights and 'Black Power' movements of the late 1960s and 1970s in the USA. In the UK the consequences of the British Empire and subsequently the Commonwealth came home (both literally and metaphorically) from the late 1950s onwards: by 1990 around five million people from the former colonies (chiefly the West Indies, Africa, India, Pakistan and Hong Kong) had emigrated to the 'motherland' in search of work and a better life. In Australia and New Zealand, meanwhile, since the 1970s at least, the position of indigenous Aboriginal and Maori peoples previously displaced or dispossessed by European settlers has been prominent on political and educational agendas (though as with their counterparts, the Native Indians of America, sometimes much more has been said than done). The most recent and radical site of postcolonial change in the English-speaking world is South Africa. The system of 'apartheid' (a Boer word meaning 'separation/segregation') was formally overthrown in 1994.

Such prodigious changes have important implications for English Studies. We are experiencing a huge shift in the ways we construct and approach our **subjects** of study, as well as in the ways we perceive ourselves as certain kinds of ideological subject, geographically and historically. Along with FEMINISM and GENDER STUDIES, postcolonialism and multiculturalism have arguably done more to transform our sense of what we are about than any other recent intellectual and political movements. Throughout the English-speaking world debates about the role of

English in education (as well as the functions and effects of education through English) regularly become embroiled in arguments about 'national' or 'regional' identity, 'mono-' or 'multi-' culturalism, majorities and minorities. In every domain of language, literature and culture there is an acute tension and sometimes a flat contradiction between globalising processes of standardisation and localising processes of differentiation.

Thus in English LANGUAGE studies there is currently much attention to the following:

New Englishes of the former British colonies, chiefly in Africa, the Caribbean, India, Australasia and the Pacific rim. These 'new' Englishes include varieties such as *pidgins and *creoles as well as alternative national **standards** (see 5.1.9, 5.3.4 c), and in fact most of them have been around for a long time. The most notable and powerful 'new' English is none other than American English, which has its roots deep in colonial history and its branches moving in a palpably multicultural atmosphere.

World or International English as a kind of global standard. This is primarily written and printed, and substantially American in spelling, vocabulary and grammar. It is commonly used for international communication in science, technology, business and education, and has a kind of colloquial counterpart in the voice of the American popular media (notably Hollywood films, TV, adverts and *pop songs). These too have a remarkably global reach.

Kinds of il/literacy. In so-called 'Third World' or 'developing' countries the ability to read and write, often in English, is a rare skill and a prized commodity. Basic illiteracy is a continuing problem. Meanwhile, in so-called 'First World' or 'developed' countries there are signs that literacy (i.e., reading and writing skills, as such), may be decreasing both in practice and prestige. Partly this is a result of cuts in education funding worldwide. Partly it is a consequence of an increasing emphasis on visual and audio-visual modes of COMMUNICATION, rather than on the written and printed word alone. The gulf between the barely literate and the sophisticatedly 'computer literate' continues to widen.

In LITERARY studies, too, postcolonial and multicultural agendas are having profound effects:

'English Literature' is currently being transformed into 'Literature in English' – or 'Literary Studies' or 'Literary and Cultural Studies', dropping the 'English' completely (see 1.5.8). This tends to happen even where there is no formal change of departmental name or programme title.

The conventional Anglocentric and Anglo-American **canons** *of literary* **classics** *are being recast in the shapes of a wide variety of national and regional cultures.* Caribbean, African, Australian, New Zealand, Canadian and other 'literatures' (themselves always *hybrid) now commonly feature as courses and programmes in their own rights. So too do national, regional and ethnic writings in English from *within* the British Isles, from Ireland, Wales, Scotland and indigenous Caribbean and Asian communities; as do the work and traditions of Black American, Spanish, Chicano, Jewish and other groups of writers *within* the USA.

Displacement of narrow notions of 'literature' and an increasing recognition of non-Western-European **genres** *of writing, oral performance and cultural production.* Legends, histories, laws, fables, anecdotes, oratory, song, chant, song-and-dance are all making their way on to a transformed literary/cultural agenda, and thereby challenging the dominant Western neo-classical division of literature into the mega-genres of **poetry**, *prose and **drama**. The latter simply don't fit many of the hybrid forms of oratory, writing and performance that characterise much pre-colonial, colonial and post-colonial verbal arts. The printed **novel**, for instance, is being recognised as just one, distinctively Western form of **narrative**. All this is also prompting a revised awareness of the nature of pre-print oral and manuscript cultures within the Old and Middle English periods. Anglo-Saxon oral-formulaic elegies and battle-poems turn out to have a surprising amount in common with modern Caribbean 'dub' poetry.

*Texts in *translation are now much more likely to be 'set' in English and Literary Studies.* Classic writers of the modern Western European theatre such as Ibsen, Pirandello and Brecht have been 'naturalised' as legitimate 'Eng. Lit.' subjects for quite a while. More recently, much attention is being paid to translations of the works of such writers, chiefly novelists, as Allende and Márquez from Central and South America, Kundera and Havel from Eastern Europe and Chang from Asia. The challenge in all these cases is to grasp the nature of 'translation' as, in its broadest sense, an activity of transformation: between languages and/as cultures. Easy access can lead to appropriation as well as assimilation. The possibility of radical misinterpretation because of an ignorance of local social and historical conditions has to be recognised and tackled.

In terms of broader CULTURE there is a corresponding relativising, and to some extent a challenging, of exclusively Western European models:

*The **classical** heritage of Greece and Rome now tends to be seen alongside or mixed up with (rather than above or instead of) the many other, sometimes older 'classical' cultures.* The Middle and Far East, India, China and Japan, as well as the largely oral cultures of Africa and the Americas (North, Central and South) also have their highly elaborate, distinctive and often extremely powerful philosophies, sciences and world-views.

*Christianity and the **Bible**,* in particular, must be seen in relation to other religions and their associated stories, symbolism, belief systems and holy books. There is especial interest in and investigation of those forms of religious organisation and spiritual insight which were displaced by the deliberate dissemination of the Bible as part of the 'civilising' project of colonisation.

Overall, then, postcolonial and multicultural perspectives entail a radical reconfiguring of English Studies, not a mere tinkering with it. (We may draw comfort and inspiration from the fact that such a changing state of affairs is the rule rather than the exception in English Studies: see 1.2.) The following are some of the most persistent questions and the most prominent figures in this lively and important area of debate (for references see Reading, p. 153):

- *How deep is skin-deep?* When does ethnicity become racism? When does patriotic pride become nationalist paranoia? (Fanon, Gates, Young).
- *What happens when 'the empire writes back'?* Or when people(s) attempt to forget or reclaim some of their many pasts? (Rushdie, Ashcroft, Griffiths *et al.*, Gates).
- *Where and how are we to locate the many and various 'centres' and 'margins' of culture?* Can we ever expect these to be more than provisional and contested? (Bhabha, Said).
- *What desires and dangers are involved when we try to recognise people(s) as **other**?* Can we be so sure our **selves** are unitary and stable in the first place? And when does a respect for cultural **difference** tip into a covert sense of separation/segregation? (Kristeva, Morrison, Spivak).

◆   *Can anyone ever 'speak for' and in every sense* **represent** *someone else?* (a member of
     one ethnic group representing another, for instance?) If people aspire to look and
     sound like one another, then who is 'mimicking' whom? Whose 'mask' is in play?
     (Spivak, Minh-ha, Bhabha).
◆   *What of community and consensus, personal expression and collective celebration?* Or is
     it all division and conflict, personal repression, public oppression or secret
     suppression? Can we reject certain imperialist (and aristocratic and patriarchal)
     aspects of the Western European humanist and Enlightenment models of *human
     nature, while building on its project of justice, reason and democracy? (hooks, Hall,
     Norris).

Key terms: ENGLISH/englishes (1.1.); LANGUAGE; LITERATURE; CULTURE; *body;
absence and presence . . . centres and margins; canon and classic
(alternatives to); *colonialism (post- and neo-); **similarity and differences**; *ethnic,
*ethnocentric (e.g. Anglocentric, Eurocentric); **foreground and background**;
*literacy and illiteracy; *native; *orality; orientalism; *race, racism; . . . **self and
other**; stereotypes; **standards and varieties**; *translation.
     Also see: MARXISM, FEMINISM and *ecology.

Major issues and models

The terrain we are traversing is uneven and shifting. It can be both frustrating and
fascinating, dangerous as well as delightful. (For a white, male, middle-aged, British-
born university teacher of English there are peculiar perils as well as privileges in
this area. You will have your own.) There are, moreover, no absolutely reliable and
impartial 'maps'. I have simply set up some signposts and ask you to follow these as
long as seems helpful – then look for or set up others.

Colonisation – a varied and ongoing process

'Colonisation' is the activity of making colonies. 'Colonialism' is the state of being
a colony. Both terms ultimately derive from the Latin *colonia*, meaning 'farm'
or 'settlement'. Both therefore also share a common root with the word 'culture',
through Latin *colere* (past. part. *cultum*) – 'to grow' (see CULTURE). As currently
used, 'colonisation' (the active noun we shall stick with here) is an all-purpose term
which can embrace many different relations amongst peoples and things and places.
In British colonisation alone we may distinguish the following kinds and stages from
the twelfth to the twentieth centuries:

◆   *'internal' colonisation within the British Isles* by England of Wales, Ireland and
     Scotland, involving successive 'plantations' of English settlers and displacements or
     'clearances' of natives from the Western Isles to the Highlands; also 'enclosures' of
     common land and evictions of natives within England;
◆   *'external' colonisation beyond the British Isles* in what became successively the British
     Empire and (from 1931) the Commonwealth. External colonies may also be further
     distinguished according to the ways in which they came into being:

     ◆ initial trading relations eventually leading to imperial administration (India from
       the seventeenth-century East India Company to the twentieth-century Raj);

- dissident religious communities, primarily of tradespeople (e.g. the Pilgrim Fathers – and Mothers and Children – who settled New England in America from the 1620s);
- farming and mining communities of settlers, living and working largely on their own (as in New Zealand) or with the more or less enforced labour of natives or slaves (in South Africa, other parts of Africa and the Americas);
- slave transportation and enforced labour on a large scale (from West Africa to the Caribbean and North, Central and South America);
- convict transportation and penal colonies (e.g. Botany Bay in Australia, so-called because of an earlier natural history survey by Thomas Cook *et al.*).

It is important to recognise the shifting permutations and complex inter-dependencies of all these aspects of empire. Trading relations could lead to imperial control (as in India). A first phase of religious foundation might be succeeded by a welter of other kinds of settler, including slave and then migrant labour (as in North America). Farming and mining might initially be undertaken by white settlers, but then draw on native and slave labour (as in South Africa). Even the term 'plantation' has shifted in sense. Initially it referred to '*trans*planting of people'; only later, by association, was the sense extended to plantations of fruit, sugar cane and cotton.

The internal–external dynamic of the processes of colonisation within and beyond Britain and America must also be appreciated. Many of the people who were the first English settlers (farmers, miners, craftspeople and traders, as well as soldiers and sailors) emigrated out of necessity or compulsion, not out of choice. Often they had been dispossessed in Britain as a result of land enclosures and clearances (especially in Ireland, Scotland and the Home Counties). Alternatively, or as well, they had been left un- or under-employed during the Industrial Revolution, chiefly as a result of the mechanisation of the cotton and wool mills, the mines and farming. Religious dissenters fled persecution as much as they sought new communities. Criminals were 'transported' abroad (e.g., to Australia); and many of the soldiers and sailors of the empire were either '(em)pressed' (i.e. forced) into military and naval service, or took up arms abroad as an alternative to unemployment or starvation at home. Thus the history of empire and exploitation *beyond* the British Isles is continuous with the history of empire and exploitation *within* the British Isles. This helps explain the complex and often vexed relations between the colonisers abroad and the colonial authorities back in Britain. It was not only the colonis*ed* who had some bones to pick with their British masters and mistresses.

The slave-trade triangle

The classic British–American example illustrating the interdependencies of empire is the 'slave-trade triangle' which linked Britain to West Africa and both to the West Indies and the Americas (see Appendix A). Ships from Britain would head for West Africa with a load of supplies (including guns) for the settlers and their allies and trinkets for the natives. In West Africa, they would pick up African slaves, spices, animal skins and ivory and take them all to the Caribbean and America. Once there, the slaves would be sold and set to work on the sugar-cane, cotton and fruit plantations. Sugar, molasses and rum, as well as raw cotton, would then be taken back to Britain for manufacture, sale and 'home' consumption or export. And so back out again. The whole 'triangular' operation had, in theory at least, an elegance, simplicity and efficiency which made it a model of economic resource management. Unless, that is, you happened to be an African captured, enslaved, transported and, if you survived the appalling voyage, quite possibly worked to death. (See 5.2.2 for a cluster of perspectives on slaves and slavery. *Oroonoko* (*c*.1681) is about this very 'slave-trade triangle'.)

America, too, has thus been in both colonial *and* postcolonial states since the arrival of the Europeans, and arguably well before. Native American Indians were – and in some sense remain – the colonis*ed*; though their own earlier tribal wars and empires complicate the picture further. Meanwhile, white Western European settlers in America (notably the English and French) were colonis*ers* then changed their status by breaking away from their respective mother/father lands to set up nations of their own. They also subsequently broke away from one another, notably in French- and/or English-speaking Canada.

Colonisers, colonised and slaves

Theoretically as well as practically, it is important to distinguish the various participants in the processes of colonisation:

♦   the colonis*ers*, 'foreigners', those who initially come from elsewhere;
♦   the colonis*ed*, '*natives', those who were born in the place (from Latin *natus* – 'born'; cf. *nation*);
♦   slaves, who were often neither colonisers nor colonised but forcibly brought from elsewhere, and therefore were both 'foreign' and 'non-native' in their new place.

It is also important to observe that over time the families of colonisers may become second-, third- and fourth-generation *settlers*, and therefore are also 'natives' in that they too were 'born there'. Settlers may also have interbred with the initial natives, thus complicating issues still further. Moreover, taking a still longer historical view, we must also recognise that many of the colonis*ed* have themselves at some time been colonis*ers* (displacing and perhaps dispossessing other peoples). Colonis*ers*, too, may well have been colonis*ed* at some point in their past. Thus in Britain the Normans colonised the Germanic tribes who themselves had colonised the Celts. In South Africa the English and Dutch (Boers) colonised the Zulus, who themselves had colonised earlier tribes and nations 'native' to the southern grasslands. In this respect no people is in absolute terms either 'native' or 'foreign' to a place. We are all in some sense visitors, temporary tenants. Put another way, everybody is involved in various stages of post/colonialism, before, during or after the event. Hence the optional slashed form (/) in the term itself.

To some extent, then, the labels 'coloniser' and 'colonised' may be swapped around over time and from place to place. Colonisation is a varied and ongoing process. Yet it is crucial to recognise that, over any given period and in any given place, some people, often whole peoples, have indeed been colonis*ers* while others have most certainly been colonis*ed*, and perhaps enslav*ed* too. Thus in the past five hundred years many (native) African, American and Asian peoples have been at the sharp end of colonisation while others (chiefly Western Europeans and their descendants) have been doing the sharpening and cutting. There are, therefore, crucial distinctions to be maintained between those 'doing' and responsible for colonisation and those 'done to' and affected by it. History *does* involve actions and reactions as well as interactions and interrelation. Otherwise we could not recognise in it a meaningful 'story' (i.e. coherent **narrative**) at all. This latter point may seem to be obvious and laboured. However, it would not seem so in the context of certain kinds of NEW HISTORICIST and POSTMODERNIST approach where agency, causality and responsibility threaten to dissolve into an amorphous mass of relations without determination, direction or moral *discrimination. In short, to repeat, some people were – and are – more colonis*ing* than colonis*ed*. To pretend otherwise is in effect to tell *no* **hi/story** while affecting to tell *every* or *any* hi/story. And we always tell *some* hi/story. The point is to realise that that is precisely what we are doing, reflect upon our knowledge, remedy our ignorance, and recognise the inevitable partiality of our **points of view** and **subject** positions.

Postcolonialism, as such, can be broadly and theoretically defined as 'what grows out of and away from colonialism'. Like POSTSTRUCTURALISM and *post-*modernism, the term expresses a state which is both continuous with and distinct from that which it succeeds. Postcolonialism, more narrowly and historically defined, is usually understood to refer to those countries which achieved formal political independence from Britain (and from other Western European powers such as Spain, France, Portugal, Holland, Belgium and Germany) from the mid-twentieth century onwards. As far as Britain is concerned, many of these countries became – and some still are – members of the British Commonwealth (first recognised in 1931). However, as the above more complex and flexible definitions of post/colonialism imply (embracing the simultaneous presence of both colonial and postcolonial states) Britain and America can be characterised as being in both colonial *and* postcolonial conditions virtually since the beginning of modern history. In this respect, the most recent, successful independence movement by a British colony *within* Britain was that of Eire (Southern Ireland) in 1922. Britain's most recent colonial 'war' was with Argentina over the Falkland Islands/Malvinas in 1982. Meanwhile, in the year in which I am writing this (1997), Hong Kong was handed back to China; though the British government has again refused to give back Gibraltar to Spain.

Neo-colonialism (meaning 'new-style' colonialism) generally means the exercise of international power through economic and commercial rather than military means. The USA and Japan are currently often accused of neo-colonialism because of their dominance in world markets and their power to make other countries economically dependent. The World Banking System, especially the International Monetary Fund, is also arguably neo-colonial in its power to maintain the dependence of many 'Third World' countries through control of their debts and trade alliances.

Multiculturalism can be briefly defined as 'awareness of the distinctively plural and hybrid nature of *all* CULTURES'. I put the case like this, slightly provocatively, because it is impossible to point to any culture which has been, is or is ever likely to be, 'single and pure' (i.e. *mono*cultural). Historically, those who have seriously sought to maintain the myth of a 'pure culture' have been rabble-rousing ideologues (e.g. Hitler). There are, however, various views of what 'multicultural' can mean. It can mean:

♦ *multiracial*, in which case the emphasis is on perceived differences in people's 'colour', hair texture and physical build (white, black, yellow, etc.) **Race* is the core term here, a concept that is still heavy with nineteenth-century notions of fixed human physiological types, particularly the mistaken belief that different peoples (African, Caucasian, Asiatic, etc.) have fundamentally different physical and mental capacities. Hence the negative charge of the term 'racism'.

♦ *multi-ethnic*, where the emphasis is more on people's social organisation and cultural practices (e.g. dress and marriage customs) rather than their physiological make-up. **Ethnicity* (derived from Greek *ethnos*, meaning 'nation') therefore avoids the biological determinism of the term 'race' and recognises the fact that people can be born into a certain group but that they may subsequently take up the cultural practices of another group. 'Ethnicity' offers the possibility of cultural change and variation; 'race' implies biologically determined fixity. (Compare the crucial distinction in GENDER STUDIES between **sex (biologically determined) and **gender (socially constructed).) Ethnicity is a term which is positively valued. **Ethnocentrism*, conversely, is negatively charged because it refers to the tendency to privilege or **centre** one culture before others, which thereby become marginalised or ignored (e.g. Anglocentric, Eurocentric).

♦ *cultural* **differences** *of all kinds*, including differences of class, rank, caste, sexuality, gender, occupation, region, age, dis/ability, etc. – as well as race and ethnicity. Though broad and potentially bland, this extended sense of multiculturalism has the great advantage that it does not concentrate upon one cultural difference to the potential exclusion of others. It recognises cultural differences to be plural and complexly interrelated (also see MARXISM and FEMINISM).

Finally, it should also be noted that 'multiculturalism' is a term that can be used in a superficial, merely expedient way. It can be used to promote the sense that everyone should simply 'get on' with one another – regardless of persisting disparities in access to education, work, housing, health care, etc. Then the concept papers over the cracks in a fundamentally unequal system. Some 'multicultural' programmes may encourage a kind of sham or fragile consensus, but without addressing the real (largely economic) causes of conflict. Others, however, directly address and seek to redress the underlying causes of mutual suspicion, fear and hatred within and between communities. Thus one person's or group's version of multiculturalism may include or exclude another's. It all depends whether the defining criteria are understood to be narrowly racial, broadly ethnic or flexibly plural. It also depends upon whose interests are really being served by the maintenance or dissolution of existing cultural differences. Such, in outline, are the problems and the possibilities facing all purportedly multicultural initiatives from Northern Ireland to the former Yugoslavia, from inner city London to outer city Johannesburg.

*Literacy, illiteracy and language policies

Questions of who can read, write and speak what kinds of thing in what language ('native' and/or English and/or another) inevitably bulk large in postcolonial contexts. They did under colonialism too. However, both il/literacy and language policies are all too easily ignored or obscured in a narrowly 'literary' approach to texts. The *fact* of reading and writing is readily assumed and forgotten by those who have long been in on the act. So are the privileges and prejudices of those who routinely and perhaps exclusively use English. (I do not except myself from this charge.) Answers to such problems, as we see shortly, vary greatly from place to place. The underlying issues, however, have much in common:

- *How far are the languages of the European colonisers (English, French, Spanish, Portuguese, Dutch and German) permanently tainted in the eyes, ears and minds of colonised non-Europeans?* Can the English word 'black', for instance, ever be fully cleansed of its dominant associations with 'evil', 'dirt' and 'darkness', and the word 'white' ever be invested with dominant associations other than those of 'goodness', 'innocence', 'light' and 'cleanliness'? What would this do to everything from pictorial representations of God as an old white man to advertising slogans for washing powders promising 'whiter than white' cleanness?
- *What are the practical alternatives to English (French, Spanish, etc.) from amongst the native languages of the various states of Africa, Asia and the Americas?* What are the immediate and the long-term dis/advantages of teaching people to read and write as well as speak these languages, especially when resources of all kinds (including those for basic literacy) are so scarce?
- *What are the 'internal' implications for regional, tribal, caste and national identity if any single language (European or indigenous) is chosen to the exclusion of others?*
- *What are the 'external' implications of a presence and voice on the international stage which is 'English' OR native?* Can a workable compromise be fashioned?

These are persistent questions facing educationists, language-planners, governments and companies worldwide. Because they cut across so many areas of language, literature and culture, refractions of them can be found elsewhere throughout the book (see 1.2; **accent and dialect** and **standards**). Figure 3 (over the page) presents a theoretically polarised view of the dilemmas. Actual instances of practical solutions, usually in the form of compromises and hybrids, are mentioned afterwards.

In practice, people invariably come up with compromises and hybrid solutions. In post-independence Tanzania, Kenya and Malaysia, for instance, English is no longer an 'official' language but it is still widely used. In India, English shares 'official' status with Hindi, Urdu and several other languages and is often valued for its external, non-sectarian status. In Nigeria English has 'official' status, along with Igbo and Yoruba; but there continues to be very pointed argument about the harm it does or benefits it brings to the literacy of indigenous cultures. In any given instance, we are likely to find a mixture of arguments from both sides. The result, in principle or practice, 'officially' or otherwise, will be a *hybrid situation. Interestingly, much the same principles apply to all kinds of bi- or multilingual groups and institutions, large and small – from individual families, schools and neighbourhoods to international companies and whole countries.

Renaming and remapping

One of the first acts of any explorer, conqueror or coloniser (the terms are at first fluidly interchangeable) is to name the places he (and it usually is a he) 'discovers'. The fact that the places he 'discovers' have been known and inhabited by native

ENGLISH	NATIVE LANGUAGE(S)
Associated with British Empire and/or American neo-colonialism	Associated with indigenous social structures and institutions
Identified with local power elite	Identified with local powerlessness
Learnt artificially through formal education	Learnt naturally through routine social interaction
Mainly for reading and writing – print culture	Mainly for speaking and listening – oral culture
Part of public, official sphere; international power	Part of personal, informal sphere; ethnic solidarity
Access to global learning and communication	Access to local learning, customs and communication

Figure 3 Postcolonial problems and possibilities with English

peoples for generations, and that many names for the places already exist, is generally overlooked or accounted of merely incidental interest. Somebody's 'New World' is always somebody else's 'Old World'. Visitors invariably 'find' what the locals had never lost – or had not lost yet anyway. The novelty of greeting any old part of the world as 'new' and then presuming to *re*name it is one of the signal acts of any explorer–conqueror–coloniser. Thus Christopher Columbus in his first voyage to what Europeans later called the 'West Indies' (because it was to *their* West) gave the names 'San Salvador' and 'Santa Maria de Concepción' to the first two islands he met, and 'Ferdinand' and 'Isabella' to the third and fourth. The first two signalled his devotion to his own religion, Christianity; the second two signalled his allegiance to his own royal patrons, the Spanish monarchy.

What *were* the many and varied names of the 'Americas' (North, Central and South) before Amerigo Vespucci's first name was applied to all of them – prefaced by some approximate longitudinal markers? 'New England' before the recently arrived Englanders named it 'New'? 'Australia' before it blew Europeans there from the north (the name comes from the Latin for 'south wind' – *auster, australis*)? And, once there, what were the tribal names of 'Aborigines' for themselves before the visiting Europeans called the natives that in the belief they had found a more 'primitive' and 'original' kind of human animal? (The European word is a conflation of Latin *ab origine*, meaning 'from the beginning'; just one of their own tribal names was 'Koori'.) Put the other way round, did you know that 'Aotearoa' was one of the Maori names for 'New Zealand' before the Dutchman Abel Tasman visited and renamed it in the seventeenth century? Or that 'Kentucky' is Iroquois for 'meadow land', and 'Kansas' and 'Arkansas' are Sioux for 'land of the South Wind people'? That 'California' and 'Texas' derive from the Spanish for, respectively, 'earthly paradise' and 'allies'? In all these ways, the suppression or the survival of particular place-names, and the ceaseless processes of renaming, give us glimpses in miniature of tiny fragments of continuing, invariably contentious, histories.

Maps, too, are symbolic as well as practical tools. For many people born in Britain in the 1950s (e.g. me) there are variously proud or perplexed memories of maps of the world liberally coloured in pink (the colour reserved for the British Empire and Commonwealth). There was also curiosity about the extremely straight, geometrical and patently non-natural, national boundaries of most of the African states. Only later did I realise just how arbitrary and 'sharp', in every sense, was the mid-nineteenth century 'carving up' of Africa by Western European powers. Now, however, I am constantly reminded of the long-term consequences for the self-(in)sufficient (non-)economic development of many of these nations in the modern world. On a still grander scale, there is the understandable but still unsettling fact that most maps of the world before the early twentieth century were made by Western Europeans with an eye to Western Europe as the **centre**, visually as well as figuratively. After all, if you think the world revolves around you, that's how you draw it. More technically, the traditional 'Mercator' (conical) projection of the globe, dominant from the seventeenth century, had a strong tendency to exaggerate the relative size of Western Europe. More recent projections such as that by Winckel represent the world more accurately in terms of actual land area. The effect has been to shrink Western Europe to less than half its former size relative to, say, Russia or Africa. On large-scale maps Britain almost disappears completely.

In all these ways, through processes of renaming and remapping, Western Europeans have left their marks, both physical and figurative, on the shape of the modern post/colonial world. To be sure, post-independence governments were often quick to *re*-rename their countries and cities, even if they couldn't always do much about the actual redrawing of their borders. Thus Rhodesia (named after Sir Cecil Rhodes) was renamed Zimbabwe; Salisbury its capital was named Harare; though these were only two of the previous local options. 'South West Africa' was named 'Namibia'; though this had no exact relation to any preceding cultural–political configuration. Each one of these acts of (re)naming and (re-)mapping, whether by colonisers or de-colonisers, is thus historically highly specific and motivated by politically distinct agendas. One thing is clear about all of these processes, however. The *signs on buildings, roads and maps may change and even 'return', but whether they change *or* return, they never point to exactly the same places or peoples. For the pointing is always going on in a different social context and historical moment. Even if the form of words (the *signifiers) looks or sounds the same, the particular times and places and people referred to (the *signifieds) are always slightly – often very – different. This is a principle of *semiotics that applies as much to actual signs as to notional ones.

White selves and black others: some cases of mis-, under- and non-representation

In general terms, we tend to brace a sense of our **selves** against our sense of everyone and everything else we are not (i.e. **others**). In *ethnic terms, this means that specific cultural groups tend to define themselves by reference to other groups they are not. Thus a Jew is aware s/he is not a Gentile; a Christian is aware s/he is not a Jew or Moslem. And countless British jokes sport with the supposed differences between 'this Englishman, this Irishman, this Scotsman and this

Welshman'. Of course, the basis of all such distinctions is ethnic stereotypes of a generally negative but occasionally positive kind: the Jew may be God-fearing or God-challenging, family-minded or acquisitive; the Scot may be wildly drunken or a hyper-sober Presbyterian, generous or mean; and so on. Add physiological features to these caricatures and you quickly get *racial stereotyping (the sallow-faced, hook-nosed Jew; the fierily red-haired Scot).

There are obviously deeply psychological as well as social dimensions to these processes. The person who reckons her- or himself to be 'pure white' has necessarily only been able to do this by taking on board an equally extreme image of 'pure black'. S/he is thus totally locked into a process of self-definition which actually needs the 'other' to maintain the fixed dynamic of that definition. The inverse applies, of course. 'Pure black' consciousness (i.e. 'negritude') actually needs an internalised and externalised sense of 'pure whiteness' to maintain *its* self-definition. Similar processes are at work when people talk approvingly or disapprovingly of someone or something as being, say, 'English through and through', 'all-American', 'genuinely Russian' or 'typically Japanese'. In all these cases, there is some strongly implied obverse ('not at all English', 'un-American', etc.) which underwrites the observation.

The model over the page (Figure 4) shows a dominant Western European mind-set and cultural frame. This model is deeply embedded in colonialism and persists in modified form into postcolonialism. Such *binary oppositions are commonly invoked or implied when people adopt a simplistically 'black-and-white' approach to ethnicity. (Some 'muted' mind-sets/cultural frames are supplied italicised in brackets. These point to alternative views that were and are available; though notice that these too may easily become polarised.) The first polarities are chiefly identified with the earlier stages of empire. The later ones are more recent and demonstrate just how remarkably resilient and pervasive such modes of thinking, seeing and saying can be.

It was a founding axiom of European colonialism, and one of the declared rationales of its 'civilising' mission, that 'the black man is the white man's burden'. The dominant polarities featured obviously underwrite this view of the coloniser as basically a helper, nurturer and guide for the colonised. Such polarities also clearly extend from the colonial to the postcolonial and neo-colonial worlds (in 'Third World/Development Aid' programmes, for instance). At the same time we must recognise the complex relations between these 'black-and-white' oppositions and those identified with, for instance, 'masculine and feminine' (see GENDER STUDIES, pp. 112–113) and 'upper (or middle) class and working class'. Thus even in terms of crudely dominant discourses, there are complications in the ways we must frame notions of race and ethnicity. These frames must be superimposed on those relating to sexuality and gender, class and rank, as well as education, religion, region, and the like. In short, even leaving aside the matter of actual times, places and names, it makes a huge difference whether we think of a white or a black person as, say, female, middle-class and Muslim or male, working-class and Christian. And of course the complications multiply prodigiously once we add in 'muted' and 'alternative' dimensions of all these superimposed and, in reality, ceaselessly shifting frames (for related work on other kinds of multicultural, political and philosophical **difference**, see MARXISM, FEMINISM and POSTSTRUCTURALISM).

'WHITE'	'BLACK'
civilisation *(corruption)*	barbarism *(innocence)*
culture *(as repression)*	nature *(back to true)*
soul (*trapped in* body)	body (*expresses soul*)
Christian (v *Christian v. Jew*)	heathen (*other religions*)
God (the *vengeful father*)	devils (*other gods*)
reason (*narrow rationalism*)	feeling (*intuition*)
intellectual (*cerebral*)	sensual (*in touch with body*)
mental activity (*white collar*)	manual activity (*worker*)
sexual restraint (*repressed*)	sexual freedom (*expressed*)
cleanliness (*obsessive*)	dirt (*natural*)
science (*inhuman*)	superstition (*folk wisdom*)
medicine (*mechanical*)	magic (*holistic*)
classical music & dance	popular music & dance
print culture (*lifeless*)	oral culture (*lively*)
reserved (*up-tight*)	savage ('*cool*')
self (*as other*)	other (*as self*)
culturally 'normal'	'ethnic'
familiar	exotic
intellectual games	athletics
'First' World	'Third' World
'Rich North'	'Poor South'
computing & hypermedia	print literacy
developed, independent	underdeveloped, dependent
future . . .	past . . .

Figure 4 Dominant post/colonial and neo-colonial mind-sets (*and their muted alternatives*)

How to practise Postcolonial approaches in a multicultural world

General frames

Begin by putting yourself 'on the map', both geographically and historically. Where in the world are you? Where did your family and people you know come from – when, where and why? What, for instance, was their likely relation to the 'slave-trade triangle' between Britain, Africa and the Caribbean/Americas? (See the maps in Appendix A and Activity (b) in 1.4 for detailed suggestions.)

More particularly, consider:

♦ *the various phases of post/colonialism (including neo-colonialism) in which you are directly or indirectly implicated.* How far do you identify yourself with colonis*er*s and/or with colonis*ed*? within and/or beyond the British Isles, Western Europe, America, Australia? within or beyond whatever **centre(s)** you identify as 'home'?

♦ *the kinds and degrees of multiculturalism in which you are directly or indirectly implicated because you live where, when and how you do.* Representatives of what ethnic and other cultural groups do you routinely (or rarely) come into contact with? Which do you only know through the media (TV, films, newspapers, magazines)?

Go on to reflect upon the kinds of LANGUAGE you use and the kinds of LITERATURE you are studying with an eye and ear to their post/colonial and multicultural implications:

♦ *What* **varieties** *of English (including accents and dialects) do you use? What* **standard** *do you identify with* – British, American, Indian, Caribbean, etc.?

♦ *Would you categorise the texts you are currently studying or interested in studying nationally, internationally or in some other way* (e.g. as 'English' or 'American' or 'Australian Literature'; 'Literature in English'; 'English Studies'; 'Comparative (Commonwealth, Postcolonial) Literature'; 'Women's Writing'; 'Literary' or 'Textual' Studies)?

Specific text

Notice that these questions can be put to any text, whether or not it has an obviously post/colonial, ethnic or multicultural dimension to it. (Revising views of 'the obvious' is itself part of the project.)

Where in the world did – and does – this text come from? Who wrote or produced it – for whom, where, when, why and how? *Is it noticeably *ethnocentric (e.g. Anglo-, Euro-, Afrocentric) in the people and places it represents, or in the communicative and media circles in which it moves?*

(All the following questions may focus initially on ethnicity; but they should be extended and complicated so as to acknowledge other **differences** of class, rank, gender, sexuality, age and education, etc.):

♦ *Which persons or peoples are* **centred**, *marginalised or ignored – geographically and socially? Do you feel that any group is over-, under-, mis- or un-***represented***?* (What if roles were reversed, say, or background figures were moved to the foreground?)

♦ *Are *racial or *ethnic stereotypes reinforced or challenged?* For instance, how far do physiological build and physical appearance (complexion, hair, bone structure, dress, *body language) support a particular cultural 'placing' and, perhaps, moral evaluation? *Who are realised as* **selves** *– near and known, familiar and perhaps 'normal'? And who are realised as* **others** *– far and foreign, unfamiliar and perhaps exotic or grotesque?*

♦ *How far does the text seem to assume or assert some of the dominant 'black-and-white' polarities presented above (e.g. culture v. nature; reason v. feeling; science v. superstition; Christian v. heathen)? And how far does it seem to offer 'muted' positions, or explore genuinely alternative possibilities* (perhaps by shifting or completely switching the terms of the argument)?

♦ *Are there any* **genres** *or cultural frames of reference which are unfamiliar to you?* For instance, are there any distinctions between or confusions of, say, literature and performance, story and history, or fiction and fact, which you find striking? And are there stories, myths, legends, religious imagery, world-views you've never encountered before?

♦ *How might you interpret (and perhaps even rewrite) the text so as to make its post/colonial and multi/cultural dimensions more – or differently – 'obvious'?* (Because every text is always already in some sense both post/colonial and multi/cultural, this is quite properly a matter not only of the initial **writing** but also of subsequent **reading** and **re-writing**.)

Example

Read Billy Marshall-Stoneking's 'Passage' (5.4.4. e) with the accompanying notes and above questions and suggestions in mind. Then compare your responses to those below.

General frame How would I put myself 'on the map'? Some brief gestures towards an autobiography are made earlier in this chapter and elsewhere in the book (see pp. 100, 138). It should be added, however, that this is far from the whole story. An earlier draft of this section contained a much fuller personal–political history relating myself, and my family and friends to a variety of specific post/colonial histories reaching far beyond Britain and way back in time. Eventually, with a mixture of reluctance and relief, the editor, pre-readers and I decided all this material, though crucial for me, might be tedious or mystifying for you. It has therefore been 'self-censored'. Nonetheless, it was well worth doing. It doubtless was for you too if you did it. All that said, here are my responses to Billy Marshall-Stoneking's 'Passage'. As usual, I have used the above 'How to practise . . .' framework flexibly rather than slavishly.

'In' but not 'of' English. The first thing that strikes me about this text is that 'English' is being talked about as an optional medium. The act of using it is commented upon explicitly and thereby foregrounded: 'The oldest man . . . speaks to me in English'; 'We speak to each other in English'. Implicitly, somewhere in the background, is the sense that another language might be used, one that that would not prompt such surprise, one that would perhaps suit 'the oldest man in the world' and the occasion better. At any rate, 'English' sticks out here. Yet we are reading and understanding it. It is still proving serviceable. It brings you and I and the narrator and the oldest man into contact. We understand them – after a fashion. But perhaps only after a fashion. The strong implication of the poem, supported by reasonable inference from the notes, is that the 'other', unmentioned yet potentially more expected, language is 'Aboriginal'. And that, clearly, as the inner narrative begins, is the culture *of* which the oldest man speaks – albeit *through* the verbal medium of another.

But there are other signs of an interplay of cultures: apparently slight yet subtle intimations of sights and sensations. From the very first line our attention is drawn to the seemingly unexceptional fact that 'The oldest man in the world wears shoes'.

To you and me, who probably wear them most of the time, this is nothing strange. Yet again, as with the insistent presence of 'English', the foregrounding of 'shoes' presence implies a significant absence. Other footwear maybe? Or perhaps rather, again taking our cue from the notes and any other cultural knowledge we have of these traditionally far-roaming, fast-moving peoples, the fact that we might expect no shoes at all. The implied absence is most likely bare feet. The same presumably goes for the fact that 'He rides in motor cars'. Notice that it doesn't say he 'drives' or 'has' (i.e. owns) a car, but that he 'rides' in them, as though there is a certain distance between him and the machine. (This distance is confirmed by the use of the more formal, now archaic phrase 'motor car'.) The oldest man's relation to motor cars evidently involves neither control nor possession – simply use. Presumably it's the poet's car. At the same time, the oldest man seems perfectly capable of handling it all. He even, in his own way, seems to be totally in harmony with the machine; or at least well able to resist and respond to it: 'He rides in motor cars. / His body: fluid, capable – a perfect shock absorber'. We might therefore say that his body is *in* the car but not *of* the car. It has its own hydraulic 'fluid' and is, in every sense, 'a perfect shock absorber'.

Re-mapping hi/story. Meanwhile, we too are in for some shocks as, in the company of this pair, 'we bounce over the dirt track in the back / of a four-wheel drive'. For this may not just be a 'dirt track' that the four-wheel drive is bouncing 'over'. The oldest man has already begun to 'name . . . Names'. Perhaps there is something we (and it) are missing – or messing up.

> 'That tree is a digging stick
> left by the giant woman who was looking for honey ants;
> That rock, a dingo's nose;
> There, on the mountain, is the footprint
> left by Tjangara on his way to Ulamburra;
> Here the rockhole of Warnampi – very dangerous – '

And so he 'names Names' and, in effect, re-maps the landscape for his listener in the car. And incidentally for us too. Perhaps *we* are the lucky ones, that this is not in an 'Aboriginal' language but in English. This way we can follow the 'Passage'. It leads us through legends otherwise almost certainly inaccessible to us; and it leads us to a vision of the landscape, both physical and mythical, we could not otherwise have. In fact here, without such help, we could not be 'other-wise': stretched beyond ourselves and wise to the other. Because for me certainly, and for you quite probably, none of these 'Names' and none of these stories is familiar. We therefore have to piece meanings together, to make some coherent sense of plants ('That tree'); minerals ('That rock'); animals ('a dingo's nose'); people ('the giant woman', 'Tjangara'); places ('Ulamburra', 'Warnampi' – or are these personal names too?). All of these are joined together by storied events *we* only have faint traces of: 'the footprint left by . . . ' and later 'the mark of his penis/dragging the ground'. To us these traces are barely decipherable. We have no frame of shared story or history in which to place them. We do not even know how many, if any, of these legends are based on what we would distinguish as story (anthropomorphic myth, folktale, fable) or history (the oral record, albeit refashioned, of some actual settlement, some actual events). Indeed, we cannot at all be sure whether or how well our conventional Western distinctions between 'story' and 'history' will hold up in this world. For this is a kind of *oral narrative, and perhaps a mix of 'hi/story'

Westerners are not now familiar with (though its principles would probably have been familiar enough to the Anglo-Saxons who knew *Beowulf*, and the Native American Indians who sang and listened to their own legends, histories and lore). Moreover, those casually assumed categories 'mineral', 'plant', 'animal', 'place', 'person', may also turn out to be inappropriate insertions and superimpositions of alien, or at least inappropriate, mind-sets and cultural frames. In fact the general drift and continuous flow of the hi/story we are being told and the whole shape and shift of the landscape we are having fashioned for us may suggest some quite different world-sense: one in which it is the intuited wholeness – not the analytical discreteness – that is being rehearsed and realised.

Tell-tale singsong. In fact, it is *through* this verbal rehearsal that all this – and this sense of 'allness' – is being realised. The world is being given coherent shape, meaning and purpose by the very act of telling the tale. The landscape is being, in every sense, 'animated' by the teller – even as the features he sees act as prompts for him in the telling:

> 'This is the power of the Song.
> Through the singing we keep everything alive;
> through the songs the spirits keep us alive.'

This, then, is a reciprocal, symbiotic relationship. The Song keeps everything alive; while the singer (and by extension singers-along and listeners) are all part of the 'us' that 'the spirits' through the songs 'keep alive'. It is a model of the world and a function of singing many people in the West are not now very familiar with. It is a hi/story within a poem – and perhaps a science within an art – that we may therefore learn a lot from.

Old worlds for new: an ol' American dream. But of course there is not one 'we' but at least two. There's the 'we' within the poem (the oldest man and his interlocutor, the poet-narrator) and there's you and I and other people outside it. Certainly, in a very crucial imaginative sense, for the duration of our reading of the poem, we all bob along as a kind of capacious, collective 'we': 'We bump along together in the back of the truck. . . . We speak to each other in English'. 'We' all do in some sense communicate, we share things. At the same time, 'we' are all of us in some crucial respects different. In the poem, for instance, 'The oldest man in the world' is distinguished from 'the newest man in the world'. And the latter acknowledges that 'my place [is] less exact than his'. Perhaps the newest man is literally on unfamiliar terrain, lost even. But perhaps, too, he feels himself to be more lost in the world – or at least less sure of his 'place' in the one they are currently in – than his older companion. And here again the supplementary notes, including a very brief biography, might help us refine, point and 'locate' our interpretation. Billy Marshall-Stoneking is an American who has adopted and adapted Australian, especially Aboriginal, ways. Perhaps, then, what he is making us privy to is his own sense of dislocation, inadequacy even, when confronted by an 'older' member of one of the ethnic groups he has a hankering after. After all, it seems that the poet-listener, like us, needs to be told these things about the land/spirit-scape he is in. Maybe he knows more of the myths, legends and hi/stories than you or I do. But he evidently knows much less than 'the oldest man' he listens to. We may therefore be left wondering a variety of things by the end of the poem. We shall almost certainly be reading the poem – and through the poem, perhaps parts of ourselves – differently. By now the last lines have built up a stronger pressure behind them, and acquired a more subtly ambiguous resonance than the first time we met versions of them near the beginning:

> We speak to each other in English
> over the rumble of engine, over the roar of the wheels.
> His body: a perfect shock absorber.

Maybe the oldest man has an effective way of dealing not only with the rumble and roar of the engine, but also with the 'rumble' and 'roar' of modern Western life. We have already been told explicitly by him that 'the Dreaming does not end; it is not like the whiteman's way.' So very likely the 'shock' his 'body' is able to 'absorb' is the 'shock of the new' (to use Toffler's phrase) as well as the literal bump and bounce of motor cars. And very likely it is this quality of resilience as well as the sense of being sure of the world and one's place in it that the poet-listener evidently admires ('a *perfect* shock absorber') and perhaps even wishes to emulate.

ACTIVITIES

(a)   Compare the ways in which ethnic **differences** are complicated and compounded by those of gender, class and age in a couple of the following post/colonial texts: Nichols's 'Tropical Death' (5.4.5 e); Shakespeare's *The Tempest* (5.3.2 b); Churchill's *Cloud 9* (5.3.4 e); Kipling's 'Muhammad Din' (5.2.4 b); Conrad's *Heart of Darkness* (5.2.4 c); Achebe's *Things Fall Apart* (5.2.4 f).

(b)   Draw on the questions and suggestions in 'How to practise postcolonial approaches in a multicultural context' to help frame a response to any text which interests you in these respects.

(c)   Rewrite the extract from Defoe's *Robinson Crusoe* (I Call Him Friday – 5.2.2 b) so as to explore alternative subject positions and perspectives. Consider changes of genre, medium and period, too, if you wish. Add a commentary on the problems and possibilities encountered. (Later, see Holdsworth (5.2.2 c) for a version done by someone else.)

DISCUSSION

Debate the following for, against, and by proposing an alternative. Support your arguments wherever possible with references to specific writers, works, genres and periods.

(i)   English the subject is the place where a fundamental question about intercultural relations is being addressed.
> Colin Evans, *English People: The Experience of Teaching and Learning English in British Universities* (1993: 213)

(ii) Post-colonialism [is] an always present tendency in any literature of subjugation marked by a systematic process of cultural domination through the imposition of imperial structures of power.
> Vijay Mishra and Bob Hodge, 'What is Post-colonialism' in Williams and Chrisman (1993: 284)

(iii)   The challenge of postcolonial literature is that by exposing and attacking anglo-centric assumptions directly, it can replace 'English literature' with 'world literature in English'.
John Docker, 'The Neocolonial Assumption in University Teaching of English' (1978) in Ashcroft *et al.* (1995: 445)

(iv)   The [Postcolonial] writer should aim at fashioning out an English which is at once universal and able to carry his peculiar experience . . .
Chinua Achebe, 'Transition' (1965) in Durant and Fabb (1990: 200; 'Postcolonial' substituted for 'African')

READING: *Introductory*: Appiah and Sollers in Lentricchia and McLaughlin 1995: 274–305; Selden *et al.* 1997: 221–42; Bhabha in Greenblatt and Gunn 1992: 437–65. *Fuller studies*: Said 1978, 1993; Brathwaite 1984; Ashcroft *et al.* 1989; Spivak 1987, 1994; Gates 1986; Bhabha 1990, 1994; hooks 1994. *Anthologies*: Walder 1990: 9–16, 171–202, 233–303; Williams and Chrisman 1993; Ashcroft *et al.* 1995; Schwarz 1996.

2.10   DEVELOPING POSITIONS AND FUTURE PROSPECTS

This brief section is for those who have worked their way through all or most of the theoretical positions and critical approaches featured in Part Two. It invites you to review what you have learnt, weigh the differences and express some provisional preferences. But it is also about opening up rather than closing down the sense of options. This is therefore an opportunity to cross-refer to approaches featured elsewhere in the book, namely, *Reception aesthetics* and *Reader-response* (see **writing and reading, response and rewriting**) and *Textual intervention* (see 4.3). It is also the time to gesture to models and methodologies it has not been possible to treat at length (or at all) in the foregoing pages.

Further approaches associated with ecology and environmentalism, English as a foreign language, editing and translation studies are available on the webpage associated with this book (see p. 5).

The following activities should help you to gauge how far you have travelled and in what directions and dimensions; also to project forward to where you (and the subject) are heading, and perhaps to see how you are going to get there, and why.

ACTIVITIES

(a)   *Return to the activity based on the cluster of 'Wordsworth' texts (5.4.3) in 'Getting some initial bearings' (2.1)*. Run through the texts and the questions again. How differently do you see them all now?

(b)   *Return to the working model of the text as products and processes (Figure 2, p. 72)*. Which areas do you currently have a greater or lesser interest in: the text as *products* (versions, notes, drafts); *producers* (authors, directors, etc.); *receivers* (readers, audiences, viewers); *relations to the rest of the world* (social and historical context, representations of life, etc.)? How far have your interests changed in these respects over, say, the last couple of years? And where do you think they may be tending?

(c)   *Read through the 'Overviews' of the various positions/approaches in sections 2.3–2.9 ('Practical criticism' to 'Postcolonialism')* Which do you now find most (i) interesting; (ii) practical; (iii) difficult; (iv) deserving of further study?

(d)   *Select a text from Part Five (or elsewhere) and briefly consider how each of the major approaches featured here in Part Two might deal with it.* What questions would each ask? What other materials and knowledges would each require? What kinds of answer might each come up with? (Use the 'How to practise . . . .' sections to help you frame appropriate questions.) Conclude by weighing which *combination* of approaches seems to work best with the particular text in hand. Would it work as well with *all* texts?

(e)   *Turn to the summary questions on the various 'fields' of* LANGUAGE, LITERATURE *and* CULTURE *in Part One (1.8)*. Which of these 'fields' do your preferred approaches relate most readily to? Are there kinds of material which you are studying that they fail to address adequately or at all?

(f)   *Turn to the 'Overview of textual activities' in Part Four (4.1)*. How might each of these be used in harness with your preferred approach(es) to explore and experiment with a text which interests you?

(g)   *Have a go at modelling the kinds of materials and methods YOU are most interested in.* Consider doing this as a diagram, picture, word-cluster, mind-map, collage, or whatever. Alternatively, remodel one of the diagrams in the present book (for a list of these see p. xiii).

COMMON TOPICS

PART THREE

PREVIEW

This consists of some twenty-five entries featuring over a hundred key terms. These are 'common' topics in that they recur in critical discussions of all kinds and are not the exclusive property of a single model or method. You will therefore find them throughout the book highlighted in bold. Indeed, words such as **author, character, image, poetry, standard(s)** and **text** are central and significant precisely because people either assume what they mean or argue about what they can mean. Paradoxically, then, what is 'common' about such terms is precisely their differences: the different roles they are made to play in various critical discourses. (**Difference** and **discourse** are also such terms, and therefore included too.) Each entry comprises:

♦ a preliminary definition, usually in the first sentence;
♦ an indication of the areas of LANGUAGE, LITERATURE and CULTURE, and the various theoretical positions and critical approaches to which it most readily relates (keyed to Parts One and Two);
♦ further distinctions and qualifications;

♦   illustrations and activities framed so as to be applicable to any text, but also keyed to
        the anthology of sample texts in Part Five;

♦   points for discussion and further reading.

At the close of this part you are invited to gather further entries and build a critical
dictionary of your own.

ABSENCE AND PRESENCE, GAPS AND SILENCES, CENTRES AND MARGINS

All the concepts gathered here have to do with the fundamental matter of understanding what *is* there in terms of what *isn't*: gauging the 'thisness' of something
against all the 'thatnesses' which it is not. In dialectical terms, this is called the
activity of *negation. Arguably, all thought involves some such process organised
round the double-edged question 'What is/n't it?' However, the concepts featured
here have become especially prominent in POSTSTRUCTURALISM and the activity of
*deconstruction in particular.

*Derrida has argued that Western thought systems are dominated by the notion
of ultimate 'presence' and 'essence'. That is, 'truth' and 'facts' are treated as
phenomena that can be positively identified and known. This contrasts with Eastern
thought systems (and some Western philosophical and mystical traditions) where
there is greater emphasis on what can*not* be identified and is ultimately *un*knowable.
Derrida illustrates this Western preoccupation with 'presence' by observing that
most Western philosophers of language, and indeed most linguists, tend to privilege
speech before **writing**, as though speech is a primary and writing a secondary
manifestation. They imply that speech is more obviously tied to an authenticating
source and palpable presence (the speaker), whereas writing can more readily exist
without the writer present. Derrida challenges this conventional wisdom by insisting
that it is writing – not speech – which is the more characteristically linguistic mode.
For, he argues, all words are always by definition *not* the things they refer to, but
substitutes for them. The word 'tree' is not a tree, but stands in for it. Language is not
primarily about presences at all, but about absences. Moreover, as many writers on
COMMUNICATION are quick to add, there is no such thing as a pure unmediated
event, 'the event in itself'. The apparently simple matter of being 'present' at an event
is no guarantee that a participant will have a full, let alone an impartial, grasp of what
is going on. Given their personal histories and temperaments, as well as their
immediate aims and expectations, participants are never strictly present in the same
way.

In PSYCHOLOGICAL terms, too, the absence of our unconscious from our conscious
selves ensures that we are never completely 'self-evident'. We are more than and
different from what we know. With this in mind, the notion of **gaps and silences**
was developed by *Macherey in his *A Theory of Literary Production* (1966). For
Macherey the primary focus of textual study is what the text *does not* or *cannot* say
(the 'non-dit'). That is, every text can be characterised not only by its *expressed
subject matter (its presences) but also by what it *represses psychologically and
suppresses politically (its absences). The role of the critical reader, therefore, is to
search for the 'gaps and silences': reading between the lines and filling the
embarrassed or pregnant silences. What figures and events have been quickly
passed over or ignored? What other stories and histories have been partially

displaced or utterly replaced by the very act of telling *this* story (or history) *this* way? Macherey explores the 'unsaid' or 'unsayable' in, for instance, *Robinson Crusoe* (see 5.2.2 b–c), tying this work in with the construction of a white colonising **self** (Crusoe) established at the expense of a a black colonised **other** (Friday). He also gestures towards hi/stories of empire and slaves either inevitably unwritten or deliberately ignored. Jameson develops related insights in *The Political Unconscious* (1981).

The concept of **centres and margins**, along with the activities of decentring and recentring, can be usefully introduced at this point. MARXISTS, FEMINISTS and others have long talked about 'marginalised' as opposed to 'dominant' groups. However, it is to POSTSTRUCTURALIST writers such as Derrida that we chiefly owe an interest in the activities known as decentring and, by extension, recentring. The basic principles are simple and follow from the previous explication of 'absences and presences' and 'gaps and silences'. By *centring* we mean the act of placing certain persons, places, times, issues and perceptions at the centre of attention – and thereby marginalising or ignoring others. By *decentring* a text, critical readers and writers actively dislocate what was assumed to be at the centre of attention and draw attention to something, inside or outside the text, which they feel throws a revealing light across it. In *Hamlet* an instance of such 'internal' decentring might mean drawing attention to the go-betweens Rosencrantz and Guildenstern (as Stoppard does in his play) or to Ophelia and Gertrude (as do many FEMINISTS). 'External' decentring might mean turning to critical receptions of the play or, say, investigating, the role of actual gravediggers (featured theatrically in Act V sc. i) in the early seventeenth century – or even analysing a series of TV ads for some cigars called 'Hamlet'. Another instance of de- and recentring is Jean Rhys's *Wide Sargasso Sea*. This centres attention on the earlier life of the mad and largely absent Mrs Rochester of Charlotte Brontë's *Jane Eyre* (see 5.2.3 d–e).

The theoretical terminology of de- and recentring, like that of *deconstruction in general, can be forbiddingly dense. But the practice can be both simple and powerful. Here's a suggested procedure:

DE- AND RECENTRING TEXTS (cf. discourse questions, p. 189)

1 *Identify the presumed centre of the text*: the one the author seems to be preoccupied with, or the one critics invite you to concentrate on.
2 *DEcentre it so as to draw attention to marginal or ignored figures, events and materials.* Try decentring in two dimensions, *internally* and *externally*, drawing attention to other possibilities within and outside the text in hand.
3 *Recognise that you have thereby REcentred the text.* Weigh the implications of what you have done for an understanding of the text as you first found it. Also notice that you have produced another configuration which can itself be challenged and changed, and further de- and recentred in turn.

There is, of course, no single 'end' or ultimate 'point' to the process of de- and recentring: there are always multiple 'absences' which will help us realise a 'presence'. Nor is there just one 'gap' or 'silence' which can be detected within the noisy fabric of a text. The value of such an activity, however, is that it encourages us to grasp texts creatively as well as critically. We weigh what they are or seem to say in relation to what they are not or might have said differently. We grasp texts not only as 'wholes' but also as configurations of 'holes'.

ACTIVITY

Consider how far a text which interests you is in some sense about the tension between 'absence' and 'presence'. Go on to apply the three-part procedure for *de- and recentring*. (Suggested focuses in Part Five: 'They flee from me' (5.1.3 a); *How late it was, how late* (5.2.6); *Not I* (5.3.4 d).)

DISCUSSION

(i) Play is the disruption of presence. [. . .] Play is always play of absence and presence.
> Jacques Derrida, 'Sign, Structure and Play in the Discourse of the Human Sciences' (1978) in Lodge (1988: 121)

(ii) Things fall apart; the centre cannot hold;
> William Butler Yeats, 'The Second Coming' (1921); also in the title of Achebe's novel (see 5.2.4 f)

Also see: POSTSTRUCTURALISM; **foreground, background**; **difference and similarity**.

READING: *Introductory*: Hawthorn 1994: 1–2; Moon 1992: 30–3, 152–5; Pope 1995: 14–30, 162–80. *Advanced*: Macherey 1966; Derrida 1978 in Lodge 1988: 107–23; Jameson 1981; Spivak 1987; Bhabha 1994.

ACCENT AND DIALECT

Accent and dialect are aspects of language **variety**. They therefore vary from place to place, over time, according to social context and depending on medium (see 1.2.1–4). Speaking 'with an accent' means pronouncing words in a way which is nationally, regionally or socially distinctive; hence speaking English with a Russian, Irish, New York or upper-class accent. In this respect everyone has an accent. Speaking or writing 'in dialect', however, is more than a matter of accent alone. It also involves choices and combinations of words which are distinctive, if not peculiar, to the vocabulary and grammar of a particular region or social group. Thus speakers of English will pronounce the same words ('How are you?', for instance) with a variety of accents. However, only when they use distinctive choices and combinations of words would we describe them as using dialectal forms (stereotypically, such greetings as 'G'day' in Australia; 'Wotcha!' in parts of London). For a fuller sense of dialectal variation in English across the whole range of word choice and word combination, as well as accent/pronunciation (here represented by variations in spelling), see the versions of 'Humpty Dumpty' (5.4.1) and the poems by Barnes (5.1.6), Chan Wei Meng (5.1.9 b); Harrison (5.4.5 c), Collins (5.1.9 c) and πO (5.1.9 a).

Accents and dialects sometimes get ranked hierarchically in relation to a socially privileged **standard**. In Britain it is common to place accents against 'Received Pronunciation' (RP) and to place the language as a whole (including dialects) against 'BBC English' or, more archaically, 'the Queen's English'. In the USA and Australia, however, there is far less identification of a specific regional accent with power, privilege and status. No one state tends to dominate the various 'network' (i.e. media) standards which operate. In any case, people everywhere routinely switch from one variety to another, depending on the social situation and topic. The 'local' variety tends to be used in informal conversation and implies a sense of solidarity. Meanwhile the 'standard' variety tends to be used whenever there is an increase in formality, where printed documents are involved and where there is a stronger sense of power. In this respect, most speakers of English and other languages are at least *di-glossic*, routinely switching between two varieties: 'local' and 'inter/national'. Indeed, most speakers are *multi-glossic* in that they readily switch amongst many varieties, depending on age, education, peer group, gender, class and ethnicity, as well as on region. The term *sociolect is sometimes used to to refer to all these other kinds of social language variety, the term 'dialect' being reserved for purely regional variety.

Selected versions of accents, dialects, sociolects and even instances of other languages are often used in novels, plays, films, adverts and songs. They signal a specific regional, class, national or ethnic **identity**. Perhaps the most persistent and predictable instances occur in TV and radio adverts. On British TV and radio, for instance, upper-class and markedly 'Queen's English' accents are used to sell insurance, banking, lean cuisine and expensive cars; 'regional' and working-class accents are used to sell beers (Australian matiness an optional extra), junk food and washing powders (though even then the sales pitch is often clinched by a final voice-over invoking the **authority** of another, more 'standard' variety). Plays, novels and stories, too, often give at least a passing flavour, and sometimes a full taste, of people speaking and writing in ways which are 'other-than-standard' (though even then they are usually braced against a standard printed or spoken form which is assumed to be the norm). Classic examples include: Shakespeare's *Henry V* (for 'stage' Welsh, Scots, Irish and French); Gaskell's *North and South*, Dickens's *Hard Times*, Lawrence's *Sons and Lovers* (for Northern English working class); Hardy's 'Wessex' novels (for rural West Country); also Faulkner's *As I Lay Dying*, Hurston's *Their Eyes Were Watching God* (5.2.4 d), Walker's *The Color Purple* and Morrison's *Beloved* (5.2.2 e) (for varieties of 'black' and 'white' Englishes from the American Southern States; also see Bambara 5.3.5 a). Synge's *Playboy of the Western World* and Thomas's *Under Milk Wood* have been especially influential stage and radio play versions of respectively, Irish and Welsh varieties of English (see 5.3.4 a–b). For current Irish and Scots varieties, see Doyle (5.2.5 e), Leonard (5.2.5 d) and Kelman (5.2.6).

In contemporary Britain, novels, plays and films by Roddy Doyle, James Kelman, Mike Leigh and Hanif Kureishi have done much to put contemporary urban Irish, Scottish, London-based and Asian varieties on the literary and media map. Soap operas, comedy programmes and other TV series such as *Coronation Street*, *Brook-side*, *EastEnders*, *Ralph Nesbitt* and *The Bill* have done something similar, though with different degrees of stereotyping. Meanwhile, the accents of *Neighbours* and *Home and Away* virtually *are* Australian English for legions of TV-watching non-Australian English-speakers the world over. Bands such as Simply Red and the Cranberries as well as comedians such as Billy Connolly, Victoria Wood, Jasper Carrott, Max Boyce and Ben Elton all have (or have had) noticeably 'regional' accents and images. Many Hollywood films also include voices other than those of white Anglo-Saxon Americans, notably black, Hispanic and Native American Indian. Remarkably few, however, get beyond stereotyped roles and marginal or token presences.

Finally, it should be noted that each one of us has a particular *idiolect. An idiolect is the distinctive and to some extent unique configuration of language varieties peculiar to each person. It is our personal repertoire – a kind of verbal fingerprint – with the difference that our *verbal* resources not only grow but also change in pattern over the course of our lives.

(For the specialised meaning of 'accent' as the accentual stress in verse, see **versification**. Translators of *Bakhtin, meanwhile, use the term 'multiaccentuality' quite differently, to refer to the capacity of words to mean rather different things every time they are used.)

ACTIVITY

Consider how regional accents and dialects (or sociolects) are represented and what they signify in a novel, poem, play, film, TV programme or advert with which you are familiar. Alternatively, concentrate on one of those referred to above or featured in Part Five: e.g., versions of 'Humpty Dumpty' (5.4.1); Barnes's 'Woak Hill' (5.1.6); Leonard's 'This is thi . . . news' (5.2.5 d); Synge's *Playboy* (5.3.4 a); Nichols's 'Tropical Death' (5.4.5 e); 'πO's '7 DAIZ' (5.1.9 a). How far are the formal differences simply matters of pronunciation/spelling or of word choice and combination? Go on to consider what kinds of social and cultural identity are being projected, against what kinds of assumed or asserted background.

DISCUSSION

> Mrs Durbeyfield habitually spoke the dialect [Dorset]; her daughter, who had passed the Sixth Standard in the National School under a London-trained mistress, spoke two languages: the dialect at home, more or less; ordinary English abroad and to persons of quality.
>
> Thomas Hardy, *Tess of the d'Urbervilles* (1891: Ch. 3)

Also see: 1.2.1–4; 1.8.1; **discourse**; **standards and . . . varieties**.

READING: *Introductory*: Montgomery *et al.* 1992: 46–51; Carter 1995: 1–4, 37; McCrum *et al.* 1992: 21–36; Freeborn *et al.* 1993: 1–75; Crystal 1995: 298–363; Wright in Graddol *et al.* 1996: 259–300. O'Donnell and Todd 1992. *Advanced*: Trudgill 1990; Trudgill and Hannah 1982; Görlach 1991.

ADDRESSER, ADDRESS, ADDRESSEE

This is a handy way of distinguishing the three main components in any act of communication: someone (addresser) communicates something (address) to someone else (addressee). In terms of **subject** positions and personal *pronouns, we may say there is the 'speaking subject' (first person 'I/we'); the 'spoken-about subject' (third person 'she/he/they/it') and the 'spoken-to subject' (second person 'you'). We may also re-express the addresser–address–addressee distinctions in a variety of ways, depending on the medium: *speaker–speech–audience* (for **speech**); *writer–text–reader* (for **writing** and print); *performer–play–audience* or *producer–programme/film–viewer* (for **theatre**, **film** and **TV**). But whatever terms we use, the advantage of an addresser–address–addressee model is that it insists we see speeches, texts and other artefacts as intermediary products caught in the process of communication between a producer and receiver. We are thereby discouraged from concentrating exclusively on 'the words on the page' (in NEW CRITICAL fashion) or 'the form and structure of the text in itself' (in FORMALIST fashion), as though these could be fully grasped independently of the relationship between the participants. We are thus encouraged to adopt a FUNCTIONALIST and **contextual** approach to COMMUNICATION.

*Jakobson developed an influential version of this addresser–address–addressee model by drawing attention to other components of the communicative event. These are represented diagrammatically in Figure 5.

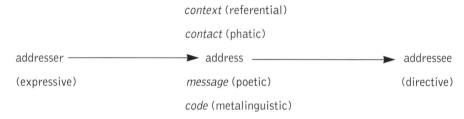

Figure 5 Jakobson's model of communication

Thus the address as a whole:

♦ takes place in some general *context* (e.g., late nineteenth-century Nigeria, America last week);
♦ involves a specific moment of *contact* (e.g., a chance encounter in a particular bar);
♦ takes the form of a specific *message* (e.g., a particular sequence of words or images);
♦ draws on the general resources of a particular *code (e.g., spoken or written English, photography, film).

Jakobson also argues that every communicative act tends to emphasise one or more of its constituent dimensions:

Address*er*-centred communication is *expressive* (e.g., 'I feel I need to tell someone').
Address*ee*-centred communication is *directive* (e.g., 'You, tell him!').
Context-centred communication is *referential* (e.g., 'That is what she said').
Contact-centred communication is *phatic and checks that channels are kept open (e.g., 'You know she said that, OK?').
Message-centred communication is *poetic and plays around with the materiality of the message (e.g., '*Telling-schmelling*! I'm telling *yoooouuuuu*!').
Code-centred communication is metalinguistic, a comment on language in language (e.g., 'I'm telling you *in her very words*').

This model has been used to frame a wide range of analytical and theoretical projects. It is particularly useful when trying to break down a communicative act into its constituent layers or levels and then relating these to functions. A big disadvantage, however, is that this is essentially a **monologic** (one-way and linear) model. It emphasises a unidirectional flow of information *from* addresser *to* addressee. As a result it tends to ignore or misrepresent **dialogic** (two- and many-way) models of communication. In fact, in most actual communicative events addressers and addressees are constantly changing places. There is a process of exchange and interaction, not simply transmission of unchanged information. We must thus acknowledge the kind of fluid swapping of roles and switches of topic found in both spontaneous **conversation** and play scripts. We also need to distinguish between 'actual' and 'implied' addressers and addressees: who actually tells or is told something as distinct from who it appears to be delivered by and for (see *narration). We also need to be careful to specify various moments of address; for there is invariably more than one moment of production, reproduction and reception involved (see 2.2). Nonetheless, if we bear all these things in mind, the model of addresser, address and addressee proves to be remarkably durable and serviceable.

ACTIVITY

Addressing the text
Apply the above model of addresser, address and addressee to a text you are studying or one from Part Five (comparison of the first three texts in the 'Versions of age' cluster (5.4.4 a–c) is especially fascinating). How useful do you find Jakobson's further distinctions (contact, code, expressive, directive, etc.)? Go on to consider the fact that you, the reader, are both being addressed and in your turn addressing the text. How does this complicate the analysis?

DISCUSSION

A letter does not always reach its destination . . .
                                        Edgar Allan Poe, 'The Purloined Letter' (1848)

Also see: COMMUNICATION; model of text in 2.2; FORMALISM INTO FUNCTIONALISM; **speech and conversation, monologue and dialogue; narrative . . . ; writing and reading**

READING: *Introductory*: Wales 1989: 9–10; Hawkes 1977: 82–6; Selden and Widdowson 1997: 3–5. *Advanced*: Jakobson in Lodge 1988: 32–56; Fiske 1990: 6–42.

AESTHETICS AND PLEASURE, ART AND BEAUTY

In casual usage if we say a poem, picture or landscape is 'aesthetically pleasing', we generally mean that it gives us a refined sense of pleasure: it is 'artistically beautiful'. In this respect the sense of 'aesthetic' (also spelt 'esthetic') is loosely synonymous with that of 'artistic'. We start with such broad generalities and potential confusions because that is precisely where these terms and concepts are in most people's minds. 'Aesthetics = refined pleasure = art = beauty' is therefore the formula we shall explore and, to some extent, explode. The result should be a sharper sense of the distinctions as well as the connections amongst all these terms.

Aesthetics derives from a Greek word meaning 'things perceptible to the sense', 'sensory impressions'. At its broadest, anything could have an aesthetic effect simply by virtue of being sensed and perceived. From the late eighteenth century, however, aesthetics became narrowed to mean not just sense perception in general but 'perception of the beautiful' in particular. Thus by the late nineteenth century aesthetics was chiefly identified with the cultivation of 'good taste' in anything and everything from fine wine and clothes to literature, painting and music. As such, it melded with highly idealised and often socially elitist notions of 'the sublime' and 'the beautiful'. At its crudest, an aesthetic sense was simply a sign of good breeding.

Art, meanwhile, was undergoing a corresponding process of narrowing in meaning and elevation in social status. Initially, the term 'art' had derived through French from a Latin word (*ars/artis*) meaning 'skill', 'technique' or 'craft'. At this stage anything requiring practical knowledge and technical expertise could be an art, from the arts of husbandry (i.e. farming and housekeeping) to the arts of writing and building. Moreover, the 'seven arts' of the medieval universities (later called the Seven Liberal Arts) did not recognise modern distinctions between sciences on the one hand and arts and humanities on the other. The seven arts thus comprised Grammar, Logic and RHETORIC (the trivium) along with Arithmetic, Music, Geometry and Astronomy (the quadrivium). But all were 'arts' in that they required technical knowledge. By the mid-nineteenth century, however, 'Art' was increasingly being used as a singular and with a capital letter. Art was also being used as an umbrella term for what were now being called the *fine* (as distinct from the *applied*) arts: architecture (as distinct from building); sculpture (as distinct from carving), chamber and orchestral music (as distinct from popular singing and playing), ballet (not just any dance), painting on canvas (rather than, say, house-painting); **poetry** (as distinct from verse and song) and LITERATURE in the sense of 'belles lettres' (as distinct from **writing** in general). Significantly, at the same time, the sciences were also tending to be split into *pure* and *applied* (e.g., physics as distinct from engineering).

The overall result was that henceforth 'Art' was increasingly distinguished from other forms of representation and signification. By the same gesture, *artists* (who were supposedly preoccupied with the sublime) were carefully distinguished from their more humble and practical counterparts, *artisans*. The former, it was argued, made *beautiful* things; the latter made *useful* things. (Incidentally, it was precisely against this divisive state of affairs that William Morris and Company and the related 'Arts and Crafts' movements came into being. They resisted the split between fine and applied art, as well as that between artist and artisan.) At any rate, notwithstanding the efforts of Morris and Co, from the late nineteenth century to the present it has been common to assume that art is ultimately a matter of 'art for art's sake', and that it is either fine and pure or impractical and useless, depending on your point of view. At the same time 'the aesthetic' is assumed to be nothing more nor less than a sensitivity to the sublime and the beautiful and an aversion to the ordinary and ugly.

For English Studies, especially for the study of Literature, the legacy of such a division has been profound. Many traditional English Literature courses still concentrate substantially on just one side of the divide: on a **canon** of literature treated as high art (poems, plays and novels revered as **classics**), as distinct from *popular writing and mass media production in general (magazines, news stories, songs, soap operas, adverts, etc.). All the latter tend to be treated as artisanal, applied, commercial and ephemeral, and therefore left to courses in CULTURAL, COMMUNICATION, AND MEDIA Studies (see 1.5.10). The former, meanwhile, are treated as artistic, fine, sublime and timeless, and appropriated as certain kinds of aesthetic literary object. The narrowed sense of 'aesthetic', meaning tasteful, refined and *discriminating (rather than 'sense perception in general') has played a crucial role in maintaining the boundaries. So has a willingness to play down the fact that many works currently canonised as timeless classics (e.g., Shakespeare's and Dickens's) were highly popular and commercial and designedly ephemeral in their own day.

Contemporary understandings of both aesthetics and art are thus far more various and contentious than one might expect. In English and Literary Studies, for instance, the two dominant aesthetics of the first half of the twentieth century have been effectively challenged. NEW CRITICS had approached texts as semi-sacred art objects ('verbal icons') and had asserted an aesthetics which resolves tensions and ambiguities and celebrates organic unity, balance and harmony (see 2.3). FORMALISTS had concentrated on *literariness and *poetics in so far as these *defamiliarise routine language and sharpen dulled perceptions (see 2.4). Both these critical movements, for all their differences, were therefore upholding positions consistent with late nineteenth-century versions of aesthetics and art. Nowadays, however, such positions are much harder to maintain and in many areas have been substantially superseded. FUNCTIONALISTS and *reader-reception critics, for instance, argue that every period or culture develops its own aesthetic principles, often defined against those which precede or surround it. They point out that the *Romantics challenged an earlier eighteenth-century *neo-classical aesthetic based upon symmetry, variety within unity and the reasoned subservience of parts to whole. In its place Romantic artists and writers developed an aesthetics based upon dislocation, multiplicity as it exceeds unity, and the emotional power of parts to shatter wholes. In a similar way, *Modernism then POSTMODERNISM challenged and changed the dominant tenets of **realism**. We are thus left with competing aesthetics (plural), not just one.

Many modern views of aesthetics are also politically charged and reject the view that art is somehow above or to one side of social struggle. MARXIST, FEMINIST and POSTCOLONIAL writers, especially, all insist in their various ways that a traditional aesthetics of harmony, balance and unity is often maintained only by ignoring or playing down potentially disruptive issues of class, gender and race. They point to the existence of opposed and alternative aesthetics based upon different versions of beauty and visions of pleasure (e.g., representations of labourers, women, people of colour and the family that resist or replace stereotypes based upon Western European aristocratic, bourgeois and patriarchal values). Often, too, there is a radical revision of what we understand by desire and pleasure. *Desire, for instance, may be perceived as a power which blasts apart stale social forms, not simply as something to be restrained by reason or religion. **Pleasure**, meanwhile, may entail participation and collaboration (in its extreme form *Barthes's ecstatic 'jouissance') rather than a sensation derived from mere spectating and voyeurism.

It is also now commonly insisted that 'the aesthetic' is not an inherent property of objects at all – artistic or otherwise. Rather, it is argued, an aesthetic experience is what is generated in the encounter between specific artefacts and specific readers, audiences and viewers in specific conditions. Different aesthetics are thus conceived as dynamic relationships not intrinsic essences: ongoing **dialogues**, not the observance of fixed codes. POSTMODERNISTS, moreover, point to the commodification and globalisation of *all* cultural products and processes. They observe that modern technologies of reproduction and communication are effectively abolishing any final division between 'high' and 'low', 'elite' and 'popular' arts. In fact the dominant characteristic of postmodernist aesthetics is its *hybridity and changeability. It is therefore, arguably, not a distinct aesthetics at all. If everything can be art, then perhaps nothing is.

ACTIVITY

Aesthetics (plural)
Identify two or more texts which seem to be constructed according to different aesthetic principles: perhaps one which appears to celebrate order and wholeness, harmony, balance and variety within unity; and another which appears to celebrate disorder and fragmentation, cacophony, imbalance and variety beyond unity. Also consider the possibility that these categories are themselves – along with notions of 'beauty' – partly in the eye, ear and mind of the reader, audience or viewer. (Texts which have worked well here, singly or in combination, include the 'Daffodils' materials (5.4.3), epitaphs (5.4.5), Queen's 'Bohemian Rhapsody' (5.1.10), Austen (5.2.3 b), Beckett (5.3.4 d), Theatre Workshop (5.4.6 f).)

DISCUSSION

(i)   In any period it is upon a very small minority that the discerning appreciation of art and literature depends.
         F.R. Leavis, *Mass Civilisation and Minority Culture* (1930) (1979: 3)

(ii) [There are] two opposing notions of the aesthetic, one figuring as an image of emancipation, the other ratifying domination.
         Terry Eagleton, *The Ideology of the Aesthetic* (1990: 411)

Also see: LITERATURE; CULTURE; FORMALISM INTO FUNCTIONALISM; **author and authority; canon and classic; poetry and word-play; difference . . . re/valuation**.

READING: *Introductory:* Abrams 1993: 2–4; Cuddon 1992: 12–14; Williams 1983: 31–3, 366–417; O'Sullivan *et al.* 1994: 6–7. *Advanced*: Mukarovsky 1936; Garvin 1964; Benjamin 1970; Bourdieu 1984; Eagleton 1990: 1–30, 366–417; Regan 1992.

AUTHOR AND AUTHORITY

'Author' is now commonly used to refer to an individual writer who is supposed to be the ultimate creator of some especially valued text, often of a LITERARY kind. A more all-purpose and less prestigious term is **writer**. Generally speaking, 'author' is to 'writer' as **artist** is to 'artisan': authors and artists are assumed to be supreme and sublime individualists; writers and artisans to be practical, humdrum and generally serviceable (see previous entry). Such a view of the author/artist is problematic, however. It is also a relatively modern and in some respects predominantly Western view. In earlier periods, as in many other cultures today, we find that the concept of authorship was and is far more tied up with notions of collective 'authority' and received wisdom. In Chaucer, for instance, 'auctors' (authors) were those who followed and in large measure *translated previous 'auctoritees' (authorities, sources). Meanwhile, many contemporary African, Caribbean and Australasian writers draw upon corresponding traditions and roles voicing public rather than private concerns. The dominant modern Western view of 'the author' must therefore be seen relatively, both historically and cross-culturally. It is characterised by five main assumptions:

1   the assumed primacy of the individual and of her or his experience as a guarantee of authenticity and authority (this is often expressed in the popular belief that each author works in splendid or miserable isolation);

2   an emphasis on the written word, as well as a generally 'logocentric' view of the creative process of composition;

3   the belief that authors make things up out of their own heads and in that sense are 'original';

4   the related belief that authors are very special, talented people and in extreme cases 'geniuses';

5   the view that all readers have to do is be receptive and reverential.

Some people, however, hold quite different views of the nature and function of authorship in particular, and of the processes of creativity and cultural production in general. They would counter each of the above assumptions by emphasising:

1a   the primarily social role of the author/artist in representing common and collective experiences, often appealing to precedent and tradition; also the fact that writers, performers and artists may work in close association with other people (editors, directors, etc.), even to the point of joint production;

2a   the pervasive interpenetration of cultural activities across many media (e.g., illustrated book, performance pieces, theatre, film), with the written word sometimes playing a minor role;

3a   the fact that authors are *reproducers* and always in some sense inherit, *mediate and transform previously existing materials (i.e. the current resources of language, literature and culture); they do not create out of nothing or simply 'out of their heads';

4a   the belief that everyone constantly communicates things of significance and worth – they do not need to be special to do this;

5a   an insistence that readers, audiences and viewers also have a crucial role to play in the negotiation and construction of meanings and values – they can be active participants too.

POSTSTRUCTURALISTS, moreover, would argue that there is never a fixed, ultimately identifiable 'source' or 'origin' for anything. There is therefore no single 'author' or absolute 'authority'. POSTMODERNISTS, meanwhile, would add that the very notion of 'authorship' has a narrowly literary as well as quaintly archaic ring to it: most media production now is palpably collaborative and decreasingly dependent on the written or printed word. 'Authenticity' (i.e. genuineness), they would further claim, has been dissolved into a succession of competing images and persistently plural points of view.

For all the above reasons, the question of whether the author (i.e., the concept of the author) is 'dead' or 'alive' is frequently raised in contemporary literary and cultural studies. Viewing the matter historically, we are also obliged to think about such matters as the impact of literary copyright and the nominal ownership of printed works from the seventeenth century onwards. Before that, writers did not 'own' their printed words and consequently could not derive direct profit from them. More recently, we may wonder what place 'authors-as-individual-creators' have in the collaborative wor(l)ds of the Internet and the hypermedia. This in turn may prompt us to revalue traditional, anonymous or collective cultural practices such as folktales, oral histories and anecdotes. In social and political terms, we may ask how far we see writers as isolable and self-creating individuals or as social roles and ideological **identities** interacting with others. In PSYCHOLOGICAL terms, we may ask how far we see writers as sources of *expression or sites of *repression. Related questions arise about LANGUAGE in particular and CULTURE in general. How far are we the active users (the 'authors') of our own words and worlds, and how far do they use and in effect 'author' us?

ACTIVITY

Authors, Writers, Producers, Directors, Performers, Practitioners ... ?
Which of the following are commonly thought to be produced by 'an author':
(a) classic novel; (b) pulp fiction; (c) computer manual; (d) sonnet; (e) magazine advert; (f) TV soap opera; (g) theatrical performance; (h) movie; (i) news story; (j) greetings card message; (k) your last essay? In each case consider everyone who might be involved in the processes of (re)production and what other terms might be substituted or added.

Go on to select one anonymous work and one work with a known author and consider how important it is to know precisely who wrote or performed it. Do you put different questions to or expect different things from work by A. Nonymous?

(Comparison between 'Maiden in the mor lay' (5.1.2 a) and Wordsworth's 'I wandered lonely . . . ', (5.4.3 a) works well here.)

DISCUSSION

the birth of the reader must be at the cost of the death of the author.
Roland Barthes, *The Death of the Author* (1968) (1977: 148)

Also see: 2.2; PSYCHOLOGICAL; POSTSTRUCTURALIST and POSTMODERNIST; **addresser**; *artist; **auto/biography**; **canon**; *narrator; **subject . . . role**; **writing . . . rewriting**.

READING: *Introductory:* Fowler 1987: 15–17; Moon 1992: 1–2; Hawthorn 1994: 11–12; Graddol and Boyd-Barrett 1994: 161–99. *Advanced:* Barthes 1977: 142–8; Barthes and Foucault in Lodge 1988: 167–72, 196–210; Parrinder 1991.

AUTO/BIOGRAPHY AND LIFE-WRITING: SELF AND OTHER

It is conventional to distinguish between *auto*biography (a life of the *self*) and biography (a life of an*other*). Conventional, too, is the expectation that autobiography will be written in the first person singular by an 'I' who is both subject and object of the narrative, while biography will be written about a third person 'she' or 'he' who is quite distinct from a more or less invisible narrator. Often such conventional distinctions hold: the autobiography and biography sections of large bookstores are full of examples. However, there are also plenty of instances where writers choose to write about themselves as or through third persons (James Joyce's *A Portrait of the Artist* and Gertrude Stein's *The Autobiography of Alice B. Toklas* are famous modern examples). It is therefore important to recognise that there is a continuous and complex relationship between writing about oneself and writing about another. The processes are closely analogous, even if not identical. Both autobiographers and biographers select and combine elements as they see fit. The result in both cases is '*a* life' (i.e., one of many possible lives) not '*the* life' (i.e., the one and only definitive life). Nor is autobiography necessarily any more 'subjective' and biography any more 'objective': both can be equally (un)reliable and (im)partial. There is thus no necessary link – though one is often assumed – between literary fiction and auto-biography on the one hand and historical fact and biography on the other hand. It all depends upon what kind of 'truth' the reader is prepared to accept.

More generally, it also depends upon the notion of **self** and **other** in play. In PSYCHOLOGICAL terms, for instance, the self is split into a variety of roles: *conscious and *unconscious, *expressive and *repressive. In later Freudian terms there is ceaseless negotiation between the 'I', the 'above-I' and the 'that (other)' (ego, super-ego and id). *Lacan characterises the psyche as a site of 'lack', Kristeva sees it as a place of *desire. Meanwhile, in socio-political terms the person can be seen not as a fixed entity but as a changing and changeable **identity** (see **subject**). Who 'I am', 'we are' and 's/he is' then depends as much upon social-historical conditions as upon psychological predispositions. Most pointedly, in a 'them and us' situation, this comes down to who counts as one of us (identified with self) and who counts as one of them (identified as other).

For all the above reasons, many contemporary theorists and practitioners prefer to talk more capaciously of **life-writing** or use the slashed form 'auto/biography'. Both leave open the matter of precisely who is writing whose life. (For much the same reasons, some POSTMODERNIST writers and discourse analysts prefer to talk of all writing as **faction** rather than some as 'fiction' and some as 'fact' (see **realism**); or of **hi/story** so as to suggest the radical continuity between forms of 'story' and 'history' (see **narrative**).) The term 'life-writing' also has the advantage of all verbal nouns in that it implies an activity as well as a thing: lives in the writing as well as already written. An emphasis on 'lives' as things we actively construct and do not just have constructed for us is especially important in the increasing numbers of critical-creative courses in life-writing. These encourage participants to write their own and other people's lives even while they analyse previous attempts at auto/biography.

The latter may range from St Augustine's or Rousseau's *Confessions* to magazine 'True Life Confessions', and from Johnson's *Lives of the Poets* through Pepys's *Diary* to Frame's *To the Is-land* (see 5.2.1 d). Letters and postcards, and even personal ads, c.v.s and interviews may also be grist to the auto/biographical mill. All these may be recognised as actual and potential 'lives', however apparently finished or fragmented. They also supply abundant models for imitation and adaptation as well as analysis.

The implications of life-writing for English, Literary and Cultural Studies are profound. Whereas earlier PRACTICAL and NEW CRITICS assiduously rejected both the autobiographical and biographical dimensions of a work as irrelevant (instances of an 'intentional fallacy'; see p. 79), many modern critics insist on the complex interconnectedness of the lives and works of both writers and readers. FEMINIST and POSTCOLONIAL writers, in particular, are committed to rediscovering, recovering and, if necessary, *revisioning previously neglected or marginalised lives. In this they are often indebted to PSYCHOLOGY for interiorised images of selves which lay claim to kinds of anthropological and historical truth, even where an actual person has been 'hidden from history'. The current resurgence of novels styled on journals and letters is one symptom of this. Increased attention to *slave narratives is another (see 5.2.2). In fact, auto/biography and life-writing are probably among the most lively (and lucrative) of contemporary **genres**, both inside and outside academic circles.

ACTIVITY

Whose 'life' is it anyway?
It is possible to look for and find (or avoid and ignore) 'autobiographical' aspects of any writer's work. It is also possible to recognise or resist the 'autobiographical' dimension of any reader's reading. With these propositions in mind, consider the various auto/biographical criteria involved in your own reading of a specific text by an identified author. Who is writing and reading whom? (Suggested focuses in Part Five include: Clare (5.1.5); Freud and 'Dora' (5.3.1 d); Dickinson (5.4.5 d); letters and diaries (5.2.1) slave narratives (5.2.2) and contemporary 'i'dentities (5.4.7 g).)

Go on to reflect upon the various constructions of your own 'selves' for 'others' when writing in genres such as diary, letter, postcard and academic essay, or when talking over coffee with friends, in seminar or interview. Who is it that writes and speaks your 'lives'?

DISCUSSION

An individual's origin is of great relevance to the way he or she experiences the subject [English] [. . .] but for many the formative experience is of discovering identity by crossing boundaries.
Colin Evans, *English People: The Experience of Teaching and Learning English in British Universities* (1993: 194)

Also see: 1.5.6; PSYCHOLOGICAL; **addresser . . . addressee; author; narrative in hi/story . . . ; realism . . . metafiction; subject . . . identities**.

READING: *Introductory:* Cuddon 1992: 68–73; Abrams 1993: 14–16; Wellek and Warren 1963: 75–93; *Advanced:* Spengemann 1986; Benstock 1988; Ward-Jouve 1991; Marcus 1994; Plasa and Ring 1994.

BIBLES, HOLY BOOKS AND MYTHS

The word 'bible' derives from Greek *biblia*, meaning 'little books'. The Bible (definite article, capitalised and singular) is the name of a particular – though to some extent variable – collection of books bearing witness to Jewish (Old Testament) and Christian (New Testament) history and belief. Both parts of the Bible have supplied myths, stories, topics, themes and allusions which pervade Western, Eastern and global literature and the arts. They have been used as the primary texts for teaching *literacy and, indeed, have often been its main object. They have been *translated from and into more languages than any other books in the world. And they have been used to underpin and **authorise** a wide variety of belief systems and social orders, not all of which are consistent with one another. (For instance, Jews see Jesus Christ as simply another prophet not the son of God; while Catholics, Protestants, Liberation Theologists, Jehovah's Witnesses and assorted tele-evangelists cite the same or different parts of the New Testament to very various social and spiritual ends.) At any rate, the Jewish and Christian faiths have been so culturally pervasive and politically contentious that it is almost impossible to read anything in English from before the mid-twentieth century (and much after it), whether from Britain, America, Africa, the Caribbean or Australasia, without encountering direct or indirect evidence of biblical influence. From the early seventh-century 'Dream of the Rood' and the fourteenth-century 'Maiden in the mor lay' (5.1.2 a – a song about Mary?), through Chaucer, Shakespeare, Milton, Behn, Defoe, Austen, Byron, Dickens and T.S. Eliot, up to and beyond Queen's 'Bohemian Rhapsody' (5.1.10 – 'Beelzebub has a devil set aside for me . . . '), the strains and stresses of two of the world's major religions and their founding books can be heard.

The implications for students of English LANGUAGE, LITERATURE and CULTURE are prodigious. It is necessary

♦   to be at least acquainted with such biblical stories as the creation of the world and of Adam and Eve, Cain and Abel, Abraham and Isaac, Noah's Flood (e.g., 5.3.2 a), the Nativity, Crucifixion and Resurrection of Christ, all the way through to the Last Judgement ('Doomsday');

♦   to recognise that myriad phrases such as 'Let there be . . . ', 'In the beginning was . . . ' and being 'worth one's salt', as well as whole styles of speech, derive from the Bible (often from specific *translations such as the Tyndall or the 'Authorised' versions);

♦   to be aware that many of the dominant models of oppositions between good and evil, heaven and hell, body and soul, light and dark – as well as dominant representations of men and women, believers and pagans/heathens – are based upon appeals to biblical authority and Judaeo-Christian doctrine.

At the same time it is important not to concentrate exclusively on the Bible. There are many other 'holy books' as well as whole oral and artistic traditions which celebrate other religious systems and social moralities. Myths, stories, rituals and representations may also be identified with specifically Greek, Roman, Germanic, Hindu, Muslim, Buddhist, African and Aboriginal belief systems. These too have impinged upon and helped configure the languages, literatures and cultures we call 'English', as they have many others. So these too at least need to be acknowledged as relevant for all of us engaged in English Studies. Such adjustments are especially important in that the subject is still sometimes casually assumed to have a Christianising mission as well as a partly Christian history. After all, English as an educational subject cultivated by Church and state partly grew out of Christian theology and Sunday and Mission schools as well as Dissenting academies. It has thus often been identified with various forms of Christian humanism, from Matthew Arnold to the NEW CRITICS (see 1.5.1 and 1.5.4). As far as the Bible and English Studies are concerned, a number of further distinctions and qualifications therefore need to be made.

'The Bible' is itself not one but many languages, literatures and cultures. (Remember *biblia* = 'books'.) The Old Testament, initially written in Hebrew, consists of a wide range of **genres** representing the historic mission of the Jews: mythic and epic narratives (Genesis to Exodus); chronicles (Kings); laws, moral codes and proverbs (Leviticus, Ecclesiasticus, Proverbs); prayers and love songs, sacred and erotic (Psalms, Song of Solomon); and lives of individual heroes and prophets (Job, Jonah, Ruth). The New Testament, initially written in Greek, also consists of many different genres: multiple narratives of the life of Christ (the four Gospels); extended letters (the epistles of St Paul to the early churches), and a mystical and highly poetic vision of apocalypse (the Book of Revelations). Moreover, various other books have been hailed as either *authentic or 'apocryphal' by different sects at different times. They have accordingly been counted in or out of various **canons** of holy books. The so-called Gospel of Nicodemus, for instance, was accepted as a faithful account of Christ's harrowing of hell during the early Middle Ages, only to be dropped later. Roman Catholics still accept more books as canonical than do Protestants. Meanwhile, the Church of Jesus Christ and Latter Day Saints has its own special Bible-sized extra book, the *Book of Mormon* (1830).

*Bibles have existed in many different *translations and adaptations and have served many different functions.* The Bible exists primarily as 'holy *scripture*' (i.e. sacred *writing*). Consequently, for much of its history, most people have not actually *read* the Bible at all. The *illiterate majority have had selections from it read *to* them, and represented *for* them by clerics and artists in sermons, prayers, hymns, paintings, stained glass and carvings. The medieval Mystery Plays were one such highly dramatic and visual representation (see 5.3.2 a). Indeed, the story of the Bible's transmission is generally one of a tension between a literate priestly caste and a more – or increasingly less – illiterate populace. The chief Bible of the Middle Ages, for instance, was called the Vulgate (i.e. Common) Bible of St Jerome (AD 405). However, this was in Latin and only 'common' to those educated in reading that language. Thereafter Bibles in the various European vernaculars began to appear: in England, notably, the Wycliffite version (*c.*1380); Tyndale's and Coverdale's (1526, 1535); the 'Geneva' Bible (1560) the so-called 'authorised' King James version (1611; largely based on the three former versions and itself revised 1881–5); and the New English, Good News (American) and New International versions (1970, 1976, 1979). Parts of the Gospels in particular have also been translated into varieties ranging from Glaswegian **dialect** to Jamaican *creole. Musical, stage and film adaptations range from Handel's *Messiah* (1742) to the 1960s' rock musicals *Joseph *and his Amazing Technicolor Dreamcoat* and *Godspell*, and Monty Python's parodic *Life of Brian* (1979). (For translations and versions of Psalm 137, see 5.4.2.)

There are many other 'holy books', myths and belief systems that we also need to acknowledge. English Literature – and even more so Literature in English – is far from exclusively Christian in its religious roots and emphases. It is more properly conceived as a cross-cultural, and specifically cross-religious, hybrid. Earlier English texts are teeming with CLASSICAL gods and heroes and their associated myths, legends and stories, from Mars and Venus to Zeus and Leda (e.g., 5.1.7). The chief sources are Ovid's *Metamorphoses*, Homer's *Iliad* and *Odyssey* and Virgil's *Aeneid*. Germanic and Celtic gods and heroes also have a large part to play, notably in Anglo-Saxon poetry (e.g., the epic *Beowulf*) and in later medieval Arthurian legends. From a narrowly Christian point of view all these materials are pagan or heathen. Nonetheless, they freely blend and sometimes contend with the official religion of court, church and state. Evidently they supplied people with imaginary resources for exploring other world-views and other moral frames. A few instances from Part Five will help confirm how various these are. Chaucer shows himself well aware of the presence and obviously felt the threat of 'hethen' religions to the east (5.1.2 b). Shakespeare attempts to represent an encounter between a Western European Christian gentleman-cum-magician (Prospero) and various benign and malign nature spirits from the Americas (Ariel and Caliban; 5.3.2 b). Defoe and Behn bear witness to the collisions and coalescences of Western European, African and American cultures, religions and il/literacies (5.2.2 a–b). Pope reveals how the outward shows and tokens of Christianity may be commodified along with the trappings of any other religion or ritual (5.1.4 b). Byron blithely mimics and mocks religious forms that Milton took so seriously – yet himself assiduously blended with elements of classical mythology (5.1.4 a and d). Kipling shows himself both fascinated by and excluded from Muslim funeral practices (5.2.4 b). Conrad is both attracted and appalled by the image of African rites he conjures up at the 'heart of darkness' (5.2.4 c) – an image which is grotesquely inverted and inflated by Caryl Churchill some time later (5.3.4 e). More recently, we may readily turn to a widening array of writings which openly celebrate and revalue religions and belief systems which the colonial imposition of Christianity had obscured or downgraded. Examples represented here include: Nigerian Igbo and Caribbean funeral rites (Achebe and Nichols, 5.2.4 f and 5.4.5 e); myths and legends from Australian Aborigine/Koori (Marshall-Stoneking, 5.4.4 e); New Zealand Maori (Frame 5.2.1 d); the Caribbean (Scott, 5.4.4 d) and Nigerian Yoruba (Tutuola, 5.2.4 e). The palpably *oral and *performance aspects of many of these pieces also remind us that many of these religions and cultures have not depended upon scriptures and 'bibles/books' at all.

*The religious beliefs and *ideological positions of readers and critics necessarily affect what books they *value* – 'holy' or otherwise. Many of the first New Critics were Christians based in the American Southern States. They tended to assume the centrality of the Bible along with the authority of its ultimate **author**, God. All this is in line with their devotion to literary texts as 'verbal icons' and their commitment to a traditional canon. Many later critics take issue with them, however. POST-STRUCTURALISTS contest the absolute authority of all books and would tend to celebrate the sheer plurality of materials and the plethora of discontinuous historical moments which make the Bible not one but many. MARXISTS may see the Bible as an instrument of social control wielded by a privileged caste of literate clergy complicit in the maintenance of social hierarchy. But they may also recognise its potential for constructive dissent and emancipation, especially as invoked by political radicals outside as well as within the ranks of the clergy. FEMINISTS would add that most of the clergy were male and the social hierarchy was patriarchal, even while recognising that the Church often offered one of the few opportunities for women to get formally educated and organised. Feminist readings of the Bible therefore tend to draw attention to the ways in which female stereotypes are, for better and worse, reinforced or revised: Eve, Delilah and Jezebel as temptresses and deceivers; Noah's wife as shrewish gossip or faithful female companion (see 5.3.2 a); Mary as patiently suffering mother; Martha as a good housewife; Ruth as patient servant and wife; the whore of Babylon, etc. Feminists also look to other religious traditions and myths for more powerful role models, e.g., Lilith, who according to the *Talmud* was the strong-willed wife of Adam before Eve, or Cassandra, the female prophetess of Troy. POSTCOLONIAL critics also have their say. They often observe the 'white mask' routinely placed by Western European writers and artists upon the faces of Christ and his parents, notwithstanding the fact the holy family were Palestinian Jews and presumably dark-skinned and perhaps African by background. But such critics may also draw attention to the potentially productive and emancipatory aspects of the Christianising mission: its resistance to as well as complicity with slavery; and its double-edged legacy of *literacy, spreading the power of a printed word that was not always wielded by the black reader in her or his own right/write. Meanwhile, the continuing case of Salman Rushdie is a stark reminder that none of this is a simple matter of black and white. As I write, the author of *The Satanic Verses* (see 5.4.2) is still under sentence of death by Muslim fundamentalists because of alleged blasphemy against the word and spirit of *their* holy books (the Koran and associated apocrypha). This too is a part of the ongoing history of writing in English.

ACTIVITIES

(a)   *Same Psalm?* Compare the various translations and adaptations of the opening of Psalm 137 (5.4.2). Add a version of your own if you wish.

(b)   *The Bible as Literature.* Select a passage from the Old or New Testaments and analyse it in terms of language, genre and narrative or dramatic structures.

(c)   *Un/authorised versions.* Investigate the precise handling of the material in a text which has an overtly biblical theme or frame of reference (e.g., *Noah's Flood* 5.3.2 a; *Paradise Lost* 5.1.4 a; *The Vision of Judgement* 5.1.4 d). What has been added, removed or modified compared with the Bible?

(d)   *Cross-cultural tensions.* Concentrate on a text which exposes the tensions between one religion or belief system and another (e.g., Chaucer 5.1.2 b; Shakespeare 5.3.2 b; Kipling 5.2.4 b; Nichols 5.4.5 e) or a text which explores a religion or belief system unfamiliar to you (maybe Tutuola 5.2.4 e, or Marshall-Stoneking 5.4.4 e).

DISCUSSION

    (i)   You just can't expect knowledge of the Bible any more. Adverts, pop and sport, sure – and maybe the odd Maori myth. But not the Bible . . .

Retiring university English lecturer, New Zealand 1996

    (ii)   Bibles are, by their very nature, partisan. As that plural suggests, there are many bibles, even in English, and each is the product of a particular interest group – whether religious, commercial or, increasingly nowadays, both.

Robert Carroll and Stephen Prickett (eds) The Bible: Authorised King James Version with Apocrypha (1997: preface)

Also see: CLASSICS; THEOLOGY; POSTCOLONIALISM AND MULTICULTURALISM; **author(ity)**; **canon**; **discourse**; **narrative in hi/story**.

READING: *Introductory:* Wynne-Davis 1989: 353–4; Ousby 1992: 83–5; Prickett in Coyle *et al.* 1990: 653–64, 951–62; Carroll and Prickett 1997. *Advanced:* Frye 1957; Barthes 1957; Said 1978, 1993; Spivak 1987; Bhabha 1994.

CANON AND CLASSIC

'The canon' refers to a body of privileged and prescribed texts which are assumed to be of 'classic' status and therefore automatically worthy of study. The matter of what texts are to be admitted to the canon, or of whether there ever has been or should be a fixed canon at all, has become especially contentious in English Studies over the past two decades. So, relatedly, has the matter of whether texts can be distinguished as 'classic' and/or 'popular'. Often this comes down to the matter of what counts as LITERATURE, and whether we need that category either.

    Canon derives from a Greek word meaning either 'measuring rod' or 'list'. Both meanings were taken over and eventually conflated by early Christianity. 'Canon law' referred to rules or decrees of the Church; 'the canon' was a list of those books of the Bible officially accepted as genuine along with, later, those works of the Church fathers approved as **authoritative** and orthodox. All these were studiously distinguished from *apocryphal* works, which were reckoned to be fake, and *heretical* works, which were reckoned blasphemous and put on 'the forbidden list'. Since the split at the Reformation, the Roman Catholic Church has continued to recognise as canonical eleven books of the Bible that Protestants reject as apocryphal. Saints, meanwhile, are formally 'canonised' once they are added·to the official list of the (s)elect. From the outset, then, whether conceived as official rules or as lists, canons and canonisation are characterised by at least two features: concerted institutional control and a high degree of inclusivity/exclusivity.

    The notion of the canon as a list of *secular* privileged books dates from the seventeenth century. Initially it referred to those works accepted as genuinely by a particular author (e.g., 'the Shakespeare canon'). More recently, debate over what shall be recognised, celebrated and taught as 'the canon of English Literature' has generated a great deal of heat if not always a lot of light. Most immediately, this comes down to the practical matter of who and what shall be 'set texts' on courses in schools, colleges and universities. The institutions involved include:

1) exam and syllabus-setting committees, 2) lecturers and teachers
3) publishers, editors, marketing managers, 4) librarians and stock-purchasers
5) critics and reviewers, 6) students and other book purchasers

At the critical and *ideological core there is invariably a complex of debates over what shall be deemed to constitute the national heritage or international identity of England, Britain, America or Australia. At the same time there are contributory, often conflicting, debates on the nature of the ENGLISH language, **standard** or otherwise, as well as argument over precisely what literature might or should be. The outcome of all these debates varies greatly. It very much depends on whether there is a predominantly monocultural or MULTICULTURAL conception of what it means to be 'English', 'American', 'Australian', etc. It also depends upon how capacious is the notion of 'standards' and 'literature' in play. There are pressingly practical dimensions to the problem too. On the one hand, considerations of cost, copyright, availability and sheer familiarity often weigh heavily in favour of the well-known (if not always well-loved) text. On the other hand, fresh texts (old as well as new) are brought to prominence and people do welcome a change if it seems to be in a promising direction. Either way, the assumption or assertion that 'the canon' (singular and definitive) has always simply been 'there', a universal and timeless entity, is a convenient but misleading myth. 'English Literature' itself has hardly been around as an educational subject for more than a century (see 1.5). How could any of its texts be that 'set'?!

The concept **classic** tends to work in tandem with that of canon. Writers and their works get dubbed 'classic(s)' when they are reckoned first- (not second- or third-) class. It is also usually insisted that they have 'stood the test of time' (though this still leaves us the question of precisely how long, whose time, and what kinds of test). Moreover, 'classics' invariably tend to be defined in contradistinction to other work which is labelled variously as 'minor', 'common' or (underscoring an implied elitism) *popular. The ancient writer Gellius, for instance, talks of the *classicus scriptor* (classic writer) who by definition is *non proletarius* (not common/proletarian) (see *OED* 'classic'). In fact, this value-laden and socially hierarchical sense of classic was carried over from Greek and Latin so that from the sixteenth century onwards 'the Classics' became the usual term to refer to the study of Greek and Latin culture as a whole (as distinct from later vernacular cultures). Thus in many a neo-classical battle of the books, 'classics' were invariably identified with 'the ancients' as opposed to 'the moderns'. However, it was not long before vernacular writers such as Dante in Italy and Chaucer, Spenser, Shakespeare and Milton in England were also hailed as classics. This especially tended to happen with poets in so far as they could be shown to use 'classical' (i.e. Greek and Latin) models *and* to represent the beginnings of modern national literary traditions. In this way the appearance of a continuous tradition was forged between older and newer literatures and social orders.

FEMINISTS, however, have been quick to point out that these were largely patriarchal orders; and POSTCOLONIAL critics have added that they were white and Western European too. For, until very recently, the charge that the traditional literary canon was largely stocked with classics by '*Dead White European Males*' (*DWEMs* for short) was hard to deny. MARXISTS, meanwhile, would insist on inserting a class component into the equation (perhaps 'DWE Middle-to-Upper Class Males'). In all these cases the results have been both radical and far-reaching. Not only have there been concerted critiques of previously established writers with respect to gender, ethnicity and class; there has also been a prodigious amount of work in the rediscovery and reappraisal of neglected traditions of women's, black and working-class writing (For further information on these, turn to sections 2.6, 2.7. and 2.8.) At any rate, it is now necessary to think in terms of opposed or alternative traditions, and to talk of *plural* or *open canons*: lists of texts and lines of development which were previously ignored or crossed out and now cross and re-cross according to the logics of **difference and similarity** and **self and other**.

But even this is only one side of the canon debate. Strictly, the other side is no canon at all. A symptom of this is that during the twentieth century it has become increasingly common to talk of many more things than authors and books as 'classics'. In the MEDIA and in *popular CULTURE generally, we readily speak of 'classic' cars, races, films, pop songs and soap operas. Indeed, in POSTMODERN discourses 'classic' has come to mean little more than 'something that used to be popular' (or more cynically, 'something being commercially recycled'). However, in principle, such a charge may be as easily levelled at the 'recycling' of Shakespeare on stage and course syllabus as at the latest TV re-run of *Roseanne* or a re-mix of 'Bohemian Rhapsody'. Indeed, whether you are inclined or required to treat any of these materials as 'canonical', 'classic' or otherwise is very much the point at issue. It is also the point of the openly ambiguous invitation to 'fire canons yourself' in the activity which follows, and again at greater leisure in section 4.6.

ACTIVITY

What *ten* texts would *you* put in a first-year course introducing a degree programme called 'English Literature', 'Literature in English', 'English Studies' or 'Literary and Cultural Studies'? (You choose the course title and emphasis too.) Go on to review and perhaps revise your choices and combinations of text in the light of the criteria below. Have you 'covered' or sought to represent instances of:

♦   mega-genres such as poetry, drama and prose (including the novel and short story)?
♦   genres ancient and modern such as comedy and tragedy, epic and lyric; auto/biography, science fiction and romance?
♦   writings and performances in English from, say, Australia, New Zealand, India, Africa, America, the Caribbean, England, Ireland, Scotland, Wales?
♦   influential texts in English translation; e.g., by Ibsen, Brecht, Allende, Márquez?
♦   various periods and movements: fifth century to the present, Anglo-Saxon to postmodern?
♦   various social groups distinguished by gender, class and ethnicity?
♦   various media – spoken, written, printed, audio-visual?
♦   any other category you consider important?

Go on to consider the possibility of introductory courses based not so much on 'set' texts but on, say, skills and knowledges, techniques, theories, approaches, practices of reading and writing and research (see Part Four for some possibilities).

DISCUSSION

(i)   The great English novelists are Jane Austen, George Eliot, Henry James and
       Joseph Conrad – to stop for the moment at that comparatively safe point in
       history.
               Frank R. Leavis, *The Great Tradition* (1948) (1972: 9, opening sentence)

(ii) The challenge, then, is not simply to supplant the 'ecclesiastical' canon with the
       'emergent' transgressive canon, but to rethink the relation of both on the basis
       of what it means to be 'cultured' or indeed educated.
               Homi Bhabha, *Times Higher Education Supplement* (24 January 1992)

Also see: 1.5.3; 1.5.10; 1.6; LITERATURE; **genre; poetry and word-play**.

READING: *Introductory:* Durant and Fabb 1990: 9–13; Sanders 1994:1–15; Guillory in
Lentricchia and McLaughlin 1995: 233–49; Strickland in Coyle *et al.* 1990: 696–707;
Maybin and Mercer 1996: 235–74; Butler *et al.* in Walder 1990: 9–41. *Advanced:* Lauter
1991; Gates 1995.

CHARACTER AND CHARACTERISATION

Character can be provisionally defined as 'the construction of a fictional figure', and
characterisation as 'the literary, linguistic and cultural means whereby that figure is
constructed'. Character is a central concept in traditional approaches to narrative,
especially novels, plays and film. That is why the meaning and value of the term are
often merely assumed or asserted. There is also a common tendency simply to
describe fictional characters as though they really existed and to forget that the
matter at issue is often the *kinds* of character represented and the *process* of
characte*risation*. For all these reasons it is important to grasp the various things
that may be implied by character, and to recognise that characterisation is both a
creative and a critical activity. It is also important to know that many approaches are
critical of the very concept of character as such.

   Character derives from a Greek word meaning 'to engrave, to inscribe' and
currently has three main meanings:

1   the distinctive nature, disposition and traits of a real person (e.g., 'My children
       have/are quite different characters');
2   the particular role played by a fictional figure in a novel, film or play (e.g., 'Hamlet
       is a character in Shakespeare's play of that name');
3   a letter of the alphabet or other graphic device (e.g., 'The printer picked up each
       character and put it in its box').

Together, all three meanings remind us that 'a character' can be everything from a
real person (whatever we mean by that) to a fragment of printed language – a
personal identity and/or a textual entity. The first two definitions also remind us that
discussions of character inevitably require us to negotiate the relation between **real**
and **imagined** persons, and between **fact** and **fiction**. One answer is to treat all

characters, 'real' or 'imagined', as the products of **discourse** and **representation**. It then depends upon the precise frames of reference (physical, biological, psychological, social, historical, philosophical, etc.) within which we construct our notions of reality and what it is to be a person. And this in turn obliges us to review the relations between words and the world, and between people and their environments. More particularly, it obliges us to engage with relations between people's personal **stories** (including **auto/biographies**) and more public and general **histories**. Indeed, if people are in reality already 'playing parts' and adopting psychological and social **roles**, it becomes a fascinating question just how far we can distinguish characters in LITERATURE from characters in the rest of life. What *are* the differences between playing the roles of, say, father, son, partner and lecturer in a film and playing those roles in fact? To be sure, there are crucial differences of consequence and responsibility. But formally and ideologically – in terms of how and why we play these roles – there is obviously much interdependence and mutual influence. 'She feels as if she's in a play – she is anyway', as the Beatles put it in 'Penny Lane'.

For these reasons not all critics are happy with the notion of 'character', as such. MARXIST, FEMINIST and POSTCOLONIAL critics often prefer to to talk about people more as 'sites of struggle', 'subjectivities', 'ideological subjects', 'identities', 'representatives of dominant or muted positions', 'instances of competing discourses', 'voices', 'bodies', 'stereotypes', 'antitypes', etc. Character in a traditional sense is not a central and effective part of their critical lexicon. Indeed, for many contemporary critics the term and concept 'character' is far too tainted by assumptions about the unity and sanctity of 'the individual' and the alleged universality of *human nature to be of much use. For such critics the concept character may serve as a point of departure, but it is rarely a point of arrival. Resistance to and *deconstruction of 'character' is even more emphatic among writers with a POST/STRUCTURALIST or a POSTMODERNIST bent. They have little time for a construct so tied to notions of the individual as a pre-given centre or for notions of 'convincing characters' tied to limiting notions of **realism**.

Notwithstanding such a barrage of alternatives, certain traditional ways of describing character and characterisation prove remarkably resilient and, if handled with care, serviceable. Characters may thus still be described as:

- *rounded or flat*, following E.M. Forster's *Aspects of the Novel* (1927): 'rounded' characters are interiorised, psychologically complex and develop (e.g., Paul Morel in *Sons and Lovers*, Seth in *Beloved*); 'flat' characters are known through exterior appearance, are apparently simpler and perhaps predictable – they are often also called *caricatures* (e.g., Jonson's Volpone, Dickens' Mr Pickwick).
- *individuals* and/or *types* (on closer inspection, most characters turn out to be of various kinds). Chaucer's and Shakespeare's major characters are often described as a mixture.
- *character-narrators* and/or *character-actors*: telling the tale and/or being told by it (Jane in *Jane Eyre* is a character-narrator, whereas Edward Rochester is a character-actor; these relations are reversed in *Wide Sargasso Sea*: see 5.2.3 d–e).
- **points of view** that switch, get mixed or compounded, according to the various narrative and dramatic strategies in play (Jane Austen and Beckett represent what may be termed, respectively, 'realist' and 'modernist' ways with character, narration and point of view).

But whatever terms you use to describe characters, it will be clear that the emphasis should largely be on character*isation*: the *kinds* of character and the *ways* in which characters are constructed. Crucially, from a critical point of view this is as much a matter of how the reader *sees* the characters as how the writer *says* them. Meanwhile, as many of the approaches referred to earlier suggest, it is sometimes arguable whether we should talk of 'characters' as such at all.

ACTIVITY

Concentrate on a group of figures from a novel, play, film, auto/biography, history or news story and suggest how they might be approached by (a) a MARXIST; (b) a FEMINIST; (c) a POSTCOLONIAL critic. How compatible are such approaches with analyses of characterisation based upon, say, 'rounded' and 'flat' characters, 'caricatures', 'individuals' and 'types', 'point of view' (see above)? Which critical terms and frames do you prefer?

(Kipling's 'Muhammad Din' is a suggested focus in 5.2.4 b.)

DISCUSSION

(i) Character is arguably the most important single component of the novel.

David Lodge, *The Art of Fiction* (1992: 67)

(ii) Characters are imaginary identities constructed through reports of appearance, action, speech and thought.

Brian Moon, *Literary Terms: A Practical Glossary* (1992: 10)

Also see: **auto/biography; narrative; foreground . . . point of view; subject . . . role**.

READING: *Introductory:* Fowler 1987: 27–9; Lodge 1992: 66–9; Moon 1992: 7–10; Forster 1927. *Advanced:* Booth 1961; Culler 1975: 230–40; Toolan 1988: 90–148.

COMEDY AND TRAGEDY, CARNIVAL AND THE ABSURD

Briefly, comedy is what makes us laugh and has a happy ending; tragedy is what makes us sad and has an unhappy ending; carnival is a kind of riotous festival, and the absurd is what perplexes and confounds us. All these terms offer ways of categorising *kinds* or **genres** of experience. They are applied chiefly but not exclusively to LITERATURE, and chiefly but not exclusively to **drama**. Comedy and tragedy are primarily associated with CLASSICAL and *neo-classical approaches to drama derived from Aristotle's *Poetics* (*c.* 330 BC). 'Carnival' and 'the absurd' have more specifically modern antecedents. Carnival and the carnivalesque owe their critical currency to *Bakhtin's interest in popular festival forms in literature, notably in his *Rabelais and his World* (1968). The absurd and absurdism are most often encountered in the phrase 'the theatre of the absurd' and still owe their currency to a highly influential book of that name by Martin Esslin (1961). The three kinds of concept gathered in this entry are on different trajectories in different frames of reference. They therefore entail different **aesthetics** and politics. Nonetheless, it is highly instructive to approach them as a relatable cluster; for they are commonly used to map, and sometimes to redraw, the same textual terrain.

Comedy and tragedy are braced against one another in a clear hierarchy by Aristotle: comedy inferior, tragedy superior. This order and emphasis are deliberately reversed in the present entry. **Comedy** derives from Greek *komos-oidos*, meaning 'revel-song', and initially referred to events associated with fertility rituals and the festival of Dionysus. According to Aristotle, who treats it slightly and slightingly (*Poetics*, Chapters 4 and 5), comedy has the following ingredients:

- *happy endings* and an overall progression from disorder to order, chaos to harmony;
- *characters of inferior moral quality, usually of lower social status* (slaves, artisans, traders, etc.);
- *a spectacle of what is ridiculous but laughable*, and therefore causes no pain.

To this must be added a catalogue of comic sub-genres which have subsequently been developed and distinguished (even though in any particular instance we invariably meet a mixture):

- *comedy of humours*, based on exaggeration of supposed physiological types: sanguine, melancholic, phlegmatic, choleric (hence 'humorous' = 'funny');
- *comedy of manners*, based on affectations in social appearance and behaviour;
- **romantic comedy*, involving fantastic adventures and/or a love interest;
- **pastoral comedy*, invoking idyllic or idiotic images of country living, especially amongst romantically prettified or grotesquely uglified shepherds;
- **satiric comedy*, exposing and censuring faults, usually involving sex and acquisitiveness, often set in a corrupt city or household;
- *black comedy*, a dark kind of satire, often with an uncertain sense of morality and a sharp sense of *absurdity* or a *carnivalesque* feel (see below).

Comedy is not limited to plays or to literature. Comedy was and is a common feature of the **novel** well before and after Fielding's witty characterisation of his *Tom Jones* (1749) as 'a comic epic poem in prose'. Meanwhile, comedy in verse – sometimes softened to **irony*, sometimes sharpened to **satire* – is evident in English from well before Chaucer to well after Byron (e.g., 5.1.4 b–e). **Comics* (plural), we should also note, refers to a couple of popular and until recently academically neglected genres: comic strips and comedians. Printed *comic strips* appeared in newspapers during the late nineteenth century and soon grew to occupy whole publications (i.e. full-blown comics) in their own right. Though long associated with children's or childish reading, neither the comic nor its descendant the modern graphic novel/book is necessarily trivial or even funny. In fact, much of the best contemporary work on **narrative** and popular verbal-visual culture concentrates on precisely these genres. 'Comics' in the sense of *comedians* ('stand-up', 'alternative' or otherwise) are also increasingly recognised as significant focuses of study. Along with TV 'sitcoms' (i.e. situation comedies), they often foreground and sport with shifts in contemporary **discourse**. The study of jokes in particular has featured centrally in various kinds of PSYCHOLOGICAL analysis virtually since its inception (e.g., Freud's *Jokes and their Relation to the Unconscious*, 1905). It is also a focus for much significant work in discourse analysis (e.g., Chiaro 1992). All in all, then, Aristotle may have had the first word on certain aspects of comedy. But he doesn't necessarily have the last laugh.

Tragedy derives from the Greek *tragos-oidos* ('goat-song') and initially referred to festivals to Dionysus in which a he-goat was sacrificed. Tragedy is treated at much greater length and with much greater seriousness than comedy by Aristotle (*Poetics*, Chs 6–19). According to him, it has the following characteristics (notice that the first three are directly antithetical to those of comedy above):

- unhappy endings and an overall progression from order to disorder, harmony to chaos;
- characters of superior moral quality, usually of higher social status: kings, generals, nobles, etc.;
- a spectacle which 'arouses pity and fear' but which, being a dramatic **representation**, not a reality, 'purges' these emotions harmlessly (a process called *catharsis*);
- a plot built around a 'downturn' (*cata-strophe*) and eventual recognition of a true, appalling state of affairs;
- a hero or heroine (the *protagonist*) who is basically noble but eventually undone by some tragic flaw (*hamartia*), often in the form of excessive pride (*hubris*), as well as by some implacable force such as destiny or fate, usually represented by the gods;
- a figure who stands out against the protagonist (the *antagonist*) as well as a chorus which comments morally, often prophetically, upon the unfolding action;
- 'the representation of an action that is complete and whole' (Ch.7).

Legions of critics (including droves of students) have sought to apply Aristotle's criteria to plays called 'tragedies'. The results range from the brilliant to the banal. Routine analyses dutifully plod through the play in hand duly noting the presence – or lamenting the absence – of 'catharsis', 'hamartia', 'hubris', 'catastrophe', etc. (invoking the Greek names seems to give the stamp of authority). However, more adventurous and genuinely critical analyses tend to brace themselves *against* the framework supplied by Aristotle. They probe the concepts themselves and ask such questions as: precisely who or what is responsible for the 'catastrophe'? Why is pride accounted a fault? What would happen if pity and fear were redirected rather than 'purged'? What social and political forces are being passed off as fate or the will of the gods? In this way the nature and function of tragedy may be identified not simply with the play itself, treated as an isolated artefact, but with specific social-historical conditions and ideological frameworks (e.g., particular state and family structures, the relative positions of nobles, citizens and slaves, men and women, natives and foreigners) as well as with specific kinds of **myth**, religion and morality.

Another important consideration is the fact that most post-classical plays are palpably 'mixed' in mode. They commonly alternate and often fuse elements of tragedy and comedy so as to produce **tragi-comedy**. For instance, Shakespeare's *Hamlet*, though nominally a tragedy, includes comic gravediggers/clowns, a fussy and funny old pedant (Polonius), as well as a protagonist, Hamlet himself, who ceaselessly sports with sense and bitterly plays the fool. Conversely, tragi-comic mixtures and fusions characterise nominal 'comedies' such as *As You Like It* and *The Tempest*. Another matter that plays havoc with classical distinctions between tragedy and comic has to do with changes in underlying social structure. For obviously, an aesthetic hierarchy based upon a distinction between the tragically noble high life and the comically ignoble low life can only hold as long as it is underwritten by a corresponding political hierarchy. Once the middle and working classes become socially prominent and politically aware, the old model becomes a strait-jacket or is irrelevant. We see this happening in Ibsen's *A Doll's House* (see 5.3.3). There the focus is on stresses and strains within the bourgeois family and the ending is left optimistically or pessimistically open, depending how you see Nora's departure. Classical distinctions between comedy and tragedy, along with their associated aesthetics and politics, simply do not apply.

The absurd, following Esslin's *The Theatre of the Absurd* (1961), refers to a group of mid-twentieth-century playwrights, notably Ionesco, Beckett, Pinter and Albee. These writers exploit silence as much as speech, absence as much as presence, and incoherence rather more than coherence. Esslin emphasises the ways in which they all explore kinds of il/logic and non/character, actionless plot and indeterminate setting, especially by comparison with the then-dominant form of 'well-made play'. (The latter characteristically had a clear beginning, middle and end, a readily recognisable theme, and often presented 'realistic' figures in middle-class surroundings such as drawing-rooms.) Beckett's *Not I* (5.3.4 d) is an instance of absurdist theatre. It shows a spotlit 'Mouth' pouring forth a continuous monologue on a minimally set stage while a shadowy figure ('the Auditor') looms to one side. However, explorations of 'the absurd', generally conceived, extend much wider and much further back than certain kinds of mid-century drama. The movement has close aesthetic links with Surrealism and Expressionism (notably Kafka) and philosophical links with the existentialism of Camus and Sartre. All these movements can be characterised by their scepticism about conventional reason and their attempts to embrace, and sometimes celebrate, 'meaninglessness' as a condition. In fact, we can readily see absurdism as part of the general il/logic of *modernism where the supposed certainties of family, state and religion are crumbling and isolated individuals are trying to piece together some sense against an ostensibly nonsensical background. In this respect, Eliot's *The Waste Land* (1922) and Joyce's *Ulysses* are not a little 'absurd'. And so, in quite different veins, are Heller's *Catch 22* (1961) and Irving's *The World According to Garp* (1978). *'Nonsense verse', and 'nonsense writing' in general, may also be cited at this point. Lewis Carroll's *Alice* books (1865, 1871; see 5.4.1) are amongst the most famous fictionalised celebrations of *paradox and nonsense. *Deconstructive critics have an especial interest in these works, as in forms of paradox and absurdism generally. They argue – and often seek to demonstrate in their own manner of writing – that every model of reason depends upon the covert release and control of its opposite (unreason, nonsense, absurdity). In effect, we cannot see or say the one without at least implying the other. In this sense, we are always speaking non/sense.

Carnival and 'the carnivalesque' are concepts identified with more socially and politically engaged, less philosophically detached, kinds of nonsense. The term derives from the Italian *carne-vale* (literally 'a farewell to flesh') and primarily refers to the Shrovetide festival in which Christians feast and revel before Lent and a period of enforced abstinence. In Europe during the Middle Ages and the Renaissance, as in South American and some other countries now, carnival was an occasion for street parties and pageants. Sometimes these led to riots and uprisings. This is how *Bakhtin defines 'carnival' as a critical concept in his *Rabelais and his World* (1968: 10):

> [C]arnival celebrates the temporary liberation from prevailing truth and from the established order: it marks the suspension of all hierarchical rank, privileges, norms and prohibitions.

Politically, carnival is seen as an expression of *popular culture opposed or alternative to an official order which it inverts and sports with. Physically, it is the celebration of the *body over all that habitually constrains it. This aesthetically and politically charged notion of carnival has had considerable impact in many areas of literary and cultural studies, especially those where popular forms and practices are braced against (or within) elite structures and contexts. Indeed, the key critical and political question is just how far carnivalesque elements are contained by – or exceed and break open – the frames within which they operate. (Broadly speaking, NEW HISTORICISTS tend to concentrate on 'containment' while MARXISTS and CULTURAL MATERIALISTS point to the possibilities of radical rupture, even revolution; see 2.6).

Texts of an obviously carnivalesque nature featured in Part Five include:

♦ the Chester *Noah* (5.3.2 a), where Noah's wife carouses with her friends before the Flood and laughingly flouts the authority of her husband;
♦ Synge's *Playboy* (5.3.4 a), where the apparent murder of a father (and the overthrow of an old version of rural Ireland) is carried through with the panache of pantomime;
♦ Theatre Workshop's *Oh What a Lovely War* (5.4.6 f), where war is presented in a music-hall frame and its horrors and heroics jostle with both sentimental songs and documentary realism;
♦ Churchill's *Cloud 9* (5.3.4 e), where men and women cross-dress, actors ostentatiously play stereotypical roles and the overall effect is one of grotesque parody;

Arguments could also be made for at least some 'carnivalesque' elements in:

♦ Shakespeare's 'My mistress' eyes' (5.1.3 b), which inverts romantic expectations about female beauty and institutes a grotesque yet lovable antitype;
♦ Swift's *A Modest Proposal* (5.2.4 a), where the grotesque metaphor of 'eating children' is turned into a satirical point about English policy in Ireland;
♦ Pope's and Byron's versions of *mock-heroic (5.1.4 b and d), where heroic pretensions are both undercut and celebrated;
♦ the extracts from Dickens's *Great Expectations* and Harrison's *v.* (5.4.5 b and c) as playfully irreverent forms of 'grave humour';
♦ Nichols's 'Tropical Death' (5.4.5 e), where the darkly negative solemnities of north-western European funeral rites are blown apart by 'a brilliant tropical death yes'.

Meanwhile, what we might call the 'mock-carnivalesque' is rampant in TV advertising, pop videos and many other forms of POSTMODERN cultural activity. But there the fantasy offer of individual freedom, bodily fulfilment and a universal utopia is always a prelude to purchase. We are only invited to play if we can pay.

ACTIVITY

(a)   *Explore a text which is nominally a comedy and/or a tragedy with Aristotle's criteria in mind (see above). How helpful or inhibiting do you find these criteria as points of departure? What aspects of the text tend to get neglected or ignored by starting at these points?*

(b)   *Drawing on the above definitions, identify a text which you consider in some way 'absurd' or in some way 'carnivalesque'.* Would it be just as useful to call them, say, 'comic', 'tragic' or 'tragi-comic'? (Likely texts from Part Five are listed above.)

DISCUSSION

(i)   The tragedy of [any] period lies in the conflict between the individual and the collectivity, or in the conflict between two hostile collectivities within the same individual.
Leon Trotsky, *Literature and Revolution* (1924: Ch. 8; 'any' replaces 'our')

(ii)   [A]t the centre of European man, dominating the great moments of his life, there lies an essential absurdity.
André Malraux, *The Temptation of the West* (1926) (see Cuddon 1992: 968)

Also see: CLASSICS; **aesthetics**; **drama**; **genre**; **poetry and word-play**.

READING: *Introductory – chiefly on comedy and tragedy:* Cuddon 1992: 119–20, 157–72, 967–8, 983–93; Abrams 1993: 1–2, 28–32, 212–15. *Advanced on comedy and tragedy:* Aristotle 1965: 29–76; Frye 1957: 33–51; Williams 1966 (modern tragedy); Purdie 1993 (modern comedy). *On the absurd:* Esslin 1961; Hinchcliffe 1969. *On carnival:* Bakhtin 1968, 1981: 41–84; Stallybrass and White 1986; Hirschkop and Shepherd 1988; Purdie 1993. *On jokes:* Freud 1905b; Chiaro 1992.

DIFFERENCE AND SIMILARITY, PREFERENCE AND RE/VALUATION

All the terms in this entry have to do with perceiving similarities and differences and expressing preferences. These are basic operations of analysis and evaluation. Hence the persistence in essay questions of such formulas as 'Compare and contrast …' and 'How far do you agree …?' Moreover, because different people – or we ourselves at different moments – may perceive other differences and express other preferences, these are also operations that involve forms of *re*valuation.

In LANGUAGE, **similarity and difference** are fundamental principles at every level because we only know one sound, word or structure to the extent that it is more or less similar to or different from others. Thus in terms of sound 'pin' is almost the same as 'bin': there's just one phoneme different, and a voiced/unvoiced difference between /b/ and /p/. But at the same time, in terms of meaning, 'pin' is almost the same as, say, 'needle' but very different from 'bin'. In this way language offers an interplay of similarities and differences at a variety of levels. When actually using language, we select from the available resources: we in effect choose one sound, meaning, word or structure rather than another.

In LITERATURE, similarity and difference are also fundamental concepts. First, in order even to construct a category of texts called 'Literature', we need to posit some kind of similarity amongst all the items included. Inevitably, at the same time, this means deciding which items are to be excluded. We thus construct the categories 'Literature/Non-literature' by a dialectical principle of '*is*' (similar to, includes) versus '*is not*' (different from, excludes). Hence fundamental arguments about whether Literary Studies should include or exclude drama, performance, TV, advertising, news reporting, etc. (see 1.8.2). Another area where the play of similarity and difference is crucial is that of **genre**. Whether we are sorting texts into the categories of **comedy and tragedy** or 'shopping lists' and 'answer-phone message' (see 5.4.7 e), the same analytical and dialectical operations apply: is this (but not that); includes this (but not that); similar to this (but different from that).

The matter of **re/valuation** most obviously comes into notions of Literature when we are constructing a **canon** of great, classic works or, more pragmatically, a syllabus built round 'set' texts. For at that point all the potential similarities and differences must be resolved into provisional preferences. What shall be read and why? Answers vary, of course. Similarities and differences perceived and preferred by one person or group may be challenged and changed by another (hence counter- and alternative canons, traditions and courses of women's, black, POSTCOLONIAL writing, etc).

CULTURE is also constructed from the perception of myriad permutations of similarity and difference.

- A '*sameness*' *concept of culture* tends towards the view that globally or nationally there is one model to which all aspire and against which all others can be placed and graded. Hence such monolithic notions as Civilisation and English Culture (capitalised and singular). An emphasis on sameness generally entails *mono-culturalism*, homogeneity, centrality and unity – what *Bakhtin terms a *centripetal force.
- A '*differences*' *concept of culture* tends towards the view that globally, nationally or locally there are many models to which different people aspire and relate, and that there is no overarching model within which cultures (lower case and plural) can be placed. Such MULTICULTURALISM is usually expressed in terms of variety and variation, multiple centres and *hybridity. Bakhtin terms this a *centrifugal force.

Not surprisingly, all genuinely dynamic conceptions of culture tend to move between and beyond these polarities. Though even then they may stress difference *within* sameness (i.e. variety within unity) as well as difference *beyond* sameness (i.e. variation which exceeds unity). It all depends how closed or open, finished or in process, the system(s) of culture(s) are reckoned to be.

Difference is a term that has become very prominent in critical theory over the last thirty years. It derives from Latin *differre*, meaning 'to move in two directions' or 'to carry away', and both senses can be traced in current usage of the term. Two distinct traditions converge to make difference a key concept: one political, the other philosophical. First, there is the political pressure of FEMINIST and POSTCOLONIAL approaches. In these cases it is the fundamental differences between 'female' and 'male' (in gender terms 'feminine' and 'masculine') and between 'black' and 'white' that constitute the initial parameters of critical discourse. In sophisticated models these differences are always recognised as shifting and *plural* rather than static and *binary*. That is, there are many more permutations of gender and shades of colour than two. It is also recognised that differences of gender and ethnicity interact with one another and with other differences based upon class, education, religion and region.

The second major force behind contemporary interest in differences derives from POSTSTRUCTURALIST philosophy, especially the writings of *Derrida. Drawing on the ambiguity of the French verb *différer* (which means both 'to be different from' and 'to delay/defer'), Derrida, proposes that *différance* be conceived as an activity whereby terms and concepts not only differ from one another but also engage us in an endless process of deferral or delay. Every act of 'differentiation' is, in effect, a delaying tactic. At its most basic, the principle of *différance* is confirmed by the fact that one dictionary definition leads to another, which leads to another, then another – and so on. Eventually, it may well come back to the term with which you started (look up 'language' and 'words' to see this circularity in motion).

Significantly, the only way to arrest the potentially infinite 'play of difference/ deferral' in language is to insist upon a *reference* in the non-verbal world; and that in turn means expressing a *preference* for certain ways of saying and seeing the world. For instance, I (like you) may be known by all sorts of *different* labels: in my case 'father', 'husband', 'son', 'lecturer', 'citizen', 'patient', 'cyclist', 'guitarist', and so on. But which one is actually used at any one time will depend upon which aspect of me is being *referred* to (and whether I'm on a bike, in a lecture theatre or a hospital, say). It will also depend upon which aspect I and other people prefer to draw attention to. **Preference** *may therefore be defined as the resolution of differences and the fixing of references.* (A related but somewhat narrower sense of preference is current in MEDIA studies. *Preferred readings* are those interpretations which appear to be offered by the text as 'natural' or 'neutral'; e.g., a right-wing account of a political demonstration in terms of a challenge to law and order – rather than as legitimate protest or a fun day out.)

Discrimination is another concept which implies both differentiation and the exercise of preferences. The term has a complex and significant history and, as it frequently figures in critical discourses, we shall note the salient points here (see *OED* and Williams 1983: 313–15). The root of 'dis*crimin*ation' derives, via Latin *crimen*, from the same root as that for *critic: Greek *krinein*, meaning 'to separate' and, by extension, 'to judge'. In a strictly legal sense, the process of 'dis-criminating' also initially meant separating out those who were 'criminals' from those who were innocent (as in 'incriminating evidence'). In both senses, then, we have a clear continuity between the activity of establishing differences (separating) and that of instituting a preference (judging). 'Discrimination' was given a decidedly upper-class spin during the late eighteenth and nineteenth centuries. To make fine discriminations and to be discriminating came to be associated with an upper-class elite as opposed to a lower-class mob. However, this usage was partly challenged in the first half of the twentieth century. The literary critic F.R. Leavis, for instance, defined 'discrimination' in terms of 'intelligence' and 'sensitivity' and to some extent wrested the term back from its exclusive association with an upper-class and dilettantish approach to literature as 'belles lettres' (see 1.5.7). Nonetheless, Leavis still identified powers of discrimination with what he termed 'Minority Culture' rather than with 'Mass Civilisation' (to pick up the two leading terms of his pamphlet of 1930). He therefore insisted on maintaining a sharply critical distance from *popular CULTURE at large (see Discussion (ii) on p. 188). This emphasis was sustained in the substantially Leavisite and highly influential collection of essays *Discrimination and Popular Culture*, edited by Denys Thompson (1964, 2nd edn 1973).

Since the 1970s the concept of discrimination has been subject to yet further pressures. Increased awareness of unequal treatment of women and of various ethnic and religious groups led to a whole host of laws on sexual, racial and other kinds of 'discrimination'. In this sense discrimination was seen *negatively*, as something to be avoided. More recently, however, it has become common to talk more assertively of '*positive* discrimination'. This applies whenever there is a concerted attempt to redress the social balance, e.g., by deliberately appointing women and members of other social groups to positions from which they were previously excluded. The net result is that we can now *discriminate* in at least four senses:

1   analytically, in the sense of perceiving differences;
2   judgmentally, in the sense of implying or stating preferences;
3   negatively, against certain social groups (e.g., sexual or racial discrimination);
4   positively, for certain groups (e.g., proactive employment and access policies).

Crucially, in actual critical and political practice, all these meanings tend to get mixed up without people being fully aware that this is happening. What is offered as a natural and neutral distinction (and perhaps a refined act of analysis) may therefore turn out to be based upon all sorts of negatively and positively charged judgements, for or against certain groups. It may even be argued that there are *no* natural or neutral discriminations. Every act of discrimination is loaded. (Similar problems and possibilities, and largely parallel histories, characterise the concepts 'distinction' and 'taste'. Both invariably turn out to be aesthetically and politically loaded. See Williams 1983: 313–15 and Bourdieu 1984.)

   Re/valuation is the term preferred here to introduce the tricky concept of *value (literary and otherwise). This is because *re-valu-ation* puts the emphasis on evaluation as a continuing process rather than on 'value' as an intrinsic property. It also draws attention to the revisionary nature of a process in which values are constantly challenged and changed, never simply enshrined and accepted (hence *re*-valuation). *Value* may be understood in at least three senses:

1   the intrinsic worth and essential quality of something (in some absolute scale of 'universal values');
2   the relative worth or usefulness of something in variable conditions (hence 'exchange value');
3   the relative significance of one *sign with respect to others within the same *sign-system (this is a specialised sense translated from *Saussure's 'valeur').

Clearly, the last two, *relative* senses of value do not sit easily with the first, *absolute* one. Do we, for instance, treat Shakespeare's *Hamlet* as though it has intrinsic qualities and embodies universal values (e.g., 'the human predicament', 'human nature')? Or do we treat *Hamlet* as something caught in shifting patterns of exchange, always open to renegotiation and revaluation? (See 2.2.) In this respect, it is worth adding that what is considered 'valid' or to 'have validity' in interpretation (both these terms are directly related to 'value') may have as much to do with the status and role of the valuer as with any intrinsic property of the thing being valued. The question 'Is this a valid interpretation?' therefore leads to further questions: for whom? for what purpose?, when, where and why?

ACTIVITIES

(a) *Similarities and differences.* Concentrate on a single short text and consider all the ways in which you might apply to it the principles of 'similarity' and 'difference'. What other texts is it similar to and different from with respect to form, subject matter and genre? How are patterns of similarity established in the areas of sound, visual presentation, word choice and word combination – and where are differences introduced which break or extend those patterns? How are differences of, say, gender, class, ethnicity and education represented (or ignored) within the text? Finally – or perhaps first – how far are the wor(l)ds offered by the text similar to or different from your own? (Suggested focuses in Part Five are: Shakespeare's 'My mistress' eyes' (5.1.3 b) or Nichols's 'Tropical Death' (5.4.5 e); Churchill's *Cloud 9* (5.3.4 e); The *Sun* '20 Yobs . . .' (5.2.5 a).)

(b) *Validity and revaluation.* Analyse and evaluate the same text using two of the approaches featured in Part Two. Which of the 'How to practise . . .' methods do you consider most valid and why?

DISCUSSION

(i) texts, like all the other objects we engage with, bear the marks and signs of their prior valuings [. . .] and are thus, we might say, always to some extent pre-evaluated for us.

> Barbara Herrnstein Smith, 'Value / Evaluation' in Lentricchia and
> McLaughlin (1995: 182)

(ii) But the modern [man] is exposed to a concourse of signals so bewildering in their variety and number that, unless he is especially gifted or especially favoured, he can hardly begin to discriminate.

> F.R. Leavis, *Mass Civilisation and Minority Culture* (1930) (1979: 19–20)

Also see FEMINISM; POSTCOLONIALISM; POSTSTRUCTURALISM; **absence and presence; aesthetics; foreground, background and point of view; writing . . . rewriting**.

READING: *Introductory:* O'Sullivan *et al.* 1994: 89–90; Williams 1983: 313–15; Herrnstein Smith in Lentricchia and McLaughlin 1995: 177–85; Richards 1924: 24–43, 229–30; Brooker and Humm 1989: 106–18; Hirsch in Rylance 1987: 172–81. *Advanced:* Mukarovsky 1936; Leavis 1936: Derrida 1978; Bourdieu 1984; Spivak 1987; Attridge 1988; Weedon 1996.

DISCOURSE AND DISCOURSE ANALYSIS

'Discourse' is now a commonly, sometimes casually, used term in the humanities and social sciences. It can mean everything from 'language understood as a form of social interaction and power' to 'a distinctive way of seeing and saying the world';

from 'dialogue in general' to 'conversation in particular'. As far as English Studies is concerned, use of the term discourse (along with **text**) has at least served to cut across conventional distinctions between LANGUAGE and LITERATURE. Both, it is strongly implied, can only be grasped in relation to one another and as forms of COMMUNICATION in specific CULTURAL contexts. Talk of language and literature (or, say, film and TV) as discourse therefore tends to occur in approaches which are socially and historically oriented, and often politically motivated (e.g., MARXISM, FEMINISM, POSTCOLONIALISM). 'Discourse' also tends to cut across conventional **fact/fiction** distinctions, encouraging us to treat all texts as in some sense **factional** (see **realism and representation**) and all **hi/stories** as potentially related (see **narrative**). Discourse is therefore one of the common terms which points to closer relations between HISTORY AND ENGLISH as subjects (see 1.5.6).

For the sake of clarity, I shall distinguish five main meanings of 'discourse':

1   a formal treatise or dissertation (archaic); e.g., Descartes's *Discourse on Method*;
2   stretches of language above the level of the *sentence (i.e. paragraphs, whole **texts**), with the emphasis on verbal *cohesion and perceptual coherence;
3   **dialogue** in general or **conversation** in particular, primarily associated with the kind of discourse/conversation analysis currently extended into work on *pragmatics and *speech acts;
4   communicative practices and 'ways of saying' which express the interests of a particular social-historical group or institution. In this case we tend to speak of discourses (plural) as distinct and often competing forms of knowledge and power; examples would be discourses of the law, medicine, science, education and 'the family';
5   *discours'* as used by theorists of **narrative** to refer to the narrational process of the story, especially the interaction between narrator and narratee, as distinguished from the *histoire'*, the narrative product as though it exists independently of the telling.

Given such a variety of potential meanings and applications, it is not surprising that people sometimes use the word discourse vaguely or confusedly. We shall concentrate on senses (3) and (4); for these are the most common senses in contemporary Literary and Cultural Studies. They may be summed up by the formula: *Discourse = text in context = power in action*. (Sense (2) will be invoked in so far as it encourages us to explore actual whole texts or interactions in detail.) The main issues can be framed as a series of questions to be put to any text.

DISCOURSE QUESTIONS

♦ What ways of saying and seeing the world are being assumed or asserted?
♦ What power relations are in play within and around the text in context?
♦ What alternative ways of saying and seeing the world are thereby being marginalised or ignored?
♦ What if the whole text-in-context were said, seen and done differently?

Thus we may consider the words and music of the British national anthem as an instance of intertwined discourses. Take the first line: 'God save our gracious queen'. This is marked in terms of religion ('God'), aristocracy ('queen'), social decorum ('gracious') and gender ('queen' again). In terms of context, the anthem as a whole is sung chiefly at the openings of national sporting and ceremonial occasions connected with Britain. All these features combine to make this a particularly powerful and privileged instance of language-in-action, text-in-context. We might call this a 'nationalistic' or 'patriotic' discourse. In order to explore and expose this discourse more fully, we might then consider whose ways of saying and seeing are *not* being represented in the British national anthem, and how *else* sporting and other public events might be – and indeed are – celebrated. For clearly there are many who would resist using or refuse to use the configuration of religion, monarchy, nationalism, gender and social decorum that it offers. Muslims, Buddhists, atheists, republicans, socialists, anarchists, internationalists, feminists, gays, and many others – all might (and often do) have different songs to sing and and occasions to celebrate. Notice, too, that even if we stick with the *words* of the national anthem (the 'text itself') but put them in a different context, their function and value can change dramatically. This happens with versions of 'God Save the Queen' by the punk group the Sex Pistols as well as by the rock group Queen. The former version was banned by the BBC (much as Roseanne Arnold's version of 'The Stars and Stripes' caused an uproar in America), while Queen's version drew attention to the band themselves along with gay politics (i.e. 'Queen(s)'). In all these ways we can see discourse as a function of language-in-action and text-in-context. And arguably we can only fully grasp this process if we also see the possibility of language activated differently, in different contexts and serving different interests. This is precisely why texts are organised in clusters rather than singly in Part Five (especially section 5.4). Comparing and contrasting interrelated texts or texts on the same theme encourages us to see the distinctive discourses in play in each. We more clearly perceive one way of seeing and saying, and one set of power relations, by recognising others which it is not.

A further brief example will help clarify what is meant by **discourse analysis** when applied to **speech and conversation** (more analytical detail can be found in that particular entry and in section 4.2). In the 'Supermarket exchange' (5.3.1 a) the following features would be observed:

- *At the macro-textual level*, the social roles and power relations in play between the customer and the cashier: these would be analysed in terms of sex, age, ethnicity, class, education and personal temperament, as well as the general historical context and the immediate occasion of the encounter (Friday night shopping in central Oxford is obviously very different from Sunday morning shopping in downtown Johannesburg).
- *At the micro-textual level*, the specific alternations of elicitation (the customer seeking a response) and silence (the cashier failing or refusing to respond); more particularly, the customer's gradual progression from relatively depersonalised and indirect statements ('There's a mistake here') to pointedly personal accusation (notably, the shift from passive to active structures in the last two moves: 'A mistake has been made' to 'You've made a mistake').

Taken together, these two macro- and micro-textual approaches to the text would provide the basic framework within which a more extensive and intensive discourse analysis could be developed. And again there would be attention to text in context and language in action. The analysis would therefore be *functional, not simply formal.

ACTIVITIES

(a)   *Put the above 'Discourse Questions' to a cluster of texts which treat ostensibly the same topic* (e.g., nature, love, war, death, marriage, the family, colonialism). How far do the various discourses in play in effect constitute a variety of subjects?
        (Suggested focuses in Part Five are: 5.4.3 (nature); 5.4.6 (war); 5.4.5 (death); 5.2.4 (colonialism).)

(b)   *Analyse an instance of conversational exchange, scripted or unscripted, for the ways in which it constitutes power relations* (e.g., the factory commissioner–millhand interview (5.3.1 c); Prospero and Caliban (5.3.2 b); King Henry and his troops (5.4.6 a); Freud and 'Dora' (5.3.1 d); *Educating Rita* (5.3.5 c)).

DISCUSSION

    (i)   But discourse is just a fancy name for language, isn't it?
                    First-year student on 'Language, Literature, Discourse I', Oxford, 1994

    (ii) this model of literature as social discourse [is] . . . socially responsible and
          progressive, and educationally useful.
                    Roger Fowler, *Literature as Social Discourse* (1981:199)

Also see: LANGUAGE; 4.2; **addresser–address–addressee**; **genres**; *ideology; **speech and conversation; subject . . . role**.

READING: *Introductory:* Carter and Simpson 1989: 8–17; O'Sullivan *et al.* 1994: 29–31; Fowler 1981: 180–200; Fowler 1987: 62–6; Kress 1989: 5–10; Lentricchia and McLaughlin 1995: 50–65 Pope 1995: 122–7; Coulthard 1985. *Advanced:* Foucault 1986; Voloshinov 1973: 83–98; Bakhtin 1981: 259–422; Cook 1994.

DRAMA AND THEATRE, FILM AND TV

All these areas prove both attractive and awkward for students of English, especially of English LITERATURE as traditionally conceived. They are attractive because they challenge the exclusivity of the 'words on the page' notion of textuality and draw attention to spoken words, (along with moving bodies, music and many other things) on the stage and screen. They are awkward for the same reason, because they are not primarily written or printed texts but audio-visual performances, live or recorded. The institutional framing of this situation in English Studies is sketched in 1.5.9–10. Its intellectual ramifications are explored in the entries on **speech**, **text** and **writing**.

We begin with some general distinctions and connections between drama and narrative. It is conventional and often convenient to contrast *drama* (the activity of acting, showing and presenting) with *narrative* (the activity of telling, reporting and representing). This can also be put in terms of who talks to whom. In drama we are most conscious of an **addresser–addressee** relation, persons speaking and spoken to. In narrative we are most conscious of the **address** itself, what is being related and spoken about. Basically, then, we may say that drama operates on an 'I/we–you' axis, while narrative focuses on 's/he', 'they' or 'it'. Characters are *dramatised* in so far as they appear to speak in their own persons; they are *narrated* in so far as someone else (a narrator) speaks for and of them. Some modern theorists, prompted by Aristotle, distinguish *mimesis* (drama) and *diegesis* (narrative).

At the same time it important to recognise drama and narrative as points on a continuum rather than mutually exclusive categories. Narrators may be visible 'up front' (and therefore dramatic), most obviously in first person narratives such as **autobiography** and in dramatic monologues (e.g., Robert Browning's). Conversely, dramatised characters constantly report on (and therefore narrate) various aspects of their own and other people's experience. Figure 6 summarises both the distinctions and connections between drama and narrative:

DRAMA << >>	First person narration << >>	*NARRATIVE*
acting, showing,	dramatic monologue	telling
reporting, presenting,	autobiography	representing
addresser–addressee		address
'I/we – you'		's/he, they, it'
mimesis		diegesis

Figure 6 Distinctions and connections between drama and narrative

We now turn to drama, theatre, film and TV in turn.

Drama derives from Greek *draein* (to do, to act) and means any kind of 'acting'. 'Acting', notice, has the dual sense of 'playing **roles**' and 'performing an action'. Acting can therefore take place on *and* off the stage/screen, in *and* out of a specially designed play or performance space. In short, 'dramas' can happen in **fiction** *and* in **fact**. Hence the common yet potentially confusing reference to 'real-life dramas' and 'dramatic rescues', where actual events are being referred to and simply heightened through an implicit appeal to fictional genres. Conventional Literary Studies courses often 'do drama', but they usually do so in a substantially text-based sense, and concentrate on **classic** plays for the stage. (See Godber's *Teechers* (5.3.5 b) for a humorously enlightened view of alternatives.) 'TV and radio drama' may be familiar enough categories in programme guides; but in the UK at least they rarely feature beyond the occasional recognition of Dylan Thomas's *Under Milk Wood* as a radio play (see 5.3.4 b), and passing recognition of Denis Potter and Mike Leigh as TV dramatists. In fact, drama is often the last and least fully represented element in the traditional lit. crit. trinity of 'poetry, prose and drama'. (Arguably, the anthology of tran/scripts in Part Five (5.3) is no exception.)

Theatre derives from Greek *thea* (spectacle) and *theon* (spectator). So does *theory which is also a kind of 'spectator sport' (see 2.2). Specifically, theatrical events always require a special 'play space' where the significantly named 'show' can take place. Theatre also invariably entails some division between actors and audiences, players and spectators. This is the case even if the boundary is sometimes blurred or deliberately transgressed, as with bouts of 'audience participation'. Theatres and the theatrical events played in them are commonly distinguished in terms of their staging: *arena, in the round, thrust, proscenium arch (also-called 'picture book' and 'fourth-wall removed')*, **Brechtian* (e.g., with staging devices and stage-hands open to view), *studio* and *promenade*. All these practical considerations of building and space feature prominently in full-blown Theatre Studies courses, as do the economic as well as the aesthetic dimensions of scenery, lighting and costume. So do economic considerations of location, access and cost, along with the precise social composition of actors and audiences. These aspects of theatre may be treated cursorily or not at all in specifcally literary courses.

Film is the name for particular MEDIA products (i.e. individual films) as well as the material from which they are made (i.e. film). Films are usually further distinguished according to a variety of criteria:

- *director and/or main actor*, e.g., Eisenstein's *Battleship Potemkin*, Chaplin's *Modern Times*, Ridley Scott's and/or Harrison Ford's *Blade Runner.*
- *technology*, e.g., celluloid or plastic film; 8mm, 16 mm or 36mm film width; silent movies, 'talkies', fully synchronised sound-track, computer-assisted effects, etc.
- *country and period*, e.g., Hollywood 1940s, French 1960s, contemporary Chinese.
- **genre**, e.g., cowboy, disaster, B movie, *film noir*, teen, spoof, art, porn, science fantasy, road, 'feel good', etc.

Notice, too, that 'film' can be both noun and verb. Like 'writing' (but unlike 'literature') 'film' can therefore more easily designate a process as well as a product. This is convenient because many courses in film emphasise the making and the viewing of films as cumulative activities.

Film is now widely recognised as an important element in English Studies. Often this is at the level of film adaptations of literary classics: Olivier's and Branagh's versions of Shakespeare's *Henry V*, Passolini's and Kurosawa's versions of *Macbeth*, Lean's versions of Dickens's *Great Expectations* and Forster's *A Passage to India*, Hepburn in Brontë's *Jane Eyre*, etc. However, increasingly (albeit belatedly), it is being recognised within English Studies that film is a medium, mode of representation and art form in its own right; as are the implications of the fact that much of world cinema is either produced in English (notably in Hollywood) or is available dubbed in English or has English subtitles. All this makes for variously close, tense or suspicious relations amongst practitioners of English and Film Studies. The materials and methods of these subjects can be seen as complementary or incompatible (see 1.5.9).

Television (Greek–Latin for 'far-seen') has been a major and growing component in both students' and teachers' leisure-time experience since the 1950s. Along with films, pop music, magazines and newspapers (all the chief elements of the **popular MEDIA*), TV constitutes probably the most common source of information and entertainment, and the most common frame of CULTURAL reference for most people in contemporary Western (and many non-Western) societies. And again, like film, a great deal of TV is produced in English (notably in the USA, UK and Australia) or is readily dubbed in English. There are therefore all the attractions – as well as the perils – of a kind of 'English-speaking-media-imperialism'. In fact, for a long time many people professionally involved in English Literature have adopted a posture of indifference or downright hostility to TV and the other popular media. NEW CRITICS in America and *Leavisites in Britain all basically agreed that 'TV was bad for you' (see *discrimination). 'Watching too much TV' was (and is) held responsible for everything from alleged illiteracy and inarticulacy to passivity and time-wasting, as well as general irreverence for authority and a supposed decline in moral standards. The fact that television was also at least potentially responsible for wider participation in democracy, visual literacy, greater awareness of other regions and nations, and offered a rich array of new genres of information and/as entertainment was not always recognised.

TV and film are readily confused because of their reliance on similar audio-visual media, and the fact that plenty of films are shown and seen on TV. However, TV is distinct from film in a number of crucial respects (just as handwriting is similar to but distinct from print) . These differences are worth pointing up.

Mode of production: TV uses video or live-relay cameras rather than film cameras: the audio-visual quality and texture are different. TV studios tend to work on series rather than one-offs; they have relatively stable teams and predictable products.

Mode of transmission: TV is characteristically *broadcast ('over the air') rather than *narrow-cast' – even though satellite and cable TV are modifying these patterns of distribution.

Mode of reception: TV is commonly part of the routine hubbub at home and, like radio and music, may be part of the background 'noise'. It is not a special spectacle received publicly in the darkness and silence of the cinema. The 'viewing unit' for TV is often, say, part of an evening rather than a specific item. Meanwhile, 'channel hopping' is not an option in the cinema – though concentrated, uninterrupted viewing is.

Genres. TV **genres** are remarkably various; they include soap operas, game and chat shows, phone-ins, police- and hospital-based series, situation comedies, sports, documentaries, nature programmes, news, pop, adverts and recyclings of cinema films. TV genres are typically 'open' and 'continuing' (rather than 'closed' and 'one-off') because of their programming in series and serials. They are also remarkably *hybrid in form and function (e.g., 'Crime-watch' programmes = police thriller + *faction (reconstructed crimes) + phone-in; 'TV evangelism' = religion + advertising + fund-raising).

ACTIVITIES

(a)   *Showing and/or telling?* Use the above 'Drama>><<Narrative' model (Figure 6) to explore the ways in which a particular text may be considered 'dramatic' and/or 'narrative', depending on how you look at it. (Suggested focuses in Part Five are: Wyatt's 'They flee from me' (5.1.3 a); Austen's *Pride and Prejudice* (5.2.3 b) and Godber's *Teechers* (5.3.5 b).)

(b)   *Cross-media and cross-genre adaptation.* Try adapting part of a novel or short story into a script for stage, radio, TV or film. Alternatively, do the reverse. Either way, add a commentary explaining your decisions and exploring the problems and possibilities encountered. Include comment on the following aspects:

- what is 'medium-specific' to each version and what 'translates' fairly easily;
- how far the switch in medium prompts a shift in genre;
- who is speaking, thinking, feeling and looking at corresponding moments;
- how far there is a discernible authorial 'voice' or directorial 'presence'.

(Suggestions in Part Five: Kipling (5.2.4 b); Ibsen (5.3.3); Theatre Workshop (5.4.6 f).)

DISCUSSION

(i)   Deadly Theatre approaches the classics from the viewpoint that somewhere, someone has found out and defined how the play should be done.
Peter Brook, *The Empty Space* (1968) (1972: 17)

(ii)   It will never be adequate simply to impose a literary analysis on television entertainment without fully understanding the institutions of television, its mode of address and how it is received.
Ros Coward, 'Come Back Miss Ellie: on Character and Narrative in Soap Operas', in MacCabe (1988: 169–70; substitute 'film' or 'drama' for 'television' if you wish)

Also see: 1.5.9; MEDIA; 5.3; **addresser–address–addressee; comedy and tragedy, carnival and the absurd; narrative; speech and conversation, monologue and dialogue**.

READING: *Drama:* Makaryk 1993: 133–8; Burton and Carter 1982: 86–115; Brook 1968; Brecht 1964; McGrath 1981 in Walder 1990: 257–63; Elam 1980; Aston and Savona 1991; Pavis 1991, Boal 1992. *Film:* Chatman 1978; Bordwell and Thompson 1993: 64–143; Giddings *et al.* 1990 and McFarlane 1996 (these last two on novel–screen adaptation). *Television:* Coward in MacCabe 1988: 171–8; Allen 1987; Fiske 1987; Selby and Cowdrey 1995.

FOREGROUND, BACKGROUND AND POINT OF VIEW

All of these terms have to do with visualising a text from a variety of perspectives and in a variety of dimensions. The **foreground** is what appears closest and most prominent to someone; the **background** is what appears remotest and most inconspicuous. **Point of view** refers to the vantage point from which a particular event is seen and, by extension, heard, felt and otherwise perceived. Partly relatable concepts, though with a decidedly POSTSTRUCTURALIST turn, can be found in the entry on **absence and presence . . . centres and margins**. The terms featured in the present entry derive chiefly from the theory of perspective in art and architecture and from the psychology of visual perception. As we shall quickly 'see', a 'way of seeing' invariably turns out to be a 'way of saying', and vice versa.

First, a couple of simple – or apparently simple – illustrations. In Leonardo da Vinci's *Mona Lisa* we might say that the top half of a woman is in the foreground, and a dark landscape is in the background. In Shakespeare's *Hamlet*, we might say that the prince of that name is in the foreground (and literally front-stage in the soliloquies) while the go-betweens Rosencrantz and Guildenstern are in the background. Ophelia, we might add, occupies a kind of middle ground. However, a little further reflection confirms that the foreground–background relation is not quite as simple and stable as it first seems. What we see in a picture (or text) is partly what we are predisposed to see or 'read into it'. It also depends how we are inclined to 'frame' the picture, physically and ideologically. Thus what is firmly in the foreground for one reader, viewer or audience – or for one period or social group – may not be for another. Reconsider Leonardo's *Mona Lisa*, also called *La Gioconda*. If you were interested in landscape rather than portraiture you would concentrate on – and thereby foreground – the background. If you were a dressmaker or historical costumier you might ignore the famous smile, but concentrate on the clothes. A MARXIST could look at the painting and the main thing at the front of his or her mind might be the painter's dependence on wealthy patrons both for subjects and support (La Gioconda was the wife of a rich merchant Zanoki del Giocondo). Alternatively, all sorts of NEW HISTORICISTS might be taking a sideways glance at the rest of the Louvre (where the painting hangs) and contemplating its shift in function from royal palace to state museum. A FEMINIST, meanwhile, might be vigorously wrestling with and trying to *re-vision one of the most teasing instances of woman as a 'specular subject/object' – both gazing and being gazed at. A POSTMODERNIST, however, might be busily comparing 'the original' with all the versions of the painting reproduced in books and magazines and on T-shirts; for **images** of the Mona Lisa are used to help sell everything from Italian spaghetti (she eats it in one advert) to a British TV arts programme (*The South Bank Show*, where she makes a cartoon appearance in the credits): 'Will the 'real' Mona Lisa stand up please . . . !' (One of the main things 'she' stands for is, of course, Paris as a centre of Western high art – and a major tourist attraction.)

Similarly revised observations might be made about the apparently simple foreground–background relation in *Hamlet*. For one thing, a specific critic or director might actually draw attention to Rosencrantz and Guildenstern, or to Ophelia, and thereby put them in the foreground and 'in a spotlight'. In fact this is precisely what Stoppard does in his play *Rosencrantz and Guildenstern are Dead* (1966) and Jean Betts does in her *Ophelia* (1995). Meanwhile, critics of all hues and persuasions do much the same in their 'rewrites' of Hamlet (as of other texts); for what are most critical essays but the highly selective quotation and fore-grounding of certain 'aspects', 'dimensions of' and 'perspectives on' the play? Here, then, are some general questions which can be put to any text. They help to draw attention to the *perceptual* and *cultural* dimensions of what is never a merely visual issue.

FOREGROUNDS, BACKGROUNDS AND POINTS OF VIEW

♦ Who and what stands out? What people and events? What linguistic features and textual structures? (Standing out against what assumed backgrounds: social and historical; linguistic and literary?)

♦ Whose points of view and which perspectives seem to be preferred? Whose and which seem to be marginalised or ignored? And what shifts and switches in point of view do you experience between, say, narrator and characters, and between both of them and you as an actual reader?

♦ How do foreground–background relations change over the course of the text? And in what contexts has the text itself been seen and used at different moments of reception and reproduction?

♦ Is there anything which *you* would actively like to *direct* attention to – even if the text itself does not seem to *draw* attention to it?

Background is also familiar to students of English Literature in the phrases 'the historical (or social) background' and 'background reading'. In both cases there is a strong implication that LITERATURE is somehow distinct or detachable from the social and historical conditions in which it is produced and received; also that the primary object of study is 'the **text** in itself', with the **context** (including **intertextual** relations) being treated as merely secondary or even optional. Clearly, a case can be made for the usefulness of such distinctions. NEW CRITICS and FORMALISTS assert or assume them all the time. However, it should be noted that the equations 'foreground = literature = primary text' and 'background = society/history = context' *is* a position, and is in fact just one position amongst many. Virtually all the other positions and approaches surveyed in Part Two would challenge those equations and the oppositions and hierarchies they presuppose. MARXISTS, FEMINISTS and POSTCOLONIAL critics, in particular, would insist on seeing all writing (not just that privileged as 'literary') as being produced and received *in* – not above, to one side or in front of – history and society. Nonetheless, the practical necessity of having to focus on *some*thing (not just *any*thing) inevitably means that some kind of foreground–background relation is implied. The point, therefore, is to decide which one, and as far as possible to make the theoretical 'grounds' of our particular 'fore-' and 'back-' explicit.

Foreground and the activity of **foregrounding** were concepts given prominence and a particular twist in *stylistics by Paul Garvin (1964). He used these words to translate Czech *aktualisace* (literally 'actualising'), as used by the 1930s' Prague School (see 2.4). For *Mukarovsky and Havranek, 'foregrounding/*aktualisace*' occurs whenever a linguistic item, device or strategy draws attention to itself against the assumed 'background' norms of the language. The result is a fresh perception both of the event represented and of the nature of language itself. Foregrounding is thus the textual mechanism whereby *defamiliarisation occurs. Routine examples of foregrounding abound in jokes and puns where the ambiguity or incongruity of a particular item suddenly draws attention to itself (e.g., 'A: But I am trying. B: Yes, very!' or 'A: My dog smells awful. How does yours smell? B: With his nose', or such quips as 'Today I got up at the crack of lunchtime'). Another, more structural kind of foregrounding can be equated with rhymes, songs and **poetry** in general, in fact wherever there is some heightening of sound-pattern (see **versification**). In the written or printed word, visual presentation and punctuation can also be foregrounded by, for instance, omitting commas and full stops and using line-breaks to control the reader's attention instead.

The term *deviation is also sometimes used to describe instances where the routine norms and expectations of the language are deliberately bent or broken (e.g., e e cummings 'anyone lived in a pretty how town' or my 3-year-old daughter's 'Mummy has *her*-grain' – modelled on '*mi*graine'!). The problem with 'deviance' analysis, however, is that it presupposes that people have the same norms and expectations. For instance, consider Nichols's lines 'The fat black woman want / a brilliant tropical death . . . some bawl / no quiet jerk tear wiping . . .' (5.4.5 e). This might strike you as a refreshingly lively evocation of funeral rites, especially if you are used to funerals in 'some North Europe far/forlorn'. However, if you are sensitive to and insistent on the maintenance of grammatical norms based on **standard** UK and US usages, you are more likely to be struck by the fact that the third person singular 'want' has no final 's' (even though this is a routine feature of both Caribbean 'Nation language' and black Afro-American Englishes generally). You might also be anxious about the noun 'some bawl' (which may be a one-off coinage by Nichols) as opposed to the more expected 'some bawl*ing*'. In other words, what we see in the foreground (including what we see as 'deviant') will depend as much upon our own linguistic and cultural expectations as upon the text in itself. The fact is that readers, audiences and viewers are also a crucial part of 'the larger picture'.

Points of view can also be identified with a variety of positions 'within' and 'outside' the text. It is useful to distinguish the following (cf. *narration):

- actual **author**'s attitudes and values, e.g., Defoe's, Brontë's;
- **narrator**'s point of view, e.g., Robinson Crusoe's, Jane Eyre's;
- **character**'s point of view; e.g., Friday's, Rochester's;
- implied **reader**'s point of view, most overtly in the 'dear reader' mode of address;
- actual reader's responses, e.g., what you and I actually see or look for.

However, what most engages us as readers or viewers is usually *shifts or switches in point of view*: the ways in which the attitudes and values of author, narrator, characters and readers (actual as well as implied) ceaselessly diverge or converge, collide or coalesce.

ACTIVITIES

(a) Put the questions on 'Foregrounds, Backgrounds and Points of View' (pp. 196–7) to a text you are studying. (Suggestions from Part Five include: Manley's *The New Atalantis* (5.2.3 a); Kipling's 'Muhammad Din' (5.2.4 b) and Freud's 'Dora' (5.3.1 d).)

Go on to read the entry on **absence and presence, gaps and silences, centres and margins** and consider whether anything is lost or gained by this switch in critical perspective.

(b) Think of an alternative title or caption for a text, painting or photo with which you are familiar. Consider how far you have realigned the implied foreground–background relations and the implied points of view compared with the actual title or caption.

DISCUSSION

(i) Saying what happened is an angle of saying.

Seamus Heaney on *The South Bank Show* (1991)
(cited in Simpson 1993: 1)

(ii)   the function of poetic language consists in the maximum foregrounding of the
       utterance.

Jan Mukarovsky and P. Havranek, 'Standard Language and Poetic
Language' in Garvin (1964: 19)

Also see: FORMALISM INTO FUNCTIONALISM; **absence and presence . . . centres
and margins; character; narrative; subject . . . role**.

READING: *Introductory:* Wales 1989: 181–3; Moon 1992: 49–51; Berger 1972.
Advanced: Garvin 1964: 3–30; Booth 1961; Bal 1985: 100–15; Simpson 1993; Fowler
1996: 160–84.

GENRE AND KINDS OF TEXT

Genres are kinds, categories or types of cultural product and process – including
texts. (The word 'genre' derives, through French, from Latin *genera* (pl.), where it
simply means 'kinds' or 'types'.) Love sonnets, absurdist drama, shopping lists
and disaster movies are all genres of text. By extension, we can also talk about
genres of everything from chats over coffee to job interviews, and pizza packaging
to shopping malls. The main thing is that there should be some basic similarity of
form and function in the kinds of cultural product or activity, notwithstanding
all the differences there inevitably are between one item and another. At the
broadest, then, analysis of genre has to do with the fundamental activity of perceiving
similarities and differences (see **difference**). For students of English it mainly
has to do with perceiving the relations between one text and another (i.e. **intertextuality**), including the pressure of different **contexts** on apparently similar texts
(see **text**).

Genre as a term and concept is chiefly known to students of LITERATURE through
such traditional categories as **poetry**, **novel** and **drama**. These are best seen as
capacious and flexible super- or mega-genres. Each can be broken down into sub-
genres:

* poetry into epic, lyric, ballad, sonnet, haiku, epigram, free verse and 'concrete
  poetry' etc. (see **versification**);
* novel into picaresque, epistolary, journals, *realist (social or 'magical'), 'stream of
  consciousness', etc. (see **narrative**);
* drama into **comedies**, **tragedies**, melodrama (initially meaning 'sung drama'),
  street theatre, naturalist, **absurdist**, etc.

Such labels are a recognised and useful part of the vocabulary of literary
criticism. Thus, it is helpful to recognise that the poems by Shakespeare (5.4.4 c)
and Brooke (5.4.6 d) are both *sonnets, that Beckett's *Not I* (5.3.4 d) is an instance
of absurdist drama, and that what links the otherwise highly diverse writings of
Defoe (5.2.2 b) and the Grossmiths (5.2.1 c) is that they are both novels in the form
of diaries. Some important qualifications and extensions need to be made, however;
for the whole matter of genres and sub-genres is a much more fascinating and
volatile area than these relatively familiar and apparently fixed categories seem
to imply.

RE-GENERATING GENRES IN THE ANTHOLOGY

Several deliberate decisions were made about the gathering and sorting of texts in Part Five. All have some bearing on matters of genre.

♦ The recognised mega-genres of poetry, prose and drama are respected but also stretched and supplemented in the three parts; hence, respectively, Poetry, song and performance (5.1); Prose fiction, journals and news (5.2); Scripts and transcripts – conversation, interview and drama (5.3).

♦ There is a recognition of relatively established generic classifications (e.g., Heroic and mock-heroic verse, 5.1.4) as well as more recent classifications (e.g. slave narratives, 5.2.2).

♦ The Intertextual clusters section (5.4), including current genres of small text (5.4.7), is an attempt to demonstrate that gathering and grouping texts is a matter of making as well as finding relations. 'Genre' is something we *do* as well as *see*.

(See the Preview to Part Five and 'Making anthologies and firing "canons" yourself' (4.6) for further explanations and experiments in all these areas.)

Any named instance of a genre always turns out to be in some sense 'mixed', *hybrid or 'impure'; at the very least it can always be categorised in variety of ways. Thus Shakespeare's 'My mistress' eyes' can be characterised and categorised not only as a sonnet but also as a *satire on women, a *rhetorical display and a *parody; Beckett's *Not I* might also be categorised as comedy and/or tragedy (depending how it is performed and interpreted), minimalist theatre or an instance of modernist stream of consciousness.

Genres are constantly changing so as to produce new variations on old modes as well as substantially new configurations. Thus the *romance* was initially a chivalric tale of love and war in the Romance languages (hence the name); but subsequently it came to be the name for any story with a love (but not an erotic or pornographic) interest. Romances can now take forms as various as sentimental Mills and Boon novelettes, A.S. Byatt's highly meta- and intertextual period piece *Possession* (1990) and most of the films featuring Meryl Streep. Meanwhile, the relatively modern genre of *science fiction* has moved from being the apparently exclusive preserve of what has been called the 'men and machines' movement (Verne, Wells, Asimov, Aldiss; latterly *Star Wars*, and *Blade Runner*) towards what might be more properly, though still inadequately labelled, *fantasy fiction*. For now the emphasis tends to be on FEMINIST and/or ecological agendas, often mixed in with variously *utopian* or *dystopian* visions of the future and meditations on the present. Examples include work by Le Guin, Lessing, Piercy, Russ and Carter; and early precursors include Mary Shelley's *Frankenstein* (1818; see 5.2.3 c).

Such constant generation of old/new genres should not surprise us. *Gen*re shares its root 'gen-' (meaning 'growth', or 'creation') with such words as *gen*erate, *gen*eration, and *gen*der. Genres which didn't come and go, change and grow, wouldn't be proper genres at all. (Other radical and ongoing shifts in generic classification are recorded in the entries on **auto/biography and life-writing, comedy and tragedy, carnival and the absurd** and **fiction, fact, faction and metafiction** (see **realism**) and **hi/story** (see **narrative**).)

Genres are by no means limited to LITERATURE *narrowly conceived, or even* LANGUAGE *broadly conceived: they are a characteristic of all kinds of* CULTURAL *product and* COMMUNICATIVE *activity.* Thus we routinely recognise and speak of different genres of *music as, say, 'pop', 'folk' and 'classical'. And then, once more, we can go on to subdivide, blend and extend these 'kinds' so as to produce or recognise sub-genres. For pop perhaps: rock 'n' roll, rhythm 'n' blues, soul, punk, funk, rap, heavy metal, etc; as well as compounds such as 'folk-rock' or – an off-the-cuff coinage I overheard recently – 'rap and roll with a funky rhythm and a touch of Jah Wobble'. (You can doubtless think of and make up many more. DJs do all the time.) In the same fertile and potentially highly nuanced vein, we can talk about different genres, sub-genres and 'cross-genres' of soap opera, game or chat show, police series, news programme, disaster movie, dance craze, and so on. (For some current genres of small text, including technologically driven new genres such as answer-phone and cashpoint messages, as well as e-mail conferencing, see 5.4.7.)

The basic principles relating to genre are therefore few and simple, even though the instances always turn out to be complexly variegated. They can be summarised as follows:

♦ One instance of a text (artefact or activity) is or is not like others in certain respects.
♦ One instance is mixed or fused with others in certain respects.
♦ One instance is always on the point of turning away from or back towards another.
♦ Genres are very much alive and, well, . . . coming and going, changing and growing. (For a relevant overview of *change – social, historical and technological – see LANGUAGE.)

ACTIVITIES

(a)   Concentrate on one of the texts you are studying (or a text featured in Part Five) and consider some of the ways in which it can be categorised. How stable or debatable are these categories? And which would you say are recognised *genres*?

(b)   *Re-genring.* Try interpreting the same short text as though it belonged to quite different genres and could therefore be 'placed' in quite different contexts and intertextual relations. (Suggestions from Part Five include all or any of the texts in 'Some Contemporary 'I'dentities' (5.4.7 g) read as science-fiction fantasy, schizo-phrenic's revelation, children's poem; Freud's 'Dora' (5.3.1 d) read as detective story, patriarchal classic, psychiatric case-history; and *all* the texts in either 5.4.3 or 5.4.5 read as though they belonged to the *same* fictional, factual or factional world.)

DISCUSSION

(i)   Genre is reborn and renewed at every new stage in the development of literature, and in every individual work of a given genre.
                              Mikhail Bakhtin, *The Dialogic Imagination* (1981: 321)

(ii)   Genres are popular when their conventions bear a close relationship to the
       dominant ideology of the time.

John Fiske, *Television Culture* (1987: 112)

Also see: **auto/biography and life-writing; comedy and tragedy, carnival and the absurd; drama and theatre; narrative in hi/story . . . ; text, context and intertextuality**.

READING: *Introductory:* Wellek and Warren 1963: 226–37; Preminger and Brogan 1993: 456–8; Branston and Stafford 1996: 54–77; Fiske 1987: 108–15; Feuer in Allen 1987: 113–33; Bhaya Nair in Toolan 1992: 227–54; Makaryk 1993: 79–85; O'Sullivan *et al.* 1994. *Advanced:* Culler 1975: 226–37; Bakhtin 1981: 41–258; Todorov 1990; Bex 1996.

IMAGES, IMAGERY AND IMAGINATION

An **image** can be strictly visual (e.g., a painting, a photo) or, by extension, it can be a verbal representation of something visual (e.g., a description in a novel). **Imagery** refers to figurative or metaphorical language invoking a comparison or likeness, chiefly in poetry or 'poetic' writing. **Imagination**, meanwhile, can be provisionally defined as the capacity to conceive, 'grasp' or 'see' things, both in a visual and in a more general intellectual sense. Taken together, then, all the terms in this entry have something to do, at least initially, with ways of seeing and saying, and with issues of **representation**, verbal, visual and otherwise. The terms 'image', 'imagery' and 'imagination' are also obviously central to many people's idea of what is going on in LITERATURE and the arts in particular, as well as CULTURE in general. They crop up regularly in discussions of everything from **poetry** and **film** to LITERARY and CULTURAL theory, and in the latter they arise in everything from CLASSICAL to PSYCHOANALYTICAL approaches. What follows is a historical overview of the interrelations among the terms image(s), imagery and imagination (including imaginative and '(the) imaginary'). This is framed so as to encourage inter-disciplinary and multimedia perspectives, while also observing the specificity of these terms in distinct discourses. (For other 'visualising' metaphors, see **foreground, background and point of view**; also **absence . . . centres and margins**.)

   Image came into English, via French, from Latin *imago* during the thirteenth century. The word already had various potential meanings, each of which has been realised and become prominent in English at successive historical moments. The cumulative result is that 'image' can now mean at least five things: *physical likeness*; *mental construct*; *figurative language* (i.e. imagery); *optical effect* and *perceived identity*. We shall consider each of these in turn.

   Image as physical likeness or visible copy, e.g., a painted or photographic representation of people and places, or a perceived resemblance ('She's the very image of her mother').

   Image as mental construct or 'idea', usually of something which only really exists *as* an idea, and may therefore be an illusion or (more negatively) a delusion. This divided sense relates to a variety of persistent debates in aesthetics, philosophy and religion about the nature of images: are they pleasing or harmful? true or false? divinely or diabolically inspired?

Image as 'imagery' – figure of speech, trope ('turn', 'twist'), figurative language in general. **Imagery**, as such, is usually further distinguished in terms of *metaphor*, *simile* and *personification*:

♦ **metaphor* (from Greek *meta-pherein* – 'over-carry'), the implicit 'carrying over' of sense from one area to another, implicitly talking about one thing in terms of something else (e.g., 'She's a doll', 'He's a real pig' – when said of a person, not of a real pig!). Metaphors are themselves further distinguished as

   – *dead* and (relatively) *routine*, e.g., 'He's hard-faced', 'Think straight!'
   – *live* and *striking*, e.g., 'He's marble-eyed', 'Think bent for a change!'
   – *extended* and perhaps *mixed* or *compounded*, depending how coherent and successful the extension is judged to be: e.g. Hamlet's 'To be or not to be' speech: 'Whether 'tis nobler in the mind to suffer / The slings and arrows of outrageous fortune / Or to take arms against a sea of troubles, / And by opposing end them' (Act III, sc i).
   – **metonymic*, in so far as there is a substitution of a part for the whole (e.g., 'motor' when used to mean 'car', 'hand' meaning 'worker') and where something physically connected is involved (e.g., 'the White House', 'the Kremlin' and 'Downing Street' when used to refer to the US, Russian and British governments).

♦ **simile* (from Latin *similis* – 'like'), an explicit and overtly controlled comparison, characteristically signalled by such words as 'like', 'as', 'seems', 'appears', 'compare', 'recalls' (e.g., 'Like a ferret up a drain-pipe', 'as happy as the day is long', 'Shall I compare thee to a summer's day?'). Similes may also be dead, live and extended.

♦ **personification*, conferring human attributes and identities on inanimate or non-human entities (e.g., 'This is a friendly (threatening, snobbish, etc.) place'; 'That vodka grabs you by the throat'). When personification involves an address *to* something as though it were a person, the device is called **apostrophe* (e.g., in **odes* such as Shelley's 'O wild West Wind, thou breath of Autumn's being'). When personification involves an address *by* some non-human speaker, the device is called *prosopopoeia* (e.g., the speaking cross in the Anglo-Saxon *Dream of the Rood*, as well as riddles of the 'I am . . .' type). Sustained personification can result in **allegory* (e.g., the Giant Despair and Hopeful in Bunyan's *The Pilgrim's Progress*, or Grumpy, Bashful, Dopey and Co. in Disney's *Snow White and the Seven Dwarfs*).

All these aspects of 'imagery' are fundamental to LANGUAGE of all kinds, spoken and written. They are not limited to poetry in particular or literature in general. Thus for a long time they were studied as aspects of RHETORIC (see 1.5.5) and drew on neo-classical models (see 1.5.3). In fact it was only NEW CRITICS and some FORMALISTS during the earlier twentieth century who tended to limit the study of 'imagery' to specifically **literary texts, especially poetry (see 2.3–2.4). Modern **discourse analysis** and a renewed interest in rhetoric is resulting in a much greater attention to 'imagery' and the metaphorical nature of non-literary texts, including conversation (see READING below).

Image as a specifically technical, optical effect. The sense here is of what results from the projection of light through a lens and/or film on to paper or a screen, or the assembly of pixels on a TV screen. This sense of image is obviously tied up with transformations in visual technology from the mid-nineteenth century onwards, notably **photography, **film, **television, **video and, latterly, computerised multimedia.

Image as projected or perceived identity, public reputation (as in 'brand image', 'company image', 'creating the right image'). This usage has become current, and in some areas of life dominant, largely through the huge growth in the institutions of *advertising, marketing and public relations. These discourses permeate many areas of life, especially in the 'postindustrial' societies. It is also common to talk of '**self**-image', largely because of the influence of popular PSYCHOLOGY.

Finally, in a specifically academic context, it is interesting to note that the plural '*images*' often occurs in the titles of books, courses, conferences and exhibitions. Hence 'Images of Women (or Men) in . . . ' or 'Images of Work (or Nature, or Hong Kong . . .)'. This usage generally draws on a combination – and sometimes a confusion – of all the above senses of image. It may therefore be unclear whether we are talking about physical likenesses and/or mental conceptions, the 'truth' or 'falseness' of these images, and who is projecting or perceiving them. Then again, unpicking and re-weaving these strands may be precisely the point of the book, course, conference or exhibition in question. (Notice that much the same confusions and challenges can arise even if we choose to talk not of 'Images' but of '*Constructions*' or '**Representations**' or 'The **Subject**' or '**Identities**' of women, men, work, nature, Hong Kong or whatever. It's just that the latter belong to currently favoured and apparently more technical-sounding critical discourses. As did image, imagery and the next term we now turn to . . .)

Imagination is a term somewhat out of favour in critical circles now. (Many critics currently prefer to talk of *signification, *signs and *sign-systems.) However, imagination is a concept with a complex history and constantly renegotiated meanings so there is every reason to believe that (like the related, equally out-of-favour but resilient term *creativity) it will have a valuable future too. 'The Imagination' has at various times been visually likened to a mirror, window, lens and eye – all-seeing, opaque, partially sighted or blind. It has also been hailed as the site or source of everything from utter delusion to sublime revelation (see Selden 1988: 9–39). The huge problem – and fascinating challenge – is of course that we are trying to define an object by means of the tool which is that object. We are trying to imagine imagination! It's like trying to define 'reason' rationally, 'comedy' with tears of laughter, and 'tragedy' with tears of grief. Most immediately, it involves trying to do what we're trying to do throughout this book: define language with language. The most famous and influential attempt at a verbal definition of imagination in English Literature is doubtless that offered by the poet and philosopher Samuel Taylor Coleridge in his *Biographia Literaria* (1817: Ch. 14). There Coleridge explains, at length, that by 'the name of imagination' he means:

> the balance or recognition of opposite or discordant qualities: of sameness, with difference; of the general, with the concrete; the idea, with the image; the individual, with the representative; the sense of novelty and freshness, with old and familiar objects; a more than usual state of emotion, with more than usual order, judgement ever awake and steady self-possession, with enthusiasm and feeling profound or vehement; and while it blends and harmonizes the natural and the artificial, still subordinates art to nature; the manner to the matter; and our admiration of the poet to our sympathy with the poetry.

Many things can be said about Coleridge's definition of imagination. One is that it was much prized and promoted by NEW CRITICS (e.g., Brooks 1947: 12). Such an elegant array of balanced antitheses admirably suited their views of both **aesthetics** and politics as processes of resolving tension through *paradox. Another is that this vision of imagination (and by extension of 'emotion', 'order', 'poetry', 'art' and 'nature') would be substantially challenged, or at least radically reformulated, by critics engaged in developing more conflictual, oppositional – or simply alternative – models of aesthetics and politics. In short, MARXIST, FEMINIST, POSTCOLONIAL, POSTSTRUCTURALIST and POSTMODERNIST writers would all tend to imagine the form and the function of imagination differently. (Hence the invitation to critique Coleridge and imagine some other possibilities in Activity (b) below.) Here just a couple of brief notes will be added to bring the story of images and the imagination up to date.

The Imaginary (*l'Imaginaire*) is given a special status in the PSYCHOANALYTICAL model developed by *Lacan. For him the Imaginary is the name of the non-differentiated state (and stage) of the unconscious before the psychological **subject** enters into language and the symbolic order. For Lacan, in the Imaginary there is not yet a clear distinction between, for instance, 'I' and 'you', 'subject' and 'object', person and thing, child and mother, masculine and feminine, body and mind, physical image and conceptual idea. The Imaginary is also a kind of reservoir of the unconscious which the psyche may draw upon throughout life, chiefly in the form of 'images'; though these are always a skewed refraction (never a direct reflection) of the psyche's 'imaginary' resources.

Meanwhile, *Baudrillard, a postmodernist philosopher and cultural critic, has effectively abolished 'images' in any traditional sense. He insists that we now live in an age when the whole concept of the image is in crisis. Because of the sheer speed, accuracy and proliferation of images in the modern audio-visual media, and because of the incredibly enhanced editing techniques of the computer-assisted multimedia, we have reached a point when it becomes hard to be sure that the image is a copy of anything in the rest of the world, or that there is an 'original' version of the image itself. This concept of the 'image-without-reference' and the 'image-without-an-original' Baudrillard calls a *simulacrum* (cf. Benjamin 1970: 219–53). Thus Baudrillard argues that we may have seen and heard countless 'simulacra' of the 1992 Gulf War in the media (e.g., 5.2.5 c). But they were so highly *mediated at every stage (from computer-guided and camera-tracked missile systems to computer-simulated reconstructions in the media) that we could easily be lulled into believing that a war was not really going on: that the whole thing was a military exercise or another hi-tech disaster movie. It all depends how we really imagine – and image – the deaths of those we do not know. Really?

ACTIVITIES

(a)   *Ways of saying and seeing.* Compare a poem with an advert, or an extract from a novel with a news report, and consider the various kinds of 'image' and/or 'imagery' in play. What are the relations between the verbal and the visual? When does a 'way of saying' become a 'way of seeing', and vice versa?

(Suggestions for comparison in Part Five are the 'Daffodils' texts (5.4.3); the Clarins advert and the other (anti-)ageing texts (5.4.4), and the news reports (5.2.5).)

(b)   *Rewrite Coleridge's definition of 'imagination'* (see above) so as to challenge his assumptions about aesthetics and politics. How, for instance, might some of the writers referred to in Part Two *other than* New Critics view the roles and resources of the imaginative writer or artist? (Suggestion: place Coleridge's pronouncements alongside one or two of the 'How to practise' sections in sections 2.4–2.9.)

DISCUSSION

(i)   Some readers are constitutionally prone to stress the place of imagery in reading [. . .] and even to judge the value of the poetry by the images it excites in them.

I.A. Richards, *Practical Criticism* (1929: 15)

(ii)   You can never stand back and scrutinize a mental image, since you are fully occupied in creating it – it represents your consciousness in action.

P.N. Furbank, *Reflections on the Word 'Image'* (1970, Ch. 1)
in Butler and Fowler (1971: 231)

Also see: 2.3; **foreground, background and point of view; realism and representation**; *sign and *sign-system.

READING: *Introductory:* Moon 1992: 66–8; Wellek and Warren 1963: 186–211; Preminger and Brogan 1993: 556–75; Lentricchia and McLaughlin 1995: 80–90; Williams 1983: 158–9; Montgomery *et al.* 1992: 127–37. *On metaphor:* Empson 1930; Hawkes 1972; Lakoff and Johnson 1980; Jakobson and Lacan in Lodge 1988: 57–61, 79–106. *On imagination:* Selden 1988: 9–39, 123–49. *On the visual image:* Benjamin 1970: 219–53; Barthes 1977: 32–51; Baudrillard 1995; Branston and Stafford 1996: 5–25, 123–49.

NARRATIVE IN HI/STORY, NOVEL, NEWS AND FILM

Narrative can be provisionally defined as 'telling stories, true or false, factual or fictional, in any medium'. The term *narration* is sometimes reserved for the *process* of telling stories, as distinct from the product of the activity, the narrative proper. Such capacious definitions are handy because they encourage us to recognise as narratives (and narrations) all sorts of products and processes: from anecdotes and jokes to adverts and news stories, from short stories to blockbuster novels, from comic strips and cartoons to full-length feature films (and their sequels), from your most recent account of 'what happened yesterday' (in conversation or diary) to full-blown printed histories, auto/biographies and TV documentaries. Narrative is any activity which results in a story being told and an event represented and reported. Such a perspective therefore allows us to see the printed novel and short story (the narrative **genres** most often featured in LITERATURE courses) as simply two amongst many story-telling modes. To offset exclusively literary and verbal emphases, we also look at narrative in history and news, including film, TV and video.

Narration, as already mentioned, is the term sometimes used to refer to the actual process of narrating, the telling as distinct from the tale. The following model is useful when approaching any instance of narrative as part of a communicative process of narration.

actual ⟷ 'external' narrator ⟷ character as narrator ⟷ narratee ⟷ actual
writer   reader

This may be explained as follows. The *actual writer* is the historical person as we conceive of him or her independently of the text s/he wrote (e.g., the living, breathing Dickens, Brontë). The *'external' narrator* is the selective image of her or himself the writer projects in the text (how Dickens or Brontë chooses to present him/herself). The *character-as-narrator* is a figure who both relates and participates in the action (e.g., Pip in *Great Expectations*, Jane in *Jane Eyre*; also see **character**). The *narratee* is the implied addressee of the narrative, the kind of person it appears to be primarily directed at (most explicit in the 'dear reader' mode of narrative, but implicit in every narrative). *Actual readers* are you and me and anyone else every time we engage with a particular narrative. The *two-way arrows* (↔) are important. They remind us of the potential bi- or multidirectionality of all acts of writing and reading. Thus, 'actual writers' define themselves through dialogue with their 'narrators', while 'actual readers' may or may not cooperate with the role of 'narratee' they are offered. A narrative is therefore not so much a given 'thing' as the constant negotiation and realignment of a variety of actual readers and writers through a variety of narrators, characters and narratees. This means that the **points of view** and **centres** of attention of a narrative are never absolutely fixed. The teller tells the tale; but no-one ever puts up with simply being 'told'. The reader, audience or viewer has a part to play too.

NARRATIVE TELLING AND DRAMATIC SHOWING

The basic distinction between *narrative* (what is told, reported and represented) and *drama* (what is shown, enacted or presented) is reviewed under **drama**. So is the fact that, characteristically, narrative emphasises the **address**: what is spoken about, the **subject** positions 'she', 'he', 'they' and 'it'. Drama, meanwhile, emphasises the **addresser–addressee** relation: people speaking and spoken to, the subject positions 'I', 'we' and 'you'. Turn to that entry for a sense of the interrelations of these two modes.

Structural aspects of narrative

Many of the most valuable terms and techniques for the analysis of narrative structure have been provided by FORMALIST and STRUCTURALIST approaches. The most common are listed below. A few words should be added by way of caution, however. Not all of these terms are mutually compatible nor are they always glossed in the same way. The very emphasis on structure as something supposedly 'whole' and 'neutral' would be challenged by many POSTSTRUCTURALIST critics, as well as by those who occupy politically explicit positions. That said, the following distinctions still prove both valuable and durable:

Story and plot. *Story* is *what* is told, the abstractable subject matter. *Plot* is *how* it is told, the actual treatment given to the material. Thus we might list the main characters and events of *Great Expectations* or *Blade Runner*, but that would not tell us how they were actually put together. The plot is what motivates and organises the raw story material.

Fabula and sjuzet (from early Formalist approaches). *Fabula* is the raw narrative events as they would usually be chronologically sequenced outside a particular telling. *Sjuzet* is the particular chronological sequencing and structural logic of a specific telling.

Discours and skaz. Discours (French) and *skaz* (Russian) are tales where the teller is prominent and openly acknowledged (e.g., in the first person and/or with a character-as-narrator). Both are distinct from *histoire* (French) or *historia* (Russian), which are narratives where the presence of the narrator is invisible or unacknowledged. Approximate English equivalents are, respectively, 'yarn' or 'anecdote' as distinct from (impersonal) 'report' or 'account'.

Narrators (also see 'narration' above) are commonly distinguished as:

♦ *first person* (speaking as an 'I') or *third person* (speaking only of others, as 'she', 'he', 'they');
♦ *omniscient* (all-knowing) or *partial / limited*;
♦ *reliable* or *unreliable*, projecting themselves as trustworthy or not.

Narrative episodes are commonly distinguished as:

♦ *beginnings*, *middles* and *ends* – points of opening, development and closure;
♦ *essential* ('kernels', 'nuclei'), i.e. episodes which substantially advance the action;
♦ *optional* ('catalysers', 'satellites'), which elaborate but do not advance action;
♦ *kinetic* – concentrating on movement and transformation;
♦ *static* – concentrating on state and atmosphere.

Characters are commonly distinguished in terms of the ways they are constructed, how far they are: individuals or types; 'rounded' or 'flat'; psychologically interiorised or externally observed (see **character and characterisation**).

Points of view are usually initially identified with specific narrators and characters, but always eventually involve exploration of the positions and values held by actual writers and readers (see 'narration' above). Critical attention is frequently trained upon *shifts and switches in perspective*, and *collisions and coalescences of identity* against a variety of frames of reference which may be internal or external to the text (see **foreground, background and point of view**).

All of the above terms can be used to analyse the structural aspects of narrative in a variety of verbal and visual media, whether in stories or histories, novels or news reports. Care must be taken, however, to respect the structural capacities and generic traditions of the medium (see **drama and theatre, film and TV**); also to recognise that a formal analysis must ultimately take account of *functions if it is to engage with **texts** in **context** (see 2.4).

We now turn to particular kinds or modes of narrative: history, the novel and film. Clearly, these are not mutually exclusive categories. There are plenty of historical novels and historical films (e.g., period pieces and documentaries). Meanwhile, both the novel and film have their own histories implicated in various media and social-historical moments: the novel arose from print technology and culture during the early modern period; film arose from photographic and audio-visual culture over the past century. In this entry we concentrate on the narrative dimensions of history, the novel and film. At what points do they converge and diverge as kinds of story?

History and **story** derive from exactly the same root, Latin *historia*. That in turn derives from the Greek *histor*, meaning 'a form of knowing'. This joint derivation points to an underlying sense in which 'history' and 'story' are basically two aspects of the same process. Both involve the fashioning of narratives which form ways of 'knowing' the world. Indeed, in English and other European vernaculars it is only from the sixteenth century onwards that 'history' begins to be systematically distinguished as a way of knowing the actual past through factual narratives as opposed to 'story' which was a way of knowing everything else through fictional narratives. Concurrently, **fact** and **fiction** were themselves being more rigorously distinguished (see **realism and representation**). Before that, the words 'histoire', 'historie' and 'storie' were used almost interchangeably. If one looks for a modern equivalent it is most likely to be the coinage **faction**. All this may strike modern readers as less strange if it is recalled that most medieval and many classical histories, chronicles and annals began with references to, respectively, Christian and pagan gods, **myths** and legends, then ran up to their own present through more recognisably 'historical' materials, often rounding off with a moral or divine vision of the world to come. The same ample view of history (including what to non-believers are fictional myths and legends) characterises the **Bible**, especially the Old Testament as a history of the Jews. All that need be added here is that there is a growing recognition that the writing and reading of histories (i.e. narrative accounts of what supposedly actually happened) have a great deal in common with the writing and reading of narratives of all kinds, whether supposedly true or not. In fact, an interdisciplinary grasp of **discourse**, **genre** and RHETORIC – *along with narrative* – has recently done much to reconfigure relations between English and History as academic subjects (see 1.5.6).

The **novel** was so called because of the perceived 'newness' of the genre in the eighteenth and nineteenth centuries. Novels can be broadly characterised as 'long narratives in prose dealing chiefly with contemporary life'. All these features together distinguished it from the main literary genres recognised previously by neo-classical writers, namely, drama (comedy and tragedy) or poetry (epic and lyric). Prose *romance was well developed earlier (e.g., Malory's *Morte D'Arthur*); but this dealt with fantastic, usually mythic or legendary materials. In fact, the formal 'newness' of the novel consisted largely in its capaciousness and flexibility: it accommodated all or flouted any of the previously recognised genres. Socially, the novel was tied to the rapid consolidation of a new class of readers, the bourgeoisie. Technologically, it was deeply dependent upon the consolidation of print culture. In all these respects (formally, socially and technologically) the rise of the novel is therefore best seen in conjunction with the rise of that other relatively 'new' phenomenon, *newspapers*. These too came into their own in the eighteenth and nineteenth centuries. These too were built from narratives in prose, appealed to much the same readership and depended upon the same print technology. The crucial and constitutive difference was that whereas novels were presumed to be broadly fictional, newspapers were presumed to be broadly factual (see **realism**).

Most early and many later novels can be further categorised in terms of:

♦ *the established literary genres they adapt and blend* (often *parodically), notably, *romance, **comedy**, **tragedy** and *heroic drama (e.g., Behn, Manley, Fielding, Sterne, Richardson, Dickens);

♦ *the extra-literary genres they draw upon and mimic* (and thereby eventually **canonise** as *literary modes), notably, journals, diaries, letters, travelogues, confessions, conduct books of manners (e.g., Defoe, Richardson, Smollett, Austen);

♦   *formal devices and structural strategies* (see 'Structural Aspects of Narrative' above and the highlighted entries), namely, first or third person, partial or omniscient and un/reliable *narration; **point of view**; emphasis on action or states, plot or **character**; techniques of **realism and representation** (e.g., 'classic realist', 'stream of consciousness', etc. (see above and separate entries).

Film and TV are sequential visual media, unfolding in time as well as in space. They are therefore especially amenable to narrative. Film is built up out of discrete frames which are then shown rapidly so as to provide the impression of continuous movement. In this respect films are like moving strip cartoons (which are themselves a significant narrative form – see *comics – as are animated films as such. TV is formed from patterns of electro-magnetic impulses (now usually stored on video-tape) which produce a continuous 'flow'. Both film and TV are now accompanied by sound-tracks which enable the synchronised reproduction of images, speech, music and sound effects. The overall consequences for the representation of narrative are profound. *Image–music–word* is the larger parcel we must learn to unpack when analysing story-telling in these media. And again it is convenient to distinguish technical, formal and social dimensions of the narrational process. (The emphasis here is upon film; so also see **drama . . . TV**.)

Technically, the basic minimum filmic unit is the *frame*, a continuous series of which builds up into a single *shot*. Shots are variously distinguished as 'still', 'panning', 'tracked' or 'hand-held'; 'long', 'medium', 'medium-close' or 'close-up'; 'full-body', 'half-body' or 'talking-head'; 'shot–reverse shot' (i.e. 'action–reaction'); from 'above', 'below' or 'eye level'; etc. All this material is edited by *cutting* and *splicing* with other shots from the same or different cameras so as to produce a *sequence*. A series of sequences makes up the film as a whole. Technical complications include the fact that a single finished frame can be a composite superimposition of several frames or be modified by computer graphics (in the case of TV 'de- and re-pixillated'). Meanwhile, the 'whole film' may exist in a variety of cut and uncut versions – thus making it a series of 'holes' too.

Formally, like all narratives, films are characterised by shifts and switches in time, place and participants. Development is only rarely strictly chronological and almost never limited to a single scene and a single perspective. Much more often the narrative proceeds through jumps in time and space (ellipsis); perhaps includes flashback, flash-forward or repetition; and generally establishes a variety of points of view – identifying with certain camera positions, focusing on certain figures, etc.

Socially, film is distinguished by specific modes of production and distribution and specific moments of reception. In the cinema proper, these include high-street general release cinema chain or specialised studio cinema. Films on TV get around differently, of course – through commercial or public broadcast; satellite or cable narrowcast; in certain scheduled slots; on or off peak, etc. There is clearly a big difference between watching a big screen from a row of special seats in the dark and lounging around amongst the clutter and clamour of a domestic front room. All these contexts fundamentally affect both the kinds of story that get told in various kinds of film and TV, and the ways in which viewers engage with those stories. Basically, TV narratives tend to be more open-ended, recursive and diffuse (soap operas and situation comedies are the classic case). Meanwhile cinematic film narratives tend to be more closed, progressive and concentrated (one-off feature films are the model here).

Finally, brief mention will be made of two very different models that have proved particularly useful in the study of *popular narratives of all kinds – whether spoken or printed, on film or TV.

Vladimir *Propp, in his influential *Morphology of the Folktale* (1928), developed a model of thirty-one narrative 'functions' (in effect stereotypical actions) based on the analysis of a corpus of Russian folktales. He distinguished such roles as 'hero', 'helper', 'dispatcher', 'villain' and 'princess' and argued that these commonly function in folktales in predictable ways. Typical examples are:

function 25 – A difficult task is proposed to the hero.
function 26 – The false hero or villain is exposed.
function 31 – The hero is married and ascends the throne.

Similar roles and functions have been found in popular narratives from Superman comics to feature films such as *Star Wars* and *Crocodile Dundee* and TV soap operas such as *Dallas* and *Santa Barbara*. This supports the view that popular narrative is substantially formulaic in nature. It perhaps also underwrites the general observation that 'there are only six or seven basic plots in the world' (though, significantly, people tend to disagree on precisely which these are!). (For fuller illustration and discussion, see Fiske 1987: 135–9 and Kosloff in Allen 1987: 47–51.)

William *Labov, in his *Language in the Inner City* (1972), developed a simple yet remarkably durable model for describing the structure of oral narratives. He studied the story-telling patterns of chiefly black vernacular culture in inner city New York and developed a schema that has been widely observed in many kinds of narrative, oral and otherwise. Labov observes that every act of story-telling tends to involve six stages. These are, in order, abstract, orientation, complicating action, evaluation, resolution, coda. Here they will be illustrated by snatches from a story I recently heard in a pub:

1 *Abstract* (preface, link in) – 'Yeah. Something like that happened to me.'
2 *Orientation* – 'There was this guy who lived by the works . . . '
3 *Complicating action* – 'But then you know what happened . . . '
4 *Evaluation* (can be pervasive) – 'He was sooooo stupid . . . '; 'Isn't that cool!'
5 *Resolution or result* – 'Anyway, no one saw him again.'
6 *Coda* (link out) – 'So there you go. Whose round is it?'

(Fuller applications and discussion can be found in Brumfit and Carter 1986: 119–32 and Toolan 1988: 146–76.)

ACTIVITIES

(a) *Draw on one or more of the models/checklists supplied above to help analyse a narrative and a process of narration which interests you.* That is, use one of these: narration as process (actual writer . . . actual reader); structural aspects of narrative; narrative in film and TV (technical, formal and social); Propp's model of popular story; Labov's model of oral story-telling. (Suggestion: Kipling's 'Muhammad Din' (5.2.4 b) or Bambara's 'The Lesson' (5.3.5 a).)

(b)   *That's history! What's news?* Compare two news reports of ostensibly the same event (e.g., 5.2.5 a and b). How precisely does each build it into a different news *story*, and in effect construct a different event? In particular, compare the ways in which these stories begin, develop and close; what arguments or agendas they address; and how they handle people, places and time as well as action, speech and evaluation. Which account would be of greatest value as a 'historical' document? Writing a history of what?

(c)   *Adapting beginnings and endings* Speculate how you would film and edit the opening and closing sequences of a novel or short story with which you are familiar. Be sure at some point to consider all the main *technical, formal* and *social* dimensions referred to above. (See reading below for further guidance.)

DISCUSSION

(i)   Caring nothing for the division between good and bad literature, narrative is international, transhistorical, transcultural.
Roland Barthes, 'Introduction to the Structural Analysis of Narratives'
(1977: 79)

(ii)   There is the time of the thing told and the time of the telling . . .
Christian Metz, *Film Language: A Semiotics of the Cinema* (1974: 18)

Also see: 1.5.6; FORMALISM INTO FUNCTIONALISM; POSTSTRUCTURALISM; POST-MODERNISM; **auto/biography; character; drama and theatre, film and TV; foreground, background and point of view; realism and representation: fiction, fact, faction and metafiction**.

READING: *Introductions to narrative in general, chiefly in literature*: Stubbs in Carter and Burton 1982: 57–85; Moon 1992: 77–9; Hillis Miller in Lentricchia and McLaughlin 1995: 66–74; Montgomery *et al.* 1992: 169–219; Pope 1995: 70–119; Branston and Stafford 1996: 26–47; also Booth 1961: 149–65; Wellek and Warren 1963: 212–26. *Fuller studies:* Propp 1928; Labov 1972; Barthes 1977: 79–124; Chatman 1978; Rimmon-Kenan 1983; Bal 1985; Toolan 1988; Prince 1987 (reference); Stibbs 1991; *Specifically in film:* Metz 1974: 16–28, 185–227; Chatman 1978; Bordwell 1985; Bordwell and Thompson 1993: 64–114; Turner 1993: Ch. 4. *Specifically in TV*: Fiske 1987: 128–48; Kosloff in Allen 1987: 42–73; Selby and Cowdrey 1995: 64–190. *On screen adaptation of novels:* Giddings *et al.* 1990; McFarlane 1996. *Advanced theory:* Jameson 1981; Bhabha 1990; Onega and Landa 1996 (anthology).

POETRY AND WORD-PLAY

This entry is in part a plea for 'play' in tertiary English Studies, both as something we study and something we do. It focuses in particular upon *word-play*, that is, play within and around language. It also proposes that *poetry*, though certainly the most prestigious and sometimes the most complex form of verbal play, is still just one of the many forms that it can take. Jokes and witty remarks (including puns and *figurative language) are obvious instances of word-play in which most of us routinely engage. But it is also possible to regard a large part of all language use as a form of play. Much of the time speech and writing are not primarily concerned with the instrumental conveying of information at all, but with the social *inter*play embodied in the activity itself. In fact, in a narrowly instrumental, purely informational sense most language use is no use at all. Moreover, we are all regularly exposed to a barrage of more or less overtly playful language, often accompanied by no less playful images and music. Hence the perennial attraction (and distraction) of everything from advertising and pop songs to newspapers (especially the tabloids), panel games, quizzes, comedy shows, crosswords, Scrabble and graffiti. Much of this language has designs upon us as well as itself: the play is ultimately designed to make someone pay. There is a commercial as well as an **aesthetic** incentive. For all these reasons, this entry does not concentrate upon poetry narrowly conceived, but on word-play broadly conceived (including poetry). More specific attention to poetry as a **genre, versification** and **imagery** will be found in those entries.

Word-play can occur at all levels of LANGUAGE: sound, visual presentation, word, grammatical structure, genre and context. It also occurs in all areas of **discourse**: the media, education, law, medicine, the family, etc. Indeed, in so far as discourses are conceived, following Wittgenstein (1953) and Lyotard (1979), as distinct kinds of 'language game' (however seriously played), certain kinds of 'word-play' are constitutive of discourses as such. We shall therefore review each of the levels of language in turn, even though in any given instance we usually find more than one level in play at once (see 4.2 for a corresponding linguistic checklist and Part Six for definitions).

Sound-play (using *phonology) arises whenever the sounds of the language become a source of pleasure in themselves, usually through repetition with variation. In simple cases the result is a kind of 'word-music' with a strong rhythm but with little semantic sense, e.g., 'Hickory, Dickory, Dock', 'Humpty, Dumpty . . . ', 'With a hey-nonny-no', 'Oop-oop-be-doop', 'Bee-bop-a-lula', 'Showaddywaddy'. Commonly these elements function as refrains or choruses: they offer points where everyone can join in. Hence their frequency in popular songs and children's rhymes. More elaborate and extended sound-play usually entails complex relations with word meaning and grammatical structure. *Alliteration, *assonance, *stress, **rhythm**, **rhyme** and **metre** may then supply a framework of sound-patterning which underpins or counterpoints everything else (see **versification**). Poetry and song offer the most complex and varied examples (see Shakespeare's 'My mistress' eyes' (5.1.3 b) and, if possible, listen to Queen's 'Bohemian Rhapsody' (5.1.10), for instance, and see section 5.1 generally). But advertising, too, draws upon many of the same playful features: e.g., 'Beanz Meanz Heinz', 'You can with a Nissan'; 'Lipsmackinthirst-quenchinacetastin . . . Pepsi!'; 'Coke. It's the Ree-a-l thing' (sung variously). The main difference is in the kinds and degrees of sophistication involved, and the 'games' we feel we are being invited to play. After all, it's not only Coke, Heinz and Queen who have 'designs' on us. So has Shakespeare and every other writer.

Visual play uses the letters, shapes, spaces and colours on the page or screen to form patterns in their own right/write. *Punctuation, font styles, letter sizes, line breaks, overall layout and design: these are all areas where the sheer materiality of the written or printed word is what attracts or sustains our attention – from tight sonnet-nuggets (5.1.3 b–c, 5.4.4 c, 5.4.6 d) through evenly spaced quatrains (5.1.6, 5.4.5 d, 5.4.6 c) to the more flexible shapes of free verse (5.4.5 e, 5.4.6 e), magazine advertising (5.4.4 b) and newspaper – especially tabloid – copy (5.2.5 a–b). The editorial sophistication of the modern, computer-assisted multimedia also means that it is increasingly common for words not only to accompany images but actually to transform into them. 'Logos' are already a well-established area of word-as-image design. But film titles and credits also routinely superimpose upon or fade and merge into the action. So do the ceaselessly re-forming names and identities of everything from news programmes to whole TV channels (the constantly metamorphosing '2' of BBC 2 and the '4' of Channel 4 are two familiar instances from the UK). Graffiti on advertising hoardings are simply one of the more graphically resistant responses to a designedly graphic stimulus.

Lexical ('word') play arises where single words or lexical items are swapped around and even chopped up so as to remind us that they are both perpetually mobile and infinitely divisible. Crosswords, Scrabble and many TV and radio quizzes depend upon precisely this volatility and versatility at the level of 'individual' words (words which in the event turn out to be highly 'dividual'!). Characteristically, however, these tend to be framed as word-*games* (narrowly conceived) rather than word-*play* (broadly conceived). Usually the questions are of the 'who', 'what', 'when' and 'where' type and can be answered by 'slot-filling' (the quiz equivalent of linguistic 'cloze' tests). Genuinely innovative and amusing panel shows such as *Have I Got News for You* and *Whose Line Is It Anyway?* are characterised by a healthy disregard for the question as posed – as well as a healthy irreverence for the questionmaster who poses. The contributors digress at will and the final score is totally irrelevant or an utter travesty. And that, arguably, is the difference between genuine word-*play* and a (mere) word-*game*. Poetry, we may add, also only becomes really significant when it constitutes a form of *play* with words – and by extension with the world – never simply a word-*game*.

Interestingly one of the most common kinds of lexical humour, the *pun, is often looked down upon in academic discourse. Evidently this is because the pun destabilises the rules of sound-meaning, sporting in the spaces between signifier and signified (see *sign). It thereby threatens the very fabric of certain kinds of rationalistic argument. It is sigificant, therefore, that many POSTSTRUCTURALIST, PSYCHOANALYTIC and FEMINIST critics have reinvested the pun with a measure of seriousness while also striving to maintain its free-booting irregularity. Derrida's pun on *'différence/différance'* (i.e. **difference**/deferral) is perhaps the most famous example. But there are many more: Lacan's 'hommelette' / 'omelette' (little man/ scrambled egg), Cixous's 'sorties' (way(s) out), Irigaray's 'specular/speculate' and Rich's '*re-vision' are simply a few. In all these cases being 'punny' is both a happy accident and a deliberately ambiguating move. All these writers seek to disturb and re-form – not merely reflect – the polished surfaces of academic discourse. Naturally, those who admire that polish decry such writers and continue to demean the pun. Yet both Shakespeare and Joyce were utterly inveterate 'punsters', as legions of critics have noted with distaste or delight.

Structural play (sporting with *syntax and *cohesion) arises whenever there is a pleasurable sense of tension set up and maintained across larger linguistic structures, even across whole texts. Take the first few lines of Hamlet's 'To be or not to be' speech (Act III, sc. i). In this case, not only is there a sustained sound-play built upon the tension between a regular underlying pattern of pentameter blank verse and the alternately halting and flowing rhythm of the speech. There is also a complex web of *metaphors ('take arms', 'sea of trouble', 'to sleep', 'to dream') which itself threatens to come apart even as it seems to come together. Joyce's *Ulysses* and Beckett's *Not I* (5.3.4 d) also sport with expectations about conventional sentence structure and conventional perceptual coherence. They thereby **foreground** clipped and elliptical structures and in effect *defamiliarise our sense of the world.

Contextual and **intertextual** play arise whenever we recognise that a text is being sited and cited differently. For ultimately every text can be aligned with a wide and potentially contradictory range of **genres** and can be located in a wide and potentially contradictory range of **contexts**. Take Freud's 'Dora', for instance (5.3.1 d). Depending upon the critical discourse in which we wish to site/cite it, this can be categorised as: 'mystery thriller', *roman à clef* (i.e. auto/biographically coded fiction), 'interview transcript', 'interrogation record', 'psychiatric case-history', 'scholarly article' and even – most immediately – 'example in a textbook' (see 2.5. Activity (c)). By extension, we may also ask what situation or context this text is to be attached to. Do we 'place' it in Freud's consulting room in late 1900, when the interview occurred? In the medical journal of 1905 in which it was first published? Or in one of the 'here and nows' as I put it in a textbook and you pull it out? All these are instances of the ways in which there is a degree of 'play' opened up in the spaces within and around the text. Genre and context are not simply 'givens'. They are the product of a kind of 'give and take'. It is also at this point that 'word-play' most obviously gives way to what may be called 'world play' – a sense of the world as a place which is not simply found but also perpetually remade.

ACTIVITIES

(a)   *In what ways might each of the following texts be considered in some sense 'playful':* the supermarket exchange (5.3.1 a); the Clarins advert (5.4.4 b), Queen's 'Bohemian Rhapsody' (5.1.10); Harrison's *v.* (5.4.5 c)? In each case review all the main levels of language (sound, visuals, individual words, larger structures, genre and context) and keep an eye and an ear open for the various discourses being drawn upon (see 4.2. for an analytical framework and checklists).

Go on to consider any other text which interests you as in some ways 'playful'.

(b)   *Is there any common feature or quality of the various 'poems' in section 5.1 that* would allow you to say categorically 'Poetry is X and does Y' or, conversely, 'Poetry is *not* A and does *not* do B'? Weigh the implications of your answer for the study of poetry in particular and texts in general.

(c)   *Discipline or pun-ish!* Attack or defend the practice of punning in academic disciplines such as English (for instances, see above). Do so in as po-faced or punny a manner as you see fit.

DISCUSSION

(i)   Play is the disruption of presence. [. . .] Play is always play of absence and presence.
              Jacques Derrida, 'Structure, Sign and Play in the Discourse of the Human Sciences' (1966) in Lodge (1988: 121)

(ii) Not only does play with language demonstrate that it is *within* our control, but
      it is also a celebration of an infinite potential and unexpected creative power
      which, though *beyond* our control, is also the key to change and freedom *from*
      control.

Guy Cook, 'Language Play in English', in Maybin and Mercer
(1996: 226)

Also see: RHETORIC; 'Alternative modes of critical and creative writing' (4.4);
**absence and presence; aesthetics; comedy and tragedy, carnival and the
absurd; image, imagery and imagination; versification: stress, rhythm, metre
and rhyme**.

READING: *Introductory on word-play:* Crystal 1995: 394–422; Makaryk 1993: 65–9,
145–9; Nash 1992: 67–155; Pope 1995: 1–45, 183–202; Cook in Maybin and
Mercer 1996: 198–234. *Fuller studies:* Nash 1989; Chiaro 1992; Lacan, Derrida and
Bakhtin in Lodge 1988: 79–156; Kristeva 1984; Cixous in Belsey and Moore 1997.
On puns: Redfern 1984; Culler 1988; Attridge 1988. *On wor(l)d-play in general:*
Wittgenstein 1953; Winnicott 1974; Bakhtin 1968, 1981: 41–83; Lyotard 1979; Hutcheon
1985, 1989.

REALISM AND REPRESENTATION: FICTION, FACT, FACTION AND METAFICTION

All the terms featured here concern the relation between what people consider
'real' and what goes on in cultural representations of that reality. How do literature
and art relate to the rest of life? What makes one work 'fictional' and another
'factual'? Is this the same as saying works are 'true' or 'false'? And how stable are
such categories as 'fiction' and 'fact' (or 'true' and 'false') from culture to culture,
period to period and even person to person? In any case, do we always have
to measure artistic and literary works by their capacity to imitate faithfully some
supposedly pre-existent reality? Can't we also think of them as *making* their own
realities?

   In this entry, we see why it is important to distinguish 'reali*ty*' (the general and
ultimately unknowable notion of 'what is') from 'reali*sms*' (specific aesthetic
movements which at various times have claimed to represent that reality accurately).
We also see that 'fiction' and 'fact' not only turn out to be variable and mutually
interdependent categories; they sometimes even turn into one another. Hence the
use of the *hybrid term 'faction', as well as the attention to texts which flaunt their
own status as fictions (i.e. 'metafictions').

   Realism in LITERATURE usually refers to one of two things:

♦ *'classic nineteenth-century realism'*, as in novels such as Austen's *Pride and Prejudice*
   (5.2.3 b) or plays such as Ibsen's *A Doll's House* (5.3.3). Such realism usually entails
   detailed attention to the routine texture of social life, a narrator who is nominally
   invisible, and language which does not draw attention to itself. All this gives the
   impression of a direct, unmediated engagement with the characters and the action.
   This is sometimes called 'bourgeois realism' by MARXISTS because of the emphasis
   on middle-class families and values.

♦   *any movement which claims to offer a fresh, supposedly more faithful view of reality, and
     thereby replace a preceding view of reality that has become conventionalised.* In this
     respect almost every major literary or artistic movement (*Neo-classical, *Romantic,
     *Modernist or POSTMODERNIST) claims to offer a higher or deeper reality than the
     one preceding it. So invariably do the movements that supersede it.

     Clearly, it all depends what we understand by reality in the first place. '*Reality*'
     derives from the Latin word *res*, meaning 'thing'. Thus whenever we privilege one
     view of 'things' to the exclusion of all others we 'reify' it. A more productive approach
     is to recognise that a certain vision or version of reality always exists in relation to
     some conceptual *frame of reference.* This in turn presupposes some evaluative *frame
     of preference* (i.e. what we prefer to acknowledge as real – the kind of reality we
     *value as deeper or truer). An obvious example of this is the fact that the various
     critical approaches featured in Part Two (NEW CRITICAL, PSYCHOANALYTIC,
     POSTSTRUCTURALIST, etc.) all frame ostensibly 'the same thing' (a **text**) in markedly
     different ways. Moreover, not only do they see 'it' differently; they also argue about
     where 'it' ends and something else begins: where text becomes **context**, and where
     one text becomes another, **intertextually**. By extension, the kind of literary and
     aesthetic 'realism' you prefer very much depends upon the kind of reality you
     recognise and value. Thus it is perfectly possible to see 'documentary realism' in
     photography, cinema, TV, the novel and news as being utterly natural and neutral *or*
     as being utterly contrived and unconvincing. It all depends how you view the illusion
     that the camera, reporter or observer are simply there by accident, and the
     implication that there has been no selection, organisation, editing or distribution.
     Conversely, you may see Joyce's *Ulysses* or Woolf's *The Waves* (1931) or Faulkner's
     The Sound and the Fury (1929) as the most 'realistic' novels you have ever come
     across (notwithstanding their reputation as deeply difficult Modernist texts
     associated with '*stream of consciousness' techniques). Again, it all depends how
     you reckon your own *consciousness works. And in all these cases it depends what
     norm of reality you recognise as **background** to the *form of realism* in the
     foreground.
          Representation has two distinct yet connected meanings:

♦   *verbal description and visual depiction,* e.g., the pictorial representation of a
     landscape or the written representation of someone's speech (in a transcript, say);
♦   *acting on behalf of someone or something, standing in for them,* e.g., proportional
     representation as a form of government, the US 'House of Representatives', or a
     'sales rep(resentative)' who sells on behalf of a business.

It is important to grasp both the distinction and the connection between these two
meanings of representation. Painting a landscape is not necessarily the same as
acting on behalf of it. Recording someone's speech is not necessarily the same
as speaking on behalf of them. And yet, at the same time, there is clearly some sense
in which offering a certain vision of a landscape and offering a certain version of
someone's words *is* an act of standing in for or acting on behalf of that landscape or
person. The one kind of representation relates to – even if it is not identical with
– the other. The following questions are framed with this in mind. They can be
put to cultural activities and political institutions in general, as well as to texts in
particular.

QUESTIONS OF 'REPRESENTATION'

♦ Who is representing whom or what, when, where, how and why?
♦ Who or what is being *mis*represented, *under*-represented or *un*represented?
♦ Who and what is present in or absent from the text, image or institution?
♦ Who and what is treated as central, marginal or non-existent?
♦ What frames of reference (and preference) is it – and are you – appealing to?
♦ How else might ostensibly the 'same' people and things be represented?
♦ Or would a really radical re-representation put quite other people and things in play?
(Compare questions on 'De- and recentring' (see **absence**) and '**Discourse** questions',
pp. 157, 189.)

Fiction has had a complicated triple sense since its first appearance in English (from French) in the fourteenth century. It could – and still can – mean:

1   imaginative literature or creative writing in general;
2   prose narrative in particular, especially the **novel** and short story;
3   something 'made-up' in the sense of being deceptive, a counterfeit (i.e. a mere or sheer fiction).

Such an ambiguous, and on balance suspicious, attitude to the 'made-up' nature of fiction is at least as old in the West as Plato. Plato would have banished poets from his ideal republic precisely because they invented things which, strictly, never had been or could be (Greek *poeisis* simply meant 'making-up', 'fashioning'; just as 'fiction' derives from another, Latin word meaning 'to fashion' – *fingere*). Something similar happened in practice during the Stalinist era in Russia and at the time of the Cultural Revolution in China. In both cases only certain officially approved forms of '*socialist realism' were encouraged (typically, these represented heroically progressive workers and pathetically decadent bourgeois reactionaries). Everything else was dubbed 'fictional', in the negative sense of being deceptive and deluded, and promptly suppressed.

Another awkward aspect of the term 'fiction' is that, especially from the nineteenth century onwards, it has tended to be crudely set against its supposed opposite 'fact'. If something is not a 'fact' then apparently it's a (mere) 'fiction' or, by this time used almost synonymously, a 'fancy'. At the same time, and for the same reasons, '**story**' was being increasingly distinguished from *its* supposed opposite, '**history**' (see **narrative**). The problem in all these cases, of course, is precisely how far we can actually distinguish 'fiction' from 'fact' and 'story' from 'history' in any particular instance. A further twist in the tale of 'fiction' is that in twentieth-century high-street bookstores and local libraries the most fundamental division is that between 'Fiction' and '*Non*-fiction' (not between 'fiction' and 'fact'). This is presumably because in these contexts it is fiction which is the most sought-after and numerous category, so *that* becomes the privileged term. 'Non-fiction' is its merely shadowy inversion – and 'Fact' has disappeared completely.

Faction (i.e. 'fact' + 'fiction') is the term preferred by some writers when seeking to challenge casually extreme notions of fact versus fiction, truth versus falsehood, and reality versus imagination. **Hi/story** (with a slash) is sometimes preferred for the same reasons: it avoids a simplistic opposition of 'story' to 'history'. In all these cases it then becomes a matter of deciding what *kinds* and *degrees* of fiction/fact and story/history are in play in any particular instance. Questions of absolute 'truth' thus tend to modulate into questions of relative power and knowledge. 'Reality' is always already implicated in discourses. It is not a pre-existent entity.

Metafiction involves the activity of revealing and sporting with the processes of fiction-making even while you are engaged in them. It is a comment *on* fiction *in* fiction, just as *metalanguage is a comment *on* language *in* language. A famous early example of metafiction is Sterne's *Tristram Shandy* (1760–67). There the narrator constantly reminds us of the options both writer and reader have as the story is built before our eyes. Devices include a blank page for the reader to fill in, a line-drawing of how a stick was flourished (because various attempts at verbal description have repeatedly defeated the writer), and the author's constant admission that there are far more events **absent** from the novel than can possibly be represented in it. More recent examples are Fowles's *The French Lieutenant's Woman* (1969), where the novelist offers us alternative, un/happy endings from which we may choose (the film adaptation offers us a film within a film). B.S. Johnson's *The Unfortunates* (1969) is another example. It was produced in a box of twenty-seven loose-leaf sections designed so that readers can reshuffle and reread them in any order they please.

But the process of self-reflexivity in writing is by no means limited to 'fiction' in a narrow or a broad sense. What FORMALISTS call 'laying bare the device' and what *Brecht, in a more politically charged vein, calls 'making strange' occur in writing and communication of all kinds. **Theatre**, for example, is full of instances of the playwright, director and performers drawing attention to the very theatricality of the stage play. Famous instances include the play within the play in *Hamlet* ('The Mousetrap') and the plays of Brecht himself. Instances in Part Five are the open clash of media and perspectives in *Oh What a Lovely War* (5.4.6 f) and the overt cross-dressing and self-consciously stereotypical acting of *Cloud 9* (5.3.4 e). We might call this 'metatheatre': comment on the theatre in the theatre. **Poetry**, too, is virtually by definition *metalinguistic in that it calls attention to its own language through sustained processes of foregrounding, notably in **versification** and **imagery**. Narrative poets such as Chaucer and Byron also remind us of the insistent presence of their narrators.

The fact (!) is that any text which at some point calls attention to the fact (!!) that it is a made object can be called 'metatextual' (as here!!!). Even the routine apparatus of avowedly factual textbooks – the acknowledgements, preface, contents, chapter divisions and titles, notes, bibliography, the covers, the title – are constant reminders that a text cannot but expose to view some of its own processes of making. Thus, to be wholly consistent, we should perhaps recognise the category 'metafaction' as something which goes on in all kinds of text, whether they are nominally categorised as 'fiction' and/or 'fact'. (The same applies to the titles and credits of films and TV programmes – whether feature or documentary.) The text in question may or may not overtly present itself as a made-up object. But nothing can stop alertly critical readers and viewers from drawing attention to precisely these aspects of its manufacture and mediation. In this respect, metatextuality is something we do as much as something we find (see **intertextuality**).

ACTIVITIES

(a)   *Realisms (plural)*. Compare an extract from a supposedly 'classic realist' text with an extract from a supposedly 'post/modernist' text (e.g., *Pride and Prejudice* (5.2.3 b) with *How Late it Was* (5.2.6); *A Doll's House* (5.3.3) with *Oh What a Lovely War* (5.4.6 f). According to what frames of p/reference might you claim that each both is and isn't 'realistic'?

(b)   *Represented and mis-, under- or un-represented?* Put the above 'Questions of "Representation" ' to any text which interests or irritates you. (Kipling's 'Muhammad Din' (5.2.4 b) often works well.)

(c)   *Non/fiction, Faction, Hi/story, Metafiction . . .* Attack, support or suggest alternatives to these critical coinages with reference to specific texts you are studying. (By way of prelude, try visiting the 'Fiction' and 'Non-fiction' sections of a general bookstore or public library. Open a book from each section at random and try to make a case for it being in the other section.)

DISCUSSION

(i)   But realism is itself just a matter of convention [. . .] and no one device is inherently more realistic than another.
Ann Jefferson, 'Russian Formalism' in Jefferson and Robey (1986: 34)

(ii)   modern realism [. . . has] developed in increasingly rich forms in keeping with the constantly changing and expanding reality of modern life.
Erich Auerbach, *Mimesis: The Representation of Reality in Western Literature* (1946: 554)

Also see: FORMALISM INTO FUNCTIONALISM; POSTSTRUCTURALISM AND POST-MODERNISM; **absence and presence; auto/biography; discourse; foreground, background and point of view; image . . . imagination; narrative in hi/story, novel, news and film**.

READING: *Introductory:* Moon 1992: 107–9; Montgomery *et al.* 1992: 211–19; Williams in Lodge 1972: 581–91; MacCabe in Bennett *et al.*: 1981: 216–35; Mitchell in Lentricchia and McLaughlin 1995: 11–22; Branston and Stafford 1996: 78–95; Selden 1988: 9–122. *Advanced:* Auerbach 1946; Williams 1983: 134–5, 257–62, 266–9. *On metafiction:* Waugh 1984; Hutcheon 1989; Marshall 1992; Currie 1995 .

SPEECH AND CONVERSATION, MONOLOGUE AND DIALOGUE

'Speech' means both the activity of speaking and the thing which results (e.g., 'a speech'). Like **writing**, the other major dimension of LANGUAGE, speech is both process and product. It is important to stress, however, that speech and writing are analogous but not identical activities. Speech is made from sounds in air (*phonological material), while writing is made from marks on paper or plastic, etc. (*graphological material). Speech is more continuous with its **context**, whereas writing has a semi-independent existence as **text**. Speech tends to be more immediate and ephemeral, writing to be more remote and permanent. Some such broad distinctions between speech and writing are initially useful. However, they also need to be qualified in view of developments in audio-visual COMMUNICATIONS and MEDIA technology since the late nineteenth century. We now routinely use such apparatuses as the record-player or gramophone (from Greek 'mark-sound'), telephone (Greek 'far-sound'), as well as photography, radio, film, television (Greek 'far-vision'), video, and a whole host of computer-assisted interfaces including e-mail, multimedia CD Rom and the Internet. All these technologies have tended to scramble and reconstitute traditional distinctions between 'speech' and 'writing'. Speech, too, can now be recorded and *edited like any written or printed text. It too can travel or be broadcast over vast distances in space and time, and just as quickly. For this reason the lists of the properties and structures of speech that follow are carefully qualified. (Corresponding and contrasting lists can be found in the entry on **writing**.)

SPEECH IS CHARACTERISTICALLY (but not always):

- *immediate, transitory and often spontaneous*
  (unless it is scripted, recorded or broadcast and thus obviously *mediated).
- *face-to-face and tied to a single shared context*
  (but with non-shared contexts if, say, talking on the telephone or watching TV).
- *potentially dialogic, two- or many-way and interactive*
  (though ostensibly 'live' speeches in lectures, sermons and political speeches can be resolutely monologic and seem anything but 'live'; conversely, letters, magazine problem-pages and TV chat shows – including studio-audience participation and viewer phone-ins – can be palpably two- or many-way).
- *learnt 'naturally' by nearly everybody without special training*
  (though *literacy, too, can come to seem 'natural' in certain communities).

THE STRUCTURES OF SPEECH are therefore characteristically (but not always):

- *deeply embedded in other, *non-verbal aspects of face-to-face* COMMUNICATION, from eye contact, posture and gesture all the way through to the size of the room and the nature of the occasion
  (though an ostensibly 'live' speaker can still avert eyes, read the speech and ignore the audience. Conversely, professional news presenters, DJs and game-show hosts cultivate a wide range of 'face-to-face' – even 'in-your-face' – strategies).
- *heavily dependent on *context-sensitive words*, e.g., 'I', 'you', 'this', 'that', 'here', 'over there', 'now', 'in a moment'
  (though informal written communications such as postcards, personal letters and casual e-mail also exhibit many of these features, along with many of those listed below).
- *pervasively organised by variations in *stress and *intonation*, often resulting in words being drawn out or clipped; e.g., 'I r-e-e-ally like *that*! D'you?'
  (though as these printed examples show, there are partly corresponding resources available in written *spelling, *punctuation and visual presentation).
- *full of suspended, mixed or reduced grammatical structures*, often with an emphasis on loose grammatical *coordination* ('And . . . And . . . But . . .'). Other common features of spoken grammar include:

- *false-starts, back-tracking, half-formed restatements* and *reinforcements* as speakers switch structures in mid-flow (e.g., 'Perhaps, if you'd be . . . Or rather, would you like me to . . . ');
- grammatically pared down structures with routine *ellipsis* of subjects and auxiliaries (e.g., 'Going tomorrow?' rather than the fuller 'Are you going tomorrow?);
- *fillers* like 'erm' and 'ah', *phatic communicators* like 'you know' and *tag *questions* like ' . . . isn't it?' – these last two being quick checks that the listener is listening. (Again, informal writing may exhibit or mimic all these features.)

♦   *frequent sharing or interrupting by different speakers*, as the listener anticipates and 'completes' or cuts across and deflects what the first speaker was saying, e.g., 'A: He's a real . . . B: – bastard. A: Yeah.'
(though typed 'conferencing' on the Internet can be full of such things too, see 5.4.7 f.)

Speech thus characteristically features all of the above properties and structures. The fact that it doesn't always – and that writing, print and the modern audio-visual media do sometimes – simply adds richness and variety to the possibilities. We therefore have to approach each instance of speech or writing on its own terms, keeping general models in mind but also with a sensitivity to specificities. It will also be clear from the foregoing that some spoken language can be **monologic** and 'one-way' in tendency. Examples are conventional lectures, sermons, political speeches and news bulletins. Equally clearly, however, the great majority of spoken language tends to be **dialogic** and 'two-' or 'many-way'. We now concentrate on the most common and characteristic of dialogic speech modes: conversation.

   Conversation is the usual word for spoken interaction of all kinds. These range from passing banter and informal chats to formal interviews and interrogations. *Conversation analysis* concentrates on verbal interaction involving two or more present participants. The following analytical scheme is commonly used, though terminology sometimes varies. (The illustrations are drawn from the conversation at the supermarket checkout (5.3.1a), which is also analysed in the entry on **discourse analysis** p. 190.)

CONVERSATIONAL STRUCTURES, ranked from larger to smaller, are:

interaction – the encounter as a whole (customer and cashier at supermarket);
transaction – negotiation of a particular topic (the bill and change);
exchange – a minimal round of initiation and response (e.g., first two lines).
turn – one person's turn at speech (e.g., 'There's a mistake here');
move – a particular move within the turn (e.g., 'Excuse me').

CONVERSATIONAL STRATEGIES, both verbal and *non-verbal, include:

♦   who opens and who closes, and how;
♦   who nominates the topic and appears to direct the transaction;
♦   who initiates and responds, who listens and supports;
♦   frequency and fluidity of turn-taking;
♦   who interrupts or 'completes' another's words;
♦   precise patterns of question, statement, command and exclamation, as well as more indirect *speech acts (e.g., statement as query, invitation as command).

When we analyse any instance of conversation with the above structures and strategies in mind, one thing quickly become clear.

CULTURE IS A CONTINUING – SOMETIMES CONTENTIOUS – 'CONVERSATION'.
To be specific,

♦ Conversation proceeds dynamically, through divergence as well as convergence, conflict as well as cooperation.
♦ Conversation enacts the negotiation of personal relationships and relations of power.
♦ Any specific interaction is just one part of a continuing conversation which, strictly, has no absolute beginning or absolute end – only provisional, though decisive, points of opening and closure.
♦ Conversation is therefore part of that larger dialogue we call, variously, society, **history** and CULTURE.

Dialogue has two further, more specialised meanings, aside from the senses of conversation and interaction in general: (i) the fictional representation of speech in novels, plays and films (e.g., 'a piece of dialogue', 'to script some dialogue'); (ii) the dialogic principle as developed by *Bakhtin, in which every utterance or text responds to a previous one and anticipates a succeeding one. We shall briefly treat each in turn.

Dialogue as the fictional representation of conversation in novels, plays and films
The most common questions put to this kind of dialogue are 'How authentic, natural or realistic is this dialogue?' or ' How much like ordinary, non-fictional speech is it?' Some cautions need to be issued however:

1   Most fiction writers have never especially aimed to represent non-fictional speech faithfully in the first place – nor have most of their readers and audiences expected it. (This goes for most of Chaucer, Shakespeare, Milton and Dickens, to mention only 'classic' writers.)

2   Most writers and readers work quite happily within highly conventionalised expectations of how people speak (and act) in the various **genres**: romance, novel of manners, detective novel, Elizabethan tragedy or comedy, Victorian melodrama, *film noir*, cowboy film, road movie, TV police series, etc. All entail distinctive verbal and visual modes, as is confirmed by their instant recognisability and their openness to *parody.

3   There is a vast difference between a crafted *script* and a *transcript* of spontaneous conversation, as is abundantly demonstrated by comparing the transcript of spontaneous conversation (5.3.1 b) with any of the scripts in the rest of that section.

4   Even spontaneous speakers in routine conversation still speak in and through various *roles. People in 'real' life also 'play parts'. Even spontaneous discourse is in that sense already partly 'made up'.

5   We therefore need a model of conversation which is sensitive to role-playing and speech genres and discourses of all kinds – in fact as well as in fiction. That is why

the above checklists (pp. 221–222) on speech, conversation and dialogue are framed so as to be equally applicable to spoken language wherever we engage with it: in our own speech and that of others, in *and* out of fiction, on *and* off the page, on *and* off the stage or screen.

The dialogic principle as developed by Bakhtin

Bakhtin's grandest claim is that 'To *be* means to communicate *dialogically*' (*Problems of Dostoevsky's Poetics*, 1984). By this he means that everyone and everything is bound up with everyone and everything else in a ceaseless process of exchange and transformation. More specifically, Bakhtin observes that 'we always use another's words in our own language' and that 'every word is a site of struggle', a '*multiaccentual' space where many people's voices are perpetually contending with those of others (1981: 303ff.). Bakhtin also observes that 'every word is directed towards an answer and cannot escape the profound influence of the answering word that it anticipates' (1981: 280). There is always some **addressee** projected by every **addresser**. Our dialogues are therefore not only backward-looking (to other people whose words we are using and reacting to) but also forward-looking (to future responses that we expect, fear or desire). Bakhtin's especial interest in the **novel** arose because it was there that he reckoned writers were most free to experiment with the 'multi-voicedness' (*heteroglossia) of human society; there too that he traced those forms of *indirect speech whereby a narrator subtly slips into the words and **point of view** of a character. Arguably, such processes are not limited to the novel, nor even to fiction as such. They may characterise the ways in which we adopt and adapt language and sign-systems in general.

ACTIVITIES

(a)   *Monologues as dialogues, and vice versa.* Consider the ways in which any text is always in some sense a combination of monologue (one-way communication) AND dialogue (two- or many-way communication) – depending who you think is talking with or to whom, when, where and how. (Suggested focuses are Wyatt's 'They flee from me' (5.1.3 a), Kelman's *How late . . .* (5.2.6) and Freud's 'Dora' (5.3.1d).)

(b)   *Tran/scripts.* Compare a *transcript* of spontaneous conversation (e.g., 5.3.1 b) with a play, film or TV *script* (e.g., 5.3.5 c). Use the above checklists of features of speech and conversation to help you do this. Go on to consider how the transcript might be 'tidied up' so as to look like a crafted script. Conversely, consider how the script might be 'roughed up' so as to sound like spontaneous conversation.

DISCUSSION

(i)   For the smallest social unit is not the single person but two people. In life too we develop one another.

  Bertolt Brecht, 'A Short Organum for the Theatre' (1948: part 58)

(ii)   What living and buried speech is always vibrating here!

Walt Whitman, *Leaves of Grass* (1871: no. 8)

Also see: 1.2.4; LANGUAGE; COMMUNICATION; **addresser . . . addressee; drama and theatre; writing . . . response and rewriting; subject . . . role and identity**.

READING: *Introductory:* Crystal 1995: 288–97; Burton in Burton and Carter 1982: 86–115; O'Sullivan *et al.* 1994: 293–6; Hawthorn 1994: 39–40; Freeborn *et al.* 1993: 76–163. *Advanced:* Traugott and Pratt 1980: 226–71; Burton 1980; Pratt 1976; Bakhtin 1981; Sell 1990.

STANDARDS AND STANDARDISATION, VARIETIES AND VARIATION

Is there such a thing as 'standard English' or does all English change over time and vary from one place or person to another? Does 'standardisation' mean 'making uniform' or 'improving' – and can it be applied as easily to speech as to writing and print? Is one variety of language more 'correct' and 'proper' than another – or should we rather look at language in terms of 'appropriateness', 'context' and 'communicative function'? How does one variety become recognised as 'standard' and can processes of variation turn any variety into a 'standard' for certain people and certain purposes? These are the questions addressed in this entry. We start with questions rather than answers because the whole area of standards and standardisation, varieties and variation is complex and contentious. Snap answers simply increase the confusion and snappiness.

ENGLISH AND ENGLISHES – ONE AND MANY

Many of the general principles underpinning the present entry, as well as that on **accent and dialect**, are introduced in 1.2 and 1.3. Turn to those sections now if you want an overview.

Standard (noun and adjective) is a term with a complicated and potentially confusing history. The plural 'standards', for instance, is often tossed around as though it were a singular and everyone knew what it/they meant. Three basic meanings of 'standard' can be distinguished:

1   average, routine, common, without frills (as in 'standard model', 'standard fare');
2   prescribed measure of quantity or quality, degree of excellence (as in British Standards Authority, the International Gold Standard);
3   the pole holding a flag or other emblem around which people rally and express their solidarity, often in the face of an enemy (as in 'the royal standard', 'raising the standard' and 'standard bearer'). This is the earliest, twelfth-century sense.

'Standards' (plural), as already mentioned, has been loosely applied from the mid-nineteenth century onwards to everything from education and industry to appearance and morality (e.g., 'academic standards', 'manufacturing standards', 'standards of dress', 'moral standards'). This sense obviously arises from a confusion of senses (2) and (3) above. The notion of 'prescribed measure' thus gets mixed up with a notion of 'social value', as well as a general sense of people 'rallying round' something or other. Equally obviously, this new sense of 'standards' strenuously avoids sense (1), meaning average, routine or what is common.

It is against this background, then, that we must place the first explicit references and appeals to Standard *English* as well as *Received*/Standard *Pronunciation* which began to appear from the mid-nineteenth century onwards (see *OED* and Williams 1983: 296–9). In both these cases there is evidence of a concerted attempt to distinguish a certain prescribed or approved form of language (in the mid-nineteenth century principally that of the British private boarding schools and the London-based professions) from the forms used routinely and commonly by other sections of the British populace at large. Alternative names for Standard English in Britain are 'the Queen's/King's English' and 'BBC English'. (The latter refers to state-sponsored radio and TV, both of which were also massively dominated, especially in their early days, by upper-middle-class speakers from the South of England.) Clearly, then, any notion of Standard English was from the first heavily implicated in specific historical, geographical, social and technological conditions. Alternative names were *not*, for instance, 'Commoners' English' or 'Manchester Evening News English'. Similar inbuilt partialities relate to the notion of Received Pronunciation: 'received' by whom, how, when, where and why? The form of the passive participle ('received') assumes we either already know or wouldn't be so rude as to enquire.

The following brief survey will help provide a historical framework for changing notions of standard English. It supplements that in the general Chronology (Appendix B). The emphasis here is social and political. Linguistic illustrations can be found in 1.1–1.4 and throughout Part Five.

Anglo-Saxon: beginning and end of a 'King's English' (to eleventh century)

Britain's polyglot foundations are laid down at this stage: Celtic and Germanic languages and dialects meet and to some extent mingle. Latin continues to be the international language of official religion (Christianity), learning and letters as it had been previously in the Roman Empire. 'Englisc' first appears as the name applied to a group of related Germanic dialects, notably those of the Angles and Saxons, during the ninth century (see p. 10). The first 'King's English' as such is identified with King Alfred (*c.* 848–*c.* 900) and centred on his Wessex court at Winchester in Southern England. This 'Saxon' variety is braced against other, more Northerly, chiefly 'Anglian' varieties associated with the Danelaw as well as against the Celtic languages of Cornwall, Wales, Ireland and Scotland. For a time, 'Alfredian English' is consolidated through a programme of educational reform, including translations from Latin and the keeping of the *Anglo-Saxon Chronicle*. But then, as a consequence of the Norman Conquest (1066), this potentially 'standard' variety is overlaid and superseded by another based on Norman French.

Medieval many-tonguedness and a hierarchy of functions
(eleventh to mid-fifteenth centuries)

The linguistic pecking order for much of the Middle Ages in Britain is as follows:

♦ *Latin* is used in speech and writing for higher religious, educational and administrative purposes, especially in international contexts.
♦ *Norman French and then Parisian French* are used in speech and writing for national and cross-Channel administration by 'nobles' and 'royautee' at 'court(e)' and in the 'parlement' (all the highlighted words derive from early French).
♦ *English* is used chiefly in speech (rarely in writing) for immediate and local purposes amongst peasants, artisans and merchants (the majority of the populace), and is only used by the higher clergy and nobles when teaching, preaching to and administering this 'third estate' (the first two being Church and Knighthood).

In fact English only really begins to make it back on to manuscript as the written word during the fourteenth and fifteenth centuries, and then it is much 'Latinised' and 'Frenchified'. Laws and parliamentary business begin to be publicised, though not at first conducted, in English towards the end of this period. Meanwhile, Northern, Midland, Southern and other regional differences persist in both language and literary forms (see 'Pearl', Langland and Chaucer 5.1.2 b–d). But then, for technological and social reasons, everything shifts again.

Early Modern: printing, the state, and the politics of 'correction'
(late fifteenth to eighteenth centuries)

*Spelling is increasingly standardised over this period, chiefly through the influence of the *printing presses. Most of these are concentrated in London (Caxton sets up the first one there in 1476–77). Again, therefore, the Southern, London-based variety associated with court, parliament and business is the one that is adopted as a model. In *hand*writing, however, people continue to spell in a wide variety of ways, often inconsistently and idiosyncratically. Even the national bard (1564–1616), blissfully oblivious of subsequent appeals to him as an authority on all things 'English', blots his copy-book and signs himself in legal documents variously as 'Shackspere', 'Shagspere', 'Shaxper' and even 'Shaxberd'.

    The other major factors in moves both towards and (eventually) away from the concept of a single 'standard' in language are tied up with the development of Britain as a nation–state and imperial power. Britain is by now, notionally at least, a single nation–state presided over by a court and parliament based in England. It is also the centre of a rapidly growing empire, already with territories, settlements or strong commercial interests (chiefly based on slavery and plantations) in America, the Caribbean, India, Africa and, latterly, Australia and New Zealand. The internal–external tensions of this situation can be felt in the sphere of language in particular. Anxiety begins to be expressed about the 'purity' of the English language. From the late seventeenth century onwards, it becomes common, even fashionable, for middle-to-upper-class writers to declare that the language is becoming 'barbarous', 'uncivilised' and 'improper', and therefore needs 'regulating', 'correcting' and 'improving'. Printed *grammars, word-lists and *dictionaries soon appear, and there are repeated calls for the setting up of an 'Academy' to prescribe rules and to outlaw certain usages.

Later Modern: standard English, empire and an explosion of varieties (nineteenth to early twentieth centuries)

Steam printing presses pour forth more – and more diverse – materials. The United Kingdom is nominally 'United' in 1801, notwithstanding continuing pressure for various forms of regional and national devolution. Successive phases of industrial revolution prompt crises in social organisation and corresponding demands for political reform (notably through Chartism, the formation of trade unions and the Labour Party). This is also the empire upon which the sun never sets and upon which the gun – as well as legions of colonial administrators and Christian missionaries – never cease to train. It is against this social and political background that we must trace the rise, from the mid-nineteenth century onwards, of appeals to 'Standard English':

♦ 'English' is first raised as the 'standard' (flag, emblem, symbol) of empire, not so much as an actual linguistic entity, but in an ongoing attempt to confer social solidity and ideological solidarity upon an ideal. 'Standard English' is offered as something that everyone should rally round and respect or protect.

♦ Meanwhile, Queen Victoria, who has a German mother and husband (both Saxe-Coburgs), also has a strong German accent. The 'Queen's English' is therefore a notional rather than an actual model. Nor is such a state of affairs that unusual. The first languages of many of the kings and queens of England have not been English at all. The real 'King's/Queen's English' often turns out to have a strong Norse, Norman, French, Dutch or German accent.

♦ In Ireland, Wales and Scotland, there is wide-scale imposition of – as well as resistance to – 'Standard English' as a compulsory school subject. Either way, it systematically displaces other native dialects and whole languages. Beyond Britain, there is corresponding displacement of other native languages and their associated cultures, ranging from Swahili and Urdu to Navaho and Koori (an Australian 'Aboriginal' tongue).

♦ The mass of the population are offered a version of *literacy and a vision of national heritage designed to help them fulfil their roles as productive factory and office workers, and efficient colonial administrators.

♦ Inevitably, at the same time, the ground is already being prepared for the planting of other 'standards' and the unfurling of banners proclaiming other versions of civilisation.

Contemporary standards – global and local varieties (late twentieth century onwards)

America, India, the Caribbean and Australia now all boast 'standard' Englishes. Each of these is to a greater or lesser degree distinct from what must now be specified as '*British* Standard English'. The differences span the whole linguistic range from accents and spelling through vocabulary and grammar to contexts and com-municative functions. For the most part these standards are mutually intelligible and this has huge potential advantages for certain kinds of international communication (see 'Standard World English?' below). But the **differences** between these 'standards' are manifold, and an apparently slight difference can speak volumes, socially and culturally. For all these reasons, the appearance of such volumes as Webster's *American Dictionary* (1828), *Indian and British English: A Handbook* (1970) and Ramson's *Australian National Dictionary* (1988), to cite just three, is arguably as linguistically and ideologically momentous as the appearance of, say, Dr Johnson's *Dictionary of the English Language* (1755) and the *OED* (1928).

A NOTE ON NON/STANDARDS?

The crude division of English into 'standard' and 'non-standard' forms is rare in linguistic circles now. This is because the term 'non-standard' is especially inadequate when it comes to distinguishing amongst such widely different phenomena as 'colloquialism', 'swearing', **accents**, **dialects**, *pidgins and *creoles. The tendency, therefore, is to talk of forms of language (*including* 'standards') as **varieties**, and to recognise the shifts and switches from one to the other as **variation**.

Varieties are the linguistic *products* of difference; they are constituted by differences according to person, place, medium, context and function. **Variation** refers to the historical *processes* of differentiation; it embraces shifts and switches within the usage of an individual – even within a single speech – as well as large-scale change across whole language communities. Varieties and variation are therefore alternative ways of seeing the same thing as, respectively, product and process. We can explore various Englishes (those of the law or science or poetry, for instance) in space and across time. To be more precise, we can explore language at a given moment, *synchronically (e.g., now *or* at a certain moment in the fourteenth century); and we can explore them as it changes over time, *diachronically, (e.g., *between* the fourteenth century *and* now). Either way, we avoid loosely value-laden and unhistorical talk of 'standards' as though these were above the whole matter of varieties and variation. A 'standard' is itself a variety subject to continuing variation. It arises and increases or decreases in influence and prominence according to need and demand.

We therefore conclude much as we began, with problems and possibilities rather than a bogus final solution. Here the focus is on what is increasingly being talked of as a new '*global* standard' – 'World English'. Though again, as with earlier notions of the 'Queen's' or 'King's' English, it is a moot point how far this really exists as a linguistic entity or is being raised as an ideological 'standard' around which various parts of the world are supposed to rally.

'STANDARD WORLD ENGLISH'?

Good for international communication?
    Bad for local, regional and national identity?
Good for formal functions and writing in print?
    Bad for informal functions and for other dialects and languages in print?
An ideal to aspire to – a utopian dream?
    An undesirable impossibility – a dystopian nightmare?

ACTIVITIES

(a)   *Non/standard, im/proper, in/correct?* All the following texts might be cited by some people as instances of 'non-standard' or even 'incorrect' and 'improper' English: family conversation (5.3.1 b); Leonard's 'This is thi . . . news' (5.2.5 d); Harrison's *v.* (5.4.5 c); Kelman's *How late it was, how late* (5.2.6); Nichols's 'Tropical Death' (5.4.5 e); Barnes's 'Woak Hill' (5.1.6); Doyle's *Paddy Clarke* (5.2.5 e). (Add or substitute any others you wish.) In each case consider other ways in which you might describe these texts so as to be more discriminating and less judgmental. What alternatives are there to the crude dichotomies non/standard, in/correct and im/proper?

(b)   *An Un/Common Language* Use the samples of 'Current genres of small text' (5.4.7) – or any other diverse yet manageable corpus you care to put together – to try to piece together a model of English based on what is 'common' or 'shared' across a range of contemporary varieties. Do this systematically with respect to every major dimension of the language: vocabulary; grammar and word formation; spelling and visual presentation; context and communicative function (see the checklist in 4.2). How complete and coherent is the model of English you come up with? What kinds of feature and structure are common? Is there *any* single item which recurs in *all* parts of the corpus?!

DISCUSSION

(i)   Certaynly it is harde to playse eueryman by cause of dyuersitie and chaunge of langage.
William Caxton, Prologue to *Eneydos* (his translation of *The Aeneid*) (1490)

(ii)   Nationally, in Britain at least, proper English is a social view of who the proper English are; internationally, proper English cannot be divorced from a view of cultural and political domination.
Ron Carter, National Director of 'Language in the National Curriculum' Project, 1989–92, *Keywords in Language and Literacy* (1995: 123)

Also see: 1.2.1–4; LANGUAGE; **accent and dialect; canon;** *change;* **speech.**

READING: *Introductory:* Carter 1995: 111–12, 121–3, 145–52; Williams 1983: 296–9; Brooker and Humm 1989: 13–72; Crystal 1995: 298–393; Crystal 1997. *Advanced:* Graddol *et al.* 1996; Maybin and Mercer 1996: 275–310; Goodman and Graddol 1996: 141–238; Crowley, 1989, 1991.

SUBJECT AND AGENT, ROLE AND IDENTITY

All the terms featured here have to do with constructions or representations of people, in and out of language. They partly – but only partly – correspond to traditional terms such as **author, character,** *individual* and person. However, they so radically challenge and change these concepts that any grounds for comparison soon dissolve. The basic difference is that talking about people as 'subjects' and 'agents', 'identities' and 'roles' tends to emphasise the social and historical constructedness of their relations and the political power (or powerlessness) those relations entail. Talk of 'authors' and 'characters', 'individuals' and 'persons', however, tends to emphasise their uniqueness and/or their universality. This is why the former terms are often found in politically self-conscious critical discourses such as those of MARXISM, FEMINISM and POSTCOLONIALISM (usually in harness with notions of *ideology and *power); whereas the latter are often found in more overtly liberal or humanist critical discourses such as those of NEW CRITICISM and *Leavisism (usually in harness with notions of truth and *human nature). To be sure, these various critical vocabularies and the positions they represent can, for a while, be tied into the same critical project. But ultimately they are probably incompatible. They operate in different dimensions and are pulling different conceptions of LANGUAGE, LITERATURE and CULTURE in different directions.

Subject is a term with a complex history and wide range of applications. It is helpful to distinguish four meanings:

1   *subject matter* or *topic*: what a particular text, film or picture, etc. is about (e.g., 'It's about Russia!', as the speed-reader remarked of Tolstoy's *War and Peace*);

2   *academic subject* or *discipline*: the particular configuration of knowledges and skills associated with a specific area of expertise and a specific institutional slot (e.g., English Studies, Psychology, Computing, Environmental Sciences);

3   the *grammatical subject*: what controls the verb in traditional grammar, as distinct from the grammatical object ('She threw the ball', for instance, has the structure subject 'She', verb 'threw' and object 'the ball');

4   *an ideological or psycho-social subject*: someone implicated in and subjected to a particular personal-political structure and its associated world-view. Thus, archaically, we talk of people being 'royal' or 'British subjects', meaning they are subject to the power of the monarch or are British citizens subject to the laws of that country. More recently and specifically, in the contemporary usage of such Social Sciences as psychology, anthropology, sociology and politics, it is common to talk of persons being the 'subjects of' (i.e. subjected to) cultural institutions and **discourses** of all kinds. *Althusser explores the conflictual nature of this kind of subject in a political sphere (see MARXISM). *Freud and *Lacan explore it in a specifically psychoanalytic sphere (see PSYCHOLOGY). Relatedly, the linguist Benveniste was careful to distinguish two dimensions of the 'I': the 'I-who-speaks' (*le sujet d'énonciation*) and the 'I-who-is-spoken' (*Le sujet d'énoncé*). The 'I-who-speaks' is always to some extent mis- or under-represented by the 'I-who-is-spoken'. The act of going verbal inevitably both projects and refracts – but never simply reflects – the speaker's position and identity.

The fourth meaning of 'subject' (*ideological subject*) has bulked largest because it is the most complex and contentious and also perhaps the least familiar. However, it is a central term in cultural debates of all kinds, so we shall look at its precise implications more closely, as well as alternatives to it.

Subject derives from the Latin verb *subiacere*: 'to throw under' (*subjectum*, the past participle, means 'thrown under'). This derivation may help explain some people's resistance to the term. If one is 'thrown under' something by someone, then this implies a kind of passivity. Subjects are perhaps thereby cast in the roles of victims, those who are 'done to' rather than those who themselves 'do' (despite the grammatical sense of subject (3) above). For this reason some people prefer the term *participant*, which refers to anyone who takes part in an event, regardless of their activity or passivity. Still others prefer the term **agent** because it implies a degree of activity and independence, even if the agent is partly acting on behalf of someone or something else. Moreover, there is a strong tradition in philosophical discourse of agency meaning 'the power to do', 'the force that causes effects'. (The word derives from the Latin verb *agere*: 'to act, to make happen'; hence English 'agitate', employment and advertising 'agencies', and 'secret agents'.)

A handy compromise is to recognise subject and agent as the passive and active dimensions of the same process. That is, each of us is potentially a **subject/agent** (a subject *and* an agent, simultaneously or by turns). We are subjects in so far as we are 'thrown under' things – politically oppressed or psychologically repressed. But at the same time we are also agents, capable of 'doing things' and 'making things happen', politically and psychologically active in our own remaking. In terms of **history**, we may therefore see ourselves as both making and being made by it. In terms of **narrative**, we may see ourselves as both the tellers and the told. In terms of **drama** we are both the playwright/director and the players. All this brings us to a couple of further terms commonly found in critical discourses when seeking to represent people: roles and identities.

Referring to people in terms of their **roles** is another alternative. Often found in such phrases as 'playing a role', 'adopting a role' or 'role play', the concept of role obviously depends upon a dramatic or theatrical metaphor. So do the concepts 'mask' and 'persona' (e.g., 'dramatis personae' as 'persons played') when applied to non-theatrical contexts. Such analogies are most famously put by Jaques in his 'Seven Ages of Man' speech in Shakespeare's *As You Like It* (Act II sc. vii): 'All the world's a stage, and all the men and women merely players . . .'. This play/world, player/person analogy has been highly productive in many areas of thought, not only in Literary Studies. It has been especially powerful in the Social Sciences where it is now routine to talk of, say, 'roles within the family' or 'social roles', 'role models' and 'switching' or 'modifying' roles. By extension, many ethnolinguists now commonly talk of *scripts* and *scenarios* when referring to predictable **genres** of speech and other discourse activity in routine (i.e. non-theatrical and non-filmic) situations. Thus we can legitimately and quite suggestively talk of real – not just fictional – judges, police officers, students, lecturers speaking and behaving 'in role' and 'playing their parts'. Still other analysts prefer to talk of these same situations in terms of *frames*, thereby drawing on analogies with the visual arts, especially photography and cinema.

Identity is another relatable term which has achieved wide critical currency in the Humanities and Social Sciences. Philosophically and in Mathematics, the term has been around for a long time with the specialised sense of 'absolute sameness' or 'absolute equality between two equations' (see *OED*; the Latin root is *idem*, meaning 'the same one'; cf. *idio*syncracy and *idio*lect). During the past thirty years, however, 'identity' has been increasingly used to refer to the social and historical make-up of a person, personality as a construct. Sometimes such identities are conceived in narrowly psychological, individualist terms, as the cumulative result of personal experience and family history (i.e. purely autobiographically). Sometimes identities are conceived in broadly sociological, collectivist terms, as the cumulative result of public pressure and larger historical circumstance (i.e. purely biographically). However, the most subtle and resourceful approaches to identity always draw upon a fusion of – or tension between – these two approaches. Identity is thereby recognised as a product of private *and* public histories, a richly psycho-social *and* personal-political process of becoming (i.e. **auto/biography** in the fullest and most challenging sense).

Identification too, we may note, is a suggestively ambiguous process. The ambiguity hinges on the difference between the concepts 'identification *of*' and 'identification *with*'; also the distance between **other** and **self**:

♦ *Identification 'of' someone or something* entails pointing to, labelling and in effect 'naming' them as *other* (as in an 'identity parade').
♦ *Identification 'with' someone or something* entails sympathising and, in extreme cases, empathising and confusing our *selves* with someone or something else (as when we 'identify with a character/cause').

The process of identification in a fully dynamic sense therefore involves perceiving identity as other *and* as self. Arguably, something of this complexity goes on when we identify with characters in plays or novels, or when we identify with figures in life generally (by falling in love, for instance).

ACTIVITIES

(a) *A matter of people.* Choose a short story, novel or play and weigh the advantages and disadvantages of approaching the figures represented as *subjects, agents, identities* and *roles*, or as *individuals* and *persons*. What differences in emphasis and approach are entailed? Alternatively, can everything be covered by notions of **character and characterisation**? (Suggestion: Kipling's 'The Story of Muhammad Din' (5.2.4 b).)

(b) *'I'dentities in crisis.* Concentrate on a text which features a first person speaker or narrator, an 'I' (e.g., 5.2.2 or the cluster in 5.4.7 g). How would you *identify* that figure in terms of gender, class, race, education, attitudes, expectations? And how far do you *identify with* him or her? In what ways are the two processes of identification connected?

(c) *Tran/scripts and roles.* Cut a script or transcript at a potentially significant point (any of the texts in 5.3 will do). Consider the various roles in play up to that point and plot two alternative outcomes from there onwards. (Explore this through role-playing with colleagues if you wish.) Go on to discuss the nature of roles, masks, scripts, scenarios and frames on *and* off the page, stage and screen.

DISCUSSION

(i) The subject is seen no longer as the source of meaning but as the site of meaning.
Raman Selden and Peter Widdowson, *A Reader's Guide to Contemporary Literary Theory* 3rd edn (1993: 226)

> (ii)   It is not theatre that is able to imitate life; it is social life that is designed as a
>   continuous performance.
>
> > Umberto Eco, 'Semiotics of Theatrical Performance' (1977)
> > in Walder (1990: 120)

> (iii) All the world's a Visual Display Unit – and all the men and women merely
>   cyphers in cyber-space . . .
>
> > Updated version of 'All the world's a stage . . . ' (Shakespeare, *As You
> > Like It,* Act II sc. vii), members of the Language, Literature,
> > Discourse III group, Oxford, Spring 1997

Also see: 1.5.9–10; PSYCHOLOGY; POSTSTRUCTURALISM AND POSTMODERNISM; **author; auto/biography . . . self and other; character; comedy and tragedy; drama and theatre;** *ideology.

READING: *Introductory:* Moon 1992: 61–3; O'Sullivan *et al.* 1994: 157–8, 309–11; Pope 1995: 47–69; Green and LeBihan 1996: 40–3, 271–305. *Advanced:* Belsey 1980: 56–84; Mühlhausler and Harré 1990; Giddens 1991; Boal 1992.

TEXT, CONTEXT AND INTERTEXTUALITY

Briefly, a text is any instance of a verbal record; the context is everything around the text; intertextuality refers to the text's relation with other texts. The concept of 'text' is now shared by many areas of LITERARY, LINGUISTIC and CULTURAL Studies. In fact, it is one of the crucial terms which allows these subjects to interrelate and to maintain a sense of some common object of study. They are all in some sense dealing with 'texts'. The problem, as with any widely used term, is that people in different subjects tend to mean rather different things by it. We can thus distinguish two basic senses of text, one narrow, the other broad.

Text as any record of a verbal message, written, printed or otherwise recorded (e.g., electronically or audio-visually)

All the following are texts in this sense: a handwritten letter; a printed newspaper or magazine; a book of any kind; a written or printed novel, poem or play; a tape-recording or a transcript of a conversation. Texts are thereby distinguished on the one hand from *un*recorded language in the form of spontaneous **speech and conversation**, and on the other hand from messages in *non*-verbal codes such as painting, photography, music and architecture. This sense of *text as verbal record* is the one favoured by most linguists and the one favoured here. However, it should be added that some self-consciously 'literary' critics shun the term 'text' altogether. They complain of it being too indiscriminate or technical-sounding and prefer to talk more selectively and exclusively of literature in general and, of poems, novels and plays as such.

Text as any instance of the organisation of human *signs, in any *code or MEDIUM

This much-extended sense of 'text' embraces everything from poems, adverts and films to paintings, photos, shopping malls and whole cityscapes. The only limits seem to be that the 'text' in question should be a cultural object produced by people rather than a natural object untouched by human hand or mind. This definition is *not* favoured here on the grounds that if virtually everything is a text the concept has no analytical power at all.

We now turn to the relation between **texts** and their **contexts** and between one text and other texts (i.e. **intertextuality**). The intrinsic and possibly inextricable relations amongst these three concepts can be gauged by the fact that con*text* and inter*textu*ality both have the core 'text' embedded within them. Moreover, the word text derives from the Latin verb *texere* meaning to weave and the noun *textus*, meaning 'tissue', 'weaving', 'web' (hence the related English words *tex*tile and *tex*ture). Texts are therefore perhaps best conceived as intermittent and extensible structures formed by a weaving together of strands. Like the World-Wide-Web – itself a contemporary kind of electronic mega-text made up of many interweavings – texts are wholes full of holes: always apparently somewhere and at the same time both everywhere and nowhere. In fact, the harder and closer you look *at* a text (paper or electronic), the more you find yourself looking *through*, *round* and *beyond* it. Its **presence** always implies and in a sense requires its **absences**. Like a bell, it rings out by virtue of the space where it is not. More practically and pointedly, we may add that *set texts* (i.e. prescribed reading) always turn out to be far from 'set' in the sense of solid and immovable. They have always been set by somebody for specific purposes. Other texts might have been set for similar or different reasons (see **canon**).

Context (Latin for 'with-text') refers to all those physical and cultural conditions whereby a text – or, for that matter, anything else – comes into being. It is analytically convenient to distinguish four kinds of interrelated context:

♦ *context meaning immediate situation*, e.g., whenever and wherever you are reading this book, a particular course;
♦ *context meaning larger cultural frame of reference*, e.g., the society, language community and general historical moment in which that reading is taking place;
♦ *contexts of (re)production*, e.g., when, where and by whom this book was sketched, drafted, read, redrafted, edited, published;
♦ *contexts of reception*, e.g., who uses it when, where, how and why.

(Notice that the term *co-text* is sometimes used to refer to other words and images in the immediate vicinity of the text. Thus if this entry is treated as a text, the co-text is the rest of the book.)

All these overlapping yet non-identical contexts must be taken into account if we are to attempt to grasp a text fully, in actual use (see 2.2 for applications to *Hamlet*). We must therefore learn to see a text not only *in* but in some sense *as* its contexts. The same goes for the next dimension of textuality.

Intertextuality (Latin for 'between-texts') is the general term for the relation between one text and another. It is analytically useful to distinguish three kinds of intertextual relation: explicit, implied and inferrable.

Explicit intertextuality comprises all the other texts that are overtly referred to and all the specific sources that the writer has demonstrably drawn upon. Thus we might cite T.S. Eliot's *The Waste Land* with its annotated references to Shakespeare's *The Tempest* and its acknowledged debts to a mixture of Christian and Sanskrit texts as an instance of explicit intertextuality. *Implied intertextuality* comprises all those passing allusions to other texts (including texts in the same **genre**) and all those effects (especially *ironic and *satiric) which seem to have been deliberately contrived by the writer so as to be picked up by the alert and similarly informed reader. One instance might be the first line of *The Waste Land* and its ironic inversion of the opening of line of Chaucer's *General Prologue*: 'April is the cruellest month' as against Chaucer's 'Aprille with his shoures soote [sweet]'. By definition, *implied* intertextuality is always more subtle and indirect – and less easy to prove – than *explicit* intertextuality.

Inferred intertextuality refers to all those texts which actual **readers** draw on to help their understanding of the text in hand. These need not have been in the writer's mind – or even existed at the time. It is their status in the reader's mind that matters chiefly here. Thus we might compare the fragmentary *collage effects of *The Waste Land* with Cubist or Surrealist art contemporary with the poem; but we might also compare or, more likely, contrast them with analogous POSTMODERN techniques in TV advertising and pop videos (where it is precisely the recognisable rather than the recondite nature of the allusions that usually engages us). We might also choose to read the poem through Eliot's own essay-writing on Shakespeare, or bring it into collision with, say, current FEMINIST or POSTCOLONIAL readings of *The Tempest*. The fact is that we can make sense of a text by comparing and contrasting it with just about any other. The point, of course, is to make the comparison or contrast significant (see **difference and similarity**). 'Inferred intertextuality' is therefore at once the most open and the most demanding kind of textuality. It is more a critical technique than a textual object: a process of intertextual weaving rather than a finished web.

ACTIVITIES

(a)   *Is there a text in this text?!* Choose a text from Part Five (or anywhere else) and consider: (a) all the various contexts and co-texts in which it is implicated; (b) all the other texts – or kinds of text – to which it can be related intertextually. What, then, are the grounds upon which you might build a concept of 'the text itself'?

(b)   *Kinds of intertextuality.* Look at one of the clusters of texts in section 5.4 or put together a cluster of your own. Either way, try to describe the relations amongst these texts in terms of the three kinds of intertextuality distinguished above: explicit, implied and inferred. How distinguishable are they in practice?

DISCUSSION

(i)   Depending on one's position, the term 'text' either serves to democratise English Studies, which was previously dominated by a study of literary 'works', or it serves to undermine the judgments of the past, which have established a canon of literary works.

Ron Carter, *Keywords in Language and Literacy* (1995: 155)

(ii)   In our century there are people who write as if there were nothing but texts.

Richard Rorty, 'Consequences of Pragmatism' (1982: 139) in Hawthorn, 1st edn (1992: 190)

Also see: 2.2; NEW CRITICISM; POSTSTRUCTURALISM; **absence and presence**; **foreground and background**; *editing; **writing . . . rewriting**.

READING: *Introductory:* Wales 1989: 93–5, 259–60, 458–61; Moon 1992: 69–71, 121–4; Hawthorn 1994: 85–7, 188–91; Carter 1995: 155–6. *Advanced:* Barthes 1977: 155–64; Birch 1989: 5–44; De Beaugrande and Dressler 1981; Toolan 1992; Kristeva 1984.

VERSIFICATION: STRESS, RHYTHM, METRE AND RHYME

Versification covers all those aspects of the formal organisation of sounds that characterise verse. These range from localised matters of alliteration and stress through more pervasive patternings of rhythm, metre and rhyme to larger structural matters of genre (e.g., sonnet, ballad, and free verse). The principal focus here is **poetry**; but all these features grow out of the routine resources of the language. Similar devices and strategies can therefore be found in the design of speech and writing of all kinds, from oratory to advertising. 'Metrics' and 'poetics' are terms sometimes used to designate partly similar areas. *Metrics*, however, is restricted to the analysis of 'measures' or 'feet' within the line of verse ('metre' – also spelt 'meter' – derives from the Greek word for 'measure' which also gives us the *metric* units cent*imetre*, kilo*metre*, etc., and gas *meter*, i.e 'gas-measurer'). *Poetics*, meanwhile, has a more capacious sense than versification alone. It embraces formal patterning in language of all kinds, and includes *rhetorical organisation in drama and narrative (Greek *poeisis* simply meant 'fashioning', 'making').

What we 'measure' in English poetry very much depends on the basic resources of the language. ENGLISH is fundamentally a *Germanic language. Therefore, like other Germanic languages such as Dutch, German, Danish, Norwegian and Swedish, its basic sound-structure is built upon the presence or absence of stress (i.e. stressed or unstressed syllables). In this respect English differs from CLASSICAL and *Romance languages such as Greek, Latin, French and Italian, which are organised chiefly round principles of syllable length (i.e. long or short syllables). Consequently, if we return to the oldest substratum of English verse, Anglo-Saxon poetry, we find it is organised on the principle of a regular number of stresses to the line (four), regardless of the number and length of intervening unstressed syllables. Another convention was that two or three of these stressed syllables had to begin with the same sound (i.e. *alliterate). The opening lines of the poem 'Wulf and Eadwacer' (5.1.1) may therefore be measured or 'scanned' as follows (/ = stressed syllable; x = unstressed syllable; v = a marked medial pause or 'caesura'; <u>underlining</u> marks structural alliteration):

```
    /    x    /    v    / x  x  / x
   Wulf, min Wulf       wena me thine

    / x  x / x    v    / x  /  x  x
   seoce gedygan        thine seldcymas

    /  x  x  /    v    / x    / x x x
   murnende mod         nales meteliste
```

The overall result is what is called stressed (or accentual) alliterative verse. Moreover, in that such poetry was primarily performed live and drew on a repertoire of half-line units (variations on all the above half-lines appear in other Anglo-Saxon poems) it is also called *oral-formulaic poetry.

This kind of heavily stressed metre with structural alliteration was a powerful tradition in early English verse. Later medieval variations on it can be found in *Piers Plowman* (5.1.2 c), *Pearl* (5.1.2 d), and the Chester *Noah* (5.3.2 a). (Have a go at reading these pieces out loud, then mark them up for (un)stressed syllables and alliteration.) Furthermore, accentual verse – with or without structural alliteration – has been recognised as a powerful resource by many later writers across a whole range of 'Englishes'. Poets as various as Burns (5.4.5 a), Barnes (5.1.6) and Hopkins in the eighteenth and nineteenth centuries, and Dylan Thomas (5.3.4 b), Walcott, Brathwaite, Dabydeen, Hughes and Heaney in the twentieth century, have all expressly acknowledged the influence of early accentual 'makers' on their own poetic craft.

However, accentual/stressed metre is only half of the history of English verse, albeit the older half. Another principle of metrical organisation has also been at work for a long time, usually in harness and productive tension with accentual metre. This is the principle of 'syllabic' or 'quantitative' metre (often accompanied by end-rhyme) and it became part of the native tradition most obviously and influentially through the work of Geoffrey Chaucer. Unlike his contemporaries, the authors of *Piers Plowman* and *Pearl*, Chaucer mainly adopted French and Italian metrical models. The result was a verse structure based on a regular number of syllables per line (usually eight or ten syllables, hence octo- or decasyllabic) and rhyme schemes ranging from the couplet to complex patterns such as 'rhyme royal' (seven decasyllabic lines rhyming ababbcc). Here are the first two lines of Chaucer's description of the Knight (5.1.2 b). Like many of *The Canterbury Tales*, these are in decasyllabic couplets and have been marked accordingly (the caesura break/pause is again marked 'v' and rhymes are in italics; notice that the final 'e' of 'time' is sounded and that of 'Trouthe' *elides with the vowel in 'and', as is usual with adjacent vowels):

```
   1   2     3   4 v 5     6 7 8  9   10
   A Knight ther was    and that a worthy man

    1   2  3 4 5  6  7 8    9 10
   That fro the time that he first bigan

    1 2 3  4   v   5 6 7    8 9 10
   To riden out,    he loved chivalrie

     1   2     3 4  v    5 6  7   8  9 10
   Trouthe and honour,    fredom and curteisie
```

Notice that where there is alliteration it is inconspicuous and localised rather than emphatic and structural. The following couplet from Pope's *The Rape of the Lock* (5.1.4 b) has a similar underlying decasyllabic structure. Here, however, I have extended the analysis so as to register a sense of the rhythm which also informs the lines. This particular pattern of 'unstressed + stressed' syllables is called by the CLASSICAL name 'iambic', though strictly in Greek and Latin this signalled a pattern of 'short + long' syllables. (Notice, too, that the uprights, |, mark the boundary between one metrical 'foot' and another; here the basic unit is an iamb, so the whole line is called 'iambic pentameter' – five iambic feet.)

```
x    /  |x  /  |x  /  |x  /  |   x   /
1    2  3  4    5  6  7 8     9  10
And now unveiled the toilet stands displayed
```

```
x   / | x  / |  x    / |x  / |x  /
1   2  3  4  5    6  7 8 9  10
Each silver vase in mystic order laid
```

BUT WHY BOTHER TO 'SCAN' VERSE?

Marking up lines of verse in these ways initially looks cumbersome and unnecessary. However, done systematically and sensitively, 'scanning' quickly proves to be both relatively straightforward and remarkably illuminating. Certainly, it helps give visible structure to the word-musics we hear (it's a kind of metrical oscilloscope). It also provides a firm basis for more subtle explorations both analytically and in performance. See Discussion (ii), p. 242 for Dr Johnson's views on the matter.

As the above examples show, it is wisest to conclude that writers of English from the later Middle Ages to the present have had basically two principles of metrical organisation at their disposal: stressed and perhaps alliterating; and quantitative syllabic and perhaps rhymed. Indeed, more often than not, the result has been various blends of the two, and what usually goes under the handily *hybrid name of 'accentual-syllabic metre'.

Rolling everything together, we may say that most verse gives us syllabic and/or stressed regularity varied by the flexible sense of a speaking voice. At the same time, language as sound interplays with language as syntax, and both are braced against the play of meaning as such. Some such comments can be made on most kinds of verse. For verse, virtually by definition, tends to be both orderly and resourceful, economic and expressive. Something of the kind may certainly be said of just about every sample of English verse in the anthology up to the mid-twentieth century, as well as many up to the present (see 5.1.3–7; analyse some and see/hear for yourself). Moreover, absolutely any verse (including 'free verse') – if it is to be at all recognisable *as* verse – must have at least some corresponding principles of regularity and flexibility, unity and variety, order and expressiveness. The principles may be those of visual design organised for silent reading and sustained meditation. Or they may be those of sound patterning organised for live performance and immediate response. They may also be a mixture depending upon the expectations, media and resources in play. But some such general principles will be in operation, even though much of the actual appeal will always depend upon how exactly they are realised in any one instance. Hence the following guidelines for you to apply (and modify) as you see and hear fit.

FINDING YOUR 'FEET'

There are five basic measures or 'feet' recognised in the scanning of English verse. Each of them involves a particular combination of unstressed (x) and stressed (/) syllables.

        x /   x / x /   x /

Iambus – e.g., again, unveil, reverse, discuss (Think of further examples)

        / x / x   / x   / x

Trochee – e.g., happy, never, heartless, discus, etc.

        x x /   x x /   x x / x x   /

Anapest – e.g., entertain, repossess, hurry up, disapprove, etc.

        /   /   /   /   /   /   / /

Spondee – e.g., heart break, wine glass, Big Mac, Disc-world, etc.

        / x x   / x x   / x x / x x

Dactyl – e.g., happiness, pulverise, orchestra, discotheque, etc.

The art of the poet chiefly lies in getting her or his 'feet' mixed up in variously elegant or arresting ways. At best the effect is of a kind of word-dance. The art of the analyst (and the perfomer) lies in retracing the steps.

Versification checklist

What makes you think it's verse?

Appearance on the page – stacked down the middle in regular blocks, or with a freer, more 'spaced-out' look? (at any rate probably not running prose-like from margin to margin).
A kind of music to the ear, and the way it trips or tears from the tongue – a more than usual sense of sound-patterning, and perhaps more effort in articulation?

Structure of the line:

- ♦ a regular or irregular number of *stresses* per line? How many, how often?
- ♦ a regular or irregular number of *syllables* per line? What kinds, in what patterns?
- ♦ systematic and structural or occasional and opportunistic use of *alliteration*?
- ♦ systematic or occasional use of *rhyme*? Or half-rhyme (e.g., 'bend/bind')?
- ♦ regular or variable *break(s)* or *pause(s)* ('caesura(e)') within the line?

Relation between verse line and sentence structure. Is there

♦   *run-over* (enjambment) of sentence structures from one line to the next?
♦   *end-stopping* so that the line-end coincides with a clause or sentence break?
♦   *tension* between the verse music and the rhythm of the speaking voice?

Larger verse structures and patterns in groups of lines. Are there

♦   *rhyming couplets, quatrains* rhyming abab, or other configurations (e.g., abaabbcc)?
♦   eight-, ten- or twelve-*syllable* lines, repeated or alternating?
♦   two-, three-, four- or five-*stress* lines, repeated or alternating?

Recognisable **genres** and 'kinds' of verse, for instance

♦   *ballad/lyric forms* – usually in four-line verses (quatrains) with alternating rhymes (abab) and with four, three and two strong stresses per line (more 'literary' versions may be syllabically regular; e.g., Blake (5.4.6 b), Wordsworth (5.4.3 a), Barnes (5.1.6).
♦   *blank verse* – regular accentual-syllabic verse, often iambic pentameter, but without rhyme or structural alliteration; e.g., Shakespeare's *The Tempest* (5.3.2 b) and Milton's *Paradise Lost* (5.1.4 a).
♦   *sonnet* – characteristically, a fourteen-line poem (occasionally sixteen), broken into units of eight and six lines (octave and sestet) or three quatrains and a couplet. Metre is generally iambic pentameter, but rhyme-schemes can be very various; e.g., Petrarchan (abbaabba cdecde), Spenserian (abab bcbc cdcd ee), and Shakespearean (abab cdcd efef gg): see 5.1.3 b, 5.4.4 c. Brooke's sonnet (5.4.6 d), for instance, rhymes ababcdcd efgefg.
♦   *free verse* – a modern hybrid form which picks up various structural principles in passing (by turns perhaps stressed, syllabic, alliterating, (half)rhyming, end-stopped or running over) but without establishing a single consistent pattern; e.g., poems by Peters (5.4.3 c), Fanthorpe (5.4.6 e), Kazantsis (5.1.7 b), Rich (5.1.8), Nichols (5.4.5 e).
♦   *concrete poetry* and *word-as-image* – where the very shape of the words on the page or their movement on the screen imitates a particular object or action (e.g., a dove-shaped poem on a dove; a fast-moving 'express' sign). Common in TV advertising and computer-assisted text/image design, poetic precursors include work by Edwin Morgan and George Herbert.

ACTIVITIES

(a)   *Reading out, listening and analysing.* Read out loud and listen to one of the following pairs of poems (or another pair of your own choosing). Go on to analyse each poem in turn using the above 'Versification Checklist.' How far do the poems use similar or different resources for similar or different effects? (Suggested pairings are: Wyatt and Shakespeare (5.1.3 a and b); Milton and Byron (5.1.4 a and d); Wordsworth and Peters (5.4.3 a and c); Yeats and Kazantsis (5.1.7 a and b); Brooke and Fanthorpe (5.4.6 d and e).)

(b)   *Prose-poetry.* Take some short passages of prose (perhaps some of the 'Current genres of small text' (5.4.7)) and set them out on the page as different kinds of 'poem'. In each case, consider how changes in typeface, line-spacing and punctuation might reinforce the rhetorical strategies and imagery in play.

Poetry-prose. Write out the poems by Kazantsis (5.1.7 b) and Rich (5.1.8) as continuous prose stretching from one side of the page to the other. What has been lost (or at least changed) by doing this? Go on to experiment with free verse structures alternative to those in the initial poems.

Poetry-song-performance. Listen to then read the lyrics of a popular song (e.g., Queen's 'Bohemian Rhapsody' (5.1.10)) How much – or how little – of the sound-effect of the piece depends on the words on the page as distinct from the words in performance? In what ways do you need to supplement the above 'Versification Checklist' to accommodate these differences?

DISCUSSION

(i)   Having learned to use his legs, he [the poet] will discover that he can not only walk, but run; and not only walk and run, but dance. [. . .] Here we come again to the contrast between prose and poetry. Prose and poetry use the same words, the same syntax, the same forms, the same sounds or tones, but differently coordinated and differently aroused.

Paul Valéry, 'Poetry and Abstract Thought' (1939) in Lodge (1972: 260–1)

(ii)   However minute the employment may appear, of analysing lines into syllables, and whatever ridicule may be incurred by a solemn deliberation upon accents and pauses, it is certain that without this petty knowledge no man can be a poet; and that from the proper disposition of single sounds results that harmony that adds force to reason, and gives grace to sublimity.

Samuel Johnson, *Rambler* 88 (19 January 1751) cited in Butler and Fowler (1971: 348)

Also see: 4.2; **foreground, background**; **poetry and word-play**.

READING: Durant and Fabb 1990: 115–25; Preminger and Brogan 1993: 768–83; Leech 1969: 103–30; Hobsbawm 1996; Short 1996: 106–67; Fabb 1997. *Advanced:* Easthope 1983; Brathwaite 1984, Kristeva 1984.

WRITING AND READING, RESPONSE AND REWRITING

Writing can be briefly defined as the activity of making verbal marks on paper or some other substance (stone, wood, plastic, computer screen, etc.); also what results (i.e. a piece of writing). **Reading** is the activity of engaging with those verbal marks and, again, what results (i.e. a reading). **Response** is a more capacious process. It includes reading but also embraces other forms of reaction and interaction, from listening and viewing to the initiation of a counter or alternative action. **Rewriting** is a fourth term added here so as to point up the relations between the other three. It reminds us that in some sense every *writing* is a *re*writing of what has been read (heard, seen) previously; while every *reading* is a *re*writing of what has been written. All these activities involve forms of response that may be variously reactive, interactive and proactive. All these activities, including response, can therefore be regarded as part of a continuous yet differentiated process. An understanding of this dynamic interrelatedness is crucial if we are to grasp the critical-creative nature of what it is we do whenever we set pen to paper or fingers to keyboards *and* when we focus our eyes on a page or a screen. Writing and reading are often treated as relatively straightforward processes, as though it were simply a matter of 'getting words down on paper' and 'reading what's written'. This is far from the case. As already intimated, the whole business of writing and reading (and at the same time responding and, in effect, rewriting) is much more complex and fascinating than that. Some finer, further distinctions are therefore necessary before we proceed.

Writing and reading can be processes as well as products, attributes as well as events. This is evident grammatically because both these words can function as verbs *and* nouns *and* adjectives:

♦ writing and reading as *processes*, e.g., 'She's writing. I'm reading' (present progressive verbs);
♦ writing and reading as *products*, e.g., 'The writings of . . . ', 'a reading of . . . ' (nouns, plural and singular);
♦ writing and reading as *attributes*, e.g., 'A writing course', 'a reading journal' (adjectives).

Another important feature of the verbs 'to read' and 'to write' is that they can be both **transitive* and **intransitive*. That is, we can read and write something to someone (transitively, with objects and persons in mind) or we can just read and write (intransitively, as ends in themselves). Thus

♦ 'I'm writing a card to my friend', 'My daughter is reading to her dolly' (both *transitive*, with *functional structure: Participant 1 – Process – Object – Participant 2);
♦ 'I'm writing', 'She's reading' (both *intransitive*, with functional structure: Participant – Process).

All this gives us plenty of room for manoeuvre when it comes to deciding what it is we are actually doing when we read and write.

WRITING AND READING OR LITERATURE OR TEXT? Which are you doing?

Writing and reading, taken together, are extremely versatile – even volatile – concepts. As shown above, they can refer to 'things', to attributes of other things, and to activities. Meanwhile, as activities, they can be ends in themselves or have objects and aims beyond themselves.

LITERATURE however, has a narrower range of senses and grammatical functions. This may or may not be a good thing, depending on how you look at it. 'English Literature', for instance, usually refers to certain privileged kinds of fictional writing, and does not include everything written and read in English. Moreover, 'literature' can only function as a noun and an adjective – not a verb. Thus we may talk of 'great literature' and 'the scientific literature on this subject' (both nouns) and of 'Literature courses' and 'literature searches' (both adjectives). However, we cannot say 'Shakespeare *literatured* this play . . .' or 'She's *literaturing* his play and then going to *literature* an essay on it'. Be all that as it may, some people prefer to talk flexibly of 'writing' and/or 'reading', while other people prefer the apparent specificity, fixity and prestige of 'literature'. (How about you?)

'Text' too has distinctive possibilities and problems. Certainly, talk of 'texts' does not pre-empt the matter of which writings are to be privileged as 'literary'; nor does it limit discussion to the written or printed word (we can talk of audio- and audio-visual texts which may not be, strictly, 'written' or 'read' at all). Nonetheless, the term text still implies a certain fixity, an emphasis on achieved product rather than ongoing process. Partly this is because, again, like 'literature' but unlike 'writing' and 'reading', 'text' functions grammatically as a noun but not a verb. (We don't – or at least we don't yet – talk of anybody *texting* a play or essay, for instance.) 'Text' and 'literature' therefore imply a primarily object-centred subject. 'Writing(s)' and 'reading(s)', however, can embrace both object-centred and activity-based notions of the subject.

For all the above reasons, it is important to distinguish precisely what it is we think we are doing. *Writing and reading? Literature? Texts?* How we answer can make a real **difference**. It may also imply some real **preferences**. (For further implications, see LITERATURE (1.8.2) and **text**.)

---

*Writing occurs in various MEDIA: *handwriting, *print and electronic modes.* The term is here being used, as is common, to cover verbal marks in all three. However, we should remember that these are to some extent distinct COMMUNICATIVE technologies with distinct yet variable functions and values. Whether people handwrite or type a letter, for instance, makes a big difference in terms of perceived (im)personality and (in)formality. Moreover, configurations of manuscript, print and screen CULTURES are constantly shifting in relation to one another; they are not fixed. Contemporary instances would be the pseudo-handwritten mass-reproduced advert (affecting informality and intimacy); the handwritten fax to a friend (a kind of electronically mediated but still personalised letter) and e-mail conferencing (which often has the interrupted structure and interactive feel of conversation, as well as the dashingly elliptical and exclamatory style of postcards; see 5.4.7 f).

Writing and reading are activities similar to but different from speaking and listening. The written and spoken words draw on the same underlying *sign-system (i.e. verbal language); but they are realised in different materials with distinct properties and potentialities. Writing is made from *graphological material (visible marks on paper, or whatever), while speech is made from *phonological material (audible sounds in air). With these distinctions in mind, here is a review of the characteristic properties and structures of writing. This should be read in conjunction with that for **speech**, where some further qualifications are included.

WRITING IS characteristically (but not always):

- *a more permanent record* than memory alone, and often more 'finished' than speech;
- *faceless and detachable from particular occasions and places* – relatively 'context-free' (though every **text** is read in some **context** and can be placed in a variety of **intertextual** frames);
- *initially 'one-way'* (**monologic**) – only 'two-way' (**dialogic**) after a delay;
- *learnt deliberately*, usually through specialised teaching (mere exposure to writing is not enough to produce *literacy);
- *dependent on special writing materials and apparatuses* such as quills, pens, inks, animal skins, paper, printing-presses, typewriters, computers (the more techno-logically advanced the apparatus, the more expensive it is in capital terms).

THE STRUCTURES OF WRITING are thus characteristically (but not always):

- *self-sufficient and free-standing*, because the written or printed word alone has to do much of the work of contextualising;
- *dependent on full and explicit references*, with an inbuilt tendency towards the past tense (e.g., 'Claire, David and Bill were in Adelaide in June 1996') rather than their *context-sensitive equivalents dependent on the present tense (e.g., 'They're here now');
- *heavily reliant on *punctuation, visual presentation and additional words*, where stress and intonation would serve to point the sense in speech (e.g., 'He greeted the baby with a strangely cooing and sickeningly patronising "Hell-O-oo!" ');
- *ostensibly 'fully-formed' and with an emphasis on the 'finished' product*: there is usually little surviving evidence of the redrafting process (including back-tracking, hesitation and changes of direction);
- *uninterrupted and with a tendency towards monologue and a single-voiced discourse*; even though writers can and do invoke other voices and discourses – as do critical and creative readers.

This last point brings us back to the dynamic interrelation of the activities of writing and reading, particularly the fact that reading is always a form of *re*writing. The rest of this entry is devoted to variations on this theme.

Reception theorists (who explore forms of Reception **Aesthetics**) insist that a text does not simply exist in itself (as NEW CRITICS maintained) but that it exists as part of a shifting relation with readers over time. The text is a constantly re-forming construct. Thus Hans Robert *Jauss sees the text historically, on a changing '*horizon of expectation' which is defined by the meeting of the historical moments of the text and reader. As with a real horizon where sky meets land or sea, the relation between text and reader constantly changes as we travel through time and space. For Jauss, therefore, there is no single fixed point of reference, no absolutely imperative original meaning, but rather a succession of *moments of reception*, each one affected by the expectations, tastes and aims of the 'receivers' (for changing reception of *Hamlet* over time; see 2.2).

Wolfgang *Iser is another German reception theorist, but he takes a rather different tack. Iser talks more abstractly and somewhat less historically about the relations between texts and readers that share the same cultural frame. He is less interested in changes in reception over time and more interested in how a contemporary reader responds to a contemporary text. Chief among Iser's tools for modelling the text–reader relation are the following concepts (see 'narration process' under **narrative**):

♦ *implied reader* – the reader apparently intended by the author and implied by the text as a role which actual readers are invited to fill;
♦ *'blanks and vacancies'* – those areas of openness and indeterminacy in the text which actual readers fill according to their own capacities and orientations (cf. Macherey's **gaps and silences**);
♦ *affirmative *negation* – the *dialectical activity of meeting such blanks, vacancies and indeterminacies creatively as well as critically: through reading, readers make sense of them**selves**; they do not simply make sense of the text as **other**.

Iser's model of critical-creative reading has been deservedly influential. Its major drawback is that it often assumes readers who substantially share the world-view of the text they are reading. Furthermore, on closer inspection, this 'ideal reader' often turns out to be white, Western European and male. The tools of reception aesthetics can be extremely useful. But the politics which informs that aesthetics still determines what horizon is expected and what kind of material is assumed to fill the blanks and vacancies. MARXIST, FEMINIST and POSTCOLONIAL readers all tend to be 'receptive' to different possibilities.

Reader-response critics are another broadly identifiable group of (chiefly American) writers engaged with readers and ways of reading. Many of these critics have a more PSYCHOLOGICAL and less aesthetic emphasis than their German counterparts. Norman *Holland, for instance, conceives of the text–reader relation as a 'transaction' much like that between analyst and analysand. For Holland, moreover, it is as much the text which analyses the reader as the reader who analyses the text. The text is thereby seen as a site for the *projection of anxieties and hopes, and is understood in terms of its therapeutic functions and effects, not in terms of intrinsic meaning. David *Bleich, another American practitioner of reader-response, extends this 'transactive' model of response into the arena of group work. Bleich explores not only the effects of a text on individuals but also the processes whereby groups cooperate and negotiate meanings with the aim of arriving at a consensus – even if in practice this is not achieved. In these respects Bleich's models and techniques of '(inter)subjective criticism' are far more subtle and powerful than, say, Stanley Fish's notion of 'interpretive communities'(i.e. academic groups who share reading practices and values). The problem with the latter is that there is little recognition of the process whereby fundamental conflicts and **differences** arise between and within various groups of readers. Nor is much attention paid to variation in reading practice, whether from one group or person to another, or even from one reading to another by the same person. Relatedly (though he is not strictly a *reader-response* critic), Harold Bloom talks of the relation between one *writer* and another in terms of an Oedipal scenario: 'strong' writers deliberately 'misunderstand' and thereby both re-write and overthrow their predecessors (who are conceived as threatening father-figures). However, Bloom does not include readers on his 'map of misprision'. Nor does he much consider models of the individual as a social **subject**, other than those supplied by Freudian psychology.

For other models of the individual reader as a self-divided subject and an **identity** constantly involved in processes of dispersal and redefinition we must turn to POSTSTRUCTURALIST and POSTMODERNIST theorists. Meanwhile, for frames in which to practise specifically 'resistant', 'oppositional' or 'alternative' readings we must turn to Marxist, feminist and postcolonial writings (see below). All these movements in their various ways challenge politically loaded idealisations of 'the reader' or 'readers' (as though s/he or they simply exist as some undifferentiated mass in an ahistorical vacuum). Hence the framing of the following questions.

'THE READER' ... WHICH READERS?

These questions can be put to any text and to anyone reading. The insistence on past and present moments of reception is a reminder that there are always more readers and readings than one.

Who could read at all there and then? Who can read here and now? What are the implications of these kinds and degrees of *il/literacy for what got and gets written?

How were (and are) readers distinguished by class, gender, ethnicity, region, nation, religion and education? And what of the specific kinds of reading practice in play then and now (public and out loud, solitary and silent, for pleasure, instruction, analysis . . .)?

How likely was (and is) a common response given the cultural make-up of the readership? Are utterly consensual *or* utterly conflictual readings ever possible?

How does one person's reading (and one person reading) influence another? And where does this leave the notion of a 'purely personal response'?

At what point does the activity of reading turn into that of (re)writing: in the head when reading? Afterwards on reflection? In conversation when describing and evaluating? In a written essay or analysis? In selective quotation? In finding or fashioning a particular edition? In a concerted critique, adaptation, updating, parody, intervention . . .?

(For influential case studies which show how such questions can be put to a range of specific historical materials, see McGann 1988.)

The following theorists have also contributed to the notion of reading as rewriting in literary and cultural studies.

Roland *Barthes made an influential distinction between 'readerly' (*lisible*) and 'writerly' (*scriptible*) texts. Readerly texts offer the reader the pleasure (*plaisir*) of total immersion in and identification with a supposedly self-sufficient and closed fictional world (examples would be Mills and Boon romances and certain kinds of 'classic **realism**'). Writerly texts offer the reader the joy/ecstacy (*jouissance*) of participation in the construction of a fictional world which is openly in process and always in the making (examples would be everything from Sterne's *Tristram Shandy* and Joyce's *Ulysses* to interactive story-books and virtual reality games; see **metafiction**). Subsequently, however, Barthes modified this distinction. He recognised that it is also the reader (not only the author or the text) who controls how far a text shall be read as 'closed' or 'open', 'readerly' or 'writerly'. Thus even the most apparently complete, self-sufficient and non-playful text (e.g., a telephone directory) can readily be recognised as 'writerly'. We simply need to draw attention to its distinctive apparatuses and discourses and its manifold uses (from finding telephone numbers and addresses to propping up shelves and demonstrating strong-arm techniques). Conversely, even the most apparently incomplete and open text can be substantially filled in and closed down so as to be made 'readerly' (e.g., critical commentaries on Sterne and Joyce). Barthes partly covered this eventuality when he later observed that the same piece of literature could be approached as a finished 'work of art' (French *œuvre*; Latin *opus*) or as a 'text' (in this case invoking its ancient meaning of 'a tissue', 'texture', 'a web' – a fabric made up of 'holes' as well as 'wholes'; see **text**). Hélène *Cixous makes a relatable distinction with respect to what she calls *écriture féminine* ('feminine writing'). Initially she claimed that there is a kind of writing characterised by its openness, fluidity and apparent fragmentariness which can be identified with women (e.g., Woolf and Dorothy Richardson). Later Cixous allowed that such writing is gendered rather than sexed, and can be identified with the 'feminine' in men too. More recently, she and other feminists have recognised that it is not only the writer but also the reader who can in effect make the reading experience more fluid and open: there is thus an activity of *lire comme femme* ('reading as a woman') too.

RESPONSE-ABILITY IS RESPONSIBILITY

Aesthetic responsiveness = Ethical responsibility
Personal response = Interpersonal response-ability (after Bakhtin, see below)

Mikhail *Bakhtin is another critical theorist who challenges any hard-and-fast distinction between the activities of reading and writing. His insistence that words are 'sites of struggle' defined in the dialogic interplay between competing discourses and voices, means that every utterance is Janus-like. It looks both back and forwards: back to past utterances to which it is a response, and forwards to future utterances which it anticipates in response. In this way, for Bakhtin, *'response-ability'* or 'answerability' is the prerogative of both writers and readers alike. Bakhtin also stresses the ethical *responsibility* as well as the historical *response-ability* of every utterance we make (both senses are covered by Russian *otvetstvenost*). Such a view of response-ability/reponsibility has little in common with an exclusively individualist view of 'personal response'. For Bakhtin, responses can never be purely 'personal' (in the sense of being 'wholly authenticated by one's own experience' and expressed 'in one's own words') precisely because one's own experience *and* words are always already implicated in those of others (what he refers to as 'another's words in one's own language'; also see **self and other**). **Self** is always expressed *through* – never simply against – **other**. Apparently personal responses always turn out to be interpersonal too.

Jacques *Derrida is a theorist who has greatly influenced contemporary models of reading and writing in yet other ways. Above all, he insists that both writers and readers, because they use and are used by LANGUAGE, are involved in the continual displacement and deferral of meanings. The ceaseless play of differences within and between words, within and between texts, ensures that there is no fixed point of departure *or* arrival in the process of writing–reading, and therefore no stable distinction between writer and reader. Instead we are treated to a fascinating play of possibilities in interpersonal and intertextual space. Derrida also challenges one of the most commonly cherished hierarchies in Western linguistics. Traditionally, speech is privileged above writing because, it is assumed, speech is more tied up with the presence of a speaker and a listener, whereas writing can go its own way independently of either writer or reader. Derrida, however, argues that it is in fact *writing* which more nearly registers the 'languageness' of language. This is precisely because writing more obviously entails **absence**, and it is 'absence-of-things' and 'absent things' which words are best at conveying. Derrida also suggests that it is precisely the play between present words and absent things that is the motivating force informing most activities of writing and reading. Whether as writers or readers, we are all involved in the endlessly fascinating yet ultimately frustrating task of trying to knit presences out of absences: looking *at* a text only to find ourselves looking *through* it. Writing – like speech – always turns out to be full of w/holes.

Resistant readers and reading other-wise. Many overtly political writers propose strategies of reading that can be variously described as 'resistant', 'counter' or 'altern-ative'. (The mere beginning of such a list might include: hooks, Brecht, Benjamin, Bhabha, Macherey, Hall, Cixous, Eco, Fetterley, Hutcheon, Kristeva, Mills, Said and Spivak.) For convenience, three kinds of response can be distinguished, though in any particular reading or reading practice there may well be a mixture:

- *Passive or submissive reading* involves reading 'with the grain' of the text, accepting its perceived values and versions of reality. This may be more positively framed as 'receptive' reading.
- *Oppositional or counter-reading* involves reading 'against the grain' of the text, aiming to invert or subvert its meanings. This may also be termed 'aggressive' or 'assertive' reading, depending upon how negatively or positively it is valued.
- *Alternative or negotiated reading* involves reading neither 'with' nor 'against' the grain of the text, but flexibly and with a sense of challengeable and changeable critical agendas. This may also be termed 'shifty' or 'subtle' reading, depending upon what precisely goes on in practice and why.

Critical reading into critical-creative rewriting

In more radical versions of reading practice it is recognised that readings lead to rewritings in deed not just in the head. At this point, therefore, we must turn to such critical-creative genres as *adaptation, *imitation, *parody, *collage and *inter-vention. Crucially, these are not only activities which specially designated **authors**, **artists** and other kinds of *creative practitioner engage in. They are also tried and tested genres of academic writing (usually including a commentary) which can very profitably and pleasurably be used to complement the traditional academic essay and analysis. (For further guidance see 4.4: Alternative modes of critical and creative writing.) All that need be added here is that such modes of re/production encourage interpretation and performance in the fullest sense. They thereby fundamentally reconfigure the relations between reading and writing, on the one hand, and criticism and creativity, on the other. Response is thus realised as something we negotiate and make together – not simply something each of us 'has'.

ACTIVITIES

(a) *Transforming texts.* For a range of activities exploring writing as both product and process, with an end in view and as an end in itself, see:

- ◆ **speech**, activity (b) – spontaneous conversation into crafted scripts, and vice versa;
- ◆ **narrative**, activity (c) – adaptation of novels and films for screen, and vice versa;
- ◆ **versification**, activity (b) – permutations of poetry, prose and performance.

(b) *Being a responsive and responsible reader.* Apply some of the terms and techniques introduced above to a text you are studying or one from Part Five: i.e., moments of reception and horizons of expectation (Jauss); implied reader, blanks and vacancies, affirmative negation (Iser); writerly and readerly, work (of art) and text (Barthes); response-ability and dialogue (Bakhtin); feminine writing and reading as a woman (Cixous); passive, oppositional and alternative readers/readings.

(c) *Critical reading as critical-creative rewriting.* Use one or two of the 'Alternative modes of critical and creative writing' (4.4) to explore a text which interests or irritates you. Be sure to add a commentary.

DISCUSSION

(i) Writing is teachable: it is an art that can be learned rather than a mysterious ability that one either has or does not have.
Robert Connors and Cheryl Glenn, *The St Martin's Guide to Teaching Writing* (1995: v)

(ii) The word is a two-sided act [. . .] every utterance is suspended between the utterance to which it responds and the response which it anticipates.
V.I. Voloshinov, *Marxism and the Philosophy of Language* (1973: 86ff.)

(iii) The goal of literary work (or literature as work) is to make the reader no longer a consumer, but a producer of the text.
Roland Barthes,'From Work to Text' (1977: 163)

Also see: 1.5.5; LITERATURE; 2.2; 4.4; **absence and presence, gaps and silences; author and authority; speech and conversation, monologue and dialogue; text.**

READING: *Introductory:* Moon 1992: 101–6; Hawthorn 1994: 53–5; Johnson in Lentricchia and McLaughlin 1995: 39–49, 321–38; Holub 1984; Graddol and Boyd-Barrett 1994: 200–72; Crystal 1995: 256–83; Maybin and Mercer 1996: 42–83; Selden 1988: 186–221 (critical anthology). *Advanced theory:* Derrida, Bakhtin, Barthes, Foucault, Iser and Eco in Lodge 1988: 107–56, 166–228, 445–55; Jauss in Rice and Waugh 1996: 83–91; Barthes 1977: 142–216; Bakhtin 1990. *On writing:* Connors and Glenn 1995; Grabe and Kaplan 1996. *On reading and response:* Iser 1978; Jauss 1982; Eco 1978; Bleich

1978; McGann 1988; Holland 1990; Fetterley 1991; Mills 1994; Bennett 1995 (critical anthology). *On reading as rewriting:* Bartholomae and Petrosky 1986, 1996; Corcoran *et al.* 1994: 163–230; Scholes *et al.* 1995: 160ff.; Pope 1995; Nash and Stacey 1997: 182–225.

YOUR OWN ADDITIONS AND MODIFICATIONS

This is a reminder to continue adding items which you yourself find useful and necessary. For clearly there are plenty of common – and some not so common – terms not featured in this book which you may feel to be equally or more significant. There will probably be some of the definitions you would like to take issue with too. In this respect, Part Three should be regarded simply as a beginning. Extend, refine and replace it as you see fit.

There are many dictionaries as well as general guides and introductions relating to the terms and topics treated in this part of the book. In putting it together I have found the following of recurrent use, and therefore invite you to use them too.

OED (*Oxford English Dictionary*) 1989.

Literature and criticism: Wellek and Warren 1963; Fowler 1987; Wynne-Davies 1989; Lentricchia and McLaughlin 1995; Coyle *et al.* 1990; Cuddon 1992; Moon 1992; Hawthorn 1994; Ousby 1992; Montgomery *et al.* 1992; Abrams 1993; Makaryk 1993; Preminger and Brogan 1993; Holman and Harmon 1996; Green and LeBihan 1996; Selden *et al.* 1997.

Critical anthologies: Lodge 1972, 1988; Selden 1988; Waugh 1992; Selden, Widdowson and Brooker 1997; Rylance 1987.

Linguistics and discourse stylistics: Ducrot and Todorov 1972; Crystal 1996, 1997; Wales 1989; Carter and Simpson 1989; Carter and Nash 1990; Carter 1995.

Culture, communication and media: Williams 1983; Fiske 1987, 1990; Watson and Hill 1984; Grossberg *et al.* 1992; O'Sullivan *et al.* 1994; Corner and Hawthorn 1995.

Read and write on . . . !

TEXTUAL ACTIVITIES AND LEARNING STRATEGIES

PART FOUR

PREVIEW

This part surveys the principal ways in which students may learn (and by implication teachers teach) in contemporary English Studies courses. The strategies and activities featured are designed to be of use when planning new courses as well as when teaching and learning existing courses. The basic premise is that we are all, in the broadest sense, *students of English*, so these are all matters of common interest. Particular attention is paid to the many ways in which we may handle texts, other people's and our own: analytically, critically and creatively. The areas treated are as follows:

4.1 *Overview of textual activities*: summary descriptions of a range of activities from traditional extract analysis and the writing of essays and dissertations to editing and publishing projects, the use of interviews and questionnaires, presentations, translation between varieties, adaptation, parody, critical rewriting and creative writing as such.

4.2 *Frameworks and checklists for close reading*: a series of extended questions to put to any text on such matters as subject matter and subject positions, medium, genre, intertextuality, context and value; followed by checklists for systematic attention to word choice, word combination, sound-patterning and visual presentation, and textual cohesion.

4.3 *Writing and research from essays to the Internet*: initial frameworks and information sources to help with the development and drafting of essays, dissertations and projects.

4.4 *Alternative modes of critical and creative writing*: from the use of alternative 'summaries' and 're-titlings', through exercises in imitation, parody and collage to the generation of preludes, interludes and postludes (before, during and after a given text) and full-blown adaptations and interventions (retelling, recentring, switches and shifts in genre, media and discourse).

4.5 *What's (not) in a name? Changing courses*: an invitation to compare the 'labels' and 'contents' of courses (even whole programmes) and weigh the alternatives.

4.6 *Making anthologies and firing 'canons' yourself*: an invitation to do just that.

A key educational principle throughout is what can be called, somewhat cumbersomely but maybe memorably 'the four inters'. Learning and teaching should be *interactive, interpersonal, intertextual* and *interdisciplinary*. That is, as most educationists maintain, genuine learning only takes place when four conditions are met, when we:

♦ grapple with, 'grasp' and thereby internalise material for ourselves (*interactively*);
♦ share the delight and distress of working and playing together (*interpersonally*);
♦ compare and contrast texts, including ones of our own finding and making (*intertextually*);
♦ are prepared to respect but also cross and redraw the boundaries of existing disciplines and thereby realise *interdisciplinary* (and even 'other-disciplinary') possibilities.

4.1   OVERVIEW OF TEXTUAL ACTIVITIES

There is still a widespread assumption in tertiary English that 'work' means 'written work' and that written work basically means essays and analyses done by individual students for assessment. This assumption is misleading on at least five counts. First, we communicate about – and in – English through speech as well as writing. There is therefore 'spoken work' as well as 'written work', and there may be 'imaged work' and 'performed work' too. Second, even if we concentrate on written work, there are many more ways of working – and playing – with writing than the essay or analysis. Third, even essays and analyses come in many shapes and sizes and can perform many functions. Fourth, not all work needs to be done by students as individuals; it can also be done in groups. Fifth and finally, not all work need be assessed or, if it is, it need not be assessed in the same ways.

What follows is an overview of textual activities (see Figure 7). **Textual** is here intended in its broadest sense, meaning derived from and/or resulting in a verbal or visual record (in writing, print, audio- or audio-visual media). Most of these activities can be done by people working on their own or in groups, in class or out of it. They can be featured in a variety of learning and teaching contexts and may or may not be formally assessed. They can be combined to produce hybrids, and they can be supplemented by other activities.

Use this overview in two ways:

♦   to identify the activities you currently favour;
♦   to consider additional or alternative activities you might try.

DISCUSSION

Debate Doyle's proposal for the reconstitution of English study in 1.7, p. 43, Discussion (ii).

READING: A lively student-centred view of the major possibilities for teaching, learning and assessment in tertiary education (not only in English) is Saunders 1994. For English and Literary Studies in particular, see Reid 1984, Durant and Fabb 1990, Thomson 1992 and Corcoran *et al.* 1994; also Furlong and Ogborn 1995. Morgan 1992 is an inspiring example of a single project which is practically multidimensional and theoretically high-powered; also see Beetham *et al.* in Brooker and Humm 1989: 236–58, and the activities and rationales developed in Carter and Long 1987, hooks 1994, Scholes *et al.* 1995. Also see the Reading in 4.3.
    A useful handbook in Cultural, Communication and Media Studies with plenty to interest the student (i.e. learner and teacher) of English is Branston and Stafford 1996.

essays can be experimental 'assays', journalistic reviews, brief 'position papers', or full mini-theses – all on set or negotiated topics. They can involve different proportions of theory, illustration, analysis and argument; and their 'logics' can be variously linear, dialectical, metaphorical, recursive or self-reflexive. There is no such thing as '*the* essay'.

dissertations/theses (the terms are interchangeable) are in effect extended formal essays, with an emphasis on the learner's role in identifying, investigating and framing a topic of particular interest to her- or himself. The supervisor's role is to help guide the research and shape the overall result. Traditionally, dissertations begin with a speculative 'hypothesis' which is subjected to successive proof ('thesis') and disproof ('antithesis') with the whole thing leading towards an eventual conclusion ('synthesis'). Now, however, this dialectical structure is often replaced by four or five chapters on interrelated issues. These are framed by an introduction and a conclusion and supported by a full scholarly apparatus of notes, bibliography and appendices.

analyses can be of short complete texts or of extracts from longer works. The objects of study may be previously 'seen' or 'unseen', and may or may not be accompanied by supplementary information on author(s), dates, contexts and conventions, etc. What is analysed may be the state or status of the text, formal, linguistic and ideological structures, the responses of particular readers or the processes of reading and sense-making as such.

presentations can be done individually or in groups, before just one person (e.g., the lecturer in a tutorial) or before a larger group (e.g., a seminar of one's peers). There tends to be as much emphasis on how, and how well, things are presented as on the information as such. Clearly audible speech, a visibly engaged face and sheer enthusiasm are the basic keys to good presentation. These are greatly helped by well prepared and rehearsed cues and notes, perhaps on cards (*not* a verbatim script dutifully read out with head down). Handouts, overhead transparencies and posters can be a big help too. So may audio-visual and multimedia aids (though beware of all flash and no substance). Success is perhaps best judged by how much thought, discussion and other activity are generated than by how much the presenter manages to cram in or show off.

translation can be done between one language and another or between distinct historical, geographical and social varieties of 'the same language'. It operates on a continuum between literal, word-for-word substitution and fairly free recasting, depending on the relative distances between source and target languages/cultures and the functions of the translation: dependent gloss, academic 'crib', 'creative' free-standing text; for specialists or non-specialists; for instruction and/or pleasure, etc. All translation involves the tricky matter of non/equivalence: the fact that different languages may have analogous – but never identical – structures and effects. There is therefore always some measure of *transformation* (never simple transference) as well as various kinds of complex *dialogue* (never simple monologue). Such problems and possibilities can be explored in a preface, notes and commentary.

editing and publishing involve gathering, comparing, selecting and combining existing materials (manuscript, print, still or moving images, sound-recording, etc.) so as to produce old/new materials. The results can be designed and published for a wide or narrow range of readers, audiences and viewers, and may or may not be accompanied by annotation and commentary. The work of scholarly editors and, say, news editors is thus in principle similar; though their materials, tools and aims differ markedly. Either way, editing is one of the most powerful forms of criticism. Student projects generally include a commentary on criteria, procedures and projected 'public'.

INDIVIDUAL.................GROUP

SPOKEN......................WRITTEN...................PRESENTED

course journals involve a cumulative record of what is going into and coming out of a course – or even a whole programme. Informal or formal, personal or public, individual or collective, purely verbal or accompanied by other materials – a journal acts as a space where the processes of learning (and teaching) can be recorded and reviewed. The whole thing may be handed in and shared, or a selection or summary made. The journal-keeper's control of the journal and what is or is not made public is crucial. Journals often work best when required for completion of a course but not directly assigned a mark. The combined results of several journals may also be edited and 'published'. This can serve as a course souvenir for participants and as a foretaste of the course for prospective students.

creative writing, performance and production may begin with one of the other activities (e.g., imitation and parody or adaptation and intervention – or even an information search) and move towards a more free-standing text. They may also begin with a topic or format suggested by someone else (e.g., an instructor); or derive from the writer's, performer's or director's own experience; or be generated by workshops and collective improvisation round a theme or object. But in any event the results will be a compound of the 'found' and the 'made', the old and the new, the individual and the collective. The activity may be as 'critical' as it is 'creative', and again a commentary may be attached to explicate and explore the processes.

information searches involve identifying, selecting and using reference resources appropriate to a specific task such as researching an author, period, genre, social group or event. The task may be 'set' or self-selected, solo or collaborative, and the resources may be paper or electronic – and other people. Given the vast increase in the variety and quality of modern information sources, along with the relative speed and ease of retrieval, it is becoming more and more important to decide what to select and how to sort it out. The framing of provisional research questions and the selection of appropriate 'key words' are thus crucial. So is the capacity to ignore what seems to be irrelevant for one's immediate purposes.

adaptation and intervention can involve transferring – and thereby transforming – a text from one genre or medium into another (e.g., verse into prose, novel into stage play or film – and vice versa) even to the point of re-casting plot, beginnings and endings, narrators, characters, and other 'macro-textual' features. At the 'micro-textual' level this may entail tinkering with specific choices and combinations of words, sounds, images, etc. The critical-creative nature of these activities spans imitation and parody and creative writing as such. Again, a commentary can be added to explore distinctions and processes explicitly .

interviews and questionnaires can elicit information and opinion about issues relevant to a particular text, activity or event (such as a lecture, concert or TV programme). Tasks may include monitoring reader-, listener- or viewer-responses, comparing 'expert' and 'non-expert' informants, and gathering instances of oral history and story. Tools may include pen and paper, tape-recorders and videos. It's a good idea to decide what *you* want to know first, then to seek advice on how to go about gathering the information and presenting the results. Most student work in this area is best seen as small-scale 'pilot studies' rather than full-blown surveys.

imitation and parody involve writing in the manner of a specific writer (e.g., reproducing Dickinson's characteristic verse-form, imagery and punctuation; or Hemingway's characteristic dialogue and action) or rewriting one writer in the terms and times of another (e.g., Austen as though by Woolf, Ibsen as though by Brecht, Eisenstein as though by Spielberg – and vice versa). How far the results are judged to be 'imitative' or 'parodic' depends on the kinds of critical distance perceived between the model and its copy. A commentary may be added to explore such distinctions and to record the processes of re- (and de-) composition.

BEFORE.................DURING.................AFTER CLASS

Figure 7 Textual activities as learning strategies

4.2   FRAMEWORKS AND CHECKLISTS FOR CLOSE READING

The following questions and suggestions are designed to help you frame an analytical, critical and creative response to any text you meet. They should be used in conjunction with the checklist which follows and the approaches featured in Part Two.

Framing an overall response

1   Why, where and when are you reading this text? (Purpose and context of reading)

For instance, did you choose it yourself or was it chosen for you? In what kind of course or programme, with what stated or implicit aims?

2   What, basically, is the text about? (Identifying subject matters)

Attempt a couple of summaries of what the text seems to be about: one in a phrase or two; the other in a paraphrase of around thirty words. In each case consider what aspects of the text you have emphasised and which you have marginalised or excluded completely. Why, do you think? Go on to compare your summaries with other people's.

3   What kind(s) of text is it? (Medium, genre and function)

◆   *medium*: does it appear to be primarily for oral delivery or silent reading? public or private? formal or informal? What traces of this are there in the text?
◆   *genre*: what other texts does it most remind you of? Is there a mixture of types?
◆   *function*: what seem to be the chief purposes of this text – to inform, persuade, amuse, stir up, calm down, make think, make feel, answer questions, pose problems? For instance, is the text instrumental and directed towards an activity beyond itself (e.g., an advert or recipe)? Or does it appear to offer itself as an object of interest in its own right (e.g., a poem, a joke)?

4   Who is talking with whom through, within and around the text? (Addresser–addressee relations) In what ways do you respond? (Dialogue and monologue)

Notice that most texts you study involve a variety of people speaking and spoken to (addressers and addressees) and therefore a variety of one-, two- or many-way conversations. We can distinguish these as variously *external* and *internal*.

◆   'External' conversations include teacher and learner, and learner and learner; also writer and reader.

♦   'Internal' conversations include those between characters or figures within the text, as well as the 'voice' or 'persona' of any narrator.

As a result, every reading of a text, however simple, is in some sense many-voiced. One of those voices – for you the most immediate and important – is yours. What have *you* got to say?

5   What overall version or vision of experience (personal, social, historical, political, moral, aesthetic) does the text appear to offer? Are you persuaded or happy to share it? ('World-view' and value)

This last general question is a reminder to stand back and weigh the overall effect and value of the text. What does it do to you? Do you find it worthwhile?

Analysing in detail

Here is a checklist to help you turn the above general response into a fairly comprehensive analysis. It is organised in terms of *word choice, word combination, sound-patterning and visual presentation*, and *textuality – text, context, intertextuality*. To begin with, it can be a good idea to analyse a text by moving systematically through each of these categories in turn. Once you have got used to the terms and categories, you may move fairly freely from one to another, depending on the nature of the text and the purpose of your analysis. The main thing is to keep relating specific textual details to larger critical frameworks.

The present method/checklist will not tell you what to think about and how to *value a particular text. But it will help you frame a response which is both searching and critical. Notice that each of the 'positive' questions below is followed by some counter- and alternative questions. These are reminders to read creatively as well as critically: to gauge what *is* in a particular text by bracing it against what is *not* – but perhaps might have been. Treat these as invitations to *rewrite, too, if you wish. (Technical grammatical and linguistic terms are glossed in Part Six.)

Word choice

What sorts of vocabulary are being used? (What others might have been used?)
How far are the words:

short or long; monosyllabic or polysyllabic (see syllable)?
simple or complex?
concrete or abstract; particular or general?
common and everyday, or from a specific area of use (religion, technology, etc.)?
literal or figurative; plain or metaphorical?
context-sensitive (e.g., the pronouns 'I', 'she', etc., and words such as 'here' and 'now') – or relatively context-free?
heavily adjectival and adverbial – or lightly modified nouns and verbs?

Experiment by substituting, adding or deleting words.

Word combination

What are the main ways in which the words are grouped or organised? (How else might they have been structured and to what alternative effects?)
How far are there:

familiar collocations (recognisable word-clusters) – or is much of it strikingly new?
speeches quoted directly or indirectly, freely or precisely?
speech moves, turns and exchanges with specific structures (see speech acts)?
long or short sentences – and how many words on average?
'fully' or 'incompletely' framed sentences (major or minor)?
coordinated and/or subordinated structures?
repetitions of words, or parallelisms of phrase and sentences structure?
lightly or heavily modified nouns (pre- or post-modified); in/definite articles?
predominantly common nouns, proper nouns or personal pronouns?
lightly or heavily modalised verbs, with auxiliary verbs and/or adverbs?
one or more verbal tenses and aspects (see verbs), suggesting what frames of time,
     duration and frequency?
active or passive, transitive or intransitive structures (see verbs)?
favoured sentence-types: stating, questioning, commanding or exclaiming?

Again, experiment with alternatives. What combinations have not been used but might have been?

Sound patterning and visual presentation

What kinds of 'music' or visual patterns do the words make, and with what effects? (What other 'musics' and visual patterns might there have been – and with what alternative effects?)
What do you hear, see, or infer with respect to:

stress, rhythm and intonation?
repetition or near-repetition of sounds or sights?
alliteration and assonance? rhyme and half-rhyme (see **versification**)?
use of short or long vowels? plosives (e.g., /p, b, t/) or fricatives (/f, s/)?
rhythmic beats (see stress) or metrical syllables to the line?
single or many voices: alternating or overlapping, in harmony or cacophony?
distinctive features of spelling, punctuation and visual presentation?
audio- or audio-visual editing techniques?

As always, experiment with alternatives in the same, different or mixed media.

Textuality

How far does the text seem to hang together 'as a whole'? In what contexts and other texts is it implicated? (Conversely, how far is the text a series of 'holes'? Is there any end to the contexts and other texts we could bring to bear on it?)
   Would you describe the text as:

generally, unified or fragmentary? uniform or diverse?

heavily context-dependent (and thus full of personal pronouns such as 'I', 'we' and 'you', and words such as 'now', 'tomorrow', 'here', 'there', 'this') or relatively context-free (and thus full of common and proper *nouns such as 'a waiter', 'John Davies' and 'Manchester')?

an instance of certain *kinds* of texts (**genres**), with recognisable features of subject matter, form and structure?

tightly or loosely cohesive in terms of

♦ explicit links and structures between sentences, paragraphs, verses (e.g., *connectors such as 'and', 'but', 'therefore', 'however')?

♦ sustained references to the same items (e.g., 'Jane . . . the woman . . . she')?

♦ parallelisms of similar words, sounds and structures?

DISCUSSION

> The journey is one of choices, judgements, of logic – if . . . then . . . and also . . . if not . . . therefore; the small words that have little use become instruments of power.
> Janet Frame, *The Carpathians* London: Vintage, (1988: 11) also see 1.8.1,
> Discussion (ii) and (iii)

READING: This checklist can be supplemented with others in Leech and Short 1981: 75–82, Toolan 1988: 111–15, Pope 1995: 192–6 and Short 1996. For some of the precursors of 'close reading', see PRACTICAL AND (OLD) NEW CRITICISM (2.3); and for more systematic applications drawing (like those above) upon **discourse** analysis and *stylistics, see Haynes 1989 and the Readings in 1.8 and 1.8.1, pp. 48, 54.

4.3   WRITING AND RESEARCH FROM ESSAYS TO THE INTERNET

There are already some good books on writing essays and dissertations. There have also recently been some good guides to using computers for research and writing in English, as well as for learning and teaching in the Arts and Humanities in general. The main purpose of this section is simply to point to these (see below) and then pretty much leave you to get on with things yourself. Before doing that, however, it may help if I at least sketch the stages through which the writing of a good essay (or for that matter most kinds of written project) tend to go. At the same time I shall indicate the main ways in which computers tend to be used in contemporary English Studies (as in the Arts, Humanities and Social Sciences in general). The reason for embracing both kinds of activity in the same section is not far to seek. The storage and retrieval, editing and distribution of information (much of it in the form of writing) are being done increasingly through computers. Meanwhile, a greater amount of the writing being done by students and teachers is word-processed, just as information searches in most college and university libraries are electronic. With many of the latter currently being dubbed 'Information and Resource Centres', the decision to approach writing and research in the context of computing perhaps requires no further elaboration.

A 'good piece of writing' (by which I here specifically intend a piece of writing that satsfies both the student-writer and teacher-reader) usually goes through a number

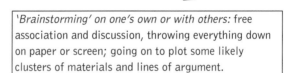

START HERE

Initial reflection upon and provisional definition of the terms of the task and the nature of the material. Note deadline and aim to meet it.

'Brainstorming' on one's own or with others: free association and discussion, throwing everything down on paper or screen; going on to plot some likely clusters of materials and lines of argument.

Library/information search (1): initial search by supplied bibliography: topic, author, periods, genres, etc., and perhaps by 'key words'.

FINISH HERE

Final draft polished off: arguments and sentences fixed up as best you can; sections finalised (perhaps adding headings for clearer signposting and refining layout for visible structure); bibliography appended; foot- or end-notes (if any), indentation and paragraph-ing regularised; spellings checked; cover page added – usually including your name and perhaps student number, course title and number; title of task; tutor's name; word-count if required and, finally, the date of submission. (With a little luck and some good management, this is on or before the one you aimed to meet at the 'START'.)

And then on to that next piece, which you'll do in a similar way but differently . . .

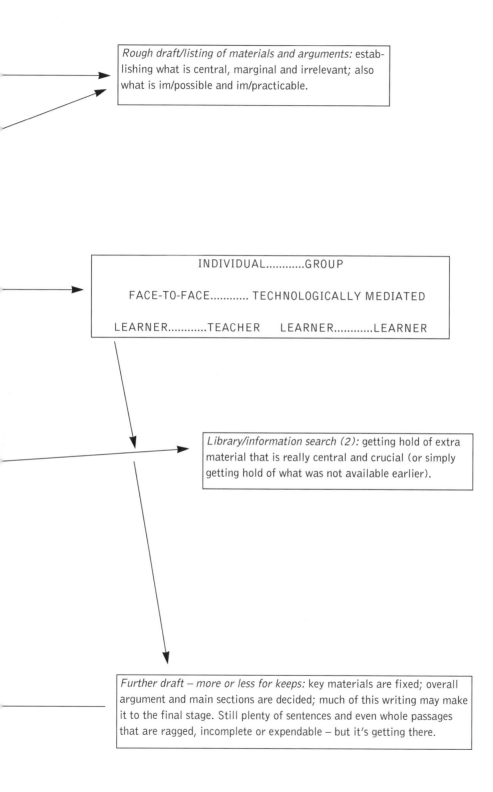

Rough draft/listing of materials and arguments: establishing what is central, marginal and irrelevant; also what is im/possible and im/practicable.

INDIVIDUAL............GROUP

FACE-TO-FACE............ TECHNOLOGICALLY MEDIATED

LEARNER............TEACHER   LEARNER............LEARNER

Library/information search (2): getting hold of extra material that is really central and crucial (or simply getting hold of what was not available earlier).

Further draft – more or less for keeps: key materials are fixed; overall argument and main sections are decided; much of this writing may make it to the final stage. Still plenty of sentences and even whole passages that are ragged, incomplete or expendable – but it's getting there.

Figure 8 Writing and research processes

of processes. These processes are themselves well enough researched and written about for at least the main elements to be agreed; even though there continues to be much disagreement about the precise models and methods and even the overall aims of academic writing. At any rate, something like the processes shown in Figure 8 are gone through before a piece of academic writing is reckoned successful.

ABOUT THE SHAPE OF *THIS* PIECE OF ELECTRONIC WRITING . . .

The open layout on pp. 262–263 is meant to suggest a process which is cyclic and recursive rather than linear and unidirectional. People may get on and off at the same points: they have assignments to do and they have to submit them. There are 'start' and 'finish' points. However, precisely where they go, what they do and the order in which they do it between these two points can differ widely – even wildly. And that makes for good writing too.

Here are the main uses to which computing is put in English Studies:

- *Word-processing:* for drafting, redrafting and final presentation;
- *Information search:* initially for finding books, journals and other materials in the library and elsewhere (in-house and on-line), but increasingly as a source of relevant information in its own right;
- *E-mail:* for contacting lecturers, fellow students and friends – just to check on course schedules or as a whole way of developing and submitting work;
- *World-Wide-Web, Internet . . . :* from casually 'surfing the net' to deliberately visiting a site – or even setting up one of your own with interested colleagues;
- *Text analysis:* everything from small-scale work on the textual variants of a single line or short poem to full-scale author, period and genre studies, including multivariate scanning of vast text corpora for word frequencies, collocations, grammatical and other structures;
- *Text manipulation:* again, from relatively localised exercises with substitutions of single words (e.g., 'cloze tests') to collaborative global projects using hypertext and multimedia facilities;
- *From hypertext to multimedia, cyberspace and beyond . . .* The sky's no limit for some. For others, however, it may still cost the earth (see *literacy, *neo-colonialism, POSTMODERNISM and World *English).

READING: *Writing essays and dissertations* for Literary Studies is excellently served by Fabb and Durant 1993; as is more *creative text composition* by Nash and Stacey 1997. For more on the contemporary theory and practice of writing, see Grabe and Kaplan 1996.

English and computing: Nash and Stacey 1997: 149–81, 231–2 is a lively and highly informed introduction; Crump and Carbone 1996 is an invaluable handbook; while Bolter 1991 and Landow 1992 situate computers in both the history and the (postmodern) theory of writing.

The following institutions and companies provide sites and services that are directly relevant to English Studies. All have ongoing development programmes:

Oxford University CTI Textual Studies Resources Guide is at http://www.ox.ac.uk/ctitext/
Chadwyck-Healey, commercial large-scale text corpora are at http://www.chadwyck.co.uk/
British National Corpus home page is at http://info.ac.uk/bnc

Academic discussion lists run by Diane Kovacsis at http://www.n2h2.com/KOVACS/

University of Virginia Electronic text centre is at http://www.lib.virginia.edu/etext/ETC.html

University of Michigan Text Initiative is at http://www.hti.umich.edu/

Wide range of online web resources for teaching at http:/www.ox.ac.uk/ctitext/service/ lectures

Voyager Company has a site at http://www.voyagerco.com/

Women Writers Project (Brown University) is at http://twine.stg.brown.edu/projects/wwp_ home.html

Online contemporary poetry at http://www.bbcnc.org.uk/online/poetry/index.html

Annotated Bibliography for English Studies at http://www.swets.nl/sps/journals/abes/ home.html

For the website associated with the present book, see p. 5.

4.4   ALTERNATIVE MODES OF CRITICAL AND CREATIVE WRITING

There are many modes of critical-creative writing other than those of the traditional academic essay, analysis or dissertation. Most of these involve some kind of *re*writing in the form of imitation, parody and adaptation of or intervention in another text. This text may be a short story, novel, poem or play; but it may also be anything from a bus ticket or snatch of passing conversation to a news report, advert or TV documentary. It is the purpose of this section to encourage the wider and more considered use of such practices of (re-)writing. All the strategies featured below are being used (often with striking success) in departments of English, Rhetoric and Composition and Professional Writing in the USA, Australia and the UK. (The fact that they may be less familiar to tertiary students of English in the UK is a special reason for me introducing them here.) Just three things need to be stressed before proceeding:

♦   *These are modes of writing ALTERNATIVE and COMPLEMENTARY to the essay, analysis and dissertation.* They are not practised instead of – and still less in opposition to – more familiar kinds of work.
♦   *Every piece of (re)writing should be accompanied by a CRITICAL COMMENTARY.* This explains the aims and explores the problems and possibilities encountered during the process. It focuses particular attention on what was learnt about the text you rewrote.
♦   *Such work is neither easier nor harder than more traditional work: it is simply DIFFERENT and, in every sense, MAKES A CHANGE.* This needs emphasis because, initially, students tend to be unsure whether they can do it, and teachers tend to be unsure whether they can mark it. In the event, especially given the crucial analytical and critical role of the commentary, these anxieties invariably prove unfounded. (For instance, reading, research and referencing are exactly the same as for more traditional work.)

Fuller explanations, rationales and guidance can be found in the Reading referred to at the end of this section.

Alternative summaries and the arts of paraphrase

Summarise the text in a variety of ways so as to draw attention to different aspects of its preoccupations or construction. In the commentary draw attention to the implication of your own methods of paraphrase. For instance, a series of summaries varying between a phrase, a sentence, 50 words, and 100 words can be very revealing in establishing what you consider progressively more or less central in terms of themes, events, figures, strategies, etc. Each of these can then be compared with those of colleagues so as to identify areas of overlap and difference. Devising posters, adverts, songs, trailers and reviews based on the text in hand is another critical-creative way of exploring summaries. Alternatively, you might 'paraphrase' the text drawing on critical discourses of one of the approaches featured in Part Two: MARXIST, FEMINIST, PSYCHOLOGICAL, POSTSTRUCTURALIST, POSTCOLONIALIST, etc. In all these ways you would in effect *translate and thereby *transform* the base text. You would also learn to treat your own apparently 'merely descriptive' summaries as forms of discourse – and your own apparently 'natural' and 'neutral' discourses as specifically value-laden ways of categorising, labelling and explaining. Paraphrase might then be recognised not so much as a 'heresy', as certain NEW CRITICS believed (see 2.3), but an 'orthodoxy'!

Changed titles, prefaces and openings

Intervene in these areas of the text so as to disturb and reorient them. Aim to cue the reader for a slightly or very different reading experience: one with slightly (or very) different expectations as to **genre**, **centre** of interest, **discourse**, readership/audience and market (e.g., 'Hamlet' as 'Ophelia's nothing' or 'A further view from the gravediggers').

Alternative endings

Alter the ending of the base text so as to draw attention to some option not explored or in some way foreclosed. Go on to explore the reasons why such an ending was not desirable, advisable or possible in the text at its initial moment of production. Then consider why you, in your own moment of reproduction, opted for it. Notice that, like all the exercises, this is an opportunity to explore historical differences and not simply express personal preferences. (What if Queen Gertrude had *not* drunk the poison? Or if Horatio were disposed to 'speak to th'yet unknowing world / How these things came about' in the manner of, say, Jane Austen, Henry James or Bertolt Brecht?)

Preludes, interludes and postludes

Extend the text 'before', 'during' or 'after' the events it represents so as to explore alternative points of departure, processes of development, or points of arrival. What overall premises, procedures and aims are highlighted by this strategy? Really 'ludicrous' preludes, interludes and postludes often sport with a variety of historical moments as well as a variety of genres and discourses, and narrative and dramatic strategies. (Notice that Rhys's *Wide Sargasso Sea* is a 'prelude' for Brontë's *Jane Eyre* (see 5.2.3 d–e) and that Stoppard's *Rosencrantz and Guildenstern Are Dead* is an 'interlude' for Shakespeare's *Hamlet*.)

Narrative intervention

Change some 'turning point' in the **narrative** so as to explore alternative premises or consequences. Also consider ways of reframing the narrative so that the very process of narration is reoriented (e.g., by adding another narrator). This method of exploring continuities and discontinuities, kinds of textual cohesion and perceptual coherence, can be applied to 'histories' as well as 'stories', 'factual' as well as 'fictional' narratives. (What would happen if Friday, not Crusoe, were the narrator in *Robinson Crusoe*: see Holdsworth's version 5.2.2 b–c?) Or if a woman were projected as the author, not Daniel Defoe (hence J.M. Coetzee's *Foe*, 1986?)

Dramatic intervention

Change the direction of a scripted **drama** or transcribed **conversation** by intervening in a single 'move' or 'exchange'. Also consider figures you might reorient or insert so as to alter the emphasis or choice of topic and the course of the action. (Thus, perhaps, someone butting into or out of the supermarket exchange (5.3.1 a) or yet other twists in the tale of Ibsen's *A Doll's House* (5.3.3) as the children get up and Helmer – not Nora – leaves?)

Narrative into drama – drama into narrative

Explore 'showing' through 'retelling', and 'telling' through 'reshowing' (see **drama** and **narrative**). Thereby examine the peculiar configuration of **re/presentation** in your text. (There are plenty of adaptations of Austen, Dickens, Twain and Mary Shelley (*Frankenstein*) for stage and screen; while Shakespeare is ceaselessly 'retold' by many more people than Lamb. So why not your attempts at samples from these? Or at exploring other texts through cross-genre – and perhaps cross-media – switches?)

Imitation

Cast something in the characteristic style and form of a particular author, director, period or genre. This is no mere matter of 'slavish imitation', even if such a thing were practically or theoretically possible (which strictly it isn't). Rather, it entails transformations of fundamental issues and discourses, along with settings and contexts. For it soon becomes obvious that rewriting, say, some Shakespeare 'in the manner' of Ibsen, Brecht or Churchill (or Austen, or Dickens, or Joyce or Morrison) is no merely superficial exercise in 'style'. It also entails transformations of 'matter' as well. Another's 'word' always implies a whole 'world'. Innumerable writers from Chaucer through Pope and Byron to Tony Harrison have engaged in studied imitation. (A lively variation on this activity is to select a nursery rhyme, contemporary news item, advert or joke, then work it up in the manner and matter of, say, Gothic fantasy, women's magazine romance or postmodern collage.)

Parody

Exaggerate some features of the text, or introduce incongruous (perhaps anachronistic) frames of reference so as to throw its characteristic style or pre-occupations into relief. Crude parody is *burlesque*. Subtle parody can be so implicit and *ironic that its parodic intent may be all but invisible. Both can be critically and creatively valid – and great fun. Either way, parody can be an act of affectionate celebration of an author's work. It is not necessarily either negative or destructive. In fact, the most searching and revealing parodies are usually those grounded in a mixture of fascination and frustration with the text/author/genre being parodied. (Milton's, Pope's and Byron's mock/heroic verses are bound in peculiarly fruitful, partly parodic relations see 5.1.4 a, b, d. Kazantsis's 'Leda and Leonardo the Swan' can be read as an especially trenchant parody of the Leda myth in general, and perhaps Yeats's poem in particular (5.1.7 a–b).)

Collage

Gather a diverse and perhaps disparate range of materials directly or indirectly relevant to the text, author or topic in hand: sources; parallels; contrasts; bits of critical commentary; relatable words, images, pieces of music, etc. – often from other periods and discourses. Then select from and arrange these materials so as to make a number of implicit statements, while also opening up the possibility of other interpretations. 'Collage' is neither more nor less than the art of 'sticking together'. As always, the commentary should seek to make explicit what was implicit, and to lay bare the process of composition. Where do *you* want to take the play of **inter-textuality** (see **text**) – and why?

*Hybrids and *faction

Recast two or more related texts in a new textual mould so as to produce a compound – not merely a mixture. Compounding conventionally 'fictional' and 'factual' texts usually produces **faction** (in every sense). Alternative metaphors for this process include grafting a new plant from two 'parent' plants to generate a *hybrid; or the biological process of cross-fertilisation of species. In any event, experiment with ways of making texts coalesce as well as collide. In this respect the generation of 'hybrids' is distinct from the sticking together of 'collages'. There is more obviously in the making of a new and organic whole rather than a mechanical assemblage of old fragments. (For instance, the 'Wordsworth' material (5.4.3) might be spliced and compounded so as to produce a complexly composite text – some of it by those writers and some by you. Again, the commentary would help reinforce or tease out the various problems and possibilities of interpretation, along with the critical-historical insights the activity entails.)

Word to image, word to music, word to movement, word to . . . ?

This is a catch-all reminder that verbal texts can be very revealingly understood in the attempt to transform them into another medium, sign-system or mode of communication and expression. Film, video, photography, painting and sculpture; all kinds of music; dance, mime and numerous kinds of performance art; even clothes, architecture, smells, touches and tastes. These all offer alternative ways of 're-realising' the actual and potential meanings, effects and values of a particular string of words: long or short, epic or epigram, novel or one-liner, single sound or letter. *Translation, in the broadest sense, always entails a *transformation*, never merely a *transference*. As always, the possibilities are infinite. But it is still your business to say which you have opened up (or closed down) and why. And it is the business of the commentary to make the implications of this critical-creative process explicit.

DISCUSSION

(i)   Criticism begins with the recognition of textual power and ends in the attempt to exercise it. This attempt may take the form of an essay, but it may just as easily be textualised as parody or countertext in the same mode as its critical object. As teachers we should encourage the full range of critical practices in our students.
Robert Scholes, *Textual Power* (1985: Ch. 1); cf. 1.7, Discussion (ii)

(ii) In a post-traditional social universe, an indefinite range of potential courses of action (with their attendant risks) is at any moment open to individuals and collectivities. Choosing among such alternatives is always an 'as if' matter, a question of selecting between 'possible worlds'.
Antony Giddens, *Modernity and Self-identity* (1991: 29)

(iii) The highest Criticism, then, is more creative . . . and the primary aim of the critic is to see the object as in itself it really is not.
Oscar Wilde, *The Critic as Artist* (1891)

READING: The best place to start is with your own rewriting. Try one of the above strategies with a text you are studying. Fuller arguments, further strategies and copious illustration of the kinds of rewriting practices featured above can be found in Scholes 1985, Carter and Nash 1990, Hackman and Marshall 1990, Thomson 1992, Bartholomae and Petrosky 1986, Bassnett and Grundy 1993, Corcoran *et al.* 1994, Pope 1995, Scholes *et al.* 1995, Nash and Stacey 1997. Also see the reading in 4.3, esp. Bolter 1991, Landow 1992; also Kress 1995.

4.5   WHAT'S (NOT) IN A NAME? CHANGING COURSES

English Studies courses are currently organised according to a variety of principles. However, we do not always explicitly debate and consciously decide what these are. This section is designed to help in this process. It is aimed at teachers *and* learners because we all have an interest in the present shape as well as the future transformation of the subject.

Individual 'English' courses tend to be framed in terms of one or more of the following: *author*; *period*; *country or region*; *movement or 'school'*; *social group*; *genre*; *medium*; *technique or approach*; *event*. The frames or categories are few and often overlap. But their permutations are numerous and in practice virtually infinite. Often the underlying principles of a course are signalled by its title. Scrutinising the title of a course is therefore a good way of gauging the assumptions that underpin that course's design, even though what actually happens during the course may turn out to be different. Course titles are particularly important because for most prospective students they afford the only point of contact with a course before actually taking it. Like labels on products, or the titles of books and films, course titles both inform and advertise. They may also attract or repel – and sometimes they deceive. At any rate, they set up expectations which may subsequently be exceeded, thwarted or diverted. Below are some fuller explanations and illustrations. As you read through them, bear in mind the following questions:

- What do the titles of *your* courses focus upon, and what do they propose as significant or self-evident?
- What other courses on similar or related materials might be signalled by using other titles and, by implication, other categories?
- Which overall principles of organisation does the programme that you are on favour?

In practice, as you will be aware, many courses have titles which combine two, three or more of the above categories (e.g., 'New Zealand Film' = Country + Medium; 'Women's Poetry of the seventeenth and eighteenth centuries' = Social Group + Genre + Period). Some course titles, however, rely on single categories (e.g., 'Tragedy', 'Critical Theory', 'Milton'). More detailed explanation of aims, course content and learning and assessment patterns is invariably supplied in accompanying descriptions and syllabuses. Nevertheless, course titles exert a strong and pervasive pressure on how we, as teachers and learners, conceive the outlines of what we are doing. Cumulatively, they also affect the overall 'look' and 'feel' of a whole programme. For that reason, you may wish to conclude (or even begin) by considering:

- What is implied by the name of the department and/or overall programme in which you are studying? (What, implicitly, are you not studying?)

AUTHOR – by person (e.g., 'Chaucer', 'Shakespeare', 'Toni Morrison'). An **author**'s name generally serves as shorthand for her or his work, life and times. The relations amongst these aspects of auto/biography, context and culture may or may not be made explicit.

*PERIOD – by time (e.g., 'Late Medieval . . .', The Eighteenth Century', ' . . . of the 1930s', 'Contemporary . . . '). A particular span of time, long or short, vague or precise, is abstracted from the continuum of history and singled out as significant.

COUNTRY or REGION – by place (e.g., 'American . . .', 'New Zealand . . .', 'Caribbean . . .', ' . . . of Northern England', 'New York . . .'). A specific place is often associated with a specific cultural identity, and the relation between them may be assumed, asserted or contested in the course which follows. (Notice that 'English' is often used in a geographically non-specific way, and may or may not relate to 'England' the country; see 1.1.)

MOVEMENT or 'SCHOOL' – by common tendency or interest (e.g., 'Augustan . . .', 'Romanticism', 'The Beats', 'Post/Modernism'). Notice that such labels are rarely proposed by the subjects themselves but usually superimposed retrospectively by subsequent commentators.

GENRE – by 'kind' of text (e.g., 'The Novel', 'Autobiographical . . .', 'Tragedy', 'Science Fiction', 'Narrative', 'The Romance'). Texts are grouped according to perceived similarities of form and substance, and there is concentration on variations within **genres**, the mixing of existing genres and the generation of new ones.

SOCIAL or CULTURAL GROUP – by perceived collective identity (e.g., 'Women's . . .', 'Black . . .', 'Working class . . .'; also 'Representations of Women/Manual Labourers . . .'). Here it is the shared identity of those producing and/or being represented in the work which is the organising principle and where, again, it is the in/stability or dis/continuity of this identity which may be at issue. (Notice that 'White', 'Men' and 'European' are often the un(re)marked and assumed social and cultural groups unless the titles expressly say otherwise.)

MEDIUM – by mode of communication (e.g., 'Manuscript to Print', 'Theatre and Performance', 'Film', 'Orality and Literacy'). In this case the material of the message and its associated codes are primary. Some genres are closely identified with certain media (drama with theatre, the novel with print).

TECHNIQUE or APPROACH – by skills or models (e.g., 'Stylistic Analysis', 'Critical Theory', 'Feminist/Marxist/Deconstructive Readings of . . .', 'Creative Writing'). Here there is an emphasis on the ways of handling and framing materials.

TOPIC or EVENT (e.g., 'Landscape and Cityscape', 'The Body in . . .', 'The Great Exhibition', ' . . . of Vietnam/the Gulf War'). In these cases it is some feature of subject matter which supplies the grounds for comparison and contrast between a variety of materials, often of an interdisciplinary nature.

READING: See Berlin 1996, Kress 1995; also see: 1.5 and **author**, **canon and classic**, **genre** and *period.

4.6   MAKING ANTHOLOGIES AND FIRING 'CANONS' YOURSELF

Many courses are organised round a specific anthology as a set text. This may be an anthology of literary texts, a 'reader' in critical theory, or a collection of critical essays on a particular author or work. The present book includes a short anthology too (Part Five). In fact, anthologies of one kind or another are such a common feature of courses that their existence is often assumed to be 'natural'. They are also often, in that significantly fixed phrase, 'set texts'.

Anthologies do not simply materialise out of thin air, however. They are *made* not simply *found*. Moreover, their making depends upon certain people (e.g., editors, publishers, course-designers, teachers, learners) deciding what to include or exclude, and how to organise and present what they have chosen. The purpose of this section is to explore these processes of 'anthologising'. Also to remind ourselves that these are processes to which we can contribute – even if we cannot entirely control them. First, we'll get a general sense of what is currently going on in this area.

The principles informing the anthology in the present book are set out in the preview to Part Five. Perhaps acquaint yourself with them at this point. Then go on to consider the following checklist, which can be used in at least four ways:

♦   to analyse the present anthology;
♦   to analyse any other anthology, collection or reader you may be using;
♦   to research other kinds of anthology which already exist;
♦   to reflect upon – and perhaps begin to put together – some other kind of anthology (however small-scale) which answers to your interests and needs.

General aim and function

Who is putting the anthology together for whom, when, where and why? (Is it for concentrated study or casual reading, for instance? For use inside and/or outside formal education?) Conversely, what sort of people are *not* putting the anthology together? And are the same kind of people making the anthology as are featured in it?

Media and genres

What kinds or categories of text are represented, communicated through what media? Is there an exclusive emphasis on writing and print – or are, say, speech, performance, painting, photography, film and TV included? Verbally, if the categories **poetry**/verse, prose or *drama/*theatre are used, how mutually exclusive or flexibly are they construed? What is understood by **drama** or **narrative**?

Persons

Does the anthology have a marked emphasis on women or men, social classes, age (children's and/or adult), regional or national groups, ethnicity, mono- or multiculturalism? Is there attention to named writers/producers as individuals or as representatives of social groups? How are they *identified?

Times

What time-span does the anthology cover, and is time conceived in terms of precise dates (1340–1580, post-1968) or centuries (eighteenth, nineteenth, twentieth century) or persons – often monarchs ('Elizabethan', 'Victorian') or *periods

('Renaissance', 'Early Modern', 'Contemporary') or movements ('Romantic', 'Modernism')?

Places

Is there an explicit or implicit concentration on a single place (England, Britain, America . . .) or are many **centres** recognised? Either way, is this place – are these places – understood in geographical, political and/or broadly cultural terms? Would you describe the emphasis as 'local', 'regional', 'national', 'international', 'global' – or a mixture? What are the strengths and weaknesses of this?

Language(s)

Is all the material in the same language in which it was initially written or performed or is some or most in *translation? What are the implications of this for your understanding of the specific cultures involved?

Thematic and other groupings

Is there some overall theme or topic (other than those implied above) that is offered as an organising principle (e.g., 'Love Poetry', 'City and Country', 'Nonsense', ' . . . of Death'?) And are parts or subsections designated in terms of specific topic, angle or attitude (apart from or in addition to period, author, genre, etc.)?

Textual apparatus

What do the cover blurb, preface and introduction lead you to expect, and are these expectations fulfilled? In what ways are the contents identified (e.g., by author/ producer, time, place, genre)? How exactly are texts presented and annotated? What observations and evaluations are you encouraged to make about the materials featured?

Off-the-peg and Internet anthologies?

Modern computer and reproduction technology is beginning to make the possibility of one-off or 'bespoke' anthologies a reality. English departments, like many others, have for some time been putting together anthologies of 'primary' texts and collections of 'secondary' materials to suit their own needs. The pressures to do this are invariably a mixture of the academic (lecturers like to control what they teach) and the economic (students can't afford to buy lots of books). However, copyright, especially for recent material, remains a thorny problem in this area. So, too, eventually, do cost and quality. Recently, however, there are signs that publishers are prepared to put together 'made-to-measure' anthologies for just a few institutions – as long as they are sure they can guarantee a return.

Meanwhile, yet other possibilities are being opened out by the use of CD-Rom and, more widely, the Internet. Copyright problems, as well as cost and quality, are problems in this area too. Nonetheless, it seems likely that in the quite near future the 'open, electronic anthology' will become a reality. Of course, the materials it can involve and the shapes it may evolve will still ultimately depend upon what is available within the system and who can access it. Modern tele- and multi-media communications simply modify and sometimes accelerate (they do not abolish) the problems and possibilities of information selection, storage, retrieval and combination.

DISCUSSION

(i) Browning, in this editor's judgement, is the most considerable poet in English since the major Romantics, surpassing his great contemporary rival Tennyson, and the principal twentieth-century poets, including even Yeats, Hardy and Wallace Stevens, let alone the various fashionable modernists whose reputations now are rightly in decline. But Browning is a very difficult poet, notoriously badly served by criticism . . .
Oxford Anthology of English Literature, Vol 2, ed. John Hollander and Frank Kermode (1973: 1279; first published 1973, unrevised since)

(ii) During the years of his marriage Robert Browning was sometimes referred to as 'Mrs. Browning's husband'. Elizabeth Barrett, who has been regarded in the twentieth century as a lesser figure, was at that time a famous poet, while her husband was a relatively unknown experimenter whose poems were greeted with misunderstanding or indifference.
Norton Anthology of English Literature Vol. 2, ed. M.H. Abrams *et al.* (6th edn, 1993: 1182)

Also see: **author, canon and classic, genre** and *period.

READING: See reading in 4.5.

ANTHOLOGY OF SAMPLE TEXTS

PREVIEW

This part of the book consists of short texts and extracts for discussion, analysis and other activities. A wide variety of Englishes is represented, past and present, 'literary' and 'non-literary', spoken, written and otherwise recorded. The aim is to provide handy resources for a variety of courses and to encourage interdisciplinary study. All these materials are featured in the illustrations and activities in the other parts of the book. A list of authors, texts and topics is supplied on the Contents page, and these can be followed up further in the Index. Much of the material is organised in three areas:

- *Poetry, song and performance* (5.1)
- *Prose fiction, journals and news* (5.2)
- *Scripts and transcripts – conversation, interview and drama* (5.3)

There is therefore a recognition of the traditional and still serviceable distinction between poetry, prose and drama. At the same time there is an attempt to extend and complicate these categories. We recognise other, relatable kinds of text and performance which are often treated separately or excluded altogether.

The remaining material is organised in groups of texts by topic or theme. It consists of

♦   *Intertextual clusters* (5.4)
     All texts are identified by author(s) or producer(s), date of first publication and date of composition where this is significantly different and known. As far as possible, texts are complete. Extracts from longer works are briefly contextualised. The accompanying notes supply further information on context as well as cross-references to particularly relevant terms, issues and approaches featured elsewhere in the book. All this supporting apparatus is important, it is suggested, if we are to *study* texts and not just *read* them.

Elsewhere in the book (4.6), you are encouraged to scrutinise the rationale informing all kinds of anthologies, including the present one. You are also invited to make anthologies and 'fire canons' yourself.

5.1.   POETRY, SONG AND PERFORMANCE

5.1.1   *Anglo-Saxon poem:* ANONYMOUS, untitled ('Wulf and Eadwacer') before 975

> Leodum is minum swylce him mon lac gife;
> willao hy hine þecgan, gif he on þreat cymeð
> Ungelic is us.
> Wulf is on iege, ic on oþerre.
> Faest is þaet eglond, fenne biworpen.   5
> Sindon waelreowe weras þaer on ige
> willao hy hine a þecgan, gif he on þreat cymeð
> Ungelic is us.
> Wulfes ic mines widlastum wenum dogode;
> þonne hit waes renig weder and ic reotugu saet,   10
> þonne mec se beaducafa bogum bilegde,
> waes me wyn to þon, waes me hwaeþre eac lað
> Wulf, min Wulf, wena me þine
> seoce gedydon, þine seldcymas,
> murnende mod, nales meteliste.   15
> Gehyrest þu, Eadwacer? Uncerne earmne hwelp
> bire wulf to wuda
> þaet mon eaþe toslite þaette naefre gesomnad waes,
> uncer giedd geador.

Translation:
> For my people it is like a present.
> They will capture him if he comes with a troop.
> We are apart.
> Wulf is on one island, I am on another.
> It is an island stronghold wrapped round by the fens.   5
> Fierce and cruel are the people there on that island.
> They will capture him if he comes with a troop.

We are apart.
For my Wulf I have sorrowed from afar.
When it was rainy weather, and I sat bereft.   10
When the bold warrior laid his arms about me.
it was a joy to me, and it was also a pain.
O Wulf, my Wulf, my longing for you
and the rareness of your coming has made me ill.
My spirit grieves me more than the lack of food.   15
Eadwacer, do you hear me? A wolf will carry
our sorry whelp to the woods.
That may easily be sundered which was never solemnised
Our song together.

This *oral-formulaic poem may be just a fragment of a larger, lost whole. It is in alliterative, stressed metre (see **versification**) and West-Saxon dialect, and survives in a single manuscript in one of the four main *Anglo-Saxon poetry anthologies, the 'Exeter Book' (compiled *c*. 975). Interpretations and *translations vary markedly, largely depending on whether the poem is read as a **monologue** or a **dialogue**, and whether there is judged to be the same or a new speaker from line 16. It used to be assumed that Anglo-Saxon poets were all men; but this belief has recently been challenged. As a **genre** this poem can be categorised as 'complaint', 'elegy' and 'riddle'. The 'ƀ' (symbol) (a 'thorn') is derived from the Germanic runic alphabet and had the sound 'th', so had the modified Anglo-Saxon ð. Both persisted to the fifteenth century.

    Compare: 5.1.2 a, c, d; 5.1.3 c and 5.1.8. Also see: 1.2.1; **absence and presence**; **author**. (For a parallel text with a somewhat different translation, see Richard Hamer, *A Choice of Anglo-Saxon Verse*, London, 1970: 82–5.)

5.1.2   Fourteenth-century verse

5.1.2 a ANONYMOUS, untitled ('Maiden in the mor lay'), *c*. 1320

Maiden in the mor lay,
In the mor lay;
Sevenight fulle,
Sevenight fulle,
Maiden in the mor lay;   5
In the mor lay,
Sevenightes fulle and a day.

Welle was hire mete.
What was hire mete?
The primerole and the –   10
The primerole and the –
Welle was hire mete.
What was hire mete?
The primerole and the violet.

Welle was hire dring.   15
What was hire dring?
The chelde water of the –
The chelde water of the –
Welle was hire dring.
What was hire dring?   20
The chelde water of the welle-spring.

Welle was hire bowr.
What was hire bowr?
The rede rose and the –
The rede rose and the –   25
Welle was hire bowr.
What was hire bowr?
The rede rose and the lilye flour.

1. mor – moor, wilds. 8. Welle – (pun here?) good / the well; mete – food. 10. primerole – primrose. 15. dring – drink. 17. chelde – chilled, cold. 22. bowr – abode.

This enigmatic poem survives in a single manuscript from the early fourteenth century. It looks and sounds to have been composed for *song and perhaps *dance, maybe as a 'carole' to be joined in at various moments by different people (part song refrain, 'round', etc). Interpretations vary widely. The 'maiden' has been seen as pagan fertility goddess, nature spirit, the Virgin Mary and a dead woman, real or imagined. At any rate, the bishop of Ossory in Ireland declared it was not suitable for singing by any of his priests.

Also see: **absence and presence**; *anonymous; **author and authority**; **imagery**; *music; **myth**; *nature; *oral; **versification**. *Compare:* 5.1.1 above; Wroth 5.1.3 c; Death (5.4.5). (For text and notes, see R.T. Davies (ed.) *Medieval English Lyrics*, London 1966: 102, 320–1.)

5.1.2 b GEOFFREY CHAUCER, from 'The General Prologue to the Canterbury Tales', *c.* 1385–92, ll.43–72 [The Knight is the first of the pilgrims to be described.]

A KNYGHT ther was, and that a worthy man,
That fro the tyme that he first bigan
To riden out, he loved chivalrie,   45
Trouthe and honour, fredom and curteisie.
Ful worthy was he in his lordes werre,
And therto hadde he riden, no man ferre,
As wel in cristendom as in hethenesse,
And evere honoured for his worthynesse;   50
At Alisaundre he was whan it was wonne.
Ful ofte tyme he hadde the bord bigonne
Aboven alle nacions in Pruce;
In Lettow hadde he reysed and in Ruce,
No Cristen man so ofte of his degree.[. . .]   55
At mortal batailles hadde he been fiftene,

And foughten for oure feith at Tramyssene
In lystes thries, and ay slayn his foo.
This ilke worthy knyght hadde been also
Somtyme with the lord of Palatye   65
Agayn another hethen in Turkye;
And everemoore he hadde a sovereyn prys.
And though that he were worthy, he was wys,
And of his port as meeke as is a mayde.
He nevere yet no vileynye ne sayde   70
In al his lyf unto no maner wight.
He was a verray, parfit gentil knyght.

49. hethenesse – heathen lands. 51. Alisaundre – Alexandria. (All the places named
in lines 51–66 were places in what is now the Middle East and Eastern Europe where
English knights campaigned in the fourteenth century.) 52. bord bigonne – sat in the
place of honour. 63. In lystes – in formal duels; ay – always. 64. ilke – same. 66. Agayn:
against. 70. vileynye – rudeness, like a 'villein' / peasant. 71 no maner wight – any
sort of person. 72. verray – true; parfit – perfect (complete); gentil – noble (of spirit
and/or rank).

Chaucer (*c*.1343–1400) was variously courtier, squire, tax-collector, court poet, and
knight of the shire and member of parliament for Kent. His patrons included John
of Gaunt, Richard II and Henry IV. 'The General Prologue' survives in over eighty
manuscripts from before the mid-fifteenth century. It is written in a South-East
Midland, London-based **dialect** that is relatively familiar to modern readers because
it came to underpin the printed **standard** favoured at court and in the capital. The
versification in decasyllabic rhyming couplets was influenced by later medieval
*French and was quite new in English at the time. Now, however, such a verse-form
is more familiar than those in (c) and (d) (below), which in fact follow an earlier,
*Germanic, alliterative and stressed tradition. Chaucer's knight has been variously
interpreted as chivalric ideal, mercenary and representative of Western European
Christian civilisation and/or barbarism.

Also see: MARXISM, Example pp. 109–110; *ethnicity, *romance. (For text and
notes, see L.D. Benson (ed.) *The Riverside Chaucer*, Oxford, 1988: 22, 800–2.)

5.1.2. c WILLIAM LANGLAND, from *Piers Plowman*, before 1387

In a somer sesoun, whan softe was the sonne,
Y shope me into shroudes, as Y a shep were,
In abite as an heremite, vnholy of werkes,
Wente forth in ƀe world wondres to here,
And saw many selles and selkcouth thynges.   5
Ac on a May mornyng on Maluerne hulles
Me biful for to slepe, for werynesse of-walked;
And in a launde as y lay, lened y and slepte,
And merueylousliche me mette, as I may telle.
Al ƀe welthe of the world and ƀe wo bothe   10
Wynkyng, as hit were, witterliche y sigh hit,
Of treuthe and tricherye, tresoun and gyle,
Al I saw slepynge, as y shal telle.

2–3. 'I dressed myself in rough clothes, like a shepherd, in the garb of a hermit of secular life.' 5. 'And saw many marvels and strange things'.

Piers Plowman survives in three different versions from the late fourteenth century (here from the third, C-text, completed by 1387). It is written in a more northerly, Midland **dialect** than Chaucer's and composed in a loosely popular alliterative **verse**. It may be by an un- or under-employed freelance cleric called William Langland.

Compare: 5.1.1; 5.1.2 d below. (Text and notes in D. Pearsall (ed.) *Piers Plowman: the C-text*, London, 1978: 27–8.)

5.1.2 d ANONYMOUS, untitled (usually called *Pearl*) first verse, c. 1380

Perle, plesaunte to prynces paye
To clanly clos in golde so clere:
Oute of oryent, I hardly saye,
Ne proved I never her precios pere.
So rounde, so reken in uche araye,   5
So smal, so smothe her sydes were,
Quere-so-ever I jugged gemmes gaye,
I sette hyr sengeley in synglere.
Allas! I leste hyr in on erbere;
Thurgh gresse to grounde hit fro me yot.   10
I dewyne, fordolked of luf-daungere
Of that pryvy perle wythouten spot.

Translation: 'Pearl, pleasing for a prince's treasure / Utterly flawlessly clasped in gold so bright: / from the orient, I confidently say, / I never came upon her precious equal. / So round, so fine in every respect, / so neat, so smooth were her sides / Wherever I have judged gorgeous gems / I would set her apart as unique. / Alas, I lost her in an arbour (garden); / Through grass to the ground it went from me. / I am pining away, utterly done for by the power of love / for that cherished pearl without a blemish'.

Pearl is a poem of 1212 lines and survives in a single manuscript. This is written in a northerly (Lancashire?) **dialect** and composed in a tightly structured **versification** combining alliteration, stress and rhyme. The present poem is almost certainly by the same *anonymous **author**, probably court poet and/or cleric at a northern baronial court, who composed *Sir Gawain and the Green Knight*, which is also found in this manuscript. The pearl may be variously interpreted as an actual jewel, a dead infant daughter, lost innocence and the promise of heaven.

Also see: *Christianity, **myth**; **imagery**. Compare: 5.1.2 c above; 5.1.1; Death (5.4.5); (For full text, see A.C. Cawley (ed.) *Pearl, Cleanness, Patience and Sir Gawain and the Green Knight*, London, 1976.)

5.1.3 Renaissance lyric and sonnet

5.1.3 a SIR THOMAS WYATT, 'They flee from me', c.1535

They flee from me, that sometime did me seek,
With naked foot stalking in my chamber,

I have seen them, gentle, tame and meek,
That now are wild, and do not remember
That sometime they put themselves in danger   5
To take bread at my hand; and now they range,
Busily seeking with a continual change.

Thanked be fortune it hath been otherwise,
Twenty times better; but once in special,
In thin array, after a pleasant guise,   10
When her loose gown from her shoulders did fall,
And she me caught in her arms long and small,
Therewith all sweetly did me kiss
And softly said, 'Dear heart, how like you this?'

It was no dream, I lay broad waking,   15
But all is turned, thorough my gentleness,
Into a strange fashion of forsaking;
And I have leave to go, of her goodness,
And she also to use newfangleness.
But since that I so kindly am serv'd,   20
I would fain know what she hath deservèd.

Wyatt (*c.* 1503–42) was an influential courtier and diplomat at the court of Henry VIII. He was twice imprisoned in the Tower of London (1536, 1541), the first time possibly for an affair with Anne Boleyn, the king's wife. This poem may allude to that incident. The text used here is taken from the Egerton MS (*c.* 1536) which is probably written in the **author**'s own hand. The poem may initially have been a *song for *musical accompaniment by lute. The poem was later *anthologised in Tottel's influential miscellany *Songs and Sonets* (1557). There it is given the title 'The Lover Showeth How He is Forsaken of Such as He Sometimes Enjoyed'. Tottel's last line reads 'How like you this, what hath she now deserv'd?'

Also see: **auto/biography**; **absence and presence**; **versification**. Compare: 5.1.3 b below; Clare 5.1.5. (For both versions, see Abrams 1993, Vol. I: 443–4.)

5.1.3 b WILLIAM SHAKESPEARE, 'My mistress' eyes' (Sonnet 130), written *c.* 1594–9, pub. 1609

My mistress' eyes are nothing like the sun;
Coral is far more red than her lips' red;
If snow be white, why then her breasts are dun;
If hairs be wires, black wires grow on her head.
I have seen roses damasked, red and white,   5
But no such roses see I in her cheeks;
And in some perfumes is there more delight
Than in the breath that from my mistress reeks.
I love to hear her speak, yet well I know
That music hath a far more pleasing sound;   10
I grant I never saw a goddess go;
My mistress, when she walks, treads on the ground.
   And yet, by heaven, I think my love as rare
   As any she belied with false compare.

William Shakespeare (1564–1616) – successful theatre shareholder, director, actor and playwright – only seems to have cared to see his **poems**, not his plays, through the press (e.g., *Venus and Adonis* (1593) and *The Rape of Lucrece* (1594) as well as *Sonnets* (1609)). At that time printed plays had little prestige as LITERATURE. In the 1590s, when *sonnets were a very fashionable **genre**, Shakespeare was well known for 'his sugared sonnets' among private friends, according to a contemporary, Frances Meres. A decade later Shakespeare had them printed, with an enigmatic dedication: 'To the onelie begetter of these ensuing sonnets, Mr W.H . . . '. This particular sonnet is about the so-called 'Dark Lady', as are most of sonnets 127–54. The other sonnets are addressed to or are about one or more male youths (e.g., 5.4.4 c). Compare: 5.4.4 c; 5.1.3 c; 5.4.6 d; and for Shakespeare's verse drama (see 5.3.2 b; 5.4.6 a). Also see: FORMALISM, Example pp. 89–90; FEMINISM AND GENDER STUDIES; **difference and similarity; foregrounding; image(ry); text, context and intertextuality; versification**.

5.1.3 c LADY MARY WROTH, from *The Countess of Montgomery's Urania*, Book. I, 1621

[Urania, a foundling adopted by shepherds, begins to realise she is not of shepherd stock. She eventually finds out she is a daughter of the king of Naples.]

> By this [time] were others come into that mead with their flocks: but she, esteeming her sorrowing thoughts her best and choicest company, left that place, taking a little path which brought her to the further side of the plain, to the foot of the rocks, speaking as she went these lines, her eyes fixed upon the ground, her very soul turned into mourning.

> Unseen, unknown, I here alone complain
>   To rocks, to hills, to meadows, and to springs,
> Which can no help return to ease my pain,
>   But back my sorrows the sad echo brings.
> Thus still increasing are my woes to me,   5
>   Doubly resounded by that moanful voice,
> Which seems to second me in misery,
>   And answer gives like friend of mine own choice.
> Thus only she doth my companion prove,
>   The others silently do offer ease.   10
> But those that grieve, a grieving note do love;
>   Pleasures to dying eyes bring but disease:
> And such am I, who daily ending live,
> Wailing a state which can no comfort give.

Wroth (*c.* 1587–*c.* 1651) moved in aristocratic, literary circles. Her uncle was Sir Philip Sidney and her aunt was Mary Sidney Herbert, countess of Pembroke. In manner, matter and name, Wroth's *Urania* is partly modelled on Sidney's *pastoral *romance known as *The Countess of Pembroke's Arcadia* (1590–93) (so called because it was edited after Sidney's death by the countess). But *Urania* is also distinctive in tone and approach, and some FEMINIST critics have discerned in its attention to both 'interiority' and 'intrigue' an early instance of women's writing that until recently has largely been ignored. There appears to be much coded reference (now lost) to contemporary goings-on at court, for the work caused an outcry there on its first publication.

Also see: CLASSICS; **canon**; **versification**. Compare: 5.1.3 a and b above, and for another sonnet 5.4.6 d. (For text and notes, see Abrams *et al*. 1993: 1687–8.)

5.1.4 Heroics and mock-heroics: seventeenth–twentieth centuries

5.1.4 a JOHN MILTON, from *Paradise Lost* Book IV, ll.549–81, 1667

[At the gates of heaven, the angel Uriel is telling the archangel Gabriel that a devil (Satan) seems to have escaped from hell.]

Betwixt these rocky pillars Gabriel sat
Chief of the angelic guards, awaiting night   550
About him exercised heroic games
The unarmed youth of heaven, but nigh at hand
Celestial armoury, shields, helms, and spears,
Hung high with diamond flaming, and with gold.
Thither came Uriel, gliding through the even   555
On a sunbeam, swift as a shooting star
In autumn thwarts the night, when vapours fired
Impress the air, and shows the mariner
From what point of his compass to beware
Impetuous winds: he thus began in haste.   560
      Gabriel, to thee thy course by lot hath given
Charge and strict watch that to this happy place
No evil thing approach or enter in;
This day at height of noon came to my sphere
A spirit, zealous, as he seemed, to know   565
More of the almighty's works, and chiefly man
God's latest image: I described his way
Bent all on speed, and marked his airy gait;
But in the mount that lies from Eden north,
Where he first lighted, soon discerned his looks   570
Alien from heaven, with passions foul obscured:
Mine eye pursued him still, but under shade
Lost sight of him; one of the banished crew
I fear, hath ventured from the deep, to raise
New troubles; him thy care must be to find.   575
To whom the winged warrior thus returned:
      Uriel, no wonder if thy perfect sight,
Amid the sun's bright circle where thou sit'st,
See far and wide: in at this gate none pass
The vigilance here placed, but such as come   580
Well known from heaven;

Milton (1608–74) – poet, pamphleteer, and classical and biblical scholar – was also a staunch Protestant, parliamentarian and anti-royalist. He probably began composing *Paradise Lost* when he was Secretary of Foreign Tongues to the Council of State, between the period of the 'Commonwealth' and before the Restoration of the monarchy (1660). Milton regularly wrote in and *translated from Latin, Italian and English. He composed most of his *hybrid Christian and neo-classical *epic *Paradise Lost* in his head, when he was blind. The text was written down by his wives Katherine (d.1658) and Elizabeth and by his daughters (cf. William Wordsworth and his female amanuenses, 5.4.3 a and b). Milton's heroically **biblical** and neo-CLASSICAL manner, *Latinate diction and sentence-structure, as well as his blank **verse** were to prove very influential.

Compare: 5.1.4 b–d below; Blake 5.4.6 b.

5.1.4 b ALEXANDER POPE, from *The Rape of the Lock*, Canto 1, ll.121–48, pub. 1714

[A young woman of high society – Belinda ('Betty') – does her make-up, assisted by her maid. 'Toilet' refers to 'toilette', the contents of the dressing-table.]

```
And now, unveiled, the toilet stands displayed,
Each silver vase in mystic order laid.
First, robed in white, the nymph intent adores,
With head uncovered, the cosmetic powers.
A heavenly image in the glass appears;                      125
To that she bends, to that her eyes she rears.
The inferior priestess, at her altar's side,
Trembling begins the sacred rites of Pride.
Unnumbered treasures ope at once, and here
The various offerings of the world appear;                  130
From each she nicely culls with curious toil,
And decks the goddess with the glittering spoil.
This casket India's glowing gems unlocks,
And all Arabia breathes from yonder box.
The tortoise here and elephant unite,                       135
Transformed to combs, the speckled and the white.
Here files of pins extend their shining rows,
Puffs, powders, patches, Bibles, billet-doux.
Now awful Beauty puts on all its arms;
The fair each moment rises in her charms,                   140
Repairs her smiles, awakens every grace,
And calls forth all the wonders of her face;
Sees by degrees a purer blush arise,
And keener lightnings quicken in her eyes.
The busy Sylphs surround their darling care,                145
These set the head, and those divide the hair,
Some fold the sleeve, whilst others plait the gown;
And Betty's praised for labours not her own.
```

Pope (1688–1744) was one of the first professional **authors** to make a living, eventually, as a poet and *translator (notably of **classical** *epics, *satires and *pastorals from Latin and Greek). He was famous for his satires on the contemporary literary scene and on fashionable London life (London was already the centre of a fast-growing empire based on trade and slavery). These satires were generally *mock-heroic in manner and often used decasyllabic couplets (see **versification**). The immediate occasion of *The Rape of the Lock* was the uninvited cutting of a lock of hair belonging to an aristocratic 'belle' (Lady Arabella Fermor) by an aristocratic 'beau' (Lord Petre). The action caused a feud between the two families and the poem was designed to help effect a reconciliation; also to demonstrate 'What mighty contests rise from trivial things.' First published in a two-canto version in 1712, the success of the piece prompted Pope to expand it into a five-canto version (pub. 1714). The above passage is from the latter.

Compare: 5.1.4 a, c–e; Clarins skincare advert 5.4.4 b.

5.1.4 c ELIZABETH HANDS, 'A Poem, on the Supposition of an Advertisement appearing in a Morning Paper, of the Publication of a Volume of Poems, by a Servant Maid', 1789.

The tea-kettle bubbled, the tea things were set.
The candles were lighted, the ladies were met;
The how d'ye's were over, and entering bustle,
The company seated, and silks ceased to rustle:
The great Mrs. Consequence opened her fan,   5
And thus the discourse in an instant began
(All affected reserve and formality scorning):
'I suppose you all saw in the paper this morning
A volume of *Poems* advertised – 'tis said
They're produced by the pen of a poor servant-maid.'   10
'A servant write verses!' says Madam Du Bloom:
'Pray what is the subject – a Mop, or a Broom?'
'He, he, he,' says Miss Flounce: 'I suppose we shall see
An Ode on an Dishclout – what else can it be?'
Says Miss Coquettilla, 'Why, ladies, so tart?   15
Perhaps Tom the footman has fired her heart;
And she'll tell us how charming he looks in new clothes,
And how nimble his hand moves in brushing the shoes;
Or how, the last time that he went to May Fair,
He bought her some sweethearts of gingerbread ware.'   20
'For my part I think,' says old Lady Marr-joy,
'A servant might find herself other employ:
Was she mine I'd employ her as long as 'twas light,
And send her to bed without candle at night.'
'Why so?', says Miss Rhymer, displeased: 'I protest   25
'Tis pity a genius should be so depressed!'
'What ideas can such low-bred creatures conceive?'
Says Mrs Noworthy, and laughed in her sleeve.
Says old Miss Prudella, 'If servants can tell
How to write to their mothers, to say they are well,   30
And read of a Sunday *The Duty of Man*,
Which is more I believe than one half of them can;
I think 'tis much properer they should rest there,

Than be reaching at things so much out of their sphere.'
Says old Mrs Candour, 'I've now got a maid   35
That's the plague of my life – a young gossiping jade;
There's no end of the people that after her come,
And whenever I'm out, she is never at home;
I'd rather ten times she would sit down and write,
Than gossip all over the town every night.'   40
'Some whimsical trollop most like,' says Miss Prim,
'Has been scribbling of nonsense, just out of a whim,
And, conscious it neither is witty or pretty,
Conceals her true name, and ascribes it to Betty.'
'I once had a servant myself,' says Miss Pines,   45
'That wrote on a wedding some very good lines.'
Says Mrs Domestic, 'And when they were done,
I can't see for my part what use they were on;
Had she wrote a receipt, to've instructed you how
To warm a cold breast of veal, like a ragout,   50
Or to make cowslip wine, that would pass for Champagne,
It might have been useful, again and again.'
On the sofa was old Lady Pedigree placed;
She owned that for poetry she had no taste,
That the study of heraldry was more in fashion,   55
And boasted she knew all the crests in the nation.
Says Mrs. Routella, 'Tom, take out the urn,
And stir up the fire, you see it don't burn.'
The tea things removed, and the tea-table gone,
The card-tables brought, and the cards laid thereon,   60
The ladies, ambitious for each others' crown,
Like courtiers contending for honours, sat down.

Hands (flourished *c.* 1789) had herself been a servant maid and subsequently a blacksmith's wife. The present poem may therefore be in part **autobiographical**. It appeared in a collection of her verse, much of which is also *mock-heroic in manner and coupleted in verse form, that was published by private subscription in Coventry in 1789. Little else is known about her.

Also see: MARXISM; FEMINISM; **foreground, background and point of view**; *literacy. Compare: 5.1.4 b above and Peters 5.4.3 c. (The present text comes from R. Lonsdale (ed.) *Eighteenth-century Women Poets*, Oxford, 1990: 425–6.)

5.1.4 d GEORGE GORDON, LORD BYRON, from *The Vision of Judgement*, 1822, ll.121–44.

[Sitting by the gate of heaven, Saint Peter is told of the recent death of King George III].

XVI

Saint Peter sat by the celestial gate,
    And nodded o'er his keys; when lo! there came
A wond'rous noise he had not heard of late –

A rushing sound of wind, and stream, and flame;
In short, a roar of things extremely great,
    Which would have made aught save a saint exclaim;
But he, with first a start and then a wink,
Said, 'There's another star gone out, I think!'

XVII

But ere he could return to his repose,
    A cherub flapp'd his right wing o'er his eyes –
At which Saint Peter yawn'd, and rubb'd his nose:
    'Saint porter,' said the Angel, 'prithee rise!'
Waving a goodly wing, which glow'd, as glows
    An earthly peacock's tail, with heavenly dyes;
To which the Saint replied, 'Well, what's the matter?
Is Lucifer come back with all this clatter?'

XVIII

'No,' quoth the Cherub; 'George the Third is dead.'
    'And who is George the Third?' replied the Apostle;
'*What George? what Third?*' 'The King of England,' said
    The Angel. 'Well! he won't find kings to jostle
Him on his way; but does he wear his head?
    Because the last[1] we saw here had a tussle,
And ne'er would have got into heaven's good graces,
Had he not flung his head in all our faces.'

---

[1]   Louis XVI of France, who was guillotined in 1793 during the Revolution.

Byron (1788–1824) – aristocrat, traveller, part-time revolutionary, sensualist and poet – is very difficult to disentangle from the madcap myth of himself which he so assiduously cultivated. Hence the notion of the 'Byronic hero'. Byron is still by far the best known of the English *Romantic poets in mainland Europe, where he, like the Shelleys, travelled extensively. In Britain, however, he is now relatively under-studied compared to Wordsworth, Coleridge and Keats – who are much less well known elsewhere. Byron had an 'insider-outsider' view of the British ruling elite: 'insider' because he was himself an aristocrat and once member of the House of Lords; 'outsider' because he was an avowed republican and never returned to England after 1816. Byron's *The Vision of Judgement* was a *satiric **response** to the British Poet Laureate, Robert Southey's poem of the same name. Southey had both elegised and eulogised the mad, blind, tyrant King George III upon the latter's death (1820). In the preface, the Poet Laureate had also attacked Byron, along with Percy Shelley, as members of 'the Satanic School' of poets.

   Also see: **Bibles . . . myths; comedy . . . carnival; versification**.
   Compare: 5.1.4 a–c above.

5.1.4 e TERRY PRATCHETT and NEIL GAIMAN, opening of *Good Omens*, 1991

> The Oxfordshire plain stretched out to the west, with a scattering of lights to mark the slumbering villages where honest yeomen were settling down to sleep after a long day's editorial direction, financial consulting, or software engineering.
>
> Up here on the hill a few glow-worms were lighting up.
>
> The surveyor's theodolite is one of the most direful symbols of the twentieth century. Set up anywhere in open countryside, it says: there will come Road Widening, yea, and two-thousand-home estates in keeping with the Essential Character of the Village. Executive Developments will be manifest.
>
> But not even the most conscientious surveyor surveys at midnight, and yet here the thing was, tripod legs deep in the turf. Not many theodolites have a hazel twig strapped to the top, either, or crystal pendulums hanging from them and Celtic runes carved into the legs.
>
> The soft breeze flapped the cloak of the slim figure who was adjusting the knobs of the thing. It was quite a heavy cloak, sensibly waterproof, with a warm lining.
>
> Most books on witchcraft will tell you that witches work naked. This is because most books on witchcraft are written by men.

Pratchett, as it says on the inside **auto/biographical** blurbs of several of his **comic** *fantasy novels: 'was born in 1948 and is still not dead [. . . He is] on average a sort of youngish middle-aged. He lives in Somerset with his wife and daughter, and long ago chose journalism as a career because it was indoor work with no heavy lifting. Beyond that he positively refuses to be drawn. People never read these biographies anyway, do they? They want to get on with the book, not wade through masses of prose designed to suggest that the **author** is really a very interesting person [. . .] He grows carnivorous plants as a hobby; they are a lot less interesting than people believe [. . .] Occasionally he gets accused of literature.' Pratchett is also the author of the hugely *popular *Discworld* series. Gaiman, Pratchett's co-writer here, has much less to say for himself but is no doubt equally un/interesting as a person.

Compare: 5.1.4 d. Also see: LITERATURE; FORMALISM, Example p.90; **discourse**.

5.1.5   JOHN CLARE, 'I am' composed *c*. 1844, published 1865

> I am – yet what I am, none cares or knows;
>   My friends forsake me like a memory lost;
> I am the self-consumer of my woes –
>   They rise and vanish in oblivion's host
> Like shadows in love-frenzied stifled throes   5
> And yet I am, and live – like vapours tost
>
> Into the nothingness of scorn and noise,
>   Into the living sea of waking dreams,
> Where there is neither sense of life or joys,
>   But the vast shipwreck of my life's esteems   10
> Even the dearest that I love the best
> Are strange – nay, rather, stranger than the rest.

I long for scenes where man hath never trod
   A place where woman never smiled or wept
There to abide with my Creator, God,   15
   And sleep as I in childhood sweetly slept,
Untroubling and untroubled where I lie
The grass below – above the vaulted sky.

Clare (1793–1864) was the son of an agricultural labourer and himself one in youth. At that time the village of Helpston, Northamptonshire, where they lived, was 'enclosed' (i.e. parcelled up into private fields for farming and parkland) and the Clares were uprooted and left without regular work. Also at that time, Clare's relationship with a local farmer's daughter, Mary Joyce, was ended by her father. Clare apparently never adjusted to these calamities, even though he subsequently married, had children and achieved a passing literary success as a 'peasant poet'. *Literacy was elementary or non-existent amongst farm labourers. '*Literariness' in such a person was judged remarkably quaint. From 1837 to 1841 Clare was in a private asylum in Epping. He escaped and walked back to Northampton, believing he was married to Mary Joyce. From 1841 till he died he was confined to Northampton General Lunatic Asylum. There he wrote this poem, which was posthumously published.

    Also see: PSYCHOLOGICAL APPROACHES, Example, pp. 98–100; MARXISM; **auto/biography**; *imaginary; **subject . . . identity**. (Text from G. Summerfield (ed.) *John Clare: Selected Poems*, London, 1990: 311.)

5.1.6   WILLIAM BARNES, 'Woak Hill', from *Poems in Dorset Dialect*, 1844–62

[Tips on reading and pronunciation: expect 'a-' prefixed to participles; 'v' for 'f' and 'z' for 's'; some ellipses (o' – of; wi' – with, etc.) and some unfamiliar vowels. 'Woak' is an 'oak'. Most of this become obvious when read aloud.]

When sycamore leaves wer a-spreaden,
   Green-ruddy, in hedges,
Bezide the red doust o' the ridges,
   A-dried at Woak Hill;

I packed up my goods all a-sheenen   5
   Wi' long years o' handlen,
On dousty red wheels ov a waggon,
   To ride at Woak Hill.

The brown thatchen ruf o' the dwellen
   I then wer a-leèven,   10
Had shelter'd the sleek head o' Meèry,
   My bride at Woak Hill.

But now vor zome years, her light voot-vall
   'S a-lost vrom the vlooren,
Too soon vor my jay an' my children,   15
   She died at Woak Hill.

But still I do think that, in soul,
　　She do hover about us;
To ho vor her motherless childern,
　　Her pride at Woak Hill.   20

Zoo-lest she should tell me hereafter
　　I stole off 'ithout her,
An' left her, uncall'd at house-ridden,
　　To bide at Woak Hill –

I call'd her so fondly, wi' lippens   25
　　All soundless to others,
An' took her wi' avòr-reachen hand,
　　To my zide at Woak Hill.

On the road I did look round, a-talken
　　To light at my shoulder,   30
An' then led her in at the door-way,
　　Miles wide vrom Woak Hill.

An' that's why vo'k thought, vor a season,
　　My mind wer a-wandren
Wi' sorrow, when I wer so sorely   35
　　A-tried at Woak Hill.

But no; that my Meèry mid never
　　Behold herzelf slighted,
I wanted to think that I guided
　　My guide vrom Woak Hill.   40

5. a-sheenen – shining. 11. Meèry – Mary. 14. jay – joy. 19. To hor vor – to care for. 23. house-ridden – house-warming. 27. avòr-reachen – forward reaching. 37. Meèry mid never – Mary might never.

Barnes (1801–1886) was a Dorset schoolteacher and parish priest with a strong interest in the history of the English Language, especially its *Germanic roots. Barnes's use of Dorset **dialect** was deliberate. He also wrote poems, and much else, in **standard** varieties. It is usually assumed that he composed this poem some time after he moved house following the death in 1832 of his wife, whose name was in fact Julia. The difference of names (here 'Meery'/ Mary) may put this in doubt. The poet and novelist Thomas Hardy, who lived close by, wrote a praising obituary of William Barnes and edited a selection of his poems in 1908.

　　Also see: 1.2.2; **absence and presence; auto/biography**. Compare: 5.4.5. (Text from N.P. Messenger and J.R Watson (eds) *Victorian Poetry*, London, 1974: 14.)

5.1.7 a WILLIAM BUTLER YEATS, 'Leda and the Swan', 1923, as pub. 1928

[In **classical** Greek *mythology, the god Zeus took on the *body of a swan in order to trap then rape the water-nymph Leda. Helen of Troy and Clytemnestra were

among the offspring that resulted from this forced union. Both were held responsible for subsequent violent disasters: the fall of Troy and the death of Agamemnon.]

> A sudden blow: the great wings beating still
> Above the staggering girl, her thighs caressed
> By the dark webs, her nape caught in his bill,
> He holds her helpless breast upon his breast.
>
> How can those terrified vague fingers push   5
> The feathered glory from her loosening thighs?
> And how can body, laid in that white rush,
> But feel the strange heart beating where it lies?
>
> A shudder in the loins engenders there
> The broken wall, the burning roof and tower   10
> And Agamemnon dead.
>   Being so caught up,
> So mastered by the brute blood of the air,
> Did she put on his knowledge with his power
> Before the indifferent beak could let her drop?

Yeats (1865–1939) – at various times, Irish nationalist, supporter of Fascist
Blueshirts in Dublin, founder of the Irish Academy of Letters, devotee of esoteric
*mythologies (CLASSICAL, Celtic and invented), as well as poet, playwright and
visionary – lived two thirds of his life outside Ireland and was awarded the
Nobel Prize for Literature in 1923. That was also the year he started to draft, and
subsequently repeatedly redraft, 'Leda and the Swan'. It was initially called
'Annunciation'. Yeats may have had in mind the scene as depicted in the neo-classical
*paintings by Leonardo da Vinci or Michelangelo.
    Compare: 5.1.7 b below. (For drafts, see Abrams *et al.* 1993, Vol II: 2463–5.)

5.1.7 b JUDITH KAZANTSIS, 'Leda and Leonardo the Swan', 1980

[See preliminary note in 5.1.7 a for mythological and artistic references.]

> Leda, the inside out lady of the swan
>   wants to knuckle the cold
> rotter who fluttered her to bed.
>
> Caught in the infinite wiggle
> in a mesmerization of paint   5
>   here she is, propped in her voluptuous stay
>   maddened
> for all who like a good sex object
> shielding her feathered friend.
>
> His beak pinches her demonstrable little   10
> breasts, quacking all mine

> her plump pubic mound pretty and public
> her eyes abashed
> how she blushes, the mystery!
>   my corrected darling!   15
>
> The silent curly face
> carries on talking backwards to the wall
> no no no no

Kazantsis (1940—) is a poet, painter and scholar from a Greek-British background. This poem is from the collection *The Wicked Queen* (1980, with Michèle Roberts and Michelene Wandor) and seems to be primarily directed at the *painting of the scene by Leonardo da Vinci (1452–1519). But she may also have had the above poem by Yeats (5.1.7 a) in mind.

Also see: CLASSICAL; FEMINISM AND GENDER STUDIES; **Bibles, holy books and myths**; *body; **foreground, background and point of view**; **difference . . . re/valuation**; **writing . . . rewriting**. (Text from Kazantsis 1995: 18.)

5.1.8   ADRIENNE RICH, 'Dialogue', 1967

> She sits with one hand poised against her head, the
> other turning an old ring to the light
> for hours our talk has beaten
> like rain against the screens
> a sense of August and heat-lightning   5
> I get up, go to make tea, come back
> we look at each other
> then she says (and this is what I live through
> over and over) – she says: *I do not know*
> *if sex is an illusion*   10
>
> *I do not know*
> *who I was when I did those things*
> *or who I said I was*
> *or whether I willed to feel*
> *what I had read about*   15
> *or who in fact was there with me*
> *or whether I knew, even then*
> *that there was doubt about these things*

Rich (1929—), born in Balitmore, USA, has been strongly influential as poet, essayist and political commentator in the development of radical FEMINIST, and latterly *lesbian feminist, writing. Her work is marked by a special interest in reclaiming LANGUAGE, exploring oppressive and repressive **silences** and in urging a *re-vision of past, present and future hi/stories.

Also see: FEMINISM, Example pp. 121–122; **speech . . . dialogue**; **versification** (free verse). Compare: Clare 5.1.5; Dickinson 5.4.5 d; Contemporary 'I'dentities 5.4.7 g. (Text from C. Rumens (ed.) *Making for the Open: Post-feminist Poetry*, 2nd edn, London, 1987: 73.)

5.1.9   Some 'New' English varieties

5.1.9 a π0, 7 DAIZ, 1996

Wun e-wa mor.
Wun e-wa mor
Wun e-wa mor Finish.
No hev kuppachino.
No hev kuppachino hee-a.   5
Nex' shop.
Nex' wun.
Wayt-kofi onli.
You Grik unch-ya.
0 – gee. 0 —gee-z!   10
Yoo awl da taym brok Ali.
Yoo awl da taym brok.
No unyon. No letus. No baykon.
No munni.
Yoo awl da taym brok Ali.   15
Yoo awl da taym brok.
Wotz yoo o'ra?
Yes pliz —thair?
Wotz yoo o'ra?
Bool-shee'!   20
Toogeta?
O'sep-aat?
On da rol?
On da bret?
Solt on? Solt on?   25
Poot solt on?
Liv it.
Liv it. Loo-i!
Liv it.
Detz yooz.   30
Da udda wun not yooz.
O'rayt. O'rayt.
Wun e-wa mor.
Wun e-wa mor Finish
Aagen. Aaagen.   35
Toomoro.

'π0' (1951—) is a Greek-Australian *performance poet who lives and works in Melbourne. For all its initial strangeness on the page, the whole thing quickly becomes clear if you try to read it out loud. Its *graphology is an attempt to represent a distinctive English *phonology. The differences from **standard** Australian, British or American **varieties** are wholly matters of **accent** not **dialect**: pronunciation not vocabulary or grammar. In terms of **genre**, this is a dramatic **monologue**.

Compare: 5.1.9 b and c below; supermarket checkout 5.3.1 a and Leonard 5.2.5 d. (Text from MacFarlane and Temple 1996: 194–5.)

5.1.9 b CHAN WEI MENG, 'I spik Ingglish' previously unpublished, 1996

I speak English
To a foreign friend —
'I don't understand what you're trying to say!'
'How come? I spik Ingglish what!'

I spik Ingglish   5
In Home —
'Hungry? You want fried lice or mee?'
'I eat Can-tucky cheeken, can or not?'
'Listen! Study Ingglish, earn more manee.'

I spik Ingglish   10
In School —
'Everybody read – sing sang sung.'
'I sing Maly hab a litter lamb.'
'Attention! School close at one.'

I spik Ingglish   15
In Work —
'You know, the komputer cannot open, izzit?'
'I donno, got pay or not?'
'Remember – customer is always light, pease.'

I spik Ingglish   20
In Shop —
'Hello, can I hepch you?'
'I looksee first'
'Buy now! they is vely cheep and new.'

I spik Ingglish   25
Everywhere
Understand?

Chan Wei Meng (c. 1975—) was a student from Singapore studying English in
New Zealand at the University of Otago in 1996. She wrote this as part of her
response to the mixture of **standard** and *creolised **varieties** encountered in a
course on Caribbean-British poetry, including the poem by Merle Collins below.

Also see: 1.2.1–1.2.4; POSTCOLONIALISM. Compare: 5.1.9 a and c; Leonard 5.2.5 d.
(Published by kind permission of the author.)

5.1.9 c MERLE COLLINS, 'No Dialects Please', performed 1970s, pub. 1987

In this competition
dey was lookin for poetry of worth
for a writin that could wrap up a feelin

an fling it back hard
with a captive power to choke de stars   5
so dey say
'Send them to us
but NO DIALECTS PLEASE'
We're British!

Ay!   10
Well ah laugh till me bouschet near drop
Is not only dat ah tink
of de dialect of de Normans and de Saxons
dat combine an reformulate
to create a language-elect   15
is not only dat ah tink
how dis British education mus really be narrow
if it leave dem wid no knowledge of what dey own history is about
is not only dat ah tink
bout de part of my story   20
dat come from Liverpool in a big dirty white ship mark
AFRICAN SLAVES PLEASE!
We're the British!

But as if dat nat enough pain
for a body to bear   25
ah tink bout de part on de plantations down dere
Wey dey so frighten o de power
in the deep spaces
behind our watching faces
dat dey shout   30
NO AFRICAN LANGUAGES PLEASE!
It's against the law!
Make me ha to go
an start up a language o me own
dat ah could share wid me people   35

Den when we start to shout
bout a culture o we own
a language o we own
dem an de others dey leave to control us say
STOP THAT NONSENSE NOW   40
We're all British!
Every time we lif we foot to do we own ting
to fight we own fight
dey tell us how British we British
an ah wonder if dey remember   45
dat in Trinidad in the thirties
dey jail Butler
who dey say is their british citizen
an accuse him of

Hampering the war effort   50
Then it was
FIGHT FOR YOUR COUNTRY, FOLKS!
You're British!

Ay! Ay!
Ah wonder when it change to   55
NO DIALECTS PLEASE!
WE'RE British!
Huh!
To tink how still dey so dunce
An so frighten o we power   60
dat dey have to hide behind a language
that we could wrap roun we little finger
in addition to we own!
Heavens o mercy!
Dat is dunceness oui!   65
Ah wonder where is de bright British?

11. Bouschet – mouth

Merle Collins is from Grenada. She has worked as a teacher, a research officer
on Latin American affairs, a solo *performance poet and a member of the group
'African Dawn'. The Afro-Caribbean tradition of poetry as *oral **hi/story**, social
celebration and political complaint is strong in her work. This piece is not difficult
to grasp if you try it out loud.

Also see: 1.2.1–1.2.4. HISTORY; POSTCOLONIALISM; **accent and dialect; standards . . . varieties**. Compare: 5.1.9 a and b; Leonard 5.2.5 d. (Text from Couzyn
1989: 51–3.)

5.1.10 QUEEN, 'Bohemian Rhapsody' (EMI) 1975, re-released 1991

Is this the real life
Is this just fantasy
Caught in a landslide
no escape from reality
open your eyes
look up to the skies
and see . . .
I'm just a poor boy   poor boy
I need no sympathy
because I'm easy come easy go
little high little low
any way the wind blows
doesn't really matter to me
to me . . .
Mama. Just killed a man. Put a gun against his head. Pulled my trigger. Now he's
    dead
Mama. Life'd just begun. But now I've gone and thrown it all away
Mama. oo-oo-oo-oo. I didn't mean to make you cry .

If I'm not back again tomorrow. Carry on carry on. Nothing really matters
Too late. My time has come.
sends shivers down my spine. Body's aching all the time
Goodbye everybody. I've got to go.
gotta leave you all behind and face the truth
Mama. oo-oo-oo-oo (anyway the wind blows). I don't want to die.
I sometimes wish I'd never been born at all

    [*Instrumental*]

I see a little silhouetto of a man
          scaramouche scaramouche
          will you do the fandango
          thunderbolt and lightning
          very very frightening me
          Galileo Galileo
          Galileo / Galileo
          Galileo piccolo
          magnifico-o-o-o-o
I'm just a poor boy
nobody loves me
          He's just a poor boy
          from a poor family
          spare him his life
          from this monstrosity

Easy come easy go
will you let me go
          dissmillah no
             we will not let you go
          let him goooooo . . .
             dissmillah no we will not let you go
          let him goooooo . . .
             dissmillah no we will not let you go
let me go   will not let you go
let me go   let you go
            never never never never never
            never never let me go-o-o-
            no no no no no no no no no
Oh mama mia, mama mia, let me go

          Beelzebub has a devil set aside for me, for me, for MEEEEE

    [*Instrumental*]

So you think you can stone me and spit in my eye
So you think you can love me and leave me to die

Oh baby
Can't do this to me baby
just gotta get out
just gotta get right out of here

[*Instrumental*]   Oh yeah Oh yeah Oh yeah . . .

Nothing really matters
anyone can see
nothing really matters
nothing really matters
to me . . .

any way the winds blows. . . .

'Bohemian Rhapsody' (1975) is a six-minute rock opera and now recognised as a pop **classic**. It has been continuously available for two decades (*Queen's Greatest Hits*, including this track, was in the UK charts for eleven years). This song was re-released in 1991, the same year it was featured in a famous 'singalong' scene in the film *Wayne's World*. This was also the year the lead singer, Freddie Mercury, died of AIDS, thereby reinforcing the **tragic** and **mythic** status of the song. The fact that many people reading the above words will 'hear' 'Bohemian Rhapsody' and perhaps even 'see' Queen (in video promo or in concert) is a measure of just how deeply this piece is embedded in *popular, POSTMODERN CULTURE (see Example, pp. 132–134).

Compare: Contemporary 'I'dentities 5.4.7 g; Wyatt 5.1.3 a; Wroth 5.1.3 c; Dickinson 5.4.5 d.

5.2   PROSE FICTION, JOURNALS AND NEWS

5.2.1   Letter, diary and life-writing

5.2.1 a MARGERY BREWS to John Paston III, A Valentine, February 1477

1   Unto my ryght welbelovyd Voluntyn, John Paston, Sqyuer, be this bill delyvered, etc. Ryght reverent and wurschypfull and my ryght welebeloved Voluntyne, I recommande me unto yowe full hertely, desyring to here of yowr welefare, whech I beseche Almyghty God long for to preserve unto hys plesure and yowr hertys desyre. And yf it please yowe to here of my welefare, I am not in god heele of body ner of herte, nor shall be tyll I here from yowe:

For ther wottys no creature what peyn that I endure,
And for to be deede, I dare it not dyscure.

And my lady my moder hath laboured the mater to my fadure full delygently, but
10   sche can no more gete then ye knowe of, for the whech God knoweth I am full sory.
But yf that ye loffe me, as I tryste vere'ly that ye do, ye will not leffe me therfor; for if that ye hade not half the lyvelode that ye hafe, for to do the grettyst labur that any woman on lyve myght, I wold not forsake yowe.

And yf ye commande me to kepe me true wherever I go,
iwyse I will do all my might yowe to love and never no mo.
And yf my freendys say that I do amys, thei shal not me let so for to do,

Myn herte me byddys ever more to love yowe
truly over all erthely thing.

20   And yf thei be never so wroth, I tryst it schall be bettur in tyme commyng.

No more to yowe at this tyme, but the Holy Trinite hafe yowe in kepyng.
Ande I besech yow that this bill be not seyn of non erthely creature safe only your
selfe, etc. And thys lettur was indyte at Topcroft with ful hevy herte, etc.

Bi your own M.B.

This is one of the many letters surviving from the fifteenth century associated with
the well-to-do Norfolk family, the Pastons. It is reproduced here for various reasons.
It is an instance of relatively informal *prose from the period between Chaucer and
Shakespeare. It shows the flexibility of *spelling, especially of vowels, before the
onset of print culture (e.g., 'welbelovyd Voluntyn', 'welebeloved Voluntyne'). It
reminds us that **real** life **discourses**, whether public or personal, are informed by
both feeling and convention, and in this case by **poetry**. It also throws a sidelight
on *literacy at the time; for this letter was dictated by Margery and written down by
Thomas Kela, a servant of the Brews family. Margery herself, as was common, could
not write.

Also see: **auto/biography and life-writing**. Compare: Peters 5.4.3 c. (Text from
D. Gray (ed.) *Late Medieval Verse and Prose*, Oxford, 1985: 42–3, 428.)

5.2.1 b SAMUEL PEPYS, *Diary*, entry for 13 November 1664

13 Lord's Day. The morning to church, where mighty sport to hear our Clerk sing out
of tune, though his master sits by him that begins and keeps the tune aloud for the
parish. Dined at home very well. And spent all the after-noon with my wife within
doors – and getting a speech out of Hamlett, 'To bee or not to bee,' without book. In
the evening, to sing psalms; and in came Mr. Hill to see me, and then he and I and
the boy finely to sing; and so anon broke up after pleasure. He gone, I to supper and
so to prayers and to bed,

Pepys (1633–1703) kept his diary in code and the whole six volumes were only
finally deciphered and transliterated in 1983 by R. Latham and W. Matthews. The
part from which the above is taken was deciphered by John Smith, a Cambridge
undergraduate, and published to great acclaim in 1851. Pepys was a senior civil
servant and many of his observations were personally compromising or publicly
scandalous.

Also see: **auto/biography; Bibles; canon**. Compare: 5.2.1 c; 5.4.2.

5.2.1 c GEORGE and WEEDON GROSSMITH, from *The Diary of a Nobody*, 1892

DECEMBER 26. I did not sleep very well last night; I never do in a strange bed. I
feel a little indigestion, which one must expect at this time of the year. Carrie and
I returned to Town in the evening. Lupin came in late. He said he enjoyed his
Christmas, and added: 'I feel as fit as a Lowther Arcade fiddle, and only require a
little more "oof" to feel as fit as a £500 Stradivarius.' I have long since given up
trying to understand Lupin's slang, or asking him to explain it.

George (1847–1912) and Weedon (1854–1919) Grossmith wrote a highly successful diary of a fictional late Victorian civil servant called Mr Pooter, partly modelled on Pepys's diary (see 5.2.1 b). A fashionable and wayward son, Lupin, is often featured.

5.2.1 d JANET FRAME, from *To the Is-Land*, 1982, opening

In the Second Place

From the first place of liquid darkness, within the second place of air and light, I set down the following record with its mixture of fact and truths and memories of truths and its direction always toward the Third Place, where the starting point is myth.

Toward the Is-Land

The Ancestors – who were they, the myth and the reality? As a child, I used to boast that the Frames 'came over with William of Orange'. I have since learned that this may have been so, for Frame is a version of Fleming, Flammand, from the Flemish weavers who settled in the lowlands of Scotland in the fourteenth century. I strengthen the reality or the myth of those ancestors each time I recall that Grandma Frame began working in a Paisley cotton mill when she was eight years old; that her daughters Polly, Isy, Maggie spent their working lives as dressmakers and in their leisure produced exquisite embroidery, knitting, tatting, crochet; and that her son George Samuel, my father, had a range of skills that included embroidery (or 'fancy-work', as it was known), rug making, leatherwork, painting in oils on canvas and on velvet. The Frames had a passion for making things. Like his father, our Grandad Frame, a blacksmith who made our fire pokers, the boot-last, and even the wooden spurtle smoothed with stirring the morning porridge. My father survives as a presence in such objects as a leather workbag, a pair of ribbed butter pats, a handful of salmon spoons.

Frame (1924–) is a writer who often mingles **auto/biography**, **fiction** and **myth**. She was born in Dunedin, South Island, New Zealand – a city which proclaims its Scottish roots in its name (the Gaelic name for Edinburgh). Frame is highly conscious of both the *hybridity and the volatility of notions of **hi/story** and CULTURE. The first section above is loosely based on Maori myth. The 'Is-land' is both New Zealand and 'what is'.

5.2.2   Slave narratives, seventeenth–twentieth centuries

5.2.2 a APHRA BEHN, from *Oroonoko, or The Royal Slave*, 1688

[The narrator is a young white woman who is the daughter of a man appointed to be Lieutenant General of (British) Surinam, later (Dutch) Guyana.]

I ought to tell you that the Christians never buy slaves but they give 'em some name of their own, their native ones being likely very barbarous and hard to pronounce; so that Mr. Trefry gave Oroonoko that of Caesar, which name will live in that country as long as that (scarce more) glorious one of the great Roman; for 'tis most evident, he wanted no part of the personal courage of that Caesar, and acted things as memorable, had they been done in some part of the world replenished with people and historians that might have given him his due. But his misfortune was to fall in an obscure world, that afforded only a female pen to celebrate his fame; though I doubt not but it had lived from others' endeavors, if the Dutch, who immediately after his time took that country, had not killed, banished, and dispersed all those that were capable of giving the world this great man's life, much better than I have done. And Mr. Trefry, who designed it, died before he began it, and bemoaned himself for not having undertook it in time.

For the future, therefore, I must call Oroonoko Caesar, since by that name only he was known in our western world, and by that name he was received on shore at Parham House, where he was destined a slave. But if the King himself (God bless him) had come ashore, there could not have been greater expectations by all the whole plantation, and those neighboring ones, than was on ours at that time; and he was received more like a governor than a slave.

Behn (1640–89) was one of the first women writers in English to make a living as a professional writer, chiefly of plays such as *The Rover* (1677) and of prose **fiction** such as *Oroonoko*. The latter begins as a harem *romance on the west coast of Africa and ends as an indictment of slavery in the West Indies and the Americas. Its narrative as told by a white English woman thus retraces the contemporary *slave-trade triangle. Behn was herself probably in the West Indies and Surinam in earlier life, and there is much that is **hi/storical** and **factional**, as well as perhaps **autobiographical**, about her account. Compare: 5.2.2 b–e; Rhys 5.2.3 e. (For a full text, see Abrams 1993, Vol. I: 1864–910.)

5.2.2 b DANIEL DEFOE, from *Robinson Crusoe*, 1719, Ch. 24: 'I Call Him Friday', 1719

[The shipwrecked hero records his first encounter with the man who is to become his servant.]

His face was round and plump; his nose small, not flat like the Negroes', a very good mouth, thin lips, and his fine teeth well set, and white as ivory. After he had slumbered, rather than slept, about half an hour, he waked again, and comes out of the cave to me, for I had been milking my goats, which I had in the enclosure just by. When he espied me, he came running to me, laying himself down again upon the ground, with all the possible signs of an humble, thankful disposition, making a many antic gestures to show it. At last he lays his head flat upon the ground, close to my foot, and sets my other foot upon his head, as he had done before; and after this, made all the signs to me of subjection, servitude, and submission imaginable, to let me know know how he would serve me as long as he lived; I understood him in many things and let him know I was very pleased with him; in a little time I began to speak to him and teach him to speak to me; and first, I made him know his name should be Friday, which was the day I saved his life; I called him so for the memory of the time; I likewise taught him to say 'Master,' and then let him know that was to be my name; I likewise taught him to say 'yes' and 'no' and to know the meaning of them; I gave him some milk in an earthen pot and let him see me drink it before him and sop my bread in it; and I gave him a cake of bread to do the like, which he quickly complied with, and made signs that it was very good for him.

Defoe (1660–1731) – journalist, novelist, tradesman and travel-writer – wrote the highly successful *Robinson Crusoe* and quickly followed it with the *Further Adventures of Robinson Crusoe* (1720) and *Moll Flanders*, the story of a (repentant) thief, prostitute and opportunist (1722). Along with the Bible and Shakespeare, *Robinson Crusoe* became one of the favourite and **classic texts** of the British Empire and was, until recently, read by most English children in full or in one of the many abridged versions. Defoe is also recognised as one of the 'fathers of the English novel'.

Compare: 5.2.2 a, c–e; Conrad 5.2.4 c; Shakespeare 5.3.2 b; Rhys 5.2.3 e; Churchill 5.3.4 e.

5.2.2 c GEOFF HOLDSWORTH, 'I call him Tuesday Afternoon', 1994

He was a strange, comical fellow, an ungainly, rather squat figure with plump limbs, and, as I estimated, in his early forties. He was possessed of an arrogant countenance and showed little warmth of spirit, and yet, he seemed to have traces of femininity in his face, and elements of the assertive independence of an African about his countenance, especially on those rare occasions when he smiled. His hair was thin and wispy, not dark and thick; his forehead was narrow and creased from squinting into the sun, and his small pig-eyes were a dull lifeless grey. His skin was white; not the pleasing tinted offwhite of the Spanish visitors I had encountered, but an alarming, sickly white, interspersed with patches of bright red. His face was round, yet long; his nose short and sharp as an arrow head, and his large lip-less mouth revealed crooked yellow and brown teeth.

Having narrowly escaped the head hunters' attack of last week, it was only a matter of time before their return, but Tuesday Afternoon (the first time I set eyes on him, and thereafter, my nick-name for this simpleton) seemed oblivious to this threat. Observing this odd fellow's strange behaviour for over a week, I was convinced that, unless I made an effort to warn him of the impending danger, he was doubtless going to die. As my previous attempts at communication had proved disastrous, I took it upon myself to attempt some form of sign language. When I approached him he was doing something to one of his goats which defies description. Thankfully, on seeing me he stopped what he was doing and made some incomprehensible noises which I took to be a form of greeting. In an effort to instill a sense of urgency and warn him his life was threatened, I mimicked the warlike gestures of the head hunters and prostrated myself on the ground before him in the manner of someone who had been mortally wounded. This was obviously not working: his only reaction was to smile like an imbecile, point to himself and mumble something like 'masta'. Frustrated, yet undeterred, I gesticulated further by grabbing one of his feet, setting it on my head and drawing my forefinger across my throat to indicate exactly what would happen to him should he remain. My exhortations were, however, all in vain. Again he grinned like an idiot, repeatedly pointed to himself and said 'masta' over and over. He then offered me some disgusting bread and warm white liquid which, just to humour him, I ate. Realising that any further attempts at communication would be futile, and that 'I masta' in his strange language probably means 'I am an idiot', I reluctantly left Tuesday Afternoon to his fate.

Holdsworth (1948—) was an undergraduate student at Oxford Brookes University. He wrote this in 1994 as part of a textual *intervention (plus commentary) on the preceding passage from *Robinson Crusoe*, 5.2.2 b.

Also see: 4.4 and Pope 1995: 99–113.

5.2.2 d FREDERICK DOUGLASS, from *The Narrative and Life of Frederick Douglass, an American Slave, Written by Himself* (1845: 49)

> Very soon after I went to live with Mr and Mrs. Auld, she very kindly commenced to teach me the A,B,C. After I had learned this, she assisted me in learning to spell words of three or four letters. Just at this point of my progress, Mr. Auld found out what was going on, and at once forbade Mrs. Auld to instruct me further, telling her, among other things, that it was unwise, as well as unsafe, to teach a slave to read. To use his own words, further, he said, 'If you give a nigger an inch, he will take an ell. A nigger should know nothing but to obey his master – to do as he is told to do. Learning would *spoil* the best nigger in the world. Now,' said he, 'if you teach that nigger (speaking of myself) how to read, there would be no keeping him. It would forever unfit him to be a slave. He would at once become unmanageable, and of no value to his master. As to himself it could do him no good, but a great deal of harm. It would make him discontented and unhappy.' These words sank deep into my heart, stirred up sentiments within that lay slumbering, and called into existence an entirely new train of thought. It was a new and special revelation, explaining dark and mysterious things, with which my young understanding had struggled, but struggled in vain. I now understood what had been to me a most perplexing difficulty – to wit, the white man's power to enslave the black man. It was a grand achievement, and I prized it highly. From that moment I understood the pathway from slavery to freedom.

Douglass (1817–95) was born into slavery on a plantation in Maryland. After learning the power of *literacy he taught fellow slaves before escaping to Massachusetts in 1838. Douglass became one of the most powerful orators, writers and campaigners for the anti-slavery movement. He enlarged his *Life* twice (1855, 1881), thereby amplifying a tradition in which **auto/biography** can be conceived as a personal-political tool.

Compare: 5.2.2 a–c, e; 5.2.4 d. (For this and other narratives by slaves themselves, see Gates 1986.)

5.2.2 e TONI MORRISON, *Beloved* (1987: 5)

[At this point, early on in the novel, a destitute black woman woman (Sethe) is reflecting on how she bartered her body for the carving of the single word 'Beloved' on her daughter's tombstone.]

> Ten minutes for seven letters. With another ten could she
> have gotten 'Dearly' too? She had not thought to ask him and
> it bothered her still that it might have been possible –
> that for twenty minutes, a half hour, say, she could have
> had the whole thing, every word she heard the preacher say
> at the funeral (and all there was to say, surely) engraved
> on her baby's headstone: 'Dearly Beloved'. But what she got,
> settled for, was the one word that mattered. She thought it
> would be enough, rutting among the headstones with the
> engraver, his young son looking on, the anger in his face

so old; the appetite in it quite new. That should certainly
be enough. Enough to answer one more preacher, one more
abolitionist and a town full of disgust.

Morrison (1931—) – novelist, university teacher and editor – makes **narratives** that
may properly be regarded as **hi/storical** and **factional**: she both researches and,
in Rich's phrase, *re-visions the past. *Beloved* explores the conditions and consequences of slave infanticide through a woman who kills her own child ('Beloved')
rather than see her born into the misery of slavery. This novel won the Pulitzer Prize
in 1987 and its author won the Nobel Prize for Literature in 1993.
    Compare: 5.2.2 a–e, 5.4.5.

5.2.3   Romance, seventeenth–twentieth centuries

5.2.3 a DELARIVIER MANLEY, from *The New Atalantis*, 1709

[An ageing Duke is showing Charlot, a young girl in his charge, one of the tales from
Ovid's *Metamorphoses* in which a girl Myrra falls in love with her father.]

She took the Book, and plac'd herself by the Duke. His Eyes Feasted themselves upon
her Face, thence wander'd over her snowy Bosom, and saw the young swelling
Breasts just beginning to distinguish themselves, and which were gently heav'd at the
Impression *Myrra's* Sufferings made upon her Heart. By this dangerous reading, he
pretended to shew her, that there were Pleasures her Sex were born for, and which
she might consequently long to taste! Curiosity is an early and dangerous Enemy to
Virtue. The young *Charlot*, who had by a noble inclination of Gratitude a strong
propension of Affection for the Duke, whom she call'd and estem'd her *Papa*, being a
Girl of wonderful reflection, and consequently Application, wrought her Imagination
up to such a lively heighth at the Fathers Anger after the possession of his Daughter,
which she judg'd highly unkind and unnatural, that she drop'd her Book, Tears fill'd
her Eyes, Sobs rose to oppress her, and she pull'd out her Handkerchief to cover
the Disorder. The Duke, who was Master of all Mankind, could trace 'em in all the
Meanders of Dissimulation and Cunning, was not at a loss how to interpret the
Agitation of a Girl who knew no Hipocrisy, all was Artless, the beautiful product of
Innocence and Nature; he drew her gently to him, drunk her Tears with his Kisses,
suck'd her Sighs and gave her by that dangerous Commerce (her Soul before
prepar'd to softness) new and unfelt Desires; her Virtue was becalm'd or rather
unapprehensive of him for an Invader; he prest her Lips with his, the nimble beatings
of his Heart, apparently seen and felt thro' his open Breast! the glowings! the
tremblings of his Limbs! the glorious Sparkles from his guilty Eyes! his shortness of
Breath, and eminent Disorder, were things all new to her, that had never seen, heard,
or read before of those powerful Operations, struck from the Fire of the two meeting
Sex; nor had she leisure to examine his disorders, possess'd by greater of her own!
greater! because that Modesty opposing Nature, forc'd a struggle of Dissimulation.
But the Duke's pursuing Kisses overcame the very Thoughts of anything, but that
new and lazy Poison stealing to her Heart, and spreading swiftly and imperceptibly
thro' all her Veins, she clos'd her Eyes with languishing Delight! deliver'd up the
possession of her Lips and Breath to the amorous Invader; return'd his eagar grasps,
and, in a word, gave her whole Person into his Arms, in meltings full of delight! The

> Duke by that lovely Extasie, carry'd beyond himself, sunk over the expiring Fair, in Raptures too powerful for description!

Manley (1663–1724) wrote novels of the secret lives of high society which were both erotic and scandalous. Her work bears comparison with that of Jackie Collins and modern magazine treatments of Hollywood stars and, in Britain, royalty. The scandal of the present extract is that it alludes to the first Earl of Portland who was said to have seduced and subsequently abandoned a friend's daughter in just such a way. There may also be an **autobiographical** dimension in that Manley claimed she too had been lured into a bigamous marriage by her guardian. Liberally capitalised nouns were a regular feature of *spelling from the seventeenth to the nineteenth centuries. (Text in D. Spender and J. Todd (eds) *Anthology of British Women Writers*, London, 1989: 165–6.)

5.2.3 b JANE AUSTEN, opening of *Pride and Prejudice*, 1797, pub. 1813

> It is a truth universally acknowledged, that a single man in possession of a good fortune, must be in want of a wife.
>
> However little known the feelings or views of such a man may be on his first entering a neighbourhood, this truth is so well fixed in the minds of the surrounding families, that he is considered as the rightful property of some one or other of their daughters.
>
> 'My dear Mr. Bennet,' said his lady to him one day, 'have you heard that Netherfield Park is let at last?'
>
> Mr Bennet replied that he had not.
>
> 'But it is,' returned she; 'for Mrs Long has just been here, and she told me all about it.'
>
> Mr Bennet made no answer.
>
> 'Do you not want to know who has taken it?' cried his wife impatiently.
>
> 'You want to tell me, and I have no objection to hearing it.'
>
> This was invitation enough.
>
> 'Why, my dear, you must know, Mrs Long says that Netherfield is taken by a young man of large fortune from the north of England; that he came down on Monday in a chaise and four to see the place, and was so much delighted with it that he agreed with Mr Morris immediately; that he is to take possession before Michaelmas, and some of his servants are to be in the house by the end of next week.'

Austen (1775–1817) was a rector's daughter who lived most of her life in moderately well-to-do circumstances in Hampshire. According to one commentator, 'Her life was inconspicuous for its lack of event – allowing **biographers** to make it a study in quiet contemplation or quiet frustration' (Ousby 1992: 49). Her novels are sometimes referred to as 'classic **realist**', but are notable for their subtle shifts in **point of view**, *irony and their 'rounded' **characterisation**.

5.2.3 c MARY SHELLEY, from *Frankenstein, or The Modern Prometheus*, 1818, Ch. 17

[The 'fiend' continues to reproach his creator for making him what he is and then disowning him; also for failing to make him a mate.]

'You are in the wrong,' replied the fiend; 'and, instead of threatening, I am content to reason to you. I am malicious because I am miserable. Am I not shunned and hated by all mankind? You, my creator, would tear me to pieces, and triumph; remember that, and tell me why I should pity man more than he pities me? You would not call it murder if you could precipitate me into one of those ice-riffs, and destroy my frame, the work of your own hands. Shall I respect man when he contemns me? Let him live with me in the interchange of kindness; and, instead of injury, I would bestow every benefit upon him with tears of gratitude at his acceptance But that cannot be; the human senses are insurmountable barriers to our union. Yet mine shall not be the submission of abject slavery. I will revenge my injuries: if I cannot inspire love, I will cause fear; and chiefly towards you my arch-enemy, because my creator, do I swear inextinguishable hatred. Have a care: I will work at your destruction, nor finish until I desolate your heart, so that you shall curse the hour of your birth.'

A fiendish rage animated him as he said this; his face was wrinkled into contortions too horrible for human eyes to behold; but presently he calmed himself and proceeded – 'I intended to reason. This passion is detrimental to me; for you do not reflect that you are the cause of its excess. If any being felt emotions of benevolence towards me, I should return them an hundred and an hundredfold; for that one creature's sake, I would make peace with the whole kind! But I now indulge in dreams of bliss that cannot be realised. What I ask of you is reasonable and moderate; I demand a creature of another sex, but as hideous as myself; the gratification is small, but it is all that I can receive, and it shall content me. It is true we shall be monsters, cut off from all the world; but on that account we shall be more attached to one another. Our lives will not be happy, but they will be harmless, and free from the misery I now feel. Oh! my creator, make me happy; let me feel gratitude towards you for one benefit! Let me see that I excite the sympathy of some existing thing; do not deny me my request!'

Mary Shelley's *mythic story of science-gone-wrong and human 'progress' at the expense of a slave/worker is far different from what many modern viewers of horror films staring Boris Karloff or Peter Cushing have come to expect. It's also much tougher and more argumentative than Branagh's sentimental and misleadingly named film *Mary Shelley's Frankenstein* (1994). The above extract gives fair notice of these concerns and qualities. Both teller and tale, for long excluded from the **canon** of LITERATURE studied at college, now receive considerable attention from FEMINIST, PSYCHOANALYTIC, MARXIST and POSTCOLONIAL critics. How might *you* *adapt this passage from **novel** into **film** (or some other medium)?

Compare: Caliban and Prospero in 5.3.2 b; also Friday and Crusoe in 5.2.2 b–c.

5.2.3 d CHARLOTTE BRONTË, ending of *Jane Eyre*, 1847

[Edward Rochester and Jane Eyre are drawn together, after many trials, tribulations and separations, by hearing one another's voices calling to them from the air.

Rochester has been blinded and crippled trying to save his 'mad' first wife from a fatal fire. Jane Eyre is the narrator.]

> Reader, it was on Monday night – near midnight – that I too had received the mysterious summons: those were the very words by which I replied to it. I listened to Mr Rochester's narrative, but made no disclosure in return. [. . .]
>
> 'You cannot now wonder,' continued my master, 'that when you rose upon me so unexpectedly last night, I had difficulty in believing you any other than a mere voice and vision, something that would melt me to silence and annihilation, as the midnight whisper and mountain echo had melted before. Now, I thank God! I know it to be otherwise. Yes, I thank God!'
>
> He put me off his knee, rose and reverently lifted his hat from his brow, and bending his sightless eyes to the earth, he stood in mute devotion. Only the last words of the worship were audible –
>
> 'I thank my Maker, that, in the midst of judgement, He has remembered mercy. I humbly entreat my Redeemer to give me strength to lead henceforth a purer life than I have done hitherto!'
>
> Then he stretched his hand out to be led. I took that dear hand, held it a moment to my lips, and then let it pass round my shoulder: being so much lower of stature than he, I served both for his prop and guide. We entered the wood and wended homeward.

FEMINISTS and others have argued long and hard about the 'progressive' or 'conservative' dimensions of: Jane Eyre as a **character**; *Jane Eyre* as a **novel**, and Charlotte Brontë as an **author** (a succession of **films** further complicates perceptions). These three (or four) elements inevitably tend to get mixed up, but nonetheless need to be carefully distinguished. The first person fictional narrator, Jane, uses a classic instance of the 'dear reader' mode of **address** to an implied reader. In what ways do you, as an actual reader, **respond**?

Compare: 5.2.3 e for another view of Edward Rochester and the (not so) 'mad' Mrs Rochester.

5.2.3 e JEAN RHYS, from *Wide Sargasso Sea*, 1968, p.85

[The narrator is Edward Rochester, a well-to-do Englishman visiting the West Indies. Antoinette is his wife, a Creole woman, who gradually finds herself stretched to breaking point between two communities. She is the 'mad' Mrs Rochester whom we never see in Brontë's *Jane Eyre*, above.]

> 'Did you hear what that girl was singing?' Antoinette said.
>
> 'I don't always understand what they say or sing.' Or anything else.
>
> 'It was a song about a white cockroach. That's me. That's what they call all of us who were here before their own people in Africa sold them to the slave traders. And I've heard English women call us white niggers. So between you I often wonder who I am and where is my country and where do I belong and why was I ever born at all. Will you go now please. I must dress like Christophine said.'
>
> After I had waited half an hour I knocked at her door. There was no answer so I asked Baptiste to bring me something to eat. He was sitting under the Seville orange tree at the end of the veranda. He served the food with such a mournful expression that I thought these people are very vulnerable. How old was I when I learned to hide

> what I felt? A very small boy. Six, five, even earlier. It was necessary, I was told, and
> that view I have always accepted. If these mountains challenge me, or Baptiste's
> face, or Antoinette's eyes, they are mistaken, melodramatic, unreal (England must
> be quite unreal and like a dream she said).

Rhys (1894–1979) was herself part Creole. She was born in Dominica and came to England at the age of 16. Her 'prequel' to *Jane Eyre* is now recognised as a **classic** instance of the de- and **recentring** of a mainstream Western novel. Antoinette is in effect the **absence** of Brontë's novel turned into a **presence**: a dead **silence** endowed with speech and life.

Also see: POSTCOLONIALISM, FEMINISM. Compare: 5.2.3 d; also Defoe and Holdsworth 5.2.2 b–c.

5.2.4 Further post/colonial tales

5.2.4 a JONATHAN SWIFT, from *A Modest Proposal for preventing the Children of poor People in Ireland, from being a Burden to their Parents or Country; and for making them beneficial to the Publick*, 1729

> I shall now therefore humbly purpose my own thoughts, which I hope will not be
> liable to the least objection.
>
> I have been assured by a very knowing American of my acquaintance in London,
> that a young healthy child well nursed is at a year old a most delicious, nourishing,
> and wholesome food, whether stewed, roasted, baked, or boiled; and I make no doubt
> that it will equally serve in a fricassee or a ragout.
>
> I do therefore humbly offer it to public consideration that of the hundred and
> twenty thousand children, already computed [in Ireland], twenty thousand may be
> reserved for breed, whereof only one fourth part to be males, which is more than we
> allow to sheep, black cattle, or swine; and my reason is that these children are seldom
> the fruits of marriage, a circumstance not much regarded by our savages, therefore
> one male will be sufficient to serve four females. That the remaining hundred
> thousand may at a year old be offered in sale to the persons of quality and fortune
> through the kingdom, always advising the mother to let them suck plentifully in the
> last month, so as to render them plump and fat for a good table. A child will make
> two dishes at an entertainment for friends; and when the family dines alone, the fore
> or hind quarter will make a reasonable dish, and seasoned with a little pepper or salt
> will be very good boiled on the fourth day, especially in winter.
>
> I have reckoned upon a medium that a child just born will weigh twelve pounds,
> and in a solar year if tolerably nursed increaseth to twenty-eight pounds.
>
> I grant this food will be somewhat dear, and therefore very proper for landlords,
> who, as they have already devoured most of the parents, seem to have the best title to
> the children.

Swift's *satire is all the more savage for scrupulously observing the **discourse** of those contemporary 'projectors' (i.e. speculators) who proposed a neatly economic solution to every human ill. In this case the butt is English absentee landlords in particular and early eighteenth-century British government policy in general. Both had effectively 'devoured' the *Irish by enforced export of foodstuffs and other goods, while at the same time depriving them of self-sufficiency. The devouring of actual *bodies was the next logical step. The reference to the 'American of my acquaintance' (who presumably was also implicated in 'devouring' the land and livelihoods of the native Indians at the time) is a reminder that *colonisation was an interlinked process taking place beyond as well as within Britain. Swift (1667–1745), born in Dublin of English parents, was Dean of St Patrick's Cathedral, Dublin.

Compare: Pope 5.1.4 b.

5.2.4 b RUDYARD KIPLING, 'The Story of Muhammad Din' (entire) 1888

Who is the happy man? He that sees in his own house at home, little children crowned with dust, leaping and falling and crying –

Munichandra, translated by Professor Peterson

The polo-ball was an old one, scarred, chipped, and dinted. It stood on the mantel-piece among the pipe-stems which Imam Din, *khitmatgar*, was cleaning for me.

'Does the Heaven-born want this ball?' said Imam Din deferentially.

The Heaven-born set no particular store by it; but of what use was a polo-ball to a *khitmatgar*?

'By Your Honour's favour, I have a little son. He has seen this ball, and desires it to play with. I do not want it for myself.'

No one would for an instant accuse portly old Imam Din of wanting to play with polo-balls. He carried out the battered thing into the veranda; and there followed a hurricane of joyful squeaks, a patter of small feet, and the *thud-thud-thud* of the ball rolling along the ground. Evidently the little son had been waiting outside the door to secure his treasure. But how had he managed to see that polo-ball?

Next day, coming back from office half an hour earlier than usual, I was aware of a small figure in the dining-room – a tiny, plump figure in a ridiculously inadequate shirt which came, perhaps, half-way down the tubby stomach. It wandered round the room, thumb in mouth, crooning to itself as it took stock of the pictures. Undoubtedly this was the 'little son'.

He had no business in my room, of course; but was so deeply absorbed in his discoveries that he never noticed me in the doorway. I stepped into the room and startled him nearly into a fit. He sat down on the ground with a gasp. His eyes opened, and his mouth followed suit. I knew what was coming, and fled, followed by a long, dry howl which reached the servants' quarters far more quickly than any command of mine had ever done. In ten seconds Imam Din was in the dining-room. Then despairing sobs arose, and I returned to find Imam Din admonishing the small sinner who was using most of his shirt as a handkerchief.

'This boy,' said Imam Din judicially, 'is a *budmash* – a big *budmash*. He will, without doubt, go to the *jail-khana* for his behaviour.' Renewed yells from the penitent, and an elaborate apology to myself from Imam Din.

'Tell the baby,' said I, 'that the *Sahib* is not angry, and take him away.' Imam Din conveyed my forgiveness to the offender, who had now gathered all his shirt round his neck, stringwise, and the yell subsided into a sob. The two set off for the door. 'His name,' said Imam Din, as though the name were part of the crime, 'is Muhammad

Din, and he is a *budmash*.' Freed from present danger, Muhammad Din turned round in his father's arms, and said gravely, 'It is true that my name is Muhammad Din, Tahib, but I am not a *budmash*. I am a man!'

From that day dated my acquaintance with Muhammad Din. Never again did he come into my dining-room, but on the neutral ground of the garden we greeted each other with much state, though our conversation was confined to '*Talaam, tahib*' from his side, and '*Salaam Muhammad Din*' from mine. Daily on my return from office, the little white shirt and the fat little body used to rise from the shade of the creeper-covered trellis where they had been hid; and daily I checked my horse here, that my salutation might not be slurred over or given unseemly.

Muhammad Din never had any companions. He used to trot about the compound, in and out of the castor-oil bushes, on mysterious errands of his own. One day I stumbled upon some of his handiwork far down the grounds. He had half buried the polo-ball in dust, and stuck six shrivelled old marigold flowers in a circle round it. Outside that circle again was a rude square, traced out in bits of red brick alternating with fragments of broken china; the whole bounded by a little bank of dust. The water-man from the well-curb put in a plea for the small architect, saying that it was only the play of a baby and did not much disfigure my garden.

Heaven knows that I had no intention of touching the child's work then or later; but, that evening, a stroll through the garden brought me unawares full on it; so that I trampled, before I knew, marigold-heads, dust-bank, and fragments of broken soap-dish into confusion past all hope of mending. Next morning, I came upon Muhammad Din crying softly to himself over the ruin I had wrought. Some one had cruelly told him that the *Sahib* was very angry with him for spoiling the garden, and had scattered his rubbish, using bad language the while. Muhammad Din laboured for an hour at effacing every trace of the dust-bank and pottery fragments, and it was with a tearful and apologetic face that he said, '*Talaam Tahib*,' when I came home from office. A hasty inquiry resulted in Imam Din informing Muhammad Din that, by my singular favour, he was permitted to disport himself as he pleased. Whereat the child took heart and fell to tracing the ground-plan of an edifice which was to eclipse the marigold-polo-ball creation.

For some months the chubby little eccentricity revolved in his humble orbit among the castor-oil bushes and in the dust; always fashioning magnificent palaces from stale flowers thrown away by the bearer, smooth water-worn pebbles, bits of broken glass, and feathers pulled, I fancy, from my fowls – always alone, and always crooning to himself.

A gaily-spotted seashell was dropped one day close to the last of his little buildings; and I looked that Muhammad Din should build something more than ordinarily splendid on the strength of it. Nor was I disappointed. He meditated for the better part of an hour, and his crooning rose to a jubilant song. Then he began tracing in the dust. It would certainly be a wonderous palace, this one, for it was two yards long and a yard broad in ground-plan. But the palace was never completed.

Next day there was no Muhammad Din at the head of the carriage-drive, and no '*Talaam, Tahib*' to welcome my return. I had grown accustomed to the greeting, and its omission troubled me. Next day Imam Din told me that the child was suffering slightly from fever and needed quinine. He got the medicine, and an English doctor.

'They have no stamina, these brats,' said the doctor, as he left Imam Din's quarters.

A week later, though I would have given much to have avoided it, I met on the road to the Mussulman burying-ground Imam Din, accompanied by one other friend, carrying in his arms, wrapped in a white cloth, all that was left of little Muhammad Din.

Born in Bombay of well-to-do English parents, Kipling (1865–1936) was sent to private school in England at the age of six and had a miserable childhood. On returning to India in 1882 he worked as a journalist and short-story writer on the *Civil and Military Gazette*, which was read by the Anglo-Indian community. The above story first circulated there before being printed in the collection *Plain Tales from the Hills*. Kipling's stories, poems and novels – including *Barrack-Room Ballads* (1892), *The Jungle Books* (1894, 1895), *Kim* (1901) and the *Just So Stories* (1902) – are remarkable for their variety and versatility; also for their critical, teasing and sometimes enigmatic visions of empire and *colonialism. After 1898 Kipling visited South Africa regularly. In 1907 he became the first English writer to receive the Nobel Prize for Literature. POSTCOLONIALISM has prompted a thorough revision of Kipling's significance.

Also see: NEW CRITICISM, Example, pp. 81–82; **Bibles, holy books and myths**. Compare: Conrad 5.2.4 c; Rushdie 5.4.2.

5.2.4 c JOSEPH CONRAD, from *Heart of Darkness*, 1902

[There are inverted commas throughout the following text because it is part of a tale told by a narrator (Marlow) as he and four friends wait for the tide to turn in the Thames estuary. Marlow is telling of a trip up another ancient river, the Congo, and it is on its banks that he reports having seen the following sight.]

'Dark human shapes could be made out in the distance, flitting indistinctly against the gloomy border of the forest, and near the river two bronze figures, leaning on tall spears, stood in the sunlight under fantastic head-dresses of spotted skins, warlike and still in statuesque repose. And from right to left along the lighted shore moved a wild and gorgeous apparition of a woman.

'She walked with measured steps, draped in striped and fringed cloths, treading the earth proudly, with a slight jingle and flash of barbarous ornaments. She carried her head high; her hair was done in the shape of a helmet; she had brass leggings to the knee, brass wire gauntlets to the elbow, a crimson spot on her tawny cheek, innumerable necklaces of glass beads on her neck; bizarre things, charms, gifts of witch-men, that hung about her, glittered and trembled at every step. She must have had the value of several elephant tusks upon her. She was savage and superb, wild-eyed and magnificent; there was something ominous and stately in her deliberate progress. And in the hush that had fallen suddenly upon the whole sorrowful land, the immense wilderness, the colossal body of the fecund and mysterious life seemed to look at her, pensive, as though it had been looking at the image of its own tenebrous and passionate soul.

'She came abreast of the steamer, stood still, and faced us. Her long shadow fell to the water's edge. Her face had a tragic and fierce aspect of wild sorrow and of dumb pain mingled with the fear of some struggling, half-shaped resolve. She stood looking at us without a stir, and like the wilderness itself, with an air of brooding over and inscrutable purpose.'

Conrad (1857–1924) had himself, like the narrator of *Heart of Darkness*, served on boats up the (Belgian) Congo. Many of the events and figures in the novel are in some measure **auto/biographical** and **hi/storical**. POSTCOLONIAL and FEMINIST critics have had much to say about this and similar passages for their construction of 'female' and 'black' as **other** fixed by the gaze of a white, Western male **self**. Conrad was a Pole who became a naturalised British **subject** in 1886. For *Leavis (1948: 9), Conrad was one of the four 'great' English novelists and has been part of the **canon** ever since.

Compare: Rhys 5.2.3 e.

5.2.4 d ZORA NEALE HURSTON, from *Their Eyes Were Watching God*, 1937 Chapter 5

[The first lamp is being lit in an all-black township in the USA.]

By five o'clock the town was full of every kind of a vehicle and swarming with people. They wanted to see that lamp lit at dusk. Near the time, Joe assembled everybody in the street before the store and made a speech.

'Folkses, de sun is goin' down. De Sun-maker brings it up in de mornin', and de Sun-maker sends it tuh bed at night. Us poor weak humans can't do nothin' tuh hurry it up nor to slow it down. All we can do, if we want any light after de settin' or befo' de risin', is tuh make some light ourselves. So dat's how come lamps was made. Dis evenin' we'se all assembled heah tuh light uh lamp. Dis occasion is something for us all tuh remember tuh our dyin' day. De first street lamp in uh colored town. Lift yo' eyes and gaze on it. And when Ah touch de match tuh dat lamp-wick let de light penetrate inside of yuh, and let it shine, let it shine, let it shine. Brother Davis, lead us in a word uh prayer. Ask uh blessin' on dis town in uh most particular manner.'

While Davis chanted a traditional prayer-poem with his own variations, Joe mounted the box that had been placed for the purpose and opened the brazen door of the lamp. As the word Amen was said, he touched the lighted match to the wick, and Mrs. Bogle's alto burst out in:

We'll walk in de light, de beautiful light
Come where the dew drops of mercy shine bright
Shine all around us by day and by night
Jesus, the light of the world.

They, all of them, all of the people took it up and sung it over and over until it was wrung dry, and no further innovations of tone and tempo were conceivable. Then they hushed and ate barbecue.

Hurston (*c*.1891–1960) grew up in Eatonville, Florida, the first 'incorporated' black township in America, and it is upon this that the above civic lamp-lighting scene is based. Hurston was an eminent anthropologist, as well as a novelist, and knit many of her researches into the black *oral traditions of the American South and the Caribbean into her writing.

Also see: **auto/biography**; **hi/story**; *Christianity. Compare: 5.2.4 e–f, Douglass and Morrison 5.2.2 d–e.

5.2.4 e AMOS TUTUOLA, from *The Palm Wine Drinkard*, 1952, Section 6:18–19

[A man hears the character and destiny of his son interpreted by the Babalawo ('doctor') on the basis of the child's 'esent'aye' – literally 'footprint in the earth'. Two other 'characters' have already been predicted in this way.]

> But then it was 'the great grief which droops the heads of elders' for Kimi Adugbo when he heard the bad 'esent'aye' of his child that morning. He was so sad that his mouth rejected food and drink, and great depression overwhelmed him immediately. Even the grief was overmuch for him so that he was unable to thank the Babalawo when he was leaving for his house that morning. After a few days, however, Kimi Adugbo accepted his fate and then he continued to be as cheerful to the people as he was before the 'esent'aye' of his child was read to him.
>
> When Kimi Adugbo's child became eight days old, he reluctantly gave him a name which was ALAGEMO. The meaning of this name 'Alagemo' is chameleon worshipper. But Kimi Adugbo named this his child in proverb, 'The Agemo dancer said that he had done all he could to train his child how to dance. But if he does not know how to dance, that will be his fault.'
>
> Moreover, his child was born in the month of Agemo (July). But now it is known that the prince of Oba chose the destiny of poverty and wretchedness, the daughter of the Otun Oba chose the destiny of harmful brawls, while the boy of Kimi Adugbo chose the destiny of the multifarious evil characters from Creator before the three of them were coming to earth.

Tutuola's tales are largely based upon Yoruba traditions circulating *orally in his native Nigeria. The underlying conception of **character** and the whole pacing and texture of the **narrative** (including frequent appeals to the **authority** of proverbs) are far different from those in the Western mainstream novel. So are the **myths** and social practices referred to – here surrounding the act of *naming.

Compare: Achebe 5.2.4 f and Behn and Defoe 5.2.2 a–b.

5.2.4 f CHINUA ACHEBE, *Things Fall Apart*, 1958, Chapter 13: 84

[A death is announced in the traditional Igbo manner.]

> The first cock had not crowed, and Umuofia was still swallowed up in sleep and silence when the *ekwe* began to talk, and the cannon shattered the silence. Men stirred on their bamboo beds and listened anxiously. Di-go-go-di-go-di-di-go-go floated in the message-laden night air. The faint and distant wailing of women settled like a sediment of sorrow on the earth. Now and again a full-chested lamentation rose above the wailing whenever a man came into the place of death. He raised his voice once or twice in manly sorrow and then sat down with the other men listening to the endless wailing of the women and the esoteric language of the *ekwe*. Now and again the cannon boomed. The wailing of the women would not be heard beyond the village, but the *ekwe* carried the news to all the nine villages and even beyond. It began by naming the clan: *Umuofia obodo dike*, 'the land of the brave'. *Umuofia obodo dike! Umuofia obodo dike!* It said this over and over again, and as it dwelt on it, anxiety mounted in every heart that heaved on a bamboo bed that night. Then it went nearer

and named the village: *Iguedo of the yellow grinding-stone!* It was Okonkwo's village. Again and again Iguedo was called and men waited breathlessly in all the nine villages. At last the man was named and people sighed 'E-u-u, Ezeudu id dead'.

Achebe's reconstruction of Igbo life up to the time when Nigeria became a British colony (in 1914) has become a **classic** of African literature in English (it has been reprinted nearly forty times in as many years). For many people, its powerfully evocative images of an *oral, organic and largely male-dominated society are held to be an accurate **representation** of pre-*colonialism. Nonetheless, it must also be recognised that the novel is a **hi/story** produced from within its own moment. Written fifty years after the events it represents, but just two before Nigeria gained independence from Britain (in 1960), and nine before the Igbo nation sought independence from the rest of Nigeria as Biafra, the narrative is also about the construction of an *authentic Igbo **identity**. The title is an explicit reference to Yeats's poem *The Second Coming* (1921): 'Things fall apart; the centre cannot hold'. Achebe's **text** must therefore be read **intertextually** as well as **contextually**.

Compare: Death and (not so) grave yards 5.4.5.

5.2.5   News stories

5.2.5 a   *SUN*, 13 February 1989, front page and p.4 (entire story, re-set)

20 YOBS HOLD TRAIN TO RANSOM

By MICHAEL FIELDER

A KNIFE-WIELDING mob held a train to ransom yesterday as they robbed terrified passengers of cash and gems.

The 20-strong black gang RAMPAGED through carriages, RIPPING necklaces and rings from women.

The thugs – known as 'steamers' – SNATCHED cash, watches and other valuables from men.

Two passengers who fought back were savagely SLASHED and beaten by the balaclava-clad yobs.

Terror struck the 1.37am Bedford-to-London train after it pulled into St Albans, Herts.

BOTTLE

The gang of powerfully built West Indians piled on board, carrying knives and Stanley blades. One wielded a bottle.

Then for 16 horrifying minutes, they stormed through the train, screeching threats and abuse.

Three stops later, the mob leaped off at Hendon station in North London, clutching thousands of pounds worth of loot.

They vanished into the darkness before police arrived.

British Transport Police branded the attack 'cowardly, vicious and unpleasant'.

Inspector Martin Pring admitted: 'It caught us completely by surprise.' Officers were called in from weekend leave to join the hunt for the gang.

Police said last night that the train had been 'virtually held to ransom' by the gang in what looked like a carefully planned operation.

No ONE alerted police when the mob stormed aboard at 2.14am.

Two staff were on duty at St Albans station, but thought the youths had merely been at one of the town's discos.

No ONE on the train pulled the communication cord because they were too frightened.

No ONE leaped from the train to dial 999 when it pulled into intermediate stations.

The gang escaped at Hendon – an unmanned station.

When the train stopped at Cricklewood a passenger finally ran to tell the driver what had happened.

The driver used his cab radio to contact a signalman, who told the police.

The two injured passengers were taken to hospital when the train arrived at its St Pancras terminus.

One had stitches to a neck wound. The other was treated for cuts.

By last night, 13 victims had reported being robbed.

One admitted he was so ashamed of being afraid during the attack that he waited 12 hours before phoning the police.

The man said: 'I was disgusted with myself for not doing something, for not fighting back.'

The *Sun* was the highest circulation **news**paper in Britain at the time (advertised sales of 4.35 million per day). Its style of *popular journalism is distinguished by 'dramatic' **narratives** and sharply contrasting **roles** in terms of GENDER, *ethnicity and *class.

Also see: **discourse; realism and representation**. Compare: 5.2.5 b below; Doyle 5.2.5 e.

5.2.5 b *GUARDIAN*, 13 February 1989, front page (entire story, re-set)

BRITISH RAIL'S FIRST 'STEAMING' RAISES CALLS FOR MORE STAFF

PAUL KEEL

The first 'steaming' incident on British Rail has provoked calls for higher staffing levels and additional policing on trains.

A 25-strong gang attacked and robbed passengers early on Sunday on an InterCity train from Bedford to London which had no guard on board.

Wearing balaclavas and brandishing knives, the group snatched cash, jewellery and credit cards from travellers on the 01.37 to King's Cross.

Two passengers were taken to hospital with head and neck injuries.

British Transport Police, which has set up a special incident room to investigate the robberies, said the gang was believed to have boarded at St Albans and left at Hendon 15 minutes later after 'steaming' through the two middle carriages of the four-car-train.

Steaming, in which large groups of robbers intimidate their victims and steal while on the run, is employed increasingly by street gangs and has been used on the London Underground.

Mr John Prescott, Labour's frontbench spokesman on transport, will demand a government statement today on the incident, which he blamed on the rundown of staff.

He added: 'This is the latest outbreak of violence against the travelling public on our railway system. How many more are we going to have to accept? British Rail is becoming a soft touch for violent gangs. Too little priority is being given to passenger safety and too much to saving money.'

Mr Prescott said he would also be demanding the publication of a British Transport Police survey conducted earlier this year which revealed widespread fears of violence among passengers.

This month British Rail vetoed publication of the survey, which it said was 'unscientific' and potentially alarmist.

Detective Inspector David Scudder of the British Transport Police said the attackers used knives and bottles. 'It was a very cowardly, vicious and totally unpleasant attack,' he added.

Another spokesman for the force said: 'We believe there are other passengers who were robbed and have not yet come forward. We would like to hear from them and anyone else who witnessed the incident.'

The *Guardian* was at this time one of the lower-circulation broadsheet **news**papers (advertised sales of 380,000 per day). It is characterised, as are most broadsheets, by an emphasis on argument and institutional agendas; it is also distinguished politically by its liberal and broad left orientation.

Also see: **discourse; realism and representation**. Compare: 5.2.5 a above and 5.2.5 c below; also Doyle 5.2.5 e.

5.2.5 c HEADLINES, LEAD-INS and CAPTIONS

Consider aspects of **discourse** in the following, engaging in detailed **discourse analysis** where possible (also see frameworks and checklists in 4.2).

(i) *Broadsheet and tabloid front-page headlines on main story, 13 October 1992*

Terrorist bombers strike at pub in London's West End	*The Times*
Five hurt in IRA pub bombing	*Guardian*
NOW WE'RE ALL TARGETS	*Daily Express*
THEY RAISE THE STAKES	*Today*
BOOZER BLITZ	*Sun*
NO-CHANCE SALOON	*Daily Star*
Small item on page 2: '350 killed in Cairo earthquake'	*Daily Telegraph*

(ii) *ITV news lead-ins, 5.45 p.m., 24 June 1988*

The news at 5.45 with Fiona Armstrong
Couple change their plea and admit starving their baby to death
The King's Cross inquiry hears the fire was foreseeable
The Germans continue their attacks at Wimbledon
And Britain's Bob Hoskins finds fame and fortune just rabbiting on

(iii) *Captions, counter-captions and alternatives*

The following two captions appeared in British and American local papers during the 1992 Gulf War (19 January). Both were attached to reproductions of an identical military press-release photo.

Captured – Iraqi POWs march through the   *Oxford Mail*
   desert
Captured Iraqi soldiers are marched through   *Philadelphia Citizen's Voice*
   the desert

The captions below were generated in **response** to those above by a group of British and American undergraduates who were examining journalistic technique at the time in Oxford. (Reproduced by courtesy of members of 'Language, Literature, Discourse III', 1991–2. These **rewrites** were accompanied by analytical commentary and discussion, as suggested in 4.4.)

Heroic resistance in the 5th province against the forces of the Western capitalist
   conspiracy.
Arabs, unite to expel the aggressor! Your comrades are in chains.
It's a man's life in the modern army – Employment opportunities in the Middle East.
Desert Storm II – The final reckoning. This time it's for real!
Long shot: Americans, Iraqis, British . . . can you tell the difference at this range?

5.2.5 d TOM LEONARD, 'This is thi six a clock news' from *Unrelated Incidents*, 1983

> this is thi
> six a clock
> news thi
> man said n
> thi reason
> a talk wia
> BBC accent
> iz coz yi
> widny wahnt
> mi ti talk
> aboot thi
> trooth wia
> voice lik
> wanna yoo
> scruff. if
> a toktaboot
> thi trooth
> lik wanna yoo
> scruff yi
> widny thingk
> it wuz troo.
> jist wanna yoo
> scruff tokn.

thirza right
way ti spell
ana right way
ti tok it. this
is me tokn yir
right way a
spellin. this
is ma trooth
yooz doant no
thi trooth
yirsellz cawz
yi canny talk
right. this is
the six a clock
nyooz. belt up.

'Leonard was born in Glasgow in 1944 and still lives there.' Text and this last line
from Hulse *et al. The New Poetry* (1993: 71, 346).

5.2.5 e RODDY DOYLE, *Paddy Clarke ha ha ha*, London: Secker & Warburg, 1993: 226–7

[The story of Paddy Clarke, a ten-year-old in Dublin in 1968. Paddy/Patrick is the
narrator.]

They always talked during The News; they talked about the news. Sometimes it
wasn't really talk, not conversation, just comments.
—Bloody eejit.
—Yes.
   I was able to tell when my da was going to call someone a bloody eejit; his chair
creaked. It was always a man and he was always saying something to an interviewer.
—Who asked him?
   The interviewer had asked him but I knew what my da meant. Sometimes I got
there before him.
—Bloody eejit.
—Good man, Patrick.
   My ma didn't mind me saying Bloody when The News was on. The News was boring
but sometimes I watched it properly, all of it. I thought that the Americans were fighting gorillas in Vietnam; that was what it sounded like. But it didn't make any other
kind of sense. The Israelis were always fighting the Arabs and the Americans were
fighting the gorillas. It was nice that the gorillas had a country of their own, not like
the zoo, and the Americans were killing them for it. There were Americans getting
killed as well. They had helicopters. Mekong Delta. Demilitarised zone. Tet Offensive.
The gorillas in the zoo didn't look like they'd be hard to beat in a war. They were nice
and old looking, brainy looking, and their hair was dirty. Their arms were brilliant;
I'd have loved arms like that. I'd never been on the roof. Kevin had, and his da had
killed him when he found out about it when he got home, and he'd only been on the
kitchen roof, the flat bit. I was up for the gorillas even though two of my uncles
and aunties lived in America. I'd never seen them. They sent us ten dollars, me and
Sinbad, one Christmas. I couldn't remember what I got with my five dollars.

Doyle was born in Dublin in 1958. While lecturing he wrote his first **novel** *The Commitments* (1988), which was *adapted into a **film** with music in 1991. *Paddy Clarke ha ha ha* won the 1993 Booker Prize.

5.2.6   JAMES KELMAN, *How late it was, how late,* London: Secker & Warburg, 1994: 52–3

[The story of an unemployed ex-convict who returns to his native Glasgow, goes blind and finds himself out on the street.]

Ah fuck it man stories, stories, life's full of stories, they're there to help ye out, when ye're in trouble, deep shit, they come to the rescue, and one thing ye learn in life is stories, Sammy's head was fucking full of them, he had met some bastards in his time; it's no as if he was auld either cause he wasnay he was only thirty-eight, he just seemed aulder, cause of the life he had led; when ye come to think about it, the life he had led. [. . .] Maybe he should go to Glancy's. It was an idea. Bound to be some cunt there that would lend him a couple of quid; even auld fucking Morris behind the bar, that crabbit auld bastard, even he would help Sammy out surely to fuck. Nay eyes man know what I'm saying nay fucking eyes! Jesus christ almighty! Okay relax. The traffic was fierce but and he had to cross this road and there was nay chance of crossing this road, no on his fucking tod, it wasnay fucking possible; out the question.
   Patience was a virtue right enough.
   Patience. Come on ya bastards! He started kicking his heel against the kerb, keeping his head down for some reason. I'm blind, he said in the offchance somebody was there. Cause there was bound to be. Nay takers but. Patience, ye had to learn it. How to just bloody stand there. What was that song . . . ? Fucking song man what was it again?
   Voices at last. He kicked the kerb again. Could ye give me a hand across the street? he said.
   What?
   I cannay see. I'm blind.
   Ye're blind?
   Aye.

Kelman was born in Glasgow in 1946 and still lives there. *How late it was, how late* won the 1994 Booker Prize. This prompted much heated (but not always illuminated) comment on the novel's allegedly gratuitous swearing. There was also much more or less (c)overt disapproval of its realisation of a Glaswegian **accent** and a cry for **standards** to be maintained in language, behaviour and much else. See also 5.2.5 d, e.

5.3 SCRIPTS AND TRANSCRIPTS – CONVERSATION, INTERVIEW AND DRAMA

5.3.1 a A SUPERMARKET EXCHANGE OVER CHANGE (transcript as script)

[At a supermarket checkout.]

> CUSTOMER: There's a mistake here [*holds out hand with change in*].
> CASHIER: Pardon?
> CUSTOMER: A mistake has been made.
> CASHIER: [blank look]
> CUSTOMER: You've made a mistake.
> CASHIER: What's wrong?

Notice that the whole dynamic and significance of this **dialogue** might be changed if the participants were identified by, say, age, ethnicity, class, sex, general appearance and personal manner, and if the time, place and other aspects of **context** (from immediate situation to general social-historical moment) were specified. For **discourse analysis** of this passage see pp. 190–191.

5.3.1 b FAMILY CONVERSATION (partial transcript)

[Sasha a girl aged 4; Ivan a boy aged 8; Tania a woman aged 38; Rob a man aged 46. Pauses at one point per second; (.) indicates half a second or less. Emphasis is underlined. { marks overlap as people speak at once.]

> SASHA: dad . . . <u>dad</u> .. can you . can you give me . errr . somethin(k) for this
> TANIA: rob . can you give her a bowl for her chocolate egg
> ROB: ok . . . . what
> TANIA: never mind . {here sash . . .
> IVAN: {look mum (.) i'm on level five of the humans . i've killed all
>   the tyrannosauruses without {being killed once
> SASHA: {no they <u>aren't</u> (.) they're <u>sharks</u>
> IVAN: no they're <u>not</u> (.) <u>look</u> . . . stupid.
> TANIA: can you move (.) love . i need the table . . . what are you writing
> ROB: . . . <u>this</u>.

A fuller transcription would register *intonation (permutations of rising, falling and even tone); voice quality (quiet, loud, whispered, husky, etc.). A *phonetic transcription would use the International Phonetic Alphabet (IPA) and register more precisely the many variations in actual articulation of sounds (Sasha's faintly unvoiced 'somethin(*k*)' for our usual voiced or absent somethin(*g*) is a gesture in this direction.)

5.3.1 c FACTORY COMMISSION INTERVIEW with MILLHAND, 1852 (partial transcript for official record)

What age are you?
Twenty-three.
Where do you live?
At Leeds
What time did you begin work at the factory?
When I was six years old.
At whose factory did you work?
Mr Burk's.
What kind of mill is it?
Flax mill.
What was your business in that mill?
I was a little doffer.[1]
What were your hours of labour in that mill?
From 5 in the morning till 9 at night, when they were thronged.[2]
For how long a time together have you worked that excessive length of time?
For about a year. [. . .]
You are considerably deformed in person as a consequence of this labour?
Yes I am.
And what time did it come on?
I was about 13 years old when it began coming, and it has got worse since; it is five years since my mother died, and my mother was never able to get me a good pair of stays to hold me up, and when my mother died I had to do for myself, and got me a pair.
Were you perfectly straight and healthy before you worked at a mill?
Yes, I was as straight a little girl as ever went up and down town.
Were you straight till you were 13?
Yes I was.
Did your deformity come upon you with much pain and weariness?
Yes, I cannot express the pain all the time it was coming.
Do you know of anybody that has been similarly injured in their health?
Yes, in their health, but not many deformed as I am.
It is very common to have weak ankles and crooked knees?
Yes, very common indeed.
This is brought on by stopping the spindle?
Yes.
Where are you now?
In the poor house.
State what you think as to the circumstances in which you have been placed during all this time of labour, and what you have considered about it as to the hardship and cruelty of it.
The witness was too much affected to answer the question.

---

[1] unloading the raw flax or finished linen
[2] busy

This is one of many such transcripts in Parliamentary Commissions on factory (and mining) conditions that were instituted in the early nineteenth century. The **discourses** of male middle-class, officially 'concerned', expert **addresser** and female, working-class, personally experienced **addressee** are characteristic. But the **dialogue** is also, of course, unique (the woman's name was Elizabeth Bentley). The industrial situation had hardly changed from the time of Friedrich Engels's *Condition of the Working Class in England in 1844* (1845). Engels himself gathered some of the material for this by observing and talking with workers at his family's cotton mill in Manchester. 1844 was the year he met and started working with Karl *Marx.

Compare: Freud 5.3.1 d. (A full text can be found in J. Carey (ed.) *The Faber Book of Reportage*, 1987: 295–8.)

5.3.1 d SIGMUND FREUD, from *Fragment of an Analysis of a Case of Hysteria* ('Dora')

[Interviews 1900, case history first drafted 1901, revised version published 1905. (1905: 104–5).

'Dora' – the name Freud chose to protect the identity of his patient – is an 18-year-old woman from a well-to-do Viennese family. She has been sent to Freud by her father, who is highly upset about his daughter's anxieties. During the course of the interviews it turns out that Dora is worried about several things: her father's infidelities; also a pass made at her by her father's friend ('Herr K') by a lake at 'L——'. At this point Freud is probing Dora about the details of a dream in which her father had saved the family from a fire but her mother had attempted to return to save a 'jewel-case'.]

> Much of the dream, however, still remained to be interpreted, and I proceeded with my question: 'What is this about the jewel-case that your mother wanted to save?'
> 'Mother is very fond of jewellery and had had a lot given her by Father.'
> 'And you?'
> 'I used to be very fond of jewellery too, once; but I have not worn any since my illness. Once four years ago' (a year before the dream), 'Father and Mother had a great dispute about a piece of jewellery. Mother wanted to be given a particular thing – pearl drops to wear in her ears. But Father does not like that kind of thing, and he brought her a bracelet instead of the drops. She was furious, and told him that as he had spent so much money on a present she did not like he had better just give it to someone else.'
> 'I dare say you thought to yourself you would accept it with pleasure.'
> 'I don't know.[1] I don't in the least know how Mother comes into the dream; she was not with us at L— at the time.'[2]
> 'I will explain that to you presently. Does nothing else occur to you in connection with the jewel-case? So far you have only talked about jewellery and have said nothing about a case.'

---

[1] The regular formula with which she confessed to anything that had been repressed.

[2] This remark gave evidence of a complete misunderstanding of the rules of dream-interpretation, though on other occasions Dora was perfectly familiar with them. This fact, coupled with the hesitancy and meagreness of her associations with the jewel-case, showed me that we were here dealing with material which had been very intensely repressed.

'Yes, Herr K. had made me a present of an expensive jewel-case a little time before.'

'Then a return-present would have been very appropriate. Perhaps you do not know that 'jewel-case' [Schmuckkästchen] is a favorite expression for the same thing that you alluded to not long ago by means of the reticule you were wearing[3] – for the female genitals, I mean.'

'I knew *you* would say that.'[4]

'That is to say, *you* knew that it *was* so. – The meaning of the dream is now becoming even clearer. You said to yourself: "This man is persecuting me; he wants to force his way into my room. My 'jewel-case' is in danger, and if anything happens it will be Father's fault." For that reason in the dream you chose a situation which expresses the opposite – a danger from which your father is *saving* you. In this part of the dream everything is turned into its opposite; you will soon discover why. As you say, the mystery turns upon your mother. You ask how she comes into the dream. She is, as you know, your former rival in your father's affections. In the incident of the bracelet, you would have been glad to accept what your mother had rejected. Now let us put 'give' instead of 'accept' and 'withhold' instead of 'reject'. Then it means that you were ready to give your father what your mother withheld from him; and the thing in question was connected with jewellery.[5]

---

[3] This reference to the reticule will be explained further.

[4] A very common way of putting aside a piece of knowledge that emerges from the repressed.

[5] We shall be able later on to interpret even the drops in a way which will fit in with the context.

Freud (1859–1939) was 44 when he conducted these **dialogues**. His practice was never to take notes during them but to write them up afterwards as **narratives** and case-**histories** from memory. The interviews took place October–December 1900. His first full draft was completed 24 January 1901. It then bore the title *Dreams and Hysteria*. The above extract is from near the middle of the version Freud revised for publication in 1905 under the more familiar title presented above. The fact that this case history is avowedly 'A Fragment' (and therefore in some sense a 'hole' rather than a 'whole') has inevitably prompted many commentators to 'fill' it. PSYCHOLOGICAL and FEMINIST critics have been especially active in this area. So have **discourse analysts** of all kinds. The effect has often been to interrogate Freudian psychoanalysis in general (including the post-Freudian analyses of *Lacan) as well as the man Sigmund Freud himself. Hélène Cixous scripted a dramatic critique of Freud's 'Dora' (*Portrait of Dora*, 1976). Others **rewrites** generated by students and teachers of English in response to the above passage include: *Dora as Annotator and Translator*; *Educating Dora* (cf. Russell 5.3.5 c); *Sherlock Freud as Sigmund Holmes: The Case of Missing Genitals – sorry – Jewel-case*; *Not So Happy Families – the Group Therapy Version*. You can doubtless generate some more.

Also see: PSYCHOLOGY, Activity (c); **foreground, background and point of view**; **genre**. Compare: 5.3.1 c above; Manley 5.2.3 a; Defoe 5.2.2 b; Shakespeare 5.3.2 b.

5.3.2   Early English stages

5.3.2 a CHESTER MYSTERY CYCLE, from *Noah's Flood*, performed c.1340–c.1550, first pub. nineteenth century

[God's flood is coming, the ark is ready but Noah's wife is not prepared to leave her friends.]

NOAH: Come in, Wife, in twenty devils way,
   Or else stand there without.   220
HAM: Shall we all fetch her in?
NOAH: Yea, son, in Christ's blessing and mine,
   I would ye hied you betime,
   For of this flood I am in doubt.

           [*Song*]

GOOD GOSSIP: The flood comes fleeting in full fast,
   On every side that spreadeth full far.
   For fear of drowning I am aghast;
   Good gossip, let us draw near.
   And let us drink ere we depart,
   For oftentimes we have done so.   230
   For at one draught thou drink a quart,
   And so will I do ere I go.
NOAH'S WIFE: Here is a pottle of Malmsey good and strong;
   It will rejoice both heart and tongue.
   Though Noah think us never so long,
   Yet we will drink atyte.
JAPHETH: Mother, we pray you all together –
   For we are here, your own childer –
   Come into the ship for fear of the weather,
   For his love that you bought!   240
NOAH'S WIFE: That will I not for all your call
   But I have my gossips all.
SHEM: I faith, mother, yet thou shall,
   Whether thou will or nought. [*Drags her aboard*]
NOAH: Welcome, wife, into this boat.
NOAH'S WIFE: [*slaps him*] Have thou that for thy note!
NOAH: Aha, Mary, this is hot!
   It is good for to be still.
   Ah, children, methinks my boat remeves.
   Our tarrying here me highly grieves.   250
   Over the land the water spreads;
   God do as He will.

   [*Then they sing and* NOAH *shall speak again.*]

NOAH: Ah, great God that art so good,
   That workes not thy will is wood.
   Now all this world is on a flood.

223. hied – hurried. 224. in doubt – afraid. 225. GOSSIP – companion; fleeting – flowing. 236. atyte – together. 254. wood – mad.

This **comic** and potentially **carnivalesque** interlude with Noah's wife is not to be found in the **Bible** story of Noah's ark and the flood (*Genesis*, 5: 28–9). It shows how **drama** can be developed out of relatively fixed rituals. The Mystery cycles presented the *Christian **hi/story** from Creation through the Crucifixion to Doomsday. They were put on by city guilds and performed by amateurs as street **theatre** every Spring. This particular play was put on, appropriately enough, by the water carriers guild. Like other pageants it may have been played on a makeshift stage or a specially constructed mobile pageant wagon. (Full text in A.C. Cawley, *Everyman and the Medieval Miracle Plays*, London, 1977: 35–49.)

5.3.2 b WILLIAM SHAKESPEARE, from *The Tempest* Act I sc. ii, performed 1611, pub. 1623

[Prospero, exiled Duke of Milan and a magician, is chastising his servant, Caliban, for not working hard enough and for trying to rape his daughter, Miranda. Caliban is a native of the island and a witch's son.]

PROSPERO: Thou poisonous slave, got by the devil himself
    Upon thy wicked dam, come forth!   320

        [Enter Caliban]

CALIBAN: As wicked dew as e'er my mother brush'd
    With raven feather from unwholesome fen
    Drop on you both! a south-west blow on ye
    And blister you all o'er!
PROSPERO: For this, be sure, to-night thou shalt have cramps,
    Side-stitches that shall pen thy breath up; urchins
    Shall forth at vast of night, that they may work
    All exercise on thee: thou shalt be pinch'd
    As thick as honeycomb, each pinch more stinging
    Than bees that made them.
CALIBAN: I must eat my dinner.   330
    This island's mine by Sycorax my mother,
    Which thou tak'st from me. When thou camest first,
    Thou strok'dst me, and mad'st much of me; wouldst give me
    Water with berries in't; and teach me how
    To name the bigger light, and how the less,
    That burn by day and night: and then I lov'd thee
    And show'd thee all the qualities o' th' isle,
    The fresh springs, brine-pits, barren place, and fertile.
    Cursed be I that did so! – All the charms
    Of Sycorax, toads, beetles, bats, light on you!   340
    For I am all the subjects that you have,
    Which first was mine own king; and here you sty me
    In this hard rock, whiles you do keep from me
    The rest o' th' island.

PROSPERO: Thou most lying slave,
  Whom stripes may move, not kindness! I have us'd thee,
  Filth as thou art, with human care; and lodg'd thee
  In mine own cell, till thou didst seek to violate
  The honour of my child.
CALIBAN: Oh ho! Oh ho! – would it had been done!
  Thou didst prevent me; I had peopled else
  This isle with Calibans.
PROSPERO: Abhorrèd slave.   350
  Which any print of goodness will not take,
  Being capable of all ill! I pitied thee,
  Took pains to make thee speak, taught thee each hour
  One thing or other: when thou didst not, savage,
  Know thine own meaning, but wouldst gabble like
  A thing most brutish, I endow'd thy purposes
  With words that made them known: but thy vile race,
  Though thou didst learn, had that in't which good natures
  Could not abide to be with; therefore wast thou
  Deservedly confin'd into this rock,   360
  Who hadst deserv'd more than a prison.
CALIBAN: You taught me language; and my profit on't
  Is, I know how to curse: the red plague rid you,
  For learning me your language!
PROSPERO: Hag-seed, hence!
  Fetch us in fuel,

Late nineteenth- and earlier twentieth-century interpretations of *The Tempest* tended to conceive it in terms of a contest between **art** (Prospero) and *nature (compounded of the earthy Caliban and the more ethereal spirit, Ariel). More recently, attention has concentrated upon the *colonial dimension of the master–slave relationship; also the *class and GENDER politics of Caliban as a wildly wilful male body and Miranda as a purely demure female. There continues to be much attention to Prospero the magician as a kind of **theatrical** super-illusionist and even as an **autobiographical** projection of Shakespeare himself saying farewell to the stage. All these issues perhaps converge in notions of **identity** and **role**-playing.

Also see: **imagery** and **versification**. Compare: Slave narratives 5.2.2; Yeats and Kazantsis 5.1.7 a–b.

5.3.3   Alternative endings

5.3.3 a HENRIK IBSEN, *A Doll's House*, two endings – both by Ibsen – performed (1) in Norway 1879 and (2) in Germany 1880

[Torvald Helmer, a lawyer, and his wife, Nora, are a married middle-class couple with children. They are here reaching the climax of a long-term crisis in their relationship. Nora sees that there has never been any real understanding between them and that they have always been 'strangers'. She decides to leave.]

(1)

HELMER: This is the end, then! Nora, will you never think of me any more?

NORA: Yes, of course. I shall often think of you and the children and this house.

HELMER: May I write to you, Nora?

NORA: No. Never. You mustn't do that.

HELMER: But at least you must let me send you –

NORA: Nothing. Nothing.

HELMER: But if you should need help – ?

NORA: I tell you, no. I don't accept things from strangers.

HELMER: Nora – can I never be anything but a stranger to you?

NORA: [picks up her bag] Oh, Torvald! Then the miracle of miracles would have to happen.

HELMER: The miracle of miracles!

NORA: You and I would have to change so much that – Oh, Torvald, I don't believe in miracles any longer.

HELMER: But I want to believe in them. Tell me. We should have to change so much that – !

NORA: That life together between us two could become a marriage. Goodbye.

[She goes out through the hall]

HELMER: [sinks down on a chair by the door and buries his face in his hands] Nora! Nora! [Looks around and gets up.] Empty! She's gone! [A hope strikes him.] The miracle of miracles – ?

[The street door is slammed shut downstairs]

This ending caused a public scandal and very hostile reviews when it was first performed and printed. This was Ibsen's expressly preferred ending. (Text translated by Michael Meyer in *Ibsen Plays: Two*, London: Methuen, 1984: 103–4.)

5.3.3 b

(2)

[Read as above up until the penultimate speech, then continue:]

NORA: That our life together could become a real marriage. Good-bye.

[She starts to go]

HELMER: Go then! [He seizes her arm] But first you shall see your children for the last time.

NORA: Let me go! I will not see them. I cannot!

HELMER: [dragging her to the door on the left] You shall see them! [He opens the door and says softly] Look – there they are sleeping peacefully and without a care. Tomorrow, when they wake and call for their mother, they will be . . . motherless!

NORA: [trembling] Motherless!

HELMER: As you once were.

NORA: Motherless! [After an inner struggle, she lets her bag fall, and says] Ah, though it is a sin against myself, I cannot leave them! [She sinks almost to the ground by the door.]

[The curtain falls]

This ending was written in 1880 by Ibsen, under financial duress, for a production in Germany, so as not to cause a scandal. Ibsen himself later described it as a 'barbaric outrage'.(Text translated by Peter Watts in Ibsen, *Plays*, Harmondsworth: Penguin, 1965: 334, n. 11.)

Also see: **author and authority; drama and theatre; text, context and intertextuality;** 4.4.

5.3.4   Voices with a difference

5.3.4 a JOHN MILLINGTON SYNGE, *The Playboy of the Western World,* 1907, Act III

[The scene is a pub in a village in County Mayo on the west coast of Ireland. Christy Mahon, a stranger, has been boasting he's killed his father, and the villagers have eventually taken fright. Pegeen Mike is the publican's daughter and Shawn, her cousin, is a young farmer.]

PEGEEN: I'll say, a strange man is a marvel, with his mighty talk; but what's a squabble in your back-yard, and the blow of a loy, have taught me that there's a great gap between a gallous story and a dirty deed. [*To Men.*] Take him on from this, or the lot of us will be likely put on trial for his deed to-day.

CHRISTY: [*with horror in his voice*] And it's yourself will send me off, to have a horny-fingered hangman hitching his bloody slipknots at the butt of my ear.

MEN: [*pulling rope*] Come on, will you?

[*He is pulled down on the floor.*]

CHRISTY: [*twisting his legs round the table*] Cut the rope, Pegeen, and I'll quit the lot of you, and live from this out, like the madman of Keel. Eating muck and green weeds on the faces of the cliffs.

PEGEEN: And leave us to hang, is it, for a saucy liar, the like of you? [*To Men*] Take him on, out from this.

SHAWN: Pull a twist on his neck, and squeeze him so.

PHILLY: Twist yourself. Sure he cannot hurt you, if you keep your distance from his teeth alone.

SHAWN: I'm afeard of him. [*To Pegeen*] Lift a lighted sod, will you, and scorch his leg.

PEGEEN: [*blowing the fire with a bellows*] Leave go now, young fellow, or I'll scorch your shins.

CHRISTY: You're blowing for to torture me. [*His voice rising and growing stronger.*] That's your kind, is it? Then let the lot of you be wary, for, if I've to face the gallows, I'll have a gay march down, I tell you, and shed the blood of some of you before I die.

This play caused a riot when it was first performed at the Abbey Theatre in Dublin. The cause was the generally **carnivalesque** nature of the piece (Christy boasts – and, it turns out, lies – about killing his father, with great *rhetorical panache and freebooting **theatricality**); and more particularly the breaking of a public taboo – the mere mention of an undergarment. Synge drew upon close observation of and familiarity with the language and people of the Aran Islands and Western Ireland as a whole. He in effect constructed *authentic literary, especially stage, **representa-tions** of Irish people and their **accents and dialects**. He thereby both reflected and reinforced the movement towards national **identity** politically realised in 1922.

Compare: Leonard 5.2.5 d; Kelman 5.2.6. (For full text, see A. Saddlemyer (ed.) *The Playboy . . . and Other Plays*, Oxford, Oxford University Press, 1995.)

5.3.4 b DYLAN THOMAS, *Under Milk Wood: A Play for Voices*, performed 1953, pub. 1954

[Dreams, dreamers and voices mingle in the night sky over a Welsh seaside town.]

FIRST VOICE

From where you are you can hear, in Cockle Row in the spring, moonless night, Miss Price, dressmaker and sweetshop-keeper, dream of

SECOND VOICE

her lover, tall as the town clock tower, Samson-syrup-gold-maned, whacking thighed and piping hot, thunderbolt-bass'd and barnacle-breasted, flailing up the cockles with his eyes like blowlamps and scooping low over her lonely loving hotwaterbottled body . . .

MR EDWARDS

Myfanwy Price!

MISS PRICE

Mr Mog Edwards!

MR EDWARDS

I am a draper mad with love. I love you more than all the flannelette and calico, candlewick, dimity, crash and merino, tussore, cretonne, crepon, muslin, poplin, ticking and twill in the whole Cloth Hall of the world. I have come to take you away to my Emporium on the hill, where the change hums on wires. Throw away your little bedsocks and your Welsh wool knitted jacket, I will lie by your side like the Sunday roast.

MISS PRICE

I will knit you a wallet of forget-me-not blue, for the money to be comfy. I will warm your heart by the fire so that you can slip it in under your vest when the shop is closed.

MR EDWARDS

Myfanwy, Myfanwy, before the mice gnaw at your bottom drawer will you say

MISS PRICE

Yes, Mog, yes, Mog, yes, yes, yes.

MR EDWARDS

And all the bells of the tills of the town shall ring for our wedding.
[*Noise of money-tills and chapel bells*]

Thomas (1914–53) was a charismatic reader of his own poetry and also a script-writer for BBC *radio. *Under Milk Wood* (first broadcast 1954) is one of the **classics** of radio **drama** precisely because it blends highly visual **imagery** with highly musical **speech**. It also both reinforced and at the same time humorously mocked a stereotypical image of *Welsh people and Anglo-Welsh accents. (There is hardly any Welsh as such in the play, and Thomas lived the second half of his short life outside Wales, chiefly in London.)

Compare: Synge 5.3.4 a above.

5.3.4 c ATHOL FUGARD, from *Boesman and Lena*, first performed 1969, pub. 1973

[A coloured woman and man share the memory of an enforced eviction from *pondoks* (shanty shacks) by *donner* (bulldozers).]

LENA: It was the same story for all of us. Once is enough if it's a sad one.

BOESMAN: Sad story? Those two that had the fight because somebody grabbed the wrong *broek* [trousers]? The *ou* [guy] trying to catch his donkey? Or that other one running around with his porridge looking for a fire to finish cooking it? It was bioscope, man! And I watched it. Beginning to end, the way it happened. *I* saw it. *Me.*

The women and children sitting there with their snot and tears. The *pondoks* falling. The men standing, looking, as the yellow *donner* pushed them over and then staring at the pieces when they were the only things left standing. I saw all that! The whiteman stopped the bulldozer and smoked a cigarette. I saw that too.

[*another act [i.e. he 'play-acts' as he has previously]*]

'Ek se' [Hey, pal], my baas . . . !' He threw me the *stompie* [cigarette butt]. 'Dankie, baas.'

LENA: They made a big pile and burnt everything.

Fugard (1932—) developed his plays through 'poor **theatre**' conditions with groups from black townships in South Africa. *Boesman and Lena* was written at a time when apartheid was vicious and public criticism of injustice by blacks or whites (let alone both together) was far more dangerous to the individuals concerned than to the state. The play is a modern **tragi-comedy** of resilience in the face of systematic brutalisation. It celebrates the forging of **identity** even when people are treated as nonentities. The translated **dialect** words derive chiefly from Dutch Afrikaans. (Full text in D. Walder (ed.) *Athol Fugard: Selected Plays*, Oxford, Oxford University Press, 1987: 228.)

5.3.4 d SAMUEL BECKETT, opening of *Not I*, 1972 (1977: 376–7)

Stage in darkness but for MOUTH, upstage audience right, about 8 feet above stage level, faintly lit from close-up and below, rest of face in shadow. Invisible microphone. AUDITOR, downstage audience left, tall standing figure, sex undeterminable, enveloped from head to foot in loose black djellaba [North African cloak], with hood, fully faintly lit, standing on invisible podium about 4 feet high shown by attitude alone to be facing diagonally across stage intent on MOUTH, dead still throughout but for four brief movements where indicated. See Note.

As house lights down MOUTH's voice unintelligible behind curtain. House lights out Voice continues unintelligible behind curtain, 10 seconds. With rise of curtain ad-libbing from text as required leading when curtain fully up and attention sufficient into:

MOUTH: . . . . out . . . into this world . . . this world . . . tiny little thing . . .
before its time . . . in a godfor- . . . what? . . . girl? . . . yes . . . tiny little girl
. . . into this . . . out into this . . . before her time . . . godforsaken hole
called . . . called . . . no matter . . . parents unknown . . . unheard of . . .
he having vanished . . . thin air . . . no sooner buttoned up his breeches
. . . she similarly . . . eight months later . . . almost to the tick . . . so no
love . . . spared that . . . no love such as normally vented on the . . .
speechless infant . . . in the home . . . no . . . nor indeed for that matter
any of any kind . . . no love of any kind . . . at any subsequent stage . . . so
typical affair . . . nothing of any note till coming up to sixty when- . . .
what? . . . seventy? . . . good God! . . . coming up to seventy . . . wandering in
a field . . . looking aimlessly for cowslips . . . to make a ball . . . a few
steps then stop . . . stare into space . . . then on . . . a few more . . . stop
and stare again . . . so on . . . drifting around . . . when suddenly . . .
gradually . . . all went out . . . all that early April morning light . . . and
she found herself in the − . . . what? . . . who? . . . no! . . . she! . . . [*Pause and
Movement* [1].] . . . found herself in the dark . . . and if not exactly . . .
insentient . . . insentient . . . for she could still hear the buzzing . . .
so-called . . . in the ears . . . and a ray of light came and went . . . came
and went . . . such as the moon might cast . . . drifting . . . in and out of
cloud . . . but so dulled . . . feeling . . . feeling so dulled . . . she did not
know . . . what position she was in . . . imagine! . . . what position she
was in! . . . whether standing . . . or sitting . . . but the brain- . . . what? . . .
kneeling? . . . yes . . . whether standing . . . or sitting . . . or kneeling . . .
but the brain − . . . what? . . . lying? . . . yes . . . whether standing . . .
or sitting . . . or kneeling . . . or lying . . . but the brain still . . . still . . . in a
way . . . for her first thought was . . . oh long after . . . sudden flash . . .
brought up as she had been to believe . . . with the other waifs . . . in a
merciful . . . [*Brief laugh*] . . . God . . . [*Good laugh*] . . .

---

[1] Movement: this consists in simple sideways raising of arms from sides and their falling back, in a gesture of helpless compassion. It lessens with each recurrence till scarcely perceptible at third. There is just enough pause to contain it as MOUTH recovers from vehement refusal to relinquish third person.

Beckett (1906–89), best known for *Waiting for Godot* (1953), is commonly labelled an **absurdist** dramatist with a tendency, especially in his novels, to use *Modernist '*stream of consciousness' techniques. He is also generally considered a non- or anti-**realist** writer. Such labels are initially useful. However, they also conceal (or indirectly reveal) questions about what one considers to be 'normal' or 'real' in the first place. They also beg questions about the relations between **identities** and **roles** on and off the stage. Even an ostensibly incoherent **text** can be made sense of in some **context** and some **intertextual** frame of reference. Every **foreground** has a variety of immediate and remote **backgrounds**. Every **monologue** presupposes or prompts a **dialogue**. Beckett won the Nobel Prize for Literature in 1969.

5.3.4 e CARYL CHURCHILL, *Cloud 9,* first performed 1979; this version pub. 1985: 260–1

[Clive is a colonial administrator in Victorian Africa; Betty is his wife, played by a man; Joshua is his black servant, played by a white man; Harry is an explorer.]

CLIVE: I did some good today I think. Kept up some alliances. There's a lot of affection there.

HARRY: They're affectionate people. They can be very cruel of course.

CLIVE: Well they are savages.

HARRY: Very beautiful people many of them.

CLIVE: Joshua! [To HARRY] I think we should sleep with guns.

HARRY: I haven't slept in a house for six months. It seems extremely safe.

[JOSHUA *comes*]

CLIVE: Joshua, you will have gathered there's a spot of bother. Rumours of this and that. You should be armed I think.

JOSHUA: There are many bad men, sir. I pray about it. Jesus will protect us.

CLIVE: He will indeed and I'll also get you a weapon. Betty, come and keep Harry company. Look in the barn, Joshua, every night.

[CLIVE *and* JOSHUA *go.* BETTY *comes.*]

HARRY: I wondered where you were.

BETTY: I was singing lullabies.

HARRY: When I think of you I always think of you with Edward in your lap.

BETTY: Do you think of me sometimes then?

HARRY: You have been thought of where no white woman has ever been thought of before.

BETTY: It's one way of having adventures. I suppose I will never go in person.

HARRY: That's up to you.

BETTY: Of course it's not. I have duties.

HARRY: Are you happy, Betty?

BETTY: Where have you been?

HARRY: Built a raft and went up the river. Stayed with some people. The king is always very good to me. They have a lot of skulls around the place but not white men's I think. I made up a poem one night. If I should die in this forsaken spot. There is a loving heart without a blot, Where I will live – and so on.

BETTY: When I'm near you it's like going out into the jungle. It's like going up the river on a raft. It's like going out in the dark.

HARRY: And you are safety and light and peace and home.

BETTY: But I want to be dangerous.

Churchill (1938—) developed this play through **role** play, workshops and research with Joint Stock Theatre Group during 1978–79. In her preface (1984: 245), Churchill explains: 'Betty, Clive's wife, is played by a man because she wants to be what men want her to be [. . .] Joshua, the black servant, is played by a white man because he wants to be what whites want him to be.' FEMINIST, GENDER-based and POST-COLONIAL approaches are thus realised **theatrically**, through the palpable interplay of **presence/absence**. This is easier to grasp with actual *bodies in *performance than from the words on the page. But either way, dominant **discourses** are radically destabilised.

Compare: Slave narratives 5.2.2; Conrad 5.2.4 c; Brooke 5.4.6 d.

5.3.5   Dramatising 'English' in education

5.3.5 a   TONI CADE BAMBARA, *The Lesson*, 1984: 88–9

[A tale of a young girl's summer outing in New York.]

> So this one day Miss Moore rounds us all up at the mailbox and it's puredee hot and she's knockin herself out about arithmetic. And school supposed to let up in the summer I heard, but she don't ever let up. And the starch in my pinafore scratching the shit outta me and I'm really hating this nappy-head bitch and her goddamn college degree. I'd much rather go to the pool or to the show where it's cool. So me and Sugar leaning on the mailbox being surly, which is a Miss Moore word. And Flyboy checking out what everybody brought for lunch. And Fat Butt already wasting his peanut-butter-and-jelly sandwich like the pig he is. And Junebug punchin on Q.T.'s arm for potato chips. And Rosie Giraffe shifting from one hip to the other waiting for somebody to step on her foot or ask her if she from Georgia so she can kick ass, preferably Mercedes'. And Miss Moore asking us do we know what money is, like we a bunch of retards. I mean real money, she say, like it's only poker chips or monopoly papers we lay on the grocer. So right away I'm tired of this and say so. And would much rather snatch Sugar and go to the Sunset and terrorize the West Indian kids and take their hair ribbons and their money too. And Miss Moore files that remark away for next week's lesson on brotherhood, I can tell. And finally I say we oughta get to the subway cause it's cooler and besides we might meet some cute boys. Sugar done swiped her mama's lipstick, so we ready.

Bambara (b.1931, New York) has this to say in 'A Sort of Preface' to her collection *Gorilla, My Love* (1984: ix–x) from which the present story comes: 'It does no good to write **autobiographical** fiction cause the minute the book hits the stand here comes your mama screamin how could you [....] So I deal in straight-up **fiction** myself, cause I value my family and friends, and mostly cause I lie a lot anyway' (my emphasis).

Also see: **accent and dialect; standards . . . varieties**. Compare: Hurston 5.2.4 d; Kelman 5.2.6.

5.3.5 b   JOHN GODBER, *Teechers*, first performed Edinburgh Festival 1987; pub. 1989: 74–6

[Nixon, a beginning drama teacher, is starting his first lesson at a rough secondary school. Most of the class are only there because they are trying to avoid doing something else. Keep an eye and ear open for quick switches in voice and action.]

> NIXON: When everyone is ready . . . Good . . . I think it would be a good thing for us to start with a very important person in the world of drama. Mr William Shakespeare. And in particular a play that you've probably seen but don't realize it. *Romeo and Juliet.*
> [GAIL *and* HOBBY *groan.*]
> Which is a tragedy.
> GAIL: And it's the basis for *West Side Story*, and it's about neighbours arguing.

HOBBY: We've done it . . .

NIXON: Oh . . .

HOBBY: We did it with Mrs Hugill.

GAIL: And we did about two tramps who're waiting for somebody and he never turns up.

HOBBY: And that was boring.

GAIL: And we've done *Hamlet*. About a prince who kills his uncle. Haven't we?

HOBBY: Yeh. And two killers who are after somebody and one of em's a deaf and dumb waiter.

GAIL: And we've done *Beverley Hills Cops. Beverley Hills Cops Two* . . .

HOBBY: *Neighbours* . . .

GAIL: *EastEnders* . . . 'Hello, Arfur . . . ' 'All right, my love.'

HOBBY: Good that . . .

GAIL: What else have we done?

HOBBY: *Indiana Jones.*

GAIL: Yeh. *Jewel of the Nile* . . . We've done all there is in drama . . .

NIXON: At that moment, a giant of a lad, Peter Saxon, stood up. He must have been six feet seven, with tattoos on his arms and a line across his neck which read, 'Cut here.' 'I wanna say something,' he said. 'I've got some drama to tell you . . . ' 'Go on then, Peter,' I said, not knowing what to expect . . .

[*He becomes* PETER SAXON.]

Right, I'm Peter Saxon now . . . One day, sir, last year, it was great. Me and Daz Horne decided to run away, to seek our fortune. We was going to London. It was a Tuesday, I think. But it could have been a Thursday. No, no, it was a Tuesday, cos we had Mr Cooper for technical drawing. Mr Cooper's soft, sir, you can swear at him and all sorts. We used to call him 'gibbon head', cos he had a bald head and looked like a gibbon. Anyway, me and Daz are in his class and I throws a chair at him, so he goes and hides himself in a store room, so me and Horney lock him in the store room, and then we get a chair and stand on it and look at him through the window in the top of the store room, and I keeps shouting 'gibbon head' to him . . . Anyway, then we twags it and gets a bus to the station. I couldn't stop laughing, sir, honest, just the picture of gibbon head sat in that store room killed me off. Anyway, Horney says that we've got drama with Mrs Hugill before dinner, so we comes back to our drama lesson. In drama we did 'different visions of hell'. I was a cyclops and Horney was my mam. Anyway, me and Horney got into stacks of trouble. But I liked doing plays when Mrs Hugill was here . . . Sir, as far as I know, sir, Mr Cooper is still locked in the store room . . .

GAIL: He's a liar . . .

NIXON: That was good, Peter. The kids had raw potential, but I had to get them into plays.

This is another *script that works a treat on stage but can still be grasped on the page. Open **role** play; switches and shifts in mode of **address** (to characters and/or to audience); code-switching between **standard** and colloquial **varieties** of English; a mixture of literary and popular media **classics; theatre** about theatre (*meta-theatre); a drama within a drama lesson – within an English lesson, perhaps . . . there's plenty to play around with here.

Also see: 1.5.1, 1.5.9. Compare: 5.3.5 a and c, above and below; Harrison 5.4.5 c.

5.3.5 c WILLY RUSSELL, from *Educating Rita*, Act I, Scene 1, first stage performance Royal Shakespeare Company, 1980; film 1983 with Julie Walters as Rita and Michael Caine as Frank; here Russell 1985: 172–3

[Rita is a 'mature student' who has enrolled on an Open University course in English. Frank has been assigned as her tutor.]

RITA: You've got to challenge death an' disease. I read this poem about fightin' death . . .

FRANK: Ah – Dylan Thomas . . .

RITA: No. Roger McGough. It was about this old man who runs away from hospital an' goes out on the ale. He gets pissed an' stands in the street shoutin' an' challengin' death to come out an' fight. It's dead good.

FRANK: Yes, I don't think I know the actual piece you mean . . .

RITA: I'll bring y' the book – it's great.

FRANK: Thank you.

RITA: You probably won't think it's any good.

FRANK: Why?

RITA: It's the sort of poetry you can understand.

FRANK: Ah. I see.

[RITA *begins looking idly round the room.*]

FRANK: Can I offer you a drink?

RITA: What of?

FRANK: Scotch?

RITA: [*going to the bookcase*] Y' wanna be careful with that stuff, it kills y' brain cells.

FRANK: But you'll have one? [*He gets up and goes to the small table.*]

RITA: All right. It'll probably have a job findin' my brain.

FRANK: [*pouring the drinks*] Water?

RITA: [*looking at the bookcase*] Yeh, all right. [*She takes a copy of 'Howards End' from the shelf.*] What's this like?

[FRANK *goes over to* RITA, *looks at the title of the book and then goes back to the drinks.*]

FRANK: *Howards End*?

RITA: Yeh. It sounds filthy, doesn't it? E.M. Foster.

FRANK: Forster.

RITA: Oh yeh. What's it like?

FRANK: Borrow it. Read it.

RITA: Ta. I'll look after it. [*She moves back towards the desk.*] If I pack the course in I'll post it to y'.

[FRANK *comes back to the desk with drinks.*]

FRANK: [*handing her the mug*]: Pack it in? Why should you do that?

[RITA *puts her drink down on the desk and puts the copy of 'Howards End' in her bag.*]

RITA: I just might. I might decide it was a soft idea.

FRANK: [*Looking at her*]: Mm. Cheers. If – erm – you're already contemplating 'packing it in', why did you enrol in the first place?

RITA: Because I wanna know.

FRANK: What do you want to know?

RITA: Everything.

FRANK: Everything? That's rather a lot, isn't it? Where would you like to start?

Russell (1947–) left school at 15, saw himself as 'a kid from the 'D' stream, a piece of factory fodder' (Russell 1985: 162). He then did a variety of manual jobs, including hairdressing, but saw a play by John McGrath and decided to become a playwright. He is also the author of *Shirley Valentine* (1987) and many other scripts for stage and TV. He was awarded an honorary MA in 1983 by the Open Univeristy in recognition of his work as a playwright.

Also see 1.5.1; **classic**. Compare: 5.3.5 a–b above.

5.4.   INTERTEXTUAL CLUSTERS

[Fuller notes are supplied at the end of each cluster.]

5.4.1   Versions of 'Humpty Dumpty'

(a) Humpty Dumpty sat on a wall,
     Humpty Dumpty had a great fall:
     All the king's horses,
     And all the King's men,
     Couldn't put Humpty together again.

                         (Most widespread modern English version)

(b) Humpty Dumpty ligs in t'beck
     Wid a white counterpane aroon his neck;
     Forty doctors and forty wrights
     Will nivver put Humpty Dumpty to rights.

                   (Cumberland, UK version: line 1 = lies in the brook)

(c) Humpty Dumpty went to town,
     Humpty Dumpty tore his gown;
     All the needles in the town
     Couldn't mend Humpty Dumpty's gown.

                         (nineteenth-century American version)

(d) she [Alice] stood and softly repeated to herself:

     'Humpty Dumpty sat on a wall;
     Humpty Dumpty had a great fall.
     All the King's horses and all the King's men
     Couldn't put Humpty Dumpty in his place again.'

'That last line is much too long for the poetry,' she added, almost out loud, forgetting that Humpty Dumpty would hear her.

'Don't stand chattering to yourself like that,' Humpty Dumpty said, looking at her for the first time, 'but tell me your name and your business.'

'My *name* is Alice, but –'

'It's a stupid name enough!' Humpty Dumpty interrupted impatiently. 'What does it mean?'

'*Must* a name mean something? Alice asked doubtfully.

'Of course it must,' Humpty said with a short laugh: '*my* name means the shape I am – and a good handsome shape it is, too. With a name like yours, you might be any shape, almost.' [. . .]

'When *I* use a word,' Humpty Dumpty said in rather a scornful tone, 'it means just what I choose it to mean – neither more nor less.'

'The question is,' said Alice, 'whether you *can* make words mean different things.'

'The question is,' said Humpty Dumpty, 'which is to be master – that's all.'

(from Lewis Carroll's Alice Through the Looking Glass, 1871: Ch. 6)

(e)   The poems and the lessons they write and send from England
      Impress me they were trying to cultivate comedians
      Comic books made more sense [. . .]
      Humpty Dumpty sat on a wall
      Humpty Dumpty did fall
      Goosey Goosey Gander
      Where shall I wander
      Ding dong dell . . . Pussy in the well [. . .]
      They beat me like a dog to learn that in school
      If me head was bright I would be a damn fool

(from 'Sparrow' (Slinger Francis), Dan is the Man, c.1960,
in Brown et al. 1989: 129–30)

(f)   Humpty Dumpty was a bad egg
      Salmonella got stuck in his leg
        All the Queen's ministers
        And all the poor hens
      Couldn't put Currie together again.

(A version produced by students in Language, Literature, Discourse III, January
1989, Oxford. Edwina Currie was a junior minister who spoke out against the
Conservative government's handling of policy relating to eggs infected by
salmonella. She was forced to resign.)

(Versions (a)–(c) are from I. and P. Opie, The Puffin Book of Nursery Rhymes,
London, 1963)

5.4.2   Versions of 'Psalm 137', verse 1

(a)   Ofer flodas babilones ðer we setun
      and weopun ða ðe we gemyndge ðin sion
      in salum in midle hire
      we hengun organa ure.

(Vespasian Psalter, Mercian (Midlands), late eighth century)

(b)   On the floodis of babylone there we saten,
      and wepten; while we bithoughten on Syon,
      In salewis in the myddil therof we hangiden
      vp our orguns

(Wycliffite Bible, here Psalm 136, c.1382)

(c) By the rivers of Babylon, there we sat down, yea, we wept, when we
       remembered Zion.
     We hanged our harps upon the willows in the midst thereof.

(King James Bible, 'Authorized' Version, 1611)

(d) On the proud banks of great Euphrates' flood
       There we sat, and there we wept:
     Our harps that now no music understood
       Nodding on the willows slept,
       While unhappy, captived we,
       Lovely Zion thought on thee.

(Richard Crashaw, from *Steps to the Temple*, 1646)

(e) By the waters of Babylon
     there we sat down and wept,
     when we remembered Zion.
     On the willows there
       we hung up our lyres

(Bible, Revised Standard Version, 1952)

(f) She leaned over to the tape deck and pushed a button. Jesus, Jumpy thought,
     Boney M? Give me a break. For all her tough race-professional attitudes, the
     lady still had a lot to learn about music. Here it came, boomchickaboom. Then,
     without warning, he was crying, provoked into real tears by counterfeit emotion
     by a disco-beat imitation of pain. It was the one hundred and thirty-seventh
     psalm, 'Super flumina'. King David calling out across the centuries. How shall
     we sing the Lord's song in a strange land.
          'I had to learn the psalms at school,' Pamela Chamcha said, sitting on the
     floor, her head leaning against the sofa-bed, her eyes shut tight. By the river of
     Babylon, where we sat down, oh oh we wept . . . she stopped the tape, leaned
     back again, began to recite. 'If I forget thee, O Jerusalem, let my right hand
     forget its cunning; if I do not remember thee, let my tongue cleave to the roof of
     my mouth; yea, if I prefer not Jerusalem in my mirth.'
          Later, asleep in bed, she dreamed of her convent school, of matins and
     evensong, of the chanting of psalms.

(from Salman Rushdie, *The Satanic Verses*, 1988 (1992: 175–6);
Boney M hit, 1978)
(Versions (b)–(d) can be found in full, with other early versions, in Hollander and
Kermode 1973, Vol. I: 534–42)

5.4.3   Daffodils?

5.4.3 a WILLIAM WORDSWORTH, 'I wandered lonely as a cloud', 1804, pub. 1807

     I wandered lonely as a cloud
       That floats on high o'er vales and hills
     When all at once I saw a crowd
       A host, of golden daffodils;

Beside the lake, beneath the trees,   5
Fluttering and dancing in the breeze.

Continuous as the stars that shine
        And twinkle on the milky way,
They stretched in never-ending line
        Along the margin of a bay: 10
Ten thousand saw I at a glance,
Tossing their heads in sprightly dance.

The waves beside them danced, but they
        Outdid the sparkling waves in glee:
A poet could not but be gay   15
        In such a jocund company:
I gazed – and gazed – but little thought
What wealth the show to me had brought.

For oft when on my couch I lie
        In vacant or in pensive mood,   20
They flash upon that inward eye
        Which is the bliss of solitude;
And then my heart with pleasure fills,
And dances with the daffodils.

Wordsworth (1770–1850) dictated early drafts to Mary, his wife, and then to Dorothy, his sister, between 1802 and 1804. This poem was first published without the third verse in *Poems, in Two Volumes* (1807). According to William's own notes which were dictated to Isabella Fenwick forty years later (1842–43), 'The best two lines in it are by Mary' (quoting ll.21–22). This poem has subsequently become one of the most *popular and **classic** lyrics in English, as well one of the most influential examples of what *Romantic poets do and of what **poetry** in general is.

5.4.3 b DOROTHY WORDSWORTH, *Grasmere Journals*, Thursday, 15 April 1802

We got over into a field to avoid some cows – people working, a few primroses by the roadside, wood-sorrel flower, the anemone, scentless violets, strawberries, and that starry yellow flower which Mrs C. calls pile wort. When we were in the woods beyond Gorbarrow park we saw a few daffodils, close to the water side. We fancied that the lake had floated the seeds ashore and that the little colony had so sprung up. But as we went along there were more and yet more and at last under the boughs of the trees, we saw that there was a long belt of them along the shore, about the breadth of a country turn-pike road. I never saw daffodils so beautiful, they grew among the mossy stones about and about them, some rested their heads upon these stones as on a pillow for weariness and the rest tossed and reeled and danced and seemed as if they verily laughed with the wind that blew upon them over the lake, they looked so gay ever glancing ever changing.

Dorothy Wordsworth's *Grasmere Journals* (1800–3) were written without thought of publication and were not published till after her death in 1855. Their substance was freely shared with her brother William, often supplying him with prompts, reminders and even phrasing for his poetry.

5.4.3 c LYNN PETERS, 'Why Dorothy Wordsworth is Not as Famous as her Brother'

'I wandered lonely as a . . .
They're in the top drawer, William,
Under your socks –
I wandered lonely as a –
No not that drawer, the top one.   5
I wandered by myself –
Well wear the ones you can find.
No, don't get overwought my dear,
I'm coming.

'One day I was out for a walk   10
When I saw this flock –
It can't be too hard, it had three minutes.
Well put some butter in it.
– This host of golden daffodils
As I was out for a stroll one –   15

'Oh you a fancy a stroll, do you?
Yes all right, William, I'm coming.
It's on the peg. Under your hat.
I'll bring my pad, shall I, just in case
You want to jot something down?'   20

(from the *Virago Book of Wicked Verse*, London, 1992)

5.4.3 d TV ADVERT for lager: 'Heineken refreshes the poets other beers can't reach'

Scene: A handsome young man in a frock coat is sitting on a mound, scratching his head and trying to write.

YOUNG MAN: I was rather lonely . . . [*He crosses it out.*]
I wandered around for a bit . . . !' [*He crosses it out again.*]
  [*Pauses and reaches for a glass and drinks from it. Sudden look of inspiration.*
  Cue rapturous symphonic music with sweeping strings
  He jumps to his feet and, over the music, begins to declaim.]
I wandered lonely as a cloud
That floats on high o'er vales and hills . . .
  [*Camera pulls back and above to reveal him dancing – and still declaiming – among a field of daffodils*]
MALE VOICE-OVER: [*mature, faintly Germanic, cordial*] Only Heineken can do this.
  Because Heineken refreshes the *poets* other beers can't reach.
  [*Final close-up shot of Heineken can with glass of lager*]

One of a series of lager *advertisements developed by Terry Lovelock the advertising copywriter, and shown on British **TV**, 1974–89, continued 1991— . All are built round variations on the formula 'Heineken refreshes the parts (poets, pets, etc.) other beers cannot reach'.

Also see: 1.8, Example, pp. 45–47; MEDIA; FEMINISM AND GENDER STUDIES; POST-MODERNISM; **author; auto/biography; canon and classic;** *centring (de- and re-); **foreground, background and point of view;** *parody; *pastoral; **poetry;** *Romantic.

5.4.4   Versions of age

5.4.4 a MAY SARTON, opening of *As We Are Now*, New York, 1973

> I am not mad, only old. I make this statement to give me courage. Suffice it to say that is has taken two weeks for me to obtain this notebook and a pen. I am in a concentration camp for the old, a place where people dump their parents or relatives exactly as though it were an ash can.
>
> My brother, John, brought me here two weeks ago. Of course I knew from the beginning that living with him would never work. I had to close my own house after the heart attack (the stairs were too much for me). John is four years older than I am and married a much younger woman after Elizabeth, his first wife, died. Ginny never liked me. I make her feel inferior and I cannot help it. John is a reader and always has been. So am I. John is interested in politics. So am I.

Sarton, born in America in 1912, is a teacher, and a writer of poems, novels and autobiographical memoirs.

5.4.4 b Clarins skincare advert (with image), *Cosmopolitan*, February, 1985

> Puffy Eyes.
> Crow's Feet.
> Help is in sight!
> Your eyes are the first place to betray your age. Don't be alarmed. Let Clarins, France's premier skin care authority, come to the rescue – with effective eye contour treatments based on natural plant extracts.
> Clarins recognizes the causes.
> Squinting. Blinking. Smiling. Crying. These are constant aggressions the delicate eye contour area endures. Even the daily application and removal of makeup take a toll. Add stress, fatigue, pollution . . . and it's no wonder your eyes reveal signs of aging. Clearly, the need for special eye contour care is urgent!
> Clarins is the Problem-Solver.
> Clarins created light, non-oily products to effectively treat the fragile skin tissue surrounding the eyes. (Oily formulations actually cause eyes to 'puff-up'!) For 30 years, Clarins' gentle eye contour treatments have proven to be successful in the Clarins Parisian 'Institut de Beauté'. Based on natural plant extracts, these treatments are dermatologically and allergy-tested.

5.4.4 c WILLIAM SHAKESPEARE, 'Devouring Time' (Sonnet 19), 1609

Devouring Time, blunt thou the Lion's paws,
And make the earth devour her own sweet brood;
Pluck the keen teeth from the fierce Tiger's jaws,
And burn the long-lived Phoenix in her blood;   4
Make glad and sorry seasons as thou fleet'st,
And do whate'er thou wilt, swift-footed Time,
To the wide world and all her fading sweets;
But I forbid thee one most heinous crime,   8
O, carve not with thy hours my love's fair brow,
Nor draw no lines there with thine antique pen
Him in thy course untainted do allow,
For beauty's pattern to succeeding men.   12
    Yet do thy worst, old Time; despite thy wrong,
    My love shall in my verse ever live young.

Shakespeare (1564–1616). See 5.1.3 b note.

5.4.4 d DENNIS SCOTT, 'Uncle Time' (1973) in Brown *et al.* 1989: 32–3

Uncle Time is a ole, ole man . . .
All year long 'im wash 'im foot in de sea,
long, lazy years on de wet san'
an' shake de coconut tree dem
quiet-like wid 'im sea-win' laughter,   5
scraping away de lan' . . .

Uncle Time is a spider-man, cunnin' an' cool,
Him tell yu: watch de hill an' yu se mi.
Huhn! Fe yu yiye no quick enough fe si
how 'im move like mongoose; man, yu tink 'im fool?   10
Me Uncle Time smile black as sorrow;
'im voice is sof' as bamboo leaf
but Lawd, me Uncle cruel.
When 'im play in de street
wid yu woman – watch 'im! By tomorrow   15
she dry as cane-fire, bitter as cassava;
an' when 'im teach yu son, long after
yu walk wid stranger, an' yu bread is grief.
Watch how 'im spin web roun' ya house, an' creep
inside; an' when 'im touch yu, weep. . . .   20

Dennis Scott (b.1939, Jamaica) is a poet, playwright, director, actor and dancer.

5.4.4 e BILLY MARSHALL-STONEKING, 'Passage' (1990) in Murray
1991: 387–8

```
The oldest man in the world wears shoes.
The oldest man in the world has a cowboy hat on his head.
The oldest man in the world speaks to me in English.
He rides in motor cars.
His body: fluid, capable – a perfect shock absorber.                    5
One tooth knocked out in front, a red bandanna tied
around his neck, he names Names
as we bounce over the dirt track in the back
of a four-wheel drive.
'That tree is a digging stick                                          10
left by the giant woman who was looking for honey ants;
That rock, a dingo's nose;
There, on the mountain, is the footprint
left by Tjangara on his way to Ulamburra;
Here, the rockhole of Warnampi – very dangerous –                      15
and the cave where the nyi-nyi women escaped
the anger of marapulpa – the spider.
Wati Kutjarra – the two brothers – travelled this way.
There, you can see one was tired
from too much lovemaking – the mark of his penis                       20
dragging the ground;
Here, the bodies of the honey ant men
where they crawled from the sand –
no, they are not dead – they keep coming
from the ground, moving toward the water at Warumpi –                  25
it has been like this for many years:
the Dreaming does not end; it is not like the whiteman's way.
What happened once again and again.
This is the law.
This is the power of the Song.                                         30
Through the singing we keep everything alive;
through the songs the spirits keep us alive.'
The oldest man in the world speaks
to the newest man in the world; my place
less exact than his.                                                   35
We bump along together in the back of the truck
wearing shoes, belts, underwear.
We speak to each other in English
over the rumble of engine, over the roar of the wheels.
His body: a perfect shock absorber.                                    40
```

Marshall-Stoneking (b. America) now lives in Australia. See: POSTCOLONIALISM,
Example, pp. 149–152.
    For whole section also see: *advertising; *age; **auto/biography**; *body; **Bibles,
holy books and myths; narrative in hi/story.**

5.4.5 Death and (not so) grave yards

5.4.5 a EPITAPHS by Pope, Gray, Burns, Monty Python, *et al.*

(i)   I was as ye are nowe
      and as I ye shall be

                                        (Common late medieval epitaph)

(ii) Here lye two poor Lovers, who had the mishap
      Tho very chaste peopl, to die of a Clap.
          (Alexander Pope (1688–1744) (Epitaph on the Stanton-Harcourt Lovers')

(iii) Here rests his head upon the lap of Earth
          A youth to Fortune and to Fame unknown.
      Fair Science frowned not on his humble birth,
          And Melancholy marked him for her own.

      Large was his bounty, and his soul sincere,
          Heaven did a recompense as largely send:
      He gave to Misery all he had, a tear,
          He gained from Heaven ('twas all he wished) a friend.

      No farther seek his merits to disclose,
          Or draw his frailties from their dread abode
      (There they alike in trembling hope repose),
          The bosom of his Father and his God.
                          (Thomas Gray, 'The Epitaph' from 'Elegy Written in a Country
                                                        Churchyard', 1751)

(iv) Here lie Willie Michie's banes;
          O Satan, when ye take him,
      Gie him the schoolin' of your weans
          For clever deils he'll mak them!
                      (Robert Burns (1759–96) *Epitaph on a Schoolmaster in Cleish
                      Parish*, Kinross-shire. 3. weans – infants, children. 4. deils – devils.)

(v)   Here lies Lester Moore
      Four slugs from a 44
      No les no more

                                        (from a headstone in Tombstone, Arizona, USA)

(vi) In Memory of MARY MARIA, wife of Wm. Dodd
      Who died Dec.r 12th AD 1847 aged 27
                  also
      of their children, LOUISA, who died Dec.r 12th 1847
      aged 9 months, & ALFRED who died Jan.y 3rd AD 1848
          aged 2 years & 9 months
      All victims to the neglect of sanitary regulation
      & specially referred to in a recent lecture on

Health in this town
And the lord said to the angel that destroyed
It is enough. Stay now thy hand – Chronicles 1, xx 17
(from a tombstone in Bilston, Staffordshire, England)

(vii) CUSTOMER: Look my lad, I've had just about enough of this. That parrot is definitely deceased. And when I bought it not half an hour ago, you assured me that its lack of movement was due to it being tired and shagged out after a long squawk.

SHOPKEEPER: It's probably pining for the fiords. [. . .]

CUSTOMER: It's not pining, it's passed on. This parrot is no more. It has ceased to be. It's expired and gone to meet its maker. This is a late parrot. It's a stiff. Bereft of life, it rests in peace. If you hadn't nailed it to the perch, it would be pushing up the daisies. It's rung down the curtain and joined the choir invisible. This is an ex-parrot.

SHOPKEEPER: Well, I'd better replace it then.

(Monty Python's 'Dead Parrot' sketch: Customer – John Cleese; Shopkeeper – Michael Palin; broadcast BBC2 TV, 1969, from G. Chapman, J. Cleese, T. Jones and M. Palin, *Monty Python's Flying Circus: Just the Words,* London, Mandarin, 1990: Vol. I: 105)

Epitaphs (iv) and (v) are from Fritz Spiegel, *A Small Book of Grave Humour*, London: Pan, 1971. Also see: **Bibles; carnival; discourse; versification**. Compare: Morrison 5.2.2 e; 5.4.5 b–e below.

5.4.5 b CHARLES DICKENS, opening of *Great Expectations*, first serialised in *All the Year Round*, December 1860–1

My father's family name being Pirrip and my Christian name Philip, my infant tongue could make of both names nothing longer or more explicit than Pip. So I called myself Pip, and came to be called Pip.

I give Pirrip as my father's family name on the authority of his tombstone and my sister – Mrs. Joe Gargery, who married the blacksmith. As I never saw my father or my mother, and never saw any likeness of either of them (for their days were long before the days of photographs), my first fancies regarding what they were like were unreasonably derived from their tombstones. The shape of the letters on my father's gave me an odd idea that he was a square, stout, dark man, with curly black hair. From the character and turn of the inscription, '*Also Georgiana Wife of the Above*,' I drew a childish conclusion that my mother was freckled and sickly. To five little stone lozenges, each about a foot and a half long, which were arranged in a neat row beside their grave, and were sacred to the memory of five little brothers of mine – who gave up trying to get a living exceedingly early in that universal struggle – I am indebted for a belief I religiously entertained that they had all been born on their backs with their hands in their trousers pockets, and had never taken them out in this state of existence.

5.4.5 c TONY HARRISON, from *v.* 1985; broadcast on Channel 4 TV, 1987

The language of this grave yard ranges from
a bit of Latin for a former Mayor
or those who laid their lives down at the Somme,
the hymnal fragments and the gilded prayer,

how people 'fell asleep in the Good Lord',
brief chisellable bits from the good book
and rhymes whatever length they could afford,
to CUNT, PISS, SHIT and (mostly) FUCK! [. . .]

What is it that these crude words are revealing?
What is it that this aggro act implies?
Giving the dead their xenophobic feeling
or just a *cri-de-cœur* because man dies?

So what's a cri-de-cœur, *cunt. Can't you speak*
the language that yer mam spoke. Think of 'er!
Can yer only get yer tongue round fucking Greek?
Go and fuck yerself with cri-de-cœur

'She didn't talk like you do for a start!'
I shouted, turning where I thought the voice had been.
She didn't understand yer fucking 'art'!
She thought yer fucking poetry obscene!

I wish on this skin's word deep aspirations,
first the prayer for my parents I can't make
then a call to Britain and to all the nations
made in the name of love for peace's sake.

Aspirations, cunt! Folk on t'fucking dole
'ave got about as much scope to aspire
above the shit they're dumped in, cunt, as coal
aspires to be chucked on t'fucking fire. [. . .]

'Listen, cunt!' *I* said, 'before you start your jeering
the reason why I want this in a book
's to give ungrateful cunts like you a hearing!'
A book, yer stupid cunt, 's not worth a fuck!

'The only reason why I write this poem at all
on yobs like you who do the dirt on death
's to give some higher meaning to your scrawl.'
Don't fucking bother, cunt! Don't waste your breath!

'You piss-artist skinhead cunt, you wouldn't know
and it doesn't fucking matter if you do,
the skin and poet united fucking Rimbaud
but the *autre* that *je est* is fucking you.' [. . .]

If, having come this far, somebody reads
these verse, and he/she wants to understand,
face this grave on Beeston Hill, your back to Leeds,
and read the chiselled epitaph I've planned:

Beneath your feet's a poet, then a pit.
Poetry supporter, if you're here to find
how poems can grow from (beat you to it!) *SHIT*
find the beef, the beer, the bread, then look behind.

The poem is 132 verses long. Only 12 are reproduced here – from beginning, middle and end. It was first broadcast in 1987, in the wake of numerous pit closures, protracted industrial action by miners in Britain and persistently rising unemployment. It prompted public debate. Tony Harrison (b. 1937) is from a working-class background in Leeds, Yorkshire (the centre of a former mining area). He is also an internationally recognised poet, script-writer, literary translator and opera librettist.

Compare: Gray 5.4.5 a (iii).

5.4.5 d EMILY DICKINSON, 'I felt a Funeral', c.1861, first pub. 1896

I felt a Funeral, in my Brain,
And Mourners to and fro
Kept treading – treading – till it seemed
That Sense was breaking through –   4

And when they all were seated,
A service, like a Drum –
Kept beating – beating – till I thought
My mind was going numb –   8

And then I heard them lift a Box
And creak across my soul
With those same Boots of Lead, again,
Then Space – began to toll,   12

As all the Heavens were a Bell,
And Being, but an Ear
And I, and Silence, some strange Race
Wrecked, solitary, here –   16

And then a Plank in Reason, broke,
And I dropped down, and down –
And hit a World, at every plunge,
And Finished knowing – then –   20

Dickinson (1830–86), poet, Puritan, sceptic and recluse, was born and lived all her life in Amherst, Massachusetts.

5.4.5 e GRACE NICHOLS, 'Tropical Death', 1984

> The fat black woman want
> a brilliant tropical death
> not a cold sojourn
> in some North Europe far/forlorn
>
> The fat black woman want   5
> some heat/hibiscus at her feet
> blue sea dress
> to wrap her neat
>
> The fat black woman want
> some bawl   10
> no quiet jerk tear wiping
> a polite hearse withdrawal
>
> The fat black woman want
> all her dead rights
> first night   15
> third night
> nine night
> all the sleepless droning
> red-eyed wake nights
>
> In the heart   20
> of her mother's sweetbreast
> In the shade
> of the sun leaf's cool bless
> In the bloom
> of her people's bloodrest   25
>
> the fat black woman want
> a brilliant tropical death yes

Nichols was born in Guyana in 1950 and moved to Britain in 1977. This is one of a series from *The Fat Black Woman's Poems* (1984: 19).

Also see: **Bibles, holy books and myths; comedy and tragedy, carnival and the absurd; discourse; standards . . . varieties; versification.** Compare: Morrison 5.2.2 e; 5.4.5 a above.

5.4.6   Visions of England at war

5.4.6 a WILLIAM SHAKESPEARE, *Henry V*, Act III, scenes i & ii, 1598–9

[King Henry V of England is exhorting his men, chiefly the nobles, to carry on storming a breach in the wall of the French city of Harfleur. Not all of them, especially the non-nobles, want to.]

KING: Once more unto the breach, dear friends, once more;
  Or close the wall up with our English dead!
  In peace there's nothing so becomes a man
  As modest stillness and humility;
  But when the blast of war blows in our ears,   5
  Then imitate the action of the tiger:
  Stiffen the sinews, summon up the blood,
  Disguise fair nature with hard-favoured rage;
  Then lend the eye a terrible aspect: [. . .]
  Now set the teeth, and stretch the nostril wide,   15
  Hold hard the breath, and bend up every spirit
  To his full height! On, on, you noble English
  Whose blood is fet[1] from fathers of war-proof;
  Fathers that like so many Alexanders
  Have in these parts from morn till even fought   20
  And sheathed their swords for lack of argument.
  Dishonour not your mothers: now attest
  That those whom you called fathers did beget you!
  Be copy now to men of grosser blood
  And teach them how to war! And you, good yeomen,   25
  Whose limbs were made in England, show us here
  The mettle of your pasture. Let us swear
  That you are worth your breeding; which I doubt not,
  For there is none of you so mean and base
  That hath not noble lustre in your eyes.   30
  I see you stand like greyhounds in the slips,
  Straining upon the start. The game's afoot!
  Follow your spirit; and upon this charge,
  Cry, 'God for Harry, England and Saint George!'
          [*Exeunt. Alarum, and [gun]chambers go off.*]

Scene II, Harfleur
Enter Nym, Bardolph, Pistol and Boy.

BARDOLPH: On, on, on, on, on, to the breach, to the breach!
NYM: Pray thee, Corporal, stay; the knocks are too hot; and for mine own part, I
    have not a case of lives. The humour of it is too hot; that is the very plain-song of
    it.
PISTOL: The plain-song is most just: for humours do abound:
    Knocks go and come; God's vassals drop and die:
        And sword and shield
          In bloody field   10
        Doth win immortal fame.

BOY: Would I were in an ale-house in London! I would give all my fame for a pot of
    ale, and safety.
PISTOL: And I:
    If wishes would prevail with me,   15
    My purpose should not fail with me,
        But thither would I hie

BOY: As duly,
        but not as truly,
        As bird doth sing on bough.

[*Enter Fluellen.*]

FLUELLEN: Up to the breach you dogs! Avaunt, you cullions[2]!   20
PISTOL: Be merciful, great Duke.

1. fet – fetched. 2. cullions – bollocks.

This rousing speech by Henry V is one of the most famous passages written by Shakespeare. However, it is often quoted *out of* **context. Dramatically**, in **theatrical** context, the king's enthusiastic and idealistic **monologue** is immediately followed by a less than enthusiastic and palpably sceptical **dialogue** amongst his common soldiers. They only in fact storm the breach when forcibly driven to it by an officer, Fluellen (who is, incidentally a 'type' of the *Welshman loyal to England). The implication is that aristocrats and commoners, officers and ordinary soldiers do not necessarily share the same vision of war or of England. Nor, perhaps, do women – who are conspicuously absent from this scene except as **imagery**. Nor, we might add, do the French; for at this moment it could be argued that they were being invaded.

Also see: **absences and presences,** . . . **centres and margins; foreground, background and point of view**. Compare: Theatre Workshop 5.4.6 f.

5.4.6 b WILLIAM BLAKE, 'And did those feet', from the preface to his *Milton*, 1804–8

[Blake draws on the ancient legend that Joseph of Arimathea brought the Holy Grail carrying Christ's blood to England and builds it into his own blend of Christian **myth**.]

And did those feet in ancient time
Walk upon England's mountains green?
And was the holy Lamb of God
On England's pleasant pastures seen?   4

And did the Countenance Divine
Shine forth upon our clouded hills?
And was Jerusalem builded here
Among these dark Satanic Mills?   8

Bring me my Bow of burning gold:
Bring me my Arrows of desire:
Bring me my Spear: O clouds unfold!
Bring me my Chariot of fire.   12

I will not cease from Mental Fight,
Nor shall my Sword sleep in my hand
Till we have built Jerusalem
In England's green and pleasant Land.   16

This poem can be read, and was probably conceived, as a dissenting vision of 'England's green and pleasant land'; hence the repeated question structures, the reference to 'these dark Satanic Mills' and the fact that there is still much to *desire, fight for and build. However, since the words were set to *music by Parry in the mid-nineteenth century 'Jerusalem', as it is popularly known, has become best known as a celebratory hymn sung in British schools, at Church of England services and on the last night of the 'London Promenade Concerts'. A further twist is that the hymn is also sometimes sung by the British Labour Party and religious protest movements.

Also see: 1.2; **discourse**.

5.4.6 c PERCY BYSSHE SHELLEY, from *The Mask of Anarchy*, 1819, pub. 1832, stanzas 37–41

'Men of England, Heirs of Glory
Heroes of unwritten story,
Nurslings of one mighty mother,
Hopes of her, and one another!

'Rise, like lions after slumber
In unvanquishable number,   5
Shake your chains to earth like dew,
Which in sleep had fall'n on you!
Ye are many, they are few.

'What is freedom? Ye can tell
That which Slavery is too well,   10
For its very name has grown
To an echo of your own.

''Tis to work, and have such pay
As just keeps life from day to day
In your limbs as in a cell   15
For the tyrant's use to dwell

'So that ye for them are made,
Loom, and plough, and sword, and spade;
With or without your own will, bent
To their defence and nourishment.'   20

Written by Shelley (1792–1822) as an immediate **response** to the killing of eleven people and the maiming of hundreds when cavalry were used to break up a rally of over 50,000 at St Peter's Field in Manchester (the 'Peterloo' massacre). The crowd were demanding political and economic reform.

Compare: 5.3.1 c.

5.4.6 d RUPERT BROOKE, 'The Soldier' December 1914, pub. June 1915

> If I should die, think only this of me:
>   That there's some corner of a foreign field
> That is for ever England. There shall be
>   In that rich earth a richer dust concealed;   4
> A dust whom England bore, shaped, made aware,
>   Gave, once, her flowers to love, her ways to roam,
> A body of England's, breathing English air,
>   Washed by the rivers, blest by suns of home.   8
> And think, this heart, all evil shed away,
>   A pulse in the eternal mind, no less
> Gives somewhere back the thoughts by England given,
>   Her sights and sounds; dreams happy as her day;   12
> And laughter, learnt of friends; and gentleness,
>   In hearts at peace, under an English heaven.

Brooke (1887–1915) was educated at a public (i.e. fee-paying private) school (Rugby) and Cambridge University. He is usually referred to as a 'Georgian' poet because of his mixture of patriotism and *pastoralism. He died of dysentery and blood poisoning on a troop ship on the way to Gallipoli. Winston Churchill, in a 'Valediction' in the London *Times* (1915), used the occasion of the poet's death and the posthumous publication of his poems a month later to reinforce a recruitment drive (see Abrams 1993, Vol 2: 1826–7):

> 'The thoughts to which he gave expression in the very few incomparable war sonnets which he has left behind will be shared by many thousands of young men moving resolutely and blithely forward into this, the hardest, the cruellest, and the least-rewarded of all the wars that men have fought. They are a whole history and revelation of Rupert Brooke himself. Joyous, fearless, versatile, deeply instructed, with classic symmetry of mind and body, he was all that one would wish England's noblest sons to be in days when no sacrifice but the most precious is acceptable, and the most precious is that which is most freely proffered.'

Compare: 5.4.6 e below, and see *sonnet.

5.4.6 e URSULA A. FANTHORPE, *Knowing about Sonnets* (1986: 112)

> Lesson I: 'The Soldier' (Brooke)
> [The task of criticism] is not to redouble the text's self-understanding, to collude with its object in a conspiracy of silence. The task is to show the text as it cannot know itself.
>
>   Terry Eagleton, *Criticism and Ideology*
>
> Recognizing a sonnet is like attaching
> A name to a face. *Mister Sonnet, I presume?*
>   *If I*
> And naming is power. It can hardly
> Deny its name. You are well on the way

To mastery. The next step is telling the sonnet
What it is trying to say. This is called Interpretation.
   If I should die
What you mustn't do is collude with it. This
Is bad for the sonnet, and will only encourage it
To be eloquent. You must question it closely:
What has it left out? What made it decide
To be a sonnet? The author's testimony
(If any) is not evidence. He is the last person to know.
   If I should die, think this
Stand no nonsense with imagery. Remember, though shifty,
It is vulnerable to calculation. Apply the right tests.
Now you are able to Evaluate the sonnet.
   If I
That should do for today.
    If I should die
        And over and over
The new white paper track innocent unlined hands
   Think this. Think this. Think this. Think only this.

Fanthorpe (b.1929) was for many years an English teacher at Cheltenham Ladies' College, a prestigious private girls' school. She now lives in Gloucestershire and teaches creative writing. Eagleton (b.1943) is a British MARXIST critic and Professor of English at the University of Oxford. His *Criticism and Ideology* was published in 1976.

5.4.6 f THEATRE WORKSHOP, from *Oh What a Lovely War*, performed, 1963, pub. 1965 (1965: 75–6)

[A dramatic collage of materials presenting one of the worst battles of the First World War. Haig was the commander-in-chief of the main British army in France.]

[*Slide 40: A map of Ypres and the surrounding district, showing Kitchener's Wood, Hill 60, Passchendaele, etc.*]

BRITISH GENERAL: If we continue in this way, the line of trenches will stretch from Switzerland to the sea. Neither we nor the Germans will be able to break through. The war will end in complete stalemate.

HAIG: Nonsense. We need only one more big offensive to break through and win. My troops are of fine quality, and specially trained for this type of war.

BRITISH GENERAL: This is not war, sir, it is slaughter.

HAIG: God is with us. It is for King and Empire.

BRITISH GENERAL: We are sacrificing lives at the rate of five to sometimes fifty thousand a day.

HAIG: One battle, our superior morale, bombardment.

JUNIOR OFFICER: [*entering*] Sir, tell us what to do and we'll do it.

HAIG: We're going to walk through the enemy lines.

[*British General and Junior Officer go off.*]

Slide 40 fades into Slide 41: Tommies advancing across no-man's-land, in full battle pack, silhouetted against clouds. A man's voice, offstage, sings slowly as Haig speaks.

SONG. THERE'S A LONG, LONG TRAIL

There's a long, long trail a-winding
Into the land of my dreams,
Where the nightingale is singing
And the white moon beams . . .

[*He carries on humming the tune, ending:*]

. . . till the day when I'll be going down that long, long trail with you.

HAIG: [*during the song*] Complete victory . . . the destruction of German militarism . . . victory march on Berlin . . . slow deliberate fire is being maintained on the enemy positions . . . at this moment my men are advancing across no-man's-land in full pack, dressing from left to right; the men are forbidden under pain of court-martial to take cover in any shell hole or dugout . . . their magnificent morale will cause the enemy to flee in confusion . . . the attack will be driven home with the bayonet . . . I feel that every step I take is guided by the divine will.

[*Sounds of heavy bombardment.*]

NEWSPANEL. FEBRUARY . . . VERDUN . . . TOTAL LOSS
ONE AND A HALF MILLION MEN.

HAIG: [*looking through field-glasses*] This is most unsatisfactory. Where are the Sherwood Foresters? Where are the East Lancs on the right?
BRITISH GENERAL: [*who has entered during above speech*] Out in No Man's Land.
HAIG: They are sluggish from too much sitting in the trenches.
BRITISH GENERAL: Most of them, sir, will never rise again.

Coordinated by Joan Littlewood and Charles Chilton, this show used a mixture – and sometimes a clash – of MEDIA to draw attention to the contradictions and cruelties of war. Most of the songs, reports, back-projected slides and statistics were drawn from contemporary sources. The aim of this kind of theatre is to 'make strange' and 'shock' in the manner of *Brecht and Benjamin.
    Compare: 5.4.6 a.

For this cluster of texts, see: 'One English . . . or many' 1.2; MARXISM; POST-MODERNISM; **aesthetics**; **discourse**.

5.4.7   Some current genres of small text

5.4.7 a PUBLIC NOTICES

(i)   In the event of fire, make your way out of the building by the quickest route. Do not use the lifts. Do not stop to collect personal belongings. Go to the nearest assembly point, as shown.

(ii)   Dogs must be carried on the escalator

(iii)   Her Majesty's Government Health Warning:
        SMOKING CIGARETTES CAN SERIOUSLY DAMAGE YOUR HEALTH

(iv)   5 mg TAR 0.5 mg NICOTINE
                    SMOKING KILLS
        Health Department's Chief Medical Officers

(v)   8mg TAR 0.75 mg NICOTINE
                PROTECT CHILDREN:
                DON'T MAKE THEM BREATHE YOUR SMOKE
        Health Department's Chief Medical Officers

(vi)   The only person to get everything done by Friday was Robinson Crusoe.

(vii)   Wanted – person to work on nuclear fissionable isotope molecular reactive
        counters and three-phase cyclotronic uranium photo-sythesisers. No experience
        necessary.

(i) notice in Bodleian Library, Oxford; (ii) notice on escalator in London Underground; (iii) warnings displayed on cigarette advertising and the packs themselves
in Britain till January 1992; (iv) and (v) warnings introduced in Britain from January
1992 as a direct result of the implementation of European Community guidelines on
the advertising and sale of tobacco products; (vi) common notice in British offices;
(vii) joke notice in California employment agency window (probably a joke).

5.4.7 b   IM/PERSONAL ADVERTS

(i)   *Attractive Male*, 38, fair hair, hazel eyes, non-smoker, seeks relationship with
        warm, affectionate Lady. Photo, please.

(ii)   *WELL DRESSED*, well travelled, honest, sincere, divorced, young 41 Male
        seeks slim attractive Female for possible lasting relationship. Prove to me that
        there is life after divorce.

(iii)   *Artistic, feminine* Eurasian lady, petite, single, looking for nonsmoking man for
        lunch time Malay/Chinese meals. Go 'Dutch' maybe more if friendship develops
        . . . Box No 432.

(iv)   Mother seeking good-looking educated girl for clean-shaven Sikh male,
        cultured, US citizen, 40, 5ft 11in, divorced. Hotel management, studying
        accountancy.

(v)   Aunt invites suitable match from professional men physicians/engineers/
        scientists.

(vi)   FLOPPY OLD HOUND on long leash, bored with fantasies, seeks Earth
        mother, object letters, chats, occasional meets for sniffs and scratches.

(vii)   BRIGHTON BIKER, 36, hairy, large motor cycle, seeks bored housewife for
        wild rides while the kids are at school.

(viii) LEMON CAKETTE seeks professional man for afternoon tea.

(ix)   CZECHMATE – 500+ cultured, sophisticated ladies – doctors, teachers,
        lawyers, radio, TV producers, 'the Arts' from Czechoslovakia, seek sincere

gentlemen for marriage. As featured on BBC News, Anglia TV, BBC World Service, *Sunday Observer*.

(i) and (ii) from *Oxford Star*, 8 November 1990; (iii) from *Adelaide Advertiser*, 7 June 1996; (iv) and (v) from *India Today*, 30 April 1992; (vi)–(ix) from *Private Eye*, 27 March 1992 and 8 May 1992.

5.4.7 c MISSION AND CUSTOMER SERVICE STATEMENTS

(i)   We aim to provide quality student-centred higher education which is responsive to the needs of the community.

(ii)   Stack 'em deep and teach 'em cheap!

(iii)   . . . Their mission: to boldly go where no man has ever gone before.

(iv)   We aim for you to serve well.

(i) British university draft mission statement (1996); (ii) Unofficial mission statement reported by US university colleague; (iii) *Star Trek*, mission of *Starship Enterprise*; (iv) Sign in tennis shop.

5.4.7 d DIALOGUE WITH A CASH-IN-THE-WALL MACHINE

WELCOME!

Please insert your card

Warning – Never use a temporary card reader.

If suspicious, phone 'card loss'.

[*You insert card*]

Please wait a moment

[*You wait*]

Please tap in your personal number on keyboard

[*You quickly tap it in*]

Please tap in your personal number again

or press 'Error' to retrieve card

[*You tap it in more carefully*]

Please choose service you require

| Cash | > | < Balance |
| Order cheque book > | | < Other services |

[*Press 'Cash'*]

Sum required:

| £10 | > | < £50 |
| £20 | > | < Other sum |

[*Press '£20'*]

Your request is being attended to.

Do you require a receipt for this transaction?

| Yes | > |
| No | > |

[*Press 'No'*]

Please take card

   [*Take card*]

Please wait!

   [*Take money*]

   WELCOME!

Please insert your card

Warning – Never use a temporary card reader.

If suspicious, phone 'card loss'.

5.4.7 e ANSWER-PHONE MESSAGES

(i)   Hi! This is Alan Jenkins here. Sorry I'm not in just now – but if you'd like to
      leave your name and number after the beep, I'll get back to you just as soon as
      I can. Thanks a lot. See ya [*Pause*] Here comes the beep, I hope . . . [*Long
      pause, crackle, BANG, beeeeeeeeep*]

(ii) Thank you for calling British Aerospace, Chadderton. There is no reply from
      that number at present. For operator, please press the star on your telephone
      NOW. Otherwise please wait or try again later. [*Sound of Vivaldi's 'Four
      Seasons'*]

(iii) This is a British Telecom recorded message. You have not been charged
      for this call. The number you require has been changed. Please dial the same
      code inserting a '1' after the first '0'. This is a British Telecom recorded
      message . . .

5.4.7 f INTERNET CONFERENCING

R: This week's starter: 'I call him Friday.'

S: Oh God, not Robinson Crusoe again!!!!!!

D: I called him a lazy bastrad this morning but he still wouldn't make the tea for a
      change. Will that do? Or do you want a whole novel? A blow by blo account.

R: Not necessarily, S, not if yu don't want. What's a 'bastrad', D? It sounds
      interesting.

A: I'd call him De 'Foe' but its already been done. Can I choose the starter
      tomorrow? 'Green ideas sleep furiously' for instance. It's already half a poem.
      Any offers for another half?

D: It's a BASTARD who can't spell, something like 'yu', R. You can't ahve rapid
      response and imacualte speeling – see what i mean.

E: Hi! I reckon crusoe could have green ideas by sleeping furiously on friday
      depending what they were on apart from one another's nerves. Tournier sussed
      that in the sixties.

The prelude to a simple electronic workshop on (re)writing, London 1997. This
session opens with a cue line from *Robinson Crusoe* (see 5.2.2 b–c). In this case the
participants were at various terminals on the same institutional network. More
ambitious workshops use such things as multiple cues, variations on a theme,
renegotiated scenarios. Participants may work in sub-groups or 'cells', including
periodic loop back and 'pooling'. Previously stored materials may be accessed and

incorporated. Workshops may also involve students and teachers in different institutions and even in different countries. All or some of the resulting text should be printed out later, analysed and a critical commentary attached (see 4.3–4).

5.4.7 g SOME CONTEMPORARY 'I'DENTITIES

What do *you* think could be the various **genres**, **discourses** and **con/texts** in play? See 'I'dentifications over the page only when you have weighed some possibilities.

(i)
At night I dream of many things
Some of which I plan and save for
Some of which I achieve
When I was young I wanted to see Africa
To run away
And so I travelled but never left
my dream
changed
and I became us
became a family
And while dazzling things dazzle still
My values hold dear

(ii)
There is no gentleness,
no softness, no warmth in this deep cave.
My hands have felt along the cave's stony sides, and, in
every crevice, there is only black depth.
Sometimes, there is almost no air.
Then I gasp for new air,
though all the time, I am breathing
the very air that is in this cave.
There is no opening, no outlet.
I am imprisoned.
But not alone.

(iii)
I have a little brain
Tucked safely in my head
And another little brain
Which is in the air instead
This follows me, and plays with me
And talks to me in bed
The other one confuses me
The one that's in my head.

The texts used in 5.4.7 (g) are: (i) female voice-over from TV ad for Nationwide Anglia building society, United Kingdom, November 1990; (ii) extract from journal of schizo-phrenic in R.D. Laing *The Divided Self*, Harmondsworth: Penguin, 1968: 146; (iii) poem by Annabel Laurance, age 10, Uganda, 1975.

GLOSSARY OF COMMON GRAMMATICAL AND LINGUISTIC TERMS

This alphabetical glossary offers brief explanations and illustrations of all the grammatical and linguistic terms you are likely to meet in initial courses on English LANGUAGE. Many of them are drawn together and applied as tools in the 'Frameworks and checklists for close reading' (4.2). They are in play whenever detailed verbal analysis is needed (e.g., in 1.8).

Most of the terms featured are common and traditional (e.g., articles, noun, sentence). A few come from more specialised but increasingly influential areas such as *pragmatics and *functional linguistics. As usual, items highlighted in **bold** (e.g., **accent, subject, text**) have fuller entries in Part Three, while items marked with an asterisk (e.g., *active, *creole, *transitive) are featured elsewhere in passing in the main body of the book. Most other italicised terms can be found elsewhere in this glossary. All of these items can be followed up through the index. Fuller explanation and illustration of traditional terms can be found in Greenbaum and Quirk 1990, Crystal 1996 and Hurford 1994 (with exercises); *functional terms can be found in Halliday 1985 and Halliday and Hasan 1989. Wales 1989 is a useful reference book. Terms specifically to do with communications and with language and literacy can be followed up in, respectively, O'Sullivan *et al.* 1994 and Carter 1995. Relevant theory (with practice) can be found in Carter and Nash 1990, Hodge and Kress 1993 and Mills 1995.

Go on to extend and supplement this glossary yourself as you feel the need. Add further illustrations to the existing entries and develop new entries of your own. The above reference books can help in this respect too.

accent Features of pronunciation that identify the speaker with a particular national, regional or social group (e.g., all the ways in which different groups say the words 'Good morning'; see 1.2).

acceptable Those usages which are recognised as 'well-formed' and 'normal' by a particular group (e.g., 'She wants' in Standard British English; 'she want' in many Black Englishes and dialects; see 5.4.5 e).

*active **1** Of verbal constructions where the grammatical subject controls the verbal action (e.g., 'Iraqi soldiers march . . .'), as opposed to **passive* verbs where the grammatical subject is controlled by the verbal action (e.g., 'Iraqi POWs are marched . . .' (see 5.2.5 c). **2** Of language competence in general, distinguishing words which people actively use in their own speech and writing, and the larger range of words which people passively recognise in listening and reading.

addresser–addressee The roles and relations obtaining between speakers and listeners, writers and readers, presenters and viewers (e.g., me and you).

adjective A structurally optional class of word which modifies the meaning of a noun (e.g., 'That *beautiful tabby* cat'). Items such as 'a', 'the' and 'that' also modify the meaning of the noun but are usually distinguished as *articles* and, along with adjectives, come under the larger category of (pre-)*modifiers*.

adverb A structurally optional class of word which modifies the meaning of a verb, usually by supplying a sense of *circumstance* (e.g., 'She writes *beautifully*). An adverbial phrase could be much bigger but occupy the same structural position (e.g., 'She writes *beautifully / in the morning / at home*'). Here the / distinguishes between adverbs of, respectively, manner, time and place.

*agent **1** In functional grammar, the person or thing responsible for a dynamic process involving an affected body (e.g., '*He / The car* hit the wall'). **2** Generally, *agency* refers to the perceived causation or determined motivation of an event (see **subject**).

*alliteration Words beginning with the same sound (e.g., 'You *great galloping goon!*'). Alliteration can also function as a large-scale structural principle in poetry, usually reinforced by patterns of stress (e.g., 5.1.1, 5.1.2 c–d). Along with *assonance* and *consonance* (the repetition of, respectively, vowels and consonants within words), alliteration is frequently used for localised effects in poetry, advertising and speech.

animate One of the primary *selectional features* identified in traditional *semantics*, conventionally braced against its binary opposite inanimate. Thus 'man' and 'cat' are animate, whereas 'rock' and 'earth' are inanimate. However, a crude animate/ inanimate distinction breaks down (as do many others) if we operate in a cultural frame other than that of Western objectivist science (e.g., the earth is animate in Aboriginal and many other world-views; see 5.4.4 e). The in/animacy distinction is also dissolved or challenged in much **myth* and **poetry** (e.g., 5.4.4 d; 5.4.5 e), as in **metaphorical* usage generally (e.g., 'It's raining cats and dogs').

antonym See *synonym*.

apostrophe **1** A mark of punctuation which signals the omission of a letter (e.g., 'don't') or signals a possessive/genitive noun (e.g., 'This woman's bag', 'Ms. Howells's bag') (see *punctuation*). **2** A rhetorical figure whereby an inanimate object, idea or absent person is addressed (e.g., **odes* beginning 'O wild West Wind . . .', 'Time, blunt thou . . .!'(see 5.4.4 c)).

apposition A series of items, often nouns or noun phrases, which have the same grammatical status (e.g., a shopping list, a reference to 'Claire Woods, the director', and the sequence 'Squinting. Blinking. Crying' in 5.4.4 b).

archaism An old word or phrase no longer in common use, often added for period flavour (and perhaps humour) or belonging to some fossilised usage such as legal terminology (e.g., ' "Gadzooks!", cried Billy Bunter' or 'The plaintiff shall rise').

articles (also called pre-determiners) Distinguished as definite ('the'), indefinite ('a, some') and demonstrative ('this, these', 'that, those'). Like *adjectives*, these are items which pre-modify the meaning of nouns, in this case signalling kinds of specificity and generality, or proximity and remoteness (hence the difference between 'The / a / that man appeared').

associations Those items which commonly occur close to or in the company of one another (e.g., leaf with branch, tree, green, grow, roots, breeze; compact disc with stereo, cassette, hi-fi, insert, HMV shop). These are also sometimes called items which *collocate* or belong to the same *semantic field*. Notice that nearly all words have multiple associations and can be sited in more than one semantic field (e.g., leaf also with loose, paper and gold, turning over a new leaf; disc also with moon, computer, records, a slipped –). In PSYCHOLOGY, 'free association' is used to plot people's characteristic thought processes: cue words are supplied and the patient responds with the first words that come to mind.

auxiliary verb A secondary *verb* used to support the main verb with respect to tense or **modality*. (In 'She *will / ought to / mustn't* do that' – all the italicised verbs are auxiliary.)

bilingual, multilingual A person or speech community which uses, respectively, two or many languages. In some sense all persons and communities are bi- or multilingual in that we constantly switch amongst registers and language varieties according to situation and topic.

*binary oppositions Seeing and saying things in terms of extreme oppositions and 'either/or' (digital) logic: on or off, black or white, masculine or feminine, up or down, internal or external, subject or object, this or that, now or then, here or there, etc.

*body language Communication by means of posture, gesture, eye contact, touch and, by extension, hair design, cosmetics, clothing and personal accessories. These are all a crucial part of **non-verbal* COMMUNICATION.

*choice and combination The two major axes of LANGUAGE structure and of **sign-systems* in general; also called, respectively, *paradigmatic* and *syntagmatic* axes. Everything from traffic lights to words, and from fashion to cityscapes can be described as systems in which items are chosen and combined. Conversely, by **negation*, we can consider what has *not* been chosen and *how else* things might have been combined.

circumstance items Along with *participants and *processes, one of the three basic structural categories of functional grammar. Circumstance items are typically *adverbs* or adverbial phrases. They are often optional in terms of grammatical structure but fundamentally affect our sense of **context**. Thus in 'They will *probably* arrive *tomorrow from Cardiff*' all the highlighted items fill out our understanding of the circumstances. Remove them and we're left with a basic participant–process structure (here pronoun– verb) which can stand alone, but which tells us much less about the manner, time and place of the event: merely that 'They will arrive'.

clause A structural unit in a sentence, usually distinguished as either *main* clause (the central structure which could stand on its own) or dependent clause (which cannot). Thus in 'The fool who lives on the hill has arrived' the main clause is 'The fool . . . has arrived'; the dependent clause is 'who lives on the hill'. The latter is also called a *subordinate* clause.

closed set A part of speech or word class composed of a limited number of items (e.g., pronouns, articles, conjunctions), as distinct from an *open set* which can be virtually infinite (e.g., nouns, verbs, adjectives). Notice, however, that, historically, even 'closed' sets change and are in that sense 'ajar' if not quite 'open'. Thus the second person singular pronouns 'thou/thee/thine' were common in earlier English and now remain only in some dialects. Meanwhile, 's/he' (usually said 'he or she') is becoming current in contemporary English.

code A system of signs for transmitting messages, now usually called *sign-system. Code-switching refers to a speaker's or writer's movement between varieties or languages.

cohesion Everything which helps to hold a **text** together and thereby encourages us to perceive it as, in some sense, 'a whole'. Factors contributing to cohesion span the whole range from visual layout or intonation patterns, through logical and spatio-temporal connectors (e.g., 'However, . . . therefore, . . . Here, then, . . . '), parallelism and associations, to overarching matters of **discourse**, **genre**, **intertextuality** and **context**. Cohesion is the formal counterpart of *coherence* (i.e. what makes sense). Both are not simply intrinsic properties of the text but also a product of the reader's, audience's or viewer's perception of that text in some context.

competence An internalised sense of a particular language and, by extension, culture. This is realised concretely through specific *performances*.

connectors A general term for all those items we use to forge explicit logical and spatio-temporal links between one sentence or part of a sentence and another. These include *coordinators* ('and', 'but', 'or'), which signal basic operations of addition, negation and choice and often join elements of equivalent grammatical status, and *conjuncts* ('because', 'therefore', 'however', 'thus' 'moreover, . . . ', 'in other words, . . . ', etc.), which signal more complex kinds of causality, often with grammatical dependence. Connectors are crucial to textual cohesion.

connotation See *denotation*.

consonants Those sounds which frame *vowels* and establish *syllable* boundaries (e.g., *president*, where 'pr' and 'nt' also represent consonant clusters).

context Everything considered to be 'with-the-text', from immediate situation (including participants, occasion and medium) to larger cultural frames. Co-text specifically refers to the immediate textual environment, the other texts a text keeps company with (e.g., the surrounding items on a newspaper page).

context-sensitive words (also called 'shifters' and 'deictics', from Greek *deixis*, meaning 'pointing') These are words and phrases which are especially dependent on **context** to fix their meaning. They include personal *pronouns* ('I, me, mine, my'; 'we', 'you', 's/he', 'they', 'it', etc.); demonstrative *adjectives and pronouns* ('this/these', 'that/those', etc); relative *pronouns* ('who', 'which', 'where', 'when') and *adverbs and adverbial groups* such as 'here', 'there', 'now', 'then', 'yesterday', 'the day after tomorrow', 'abroad', etc. Thus the sentence 'I'm here now' (which contains three heavily context-sensitive words) may be said by many different people in different places at different times. By contrast, the sentence 'Rob Pope is in Oxford, Sunday, 20 October 1996' (which contains mainly proper nouns) is relatively *context-free*. Notice, however, that all words are to some extent context-sensitive. The precise meaning of that last example still depends upon what different people understand by 'Oxford', 'Sunday' and 'Rob Pope'!

conversation The construction, exchange and transformation of meanings through speech, and more generally through **dialogue** of all kinds. In speech, the characteristic levels are, larger to smaller: event, transaction, interaction, turn and move.

cooperative principle A view of COMMUNICATION, especially conversation, premised on the notion that people aim to cooperate (i.e. work together) to achieve success. Grice proposes four maxims which must be observed for such cooperation to take place. Speakers should: (1) give adequate information – neither too little nor too much (quantity); (2) not tell lies (quality); (3) be relevant (relation); (4) avoid obscurity (manner). Leech adds a fifth politeness principle: (5) be polite. Accidental failure to observe these maxims 'violates' the cooperative principle. Deliberate violations 'flout' them. Grice's and Leech's models can be aligned with a consensus model of communication and, by implication, society. In this view misunderstanding is basically the result of 'a failure to communicate'; the desire or need *not* to cooperate is treated as abnormal or *deviant. However, this emphasis can only be maintained if the persistently unequal power relations in actual societies are treated as abnormal. In a conflict model of language and society 'misunderstanding' is the systemic result of fundamental **differences** of interest. 'Breakdowns in communication' are the symptoms not the causes.

It is therefore also necessary to recognise a kind of 'non-cooperative' (or, perhaps better, 'assertiveness') principle. This occasions some supplementary maxims: (1a) ask for more or different information; (2a) don't expect to be told 'the whole truth and nothing but the truth'; (3a) ask 'relevant to whom?', whose interests are being served? (4a) look for the loose ends which must have been tied up or snipped off to achieve total clarity; (5a) be forthright and assertive – if not exactly 'impolite'!

coordination See *sentence*.

creole A more fully developed and self-sufficient form of language than *pidgin*, from which creoles in part derive. Pidgins are limited forms of secondary, supporting language used for minimal functional understanding in such areas as work, trade and religion and are often tied to specific master–slave and slave–slave relations. Pidgins have no native speakers. Creoles, however, have developed all the major features and functions of a language and do have native speakers. Many Afro-Caribbean Englishes are creoles (e.g., Collins 5.1.9 c), and these often carry traces of other languages of empire such as Spanish, Portuguese, French and Dutch as well as of many native, non-European languages. Creoles are languages palpably in the making, much as the European vernaculars formed after the Roman Empire.

declarative   A statement; also see *sentences* and *speech acts*.

deictics   See *context-sensitive words*.

denotation   What appears to be the core meaning or primary *reference* of a word, as distinct from general cultural *connotations* and personal *associations*. For instance, 'nourishment', 'food', 'grub' and 'yummies' all have something in common. They all refer to 'things to eat'. That is their shared denotation. Similarly, 'senior citizen', 'the elderly', 'OAP (old-age pensioner)', 'old fogey' and 'wrinkly' all have overlapping denotations but markedly different connotations.

*deviation   Narrowly, any localised twist or turn of the language away from what is expected (e.g., 'I got up at the crack of *lunchtime*' (expecting 'dawn'); 'lipsmackin-thirstquenchinacetastin . . . ' (expecting breaks between words)). Broadly, any way in which expected norms or rules are bent or extended. In the sense that we all constantly make more or less unique utterances, we are bending and extending the language all the time. Thus, paradoxically, some degree of 'deviance' is normal. Poets are especially prone to verbal 'deviance'. See **foregrounding**.

diachronic   (from Greek *dia-chronos* – 'across-time') To do with language change; a historical approach to language. Conversely, a *synchronic* approach (from Greek *syn-chronos* – 'together/same-time') concentrates on language at a given point in time (e.g., now, or across the fourteenth century). A diachronic perspective focuses on **variation**; a synchronic perspective focuses on **variety**. Both are ultimately, intimately interrelated.

dialect   The distinctive vocabulary choices, syntactic combinations and **accent** identified with a particular region within a national language. Some approaches distinguish **variety** according to user (dialect) and use (register). *Idiolect* is the particular and to some extent peculiar mix of varieties associated with a single person, her or his 'linguistic fingerprint'.

dialogue   (from Greek *dia-logos* – 'across-word') Verbal exchange, notably in conversation. More generally, a two- or many-way interaction as distinct from a one-way **monologue**. For *Bakhtin all language use is *dialogic* in that we are always in some sense responding to a past utterance and anticipating a future response. Words are therefore sites of struggle and celebration between **self** and **others** and are constituted by converging and diverging **discourses**.

diction   Archaic word for vocabulary or word-choice usually associated with RHETORIC and **poetry**.

*direct and indirect speech   The difference between, respectively, a supposedly accurate tran/script and an approximate report of what someone has said. Thus *'I'm coming,' he said* records direct speech, while *He said that he was coming* reports through indirect speech. Direct speech usually entails quotation marks, a separate phrase attributing the speech, and some differences in pronouns and tenses. Indirect speech usually entails the absence of quotation marks, a grammatically integrated attributing phrase and a uniform consistency of pronouns and tenses. *Free direct speech* would simply be *I'm coming* (with no framing attribution). *Free indirect speech* occurs where the distinction between speaker and reporter is blurred and there is an inexplicit conflation of personal references and temporal perspectives – when we

cannot be sure whose words are being represented (e.g., *Coming, yes. Going when?*, where who is perceived as saying or thinking these words would depend on context). All these ways of representing speech can be applied to and to some extent overlap with ways of representing thought and other perceptions (e.g., hearing and seeing). Simply substitute analogous structures using, say, 'thinks/thought that', 'sees/saw that', 'hears/heard that'.

discourse Several meanings are currently available: **1** a formal speech or treatise (archaic); **2 conversation** in particular or **dialogue** in general; **3** stretches of **text** above the level of the sentence, including **context** and **intertextuality**; **4** COMMUN-ICATIVE practices expressing the interests of a particular socio-historical group or institution. **Discourse analysis** engages with the last three in varying permutations.

elision The sliding together of adjacent *syllables* to produce a single item (e.g., 'She'll' – 'she will', 'can't – 'cannot'). Elision is a routine feature in speech of all kinds but is rarely represented in formal writing. Poets and song-writers often avail themselves of elision (as well as elongation of vowel sounds) to maintain a regular number of syllables to the line.

ellipsis Omission of items implicitly understood from the context (e.g., 'See you tomorrow!', which omits 'I/we'll'). Ellipsis is especially common in speech.

etymology The history or derivation of words and its study.

euphemism (Greek for 'well-speaking') Words and phrases which cover or obscure culturally *taboo* subjects, often associated with birth, death, war, sex, defecation and, in some contexts, money, religion and politics. *Dysphemisms* (Greek 'bad-speaking') are words emphasising unpleasantness. Most euphemisms and dysphemisms are culture-specific and express a culture's symptomatic fears and anxieties. The famous Monty Python 'Dead Parrot' sketch is constructed almost wholly of euphemisms and dysphemisms (see 5.4.5 a). Such materials are common in **comedy** and **carnival** generally.

existential subject (also called 'prop', 'empty' or 'dummy' subject) Words such as 'there' and 'it' when used as subjects of verbs without any explicit sense of what is being referred to (e.g., '*There* is every reason to believe that ...', '*It* seems certain that ...'). These devices deny or delay a sense of agency and responsibility. There is therefore every reason to believe and, indeed, it seems certain that such constructions are especially useful when one wishes to sound impersonal and authoritative (as here).

*figurative Language composed of **metaphors*, metonyms and similes (see **imagery**) and not perceived to be 'literal'. However, all language is in some sense figurative in that even the most literal word turns out to have a metaphorical aspect. For instance, the word 'literal' itself derives from *littera*, the Latin word for 'letter', and that in turn relates to a word for 'shore', 'margin' or 'boundary' – and so on.

finite and non-finite See *verbs*.

foregrounding Any linguistic feature or strategy which draws attention to itself against an assumed *background* in the text and/or the language at large. Sound patterning, visual presentation, word choice (e.g., metaphor) and syntax may all be foregrounded in this way. So may **genres** and MEDIA when there is a marked shift or switch from one to another (e.g., a sudden shift into prose during a poem, or into song during a naturalistic play).

form **1** Outward appearance or structure of words as **signifiers*, usually considered without reference to meaning, *function* and **signifieds*. **2** *Formal* language tends to be precise, impersonal and self-consciously 'proper', and to be associated with public occasions. *Informal* language tends to be looser, more personal and relaxed. **3** FORMALISM ('Russian') was the name given to an early structuralist movement by its detractors (see 2.4).

fronting In grammar, moving a feature from the middle or end to prominence at the front (e.g., '*Slowly*, she turned the page').

function **1** Language in use – what words do to us and what we do with them (cf. *form* and *grammar – functional*). **2** FUNCTIONALISM ('Czech') was a socially and historically aware development of FORMALISM (see 2.4).

genre Any 'kind' or 'category' of cultural practice; textually, any **intertextual** frame in which a text can be placed. Actual instances of genres always turn out to be **hybrid*, never pure.

*grammar Broadly, structures of LANGUAGE and their study. More narrowly and usually, grammar is synonymous with *syntax* (including *morphology*), one of the three main categories of linguistic analysis (the other two being *phonology* and *semantics*). Grammar/syntax thus conceived is concerned with the formal rules for structuring stretches of language, chiefly at the level of the *clause* and the *sentence*. The kind of grammar linguists are primarily concerned with is *descriptive* (describing what people actually do with language) rather than *prescriptive* or *proscriptive* (telling people what they should or shouldn't do measured against some normative notion of 'correctness'). In the teaching of a particular language, 'Grammars' are text-books designed to guide learners in well-formed and acceptable structuring of that language. There are two main contemporary models of grammar:

- ♦ generative-transformational grammar, which concentrates upon the mentalistic notion of a universal, inbuilt language *competence* and language as the generation of infinite 'surface' structures from finite 'deep' structures (primarily associated with **Chomsky);
- ♦ *functional* grammar, which concentrates upon how language choice and combination relate to what people actually do with language in society and history, primarily associated with **Halliday (see *participants and processes* and *circumstance*).

graphology visible verbal marks on or in some material such as wood, stone, paper, plastic, or a TV screen; also the study of those marks. Graphology includes **spelling, *punctuation*, visual layout and all aspects of visible design.

hedges, hedging Ways of playing down or weakening the impact of an utterance (e.g., by adding 'well, . . . ', 'a sort of a', 'kind of', 'perhaps', 'a little', 'in a way', etc.). Ways of playing up or strengthening the impact of an utterance include such *intensifiers* as 'certainly', 'absolutely', 'in every respect', 'always'. All are aspects of *modality*.

heteroglossia ('varied-tonguedness', the usual translation of **Bahktin's *raznorechie*) The fact that any supposedly unitary national language (e.g., ENGLISH) is actually made up of many colliding and coalescing **varieties** and is therefore inherently hetero-glossic – a *hybrid. For Bakhtin, every language is ceaselessly subject to *centrifugal forces* (tending to fragment it) and *centripetal forces* (tending to unify it). Because these forces are never equal, LANGUAGE has a constant tendency towards **variation** and change, even to the point of one language turning into another. *Polyglossia* refers to the 'external' interaction of notionally discrete national languages. Ultimately, heteroglossia and polyglossia interrelate. *Monoglossia* is the notion of a single, unitary language.

hyperbole   Emphatic exaggeration (e.g., 'There was tons to eat').

hypotaxis   The use of dependent, subordinated *clauses*; cf. *parataxis*.

idiolect   See **dialect**.

idiom   See *morphology*.

imperative   A form of command or direction (e.g., 'Go!'); see *sentences* and *speech acts*.

implicature   In *speech acts*, those subtle, indirect meanings which go beyond or even subvert a speaker's apparently literal, direct meanings. For instance, depending on the situation, 'Have you done the washing up yet?' can be intended as (1) a reproach; (2) an offer to do it oneself; (3) an invitation to come to bed; (4) any other plausibly 'indirect' meaning you come up with. Cf. *locutions*.

inference   The sense-making activity of listeners, readers and viewers: how we actually go about constructing meaning out of the materials we are given, most obviously through 'gap-filling'. Thus we may be told 'A man lived in a house'; but the precise kind of 'man' and 'house' we imagine will depend on inference. *Addressers* may imply – or indirectly *implicate* – particular meanings; but it is still up to *addressees* to make their own inferences. Cf. *locutions*.

information structure   The organisation of verbal or other information. The basic questions are:

1 What item of information is introduced first (the *theme*)?
2 What item is held over till later (the *rheme*)?
3 What knowledge and attitudes are being assumed (the '*given*' premises)?
4 What knowledge and attitudes are being offered as additional or supplementary (the '*new*')?

For instance, the headlines '19 shot in Bosnia' and 'Muslim Serbs shoot 19 Christian militia in former Yugoslavia' have different information structures. They begin and close with different information (here using, respectively, *passive* and *active* verbal structures); they make varying assumptions about and demands upon the reader's existing knowledge; and they offer (or omit) to supplement that knowledge in different ways.

intensifiers   See *hedges*.

inter-   A Latin-derived prefix meaning 'between' much favoured in contemporary criticism (e.g., interpersonal, **intertextual**, interrelation; also see the politics of *(textual) intervention*). 'Inter-' words are commonly used to mark the significance of relations *between* persons, times, places and events, and thereby resist the tendency to fix meanings and values *within* particular phenomena.

interrogative Questioning; see *sentences* and *speech acts*.

intonation A crucial *paralinguistic* aspect of speech-sound embracing pitch (relative height of voice), *stress* (relative force), and voice quality (husky, whispered, etc.). Intonation in English may be broadly distinguished in so far as it is rising (suggesting a question, exclamation or general excitement); even (suggesting a statement); or falling (suggesting an emphatic statement or disappointment). Many permutations are possible.

LANGUAGE **1** The notional totality of all verbal systems. **2** The nominal identity of particular languages (e.g., ENGLISH, Russian, Yoruba). **3** Loosely, of any COMMUN-ICATION or *sign-system (e.g., 'body language', 'the language of music').

lexical item A precise, if cumbersome, alternative to 'word or phrase'. For instance, consider the alternatives in 'she loves/adores/has a liking for/is fond of/ ice cream'. Even though the number of *words* in each case varies from one to four, there is just one structurally corresponding lexical item in each case.

locutions All *speech acts* can be broken down analytically into three components: the *illocution* (what the speaker intends or indirectly *implicates*); the *locution* (the material of the message itself); and the *perlocution* (what the listener actually *infers* and understands). Cf. (non-)*cooperative principle*.

logocentric Privileging LANGUAGE before other *sign-systems* and modes of COMMUNICATION.

MEDIUM The material means whereby messages are communicated: speech, writing, print and audio-visual (e.g., electronic) media; in paint, wood, stone, metal, plastic, etc. We also speak generally of the 'mass' or 'popular' (i.e. *broadcast) media. *Mediation* is the activity of processing materials in particular media and always results in a transformation and translation (never a mere transference) of information.

meta- A Greek-derived prefix meaning 'above' or 'over' much favoured in contemporary criticism. Metalanguage is a comment *on* language *in* language: any way in which the act of verbal communication itself is drawn attention to. Hence the metalinguistic function of the highlighted words in the following: '*You might say* it's a catastrophe, *in a sense*'. '*My reading of this* is that . . . '. All the terms in this glossary also offer a technical metalanguage, words describing and defining words. By extension, texts which **foreground** the actual process of composition and draw attention to their own 'made' status are termed metatextual.

*metaphor Talking of one thing in terms of another by implicit substitution or compression. For instance, take Walcott's densely packed lines: 'The world's green age then was a rotting lime/whose stench became the charnel galleon's text.' Here a number of usually discrete concepts and words are conflated so as to be seen in terms of one another: the world + green + age; charnel + galleon + text. However, a great deal of routine language use is also metaphorical in its tendency to colour one kind of experience with another (e.g., 'Where *in hell* (or *heaven*) is that screwdriver? I'd *dig* it out for you, but I'm not *thinking straight* this morning'). These are fairly *dead metaphors*, though even then not wholly without signs of rhetorical colour. Hamlet's 'To be or not to be' soliloquy opens with a number of *extended metaphors*, which may also be considered '*mixed*' or '*compounded*', depending how successfully integrated

you reckon them to be. Explicit comparison signalled by such words as 'like', 'as', 'compare', 'looks/seems like' is called *simile. Cf. *figurative.

*metonymy Talking of one thing in terms of some physically connected part of it; e.g., 'There was a motion from *the floor*, so *the chair* called for a seconder.' Cf. 'farm *hands*' (i.e. manual workers, who work with their hands) and 'a *motor*' (i.e. car).

*modality Those features of language which most obviously express the 'angling' of events in terms of possibility, probability, conditionality and obligation. All the highlighted alternatives in the following contribute to modality: 'I *must/may/could/ought to* say, I *certainly/really do rather/quite/perhaps* like this *very much/a little/sometimes*'. (A much more simply modalised version would be 'I say I like this'.) Typically, then, it is the *auxiliary verbs* and the *adverbs* (including *hedges* and *intensifiers*) which contribute most obviously to modality. Cf. *speech acts*.

modification, pre- and post See *noun groups*.

monoglossia See *heteroglossia*.

monologue See **dialogue**.

morphology The internal structure of words; also its study. For instance, 'reactive' consists of the *morphemes* re + act + -ive.
  ♦ 're-' is a bound prefix because it doesn't appear on its own and is attached to the front of the word;
  ♦ 'act' is a free stem because it could stand on its own and is here the core around which the word is built;
  ♦ '-ive' is a bound suffix in that it cannot stand on its own and is attached to the end of the word.
  Other ways of word-building, aside from basically adding morphemes, include:
  ♦ *mutation*, changing the shape of the root (e.g., 'mouse' plural 'mice'– not 'mouses'; 'run' past tense 'ran – not 'runned');
  ♦ *compounds*, a word made of two or more other words which combine to produce a new word with a specialised meaning; thus a 'hotdog' is not a 'hot dog'; a 'greenhouse' is not a 'green house';
  ♦ *idioms*, which are similar to compounds in that they combine a number of words to produce a larger unit with a specialised sense; thus 'to put your foot in it' or 'throw up'.

  Word-building is going on all the time. Witness this tiny sample from the hundreds of thousands of the past twenty years: 'sell-by date', 'privatise', 'prioritise', 'bio-degradable', 'trekkie', 'cyber-punk'.

multifunctionality The fact that the same word often has more than one grammatical function and can operate in various *word-classes*. Thus 'light' can function as noun, verb and adjective: 'Have you a light?' (*noun*); 'Light my fire!' (*verb*); 'What a light, airy room' (*adjective*). (Hence the possibility of the joke 'Have you got a light(,) mac?') In fact the great majority of words are grammatically multifunctional. 'Table', 'man', 'woman', 'gender', 'black', 'white', 'race', 'book', for instance, can all be used as nouns or verbs or adjectives.

multilingual See *bilingual*.

nominalisation The realisation of an event as a *noun* (and, by implication, a fixed 'thing' or *product*) rather than as a *verb* (and, by implication, an action, state or *process*). For instance, 'recession' is an abstract noun which nominalises what might otherwise be expressed verbally as 'the process whereby employment, wages, output and profits are constantly driven downwards' or (using an *active* rather than a *passive* verb) 'the process whereby certain people constantly drive employment, wages, output and profits downwards'. Notice that 'employment', 'wages', 'output' and 'profits' are also, in turn, nominalisations; as, indeed, are 'process' and 'people'. Try realising each of these nouns through a definition which involves a verb and you will see that this automatically entails a sense of process and change as well as, perhaps, responsibility and agency.

non-verbal communication A catch-all term for the multifarious ways in which people (along with other animals) communicate without using words. *Body language* is one of the most fundamental; but music, painting, architecture, land- and cityscaping might all be cited too. The problem with the 'non-verbal' tag is that it divides all COMMUNICATION into 'verbal' and 'non-', and thereby privileges a logocentric view of **sign-systems*.

nouns A *word-class* (or 'part of speech') distinguished from and braced against other word-classes such as *verb, adjective* and *adverb*. For instance, only nouns would be likely to fill the slot marked 'X' in '*X fell suddenly*' (where X might be 'Rain' 'Constantinople', 'He'). And only similar kinds of item would fill the 'Y' slot in 'Falling towards Y' (where Y might be 'home', 'happiness', 'them', 'England'). Nouns may be distinguished as:

   ♦ common nouns, which refer to types or categories of phenomena – e.g., 'table', 'bus conductor', 'atmosphere', 'truth', 'democracy' – which may themselves be further distinguished as *concrete* (e.g., 'table') or *abstract* (e.g., 'truth'), as well as *count* (e.g., 'pea/peas') or *non-count* (e.g., 'cosmos' but not 'cosmoses');
   ♦ proper nouns, which name specific persons, places and events (e.g., 'England', 'Tom Paine', 'St Petersburg', your own name and address);
   ♦ pronouns, which are a special kind of *context-sensitive* word in that they 'stand in' for a noun (hence 'pro-' noun) and can also be further distinguished, namely: the *personal* pronouns 'I, me, my, mine', 'we, us', 'you', 's/he', 'they', 'it'; the *interrogative* pronouns 'who?', 'whom?', 'what?', 'which?', 'where?', 'when?', 'how?' and 'why?'; the *relative* pronouns, which are similar to the latter except that they occur in relative or dependent *clauses* (e.g., 'I'll tell you what, the man who . . .'; also 'that' as in 'the man that arrived'); and the *demonstrative* pronouns, which distinguish 'this/these' from 'that/those' (e.g., 'This is it'). Cf. *noun groups*.

noun groups A structure built around a noun. This structure is best understood in terms of *pre- and post-modification*. Pre- and post-modifiers are items placed, respectively, before and after a *noun* (which is then called the *head* of the noun group). Traditionally, most modifiers are called *adjectives* and adjectival phrases. However, distinguishing pre- and post-modification has the advantage of allowing us to be precise about placement and also to embrace dependent phrases and *clauses* of all kinds. (*Articles/pre-determiners* are pre-modifiers that are usually distinguished separately.) We thus have an overall analytical scheme like this:

(pre-modifiers)		(head)		(post-modification)	
Those (pre-det.) magnificent	young	men	in	their flying	machines
				(pre-mod)	(head)

(Notice that the post-modifying phrase is itself composed of a noun group with 'machines' as the head and 'their' and 'flying' as pre-modifiers; 'in' is a preposition.) Thus, grammatically, we have a noun group within a noun group; while, perceptually, we have a hierarchical layering of one perception within another. Modification has a prodigious effect on the way we see what is represented by the noun. Here, for instance, is a completely stripped-down, *un*modified version of the above noun group: 'men'!

object, direct and *indirect*   See *sentences.*

open set   See *closed set.*

orthography   Letter-forms and spelling; also their study.

paradigm   See *choice and combination.*

paralinguistic features   Those aspects of **speech**-sound which tend to get left out or crudely registered in the transition to **writing**: *intonation, stress,* pitch (relative height of voice), and voice quality (tense, relaxed, whispered, husky, etc.). Along with **body language,* such features are often fundamental to the precise meaning and effect of speech.

parallelism   Repetition with variation: the most common form of textual patterning. Parallelism can be a larger structural feature of texts (e.g., repetition of the same verse form but using different words; mirroring of main plot and sub-plot; recurrence of similar motifs); or it can be highly localised (e.g., 'I am the way, the life and the truth', which has a parallel structure of definite article plus different nouns).

parataxis   The use of coordinated *clauses*; cf. *hypotaxis.*

part of speech   An archaic name for *word-class.*

*participants and **processes*   Two of the three basic structural categories in *functional grammar,* the other being **circumstances* (see Toolan 1988: 111–15 and Halliday 1985: 101–57). Typically, *participants* are expressed by *nouns, processes* by *verbs,* and *circumstances* by *adverbs.* For instance, the two following sentences have the same raw structure at a primary level of analysis:

(1)	The car	hit	the wall	at high speed
(2)	I	shall love	you	for ever
	participant 1	*process*	*participant 2*	*circumstance*
	(noun)	(verb)	(noun)	(adverb)

In each case we are left with a sense of participants ('persons' or 'things') being brought into specific relations by processes in specific circumstances.

There are many kinds of participant–process–circumstance structure in language, and each one corresponds to a particular way of verbalising experience. The main ones are:

♦   *material,* in which something is physically done or acted upon and a change is effected. Typical participants are *agent* and *affected,* e.g., 'The army / exploded / the bomb' (agent – **transitive process* – affected) and 'The bomb / exploded' (affected – **intransitive process*);

♦   *mental-perceptual,* in which participants do not so much act on materials as sense and express awareness of them through the processes 'think', 'feel', 'believe', 'know', etc. Typical participants are *senser* and *phenomenon*, e.g., 'They / know / the truth' and 'She / loves / you' (both senser – process – phenomenon);

♦ *relational*, in which one participant is defined by or relates to another through the processes 'to be' ('is', 'was', etc.), 'become', 'seem', as well as 'have', 'own', etc. Typical participants are, respectively, *identified* and *identifier* or *possessor* and *possessed*, e.g., 'Roses / are / red' (identified – process – identifier) and 'Fred / has / a whippet' (possessor – process – possessed);

♦ *verbalising*, in which the linguistic processes of 'saying', 'writing', 'reading', 'telling', 'informing', 'advising', etc. are themselves what the participants are engaged in. Typical participants are *addresser* and *addressee* (e.g., 'I / am writing / this / for you' (addresser – *transitive process – address – addressee) and 'I / am writing' (addresser / *intransitive process).

participles See *verbs.*

passive See *active* and *verbs.*

performative An utterance that overtly performs an action or constitutes a transaction (e.g., 'I hereby swear . . . ', 'I declare you man and wife', 'I name this building . . . ', 'I promise to pay . . . '). *Pragmatics* extends this insight to all *speech acts* and *discourse.*

phatic Language which maintains social contact and checks that communication channels are open (tags such as ' . . . , you know', ' . . . , isn't it?')

phoneme See *phonology.*

phonetics The study of the physical production and reception of speech sound. Much attention is paid to the articulatory mechanisms whereby speech is produced, especially those which articulate a difference between 'voiced' sounds (where there is vibration in the glottis) and 'unvoiced' sounds (where there isn't). Thus, just as a distinct contrast in sound is essential if we are to recognise different *phonemes* (see **phonology*), so there has to be a distinct contrast in the way the sounds are produced. For instance,

♦ vocal cords vibrate or they don't: /b/ contrasts with /p/; /d/ contrasts with /t/; /v/ contrasts with /f/; /z/ contrasts with /s/. Each of these pairs of sounds is produced similarly, except that in each case the first item is voiced and the second is unvoiced. (All *vowels* and *diphthongs* involve vibration of the cords in the glottis and are voiced.)

♦ air is released suddenly or continuously, thus resulting in a distinction between sudden, *plosive* sounds: e.g., /p/, /b/, /t/, /d/ and continuous, *fricative* sounds: e.g., /f/, /v/, /s/, /z/, /ʃ/. These last three (/s/, /ʃ/ and /z/) are all present, respectively, in the sounds of the word 'sessions', these are also called 'hissing sounds' or *sibilants.*

♦ the *nasal* cavity is used or it isn't: /m/, /n/ and /ŋ/ all sound in the nasal cavity. All are present, in that order, in the word *managing.*

phonology The sound-system of a particular language; also its study. A basic concept of phonology is the *phoneme.* Phonemes are the minimum distinctive **differences** of sound routinely recognised in a particular language. For instance, each of the following words, when spoken, begins with a different sound: 'bin', 'din', 'sin', 'shin', 'thin', 'tin'. Each of these sounds is an *acceptable* English phoneme at the beginning of a word. The sounds corresponding to '*ŋgin*' or '*ɀdgin*', however, are not acceptable in such a position and therefore not a part of routine English phonology. However, if we go on to include the phonological characteristics of the many **varieties** of English, including regional **dialects** and the various national **standards** (American, Caribbean, Australian, etc.), the potential sound system of the language is much more extensive and flexible. Cf. *phonetics*.

phrase A cluster of words grammatically smaller than a *clause*, often taking the form of a *noun* or *adverbial group* (e.g., 'those amazing women', 'up the road').

pidgin See **creole*.

plosive See *phonetics*.

polyglossia See *heteroglossia*.

pragmatics Broadly, study of the practical conditions relating LANGUAGE to **context**. More narrowly, systematic study of the premises, assumptions, expectations, predictions and review processes which underpin successful interaction in language. The most immediately useful work in pragmatics concentrates on 'real world' language, especially **conversation** (rather than made-up examples) and is supported by a wide range of techniques and models concerned with **dialogics, speech acts*, **genre** and **discourse**. Pragmatic studies draw attention to the ways in which people do and do not *cooperate* in producing meaning; the interplay of consensus and conflict, and '**gaps**' as well as the connections between an **addresser**'s *implicature* and an **addressee**'s *inference*. Cf. *locutions*.

pre- and post-modification See *noun groups*.

prepositions (also called *particles*) Items that typically precede nouns and noun groups and occur in phrasal *verbs*, assisting in orienting and interrelating them (e.g., 'up' and 'down' in 'up/down the road' and 'to get up/down').

*processes See **participants* and *verbs*.

progressive and non-progressive/perfective See *verbs*: aspect.

pronouns See *nouns* and *context-sensitive words*.

pronunciation See **accent** and *intonation*.

psycholinguistics Study of the relations between language and mental (perceptual, cognitive and developmental) processes, sometimes in harness with *sociolinguistics*.

punctuation A system of graphic notation developed to point up grammatical, logical or rhythmic structures in **writing** and print. The basic range of punctuation current in written and printed modern English is:

, comma – dash ; semi-colon : colon . full stop

... suspension dots ( ) brackets ' ' single inverted commas " " double inverted commas ? question mark ! exclamation mark

' apostrophe - hyphen Capitalisation, s p a c i n g , paragraphing

indentation, * asterisks, numbering and lettering 1 2 3 . . . a b c . . . (sub- and superscript), specialised symbols ($ £ % & @ etc.).

Many of these punctuation marks have become relatively **standardised** since the development of **printing*. However, like any linguistic system, that of punctuation is constantly changing and evolving to meet new needs. Ostensibly the same items also develop new functions. For instance, in the Middle Ages the punctus (.) was widely used to signal pauses, the length of pause being indicated by its height above the line. The punctus may look like a full stop but it did not, as now, signal the end of sentences. That function was signalled by spacing or another symbol that has now disappeared. From the sixteenth to the nineteenth centuries Nouns were commonly highlighted by the use of initial Capitals (as here, and in modern German). Meanwhile, in contemporary written English there are signs of a marked decrease in the use of the semi-colon (;) – which came in during the fifteenth century – and an increase in the use of commas and dashes. The history of the dash (–) is particularly interesting. Though now sometimes associated with informal writing (e.g., postcards and notes) and stigmatised as casual, the dash was widely used in writing of all kinds in the seventeenth and eighteenth centuries. It was also the most common item of punctuation in the verse of, for instance, Byron (see 5.1.4 d) and Dickinson (5.4.5 d). Apostrophes, meanwhile, are hovering on the brink of dissolution and probably eventual extinction. The fact that they signal missing letters is still obvious with, say, 'can't' (i.e. 'can(no)t' and 'it's' (i.e. 'it (i)s'); but it's hardly obvious with the possessive usage that records a form lost since the fifteenth century (e.g., 'man's' from earlier 'man(ne)s'). Meanwhile, other symbols are becoming unexpectedly current. The mark @ , for instance, was previously an accounting symbol meaning 'so many X @ (at a rate of) $Y'. But now @ has had a new lease of life and is increasingly widely recognised as meaning 'at the e-mail site of'.

reference The capacity of language to 'name' and thereby categorise phenomena in the extra-linguistic world. What is referred to is called the referent.

register A traditional term for language **variety** as it relates to use (medium, situation and purpose) as distinct from user (see **dialect**). Typical questions on register are: Is this language written, printed or otherwise recorded (e.g., electronically)? Is it for use in formal or informal, public or private situations? Is it for technical or non-technical purposes?

reported speech See *direct and indirect speech*.

rhythm Perceived regularities of *stress* in speech, poetry and song.

selectional features The attempt in traditional *semantics* to describe word-meaning through an array of *binary oppositions*: + or − *animate*; + or − human; + or − female; + or − edible ; + or − concrete, etc. Thus the word 'man' can be described as '+ human − female'; while 'bitch' (i.e. female dog) is '− human + female'. The main problem is that the great bulk of language use turns out to be figurative, idiomatic or both. *Metaphor*, too, is a routine – not an exceptional – dimension of language (e.g., the spatio-temporal metaphor 'dimension' in this very sentence). A more flexible and powerful approach to meaning is offered by *pragmatics* and the *functional* study of **discourse** in social and historical **context**.

semantics Verbal meanings and their study. Along with *phonology* and *syntax*, semantics is one of the three main areas of traditional language study. (The 'sem-' part derives from Greek *semeion* meaning *sign*, a root *semantics* shares with *semiotics*, the study of sign-systems in general). Many current approaches stress the relation between meaning and **context** and *function*. Cf. **discourse** and *pragmatics*.

sentences Several traditional definitions of 'the sentence' are current:
1 a series of words which expresses a complete thought;

2 a series of words beginning with a capital letter and ending with a full stop;

3 a grammatical structure containing, at least, a subject and main verb.

Whatever their value as rough rule-of-thumb guides, none of these definitions proves infallible as an analytical tool. After all, what *is* 'a complete thought'? Is 'Eeeee' a sentence? And isn't 'A packet of cigs, please' a passable sentence – even though there's no verb and it's hard to say whether 'a packet of cigs' is grammatically subject or object? In fact, it proves extremely difficult to describe or define the concept 'sentence' so as to cover all or perhaps even the majority of cases. For the fact remains that the majority of language use is still predominantly oral and conversational. It is rooted in *dialogic* 'give and take' and substantially shared or exchanged structures (see 5.3 throughout). Narrowly logical, typographical or grammatical conventions are painfully inadequate in these areas. Indeed, in **conversation** the nearest equivalent to the concept 'sentence' is probably the 'move'. Theoretically, then, it proves unproductive to try to define '*the* sentence', as though it were a single, uniform entity. Of much more practical use is some sense of the various types of sentence. These are:

♦ major sentences, which contain a main verb and grammatical subject and are the favoured type in formal writing and speech (e.g., 'The cat sat on the mat');

♦ minor sentences, which don't contain a main verb and are the favoured type in conversation, as well as many types of short text such as headlines, titles and captions (e.g., 'Over there', 'If you like', 'Some time in the future . . . maybe?', 'A PLJ day' (advert), 'Miners sympathy strike' (headline));

♦ simple, single-clause sentences (e.g., 'The boy's here. He brought his dog') and *complex* multi-clause sentences, which may be *coordinated (e.g., 'The boy's here *and* he brought his dog'), *subordinated (e.g., 'The boy *who brought his dog* is here') or both (e..g. 'The boy who brought his dog was here and now he's gone');

♦ declarative (stating); interrogative (questioning); imperative / directive (commanding or instructing); exclamative (expressing surprise).

Sentences may be traditionally analysed (or 'parsed') in terms of subject, verb, objects (direct and indirect), complement and adjunct/adverbial. Thus:

(1)	She	wrote	a letter	to me	in the morning
	subject	verb	direct object	indirect object	adjunct

(2)	The late train	probably	will be	an overnight sleeper	
	subject	adjunct	verb	complement	

Traditionally speaking, the subject governs or controls the verb and is typically a *noun* or noun group. The *verb* (including the verb group) is a 'doing', 'being' or 'relating' word and expresses actions, states or relations amongst the other items. The direct object is the object, focus or result of the activity and is typically a noun or noun group. The indirect object (also typically a noun or noun group) is the person or thing to or for whom the activity relates. The adjunct supplies information on the circumstances or conditions of the activity and is typically an *adverb* or adverbial group. The complement is an extension of the subject introduced by parts of such verbs as 'to be', 'seem', 'appear', etc. All these structures can be analysed in finer detail, at another level of 'delicacy', in terms of their constituent *noun, verb* and *adverbial* (group) structures, including *prepositions/particles*. For structural analysis of sentences in terms of *functional grammar*, see *participants and processes* and *circumstances*.

sibilants, sibilance The 'hissing' fricative sounds /s/, /ʃ/ and /z/ (e.g., – in that order – in 'sessions').

*sign, signifier, signified Fundamental terms in *semiotics*, the study of *sign-systems* (including language). A *sign* consists of a *signifier* (the material which does the signifying; e.g., the sounds in air or marks on paper of the English word 'tree') and a *signified* (the concept or category of experience that is signified: whatever we understand 'tree' to mean). Signifier and signified combine to make a sign. However, there is no necessary and fixed relation between signifier and signified, as witnessed by the simple fact that partly corresponding words in other languages are said and written differently and may refer to somewhat different things (e.g., French *arbre*, German *Baum* and Russian *djerevo*). There is thus an ultimate instability in the construction of verbal signs. Following Peirce, we may also distinguish three major kinds of sign:

1 *indexical*, where there is a physical connection between signifier and signified (e.g., smoke *indicates* that there is combustion);

2 *iconic*, where there is a physical resemblance between signifier and signified (e.g., all kinds of representational painting, statuary, photography and film which depict recognisable phenomena);

3 *symbolic*, where there is a purely arbitrary, learned relation between signifier and signified (e.g., traffic lights, chess, Arabic numbers (1, 2, 3, etc.) and most verbal LANGUAGE).

simile An explicitly marked comparison of one thing with another, typically involving such linking words as 'like', 'as', 'seemed', 'appeared', 'in the manner of' (e.g., *'like* a bat out of hell', *'as* happy *as* the day is long'). Cf. **metaphor*.

sociolect A linguistic **variety** defined socially in terms of, say, class, gender, ethnicity and occupation rather than by regional or national **accent and dialect** alone. Cf. *register*.

sociolinguistics Study of the relations between language and society, often in terms of functions and usages, *sociolects* and *registers*. The study of particular language communities is *ethnolinguistics* (a part of ethnography). All may be studied in harness with *psycholinguistics*.

speech Both the activity of speaking and the thing which results (i.e. a/some speech). Speech is usually braced against **writing**, the other main MEDIUM in which LANGUAGE operates. Both have analogous but non-identical structures and functions.

*speech acts What we actually do with **speech** and, by extension LANGUAGE and **discourse** in general; a part of *pragmatics*. Narrowly conceived, speech acts are *performatives*, whereby the person using certain words is deemed to be performing an action (e.g., 'I hereby *name* this ship . . . '; 'I hereby *declare* you man and wife'; 'We the undersigned *witness* this document', 'I *promise* to pay the bearer . . . ', etc.). But the notion of 'doing things with words' can be much extended. For instance, all instances of language-use (spoken or written) can be sorted into four broad categories:

♦ declaratives, which state (e.g., 'I am');

♦ interrogatives, which question ('Am I?', 'Who am I?');

♦ directives / imperatives, which command or instruct ('Be good', 'Do it');

♦ exclamatives, which express excitement ('I am!' 'Good grief!!').

Each of these four basic types can readily be combined with one or more of the others ('Am I?!' 'I *am!*'). But there are many other things we do with language over and above or in and among the business of declaring, interrogating, directing and exclaiming. We also threaten, promise, cajole, swear, wheedle, whinge, cringe, complain, protest, submit, assert, etc., etc. In fact, the list is as endless as the number, variety and permutations of social relations in which people engage.

standard In LANGUAGE, a term commonly applied to those privileged **varieties** associated with dominant social groups (e.g., 'Standard', 'Queen's' or 'BBC ENGLISH'). Globally, it is now necessary to recognise a number of 'standard Englishes', especially in **speech** (Caribbean, Indian, Australian, American and British – as well as so-called 'World Standard'). Issues often get muddied in that 'standard' can mean both 'average' (e.g., 'standard size') and 'of approved quality' (i.e. 'up to a high standard'). Meanwhile, 'standards' (plural noun, singular function) tends to be applied to everything from morals and education to dress and appearance, as well as to language. The notion of 'non-standard' English (meaning variously colloquial, **dialectal** and substandard) is a bluntly *binary* instrument to use when trying to recognise genuinely plural possibilities and fine distinctions.

stress A *syllable* that receives heavier emphasis than those immediately surrounding it (usually through a stronger pulse of air). It is helpful to distinguish three kinds of stress:
- *word stress*, where every word of two or more syllables has at least one syllable which is emphasised (e.g., *orch*estra, orch*est*ral and orche*stra*tion);
- *utterance stress*, where speakers routinely have the option of deliberately stressing one word or phrase rather than others. (Thus the words 'What are you doing here?' may mean at least five different things depending which word is stressed: '*What* are you doing here?'; 'What *are* you doing here?'; 'What are *you* doing here?', etc.);
- *rhythmic stress*, which is the pattern of stresses (usually involving *parallelism*) that occurs in a relatively dispersed fashion in casual **speech**; becomes more marked in formal speeches (e.g., lectures, political speeches, sermons); and is most marked in **poetry** and *song (see **versification**).

stylistics The study of language **variety and variation**, now usually prefaced by the epithets 'literary' or '**discourse**', depending on the primary focus.

subject Four basic meanings can be distinguished: **1** subject matter (e.g., what a book or film is about); **2** academic subject or 'discipline' ('English', 'History', 'Physics', etc.); **3** the grammatical subject: i.e. what controls the verb ('She saw it' has the subject 'she' – see *sentences*); **4** ideological subject, role and identity within a particular structure of power defined with respect to gender, ethnicity, class, religion, age, occupation, etc. (e.g., archaically, 'royal' or 'British subject'). Cf. *agent*.

subordination See *sentences*.

syllable A single pulse of speech-sound, typically built round a vowel; e.g., monosyllabic/single-syllable 'tip', 'pipe', 'Mum'; di-syllabic/two-syllable 'tipper', 'pipe-smoke', 'mother'; and so on. We can also distinguish long and short syllables (e.g., 'pip' – 'pipe' ; 'sell' – 'seal'). Analytically, we may represent raw syllable structure thus (C = consonant or consonant cluster; V = vowel or diphthong): 'library' = cvcvcv; 'junk food' = cvc-cvc. Cf. *alliteration, stress*.

synchronic See *diachronic*.

synonym A word that may be substituted for another word and, in context, has broadly the same meaning (e.g., 'food', 'nutriment', 'grub', 'nosh', etc.). However, even though the basic *denotations* or *references* of synonyms may be similar, the *connotations* and *registers* may be vastly different. There are therefore no exact synonyms. *Antonyms* are words which in some respects are 'opposites' (e.g., 'good/bad', 'up/down', 'run/walk'); though in many other respects such words must necessarily be similar for the contrast to hold; also see **binary oppositions*.

syntagmatic See *choice and combination*.

syntax See *grammar*.

tense See *verbs*.

text A recorded verbal message – written, printed or otherwise recorded (e.g., electronic-ally or audio-visually); more loosely, a message in any **sign-* or COMMUNICATION system. It is a moot point how far texts can be distinguished from **contexts** and **intertextuality**. But some such distinction is at least provisionally necessary if we are to identify a verbal object as such.

theme (linguistic) See *information structure*.

topics The various subject matters treated over the course of a conversation or text, typically involving development, shifting or switching of topic. See *information structure*.

transformation See *grammar* – generative.

*transitivity The **process* of 'carry-over' or 'extension' whereby one **participant* is held to affect or in some way relate to another (e.g., 'Pilots fly aeroplanes'; 'Writers write texts'). **Intransitivity* is a process which does not 'carry over' to something else but remains focused on the process itself (e.g., 'Pilots (or aeroplanes) fly'; 'Writers write'). Many *verbs* may be used transitively or intransitively (e.g., 'grow', 'press', 'reach', 'see', 'hear', 'read', 'write', etc.). This makes a huge difference to how we perceive the processes and participants in play: the difference between, say, 'writing and reading something' (transitively, with the emphasis on the object or product) and simply 'writing and reading' (intransitively, with the emphasis on the process). See **writing and reading**.

*translation The activity of transforming texts or utterances between one language and another and, by extension, between different varieties of what is nominally the same language; also what results from all this activity (i.e. 'a translation').

utterance General term for a stretch of spoken language or a *speech act*.

variety A capacious term embracing the many kinds of LANGUAGE according to use (see *register*) and user (see **dialect**). Notions of variety – and, more dynamically, of **variation** – are often braced against notions of a **standard** unitary language. Cf. *heteroglossia*.

verbs That class of words in which experience is most obviously conceived as *processes*, as distinct from *nouns* where experience is conceived in terms of relatively stable 'things', 'persons' or *participants*. Verbs are highly complex in form and subtle in function. Nonetheless, it is possible to identify the basic form and function of a verb at any one time using the following criteria: *tense; aspect; modality; active or passive; non/finite; in/transitive; dynamic or stative*. Here all these options are illustrated with the verb 'to win':

♦ *tense*, the basic temporal dimension ('when'); e.g., present, 'she wins'; future, 'she will win'; simple past, 'she won'. All these tenses may be further modified in terms of aspect.

♦ *aspect*, the temporal dimension of duration or frequency ('how long or how often'); e.g., instantaneous 'dramatic' present, 'She wins!' (i.e. now); generalising 'state' present, 'She wins at games' (i.e. all the time); progressive, continuous present, 'She's winning as she comes round the bend'. Taken together, the tense and aspect dimensions of the verb always result in a complex spatio-temporal orientation. This overlaps with modality.

♦ *modality*, the most obviously 'attitudinal' dimensions of the verb (including various degrees of possibility, probability, condition, concession, obligation and capacity); e.g., 'she can win', 'she must win' ('may', 'should', 'ought to' and 'did', etc.). (Notice that modality is not limited to verbs; see *modality above.)

♦ *active and passive*, respectively, the 'doing' or 'done to' dimensions of the verb; e.g., 'They won the war' (active) and 'The war was won' (passive). The former specifies a human *agent* as the grammatical *subject* ('They'); the latter deletes or delays the agent and focuses on the result as the grammatical subject. Also see *active above.

♦ *finite and non-finite*, respectively, the 'specific' and 'non-specific' dimensions of the verb: 'She won' and 'They are winning' are both *finite* in that they are marked for tense, person and number. However, 'To win, or not to win' (the infinitive) and 'winning, winning, won!' (the unattached present and past participles) are both *non-finite* in that we are not sure precisely who, what or when they apply to.

♦ *transitive and *intransitive*, respectively, verbs that do or do not 'carry over' or 'extend' from one participant to another: thus 'She won the race' is transitive in that it has a participant–process–participant structure: there is 'carry-over'. However, 'She won' and 'She is winning' are both *intransitive* in that they simply have participant–process structure: there is no 'carry-over'. Also see *transitivity above.

♦ *dynamic and stative*, respectively, the 'doing' or 'being/having' dimensions of the verb: thus 'The car hit the wall' is *dynamic* and involves some material action; but 'The car is a wreck' is *stative* in that we are presented with a state of being: no change, it just *is* wrecked. For a general overview of the main types of verbal process in functional grammar (material, relational, perceptual, etc.), see *participants and processes.

verbal group   Any phrase organised round a *verb*; as distinct from a *noun group*. A complex verbal group commonly consists of *auxiliary* verb plus *secondary verb* plus *main verb(s)*, perhaps with *adverbs* attached; e.g.,

She	has	already	missed	the train.
	aux. v.	adv.	main v.	
She	has been	trying	to buy	a ticket.
	aux. v.	sec. v.	main v.	

Particularly common in modern English and a tricky problem for both language learners and analysts alike are the phrasal or multi-word verbs (e.g., 'to go up the wall'; ' to take out a plate' (or ' to take a plate out'); 'She threw her hands up'). These have a verb + preposition structure and there is often a choice as to where the *preposition* is put.

voice Three quite distinct senses are current: **1** the difference between *active and passive* forms ('voices') of the *verb*; **2** the characteristic speech behaviour of a person, technically equivalent to *idiolect* (see **dialect**) or loosely equivalent to a person's 'verbal identity'; **3** the articulatory or vocal mechanisms whereby speech is produced (see *phonetics*).

vowels See *syllable*.

word The general term for items that are separated by spaces in writing and, at least potentially, by pauses in speech; cf. *lexical item*.

word-class Sets of words which show the same formal properties and fulfil the same grammatical functions (e.g., *nouns, verbs, adjectives, adverbs*); archaically termed 'parts of speech'.

writing The activity of making marks on or in some material such as wood, bone, parchment, paper, plastic, neon lighting, a TV or VDU screen, etc.; also what results (i.e. 'a piece of writing'). Traditionally, writing (including print) is braced against **speech** and both are conceived as analogous but non-identical uses of language. Latterly, however, it has become necessary to add a third term to the equation: the 'audio-visually recorded word' (i.e. in film, TV and audio- and video-recording, and subsequently, through computing, the *multi*-MEDIA). This third area offers a tantalising and teasing hybrid of spoken ('live') and written ('recorded') features. Writing and reading can also be viewed as *transitive* and *intransitive* processes: we can write or read something (transitively, with an emphasis on the object) and we can simply write or read (intransitively, with an emphasis on the activity).

And that brings us to . . .

NOT THE END

As mentioned at the outset, this brief glossary is merely a beginning. Extend the entries and add other terms which *you* find particularly useful.

APPENDIX A
Maps of Britain, the USA and the world

Figure A1 Varieties of English and other languages in the British Isles
Drawn by R.M. Pomfret, 1997

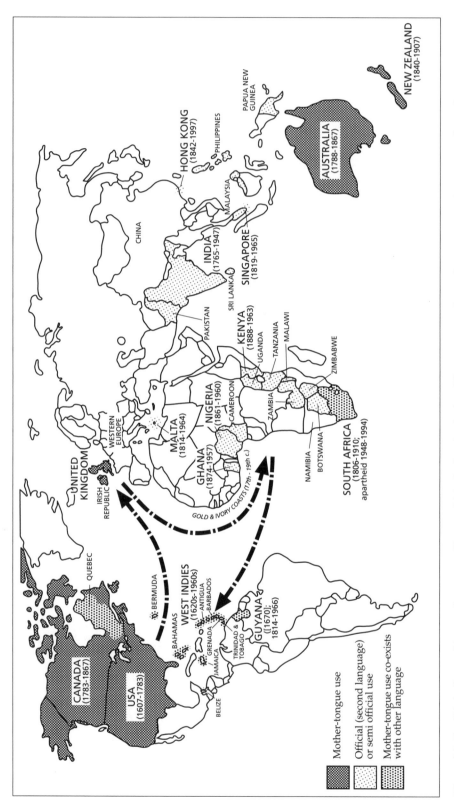

Figure A2 English in the world: a modern map with some historical underpinning. The names are those of current countries. Dates refer to formal beginnings and ends of British colonies. The arrows represent the main slave trade triangle in the seventeenth and eighteenth centuries. Shadings indicate extent and status of English, according to the key.

Drawn by R.M. Pomfret, 1997 (Conflated and adapted from Crystal, 1988: 8–9 and Leith, 1997: 195)

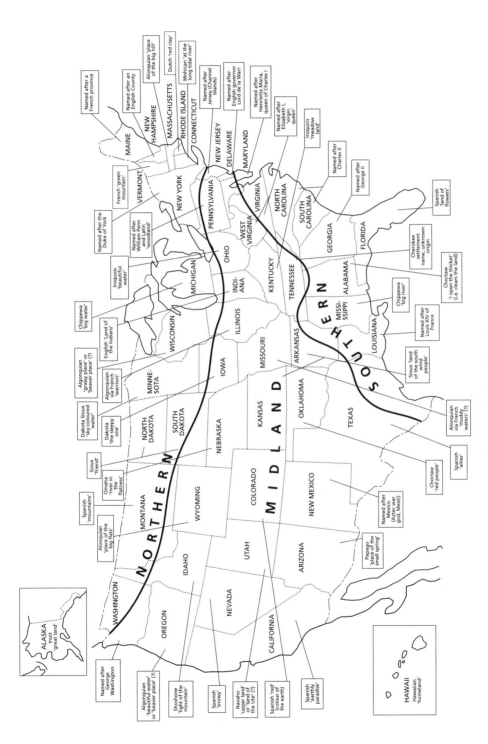

Figure A3 The USA: origins of state names with chief Northern, Midland and Southern dialect areas
Drawn by R.M. Pomfret, 1997 (Adapted from Crystal, 1995: 94, 105 and Graddol et al., 1996: 199)

APPENDIX B
A chronology of English language and literature, culture, communication and media

EVENTS	LANGUAGE & LITERATURE	CULTURE COMMUNICATION & MEDIA
AD 43 Roman invasion of Celtic Britain	Celtic languages and oratures	Celtic tribal structures, myths and art forms
410 Romans leave 432 Patrick brings Christianity to Ireland.	**Old English language** (Anglo-Saxon, Jutish and Kentish dialects): Germanic base with some traces of imperial Latin and Church Latin; highly inflected, relatively free word-order.	Germanic tribal (kin-based) society organised round house-hold, village, church and court. Heroic warrior culture with admixtures of Celtic and Roman Christianity.
597 Augustine brings Christianity to England 449–900 Romano–Celtic Britain invaded by Germanic tribes	**Anglo-saxon orature and literature** (*c.* 450–*c.* 1100): poetry – oral-formulaic and stressed alliterative, chiefly, epic, heroic, elegiac (see 'Wulf and Eadwacer' 5.1.1) and saints' lives; prose – chiefly chronicles and sermons.	Oral and manuscript (animal skin) verbal media
1066 Norman conquest 1120–80 First English 'plantations' in Wales and Ireland 1362 English first used for opening of Parliament	**Middle English language** (1066–*c.* 1450): Germanic base with French and Latin superstructure; loss of inflections, fixing of word-order; onset of vowel changes. Anglo-Norman (earlier) for local administration; Paris French (later) for court and aristocracy; Latin for learning, church and international administration **Medieval English literature:** Poetry – chiefly lyric (e.g 'Maiden in the mor lay' 5.1.2 a,	Feudal (land-based) society organised round manor, castle and court, church or monastery, town and village – gradually giving way to money-based economy centred on trade and the city. Oral and manuscript culture – gradually giving way to paper and print-based culture. Religious control of learning gradually giving way to secular. Pan-European notions of Christendom (braced against

EVENTS	LANGUAGE & LITERATURE	CULTURE COMMUNICATION & MEDIA
1384 Wyclif's Bible in English	romance, satire and saints' lives; versification variously alliterative and stressed (e.g. *Piers Plowman* and *Pearl* 5.1.2 c–d) or rhymed and syllabic (e.g. Chaucer's 'General Prologue' 5.1.2 b).	'pagan / heathen' Muslims to the East, notably in the Crusades) and international court culture.
1415 Agincourt and Henry V's victory over the French	Drama – chiefly religious Mystery Plays and some popular carnival forms (e.g. Chester *Noah* 5.3.2 a). Prose – chiefly didactic, functional, some mystical and romance.	
1476 Caxton starts first printing press in London 1525, 1535 First printed Bibles in English: Tyndale (New Testament) and Coverdale (complete), from Cologne 1534 Break with the papacy: Church of England established 1603 Union of Crowns James I of England and VI of Scotland 1607 First permanent English settlement in America 1619 First African slaves transported to America 1642–51 English Civil War 1765 Beginning of major British influence in India	**Early Modern English** (1450–1800): Germanic base with deep layers of French and Latin, and admixtures from other European and some non-European languages (ancient Greek, Dutch, Spanish, Italian . . . Caribbean and American Indian); major vowel shift effected in speech; written form gradually standardised through printing. **Renaissance / Early Modern literature:** Drama (1580s onwards) – centred on 'public' and 'private' theatres, playhouse and court – comedies, tragedies, histories, satires (e.g. Shakespeare 5.3.2 b and 5.4.6 a). Poetry – principal genres: sonnet (e.g. Shakespeare 5.1.3 b and 5.4.4 c; Wroth 5.1.3 c); lyric (e.g. Wyatt 5.1.3 a); neo-classical epic (e.g. Milton 5.1.4 a); satire and mock-heroic (e.g. Pope and Hands 5.1.4 b–c). Prose – especially the novel (e.g. Behn 5.2.2 a; Manley 5.2.3 a and Defoe 5.2.2 b); the satiric tract (e.g. Swift 5.2.4 a) and letters and diaries (e.g. Brews–Paston 5.2.1 a and Pepys 5.2.1 b).	Print-based culture gradually displaces, but does not replace, oral and manuscript-based culture. Brief yet decisive prominence of drama in Elizabethan and Jacobean periods, and intermittently thereafter. Rise of nation–states and sense of national identity. Christendom divides into (North European) Protest-antism and (South European) Roman Catholicism, as well as the Eastern Orthodox Church. Revival of classical learning and literature and (re)editing of ancient Greek and Roman texts.

EVENTS	LANGUAGE & LITERATURE	CULTURE COMMUNICATION & MEDIA
1775–82 American War of Independence 1788 Penal colony established in Australia 1789 French Revolution begins 1801 Establishment of United Kingdom (England, Wales, Ireland and Scotland) 1840 Official colony in New Zealand 1861–65 American Civil War	**Romantic & Victorian** **literature** (1790–1900): Poetry – chiefly lyric and adapted ballad (e.g. Blake 5.4.6 b, W. Wordsworth 5.4.3 a, Clare 5.1.5, Barnes 5.1.6 and Dickinson 5.4.5 d); narrative and satire (e.g. Byron 5.1.4 d and P. B. Shelley 5.4.6 c). Prose – chiefly novels of social manners, romance and realism (e.g. Austen and Brontë 5.2.3 b and d and Dickens 5.4.5 b); speculative or political tracts (cf. M. Shelley 5.2.3 c) and journals and auto-biography (e.g. D. Wordsworth 5.4.3 b and Douglass 5.2.2 d). Drama – heroic, romantic and domestic, initially in verse, latterly in prose (e.g. Ibsen 5.3.3).	Belief in scientific progress blends with egalitarian models of society leading to revolutions and reforms. Industrial Revolution sharpens division between city and country and, in Britain, between industrial North and rural South; while London grows to be Cobbett's 'great Wen' (i.e. tumour). Steam-printing presses massively increase output of print material. Newspapers and novels multiply. Demand and opportunity for literacy grow. Railways, canals and steam- ships revolutionise transport communication. First practical photograph/ daguerrotype (1837)
1870–1910 European states divide up Africa		Telegraph invented (1840) Morse Code developed (1852) Typewriter invented (1860) Telephone invented (1860) Phonograph / record-player invented (1877)
1914–18 First World War 1922 Eire / Republic of Ireland formed 1931 British Commonwealth established as British Empire disintegrates	**Modernist & Postmodernist** **writings:** non-realist fiction (e.g Beckett 5.3.4 d) or mixed realist / non-realist (e.g. Theatre Workshop 5.4.6 f and Kelman 5.2.6), variously 'high art' or 'popular' culture. **Post/modern media** **productions** for radio, film and TV (e.g. Thomas 5.3.4 b and Russell 5.3.5 c) and records and video (e.g. Queen 5.1.10; cf.	Radio developed by Marconi (1901) First one-reel 'silent' narrative film (1903) Television invented (1926) Sound-films / 'talkies' (1928) BBC's first high-definition television broadcast in the UK (1937)

EVENTS	LANGUAGE & LITERATURE	CULTURE COMMUNICATION & MEDIA
1939–45 Second World War	Rushdie 5.4.2), including advertising (e.g. Heineken 5.4.3 d and Clarins 5.4.4 b) and news (e.g. 5.2.5).	NBC begins broadcasting in the USA (1939)
1947–1980s Independence and decolonisation from India to Africa and the Caribbean to the Pacific		Audio-tape invented (1937)
	Post/colonial and multi-cultural writings, marking the passing of empire (e.g. Kipling,	Electronic computer developed (1943)
1950— Growing dominance of USA in economic, diplomatic and military power (Korea, Vietnam, Central America); neo-colonialism	Conrad, Hurston, Achebe 5.2.4 b–f, Morrison 5.2.2 e, Churchill 5.3.4 e), the resurgence of 'new' regional and national identities (e.g. Synge 5.3.4 a, Leonard and Doyle 5.2.5 d–e, Fugard 5.3.4 c,	Transistors begin to replace valves (1948) Microprocessors developed (1978—)
1950s–1975 Large-scale emigration to Britain from the Caribbean, Africa and Asia	Achebe 5.2.4 f , πO 5.1.9 a) and the possibility – or impossibility – of cross- and multicultural understanding (e.g. Rhys 5.2.3 e, Wei Meng and Collins 5.1.9	Computerised multimedia interfaces developed (1980s—) World-Wide-Web, e-mail and 'cyber-space' become widely
1973 Britain joins the European Union	b–c, Harrison 5.4.5 c and Nichols 5.4.5 e).	available (virtual) realities for those who have resources and access . . .
1989— State Communist regimes collapse in Eastern Europe Yugoslavia in protracted civil war	**'New' Englishes** recognised (African, Caribbean, Asian, Pacific) – also the promise and threat of 'World Standard English' . . .	Oral, manuscript and print cultures continue to be displaced but not replaced. Communications and media are ever more complex but also
1994 Formal end of apartheid in South Africa		potentially more homogeneous – more readily 'translatable'.
1998— Much of Africa continues in crisis Japan and Korea dominate many world markets China is poised for further change . . .		Cultures are increasingly global and local, international and national or regional; multi- and monocultural . . .

English Literary HISTORY, HISTORY of English Language, Lang. & Lit.
in HISTORY

HISTORY (social, political, inter/national, oral . . .)
ART & ARCHITECTURAL HISTORY
HISTORY OF MUSIC, DRAMA, DANCE
HISTORY OF IDEAS, PHILOSOPHY, EDUCATION, SCIENCE . . .

English LANGUAGE, Teaching & Learning English as a Foreign,
Second LANGUAGE – or for Special Purposes (technical,
scientific, etc.)

LINGUISTICS (general, applied, socio-, ethno-, psycho-, historical, etc.)
MODERN LANGUAGES – FRENCH, SPANISH, ITALIAN,
GERMAN, RUSSIAN, JAPANESE, CHINESE, AFRICAN, INDIAN, etc.
CLASSICAL LANGUAGES – LATIN, GREEK, SANSKRIT,
INDIAN, CHINESE, etc.

ENGLISH

English WRITING, SPEAKING AND PRESENTATION – for academic,
business and other purposes

WRITING FOR ACADEMIC, TECHNICAL, BUSINESS, etc. PURPOSES
RHETORIC (ancient, neo-classical, modern and 'new')
COMPOSITION (comprehension, technical, literary)
CREATIVE WRITING (adaptation, imitation, expressive; individual,
collaborative; print, multimedia)
HYPERTEXT (e-mail, World-Wide-Web, multimedia)
PUBLISHING & COMMUNICATIONS

INTERNATIONAL/WORLD English – LOCAL englishes

GEOGRAPHY (political, economic, physical, etc.)
ECOLOGY & ENVIRONMENTALISM
AREA STUDIES – BRITISH, EUROPEAN (Western, Middle,
Eastern), AMERICAN (North, Central, South), CARIBBEAN,
AFRICAN, MIDDLE EASTERN, ORIENTAL, ASIAN, PACIFIC, etc.

Figure C   English *and* or *as* other educational subjects

EDUCATION in English, English in EDUCATION

EDUCATION (theory, methodology and practice)
HISTORY OF EDUCATION (formal and informal – including that of 'English' at
elementary, primary, secondary and tertiary levels)
TEACHING, LEARNING & ASSESSMENT (individual, group; written, oral,
recorded, multimedia; other, self- and peer; 'open', 'closed' and negotiated)
EDUCATIONAL METHODS & TECHNOLOGY (strategies; audio-visual; . . .)
STAFF & STUDENT SUPPORT & DEVELOPMENT (counselling, training,
careers, etc.)

English TEXTS/INFORMATION in English

PUBLISHING (book, magazine, newspaper; paper, electronic; editing,
design, marketing, distribution; general, specialist)
BIBLIOGRAPHY & TEXTUAL SCHOLARSHIP
LIBRARY & INFORMATION SERVICES
INFORMATION SCIENCES
COMMUNICATIONS

English STUDIES

WOMEN'S STUDIES,
GENDER STUDIES,
POSTCOLONIAL STUDIES
AREA STUDIES
ENVIRONMENTAL & ECOLOGICAL

**English THEATRE AND DRAMA – PLAY(S), PERFORMANCES
AND RE/PRESENTATIONS partly in English**

THEATRE STUDIES (textual, practical, vocational)
DRAMA & PERFORMANCE (with music and dance; on page, stage
or screen; classical, contemporary; in and out of education)
VISUAL STUDIES – photography, film, video, art (fine, popular and
commercial)
FILM, TV, MEDIA & MULTIMEDIA STUDIES

**English (British, American, Australian, Caribbean . . .) CULTURE – CULTURES partly
through English**

ART, MUSIC & DANCE ('high' and 'popular')
POPULAR CULTURE
HISTORY, GEOGRAPHY, SOCIOLOGY, LAW, POLITICS, HEALTH CARE, BIOLOGY,
SCIENCES (theoretical and applied) . . .
CULTURAL STUDIES (British, American, Australian etc. models)

BIBLIOGRAPHY

Most of the following references are to books or parts of books. Relevant journals, as well as addresses of useful associations, can be found in the next section. Guidance on general reference books is offered at the end of Part Three.

Abrams, M.H. (1993) *A Glossary of Literary Terms*, 6th edn, New York: Harcourt Brace.

Abrams, M.H., et al. (eds) (1993) *Norton Anthology of English Literature*, Vols 1 and 2, 6th edn, New York: W.W. Norton.

Achebe, C. (1958) *Things Fall Apart*, London: Heinemann.

Aitchison, J. (1991) *Language Change: Progress or Decay?*, Cambridge: Cambridge University Press.

— (1996) *The Language Web* (BBC 1996 Reith Lectures), Cambridge: Cambridge University Press.

Allen, R.C. (ed.) (1987) *Channels of Discourse: Television and Contemporary Criticism*, London: Routledge.

Andersen, R. (1988) *The Power and the Word: Language, Power and Change*, London: Paladin.

Andrews, R. (ed.) (1992) *Rebirth of Rhetoric: Essays in Language, Culture and Education*, London and New York: Routledge.

Aristotle (1965) *Aristotle, Horace, Longinus: Classical Literary Criticism*, trans. T. S. Dorsch, Harmondsworth: Penguin.

Armstrong, I. (ed.) (1992) *New Feminist Discourses*, London: Routledge.

Ashcroft, B., Griffiths, G. and Tiffin, H. (1989) *The Empire Writes Back: Theory and Practice in Post-Colonial Literatures*, London: Methuen.

— (eds) (1995) *The Post-Colonial Studies Reader*, London and New York: Routledge.

Aston, E. and Savona, G. (1991) *Theatre as Sign System: An Introduction to Text in Performance*, London and New York: Routledge.

Attridge, D. (1988) *Peculiar Language: Literature as Difference from the Renaissance to James Joyce*, London: Methuen.

Attridge, D., Bennington, G. and Young, R. (eds) (1987a) *Poststructuralism and the Question of History*, Cambridge: Cambridge University Press.

Attridge, D., Durant, A., Fabb, N. and MacCabe, C. (eds) (1987b) *The Linguistics of Writing: Arguments between Language and Literature*, Manchester: Manchester University Press.

Auerbach, E. (1946) *Mimesis: The Representation of Reality in Western Literature*, trans. W.R. Trask, Princeton, NJ: Princeton University Press.

Bailey, R. (1992) *Images of English: A Cultural History of the Language*, Cambridge: Cambridge University Press.

Baker, N.L (1989) *A Research Guide for Undergraduate Students (English and American Literature)*, 3rd edn, New York: MLA Publications.

Bakhtin, M. (1968) *Rabelais and his World*, trans. H. Iswolsky, Cambridge, MA: MIT Press.

— (1981) *The Dialogic Imagination: Four Essays*, ed. M. Holquist, trans. C. Emerson and M. Holquist, Austin: University of Texas Press.

— (1984) *Problems of Dostoyevsky's Poetics*, ed. and trans. C. Emerson, Manchester: Manchester University Press.

— (1990) *Art and Answerability: Early Philosophical Works*, ed. M. Holquist, and V. Liapunov, trans. V. Liapunov, Austin: University of Texas Press.

Bal, M. (1985) *Narratology*, trans. C. Van Boheemen, Toronto: University of Toronto Press.

Baldick, C. (1983) *The Social Mission of English Criticism 1848–1932*, Oxford: Oxford University Press.

— (1996) *Criticism and Literary Theory, 1890 to the Present*, London: Longman.

Bambara, T.C. (1972) *Gorilla, My Love*, London: The Women's Press, 1984.

Barker, C. (1977) *Theatre Games: A New Approach to Drama Training*, London: Eyre Methuen.

Barricelli, J-P, Gibaldi, J. and Lauter, E. (eds) (1990) *Teaching Literature and Other Arts*, New York: Modern Languages Association.

Barry, P. (1995) *Beginning Theory: An Introduction to Literature*, Manchester: Manchester University Press.

Barthes, R. (1957) *Mythologies*, selected and trans. A. Lavers, New York: Hill and Wang, 1972.

— (1970) *S/Z*, trans. R. Miller, London: Cape, 1975.

— (1977) *Image-Music-Text*, ed. and trans. S. Heath, London: Collins.

Bartholomae, D. and Petrosky, A. (1986) *Facts, Artifacts and Counterfacts: Theory and Method for Reading and Writing*, Portsmouth, NH: Boynton/Cook.

— (eds) (1996) *Ways of Reading. An Anthology for Writers*, 4th edn, New York: St Martin's Press.

Bassnett, S. (1991) *Translation Studies*, 2nd edn, London: Routledge.

Bassnett, S. and Grundy, P. (1993) *Language through Literature: Creative Language Teaching through Literature*, London: Longman.

— (ed.) (1996) *Studying British Culture: An Introduction*, London: Routledge.

Bate, J. (1991) *Romantic Ecology*, London: Routledge.

Batsleer, J., Davies, T., O'Rourke, R. and Weedon, C. (1985) *Rewriting English: Cultural Politics and Gender and Class*, London: Methuen.

Baudrillard, J. (1995) *The Gulf War Did Not Take Place*, Bloomington: Indiana University Press.

Baugh, A.C. and Cable, T. (1993) *A History of the English Language*, 4th edn, London: Routledge.

Beckett, S. (1992) *Collected Plays*, London: Faber & Faber.

Belsey, C. (1980) *Critical Practice*, London: Methuen.

Belsey, C. and Moore, J. (eds) (1997) *The Feminist Reader: Essays in Gender and the Politics of Literary Criticism*, 2nd edn, London: Macmillan.

Benjamin, W. (1970) *Illuminations*, ed. H. Arendt, trans. H. Zohn, London: Cape.

Bennett, A. (ed.) (1995) *Readers and Reading: A Critical Reader*, London: Longman.

Bennett, T. (1979) *Formalism and Marxism*, London: Methuen.

Bennett, T., Boyd-Bowman, S., Mercer, T. and Woollacott, J. (eds) (1981) *Popular Television and Film*, London: Open University Press and British Film Institute.

Benstock, S. (ed.) (1988) *The Private Self: Theory and Practice of Women's Autobiographical Writings*, New York: Routledge.

Berger, J. (1972) *Ways of Seeing*, London: BBC and Penguin Books.

Berlin, J. (1996) *Rhetorics, Poetics, Cultures: Refiguring College English Studies*, Philadelphia: NCTE.

Bex, T. (1996) *Variety in Written English: Texts in Society/Society in Texts*, London: Routledge.

Bhabha, H. (ed.) (1990) *Nation and Narration*, London: Routledge.

— (1994) *The Location of Culture*, London and New York: Routledge.

Birch, D. (1989) *Language, Literature and Critical Practice*, London: Routledge.

Bleich, D. (1978) *Subjective Criticism*, Baltimore, MD: Johns Hopkins University Press.

Boal, A. (1992) *Games for Actors and Non-actors*, trans. A. Jackson, London: Routledge.

Bolter, J. (1991) *Writing Space: The Computer, Hypertext, and the History of Writing*, Hillsdale, NJ: Erlbaum.

Boone, J. and Cadden, M. (eds) (1990) *Engendering Men: The Question of Male Feminism*, New York: Routledge.

Booth, W. (1961) *The Rhetoric of Fiction*, Chicago: Chicago University Press.

Bordwell, D. (1985) *Narration in the Fiction Film*, London: Methuen.

Bordwell, D. and Thompson, K. (1993) *Film Art: An Introduction*, 3rd edn, New York: McGraw-Hill.

Bourdieu, P. (1984) *Distinction: A Social Critique of the Judgement of Taste*, trans. R. Nice, London: Routledge.

Bradford, R. (ed.) (1996) *Introducing Literary Studies*, Hemel Hempstead: Harvester Wheatsheaf.

Branston, G. and Stafford, R. (1996) *The Media Student's Handbook*, London: Routledge.

Brantlinger, P. (1990) *Crusoe's Footprints: Cultural Studies in Britain and America*, London and New York: Routledge.

Brathwaite, E.K. (1984) *History of the Voice*, London: New Beacon Books.

Brecht, B. (1964) *Brecht on Theatre*, ed. and trans. J. Willett, London: Methuen.

Brook, P. (1968) *The Empty Space*, Harmondsworth: Penguin, 1972.

Brooker, P. (ed.) (1992) *Modernism/Postmodernism: A Reader*, London: Longman.

Brooker, P. and Humm, P. (eds) (1989) *Dialogue and Difference: English into the Nineties*, London: Routledge.

Brooker, P. and Widdowson, P. (eds) (1996) *A Practical Reader in Contemporary Literary Theory*, Hemel Hempstead: Harvester Wheatsheaf.

Brooks, C. (1947) *The Well Wrought Urn: Studies in the Structure of Poetry*, New York: Harcourt, Brace and World.

Brown, J. and Gifford, T. (1989) *Teaching 'A' Level English Literature: A Student-centred Approach*, London: Routledge.

Brown, S., Morris, M. and Rohlehr, G. (eds) (1989) *Voice Print: An Anthology of Oral and Related Poetry from the Caribbean*, London and Kingston: Longman.

Brumfit, C.J. and Carter, R.A (eds) (1986) *Literature and Language Teaching*, Oxford: Oxford University Press.

Buell, L. (1995) *The Environmental Imagination: Thoreau, Nature Writing and the Formation of American Culture*, Cambridge, MA: Harvard University Press.

Burnley, D. (ed.) (1992) *The History of the English Language: A Source Book*, London: Longman.

Burton, D. (1980) *Dialogue and Discourse: The Sociology of Modern Drama Dialogue and Naturally Occurring Conversation*, London: Routledge and Kegan Paul.

Burton, D. and Carter, R.A. (eds) (1982) *Literary Text and Language Study*, London: Arnold.

Butler, C. and Fowler, A. (eds) (1971) *Topics in Criticism*, London: Longman.

Cameron, D. (ed.) (1990) *The Feminist Critique of Language*, London: Routledge.

—— (1992) *Feminism and Linguistic Theory*, 2nd edn, London: Macmillan.

Carey, J. (ed.) (1987) *The Faber Book of Reportage*, London: Faber & Faber.

Carroll, R. and Prickett, S. (eds) (1997) *The Bible: Authorised King James Version, with Apocrypha*, Oxford: Oxford University Press.

Carter, R.A. (ed.) (1982) *Language and Literature: An Introductory Reader in Stylistics*, London: Allen and Unwin.

—— (1995) *Keywords in Language and Literacy*, London: Routledge.

—— (1997) *Investigating English Discourse: Language, Literacy and Literature*, London: Routledge.

Carter, R.A. and Long, M. (1987) *The Web of Words: Language-based Approaches to Literature*, Cambridge: Cambridge University Press.

Carter, R. and McRae, J. (eds) (1996) *Language, Literature and the Learner: Creative Classroom Practice*, London: Longman.

Carter, R. and McRae, J. (1997) *The Routledge History of Literature in English: Britain and Ireland*, London: Routledge.

Carter, R.A. and Nash, W. (1990) *Seeing through Language: A Guide to Styles of English Writing*, Oxford: Blackwell.

Carter, R.A. and Simpson, P. (eds.) (1989) *Language, Discourse and Literature: An Introductory Reader in Discourse Stylistics*, London: Unwin Hyman.

Caws, M.A. and Prendergast, C. (eds) (1994) *World Reader*, New York: HarperCollins.

Chatman, S. (1978) *Story and Discourse: Narrative Structure in Fiction and Film*, Ithaca, NY: Cornell University Press.

Cheshire, J. (ed.) (1992) *English around the World: Sociolinguistic Perspectives*, Cambridge: Cambridge University Press.

Chiaro, D. (1992) *The Language of Jokes: Analysing Verbal Play*, London: Routledge.

Churchill, C. (1985) *Churchill: Plays One*, London: Methuen.

Coates, J. (1993) *Women, Men and Language*, 2nd edn, London: Longman.

Cohan, S. and Shires, L.M. (1988) *Telling Stories: A Theoretical Analysis of Narrative*, London: Routledge.

Colley, L. (1992) *Britons: Forging the Nation 1707–1837*, New Haven, CT: Yale University Press.

Con Davis, R. and Schleifer, R. (eds) (1994) *Contemporary Literary Criticism: Literary and Cultural Studies*, 3rd edn, New York: Longman.

Connor, S. (1996) *Postmodernist Culture*, 2nd edn, Oxford: Blackwell.

Connors, R. and Glenn, C. (1995) *The St Martin's Guide to Teaching Writing*, 3rd edn, New York: St Martin's Press.

Cook, G. (1994) *Discourse and Literature*, Oxford: Oxford University Press.

Corcoran, B., Hayhoe, M. and Pradl, G. (eds) (1994) *Knowledge in the Making: Challenging the Text in the Classroom*, Portsmouth, NH: Boynton/Cook, Heinemann.

Corner, J. and Hawthorn, J. (eds) (1995) *Communication Studies: A Reader*, 4th edn, London: Arnold.

Coulthard, M. (1985) *An Introduction to Discourse Analysis*, 2nd edn, London: Longman.

Couzyn, J. (ed.) (1989) *Singin' Down the Bones*, London: The Women's Press.

Cox, J. and Reynolds, L. (eds) (1993) *New Historical Literary Study*, Princeton, NJ: Princeton University Press.

Coyle, M., Garside, P., Kelsall, M. and Peck, J. (eds) (1990) *Encylopedia of Literature and Criticism*, London and New York: Routledge.

Critical Survey (1996) 8 (1): Diverse Communities, Oxford: Oxford University Press.

Crowley, T. (1989) *Politics of Discourse: The Standard Language Question in British Cultural Studies*, London: Macmillan.

—— (ed.) (1991) *Proper English? Readings in Language, History and Cultural Identity*, London: Routledge.

Crump, E. and Carbone, N. (1996) *The English Student's Guide to the Internet*, New York: Houghton Mifflin.

Crystal, D. (1988) *The English Language*, Harmondsworth: Penguin.

—— (1995) *The Cambridge Encyclopedia of the English Language*, Cambridge: Cambridge University Press.

—— (1996) *Re-discover Grammar*, 2nd edn, London: Longman.

—— (1997) *Cambridge Encyclopedia of Language and Linguistics*, 2nd edn, Cambridge: Cambridge University Press.

—— (1997) *English as a Global Language*, Cambridge: Cambridge University Press.

Crystal, D. and Davy, D. (1969) *Investigating English Style*, London: Longman.

Cuddon, J. (1992) *A Dictionary of Literary Terms and Literary Theory*, 3rd edn, Harmondsworth: Penguin.

Culler, J. (1975) *Structuralist Poetics*, London: Routledge and Kegan Paul.

—— (1981) *The Pursuit of Signs: Semiotics, Literature, Deconstruction*, London: Routledge and Kegan Paul.

—— (ed.) (1988) *On Puns: The Foundation of Letters*, Oxford: Blackwell.

Currie, M. (ed.) (1995) *Metafiction: A Critical Reader*, London: Longman.

Davis, L. (1983) *Factual Fictions: The Origins of the English Novel*, New York: Columbia University Press.

Davis, H. and Walton, P. (eds) (1983) *Language, Image, Media*, Oxford: Blackwell.

De Beaugrande, R. and Dressler, W. (1981) *Introduction to Text Linguistics*, London: Longman.

Derrida, J. (1976) *Of Grammatology*, trans. G. C. Spivak, Baltimore, MD: Johns Hopkins University Press.

—— (1978) *Writing and Difference*, trans. A. Bass, Chicago: Chicago University Press.

Dixon, J. (1991) *A Schooling in 'English'*, Milton Keynes: Open University Press.

Dixon, P. (1971) *Rhetoric*, London: Methuen.

Donahue, P. and Quandahl, E. (1992) *Reclaiming Pedagogy: The Rhetoric of the Classroom*, Carbondale: Southern Illinois University Press.

Doyle, B. (1989) *English and Englishness*, London: Methuen.

Doyle, R. (1993) *Paddy Clarke ha ha ha*, London: Secker & Warburg.

Dubrow, H. (1982) *Genre*, London: Methuen.

Ducrot, O. and Todorov, T. (1972) *Encyclopaedic Dictionary of the Sciences of Language*, Baltimore, MD: Johns Hopkins University Press.

Durant, A. and Fabb, N. (1990) *Literary Studies in Action*, London: Routledge.

During, S. (ed.) (1993) *The Cultural Studies Reader*, London: Routledge.

Eagleton, T. (1990) *The Ideology of the Aesthetic*, Oxford: Blackwell.

—— (1996) *Literary Theory: An Introduction*, 2nd edn, Oxford: Blackwell.

Eagleton, T. and Milne, D. (1995) *Marxist Literary Theory: A Reader*, Oxford: Blackwell.

Easthope, A. (1983) *Poetry as Discourse*, London: Methuen.

—— (1991) *Literary into Cultural Studies*, London: Routledge.

Eco, U. (1978) *The Role of the Reader: Explorations in the Semiotics of Texts*, Bloomington: Indiana University Press.

Elam, K. (1980) *The Semiotics of Theatre and Drama*, London: Methuen.

Elbow, P. (1993) *What is English?*, New York: Modern Language Association and NCTE.

Ellman, M. (ed.) (1994) *Psychoanalytic Literary Criticism: A Critical Reader*, London: Longman.

Empson, W. (1930) *Seven Types of Ambiguity*, Harmondsworth: Penguin, 1972.

Erlich, V. (1981) *Russian Formalism: History-Doctrine*, 3rd edn, New Haven, CT: Yale University Press.

Esslin, M. (1961) *Theatre of the Absurd*, Harmondsworth: Penguin.

Evans, C. (1993) *English People: The Experience of Teaching and Learning English in British Universities*, Milton Keynes: Open University Press.

Evans, C. (ed.) (1995) *Developing University English Teaching*, Lampeter: Edwin Mellen Press.

Fabb, N. (1997) *Linguistics and Literary Theory*, Oxford: Blackwell.

Fabb, N. and Durant, A. (1993) *How to Write Essays, Dissertations and Theses for Literary Studies*, London: Longman.

Fairclough, N. (1989) *Language and Power*, London: Longman.

Fanthorpe, U.A. (1986) *Selected Poems*, Harmondsworth: Penguin.

Fekete, J. (1977) *The Critical Twilight: Explorations in the Ideology of Anglo-American Literary Theory from Eliot to McLuhan*, New York: Routledge and Kegan Paul.

—— (1988) *Life after Post-Modernism: Essays on Value and Culture*, London: Macmillan.

Fetterley, J. (1991) *The Resisting Reader: A Feminist Approach to American Fiction*, Bloomington: Indiana University Press.

Fiske, J. (1987) *Television Culture*, London: Routledge.

—— (1990) *Introduction to Communication Studies*, 2nd edn, London: Routledge.

Forster, E.M. (1927) *Aspects of the Novel*, Harmondsworth: Penguin, 1962.

Foucault, M. (1986) *The Foucault Reader*, ed. P. Rabinow, Harmondsworth: Penguin.

Fowler, A. (1982) *Kinds of Literature: An Introduction to the Theory of Genres*, Oxford: Oxford University Press.

Fowler, R. (1981) *Literature as Social Discourse*, London: Batsford.

—— (ed.) (1987) *A Dictionary of Modern Critical Terms*, London: Methuen.

—— (1991) *Langage in the News: Discourse and Ideology in the Press*, London: Routledge.

—— (1996) *Linguistic Criticism*, 2nd edn, Oxford: Oxford University Press.

Frame, J. (1982) *To the Is-land*, Auckland: Random Century, 1989.

Freeborn, D., French, P. and Langford, D. (1993) *Varieties of English*, 2nd edn, London: Macmillan.

Freire, P. (1972) *Pedagogy of the Oppressed*, trans. M. Ramos, Harmondsworth: Penguin.

Freud, S. (1905a) *Case Histories I: 'Dora' and 'Little Hans'*, ed. and trans. A. Richards, Harmondsworth: Penguin, 1977.

—— (1905b) *Jokes and their Relation to the Unconscious*, trans. J. Strachey, Harmondsworth: Penguin, 1976.

Fromkin, V. and Rodman, R. (1997) *An Introduction to Language*, 5th edn, New York: Harcourt Brace Jovanovich.

Frye, N. (1957) *Anatomy of Criticism*, Princeton, NJ: Princeton University Press.

Fugard, A. (1986) *Selected Plays*, Oxford: Oxford University Press.

Furlong, T. and Ogborn, J. (1995) *The English Department: Organisation and Management*, Sheffield: National Association for the Teaching of English.

Garvin, P. (ed.) (1964) *A Prague School Reader on Esthetics, Literary Structure and Style*, Washington: Georgetown University Press.

Gates, Jnr., H.L. (ed.) (1986) *The Classic Slave Narratives*, New York: Mentor.

—— (1995) *Loose Canons: Notes on the Culture Wars*, Oxford: Oxford University Press.

Geok-Lin Lim, L. and Spencer, N. (eds) (1993) *One World of Literature*, Boston: Houghton Mifflin.

Giddens, A. (1991) *Modernity and Self-identity*, Cambridge: Polity Press.

Giddings, R., Selby, K. and Wensley, C. (1990) *Screening the Novel: The Theory and Practice of Literary Adaptation*, London: Macmillan.

Gilbert, S.M. and Gubar, S. (1979) *The Madwoman in the Attic: The Woman Writer and the Nineteenth-Century Literary Imagination*, New Haven, CT: Yale University Press.

Giles, J. and Middleton, T. (eds) (1995) *Writing Englishness 1900–1950: An Introductory Sourcebook on National Identity*, London: Routledge.

Godber, J. (1989) *Five Plays*, Harmondsworth: Penguin.

Goodman, S. and Graddol, D. (eds) (1996) *Redesigning English: New Texts, New Identities,*

London and New York: Open University and Routledge.

Görlach, M. (1991) *Englishes: Studies in Varieties of English 1984–1988*, Amsterdam: Benjamins.

Grabe, W. and Kaplan, R. (1996) *Theory and Practice of Writing*, London: Longman.

Graddol, D. (1997) *The Future of English?* London: British Council and Keltic International.

Graddol, D. and Boyd-Barrett, O. (eds) (1994) *Media Texts: Authors and Readers*, Clevedon, PA: Multilingual Matters.

Graddol, D., Leith, D. and Swann, J. (eds) (1996) *English: History, Diversity and Change*, London and New York: Routledge and the Open University.

Graff, G. (1987) *Professing Literature: An Institutional History*, Chicago: Chicago University Press.

Green, K. and LeBihan, J. (1996) *Critical Theory and Practice: A Coursebook*, London: Routledge.

Green, M. and Hoggart, R. (eds) (1987) *English and Cultural Studies: Broadening the Context*, London: John Murray.

Greenbaum, S. and Quirk, R. (1990) *A Student's Grammar of the English Language*, London: Longman.

Greenblatt, S. and Gunn, G. (eds) (1992) *Redrawing the Boundaries: The Transformation of English and American Studies*, New York: Modern Language Association.

Greenwell, B. (1988) *Alternatives at English 'A' Level*, Sheffield: National Association for the Teaching of English.

Grice, H.P. (1975) 'Logic and conversation', in P. Cole and J. Morgan (eds) *Syntax and Semantics 3: Speech Acts*, New York: Academic Press.

Griffith, P. (1987) *Literary Theory and English Teaching*, Milton Keynes: Open University Press.

—— (1991) *English at the Core: Dialogue and Power in English Teaching*, Milton Keynes: Open University Press.

Grossberg, L., Nelson, C. and Treichler, P. (eds) (1992) *Cultural Studies*, London: Routledge.

Gubar, S. and Kamholtz, J. (eds) (1993) *English Inside and Out: The Place of Literary Criticism*, New York: Routledge.

Guy, J. and Small, I. (1993) *Politics and Value in English Studies: A Discipline in Crisis?*, Cambridge: Cambridge University Press.

Hackman, S. and Marshall, B. (1990) *Re-reading Literature: New Critical Approaches to the Study of English*, London: Hodder and Stoughton.

Halliday, M.A.K. (1985) *An Introduction to Functional Grammar*, London: Arnold.

Halliday, M.A.K. and Hasan, R. (1989) *Language, Context and Text: Aspects of Language in a Social-semiotic Perspective*, Oxford: Oxford University Press.

Harland, R. (1984) *Superstructuralism: The Philosophy of Structuralism and Post-structuralism*, London: Methuen.

Harner, J.L. (1993) *Literary Research Guide: A Guide to References and Sources for the Study of Literatures in English and Related Topics*, 2nd edn, New York: Modern Language Association.

Harrison, T. (1987) *Selected Poems*, 2nd edn, Harmondsworth: Penguin.

Hawkes, T. (1972) *Metaphor*, London: Methuen.

—— (1977) *Structuralism and Semiotics*, London: Methuen.

Hawthorn, J. (1994) *A Concise Glossary of Contemporary Literary Terms*, 2nd edn, London: Arnold.

Haynes, J. (1989) *Introducing Stylistics*, London: Routledge.

Hillis Miller, J. (1992) *Illustration*, London: Reaktion Books.

Hinchcliffe, A.P. (1969) *The Absurd*, London: Methuen.

Hirschkop, K. and Shepherd, D. (eds) (1988) *Bakhtin and Cultural Theory*, Manchester: Manchester University Press.

Hobsbawm, P. (1996) *Metre, Rhythm and Verse Form*, London: Routledge.

Hodge, R. (1990) *Literature as Social Discourse: Textual Strategies in English and History*, Cambridge: Polity Press.

Hodge, R. and Kress, G. (1993) *Language as Ideology*, 2nd edn, London: Routledge.

Holland, N. (1990) *Holland's Guide to Psychoanalytic Psychology and Literature-and-Psychology*, New York: Oxford University Press.

Hollander, J. and Kermode, F. (eds) (1973) *Oxford Anthology of English Literature*, 2 vols, New York: Oxford University Press.

Holman, C. H. and Harmon, W. (1996) *A Handbook to Literature*, 7th edn, New York: Macmillan.

Holub, R. (1984) *Reception Theory: A Critical Introduction*, London: Methuen.

hooks, bell (1994) *Teaching to Transgress*, New York: Routledge.

Hulse, M., Kennedy, D. and Morley, D. (eds) (1993) *The New Poetry*, Newcastle upon Tyne: Bloodaxe.

Humm, M. (ed.) (1992) *Feminisms: A Reader*, Hemel Hempstead: Harvester Wheatsheaf.

Humm, P., Stigant, P. and Widdowson, P. (eds) (1986) *Popular Fictions: Essays in Literature and History*, London: Methuen.

Hunt, A. (1975) *Hopes for Good Happenings: Alternatives in Education and Theatre*, London: Eyre Methuen.

Hurford, J.R. (1994) *Grammar: A Student's Guide*, Cambridge: Cambridge University Press.

Hurston, Z.N. (1937) *Their Eyes Were Watching God*, London: Virago, 1986.

Hutcheon, L. (1985) *A Theory of Parody: The Teaching of Twentieth-century Art Forms*, London: Methuen.

—— (1989) *The Politics of Postmodernism*, London: Routledge.

Ibsen, H. (1965) *The League of Youth, A Doll's House, The Lady from the Sea*, trans. P. Watts, Harmondsworth: Penguin.

—— (1984) *Plays: Two*, trans. M. Meyer, London: Methuen.

Iser, W. (1978) *The Act of Reading: A Theory of Aesthetic Response*, Baltimore, MD: Johns Hopkins University Press.

Jameson, F. (1972) *The Prison-House of Language: A Critical Account of Structuralism and Russian Formalism*, Princeton, NJ: Princeton University Press.

—— (1981) *The Political Unconscious: Narrative as a Socially Symbolic Act*, London: Methuen.

Jardine, A. and Smith, P. (eds) (1987) *Men in Feminism*, London: Methuen.

Jauss, H.R. (1982) *Towards an Aesthetics of Reception*, trans. T. Bahti, Brighton: Harvester Press.

Jefferson, A. and Robey, D. (eds) (1986) *Modern Literary Theory: A Comparative Introduction*, London: Batsford.

Kachru, B. B. (1986) *The Alchemy of English: The Spread, Models and Functions of Non-native Englishes*, Oxford: Pergamon.

—— (ed.) (1992) *The Other Tongue: English across Cultures*, Urbana and Chicago: University of Illinois Press.

Kazantsis, J. (1995) *Selected Poems 1977–1992*, London: Sinclair-Stevenson.

Kershaw, B. (1992) *The Politics of Performance: Radical Theatre as Cultural Intervention*, London: Routledge.

Kinneavy, J.L. (1971) *A Theory of Discourse*, New York: W.W. Norton.

Kipling, R. (1888) *Plain Tales from the Hills*, London, Macmillan, 1982.

Knights, B. (1993) *From Reader to Reader*, Brighton: Harvester Wheatsheaf.

Kress, G. (1989) *Linguistic Processes in Socio-cultural Practice*, Oxford: Oxford University Press.

—— (1995) *Writing the Future: English and the Making of a Culture of Innovation*, Sheffield: National Association for the Teaching of English.

Kristeva, J. (1984) *Revolution in Poetic Language*, trans. M. Waller, New York: Columbia University Press.

Labov, W. (1972) *Language in the Inner City*, Philadelphia: University of Pennsylvania Press.

Laing, R.D. (1965) *The Divided Self*, Harmondsworth: Penguin.

Lakoff, G. and Johnson, M. (1980) *Metaphors We Live By*, Chicago: Chicago University Press.

Landow, G. (1992) *Hypertext: The Convergence of Contemporary Literary Theory and Technology*, Baltimore, MD: Johns Hopkins University Press.

Landow, G. and Delany, P. (eds) (1992) *Hypermedia and Literary Studies*, Cambridge, MA: MIT Press.

Lauter, P. (1991) *Canons and Contexts*, Oxford: Oxford University Press.

Leavis, F.R. (1930) *Mass Civilisation and Minority Culture*, Cambridge: The Minority Press, 1979.

—— (1936) *Revaluation*, Harmondsworth: Penguin, 1972.

—— (1948) *The Great Tradition*, Harmondsworth: Penguin, 1972.

Leech, G.N. (1969) *A Linguistic Guide to English Poetry*, London: Longman.

—— (1983) *Principles of Pragmatics*, London: Longman.

Leech, G. and Short, M. (1981) *Style in Fiction: A Linguistic Introduction to English Fictional Prose*, London: Longman.

Leith, D. (1997) *A Social History of English*, 2nd edn, London: Routledge.

Leith, R. and Myerson, G. (1989) *The Power of Address: Explorations in Rhetoric*, London: Routledge.

Lemon, L.T. and Reis, M.T. (eds) (1965) *Russian Formalist Criticism*, Lincoln: University of Nebraska Press.

Lentricchia, F. (1980) *After the New Criticism*, London: Athlone Press.

Lentricchia, F. and McLaughlin, T. (eds) (1995) *Critical Terms for Literary Study*, 2nd edn, Chicago: Chicago University Press.

Lodge, D. (ed.) (1972) *20th Century Literary Criticism*, London: Longman.

— (ed.) (1988) *Modern Criticism and Theory: A Reader*, London: Longman.

— (1992) *The Art of Fiction*, Harmondsworth: Penguin.

Lucas, J. (1990) *England and Englishness: Ideas of Nationhood in English Poetry 1688–1900*, London: Hogarth.

Lukács, G. (1962) *The Historical Novel*, trans. H. and S. Mitchell, London: Merlin.

Lynn, S. (1994) *Texts and Contexts: Writing about Literature with Critical Theory*, New York: HarperCollins.

Lyotard, J-F. (1979) *The Postmodern Condition: A Report on Knowledge*, trans. G. Bennington, Manchester: Manchester University Press, 1986.

McArthur, T. (1992) *The Oxford Companion to the English Language*, Oxford: Oxford University Press.

MacCabe, C. (ed.) (1988) *Futures for English*, Manchester: Manchester University Press.

McCrum, R., Cran, W. and MacNeil, R. (1992) *The Story of English*, 2nd edn, London: Faber & Faber and BBC Books.

McFarlane, B. (1996) *Novel to Film. An Introduction to the Theory of Adaptation*, Oxford: Oxford University Press.

MacFarlane, P. and Temple, L. (eds) (1996) *Blue Light Clear Atoms: Poetry for Senior Students*, Melbourne: Macmillan.

McGann, J.J. (1988) *The Beauty of Inflections: Literary Investigations in Historical Method*, Oxford: Oxford University Press.

Macherey, P. (1966) *A Theory of Literary Production*, trans. G. Wall, London: Routledge and Kegan Paul, 1978.

McQuail, D. and Windahl, S. (1993) *Communication Models for the Study of Mass Communication*, London: Longman.

Makaryk, I.R. (ed.) (1993) *Encyclopedia of Contemporary Literary Theory: Approaches, Scholars, Terms*, Toronto: University of Toronto Press.

Marcus, L. (1994) *Auto/biographical Discourses*, Manchester: Manchester University Press.

Markham, E. (ed.) (1989) *Hinterland: Caribbean Poetry from the West Indies & Britain*, Newcastle upon Tyne: Bloodaxe.

Marshall, B. (1992) *Teaching Postmodernism: Fiction and Theory*, London: Routledge.

Matejka, L. and Pomorska, K. (eds) (1978) *Readings in Russian Poetics*, Ann Arbor: Michigan University Press.

Maybin, J. and Mercer, N. (eds) (1996) *Using English: From Conversation to Canon*, London and New York: Routledge and the Open University.

Medvedev, P. and Bakhtin, M. (1978) *The Formal Method in Literary Scholarship: An Introduction to Sociological Poetics*, trans. A. Wehrle, Baltimore, MD: Johns Hopkins University Press.

Mercer, N. and Swann, J. (eds) (1996) *Learning English: Development and Diversity*, London and New York: Routledge and the Open University.

Metz, C. (1974) *Film Language: A Semiotics of the Cinema*, trans. M. Taylor, New York: Oxford University Press.

Michaels, L. and Ricks, C. (eds) (1990) *The State of the Language*, London: Faber & Faber.

Millroy, J. and O'Rourke, R. (1991) *The Woman Reader: Learning and Teaching Women's Writing*, London: Routledge.

Mills, S. (ed.) (1994) *Gendering the Reader*, New York and London: Harvester Wheatsheaf.

— (1995) *Feminist Stylistics*, London: Routledge.

Milner, A. (1996) *Literature, Culture and Society*, London: University College London Press.

Moffett, J. (1968) *Teaching the Universe of Discourse*, Boston, MA: Houghton Mifflin.

Moi, T. (1985) *Sexual/Textual Politics*, London: Methuen.

Montgomery, M. (1996) *An Introduction to Language and Society*, 2nd edn, London: Routledge.

Montgomery, M., Durant, A., Fabb, N., Furniss, T. and Mills, S. (1992) *Ways of Reading: Advanced Reading Skills for Students of English Literature*, London: Routledge.

Moon, B. (1992) *Literary Terms: A Practical Glossary*, London and Scarborough, WA: English Media Centre and Chalkface Press.

Morgan, W. (1992) *A Poststructuralist English*

Classroom: The Example of Ned Kelly, Melbourne: Victoria Association for Teaching of English.

Morrison, T. (1987) *Beloved – A Novel*, London: Chatto and Windus, 1988.

Mühlhausler, P. and Harré, R. (1990) *Pronouns and People: The Linguistic Construction of Personal and Social Identity*, Oxford: Blackwell.

Mukarovsky, J. (1936) *Aesthetic Function: Norm and Value as Social Facts*, trans. M. Suino, Ann Arbor: University of Michigan Press, 1970.

Mulhern, F. (1979) *The Moment of Scrutiny*, London: New Left Books.

Murphy, P. D. (1995) *Literature, Nature and Other Eco-Feminist Critiques*, New York: State University of New York Press.

Murray, L. (ed.) (1991) *The New Oxford Book of Australian Verse*, 2nd edn, Melbourne and Oxford: Oxford University Press.

Nash, W. (1982) *The Language of Humour: Style and Technique in Comic Discourse*, London: Longman.

—— (1989) *Rhetoric: The Wit of Persuasion*, Oxford: Blackwell.

—— (1992) *An Uncommon Tongue: The Uses and Resources of English*, London: Routledge.

Nash, W. and Stacey, D. (1997) *Creating Texts: An Introduction to the Study of Composition*, London and New York: Longman, Addison and Wesley.

Nichols, G. (1984) *The Fat Black Woman's Poems*, London: Virago.

Norris, C. (1991) *Deconstruction: Theory and Practice*, 2nd edn, London: Methuen.

O'Donnell, W. and Todd, L. (1992) *Variety in Contemporary English*, London: Routledge.

OED *(Oxford English Dictionary)* (1928, 2nd edn, 1989) ed. R. Burchfield, J. Simpson, *et al.*, Oxford: Oxford University Press.

Onega, S. and Landa, J. (eds) (1996) *Narratology: An Introduction*, London: Longman.

Open University (1996a), *A210: Approaching Literature*, Milton Keynes: Open University Press.

—— (1996b) *U210: The English Language: Past, Present and Future*, Milton Keynes: Open University Press.

O'Sullivan, T., Hartley, J., Saunders, D., Montgomery, M. and Fiske, J. (1994) *Key Concepts in Communication and Cultural Studies*, 2nd edn, London: Routledge.

Ousby, I. (ed.) (1992) *The Cambridge Guide to Literature in English*, 2nd edn, Cambridge: Cambridge University Press.

Palmer, D.J. (1965) *The Rise of English Studies*, Oxford: Oxford University Press.

Parrinder, P. (1991) *Authors and Authority: English and American Criticism, 1750–1900*, 2nd edn, London: Macmillan.

Pavis, P. (1991) *Theatre at the Crossroads of Culture*, trans. L. Kruger, London: Routledge.

Pennycook, A. (1994) *The Cultural Politics of English as an International Language*, London and New York: Longman.

Plasa, C. and Ring, B. (eds) (1994) *The Discourse of Slavery: Aphra Behn to Toni Morrison*, London: Routledge.

Platt, J., Weber, H. and Ho, M.L. (1984) *The New Englishes*, London: Routledge and Kegan Paul.

Pope, R. (1995) *Textual Intervention: Critical and Creative Strategies for Literary Studies*, London and New York: Routledge.

Pratchett, T. and Gaiman, N. (1991) *Good Omens*, London: Corgi.

Pratt, M.L. (1976) *Towards a Speech Act Theory of Literary Discourse*, Bloomington: Indiana University Press.

Preminger, A. and Brogan, T.V. F. (eds) (1993) *The New Princeton Encyclopedia of Poetry and Poetics*, Princeton, NJ: Princeton University Press.

Prince, G. (1987) *A Dictionary of Narratology*, Lincoln: University of Nebraska Press.

Propp, V. (1928) *Morphology of the Folktale*, Austin: University of Texas Press, 1975.

Punter, D. (ed.) (1986) *Introduction to Contemporary Cultural Studies*, London: Longman.

Purdie, S. (1993) *Comedy: The Mastery of Discourse*, Hemel Hempstead: Harvester Wheatsheaf.

Quirk, R. and Widdowson, H.G. (eds) (1985) *English in the World: Teaching and Learning the Language and Literatures*, Cambridge: Cambridge University Press and the British Council.

Redfern, W. (1984) *Puns*, Oxford: Blackwell.

Regan, S. (ed.) (1992) *The Politics of Pleasure: Aesthetics and Cultural Theory*, Buckingham and Philadelphia: Open University Press.

Reid, I. (1984) *The Making of Literature: Texts, Contexts and Classroom Practice*, Canberra: Australian Association for the Teaching of English.

—— (1992) *Narrative Exchanges*, London: Routledge.

Rhys, J. (1966) *Wide Sargasso Sea*, Harmondsworth: Penguin, 1968.

Rice, P. and Waugh, P. (eds) (1996) *Modern Literary Theory: A Reader*, 3rd edn, London: Arnold.

Rich, A. (1967) *Selected Poems*, London: Chatto and Windus.

Richards, I.A. (1924) *The Principles of Literary Criticism*, London: Routledge and Kegan Paul, 1967.

—— (1929) *Practical Criticism: A Study of Literary Judgement*, London: Routledge and Kegan Paul.

Ricks, C. and Michaels, L. (eds) (1990) *The State of the Language in the 1990s*, London and New York: Faber & Faber.

Rimmon-Kenan, S. (1983) *Narrative Fiction: Contemporary Poetics*, London: Methuen.

—— (ed.) (1987) *Discourse in Psychoanalysis and Literature*, London: Methuen.

Rushdie, S. (1988) *The Satanic Verses*, London and New York: The Consortium, 1992.

Russell, W. (1985), *Educating Rita and Other Plays*, London: Methuen, 1988.

Ryan, K. (ed.) (1996) *New Historicism and Cultural Materialism: A Reader*, London: Arnold.

Rylance, R. (ed.) (1987) *Debating Texts: A Reader in 20th-Century Literary Theory and Method*, Milton Keynes: Open University Press.

Said, E. (1978) *Orientalism*, New York: Random House.

—— (1993) *Culture and Imperialism*, London: Chatto and Windus.

Samuel, R. (ed.) (1989) *Patriotism: The Making and Unmaking of British National Identity*, 3 vols, London: Routledge.

Sanders, A. (1994) *The Short Oxford History of English Literature*, Oxford: Oxford University Press, 2nd edn, 1997.

Sarap, M. (1993) *An Introductory Guide to Post-structuralism and Postmodernism*, Hemel Hempstead: Harvester Wheatsheaf.

Sarton, M. (1973) *As We Are Now*, London: The Women's Press, 1983.

Saunders, D. (ed.) (1994) *The Complete Student Handbook*, Oxford: Blackwell.

Scholes, R. (1985) *Textual Power: Literary Theory and the Teaching of English*, New Haven, CT: Yale University Press.

Scholes, R., Comley, N. and Ulmer, G. (1995) *Text Book: An Introduction to Literary Language*, 2nd edn, New York: St. Martin's Press.

Schwarz, B. (ed.) (1996) *The Expansion of England: Race, Ethnicity and Cultural History*, London: Routledge.

Selby, K. and Cowdrey, R. (1995) *How to Study Television*, London: Macmillan.

Selden, R. (ed.) (1988) *The Theory of Criticism from Plato to the Present – A Reader* London: Longman.

—— (1989) *Practising Theory and Reading Literature*, Hemel Hempstead: Harvester Wheatsheaf.

Selden, R., Widdowson, P. and Brooker, P. (1997) *A Reader's Guide to Contemporary Literary Theory*, 4th edn, Hemel Hempstead: Harvester Wheatsheaf.

Sell, R. (ed.) (1990) *Literary Pragmatics*, London: Routledge.

Shakespeare, W. (1994) *Hamlet: Case Studies in Contemporary Criticism*, ed. S. L. Wofford, Boston and London: Bedford/Macmillan.

Shepherd, V. (1993) *Playing the Language-Game*, Milton Keynes: Open University Press.

Short, M. (ed.) (1989) *Reading, Analyzing and Teaching Literature*, London: Longman.

—— (1996) *Exploring the Language of Poems, Prose and Plays*, London: Longman.

Showalter, E. (1977) *A Literature of Their Own*, London, Virago, 1979.

Simpson, P. (1993) *Language, Ideology and Point of View*, London: Routledge.

—— (1997) *Language through Literature: An Introduction*, London: Routledge.

Sinfield, A (1992) *Faultlines: Cultural Materialism and the Politics of Dissident Reading*, Oxford: Oxford University Press.

Spengemann, W.C. (1986) *The Forms of Autobiography: Episodes in the History of a Literary Genre*, New Haven, CT: Yale University Press.

Spivak, G.C. (1987) *In Other Worlds: Essays in Cultural Politics*, London: Methuen.

—— (1994) *Outside in the Teaching Machine*, London and New York: Routledge.

Stallybrass, P. and White, A. (1986) *The Politics and Poetics of Transgression*, London: Methuen.

Stibbs, A. (1991) *Reading Narrative as Literature: Signs of Life*, Milton Keynes: Open University Press.

Stubbs, M. (1983) *Discourse Analysis: The*

Sociological Analysis of Natural Language, Oxford: Blackwell.

Tallack, D. (ed.) (1987) *Literary Theory at Work: Three Texts*, London: Batsford.

Tannen, D. (1989) *Talking Voices: Repetition, Dialogue and Imagery in Conversational Discourse*, Cambridge: Cambridge University Press.

—— (1992) *You Just Don't Understand: Women and Men in Conversation*, London: Virago.

Taylor, G. (1989) *The Student's Writing Guide for the Arts and Social Sciences*, Cambridge: Cambridge University Press.

Theatre Workshop (1956) *Oh What a Lovely War*, London: Methuen, 1965.

Thomas, D. (1995) *The Dylan Thomas Omnibus*, London: Phoenix Orion.

Thompson, A. and Wilcox, H. (eds) (1989) *Teaching Women: Feminism and English Studies*, Manchester: Manchester University Press.

Thompson, D. (ed.) (1973) *Discrimination and Popular Culture*, 2nd edn, Harmondsworth: Penguin.

Thomson, J. (ed.) (1992) *Reconstructing Literature Teaching*, Norwood, S.A: Australian Association for the Teaching of English.

Todd, L. (1984) *Modern Englishes: Pidgins and Creoles*, London: Blackwell and Deutsch.

Todorov, T. (1990) *Genre in Discourse*, Cambridge: Cambridge University Press.

Toolan, M.J. (1988) *Narrative: A Critical Linguistic Introduction*, London: Routledge.

—— (ed.) (1992) *Language, Text and Context: Essays in Stylistics*, London: Routledge.

Traugott, E.C. and Pratt, M.L. (1980) *Linguistics for Students of Literature*, New York: Harcourt Brace Jovanovich.

Trudgill, P. (1990) *The Dialects of England*, Oxford: Blackwell.

Trudgill, P. and Hannah, J. (1982) *International English: A Guide to Varieties of Standard English*, London: Edward Arnold.

Turner, G. (1993) *Film as Social Practice*, London: Routledge.

Tutuola, A. (1952) *The Palm Wine Drinkard*, London: Faber & Faber, 1987.

Tweddle, S., Adams, A., Clarke, S., Scrimshaw, P. and Walton, S. (eds) (1997) *English for Tomorrow*, Buckingham: Open University Press.

Van Peer, W. (ed.) (1988) *Taming the Text: Explorations in Language, Literature and Culture*, London: Routledge.

Veeser, H. A. (ed.) (1989) *The New Historicism*, New York: Routledge.

Voloshinov, V.N. (1973) *Marxism and the Philosophy of Language*, trans. L. Matejka and I. Titunik, New York: Seminar Press.

Vygotsky. L.S. (1934) *Thought and Language*, trans. E. Hanfmann and G. Vakar, Cambridge MA: MIT Press, 1962.

Walder, D. (ed.) (1990) *Literature in the Modern World: Critical Essays and Documents*, Oxford: Oxford University Press and Open University Press.

—— (1997) *Post-colonial Literatures in English: An Introduction*, Oxford: Blackwell.

Wales, K. (1989) *A Dictionary of Stylistics*, London: Longman.

Wall, C. (ed.) (1989) *Changing Our Own Words: Essays on Cultural Theory and Writing by Black Women*, London: Routledge.

Ward-Jouve, N. (1991) *White Woman Speaks with Forked Tongue: Criticism as Autobiography*, London: Routledge.

Warhol, R. and Herndl, D. (eds) (1991) *Feminisms: An Anthology of Literary Theory and Criticism*, New Brunswick, NJ: Rutgers University Press.

Watson, J. and Hill, A. (1984) *A Dictionary of Communication and Media Studies*, London: Arnold.

Waugh, P. (1984) *Metafiction: The Theory and Practice of Self-conscious Fiction*, London: Methuen.

—— (1992a) *Practising Postmodernism / Reading Modernism*, London: Arnold.

—— (ed.) (1992b) *Postmodernism: A Reader*, London: Arnold.

Webster, R. (1996) *Studying Literary Theory*, 2nd edn, London: Arnold.

Weedon, C. (1996) *Feminist Practice and Poststructuralist Theory*, 2nd edn, Oxford: Blackwell.

Wellek, R. and Warren, A. (1963) *The Theory of Literature*, 3rd edn, Harmondsworth: Penguin.

Widdowson, H.G. (1975) *Stylistics and the Teaching of Literature*, London: Longman.

Widdowson, P. (ed.) (1982) *Re-reading English*, London: Methuen.

Williams, P. and Chrisman, L. (eds) (1993) *Colonial Discourse and Postcolonial Theory: A Reader*, Hemel Hempstead: Harvester Wheatsheaf.

Williams, R. (1958) *Culture and Society 1780–1950*, Harmondsworth: Penguin.

—— (1966) *Modern Tragedy*, London: Chatto and Windus.

—— (1977) *Marxism and Literature*, Oxford: Oxford University Press.

—— (1983) *Keywords: A Vocabulary of Culture and Society*, 2nd edn, London: Flamingo.

—— (1989) *What I Came to Say*, ed. N. Belton, F. Mulhern and J. Taylor, London: Hutchinson.

Winnicott, D.W. (1974) *Playing and Reality*, Harmondsworth: Penguin.

Wittgenstein, L. (1953) *Philosophical Investigations*, ed. and trans. G. Anscombe, Oxford: Blackwell.

Wright, E. (1984) *Psychoanalytic Criticism: Theory and Practice*, London: Methuen.

Wynne-Davis, M. (ed.) (1989) *Bloomsbury Guide to English Literature*, London: Bloomsbury.

Young, R. (ed.) (1981) *Untying the Text: A Poststructuralist Reader*, London: Routledge and Kegan Paul.

—— (1990) *White Mythologies: Writing History and the West*, London: Routledge.

RELEVANT JOURNALS AND USEFUL ADDRESSES

Most of these associations sponsor other useful publications, many of which are of international as well as national significance.

Critical Survey (clear and lively overview of developing debates; includes creative writing), Oxford: Berghahn Publishers.

College English, National Council of Teachers of English, 1111, W. Kenyon Road, Urbana, IL 610801–1096, USA.

English Academy of South Africa, PO Box 124, Wits, 2050, South Africa; also see *Critical Language Awareness Series*, ed. Hilary Janks, Hodder and Stoughton, South Africa.

English in Australia, Journal of Australian Association for the Teaching of English, PO Box 3203, Norwood, South Australia, 5067.

English in Education, National Association for the Teaching of English, 50, Broadfield Road, Sheffield, S8 0XJ, England. Tel 44–(0)–114–255–5419. Fax 44–(0)–114–255–5296.

English & Media Magazine, English and Media Centre, 136 Chalton Street, London NW1 1RX.

English-Speaking Union of the Commonwealth, Dartmouth House, 37 Charles Street, London, W1X 8AB, UK; 16 East 69th Street, New York, NY 10021, USA.

English Today, Cambridge: Cambridge University Press.

European Journal of English Studies, journal of the European Society for the Study of English, Swets and Zeitlinger Publishers, PO Box 825, 2160 SZ Lisse, The Netherlands.

Language & Literature, journal of the Poetics and Linguistics Association, Sage Publications, 6, Bonhill Street, London, EC2A 4PU, UK.

Literature and History (old series and new series).

Literature Matters and *Journal of British Studies*: The British Council, 11, Portland Place, London, WIN 4EJ UK or 10 Spring Gardens, London, SW1A 2BN UK. Tel: 44–(0)–171–389–4451. Fax: 44–(0)–171–389–4424 or (UK Regional Services Manager) Medlock Street, Manchester M15 4AA. Specifically for: Northern Ireland – 1 Chlorine Gardens, Belfast, BT9 5DJ; Scotland – 3 Bruntsfield Crescent, Edinburgh, EH10 4HD; Wales – 28 Park Place, Cardiff, CF1 3QE.

Networking English Language Learning in Europe, Bredestraat 12, NL–6211, HC Maastricht, The Netherlands.

Open University Educational Enterprises Ltd, 13 Cofferidge Close, Stony Stratford, Milton Keynes, MK11 1BY, UK. Tel: 44–(0)–1908–261662. Fax: 44–(0)–1908–261001.

Textual Practice (sophisticated contemporary theory and practice), Routledge, 11 New Fetter Lane, London EC4P 4EE.

Wasafiri (dedicated to Caribbean, African, Asian and associated literatures in English; includes creative writing and information on cultural events, films, etc.), Dept. of English and Drama, Queen Mary and Westfield College, University of London, Mile End Road, London, E1 4NS, UK.

World Literature Written in English, Division of Literature and Drama, National Institute of Education, Buki Timah Road, Singapore 1025.

For addresses of established institutional and commercial World-Wide-Web sites, see 4.3.

More advanced resources for research and review, including annual bibliographies and volumes on specific topics, are:

Annual Bibliography of English Language and Literature, Modern Humanities Research Association, Cambridge, UK.

Modern Language Association (MLA) International Bibliography of Books and Articles on the Modern Languages and Literatures, Modern Language Association of America, New York, USA.

The Review of English Studies, Oxford: Oxford University Press, UK.

The Yearbook of English Studies, Modern Humanities Research Association, Cambridge, UK.

The Year's Work in English Studies and *The Year's Work in Critical and Cultural Theory*, Oxford: Basil Blackwell; also *Essays and Studies*, Cambridge: Brewer – all publications of The English Association, c/o University of Leicester, UK.

INDEX

This includes all significant references to terms, topics, persons and places. Highlighting is similar to that used throughout the book. Items in SMALL CAPITALS (e.g. ENGLISHES, LITERATURE, FEMINISM, POSTMODERNISM) refer to sections in Parts One and Two. Items in **bold** (e.g. **author, canon, discourse, standards,** text) refer to entries in Part Three. The only difference is that items marked with an *asterisk in the main text (referring to topics defined or illustrated in passing, as well as to significant writers) are here presented without an asterisk. All page numbers indicating the principal references – and the best places to start – are highlighted in **bold** (e.g. **accent** 18, **158–60**, 362).

Aborigine, aboriginal 38, 144, **149–52**, 171, **343**

Abrams's model of 'work' (modified) 71–3

absence 106, 128, **156–8**, 218, 249

absurd 15, **179–84**, 330–1; *also see* **comedy**

accent 18, **158–60**, 362; multiaccentual 160; accentual-syllabic measure 160, 238–9

acceptable (usage) 362

Achebe, C. (1930–), *Things Fall Apart* 18, 23, 152, 153, 172; text **313–4**; 389

active (verb) 362; *also see* verb 381

adaptation 32, 212, 249, as learning strategy 257

addresser, address, addressee 61, 64, 105–6, **160–2**, 192, **207**, 224, 258, 362

adjective 362

adverb 362

advertising 47, 53, 57, 70, 83, 125, 213, 389; examples: TV **340–1, 358**; magazine **341–2**; personal **355–6**

aesthetic(s) 35, 55, 60, 88–9, 103–4, 125, **162–5**

Africa(n) 9, 18, 20, 31, 35, 135, 138, **145**, 166, 171, 313–4, 387–9; map **384**; South 18, 135–7, 139, 140, 145, 330, map **384**, 389

age, versions of (texts) 341–3

agent, agency 105–6, **232**, **362**

AIDS 113, 132, 134, 298

Aitchison, J. 53

allegory 15

alliteration 213, **237–8**, 280, **362**

allusion 236; *also see* intertextuality

Althusser, L. (1918–1990) 88, **105–6**, 231

ambiguity 38, 69, 78, 81

America(n) 9, **13**, 18, 135, 139, 144, 151, 228–9, maps **384–5**, 387–9; American Indian 135, 140, 151, 159, map **385**; university 'English' in 29–32

analysis (textual) 45–8, **255**, 256, **258–61**, 264

Angelou, M. (1928–) 53

Anglo-Saxon 10–1, **14–5**, 26, 33, 52, 137, 151, 226, 237–8, example of **276**, 386

animate, inanimate (semantics) 362

anonymous 167, 'Wulf and Eadwacer' 276, 'Maiden in the mor lay' 277, 'Pearl' 280; 354–6

anthologies, anthologising **271–4**, 275–360

apostrophe 363, 375–6

apposition (grammatical) 363

Arab(ic) 18

archaism 363

Aristotle (384–322 BC) 29, 104, **179–84**

Arnold, M. (1822–1888) 25, 29, 78, 171

art 27, 38, 40, 55, 60, 104–5, **162–5**; artisan, artist(ic) 55, **163–4**; Art History 40, 390–1; *also see* **aesthetics**

articles, definite and indefinite 363

Asia(n) 9, 38, 140, 159, 390–1

aspect (verbal) *see* verb 381

assessment 254, 255–6, 390–1
association (of words) 363; *also see* denotation 366
assonance 213; *also see* alliteration 362
Auerbach, E. (1892–1957) 220
Austen, J. (1775–1817), *Pride and Prejudice* 23, 25, 39, 45, 83, 93, 118, 134, 165, 194, 220, text **305**, 388
Australia(n) 9, 18, 31, 60, 135, 139, **144**, 151, 158–9, 228–9, **343**; map **384**, 388
authenticity 167, 171
author 16, 39, 41, 55, 71–2, 74, 79, 108, 128, **165–8**, 172, 230–1, 270; **authority** 29, 61, **166**, 174; 'authorised' 171, 172, 173
auto/biography 34, 38, 57, 69, 98, 99–10, 118, **168–70**, 178, 192, 233; examples of 280, 288–9, 299–303, 333, 339, 341, 346–7, 352, 354, 358

background 34, 40, 91, 109, **195–9**, 217; *also see* **foreground**
Bakhtin, M. (1895–1975) 20–1, **88**, 96, 107, 160, 179, 185, 201; *also see:* **carnival** 182–3; centrifugal and centripetal 20, 185, 369; dialogic 222; heteroglossia 20, 368–9; 'response-ability' 248, 250
Bambara, T.C. (1931–), 'The Lesson' 18, 159, 211, text **333**
Barnes, W. (1801–86), 'Woak Hill' 15, 23, 53, 160, 230, 238, 241, text **289–90**, 388
Barthes, R. (1915–1980) 43, 124, **127**, 167, 212, **247–8**, 250
Baudrillard, J. (1929–) 129, 205
beauty 162–5; *also see* **aesthetics**
Beckett, S. (1906–1989), *Not I*, 83, **90–1**, 101, 134, 158, 165, 182, 199, **200**, 215; text **330–1**, 388
Behn, A. (1640–89), *Oroonoko* 23, 64, 114, 119, 122, 140, 172, text **300–1**, 387
'belles lettres', bellelettrist 35
Benjamin, W.(1892–1940) 64, 86, **104–5**, 130, 249
Benveniste, E. (1902–76) 231
Bhabha, H.K. 137–8, 177, 249
bibles 15, 25, 28–9, 137, **171–4**, 209, 337–8, 387; *also see* translations
binary 113, **128**, 131, 132, 146, 185, **363**
biography 32, 35, **168–70**; *also see* **auto/biography**
black (as cultural construct) 52, 145–7, 173, 311–2

Blake, W. (1757–1827), 'And did those feet. . . .' (*Milton*) 29, 40, **85**, 241, text **350–1**, 388
Bleich, D. 96, 246
Bloom, H. 246
body 97, **119–20**, 147, 152, 183; body language 50, 148, **363**
Brecht, B. (1898–1956) 76, 86, **103–4**, 130, 137, 218, 224, 249, 391; Brechtian 104, 193, 228–9, 354; *also see* 'making-strange'
Brews, M. (Paston letters) text **298–9**, 387
Britain, British, Briton 9, **10–5**, 22–3, 135, 138–40; map **383**, 388; British Empire 13–4, 25, 64, 114, 135, 145, map **384**; *also see* England, ENGLISH
broadcast 57, 63, 194, 210, 388–9
Brontë, C. (1816–55), *Jane Eyre* 25, 118, 157, 178, 198, 207, text **306–7**, 388
Brook, P. 195
Brooke, R. (1887–1915) 'The Soldier' 134, 199, 241, text **352**
Brooks, C. (1906–) 79, 204
Browning, E.B. (1806–61) and R. (1812–89) 273–4
Burns, R. (1759–96) 15, 238, text **344**
Byron, G.G. (1788–1824), *The Vision of Judgement* 23, 27, 172, 173, 183, text **287–8**, 388

Cameron, D. 117, 123
Canada 140, map 384
canon, canonical 35, 59, 118, 136, 163–4, 171, **174–7**, 185
Caribbean 18, 20, 38, 136, 139, 166, 194, **294–6**, 342, 348, map **384**, 389
carnival(esque) 18, 88, 91, **179–84**; *also see* **comedy**
Carter, R. 230, 236–7
catharsis 96, 181
Caxton, W. (c.1420–1491) 227, 230, 387
Celts, Celtic 11, **15**, 140, 226, map **383**, 386
censorship 94
centre 124–5, 127–8, 131, 137, 145, 148, **157–8**, 218; de- and re-centring 131, **157**; *also see* **absence** and **foreground**
centrifugal, centripetal (after Bakhtin) 20, 185, 369
change (in language) 51–2, 201
character, characterisation 80, 103, **177–9**, 208, 230–1, 233; caricature 178
Chaucer, G. (c.1343–1400), 'General Prologue' 13, 23, 25, 30, **109–10**, 172, 173, 175, 236, **238–9**, text **278–9**, 387

Chester Mystery play *see* 'Noah's Flood'
choice **85, 259–60**, 296, 363; *also see* paradigm
Chomsky, N. (1928–) 21, 125, 368
Christianity 15–6, 25, **28–9**, 110, 137, 144, 147, 148, **170–4**, 174, 283–4, 350–1, 386–7
Churchill, C.(1938–), *Cloud 9* 91, 152, 172, 183, 188, 319, text **332**, 389
Churchill, W.S. (1874–1965) text **352**
circumstance (grammatical) 364
Cixous, H.(1937–) 115, 117, 214, 248, 249, 250
Clare, J. (1793–1864), 'I am, yet what I am . . . ' 16, 83, **98–100**, 169, text **288–9**, 388
Clarins skincare advert, text **351**; *also see* advertising
class *see* MARXISM
classic 40, 63, **174–7**; *also see* **canon** and CLASSICS
CLASSICS 290–1, 387, 390; neo-classical 164, 179
code 19, 62, 127, 161, 235, 364
cohesion 189, 214, 261, 364
Coleridge, S.T. (1772–1834) 204–6
collage 125, 249, as learning strategy 268
Collins, M., 'No Dialects Please' 18, 53, 158, text **294–6**, 389
collocation 259
colonisation, colonialism 12–3, 16, 130, **138–41**; neo-colonialism 141; *also see* POSTCOLONIALISM
combination 85, **260, 363**; *also see* syntagmatic
comedy 27, **179–84**; comic(s) 159, **180**, 210
COMMUNICATION **63–4**, 79, 124, 129, 156, 161, **386–9**; COMMUNICATION STUDIES 31, **40–1**, 63–4, 164, 390–1
COMPOSITION **29–32**, 390–1; *also see* RHETORIC
condensation (psychological) 94–5
Connors, R. 250
connotation *see* denotation 366
Conrad, J.(1857–1924), *The Heart of Darkness* 53, 83, 122, 152, 172, text **311–2**, 389
consciousness 52, 92, **94**, 99, 168
content (manifest and latent) 94–5
context 215, **234–7**, 364; context-sensitive and context-free 221, 245, 259, 261, 365; *also see* **text**
Cook, G. 216
co-text 235, 364
conversation 61, 116–7, 162, 189, **222–3, 365**; examples of **320–1**; *also see* **speech** and transcripts

cooperative and uncooperative (assertiveness) principles 365
coordination (grammatical) 365
Coward, R. 198
creative writing 32, 57, **257**, 390; critical–creative re-writing 249–50, 265–9 (examples 302, 317); creativity 166, 204
creole 18, 136, 172, 229, **365**
criticism 15, **36**, 78, 186, 269; critique **36**, 69; *also see* PRACTICAL and NEW CRITICISM and creative writing (critical-creative re-writing)
CULTURE 15, 46–7, **58–61**, 64–5, 93, 102, 126–7, 137, 138, 147, 185, **386–9**; CULTURAL MATERIALISM 70, **103–4, 107–8**, 110; CULTURAL STUDIES 28, **40–1**, 164, 390–1; *also see* MULTICULTURLISM

decentring and recentring 157; *also see* **centre**
declarative 366
deconstruction 48, 79, **124–5, 127–8**, 156–8, 182
defamiliarisation 38, 56, 84, **86–7**, 89–91, 104, 164, 197
Defoe, D. (1660–1731), *Robinson Crusoe* 64, 122, 134, 152, 156, 172, 198, 199, 266; text **301–2**, 357, 387
deictics, deixis *see* context-sensitive 365
denotation 366
Derrida, J. (1930–) 21, 124, **127–8**, 134, **156–8**, 186, 214, 215, **248–9**; *also see* **centre**, deconstruction and différance
desire 99, 164, 168
deviation 197–8, 366
diachronic 366
dialect 18, **158–60**, 366; *also see* **accent** and **variety**
dialogue 61, 92, 162, 189, **222–5**, 258, 356, **366**; **dialogic** (after Bakhtin) 88, 224; *also see* **speech**, scripts and transcripts
diaries 168–9; *also see* journals
Dickens, C. (1812–70) 103, 164; *Great Expectations* 39, 40, 93, 183, 207; text **345**, 388
Dickinson, E. (1830–86), 'I felt a Funeral . . . ' 23, 83, 91, 100–1, 119, 169; text **347**, 388
dictionaries 227, 229; *also see* Oxford English Dictionary
difference 21, 92, 112–3, 127–8, 131, 132, 137, 142, 152, **184–8**; différance (after Derrida) 128, 214
directive *see* speech acts 378–9
discourse, discourse analysis 27, 34, **45–8**, 49,

54, 57, 96, 128–9, 178, **188–91**, 231, 367; 'discours' 189, 208

discrimination 186–7

displacement (psychological) 94–5

dissertation 256

Docker, J. 153

Douglass, F. (1817–95), *The Narrative of the Life* . . . 64, text **303**, 388; *also see* slave narratives

Doyle, R. (1958–), *Paddy Clarke ha ha ha* 15, 23, 159, 230, text **318–9**, 389

Doyle, B., *English and Englishness* 43, 255

drama, dramatic 38–9, 57, 137, 178–9, **191–5**, 199–200, 387–9; examples of 320–336, 340, 348–9, 353–4; dramatic intervention 267; *also see* THEATRE STUDIES and scripts

dreams, dream work 94–5

Dutch (Holland) 18, 140, 143, 144

Eagleton, T. (1943–) 58, 83, 107, 130, 165

Eco, U. (1932–) 234, 249

ecology, ecological approach 60, 108, 153, 390–1

écriture féminine 248; *also see* writing (as a wo/man)

editing 153, as learning strategy 256

Education (and/in English) **21–42**, 390–1; *also see* schools and universities

ego, super-ego (after Freud) **95–6**, 99, 168

Eikhenbaum, B. (1886–1959) 84, 86

Eliot, T.S. (1888–1965) 86, 125, 236

elision, elide 238, **367**

ellipsis 222, **367**

Emerson, R.W. (1802–92) *Circles* 48

empire *see* British Empire and colonialism

enclosure (of land) 99, 100, 139, 289

England **10–3**, 60, 138, 175, map **383**; 'England at war' 349–54

ENGLISH/englishes **8–14**, 15–24, 390–1; English Literature 25–6, 35–8, **54**, 57, 59,175, 176, 391; Literatures in English 8, **37–8**, 57, 176; English as a Foreign Language 26, 149; map **384**; English in Education 24–44; English Studies (as name) 1, 44–5, 48; Englishness 9, 23; 'King's / Queen's' English 10–2, 158–9, 226, 228; Standard English 225–30; Global/World English 13–4, **18–9**, 20–1, 229–30, 389; Old, Middle and Modern 14–8, **33–4**, 137, 386–7; New Englishes 11, **33–4**, 136, 149–51, **293–6**, 313–4, 389; *also see* African, American, Australian, British, Caribbean

epic 27, **103–4**

epitaphs, examples **344–5**

essay, essay-writing 254, 256, 261–4

ethnic(ity) 142; ethnocentric 142, 148; ethnolinguistics 390; *also see* sociolinguistics 378

euphemism 367

Europe **12–3**, 143–4, 388–9

Evans, C., *English People* . . . 8, 152, 169

existential subject 367

expression 52, 92, 93, 94, 106, 156, 168; expressive 71, 161

fabula 86–7, 208

fact, factual 55, 177–8, 209, **218–9**; **faction** 34, 131, 133–4, 168, 189, 209, **218–9**; as learning strategy 268; *also see* **realism, fiction** and **hi/story**

Factory Commission Report 83, 113, 191; text **321–2**

fantasy 200, 288, 306; *also see* **fiction**

Fanthorpe, U.A. (1929–) 'Knowing about Sonnets' 23, 241; text **352–3**

feminine (as cultural construct) 112–3

FEMINISM 48, 69–70, 97, **111–23**, 125, 164, 169, 173; *also see* writing as a wo/man and GENDER STUDIES

fiction 55, 57, 93, 177–8, 209, **218–9**; dialogue in fiction 223–4; **metafiction** 131, 219; science and fantasy fiction 200, 288, 306; for examples of prose fiction *see* **novel**; *also see* **fact** and **faction**

figurative language, figures of speech 29, **203**, 367; *also see* metaphor

film 57, 74, 191–5, **193–4**, 203, **210–1**, 335–6; FILM STUDIES **38–9**, 391; *also see* **drama** and **narrative**

finite and non-finite *see* verbs 381

Fiske, J. 130, 202

foreground 34, 40, **195–9**; foregrounding 84, 87, 89–91, 109, **197–8**, 217, **367–8**

form, formal 80, 88, 99, 210, **368**

FORMALISM ('Russian') 38, 48, 56, 69, **83–92**, 124, 164, 207–8, 218

Forster, E.M. (1879–1970) 178

Foucault, M. (1926–1984) **96–7**, 124, **128–9**

Fowler, R. 191

frame (of reference) 232

Frame, J. (1924–), *To the Is-Land* 23, 169, 172, 261; text **300**

France, French 12, 16–7, 140, 141, 227, 350, 386–8

Freud, S. (1856–1939) **92**, **94–6**, 101, 169, 180, 231; *Fragment of an Analysis . . .* (*'Dora'*) 95, 101, 122, 134, 169; text **322–3**; Freudian 111, 168, 198, 201, 215, 224, 246
fricative *see* phonetics 374
fronting 368
Fugard, A. (1932–) *Boesman and Lena* 18, 23; text **330**, 389
function (verbal) 50–1, 53, 88, 191, 258, **368**; functional grammar 368; narrative function 211
FUNCTIONALISM 50, **83–92**, 164
Furbank, P.N. 206

games (theory) 129, **214**; *also see* play and **word-play**
gaps and silences 106, 109, 110, **156–8**; *also see* **absence**
gay 112, **114–5**, 121
gender 112–3, **115–6**, 200; GENDER STUDIES **112–23**, 391
generative-transformational *see* grammar 368
genre, generic 27, 34, 40, 88, 149, 169, 179, 194, **199–202**, 209–10, 258, 271, 272, **368**; re-genreing 201; current genres of small text 354–9
geography 18, 390
Germanic (languages) 10–1, 14–7, 33, 140, 171, 226, 237, 386
Germany, German 12, 141, 143
Giddens, A. 269
global(ism) **13–4**, 37, 60, 125, 129, 131, 133, **136–7**, 144, 228–9, 389
Godber, J. (1956–), *Teechers* 192, 194; text **333–4**
grammar 10, 54, 227, **368**
graphology 368
Gray, T. (1714–71), 'Elegy in a Country Churchyard – Epitaph' text **344**
Greek 15–6, 27–8, 29, 171, 293, 387
Grossberg, L. 64
Grossmith, G. (1847–1912) and W. (1854–1919), *Diary of a Nobody* 199; text **299–300**
Guardian, The (newspaper) text **315–6**
gynocriticism 118–9

Halliday, M.A.K. 53
Hands, E. (*fl.* c.1789), 'A Poem . . . by a Servant Maid' 110, 122; text **285–6**, 387

handwriting 244
Hardy, T. (1840–1828) 159, *Tess of the Durbervilles* 160
Harrison, T. (1937–), *v* 23, 53, 158, **183**, 215, 230; text **346–7**, 389
Hawthorn, J. 134
Heaney, S. (1939–) 198, 238
Heath, S. 123
hedges, hedging 116, **368**
Heineken lager advert 46–7, 69–70; text **340–1**
heroic 209; example **283–4**; *also see* mock-heroic
Herrnstein Smith, B. 188
heteroglossia 20, 224, **368–9**
HISTORY (and English) **32–5**, 390–1; History of English Language 14–8, 33; *also see* NEW HISTORICISM and **hi/story**
hi/story 34, 55, 69, 106, 129, 131, 134, 141, 150–1, 168, 178, 189, **209**, 211, 218; *also see* **narrative** and HISTORY
Hodge, B. 152
Holdsworth, G., 'I Call Him Tuesday Afternoon' 152; text **302**
hole *see (and) hear* whole
Holland, N. (1927–) 96, 246
holy books *see* **bibles**
horizon of expectation (Jauss) 245, 250
'Humpty Dumpty' 15, 53, 158, 160, versions of **336–7**
human nature 60, 138, 231; *also see* nature
Hurston, Z.N. (1891–60), *Their Eyes Were Watching God* 18, 23, 115, 159; text **312**, 389 Hutcheon, L. 130, 135, 249
hybrid(isation) 21, 88, 136, 143, 184, 195, **200**, 369; as learning strategy 268
hyperbole 369
hypertext 41, 167, 264, 390; *also see* MEDIA, multimedia
hypotaxis 369
hysteria 95, 98, 322–3

Ibsen, H. (1828–1906), *A Doll's House* 23, **82–3**, 114, 122, 137, 182, 195, 220, 267; texts **326–8**, 388
iconic *see* sign 378
id (after Freud) **95–6**, 99, 168
identity 92, 98–9, 101, 159, 167, 168, 204, **232–3**; identification (of and with) 120, 233; *also see* **subject**
ideology **105–6**, 172, 231; dominant, residual and emergent (Williams) 106–7, 109
idiom(atic) *see* morphology 371

idiolect 51, 160, 232; *also see* dialect 366

illiteracy *see* literacy

image 125, 129, 196, **202–6**, 241; *also see* sign; **imagery** 79, **203**; *also see* figurative

imagination 57, **204–5**; 'the Imaginary' (after Lacan) 15, 95, **205**

imitation 249; as learning strategy 257, 267

imperative 369

implicature 369

indexical *see* sign 378

India, Indian 9, 18, 31, 81–2, 135–7, 138, 139, 143, 228–9; map **384**, 387, 389; *also see* American Indian

indirect speech 224, 318, **366–7**; *also see* **speech**

individual, individualism **105–6**, 166, 230–1

inference 369; inferred intertextuality 236

information search 256, 261–4; information structure 369

intensifier *see* hedges 368

inter- (prefix) 369

interdisciplinary 42, 43, 390–1

internet (use of) 261, 264, 273; site for this book 5; internet conferencing text 357–8; *also see* World Wide Web

interpersonal 50, 62, 296

interrogative 370

intervention (textual) 32, 249, 257, **265–9**

interviews, examples of 321–3; as learning strategy 257

intertextuality 45–8, 215, (explicit, implied and inferred) 234–7; examples of 'intertextual clusters' 336–60; *also see* **text** and **genre**

intonation 221, **370**; *also see* sound-structure

intransitive and transitive processes: 'change' as 51–2; 'writing' as 243–4; *also see* verbs 381

Ireland, Irish **9–12**, 15, 114, 136, 138, 139, 141, 145, 159, 228, 318–9; map 383, 386–88; *also see* Celtic

Irigaray, L. (c.1934–) 117, 214

irony 38, **79**, 110, 180, 236

Iser, W. (1926–) 88, **245–6**, 250

Italy, Italian 16, 18

Jakobson, R. (1896–1982) 84–6, 161–2

Jameson, F. (1934–) 94, 97, **106**, 107, 134, 157

Jauss, H.R. (1921–) 88, **245**

Jefferson, A. 220

Johnson, S. (1709–84) 32, 55, 169, 229, 242

jouissance (joy) *see* **pleasure**

journals, examples of 299–303, 339, 341; course journals 257; *also see* diaries

Jung, C. (1875–1961) 95

Kazantsis, J. (1940–), 'Leda and Leonardo the Swan' 122, 241, 242, 267; text **291–2**

Kelman, J. (1946–), *How late it was, how late* 15, 23, 64, 158, 159, 224, 230; text **319**, 388

Kipling, R. (1865–1936) 8; 'The Story of Muhammad Din' 23, 64, **81–2**, 110, 152, 172, 173, 179, 195, 198, 211, 220, 233; text **309–11**, 389

Klein, M. (1882–1960) 95, **96**

Kristeva, J. (1941–) 101, 115, 137, 168, 249

Labov, W. 211

Lacan, J-M. (1901–81) 92, **95**, 168, 205, 214, 231

lack (psychological) 95, 130, 168

Laing, R.D., text **358–9**

Lakoff, R. 116–7

Langland, W., *Piers Plowman* 23, 238, text **279–80**, 387

LANGUAGE 16, 45–7, **48–54** (functions **50–1**, change in **51–2**), 92–3, 136, 184, **370**, 386–9, 390; gendered languages 112–3, 115–6; *also see* ENGLISH/englishes

Latin, Latinate **15–7**, 27–8, 29, 51, 227, 386–7

Laurance, A., 'My Brain' text **358–9**

learning strategies 253–74

Leavis, F.R. (1895–1978) 25, 29, **36**, 58–9, 79, 165, 177, 186, 188, 194, 231

Leonard, T. (1944–), 'This is thi / six a clock / news' 15, 23, 159, 160, 230; text **317–8**, 389

lesbian 112, **114**, 121, 122, 123, 292

letters, example of 298–9

Lévi-Strauss, C. (1908–) 124, **126–7**

lexical item 214, **370**

life-writing 168–70; *also see* **auto/biography**

Linguistics 46–8, 56, 124, 126, 390

literacy, il/literate 10–1, 29–30, 48, 49, 55, 118, 136, **142–3**, **144**, 170–1, 173, 228, 245; texts about **300–4**

literariness 10–1, 38, 41, 49, 56, 69, 84, **87**, **89**, 164

LITERARY APPRECIATION 35–7; LITERARY CRITICISM 36–7, 78; LITERARY HISTORY **32–3**, 119, 390–1; LITERARY STUDIES **37–8**, 55–6, 136–7 literature 16, 45–7, **54–8**, 93, 102, 184–5, 243–4, 386–9; Comparative and 'World' 37; *also see* ENGLISH Literature, Literatures in English

local 60, 131, 133, 144, 159, 228–9, 389

locution, illocution, perlocution 370

logocentric 120, 166, 370

Lodge, D. 179

Lukacs, G. (1885–1971) 103, 104

Lyotard, J-F. (1924–) **129**, 213

Macherey, P. (1938–) 94, 97, **106**, **156–7**, 249

'making-strange' (Verfremdung, after Brecht); 86, 91, **104**, 219, 246, 354

'Maiden in the mor lay' 167, 170, text **277–8**, 386

Malraux, A. (1901–76) 184

Manley, D. (1663–1724), *The New Atalantis* 119, 198, text **304–5**, 387

maps 145, 149; (re-)mapping 22–3, **145**, 147, 150–1; of British Isles 383; of English in the world 384; of USA 385

margin 156–8; *also see* **centre**

Marshall-Stoneking, B., 'Passage' 23, **149–52**, 172, 173; text **343**

Marx, K. (1818–83) 102, 111

MARXISM 48, 70, 97, **102–11**, 125, 130, 164, 173, 178

masculine (as cultural construct) 112–3

medieval 63, 227; *also see* ENGLISH, Middle

MEDIUM, MEDIA 10, **19–20**, **41**, 57, 62, 70, 258, 271, 272, 370, 386–9; MEDIA STUDIES **40–1**, **63–4**, 164, 391; mediation **62–3**, 129, 166, 205, **370**; *also see* multimedia

meta- (prefix) 131, **370**; metafiction 131, **219**; metalinguistic, meta-textual 50, 161, 219, **370**

metaphor 29, 94, **203**, **370–1**

metre 27, 99, 213, **237–42**; *also see* **versification**

metonymy 203, **371**; *also see* metaphor

Metz, C. 212

Milton, J. (1608–74) 25, *Paradise Lost* 16, 27, 29, 64, 172, 173, 175, 241; text **283–4**, 387

mimesis 72, 192

Mishra, V.J. 152

mock-heroic **183**, 200, 267; examples of **285–8**

modality 371; *also see* verb 381

modernism 34, 57, 86, 90, 104, 117, 124, **125**, 164, 182, 388; *also see* POSTMODERNISM

modification (pre- and post-) *see* noun group 372–3

monologue 61, **161–2**, **222**, 224, 258, 366; *also see* **speech** and **dialogue**

Montrose, L. 102, 111

Monty Python 172, text **345**

Moon, B. 179

morphology 371

Morrison, T. (1931–), *Beloved* 64, 137, 159, text **303–4**, 389

Mukarovsky, J. (1891–1975) 84, **86–7**, **88**, 92, 197, 199

multiaccentuality 160

MULTICULTURAL(ISM) 17, 29, 135–53, **141–2**, 185; *also see* CULTURE and POSTCOLONIALISM

multifunctionality 371

multimedia 41, 129, 134, 214, 264, 389, 391

music **40**, 132–3, 201, 260, 390–1; *also see* song

mystery play, *see* 'Noah's flood'

myth 27–8, 95, **127**, **170–4**, 150–1, 209, 290–3; *also see* **bibles** and CLASSICAL

names, re-naming: of people(s) and places 105–6, **116**, **143–5**, 150; of courses 269–71

narrative 34, 57, 86–7, 137, 189, **192**, **206–12**; narration 206–7; narratee 189, 206; narrator 189; narrators and narratees (implied and actual, un/reliable, omniscient and im/partial, first or third person) 80, 81, 208; 'grand' and 'small' narratives **129**, 130, 131, 133; narrative intervention 266; for examples of narrative, *see* **auto/biography**, journals, prose, **novel**, news and slave narratives

narrowcast **57**, 63, 194, 210

native(s) 140

naturalistic 90; *also see* **realism**

nature 60; *also see* human nature

negation 106, **156**, 246

neo-classical 164; *also see* CLASSICS

neocolonialism 130; *also see* POSTCOLONIALISM

NEW CRITICISM 36, 38, 48, 56, 69, **77–83**, 104, 164, 169, 172, 204; *also see* PRACTICAL CRITICISM and criticism

NEW HISTORICISM 34, 70, **103**, **107–8**, 110, 141

news 53, 57, 83, 91, 117, **209**, 212; examples of 314–8, 353; *also see* **narrative**

New Zealand 18, 31, 135, 139, 144; map **384**, 388

Nichols, G. (1950–), 'Tropical Death' 18, 23, 53, 64, 91, 152, 160, 172, 173, **183**, 188, 198, 230, 241; text **348**, 389

'Noah's Flood' (Chester Mystery Play) 23, 29, 170, 173, 183, 238, text **324–5**, 387

nominalisation 371–2

nonsense **129**, 182; *also see* **absurd**

non-verbal communication (NVC) 50, 62, 221, **372**

nouns 372; noun-group 372–3

novel 25, 118, 137; genres of 199, **209–10**, 218, 224, 387–8; examples of 300–7, 311–4, 338, 341, 345; *also see* **narrative** and **fiction**

object (direct and indirect) *see* sentence 377

Oedipus (complex) 95, 246

other 62, 92, **95–6**, 99, 108, 137, 145–6, 147, 148, 156–7, **168–70**, 248; *also see* **self**, **absence** and **auto/biography**

oral, orality 20, 34, **49**, 57, 59, 144, **150–1**, 238, 277, 313, 386–9; *also see* **speech**

orthography 373

Oxford English Dictionary (OED) 10–1, **21–2**, 53, 55, 229

paradigm(atic) 27; *also see* choice 363

paradox **79**, **81**, 182, 204

paralinguistic features 373

parallelism 259, 373

paraphrase 79; as learning strategy 258, 266

parataxis 373

parody 32, 69, 88, 200, 209, 249; as learning strategy 257, 268; examples of 302, 340–1

participants 62, 70, 232; grammatical 243, **373**

passive *see* active 362; and verb 381

pastoral 27, **180**, 339

parts of speech 373

participles *see* verb 381

'Pearl' 23, 238; text **280**, 387

Peirce, C.S. (1839–1914) 378

Pepys, S. (1633–1703), *Diary* 169; text **299**, 387

performance 54, 57, 167, 132–4, 293, 391

performative 50–1, **374**; *also see* speech acts

period, periodisation **34–5**, 40, 270, **272**

personification 203

Peters, L., 'Why Dorothy Wordsworth is not . . . ' 46–7, 69–70, 81, 241, text **340**

phatic 161, 222, **374**

Philosophy 124, 127–8, 130, 390

phonetics 374; phonology 213, **374–5**; phoneme 184, **374–5**

photography 203, 388

pidgin 136, 229, **365**; *also see* creole

plantation 12, 138, 139, 386

play 38, 51, 96, 193, **212–5**; *also see* **poetry and word-play**

plays *see* **drama**

pleasure 162–5; *also see* **aesthetics** and desire

plosive *see* phonetics 374

plot 80, **208**

π0, '7 DAIZ' 18, 53, 158, 160; text **293**, 389

Poe, E.A. (1809–49) 162

poetry 85, 89, 199–200, 212–6, 219, **237–42**, 386–9; examples of 276–96, 338–44, 346–52, 358; poetics 54, 57, **85**, **89–90**, 137, 161, 164, 218; *also see* **versification**

point of view 80, **195–9**, 208; *also see* **foreground**

Pope, A. (1688–1744), *The Rape of the Lock* 27, 122, 172, 183, **239**; text **284–5**, 387; epitaph **344**

popular 8, 40, 57, **60**, 63, 104, 125, 136, 164, **175–6**, 183, 186, 193–4; pop song **296–8**; populist 125

pornography 114, 119

Portugal, Portuguese **18**, 141

POSTCOLONIALISM 13, 48, 60–1, 70, 97, 125, **135–53**, 141, 164, 169, 173, 389, 391; *also see* colonialism, neocolonialism, MULTICULTURALISM, slave narrative

POSTMODERNISM 21, 34, 48–9, 60, 70, 103–4, **124–35**, 141, 164, 167, 388; *also see* modernism

POSTSTUCTURALISM 21, 97, 105–6, **124–35**, 156–8, 166–7, 186; and readers 246–50; *also see* **absence** and deconstruction

power 51, 61, 102, 107, 144, 188, 191; *also see* **discourse** and ideology

PRACTICAL CRITICISM 36, 69, **77–83**; *also see* NEW CRITICISM

practice 70–1

pragmatics 50–1, 189, **375**; *also see* speech acts

Pratchett, T. and N. Gaiman, *Good Omens* 90; text **288**

preference 184–8, **186**; *also see* **difference** and **value**

preposition 375

presence 156–8, 218; *also see* **absence**

presentation (as learning strategy) 255

Prickett, S. 174

printing 52, 227–8, 244, 387–9

process (verbal and textual) 21, 243; *also see* participants and processes 373–4

producers 71–4, 154

product 21, 71–3, 154, 243

progressive and non-progressive *see* verb, aspect 381
projection (psychological) 96
pronouns 160; *also see* noun 372
pronunciation *see* **accent** and **standard**
Propp, V. (1895–1970) 87, 211
prose 80, 137, 200, 242, 386–9; examples of 288, 298–319, 338–9, 341–2, 344, 352, 354–9; *also see* **novel**
Psalm 137 53, 173; versions of **337–8**
PSYCHOLOGY, PSYCHOANALYSIS 48, 63, **92–101**, 105–6, 156, 322–3; and language 92–3, 115–6; psycholinguistics 375; FEMINIST approaches to 115–7, 120; and POSTSTRUCTURALISM 130; *also see* Freud and Lacan
publishing 256, 390
pun 214, 215
punctuation 213, 245, **375–6**

Queen, *Bohemian Rhapsody* 45, 53, 101, **132–4**, 165, 170, 190, 213, 215, 242, text **296–8**, 388
queer *see* gay
Quiller-Couch, A. (1863–1944) 35–6

race, racism 142, 148
radio 38, 330, 388
reading 78, 130, **242–51**; reader response 246–8; reception aesthetics 245–6; resistant readers 249; reading as re-writing 242–3, 247, 249; reading as a wo/man 119
realism 86, 125, 178, **216–20**; socialist realism 103, 208
receiver 71–3, 74–5, 154
re-centring *see* **centre**
reception aesthetics 73, 75, 164, **245–6**; *also see* **reading**
reference, referential 50, 72, 161, 186, **376**
register 376
relations to the rest of the world **72–3**, **75**, 102, 154
reported speech *see* indirect speech 366
representation 34, 72, 125, 138, 148, 178, **217–8**, 220; of women by men 118; non-realist 125; *also see* **realism**
repression 52, 92, 93, **94**, 106, 156, 168; *also see* expression
reproduction (textual) **73–5**, 108, 166; economic 102; sexual 113; *also see* **reading**, reception and response

research (practising) 261–4
response 242–51; reponse-ability (after Bakhtin) 100, **248**; *also see* **reading**, reception and reproduction
re/valuation 37, 64, 88–9, 112, 118–9, 184–8, **187**; *also see* **value** and **preference**
re-visioning (after Rich) 122, **123**, 169, 196, 214, 292
re-writing 101, 149, **242–51**; *also see* intervention (textual)
RHETORIC 27, **29–32**, 45–8, 54, 56, 57, 78, 390; rhetorical 30, 200
rhyme 16, 213, **237–42**; *also see* **versification**
Rhys, J. (1894–1979), *Wide Sargasso Sea* 23, 122, **157**, 178, 266; text **307–8**, 389
rhythm 213, **237–42**, 376; *also see* stress
Rich, A.(1929–), 'Dialogue' 23, 83, 101, 115, **121–2**, 123, 214, 241, 242; text **292**
Richards, I.A. (1893–1979) 64, **78–9**, 206
role 192, 232, 233; *also see* **subject** and **identity**
Roman 15, 51, 114, 226, 386–7
romance: genre 113, **200**, 209; examples of 304–8; languages 51, 237
Romantic (period, movement) 30, **34**, 39, 60, 164, 180, 339, 388
Rorty, R. 237
Rushdie, S. (1947–), *The Satanic Verses* 137, **173**; text **338**, 389
Russell, W. (1947–), *Educating Rita* 83, 191; text **335–6**, 388

Said, E. (1935–) 130, 137, 249
Sarton, M. (1912–), *As We Are Now* text **341**
satire 27, 32, 180, 200, 236, 284, 287, **308**
Saussure, F. de (1857–1913) 124, **126**
scan, scansion (metre) 239–41
scenario 232; *also see* **role** and script
Scholes, R. 269
school (English in) 24–6
Schorer, M. 80, 86
science fiction 200; *also see* **fiction**
Scotland, Scots **9–12**, 15, 30, 136, 138, 139, 145–6, 159, 317–8, 319; map **383**, 387–8; *also see* Celtic
Scott, D. (1939–), 'Uncle Time' 172; text **342**
script 31, 38, 57, 223, 224, **232–3**, examples of 324–35, 340, 348–9, 353–4 ; *also see* **drama** and transcript
Selden. R. 233
selectional features (semantic) 376
self 62, 92, **95–6**, 99, 108, 137, 145–6, 147,

148, 156–7, **168–70**, 248; *also see*
auto/biography and **other**
semantics 376
semiotics 120, 124, 145; *also see* semantics
376
sentence (types and structures) 376–7
sex, sexuality 95, 99, **112–3**, 120, 133, 147
Shakespeare, W. (1564–1616) 25, 28, 30, 32,
39, 93, 164, 175, 227, 387; *Sonnets* 83, 89,
113, 122, 134, 183, 199, 213, 241; texts
281–2, **342**; *Henry V* 110, 159, 191; text
348–50; *Hamlet* **73–5**, 77, 107, 157, 181,
187, 195–6, 214–5, 219, 266; *The Tempest*
64, 83, 152, 172, 173, 181, 191, 241; text
325–6; *As You Like It* 232, 234
Shelley, M. (1797–1851), *Frankenstein* 100,
119, 200, text **306**, 388
Shelley, P.B. (1792–1822), *The Mask of
Anarchy* text **351**, 388
Shklovsky, V. (1893–1984) 84, **86**, 92
Shaw, G.B. (1856–1950) *Pygmalion* 145–7
Showalter, E. (1941–) 119, 123
showing **192**, 194, **207**, 267
sign, signifier, signified (sign-systems) 52, 95,
120, **126–7**, 145, 204, 214, 235, **378**; *also
see* **image** and structuralism
silences 156–8; *also see* **absence**
similarity 184–8; *also see* **difference**
simile 203, **378**
simulacrum (after Baudrillard) 129, 205
Singapore 18; 'Singlish' text **294**; map 384
sjuzet **86–7**, 208
skaz 86, 208
slave narratives 169, 200; examples of 300–4 ;
slave trade 139–41, 147; map **384**
Smith, B. 123
socialist realism 103, **218**
sociolect 159, 378
sociolinguistics 378
song, examples of 277, 296–7, 337, 353–4,
349–50; *also see* **poetry**
sonnet **89–90**, 199, 213, **241**; examples of:
Shakespeare 281, 342; Wroth 282; Brooke
352; *also see* Fanthorpe 352
sound-structure, sound-pattern 213, 260; *also
see* phonetics, phonology and **versification**
Spain, Spanish 12, 18, 141, 143, 144
speech 52, 85, 156, **220–5**, 378; direct and
indirect 224, 318, **366–7**
speech acts 189, 378–9; *also see* pragmatics
spelling 227
Spivak, G.C. 107, 115, 130, 137–8, 249
standards, standardisation 10–1, 18, 24, 25, 49,

136, 148, 158–60, 198, **225–30**, **379**;
non-standards 229–30; *also see* ENGLISH
story 16, 55, **207**, 209, 218; *also see* **hi/story**
stream of consciousness 125, 200, **217**
stress 213, 222, **237–42**, **379**; *also see*
versification
structuralism 124, 126–7, 207–8; *also see*
POSTSTRUCTURALISM
style 29, 50; stylistic checklist 255–60;
Stylistics 78, 197, 379
subject 24, 41, **105–6**, 124, 131, 132, **230–4**,
379; grammatical 231
subordination (grammatical) *see* sentences 377
Sun, The (newspaper) 188; text **314–5**, **316**
Swift, J. (1667–1745), *Gulliver's Travels* 86,
100; *A Modest Proposal* 64, 91, 183; text
308–9, 387
syllable 379
symbol(ic) 60, 62, **94–5**, 115–6, 378
synchronic *see* diachronic 366
Synge, J.M. (1871–1909), *Playboy of the
Western World* 15, 159, 160, 183; text
328–9, 389
synonym 380
syntagm(atic) 363; *also see* combination
syntax 214; *also see* grammar

taboo, examples of 319–201, 346–7
taste 187; *also see* discrimination
teaching *see* learning strategies and Education
tele-communications 63; *also see*
COMMUNICATIONS
television *see* TV
telling **192**, 194, **207**, 267
tense *see* verb 381
text 49, 54, 57, 69, 71–3, **234–7**, 244, **380**,
391; textual intervention 32, 249, 257,
265–9; *also see* **context**, co-text,
intertextuality, meta-textuality
theatre 57, 71, 73–4, **191–4**; THEATRE
STUDIES **38–9**, 391; *also see* **drama**
Theatre Workshop, *Oh What a Lovely War* 91,
104, 110, 165, 183, 195, 219, 220; text
353–4, 388
THEOLOGY 27, **28–9**; *also see* **bibles** and
Christianity
theory 41–2, **70–1**, 192–3
Thomas, D. (1914–53), *Under Milk Wood* 15,
23, 159, 192, 238; text **329–30**, 388
tragedy 27, **179–84**
transaction: conversational 221; psychological
96, 100

translation 16, 25, 29, 37, 49, 53, 57, 62, 63, 82, 137, **153**, 166; of **bibles** 15, **171–2**; studying literature in 37; examples of 276–80, 322–3, 326–7, 337–8; as learning strategy **256**, **269**, 380

transcript 223, 224, 233; examples of 320–3, 356–8; *also see* script

transitive 380; *also see* intransitive

travel-writing 38

Trilling, L. (1905–75) 29, 58–9

Trotsky. L. (1879–1940) 184

Tutuola, A. (1920–), *The Palm-Wine Drinkard* 18, 23, 64, 172, 173; text **313**

TV (television) 38–9, 159, 191–5, **193–4**, 203, **210–1**, 388, 391; examples of: news 316, 318; advert 340

unconscious, the 52, 92, **94**, 99, 168; *also see* consciousness

United Kingdom **12**, 388

United States **13**, 22, 30–2, 136; map of state-names 385; *also see* America(n)

university (ENGLISH at) 26–44

utterance 380

value 25, 35, 62, 64, 88, 172, **187**, 259; validity 187; *also see* re/valuation

variety, variation (in language) 8–21, 49, 148, 158, **225–30**, 380; in Britain and USA (maps) 383, 385

verb, verb group 380–2; *also see* participants and processes 373–4

versification 99, **237–42**; *also see* poetry

video 203; *also see* TV

visual presentation (textual) 260

voice 96, 382

Voloshinov, V. 107, 250

Vygotsky, L. 96

Wales, Welsh **9–12**, 15, 136, 138, 145, 159, 228, 329–30; map **383,** 386, 388; *also see* Celtic

Wei Meng, Chan, 'I spik Ingglish' 18, 23, 53, 158; text **294**, 389

Wellek, R. (1903–) 58, 85

white (as cultural construct) 52, **145–7**, 173

Whitman, W. (1819–92) 225

w/hole (a pun I labour) e.g., 126, 131, 235, 260–1; *also see (through)* hole

Widdowson, P. 58, 233

Williams, R. (1921–88) 64, 76, 97, 102, **106–7**

Wimsatt, W.K. (1907–75) 64, 79, 83

Winnicott, D.W. (1896–1971) 96

Wittgenstein, L (1889–1951) 129, 213

word 48, 156; word choice and combination 85, **259–60**, 363; word-class 382; **word-play** 92, 212–6, *and see* **poetry**

Wordsworth, D. (1771–1855), *The Grasmere Journals* 46, 69–70, 81, 122, 134, 153; text **339–40**, 388

Wordsworth, W. (1770–1850), 'I wandered lonely . . . ' 25, 30, **45–7**, 69–70, 81, 122, 134, 153, 167, 205, 241; text **338–9**, 388

World Wide Web (WWW) 125, 235, 389, 390; site for this book 5; *also see* internet

Wright, E. 101

writing 19–20, 49, 52, 54, 57, 156, **242–51**, 382; writing essays 261–4; writing as a wo/man 117–8, 119, 248; writer 55, 165–6; **re-writing** 101, 149, **242–51**; examples of student re-writing 302, 317

Wilde, O. (1854–1900) 269

Wroth, M. (c.1587–1651) 122; text **282–3**, 387

'Wulf and Eadwacer' 237–8; text **276–7**, 386

Wyatt, T. (c.1503–42), 'They flee from me' 83, 91, 122, 158, 194, 224, 241; text **280–1**, 387

Yeats, W.B. (1865–1939), 'Leda and the Swan' 64, 122, 158, 241, 268; text **290–1**